Revolutions

Revolutions

A New History

Donald Sassoon

VERSO
London • New York

To Jake and Ryan

First published by Verso 2025
© Donald Sassoon 2025

The manufacturer's authorized representative in the EU for product safety (GPSR) is LOGOS EUROPE, 9 rue Nicolas Poussin, 17000, La Rochelle, France
contact@logoseurope.eu

All rights reserved

The moral rights of the author have been asserted

1 3 5 7 9 10 8 6 4 2

Verso
UK: 6 Meard Street, London W1F 0EG
US: 207 East 32nd Street, New York, NY 10016
versobooks.com

Verso is the imprint of New Left Books

ISBN-13: 978-1-80429-992-0
ISBN-13: 978-1-83674-021-6 (UK EBK)
ISBN-13: 978-1-83674-022-3 (US EBK)

British Library Cataloguing in Publication Data
A catalogue record for this book is available from the British Library

Library of Congress Cataloging-in-Publication Data
A catalog record for this book is available from the Library of Congress

Typeset in Minion Pro by MJ & N Gavan, Truro, Cornwall
Printed in the UK by CPI Group (UK) Ltd, Croydon, CR0 4YY

Contents

Introduction		1
1	The English Civil War	36
2	America: The Settlers' Rebellion	65
3	Debating the French Revolution	95
4	The 'National Revolutions' of the Nineteenth Century	153
5	The Rise and Fall of the Russian Revolution	184
6	The Chinese Revolution: Not a Dinner Party	259
Conclusion		324
Acknowledgements		345
Notes		346
Index		407

Introduction: Turning the World Upside Down

Eric Hobsbawm recalled how in January 1989, as the bicentenary of the Revolution approached, France's Socialist Prime Minister Michel Rocard said he hoped the commemorations would convince people 'that revolution is dangerous, and that if one can do without it, so much the better'.[1] However, matters are never that simple, even for politicians as clever as Rocard. A few months later Rocard, whose mother was a Protestant, had obviously changed his mind, since he celebrated – as one of the Revolution's central achievements – Article 10 of the Declaration of the Rights of Man and of the Citizen (26 August 1789), which established freedom of worship. 'French Protestants cannot but recognize in the French Revolution the founding moment of their freedom,' Rocard declared, pointing out that in Great Britain, Catholics were only emancipated in 1829, thirty years after the French measure. '*1789 change tout*,' he concluded.[2]

Politicians inevitably take from history what they can. Historians have to be more careful. The half-dozen revolutions which constitute the main object of this book – the English Civil War; the American War of Independence; the French, Russian and Chinese Revolutions; and what I call the 'national revolutions' of the nineteenth century – all involved the overthrow of the old regime. But old regimes do not need a revolution to be overthrown. You can have a coup d'état, which were frequent in ancient Rome and more recently; or a revolution from above, as with the Meiji Restoration in Japan; or an anti-colonial struggle, as in Algeria, Malaysia or Vietnam.

Some regimes are toppled by war, such as the Austro-Hungarian and Ottoman Empires after 1918. On the other hand, the First World War was quite finished by the time Mussolini erected his Fascist regime in Italy, and Germany wasn't at war when the Weimar Republic disintegrated, giving way to Nazism. The end of dictatorship in Greece and Spain in the 1970s wasn't due to war, though Salazar's demise in Portugal can be attributed to the country's unsuccessful wars in its African colonies. The collapse of Soviet Communism in 1991 was virtually bloodless.

To generalize is almost impossible. Regime change is, in fact, a 'normal' vicissitude of world history. We would otherwise still be in Antiquity (which, anyway, saw plenty of regime change).

For want of a definition

Like most complex phenomena, revolution is virtually impossible to categorize except in generic terms, as Theda Skocpol valiantly tries when she explains that 'social' revolutions are 'rapid, basic transformations of a society's state and class structures; and they are accompanied and in part carried through by class-based revolts from below'.[3] Was the American War of Independence, on this basis, a revolution? Patriots talked of 'independence'; however, sporadic mentions of 'revolution' were established early on. William Henry Drayton, chief justice of South Carolina, wrote a few months after the Declaration of Independence: 'This Revolution [is] ... one of the most important Epocha's [sic] in the History, not of a Nation, but, of the World', and far more significant than England's Glorious Revolution of 1688.[4] The word 'revolution' was subsequently deployed in many American pamphlets and publications. Thomas Paine used the term in 1777 and in a series of articles on 'The American Crisis', the final instalment of which was published in April 1783 as the War of Independence was ending. 'These are times that tried men's souls,' wrote Paine,

> and they are over – and the greatest and completest revolution the world ever knew, gloriously and happily accomplished. But to pass from the extremes of danger to safety – from the tumult of war to the tranquillity of peace ... requires a gradual composure of the senses to receive it.[5]

For John Adams, writing to Thomas Jefferson in 1815, the Revolution had started well before the War. It had begun in the minds of the people:

What do We mean by the Revolution? The War? That was no part of the Revolution. It was only an Effect and Consequence of it. The Revolution was in the Minds of the People, and this was effected, from 1760 to 1775, in the course of fifteen Years before a drop of blood was drawn at Lexington.[6]

But if a change in the economic power structure of society is the criterion, the War of Independence was not a revolution. This is the view of some, such as Howard Zinn, who took a somewhat radical and alternative view, making the American revolt sound almost like a counter-revolution. The settlers, Zinn wrote, found that

> by creating a nation, a symbol, a legal unity called the United States, they could take over land, profits, and political power from favorites of the British Empire. In the process they could hold back a number of potential rebellions and create a consensus of popular support for the rule of new privileged leadership.[7]

Had the War of Independence not taken place, slavery might have been abolished sooner, since it was abolished in the British Empire in 1833, though there would probably have been a rebellion in the American colonies in favour of retaining it. Ending slavery in the US, unquestionably a major radical change, required a civil war which hardly anyone has ever called revolution, although Eric Foner characterizes the postbellum Reconstruction era as an 'unfinished' one.[8]

The ambiguity of the term 'revolution' was made evident by the widely quoted response of Zhou Enlai, prime minister of China, to Richard Nixon and Henry Kissinger when asked: 'What is your view on the French Revolution?' Zhou Enlai is supposed to have answered: 'It is too early to say.' This was taken to represent, in accordance with a Western stereotype, the long-term view of a wise Chinese sage with a continuous history of over 2,000 years behind him. The reality, according to Nixon's interpreter Chas Freeman (and as Chinese archives corroborated) is that since the distinction between 'revolution' and 'revolt' is ambiguous in Chinese, Zhou Enlai thought Nixon was referring to the events in Paris in May 1968. It was, Freeman explained years later, a misunderstanding 'too delicious' to correct.[9]

Even Karl Marx, who was supposed to know a thing or two about revolutions, never produced a general theory of them, though his more political writings make some generalized statements. He seldom used the term 'bourgeois revolution'. As Perry Anderson has noted, there is very little in the works of Marx and Engels about the momentous changes which occurred under their very eyes in Europe: the unifications of Italy and Germany.[10] There is nothing about the Meiji Restoration in Japan, and Marx's writings on the American Civil War are more in the nature of intelligent journalism.

Contrary to what is commonly believed, Marx did not always think it inevitable that a transition from capitalism to socialism required a violent revolution. In a speech in Amsterdam in 1872 he said that in countries such as the United States of America and England, 'the workers can achieve their aims by peaceful means'. In a letter of 8 December 1880 to the English socialist Henry Hyndman, founder of the Social Democratic Federation, he explained that his 'party' 'considers an English revolution not necessary, but – according to historic precedents – possible. If the unavoidable evolution turns into a revolution, it would not only be the fault of the ruling classes, but also of the working class.'[11]

In *Das Kapital*, the word 'revolution' is used with the lack of precision characteristic of everyday language. We find, of course, the odd reference to the Glorious Revolution of 1688, the French Revolution and the 'revolution' of 1848, along with many more mentions of the 'agricultural revolution' and 'industrial revolution'. In an unpublished note on economists, Marx wrote that 'a change in the social relation of workers and capitalists' constituted 'a revolution in the conditions governing capitalist production'.[12] But this too isn't very exact.

Hobsbawm's book *The Age of Revolution 1789–1848* dealt with a 'dual' revolution: a political revolution in France and an industrial one in England – two quite different phenomena. The term 'industrial revolution' had already been used by Arnold Toynbee in his *Lectures on the Industrial Revolution in England*, published posthumously in 1884.

By the twentieth century, the word 'revolution', long popular in France and the US, particularly with progressives, was being embraced even by the far right. Mussolini called the March on Rome of 1922 that coincided with his appointment as prime minister 'the Fascist revolution', even though the real changes (his dictatorship) only occurred a few years later.[13] Many leading Fascists, such as Education Minister Giuseppe Bottai, continued to use 'revolution' to describe their takeover of the state and its institutions.[14] In Germany, Joseph Goebbels referred in 1933 to the National Socialist Revolution, while in 1936 Heinrich Himmler denounced the 'Jüdisch-Bolschewistische revolution des Untermenschen' (the Judeo-Bolshevik revolution of the sub-humans). The latter theme had been mentioned in various forms by people as diverse as Henry Ford and Winston Churchill, who discussed Jewish revolutionaries such as Karl Marx, Leon Trotsky, Rosa Luxemburg and others as part of a 'world-wide conspiracy for the overthrow of civilization'.[15] Hermann Rauschning, a former Nazi who turned against the regime, described Nazism as a 'revolution of nihilism'.[16]

In recent times we have used 'revolution' increasingly loosely. Post-communist Eastern Europe has been garlanded with botanically named 'revolutions', usually protests, such as the Orange Revolution in Ukraine challenging the results of presidential elections, the Rose Revolution in Georgia and the Tulip Revolution in Kyrgyzstan. The demonstrations in Maidan Square in Kyiv in 2014, which led to the establishment of a government hostile to Russia, was called the Revolution of Dignity (*Revoliutsiia hidnosti*) and was also known as the Maidan Revolution. The journalist Christopher Hitchens rather absurdly welcomed the 2003 US invasion of Iraq as 'something more like a social and political revolution than a military occupation. It's a revolution from above, but in some ways no less radical for that. I haven't seen anything like it.'[17] He could not have envisaged the disastrous consequences and the appalling mess that ensued.

Historians and social scientists have published books about the Roosevelt Revolution, the supply-side revolution, the neo-conservative revolution, and so on.[18] A revolution can now mean a watershed, turning point, or shift in behaviour and mentalities: the sexual revolution, the social media revolution. A modern use of the term can be detected as early as 1849 in Robert Owen's optimistic *The Revolution in the Mind and Practice of the Human Race; or, The Coming Change from Irrationality to Rationality*, which heralded 'a revolution from wrong to right, from falsehood to truth, from oppression to justice, from deception and misery to straightforward honesty and happiness'.[19] Today we talk of 'revolutionary' musicians, some of whom have sung about revolution themselves, from the Rolling Stones' 'Street Fighting Man' to the Beatles' more moderate 'Revolution', both released in 1968.

Revolution has also been commercialized and trivialized.[20] A beautifying face cream called the 'Revolution Pro Miracle Cream' will transform, or so the manufacturers claim, your 'tired and dull complexions in just 4 weeks!' Emmanuel Macron, a banal centrist politician, published a book in 2016 called *Révolution*, which describes his life, his wife and the great changes he had in mind, none of which he enacted. The arrival of Theresa May as British prime minister was greeted with the publication of *Theresa May: The Downing Street Revolution* by Virginia Blackburn, a columnist for the distinctly non-revolutionary *Daily Express*.[21] May lost her majority in 2017, and almost immediately both the book and the 'revolution' disappeared without a trace. During the COVID-19 pandemic, her successor Boris Johnson announced an instantly forgotten 'cycling and walking revolution', while in the same month – on the 14th of July! – the *Guardian* hailed the 'Nespresso coffee revolution'.[22] By then the term had lost any meaning, hence articles such as one in the *Daily Mirror* on 27 September 2022 which described Labour Party leader Keir Starmer as 'the quiet revolutionary'.[23]

What all this goes to show is the impossibility of offering a strong definition of revolution. Scholars such as Skocpol could have written the same interesting books without hazarding one. Of course, we use all sorts of words – such as capitalism, socialism, fascism – without feeling obliged to provide a clear definition. As Dale Yoder wrote almost one hundred years ago: 'Revolution has acquired a variety of meanings which make it as adaptable to personal purposes as is the chameleon's skin.'[24]

Saturn's children

It is often said that revolutions go bad, that they betray their original high-minded principles (when they have them) and that, in what has now become a cliché, they 'devour their children'. This expression seems to have been coined in 1793 by the journalist and essayist Jacques Mallet du Pan and used in an anti-revolutionary pamphlet where he wrote that 'a l'exemple de Saturne, la révolution dévore ses enfants' (like Saturn, the revolution eats its children).[25] The use of the guillotine had just begun: a 'humanitarian' form of execution, since hanging or the axe tended to prolong the agony of death. In January 1793, King Louis XVI was executed. Over the following eighteen months, 'only' 2,639 people, mainly aristocrats, were guillotined in Paris.[26] Many more died as a result of being shot or imprisoned, and even more died in the civil war in the Vendée and elsewhere, which had originated in peasant opposition to conscription into the French army to fight foreign enemies. Mallet du Pan, who was born in Geneva, called the revolutionaries 'butchers', 'barbarians', 'criminals', 'murderers' and 'fanatics'. The real Terror started after the publication of his pamphlet, yet the image of Saturn devouring his children contained a grain of truth, since many revolutionaries were eventually themselves victims of the revolution, as was the case during the 1930s in the Soviet Union and in China during the Cultural Revolution.

The French Revolution did not so much devour its children as forget about them. Jean-Paul Marat, Georges Jacques Danton and Maximilien de Robespierre went virtually unmentioned during the celebration for the bicentenary. They are in the strange position of being uncelebrated in a country which constantly celebrates its heroes (the Panthéon and so on) and even its quite unmemorable leaders. So in Paris, there is a Centre Pompidou, named after a half-forgotten president; an avenue named after Félix Faure, president of the Republic (1895–99) who died while having sex with his mistress in his office; and a place named after Jules Joffrin, a little-known moderate socialist who became vice-president of the Paris municipal council. But there is no rue Robespierre (though there was one until 1950, and there are many in towns all over France) or rue Marat in Paris proper (that is, within the twenty *arrondissements*), although there is a rue Danton in the Sixth Arrondissement.

Lenin has been kept in his own mausoleum in Moscow's Red Square but his statues and monuments in Ukraine have been demolished, despite the fact that he created the Ukrainian Soviet Socialist Republic in 1922. Stalin's body, which had been next to Lenin's, was removed in 1961 and re-buried in the Kremlin Wall necropolis, just outside the Kremlin walls. Ho Chi Minh has his own mausoleum in Hanoi, and Saigon has been re-baptized Ho Chi Minh City, while Leningrad was renamed St Petersburg after the fall of communism. Mao Zedong still has his own mausoleum in Beijing's Tiananmen Square. In the US, the Founding Fathers are similarly revered, with the capital and a state in the Pacific North West named for George Washington, as are bills, monuments and statues scattered through major cities.

The celebration of revolutionaries rests not on their actual achievements but on how they are regarded by posterity. Oliver Cromwell got a statue near Parliament in 1899 despite qualms over his role in the regicide of Charles I and his terrorizing of Ireland.

The spectre of comparisons

Revolutions usually start with the breakdown of the state, in the sense that state institutions (such as finance or law and order) no longer work. A period of crisis ensues and then either the state is reorganized or a new one emerges. But was Fascist Italy or Nazi Germany the product of revolution, as some of their supporters claimed? After all, the Weimar Republic and the Italian 'liberal' state both collapsed, though not particularly violently, since Mussolini and Hitler were appointed in the usual manner, according to established rules, and the violence that immediately followed was supposedly legal. Similarly, the fall of communism in Eastern Europe and the USSR, which did involve the breakdown of the existing states, though with limited popular participation, was not called a revolution except in Czechoslovakia, where the Velvet Revolution of 1989 led not only to the end of Communism, but also to the separation of Slovakia from the Czech Republic.

Is mass participation essential to a revolution? It is difficult to say. The majority of Russians did not take part in the actual revolutions of 1917, whether that of February, which ended the Romanov dynasty, or that of October which started a process leading to the victory of the Bolsheviks. Eventually the masses joined in, but as part of the ensuing civil wars, and on various sides.

How about the anti-colonial revolutions? These involved the destruction of the colonial apparatus and its replacement with a state run either by settlers (as in the Americas) or the indigenous population (as in most of Africa). Here, too, elites played the dominant role.

Then there are cases in which one state takes over other states, such as the unification of Italy (1861) and Germany (1871). These led to momentous changes of regimes including in the conquering states, Piedmont and Prussia respectively. I have included these two cases in the present work, even though they were seldom called revolutions.

If we define revolution narrowly, we end up with the two or three of the usual suspects (the French, Russian and Chinese). If the definition is broad enough, we come to an extraordinary high number of revolutions just in the twentieth century. Mark Beissinger claims that out of the 166 countries he examined, 131 'underwent at least one episode of revolutionary contention' between 1900 and 2014. Beissinger's definition of revolution is unavoidably vague, which explains the large number of cases he identified. For him, a revolution is 'a mass siege of an established government by its own population with the goals of bringing about regime-change and effecting substantive political or social change'.[27] One would, of course, need to define 'mass siege' and 'substantive' change. What minimum percentage of inhabitants would need to be involved to constitute 'the population'? And so on, ad infinitum, from definition to definition.

In one of the rare comparative analyses of revolutions – written in 1938, too early for the Communist victory in China – Crane Brinton outlined 'uniformities' of the English, French, American and Russian revolutions, noting a cyclical pattern of increasing fervour, a climax of intensity, then a period of disillusionment, followed by the restoration of order and stability.[28] Revolutions are a kind of 'fever', he wrote. Thermidor – the formal end of the radical phase of the French Revolution – signalled 'a convalescence from the fever of revolution'.[29] Such a cycle, however, is applicable to any crisis; besides, as Brinton was perfectly aware, what followed most revolutions (Napoleon, the American Civil War, Stalin) was far from any kind of stability.

In his own landmark study, Barrington Moore noted that the successful bourgeois revolutions (those that led to capitalism) were the English Puritan Revolution, the French Revolution and the American Civil War. But there also were conservative revolutions that lacked popular participation, such as the German and Japanese. And then there were the Communist revolutions in Russia and China. But such efforts to classify revolutions led him, almost inevitably, to recognize differences between them in their starting points, in their processes and in their results. In China, it was the peasants who made a revolution. In England and France, though there were peasants, there were no peasant revolutions. To establish the points of divergence that really matter is, in the end, an empirical and not a theoretical matter.[30]

Revolutions seem to occur not in the most economically advanced countries but rather in those keen to catch up.[31] England in the seventeenth century was less advanced than the Dutch Republic; France in 1789 was behind England; Russia and China lagged behind Western countries. But these generalizations seldom hold true. There was a revolution in Geneva in 1781–82, and it was called one from the beginning. Yet, far from being backward, Geneva was a major banking centre and the most important place for the highly skilled manufacture of watches. The revolt concerned the degree of equality between the local aristocracy, those born in Geneva, and those who had immigrated. The revolt failed, with the help of 'revolutionary' France, though there were some reforms.[32] Geneva was annexed to France in 1798. After Napoleon's defeat, the citizens themselves thought it would be more prudent to become part of the Swiss Confederation.[33] In spite of its conservative nature – or because of its uncommon stability – Switzerland became, throughout the nineteenth century and for part of the twentieth, a haven for refugees, from Alexander Herzen to those of the Paris Commune, to anarchists such as Pyotr Kropotkin and Mikhail Bakunin, and revolutionaries such as Vera Zasulich, Georgi Plekhanov and Vladimir Lenin.

Demagogues and Athenians

In *The Politics*, Aristotle speaks of 'revolution' as something to be avoided but does not explain what it is. We can assume, from the context, that he means a violent uprising and a consequent shift in political power. The word Aristotle uses for 'revolution' is a variant of *metabole* (μεταβολή), which is really about changing course. Today we might say 'regime change'.

Both Thucydides and Aristotle contrasted *metabole politeias* (change of constitution), which is relatively peaceful, to *metabole kai stasis* (change with uprising). The other word which could suggest revolution is *epanástasis* (επανάστασις), which means uprising, revolt or insurrection, as used by Thucydides in his examination of the rebellion of the Samians. To describe the struggle between different factions within a polis (that is, civil war), the Greeks used the term *stasis* (στάσις) or *metastasis* (μετάστασις).[34]

Aristotle thought revolutions could be caused by poverty, envy or excessive taxation: 'Many who were rich will become poor; this is a most undesirable consequence, since you can hardly prevent such persons from becoming bent on revolution.'[35] He thus linked the distribution of wealth to the possibility of civil strife. However, he also thought it 'a defect of human nature never to be satisfied', and argued that while 'there is certainly some value in equality of wealth as a safeguard against civil strife, we must not exaggerate its efficacy, which is not really very great', because the upper classes 'will think they deserve something better than equality.'[36]

In democracies, as we read in Benjamin Jowett's classic translation of Aristotle from the 1880s, the principal cause of revolution is 'the insolence of the demagogues'. Thomas A. Sinclair's 1962 Penguin translation converted 'demagogues' to 'popular leaders', and instead of being 'insolent' they are 'unprincipled'.[37] Aristotle thought that a democracy was a corrupt and unnatural regime, though better than an oligarchy, which was in turn better than a tyranny. The best regimes were those where power was constrained by rules, such as monarchy (rule by one), aristocracy (rule by the best) and the confusing term *politeia*, or rule by the many.[38] In other words, rule should always be constrained, never absolute. We should remind ourselves that when the ancient Greeks talked about democracy, they meant rule by the people (the demos). The key question, then as today, is who is to be included in the people: who are the free citizens of the polis, and how is their rule to be exercised?

In ancient Athens, women, slaves, foreigners and debtors were not part of the demos and were excluded from voting. Only one-tenth of the populace were citizens with political rights, and slaves outnumbered free citizens.[39]

In Athens, at around the same time as the establishment of the Roman Republic, the aristocratic oligarchy was replaced with a democracy, albeit one open only to free male citizens, and this is often referred to as the 'Athenian revolution'. It was a three-day leaderless event – a riot – which, however, resulted in the expulsion of King Cleomenes and his Spartan troops from Attica.[40] This is one of the few instances for which we use the term 'revolution' in the context of ancient history. The later slave rebellion of Spartacus in 73–71 BC, the last of its kind to threaten the Roman Republic, and the one so often celebrated in films and novels, was not a wholesale attempt to abolish slavery, but, as Aldo Schiavone has explained, aimed only 'to overthrow local setups, and to exact vengeance on inhuman masters, not to uproot an overall system'.[41]

The Roman Republic gave way to an empire in 27 BC, when Octavian, Julius Caesar's adoptive son, was proclaimed Emperor Augustus. No one at the time talked of revolution, and the term *novas res* (new thing) appears in Tacitus as a pejorative, as when he describes the mob of soldiers *ad pronus novas res* (ready for new things). Cicero also used the term *mutatio omnium rerum* (change in all things), often translated with a negative slant as 'revolution'.[42] The term 'Roman Revolution' did not become established even after the publication of Theodor Mommsen's multi-volume *Roman History* (1854–56), where he uses 'revolution' to describe the period from the fall of the Gracchi brothers to the advent of Julius Caesar. It did not catch on even after Ronald Syme's famous book, *The Roman Revolution* (1939), an examination and a defence of the establishment of the Roman Empire as a military dictatorship, with Octavian-Augustus seen as a restorer of public order, at a time when Mussolini, Franco and Hitler were projected in a similar vein.[43]

Commoners in arms

Throughout the Middle Ages, major political changes are referred to as 'reforms'. We talk of the Gregorian reform in the eleventh century, named after Pope Gregory VII who strengthened enormously the power of the papacy. Gregory's *Dictatus papae* of 1075 enabled the pope to appoint bishops and unseat emperors (*quod illi liceat imperatores deponere*) and ordered that 'all princes shall kiss his feet' (*quod solius pape pedes omnes principes deosculentur*).

The Christian Church had long been divided between its western branch (the Church of Rome) and the various Eastern churches. In 1054 the Great Schism between the Church of Byzantium and that of Rome led to wars, crusades (including the sacking of Constantinople) and various military conflicts, but no revolutions. Eventually the much-weakened Byzantium gave way to the Muslim Ottoman Empire of the fifteenth century. The Eastern Orthodox Church of Russia had to face, in the thirteenth century, the threat of the (Catholic) Teutonic Knights who tried to conquer the republics of Pskov and Novgorod. The Knights were defeated, and the Eastern Orthodox Church survives to this day (having even survived Soviet Russia). None of these ideological and military conflicts constituted revolutions.

Martin Luther himself did not split from Rome. His famous Ninety-Five Theses were mainly directed against what he regarded as clerical abuses. The goal was indeed a 'reformation'. In response, Pope Leo X issued a papal bull against Luther, and in 1521 a Diet (assembly) was held in Worms presided by the Emperor Charles V, who had sided with the pope. Luther was forced to attend and, having refused to recant, was declared to be a heretic. It was only then that one could speak of the birth of a new church; the word 'revolution' was not used.

Before Luther there had been other attempts to reform the Roman Catholic Church, by figures such as Arnoldo da Brescia (*c.* 1090–1155), whose writings were burned; Pierre Waldo (1140–1205), who was excommunicated; the Lollard leader John Wycliffe (fourteenth century), whose body was reburied in unconsecrated ground; and the Dominican friar Girolamo Savonarola (1452–1498), who was burned at the stake. Then, after Luther, there was the English Reformation led by Henry VIII, which was more about politics, namely the powers of the monarch, than about theology. All these dissidents, for lack of a better word, were regarded as reformers.

If there were no revolutions in the Middle Ages, there were plenty of agrarian tumults and peasant rebellions – the so-called Jacqueries, from the pejorative term used by aristocrats to describe peasants: Jacques Bonhomme, or Jack Goodfellow. The term was used by Jean Froissart in his famous *Chronique* (1369?) of the first half of the Hundred Years' War, where he explains that worse than plague and famine is the Jacquerie. He writes, mixing disdain with understanding:

Crushed by taxes ... weary of paying and suffering, the people rise up, as they always rise up, without knowing what they are doing or what they want, absurd, abominable ... Jacques Bonhomme goes off like a delirious brute ... He pillages, he burns ... he kills, and with such fury, that the cruelties of men-at-arms are nothing compared to his butcheries.[44]

Many of these rebellions had economic origins: the imposition or raising of taxes. Thus, the English Peasants' Revolt of 1381 originated as a protest against a poll tax, though subsequent accounts give a more complex narrative linking the economic causes to honour and morality: John Tyler (possibly another name of Wat Tyler, leader of the revolt) killed a tax collector who had attempted to rape his daughter. This is what sparked the Peasants' Revolt, so the story goes. It is a peculiarity of such revolts, but also of later revolutions such as the English and the American, that the original cause is linked to others, such as freedom and dignity, as if a mere economic basis is not sufficient to justify such action.[45] Even the Indian anti-colonial revolution led by Mahatma Gandhi had, as one of its crucial turning points, the massive non-violent demonstration against the salt tax in March–April 1930.[46]

Alexis de Tocqueville was quite right when he wrote that there is hardly any public affair of importance which does not arise or end with taxation.[47] In the eighth century there was the 'Abbasid Revolution (or *thawra*, uprising) whose aim was to assimilate all Muslims (Arabs and non-Arabs) in the then Arab Empire into a single Muslim community. Here too taxes were in the forefront since the 'revolution' was led by 'déclassé' Arabs and non-Arabs who resented having to pay taxes to the Umayyad Caliphate.[48]

Simple revolts are a common feature of history. The German Peasants' War of 1524–25 ended in a massacre of the peasants by the aristocracy, a far greater slaughter than that of the French Revolution. In Hungary, the 1514 peasant revolt led by György Dózsa was put down: 60,000 of his followers were killed, Dózsa was roasted alive on an iron chair and his starving comrades forced to eat him.[49] This was never called 'The Terror', as was the revolt of the Jacobins. Between 1623 and 1648 there were almost constant revolts by artisans or beggars in various parts of France. Both the revolt of the *va-nu-pieds* (barefooted ones) in Normandy and that of the *Jacquerie des croquants*, mainly in the South-east of France, were crushed. In 1675 there was, in Brittany, the so-called *révolte du papier timbre*, an anti-tax revolt against a law which required a stamped paper to authenticate official documents.

Most revolts were defeated and the leaders and their followers executed. The causes were usually taxation blended with religious elements. Revolts, however, even those as serious as the German Peasants' War, never amounted to revolutions because they did not even aim at the seizure of power or a change of regime. They were really protest movements and some, at best, achieved reforms.

In Japan, the Shimabara Rebellion (1637–38) interrupted the otherwise relative peace of the Edo period under the Tokugawa shogunate. In China, Li Zicheng led a peasant rebellion which even succeeded in overthrowing the Ming dynasty and made him emperor, but his rule lasted only a year (1644–45) and his downfall paved the way for the Qing – the last Chinese imperial dynasty. Mass rebellions were extremely frequent in China. The historian and political scientist Yuhua Wang claims that 789 have been recorded in the 2,000 years preceding the final fall of the Qing in 1911.[50] Yet China has remained a single country, unlike Europe which, after the fall of the Roman Empire, was constantly divided between various nations often at war with each other.

Not all revolts had to do with the peasants. The famous *tumulto dei ciompi* in Florence (1378–82) could be classified as a proletarian revolt (the *ciompi* were wool carders).[51] There were also revolts by the aristocracy against absolute kings, such as the one in Poland, derisively known as the 1537 Chicken War, against King Sigismund I the Old, who had attempted to establish a permanent conscription army and raise from them the required finance. The nobility successfully forced the king not to proceed without their consent.

In Russia there was the so-called Time of Troubles (1598–1613), a period of unrest and anarchy led by various pretenders or imposters claiming the title of tsar. Later in 1670 there was revolt, almost a revolution, led by the Cossack Stenka Razin; it ended the following year with Razin dismembered and then executed in Moscow near the Kremlin. In 1773, during the rule of Catherine the Great, the Cossack Yemelyan Pugachev (pretending to be her late husband, Peter III) led a major peasant revolt during which he abolished serfdom and unpopular taxes. Like Razin, he was quartered and beheaded. Pugachev's revolt was often described by Russian historians as a *perevorot* (*переворот*, overturn) or *perelom* (*перелом*, turning point).[52]

The long Dutch Revolt (1566–1648) against Spanish rule was denied the use of the term 'revolution', even though it gave birth, in J. W. Smit's words, to 'the first real capitalist and bourgeois nation'.[53] The Dutch Revolt, in a way, prefigured some aspects of the subsequent American

Revolution, since it was also a movement for national independence. Like the English Civil War and French Revolution, it resulted in a republic, also known as the United Provinces of the Netherlands. Here as elsewhere, taxation and religion mixed. The Dutch did not want to subsidize Spanish conquests or remain under Catholic rule. As Lauro Martines put it, it was 'evangelical Calvinism in all-out battle against Catholics'.[54] The aim, at first, was to have a Protestant monarch. At one stage even Queen Elizabeth was offered the Dutch crown, but she refused, being reluctant to get involved in a potential conflict with Spain. Eventually, *faute de mieux*, the Dutch Republic was born.

Had it happened in the nineteenth century, the Dutch Revolt would have been called a revolution. It contained the typical characteristics: the refusal to pay taxes without being represented, religious disputes, the implicit rejection of the divine right of kings (in this case the right of the Spanish king, formal ruler of the Low Countries), and a striving for national independence. The war with Spain ended on 30 January 1648, with the Treaty of Münster between Spain and the Netherlands – part of the Peace of Westphalia which concluded the Thirty Years' War, one of the most devastating European wars ever. The Dutch Republic was now recognized as an independent state and became a prosperous commercial and colonial power, unlike the (Catholic) Southern Netherlands which remained under Spanish rule. The paradox is that after the Napoleonic Wars, the republic was abandoned and the Netherlands became a monarchy, as it still is today.

The age of *rivoluzioni*

The term 'revolution', in the modern sense, began to appear sporadically – mainly in Italy, and very sparingly.[55] The dictionary of the Accademia della Crusca, the first in Europe and the model for dictionaries in France, Spain and England, in its first edition (1612) defined *revoluzione* (also *Rivoltura*) as 'rivolgimento, mutazione di stato' (change of state, of regime).[56]

Machiavelli uses the term only once in *Il Principe*, mainly in the sense of 'convulsions' plaguing Italy.[57] Luca Assarino, a successful Italian novelist born in Bolivia, published his *Delle rivoluzioni di Catalogna* in 1644. Placido Reina, a Sicilian, wrote *Delle rivoluzioni della città di Palermo* (1649); Giovanni Battista Birago Avogadro, a Genoese, wrote his *Turbolenze d'Europa dall'anno 1640 fino al 1650* (1654) without using the word 'rivoluzioni', but his *Historia della disunione del regno di Portogallo dalla corona di Castiglia* (1644) became *Historia delle rivoluzioni del regno di Portogallo* when his Geneva publisher inserted the term *rivoluzioni* in 1646. The 1647 tax revolt in Naples led by Masaniello against the Spaniards gave an impetus for more books on revolution: Galeazzo Gualdo Priorato, who was at the court of Louis XIV, wrote *Histoire des révolutions et mouvements de Naples* (1654), followed by Agostino Nicolai's *Historia, o vero narrazione giornale dell'ultime rivoluzioni della città e regno di Napoli*, published in Amsterdam in 1660.[58]

Of greater importance was Alessandro Giraffi's *Le rivolvtioni di Napoli* (1647), though in the text he uses the expression 'tumult', with 'revolution' appearing only in the title.[59] For the first ten days (7–17 July 1647) the Neapolitan revolt was a genuine popular rebellion. When Masaniello was murdered on 13 July, a second revolution followed. A republic was proclaimed in October but lasted only a few months. By April 1648 the Spanish crown was back in control.[60] The event appeared frequently in popular culture and famously in one of the first French grand operas, *La Muette de Portici* by Daniel Auber (1828). Its performance in Brussels was allegedly the spark for the Belgian Revolution of 1830.

In 1649, Robert Monteith of Salmonet, a Scottish Catholic exile in France, published *Histoire des troubles de la Grand' Bretagne* dealing with the years leading up to the English Civil War. He claimed that of all the revolutions of this century, the British example was the most important, the strangest and the most disastrous.[61] But 'revolution' in the political sense appears only once; instead, 'troubles' is the chosen word.

The war which enabled Portugal to re-establish its independence from Spain could have been called the Revolution of 1640 or the War of Independence, but the common term is the Portuguese Restoration War, with 'independence' occasionally added (*Guerra da Restauração da Independência*). The conflict was concluded in 1668 with the Treaty of Lisbon, which led the House of Braganza to occupy the Portuguese throne.

In 1639, the French physician and librarian Gabriel Naudé published his *Considérations politiques sur les coups d'État*, but for him 'coup d'état' did not have today's connotations. For Naudé it meant justified repression from on high, as in 'the state striking the people'. One of his many examples was the massacre of Saint Barthélemy of August 1572, when thousands of Protestants were butchered by intransigent Catholics with the encouragement of King Charles IX (or his mother Catherine de' Medici, or his brother, the future Henri III, or the Duc de Guise – there is no consensus). Naudé's criticism was that *le massacre* should have gone further: it failed to kill *all* the Huguenots.[62] Following his own interpretation of Machiavelli, Naudé urged the ruler to lie to the people in order to sway it. The common people, he explained, are 'always stupid and of weak understanding'. They easily follow 'the false prophets, the seditious, the superstitious, the ambitious', are always ready to rebel, always angry and everything they say is false and absurd, 'everything they condemn is good, everything they approve is wicked, everything they praise is disgraceful and everything they do pure folly'.[63]

'Power to the people' was a horrifying thought. An anonymous pamphlet printed in England during Cromwell's rule, *Britania Triumphalis: A Brief History of the Warres and Other State-Affairs of Great Britain*, blamed the people for the tumults while conceding the corruption, pride and avarice of the Court:

> The first and generall Cause was the Sinnes of the Pople, who ... growing wanton whereby, gaz'd after novelty (that Magneticall attraction of the Plebeian rout) ... sought felicity in things they wanted, and were still unsatisfied even in the accomplishment thereof: whence it occasioned the hatred of tranquillity, the desire of motion, the loathing of present things, and seeking after future.[64]

With the English Civil War – or to be more precise, Civil Wars, since Scotland and Ireland were also involved – we enter a more consolidated period of modern revolutions, though the term was not used in the modern sense until the Glorious Revolution of 1688, which was hardly a revolution at all. The Civil War led to the abolition of the monarchy, execution of Charles I and establishment of Oliver Cromwell's Commonwealth – by any definition a real revolution. In his speech to the first Protectorate Parliament, Cromwell described it as 'a thing of God'.[65] The historian Edward Hyde (Lord Clarendon), pro-monarchist author of one of the first texts on the conflict, called it 'rebellion'.

'All things runne around'

The seventeenth century was a period of such global conflict that historians discuss what Eric Hobsbawm called 'the Crisis of the Seventeenth Century', which, in his view, signalled the last phase of the transition from a feudal to a capitalist economy. Was it a revolution? The debate was taken up by Hugh Trevor-Roper, J. H. Elliott, Keith Thomas and others. No consensus was ever reached.[66] All agreed that the seventeenth century had been an unusually tormented century. It had seen the English Civil War, the Thirty Years' War in Europe (the bloodiest war before the Napoleonic Wars), years of virtual civil war in France between members of the nobility and Louis XIV (the so-called Fronde), revolts in Catalonia and Portugal, and in Sicily and Naples, and dramatic changes in China and Japan. Writers talk of troubles, civil war, conspiracy, revolt and upheaval, but seldom of revolution.[67]

In most European languages the term 'revolution' was, of course, originally used in the context of natural phenomena, as per Copernicus's *On the Revolution of Celestial Spheres* (1543). However, in astronomy, a revolution occurs when the body in question returns to its original position – quite unlike the modern political conception of an old world disappearing for good in favour of a new social order. In 1605 the historian William Camden, in his *Remaines of a Greater Worke, Concerning Britaine*, employed the word in a cyclical sense when he wrote: 'All things runne round; and as the seasons of the year; so men's manners have their revolutions.'[68] In 1660, on the other hand, Matthew Wren, a royalist, referred to 'waves of revolution' in the English Civil War.[69]

Then it became a metaphor for a 'world turned upside down', to use the title of Christopher Hill's classic book of 1972. Those who, in Hill's account, sought to 'turn the world upside down' in seventeenth-century England were Gerrard Winstanley's 'True Levellers' or Diggers, along with the Ranters, Seekers and other political and religious sects. They failed to change the world or turn it upside down, though their ideas outlasted them. The subtitle of Hill's book indicated that their radicalism co-existed with a wider event known as the English Revolution. As Hill explains:

> There were, we may oversimplify, two revolutions in the mid-seventeenth century England. The one which succeeded established the sacred rights of property (abolition of feudal tenures, no arbitrary taxation), gave political power to the propertied (sovereignty of Parliament and common law, abolition of prerogative courts), and removed all impediment to the triumph of the ideology of the men of property – the Protestant ethic. There was, however, another revolution which never happened, though time to time it threatened.[70]

'The world turned upside down' had a pejorative connotation, and those who sought such a goal were seen unfavourably. Even in the

Cover of the pamphlet *The World Turn'd Upside Down,* attributed to John Taylor

relatively peaceful Elizabethan era, poets such as Michael Drayton lamented the prevailing 'confusion' when one cannot know 'what to approve, or what to disallow':

> All arsey varsey, nothing is it's owne,
> But to our proverbe, all turnd upside downe.[71]

A Civil War–era ballad called 'The World Turned Upside Down' and published in 1646 had as its subtitle 'a brief description of the ridiculous fashions of these distracted times'. The cover depicts a man with gloved hands where shoes should be and boots where hands should be, while in the background, fish fly, a horse whips a cart, a cart pulls a man, and a church hangs upside down.

Hill used this image as the cover of his own book, though the pamphlet in question did not decry the rule of the rich and powerful. On the contrary, it was, presumably, a royalist protest against the puritanical decision of the Long Parliament to tone down the merriment associated with Christmas:

Listen to me and you shall hear, news hath not been this thousand year:
... Old Christmas is kicked out of Town.
Yet let's be content, and the times lament, you see the world turn'd
    upside down.
...
The wise men did rejoice to see our Saviour Christ Nativity:
The Angels did good tidings bring, the Shepherds did rejoice and sing.
Let all honest men, take example by them.
Why should we from good Laws be bound?
Yet let's be content, and the times lament, you see the world turn'd
    upside down.[72]

It was a defence of the 'old days'. We find a similar fear of the new in the Acts of the Apostles, though this fear is attributed to Jews antagonistic to a new creed, Christianity. The text tells that when Paul arrived in Thessaloniki, he argued with Jews for three weeks trying to convince them that Christ had come to redeem them and that they should embrace the new faith. Some were persuaded but others 'were jealous', and organized 'wicked fellows of the rabble' to drag some of Paul's followers before the city authorities, accusing them of having 'turned the world upside down' – which in a way was quite true.[73]

Salons and piazzas

By 1789, *révolution* was widely used by French revolutionaries as well as by their opponents. Montesquieu used the term frequently in his *De l'esprit des lois* (1758), by which he usually meant a change of regime. He writes that China had twenty-two 'revolutions' because it had twenty-two dynasties.[74]

Some reforms were heralded as revolutions before the real revolution had occurred. René-Nicolas de Maupeou, chancellor of France under Louis XV between 1768 and 1774, attempted to strengthen and centralize the monarchy against the aristocracy and judiciary. On 19 January 1771, magistrates were awakened by guards in the middle of the night and asked to sign a statement of loyalty to the king. This event, of relatively minor importance, was often referred as the Maupeon Revolution, including by Maupeon himself.[75]

Coups d'état were also dubbed revolution. In the Swedish Revolution of 1772, Gustav III re-introduced absolute monarchical rule against the

Riksdag, a representative chamber of the main estates. This ended the so-called Age of Liberty, which had been established in 1719 after a string of military defeats. Montesquieu had praised Sweden in his *De l'esprit des lois* (1748) as the home of European liberties, the 'factory of those instruments which break the shackles forged in the South', while Voltaire's *Essai sur les moeurs* (1756) called Sweden 'the freest kingdom on earth'.[76] What occurred in 1772, when Gustav took over, was seen as a bloodless coup d'état. He had become a de facto absolute monarch, though not in the juridical sense.[77] Deeply influenced as he was by Enlightenment philosophers, Gustav was an enlightened despot who oversaw a flowering of the arts and extended some limited religious toleration to Roman Catholics and Jews. He was assassinated in 1792 by a disgruntled aristocrat, an event which inspired Verdi's 1859 opera *Un ballo in maschera* (which, for censorship reasons, had to be set in colonial Boston). Popular participation in these events was minimal. It had been a *rivoluzione passiva*, to use the term of southern Italian historian Vincenzo Cuoco in his remarkable *Saggio storico sulla rivoluzione napoletana del 1799*. 'Passive revolution' was famously taken up by Antonio Gramsci in his *Prison Notebooks*, where he used the term quite differently.

Cuoco's Neapolitan Revolution of 1799 – by then the term was frequently used – could only take place because of the Napoleonic invasion of Italy. It did not last more than a few months, and Cuoco analysed the causes of the defeat. The main one is that the revolutionary elites did not even try to obtain the support of the people, the *lazzaroni* or lower orders, who instead defended the old regime. The gap between the elites and the people was enormous, Cuoco explained. The 'Neapolitan nation' was divided into two peoples, who appeared to live in different eras, even different climates. The culture of the educated classes was a mere imitation of that of foreigners, the English and French, while the people had remained Neapolitan and uneducated. Revolutions could not take place in the salons, but in the piazza, where leaders and led could bridge their differences and understand each other.[78]

Cuoco was highlighting a central peculiarity of what many call, after Marx, 'bourgeois' revolution. The bourgeoisie must dislodge the upper classes – the aristocracy, nobility, ancien régime – and to do so it must either have the clear support of the lower orders (proletariat or peasantry) or at least ensure that they will remain supine. Marx was often scathing about the possibilities that the bourgeoisie would be able to make a revolution. Even when the middle classes obtain a major reform, such as the repeal of the Corn Laws in England in 1846, they must be aware, he warned in the pages of the *New York Daily Tribune*, that while the aristocracy is the bourgeoisie's 'vanishing opponent, the working class is their arising enemy'.[79] Revolutions have hardly ever been achieved by members of the industrial capitalist class. They may have ended up benefiting the bourgeoisie, but it does not follow that the bourgeoisie made them. Their leaders were often intellectuals, merchants, professionals and aristocrats, as we will see. They did not consciously work for the establishment of capitalism, but for civil liberties and a less authoritarian form of government.

Imagining revolution

Thanks to the French Revolution, the term 'revolution' acquired a somewhat positive connotation, and during the nineteenth century its use was expanded to describe any tumultuous uprising, some of which were successful and many unsuccessful. Italy and Germany were the most successful so-called national revolutions, accomplished largely thanks to the leading states within each of the two territories, though in the Italian case with considerable help from Giuseppe Garibaldi, France and Prussia. In the rest of Europe, nationalism succeeded when the Great Powers intervened; these cannot be considered *real* popular revolutions.

In Greece there was an uprising against Ottoman rule in 1821. Success arose only when Great Britain, France and Russia intervened in 1827, yet the process was commonly referred to as the Greek Revolution, even at the time. By 1830 Greece had become an independent state, though its first king, Otto of Bavaria, was German, imposed by the British.

Leopold von Ranke reached for the term 'revolution' in his *Die Serbische Revolution*, about the First Serbian Uprising against the Ottomans (1804). It was unsuccessful, though the second uprising led to de facto independence. Full independence was obtained only in 1878 through the Congress of Berlin.

The formation of the Belgian state was also bestowed with the appellation 'revolution' by Charles Frederick Henningsen in his *Scenes from the Belgian Revolution* (1832) and by Charles White in his 1835 *Scenes from the Belgic* [sic] *Revolution*. White was English, while Henningsen had a Danish father and an Irish mother; the latter participated in revolutions and civil wars in various countries, including Spain, Hungary and the US (on the side of the southern Confederates).

The November Uprising of 1830–31 in Poland against the Tsarist

Empire was soon dubbed the Polish Revolution by contemporaries such as Joseph Hordynski, author of *History of the Late Polish Revolution* (1832) and a participant in the military campaign on the side of the insurgents. What was rebellion for opponents became revolution for supporters.

Muhammad Ali, of Albanian origin, and regarded by some as the 'father of modern Egypt' and its de facto ruler, attempted to modernize Egypt in the first half of the nineteenth century when it was under Ottoman rule. His endeavours were regarded by Andrew Archibald Paton, a diplomat and writer, as a 'social and commercial revolution'.[80] It led to a dynasty which lasted until 1952. Its history was briefly interrupted by the 'Urabi revolt (1879–82), also known as the 'Urabi Revolution, led by Colonel Ahmed 'Urabi. It failed, and Egypt remained under de facto British control. The 1952 coup d'état led by army officers under Mohammed Naguib and Gamal Abdel Nasser was sometimes referred to as 'the Egyptian revolution of 1952' because of its 'progressive look', and since it overthrew a monarch (King Farouk) and had been sparked by riots in Cairo.

The Irish War of Independence against the British was seldom called a revolution, though it had many of the characteristics of one.[81] In 1916 there was a failed Easter Rising against British rule, also known as the Irish Rebellion. In December 1918, Sinn Féin, having won the election, declared independence. A conflict with the British followed. Eventually, in 1921, a treaty was signed and Ireland was partitioned: the North with its Protestant majority (but a significant Catholic minority) remained part of the United Kingdom, while an independent Ireland was established in the South, initially called the Irish Free State. An eleven-month civil war ensued between those who accepted partition and those (including Sinn Féin under Éamon de Valera) who did not. This civil war exacted as many casualties as the actual war of independence.

The protracted Vietnamese struggle against French and American colonialism is another revolution that is rarely described as such. After Japan's defeat in August 1945, the Communists under Ho Chi Minh established themselves in the northern part of the country. A new conflict resumed against the French until the internationally recognized Geneva Accords of 1954 instituted what should have been a temporary division of the country. Soon the conflict continued between the Communist North and the Western-backed anti-Communists in the South. American intervention ensured that the Communist victory would be delayed by some thirty years. It was only in April 1975 that the country could be unified under Communist rule.

Religion and modernity

The change of regime undergone by Italy at the end of the Second World War – the passage from a monarchy to a republic – was never described as a revolution. By contrast, the events that took place in Iran in 1979, when the shah was ousted and the Ayatollah Khomeini seized power, are often referred to as the Islamic or Iranian Revolution – the first and (so far) the only modern revolution led by a religious leader. The shah himself, Mohammad Reza Pahlavi, had initiated in 1963 what he called a White Revolution, essentially a modernization of the country not so dissimilar from that promulgated in the 1920s by the Turkish leader Mustafa Kemal (Atatürk or Father of the Turks, after surnames were introduced in 1934). The latter, however, went much further.

Atatürk had come into power after the First World War when the Ottoman and Habsburg empires were dismembered and that of the tsar fell into the hands of revolutionaries. His advent to power resembled a coup d'état rather than a revolution, but one should not discount the popular support Atatürk was able to obtain and how he was able to boost the much undermined Turkish national self-esteem.[82] Kemalist anti-clericalism, though never intending to eliminate Islam, was based on the belief that civilization meant Western civilization.[83] Modernization, which had been embraced previously by members of the Ottoman elites, proceeded apace throughout the 1920s: the monarchy gave way to a republic; religious schools were abolished; the turban and the fez were outlawed; the Christian-era calendar was adopted; the Latin script was to be used instead of the Arabic; religious schools were abolished; laws favouring the emancipation of women were enacted; laws establishing Islam as the state religion were abolished; and the Swiss civil and Italian penal codes were adopted.[84] Kemal championed women's rights, presumably as a symbol of modernization. By the end of 1934, women had full political rights. The adoption of the Swiss Civil Code meant that women had relative equality with men in marriage, divorce and inheritance (though women could not vote in Switzerland until 1971, much later than in most European countries).[85] Atatürk even created an opposition party to create the semblance of a Western democracy.[86]

Modernizers sought to modernize without eradicating their own culture. In Japan, the overthrow of the shogunate – a hereditary military dictatorship – in 1868 and the development of a modernizing, Western-leaning political system was called the Meiji Restoration, and not the Meiji revolution. The actual Japanese term for "restoration", *Ishin*, originates from the two Chinese characters for continuity and renewal.[87] Japan could be turned into a modern nation-state by revitalizing its traditions in the light of Western examples, giving modernization the appearance of a return to the past. 'The Meiji Restoration was a revolution,' writes Mark Ravina, 'but its bold innovations were grounded in precedents from the ancient imperial state. The leaders of the Restoration ransacked the Japanese past in the search for the Japanese future.'[88]

The slogan of Chinese reformers at the turn of the century – 'import from the West its practice not its ideas' – is at the heart of the formula (*tǐ-yòng*) popularized by Zhang Zhidong in his *Exhortation to Learning* (1898), where he argued: 'The old learning is the fundamental thing; the new learning is for practical use.' The old learning was China's; it was fundamental (*tǐ*). The practical (*yòng*) knowledge was Western.[89] Turkey followed this near-universal model: 'A patriotic Turk should try to achieve a balance between the benefits of the West and the East by opting for adopting the science and technology of the former and the spirituality of the latter.'[90] Kemalism did not have a strong ideology, and there was no attempt to export it. It was mainly about modernity, like the Meiji Restoration, but without a clear economic programme.

The so-called Kemalist Revolution was, by the standards of the twentieth century, relatively peaceful. The number of those killed during the seizure of power and subsequently amounted to a few thousand. It was an authoritarian dictatorship, but the crushing of a rebellion in Kurdistan in 1925 or the Menemen Incident of 1930 were not particularly bloody.

What the revolutions promulgated by the shah and Atatürk had in common was, above all, the secularization of the country. The shah's modernization mainly helped the urban middle classes, but carried with it a failed land reform, increased inequality despite surging oil revenues, an unpopular pandering to the US, and repression. The shah himself had maintained his rule largely thanks to Anglo-American intervention when, in 1953, he overthrew the democratically elected government led by Mohammad Mosaddegh.

The Islamic Revolution of 1979 was the result of an unstable coalition between liberals and religious leaders, as the Ayatollah Ruhollah Khomeini had at first toned down his theocratic outlook and was backed by *bazaari* merchants. In fact, Khomeini, writing in 1988 just before his death, declared that the state had priority over Islamic law.[91] The war with Iraq (1980–88) – initiated by Saddam Hussein's Iraq with considerable Western support, including that of the US – led to a stalemate but also to the final ousting of the liberal elements in Iran and the further strengthening of Islamic state power.

The Iranian case appeared to be something more like a real revolution. The monarchy – in practice, a modern dictatorship – was abolished. The Grand Bazaar of Tehran, home of the lower-middle classes, played a central role in the revolution of 1979, since for them (and for the shah), modernity meant the end of the bazaar, while, in the early stages of the Islamic Republic, the Ayatollah Khomeini declared: 'We must preserve the bazaar with all our might; in return the bazaar must preserve the government.'[92] Today, though still an important pillar of Iranian religious conservatism, the Bazaar is a much weakened force. Such a paradox – the revolutionaries losing when the revolution is past its peak – is not uncommon. Modernization could not be avoided. The traditional Islamic government transformed the Bazaar's organization, introducing contractually based exchanges and the shift to more manufactured and standardized goods.[93]

So the Iranian Revolution managed to be a modern revolution (nationalist and republican) *and* a return to Islamic values. The contradiction between modernity and the imposition of religious precepts has been increasingly difficult to resolve, perhaps because it cannot be resolved. The ambition, as in the case of the French and Russian revolutions, was to export it to the rest of the world, or at least to the rest of the Middle East. It led to not insignificant changes in the economy and was accompanied by a major expansion of education.[94] This came, however, with the imposition of the hijab in 1983: not wearing it could lead to a punishment of up to seventy-four lashes, with jail and fines eventually replacing flogging. By 2022, such laws had led to a strong popular protest movement.

Reformism?

The question of *reform or revolution* has been part of the history of politics, and of the left in particular, since at least the days of the French Revolution. Common usage suggests that reform seeks somehow to make something better while preserving its essence. Reform appears to be peaceful and common while revolution is violent and exceptional, which is why most people would side with the reformists most of the time. As Hobsbawm remarked: 'The times when ordinary people want a revolution, let alone make one, are unusual.'[95] The appeal of reform is such that revolutionaries themselves are usually forced to advocate it, either to show that if reform fails, nothing will change without a violent upheaval, or to attract to their ranks those who are not yet revolutionaries but who want change.

Reform, of course, does not mean much without a context. It is a generic name for change. It could refer to universal suffrage, or equal rights for women, people of colour or LGBTQ people, or greater powers for parliaments, or a statutory limit to the working day, or taxing the rich, or tariffs to protect domestic industry, or free trade to help exports, or abolishing privileges of the powerful, or revitalizing a religion, or regulating (or deregulating) the economy – the list is endless. Some of these goals, such as female suffrage, were achieved with little or no violence. In some cases, to achieve greater powers for parliaments required considerable violence.

When reformists fail, revolutionaries advance, but eventually they reach a situation that might already have been achieved had reforms been implemented in the first place. This, of course, is the reformists' favourite argument: revolutions are useless. In a rather ahistorical passage, Hannah Arendt maintained that:

> To our sorrow ... freedom has been better preserved in countries where no revolution ever broke out, no matter how outrageous the circumstances of the powers that be, and ... there exist more civil liberties even in countries where the revolution was defeated than in those where revolutions have been victorious.[96]

She was obviously not thinking of Nazi Germany or Fascist Italy.

And yes – revolutions are bloody and violent affairs, but so (indeed, more so) are wars. Wars are often glorified more than revolutions, as shown by the numerous memorials in so many Western countries remembering the dead of the First and Second World Wars, or of the American Civil War.[97] People are willing to kill and to die for the cause of the revolution, but also for the motherland, or for God.

Reactionaries in the strict sense of the word will always lose, since nothing can stand still for very long. Some revolutionary changes did not last long, but there was never a return to the ante-revolutionary status. The English Civil War resulted, eventually, in a constitutional monarchical regime which Charles I could have conceded, thus saving his head. In France, after the years of Terror and the Napoleonic interlude there was a constitutional monarchy (first Bourbon, then the more liberal Orléans), a regime similar to that of Louis XVI in 1789 when he had appeared to accept a limit to his powers. In America, the Thirteen Colonies, once independent from Great Britain, did not change in a dramatic way the order of things even under a new elaborate constitution, though more states were added. The Civil War changed matters much more. In Russia, the Bolsheviks failed to establish anything resembling a socialist society, though they developed an industrial society (the purported task of the bourgeois revolution). The Chinese, after 'great leaps forward' and 'cultural revolutions', ended up with an authoritarian but thriving market economy which lifted millions from poverty, and which they called 'socialism with Chinese characteristics'.

Most of the reforms of the nineteenth and twentieth century survived: the slave trade and slavery, once abolished, never legally re-emerged; the suffrage once expanded was never restricted; once women obtained the vote, they kept it; welfare was seldom seriously retrenched; homosexuality, when legalized, was never re-criminalized; colonies, having acquired their independence, remained independent; monarchies, if abolished, usually remained obsolete (some exceptions occurred, for instance France in the nineteenth century and Greece and Cambodia in the twentieth, but republican rule returned in all of them). Eventually the French Republic was recognized by most French Catholics. In America most southerners, accepted, sometimes grudgingly, the outcome of the Civil War.

In history not that much can be undone. Change is a historical constant; it has greater appeal than stasis. If change is for the better, reformists as well as revolutionaries are encouraged; if it is for the worse, some will lament the good old days and advocate a return to the status quo ante, which isn't easily accomplished. Of course, at any given moment, some things cannot be changed. So, reformists and revolutionaries must learn to navigate between what can and can't be done, at least in the foreseeable future. Discovering one's scope for manoeuvre is central to the art of politics. Writing a few years after the start of the so-called Terror, the French politician Antoine Boulay de la Meurthe wrote, in an essay on the English Civil War: 'The great art, in revolutions, is to reach one's goal doing the least possible harm.'[98]

Those members of the establishment in Britain who supported the Representation of the People Act 1832, which extended the suffrage, argued that it was the most effective way to prevent a revolution. As the historian and Whig politician Thomas Babington Macaulay explained in the House of Commons on 2 March 1831:

Let us know our interest and our duty better. Turn where we may, within, around, the voice of great events is proclaiming to us, Reform, that you may preserve ... I oppose universal suffrage, because I think that it would produce a destructive revolution. I support this measure, because I am sure that it is our best security against a revolution.[99]

In an earlier debate the prime minister, Lord Grey, had declared: 'My great object is the desire of preventing that which ... must always be *regarded* the greatest of all possible political evils. The principle of my reform is to prevent the necessity of revolution.'[100] The need to do so was made evident by riots which took place after a suffrage bill was defeated in Parliament in October 1831.

Similar language was used in a different context by US Senator John Sherman when in 1890 he introduced the Sherman Antitrust Act to prevent the further development of large corporations. His outlook reflected that of small producers when he declared that unless one heeded the complaints of the people who were feeling the negative impact of the giant corporations, they would turn to 'the socialist, the communist, and the nihilist'.[101]

At roughly the same time, in China, the prominent reformer Kang Youwei – who was close to the young Guangxu Emperor and one of the architects of the failed Hundred Days' Reform – used the example of the French Revolution ('swimming in blood') as a warning against those who wished to block reforms.[102] In a later essay on the French Revolution written in 1906, Kang Youwei described the French Revolution as chaos, a catastrophe to be avoided by implementing reforms on time.[103]

Land reform – government expropriation of large tracts of land from the wealthy and redistribution to the rural poor – was occasionally achieved as part of a revolution, but more commonly by a state wishing to avoid troubles and tumults. Examples from elsewhere, for instance the Cuban Revolution of 1959, might occasionally have encouraged even some conservative governments to pursue land reform: the 1960s through to the 1980s saw the peak of redistributive land reform in Latin America. Most land reforms were not the results of revolutions; in fact, they were often initiated by elites, though in some cases (Mexico), a peasant uprising pushed them to start the reform.[104] The most successful instances, such as those of Taiwan and South Korea, were the result of a strong interventionist state able to act without having to face the opposition of landlords, swept from power in previous wars, unlike in Latin America where such reforms faced well-organized landed interests.[105]

The rebellions of 1837–38 in the British colonies of Upper and Lower Canada witnessed a series of armed insurrections against corrupt local governance. The uprisings were crushed, but they incentivized London to commission Lord Durham to produce the *Report on the Affairs of British North America* (1839), which led to the 1840 Act of Union and eventually to self-government and greater democratic control.[106] Would such reforms have taken place without the uprisings?

Revolutions are simply means to achieve change when mere reforms are not possible or sufficient. They are supposed to establish something entirely new, to abolish the old, to change political and economic structures in a radical manner, and they are often accompanied by a violent shock or an uprising. Though revolutions are always the work of minorities, they need to have considerable popular support to distinguish themselves from a power grab or a coup d'état. But these are vague terms: what is *new*, or *radical*? It is part of the self-congratulatory element of the common view of British history that the country has undergone major changes without a revolution, at least over the last three hundred years. Major changes, if achieved gradually, are not regarded as revolutionary. Few would argue that Britain in 2025 was only marginally different from Britain at the end of the Napoleonic Wars in 1815, or that France at the beginning of the Third Republic in 1870 was the same as France today, though it is still a republic. So what matters is not just that there should be change but that it should be tied to a radical event.

Many reformists, of course, such as the Fabians in Great Britain or Edward Bernstein in Germany or Filippo Turati in Italy, thought that capitalism could be supplanted slowly, almost imperceptibly, one step at a time. Even Karl Kautsky, Bernstein's great rival, assumed that reforms would simply bring the final collapse of capitalism nearer, and eventually capitalism would be turned into socialism. The programme of the Second International founded in 1889 had a long list of desirable reforms to be achieved before the revolution: universal suffrage; the eight-hour day; separation of church and state; and state welfare.

As Tocqueville pointed out: 'It is not always going from bad to worse that leads to revolution.' People often put up with oppressive laws without complaint, only to reject them when the burden is alleviated.

> The regime that a revolution destroys is almost always better than the one that immediately preceded it, and experience teaches that the most dangerous time for a bad government is usually when it begins to reform …

> The evil that one endures patiently because it seems inevitable becomes unbearable the moment its elimination becomes conceivable.[107]

In other words, there is a right time and speed for reforms, just as for revolution and for repression. Otto von Bismarck, as one of the most intelligent statesmen of the nineteenth century, knew only too well that occasionally it paid to pre-empt undesirable changes by taking command of them. Faced with the consequences of the liberal-national revolutions of 1848, he declared: 'Pressure from abroad will compel us to proclaim the German constitution of 1849 and to adopt truly revolutionary measures. If there is to be revolution, we would rather make it than suffer it.'[108]

Joining a revolution to stop one

No one can foresee the long-term consequences of change, not even intelligent conservatives. Take the most famous passage of the novel *Il Gattopardo* by Giuseppe Tomasi di Lampedusa – or *The Leopard*, to use its incorrect English title (a *gattopardo* is not a leopard but the African wild cat, or serval, which adorns the coat of arms of the noble Sicilian family of the Prince of Salina, the main protagonist of the novel). We are in Sicily in 1860. The country is part of the so-called Kingdom of the Two Sicilies, with Naples as its capital. Giuseppe Garibaldi has just landed with the aim of liberating the South and uniting it with the rest of Italy. The Prince of Salina adores his nephew Tancredi, whom he regards as his 'real son'. When Tancredi tells him that he is about to join the *garibaldini*, the prince is horrified: 'You are mad, my boy! Going with these people! They are all troublemakers and mafiosi.'

The prince is poised between two worlds. He is conscious that he belongs to a noble family whose privileges he enjoys, but he realizes that this age belongs to the past. So he accepts Tancredi's famous riposte: 'Unless we ourselves take a hand now, they'll foist a republic on us. If we want things to stay as they are, things will have to change.' Note the language. Tancredi does not regard himself as part of the Garibaldi forces. 'They' are there, hoping to conduct a real revolution, but when Tancredi says 'we' and 'us', he clearly defines himself as part of an aristocratic caste. He joins the revolution to stop the revolution, to make sure that 'nothing' changes. The nature of this *nothing* is obvious: it pertains to who wields political power in the real world. The author of the novel, writing in the aftermath of the Second World War, was only too aware that the power of the aristocracy had disappeared. Tancredi was unable to stop that change. Nothing remained the same.

The theme was not new. *The Viceroys* (*I Vicerè*), an 1894 novel by Federico De Roberto which obviously inspired *The Leopard*, also dealt with a dysfunctional aristocratic Sicilian family whose members are greedy, ambitious and devoid of principles or scruples, except for those who are demented (Ferdinando), self-destructive (Matilde) or mystically religious (Teresa). The desperate concluding judgement on the family by one of its members is unsparing: 'No, our race is not degenerate: it is always the same.'[109] They enter politics to keep everything as it was, to continue thieving as before and keep their power and their wealth. But eventually, their caste too is doomed. Its members may preserve positions and resources, but they do not retain power and, in the longer term, their regime does not persist.[110]

Neither revolutionaries nor reactionaries are in command of the future. Revolutionary crises happen, and some may be sparked by uprisings of one sort or another, but eventually organized revolutionaries must seize the day. If there are no organized revolutionaries, revolutions fail, as they did in Europe in 1848 and in the Middle East in 2011 (the so-called Arab Spring). As the leading American abolitionist and women's rights upholder Wendell Phillips famously declared, 'revolutions are not made, they come'; but the context of his statement made it clear that a group of people 'pledged to new ideas' is also necessary to achieve lasting change.[111] In his pamphlet on Louis Bonaparte, Karl Marx struck a middle path between voluntarism and structuralism when he wrote:

> Men make their own history, but they do not make it just as they please; they do not make it under circumstances chosen by themselves, but under circumstances directly encountered, given and transmitted from the past. The tradition of all the dead generations weighs like a nightmare on the brain of the living. And just when they seem engaged in revolutionizing themselves and things, in creating something that has never yet existed, precisely in such periods of revolutionary crisis they anxiously conjure up the spirits of the past to their service and borrow from them names, battle cries and costumes in order to present the new scene of world history in this time-honoured disguise and this borrowed language.[112]

What happens in a crisis depends on a multiplicity of factors, and not just on revolutionaries and counterrevolutionaries. Revolutions are usually initiated by a minority taking advantage of an exceptional conjuncture which they have not created. If the revolutionaries triumph, they must establish an authoritarian regime to convince others of the righteousness of their aims, or they must give power (usually through the suffrage) to the masses; but if the masses are not in tune with the revolutionary minority, a process which no one had foreseen may develop. Those who stood against Charles I did not know there would be a republic and a dictator (Cromwell), or the return of the Stuarts. The Americans who stood against the British over taxes and rights did not know the colonies would achieve independence. Those who stormed the Bastille could not possibly know that this would be the first step towards a republic, since all they wanted was the return of Jacques Necker, minister of finance, and the removal of mercenary troops from Paris. Nor could they possibly know that France, over the following century, would have to go through two dynasties, two empires and two republics before settling down with the Third Republic in 1870. Revolutions follow an unpredictable course. As the Russian novelist Mikhail Sholokhov wrote in his 1930s masterpiece *And Quiet Flows the Don*:

> When swept out of its normal channel, life scatters into innumerable streams. It is difficult to foresee which it will take in its treacherous and winding course. Where today it flows in shallows, like a rivulet over sandbanks, so shallow that the shoals are visible, tomorrow it will flow richly and fully.[113]

Seizing the state

If the state did not matter, if it were simply a superstructure full of lazy or cruel aristocrats unable and unwilling to do much for anyone, then revolutions would not have state power as an object. The seizure of power matters when government is for real: when it imposes taxes; wages wars; and seeks to maintain law and order. As David Hume explained, governments are 'one of the finest and most subtle inventions imaginable'. Thanks to governments and the finances they raise, 'bridges are built; harbours opened; ramparts raised; canals formed; fleet equipped; and armies disciplined'.[114] This is why the history of revolutions begins in earnest with the history of the state and the national economy – what we call capitalism. It is also why, in this book, revolutions are not sudden, short-lived events resolved in a few years. Instead, the purported original spark launches a process with new demands and grievances, even when the original ones have been resolved.

Thus one can argue, as I do, that the English Revolution began around 1640 when king and Parliament clashed over finance, and didn't end until around 1714 when the new monarch (George I) finally accepted that Parliament would be supreme: the monarch could 'reign but does not rule', to use the formula usually attributed to Thomas Babington Macaulay. The American Revolution originated in the 1760s when the settlers began to resist taxation from London and came to a close, if at all, with the Civil War a century later, when slavery was abolished. The French Revolution began on 5 May 1789 when the États Généraux were convened by Louis XVI at Versailles and concluded in 1870 when the Third Republic was declared, or else in 1880 when the new regime was consolidated.

Tocqueville, writing soon after the 1851 coup d'état of Louis Bonaparte made, as he often did, the right point: he thought that the advent of the liberal monarchy of Louis-Philippe in 1830 had only 'ended the first period of our revolutions, or, rather of our revolution, for there was only one – it was always the same ... whose beginnings our parents witnessed and whose end in all likelihood we will not live to see'.[115]

The Russian Revolution began in 1905 when a wave of popular unrest forced the tsar to concede some elements of parliamentary democracy. It continued in March 1917 when tsardom ended, and moved on apace in November 1917 when the Bolsheviks seized power and attempted to construct a socialist society. After seventy years this attempt was seen to have failed: in 1989–91 the Soviet Union, the continuation of the Tsarist Empire, was dismembered, and a form of capitalism emerged. This was the end of the Russian Revolution.

The Chinese Revolution can be said to start in 1911 when the Qing dynasty was overthrown and a republic established. This was followed by almost forty years of bloody internecine warfare and foreign invasions (by Japan) until the Communist People's Republic of China was declared in 1949. Successive attempts to construct a socialist society encountered severe problems, such the disastrous Great Leap Forward of 1958–62 and the quite disruptive Cultural Revolution of 1966–76. But unlike in Russia the Communist Party retained power and initiated a series of economic reforms under Deng Xiaoping aimed at developing socialism with 'Chinese characteristics' – in practice, a state-controlled market economy.

Since the term 'revolution' is so nebulous, Germans often use the equally vague term *Umwälzung* (upheaval). The view of revolutions I propose here tends to strike a middle way between the *longue durée* – the analysis of slowly evolving historical structures, imperceptibly changing over the centuries – and the *histoire évènementielle* or *le temps court*, the history of conjunctures or short burst of events. Fernand Braudel, who developed this famous analysis of historical times, disparagingly called the latter 'la plus capricieuse, la plus trompeuse des durées' (the *most capricious*, the *most deceptive* of time periods), the domain of mere chroniclers and journalists.[116] In this context Braudel explains that the French Revolution is only a 'moment' essential to the long history of the revolutionary and violent destiny of the West.[117]

My revolutions are neither the one nor the other. They are concerned with processes and structures. I am inspired by Braudel's *Plan B*, the intermediate level between *le temps court* (Plan A) and *the longue durée* (Plan C). *Plan B* deals with a longer conjuncture: ten, twenty, fifty years – perhaps more. I will try to avoid the temptation to treat the period preceding each revolution as one of *preparation*, because revolution usually arrives unexpectedly, catching the revolutionaries themselves by surprise, even though they have spent years or even decades preparing for the great moment. As Montesquieu explained, perhaps over-optimistically, any revolution which can be foreseen will never take place, for if foreseen it will be pre-empted by any intelligent politician.[118]

Revolutions are usually remembered in terms of a key date which can be celebrated, its often being established well after the event with triumphant intentions: the Fourth of July (US); the Fourteenth of July (France); the Great October Revolution (7 November, Russia); 1 October (China). One can, of course, debate dates endlessly, but they are mere indications of the possible beginning of a process or its conclusion – assuming anything in history can be said to have concluded. As the conservative historian and politician François Guizot declared to Parliament on 3 May 1819:

> Revolutions, gentlemen, take almost as many years to complete as to prepare; and well before the day they broke out, society was perturbed by a voiceless and painful struggle, and, long after revolutions seem to be finished, they disturb and torment governments and peoples.[119]

There is no date set for the beginning of the Middle Ages or its end, or the beginning of the Renaissance, or the start of capitalism. Processes, almost by definition, do not have clear beginnings, let alone clear ends.

1
The English Civil War

There is no memorable date on which to celebrate the English Civil War. There is no equivalent of 4 July (1776) when the representatives of the settlers in the American colonies convened in Philadelphia to sign the Declaration of Independence; no equivalent of 14 July (1789), the day of the *prise de la Bastille*; no equivalent of 7 November (1917) when the Bolsheviks stormed the Winter Palace in Petrograd; or of 1 October (1949) when Mao Zedong proclaimed the People's Republic of China. England lacks such foundation dates around which nationalism could fasten and the hearts of schoolchildren and patriots could flutter. The day 30 January 1649 means nothing to most people, yet on that morning Parliament, the new supreme power in England, ruled that it was henceforth illegal to proclaim a new king, thus declaring, in practice, the birth of a republic. A few hours later, Charles I, king of England, Scotland and Ireland, was executed.

Oliver Cromwell, the regicide, is not much celebrated by posterity. The monarchy returned in 1660 with Charles II, son of the executed king. Cromwell's body (along with that of John Bradshaw, president of the tribunal that convicted Charles I, and that of General Henry Ireton, Cromwell's son-in-law) was removed from Westminster Abbey in 1661, on the anniversary of Charles I's execution. The body was hanged at Tyburn near Marble Arch and the severed head was displayed on a pike above Westminster Hall, where it remained, rotting, for many years. Then, in 1899, 300 years after his birth, Cromwell was memorialized in a statue thanks to the support of Whig historians. This still stands just outside the House of Commons, near where his severed head had been exhibited. But Cromwell is still not a national hero like Garibaldi or George Washington, or Lajos Kossuth in Hungary.

In England, not even military figures such as Nelson and Wellington, or war leaders such as Lloyd George and Churchill, are remembered for specific dates. Nelson stands on a column in a square dedicated to his naval victory (Trafalgar), his 1799 massacre and crimes in Naples conveniently forgotten.[1] Wellington's famous victory is immortalized in a railway station (Waterloo), while the contribution of Prussian General Gebhard von Blücher to Napoleon's defeat on the battlefield is hardly ever acknowledged in Great Britain. At the time, Wellington had confessed: 'I shall not do justice to my feelings or to Marshal Blücher and the Prussian army, if I do not attribute the successful result of this arduous day, to the cordial and timely assistance I received from them.'[2]

In Liverpool there is John Lennon Airport, but William Ewart Gladstone, also a native of Merseyside, does not even get a bus station. Italy has airports named for Galileo Galilei (Pisa), Cristoforo Colombo (Genoa), Marco Polo (Venice) and Leonardo da Vinci (Rome). France's main airport in Paris is named after Charles de Gaulle.

Unlike France, the US, Russia and most other countries, the United Kingdom has no national day. There are religious days (Christmas, Easter), May Day and New Year's Day, and the days when banks are closed (bank holidays). No British historical date is celebrated. For almost two centuries, some royalist worshippers in England and Scotland prayed and fasted on 30 January in memory of Charles I. Then in 1859, state services and celebrations associated with 30 January were cancelled, as were those connected to the Restoration of Charles II and William of Orange's arrival in England. They had become offensive to Catholics and Nonconformists, and many Anglicans regarded them as outdated. The only historical date which has some present-day significance is 5 November, which marks the 1605 Catholic Gunpowder Plot to blow up Parliament, well before the Civil War. Guy Fawkes was tortured and, along with his fellow plotters, hanged, drawn and quartered. Children used to go door to door asking for 'a penny for the Guy'; the penny was supposed to be for the bonfire required to burn his effigy, but fortunately few children knew that.

Charles I and Cromwell

This chapter traces the long arc of English upheaval that began with the first battle of the Civil War at Edgehill in Warwickshire on 23 October 1642 and ended seven decades later with a Hanoverian prince being parachuted into an English throne on 1 August 1714, albeit with much reduced powers. I want to look at the ways contemporaries thought about these events and how they either held or shifted their ground as they navigated the tumult. I will also try to tease out the paradoxical connection between English liberties and English (later British) world power, particularly in relation to the slave trade.

At the inception of the English Revolution was a struggle between king and Parliament over taxation and finance. Since the days of Elizabeth I, the wealth of commercial interests had been increasing relative to that of the Crown, and it was widely held that the royal prerogative to raise levies was 'incompatible with popular liberty'.[3] National and religious questions also loomed large. One could almost say that the main cause of the English Civil War was the king's need to dominate Scotland (and Ireland).[4] Charles I's aim was to construct a strong unified state despite the religious differences between the Church of England and the Calvinist and Presbyterian Church of Scotland. The king antagonized Presbyterian Scotland by strengthening the High Anglican element of the Church of England, which led to open warfare. In 1640, after eleven years of personal rule, he finally convened a parliament at Westminster, hoping to obtain the necessary finance to pay for the war in Scotland. 'If the King had had money,' argued Thomas Hobbes in *Behemoth: The History of the Causes of the Civil Wars of England* (1681),

> he might have had soldiers enough in England. For there were very few of the common people that cared much for either of the causes, but would have taken any side for pay or plunder. But the King's treasury was very low, and his enemies ... had the command of the purses of the city of London, and of most cities and corporate towns in England, and of many particular persons besides.[5]

Hobbes was unambiguous: the Presbyterian merchant class of the City of London was an engine of revolution, for they hoped to build a state governed, like the Dutch Republic, by merchants for their own interests: 'The city of London and other great towns of trade, having in admiration the prosperity of the Low Countries ... were inclined to think that the like change of government here, would to them produce the like prosperity.'[6]

Christopher Hill boldly claimed that the English Civil War was 'a struggle for political, economic and religious power, waged by the middle class, the bourgeoisie, which grew in wealth and strength as capitalism developed'.[7] Of course there were capitalists in seventeenth-century England, but they were mainly agrarian capitalists. There were also tenant farmers, craftsmen and traders – a 'middling sort' who worked for their income, seen by some as a driving force behind the conflict.[8]

The issue of who were at the time the *active* popular masses has long perturbed scholars of the English Civil War. Hill noted:

> 'The people' themselves had no coherent shape or form or general will. Do they include the poor? Or only heads of households? Property owners? Freeholders? Copyholders? Vagabonds? Locke managed never to define 'the people' at all, though they are basic to his political philosophy.[9]

Conrad Russell, one of the so-called revisionist historians who have disputed any idea of a strong class basis for the Civil War, polemically entitled a collection of essays on the pre-war period *Unrevolutionary England, 1603–1642* (1990). The Civil War was in fact preceded by growing popular dissent and hostility towards the nobility, which David Cressy has termed a 'cultural revolution'.[10] And the second half of the seventeenth century saw constant social unrest, attempted revolutions and wars. This is why I argue that the English Revolution, once it gathered pace, did not truly come to a rest until the Hanoverian Succession.

In *Behemoth*, Hobbes notes the conflicting intrigues of papists who wished England to return to Rome through the king's party and of Presbyterians who thought that Parliament had a right to govern the whole nation, much as every minister should govern his parish without the interference of bishops. On 22 November 1641, Parliament, reluctant to relinquish money for the Scottish war, produced the so-called Grand Remonstrance, a list of grievances against the king.[11] While the Remonstrance, which consisted of 204 paragraphs, contained the odd conciliatory phrase – 'without the least intention to lay any blemish upon your royal person' – it also accused 'malignant parties' of working to the advantage of popery and bewailed the 'malicious designs of the Popish party'. MPs demanded that bishops should be deprived of their votes in Parliament. Twenty-two bishops constituted around one-third of the total membership of the House of Lords. The bishops, it was claimed, along with 'Jesuited Papists', councillors and courtiers, were working on behalf of foreign princes.[12]

The Grand Remonstrance insisted that Parliament should be allowed to veto royal appointments and that there should be no further sale of the land confiscated from Irish rebels. The document also contained frequent reminders of expenses paid to fight the Scottish and Irish wars. What is clear is that 'turning the world upside down' could not have been further from the intention of Parliament in 1641. MPs insisted that all they wished for was a return to ancient liberties. It is a recurrent pattern in politics: appearing to fight for something old which has been taken away. Machiavelli wrote in the *Discourse* that he who seeks to reform a state 'must at least retain the shadow semblance of the old forms; so that it may appear to the people that there has been no change ... even though in fact the new orders are in every way different from the old ones'; for, he added, 'mankind is satisfied with what appears as if it were real, and is often even moved more by the things that seem than by those that are'.[13] Marx developed the theme when, commenting on Louis Bonaparte's 1851 coup d'état, he observed how political leaders 'anxiously conjure up the spirits of the past to their service and borrow from them names, battle-cries ... in order to present the new scene of world history in this time-honoured disguise and this borrowed language'.[14]

The king replied to the Grand Remonstrance on 23 December, almost a month after it had been submitted to him. He was probably encouraged by the fact that Parliament was far from being united: the Grand Remonstrance had barely achieved a majority. He tried to appear conciliatory, re-affirming his desire to 'preserve the peace and safety of this kingdom from the design of the Popish party', but was immovable on the main demands. The bishops would remain in Parliament, which would not have the right to veto appointments by the Crown.[15] Since the two views were irreconcilable – either Parliament or the king had to have the final say – a clash was inevitable. Starting in 1642, a series of military conflicts pitted against each other those defending parliamentary power (the so-called Roundheads) and the monarchists (the Cavaliers). The Crown was weak since it did not have a standing army or even a stable bureaucracy.[16] The newly constituted New Model Army – commanded by Sir Thomas Fairfax and the politically astute Oliver Cromwell, purged of unreliable aristocratic leaders, and funded and recruited by Parliament – quickly became a formidable fighting force. By the standards of the seventeenth century, it possessed high morale strengthened by a distinctive collective religious consciousness and a novel spirit of egalitarianism.[17]

Even when defeated, Charles stubbornly refused to accept limitations to his powers, the kind of reform which would have turned the country into a constitutional monarchy. The parliamentarian forces were thus led to the brink of a real revolution, which might have occurred in 1647 when the New Model Army examined the 'Agreement of the People' proposed by John Lilburne's Agitators. The Agitators were called the Levellers by their opponents because of their egalitarianism. They mainly represented small producers (rural and urban) and were particularly strong in London. They wanted a virtually universal manhood suffrage (they would exclude servants, apprentices and labourers, all to be represented by the head of the household). Cromwell and Henry Ireton, on the other hand, wanted the suffrage to be based on landholding.

More revolutionary were Gerrard Winstanley's Diggers, who preferred the appellation of 'True Levellers'. Following their idiosyncratic interpretation of the Bible, they wanted shared ownership of land. Winstanley declared that the 'great creator' had 'made the earth to be a common treasury and man the lord was to govern this creation. But not one word was spoken in the beginning that one branch of mankind should rule over another.'[18] In the uncertain aftermath of the king's execution, Winstanley's Diggers threatened the local power bases of the landed ruling class because they addressed themselves to disaffected tenants and labourers, as well as to soldiers and Londoners.[19]

The reformists in and around Parliament were like the Mensheviks in 1917 Russia facing the more militant Bolsheviks; and in the late 1640s, these English Mensheviks prevailed. The New Model Army purged Parliament of those reluctant to condemn the king – about half the total membership of the House of Commons – giving rise to the so-called Rump Parliament. The Putney Debates were shut down by Cromwell and Ireton. The handful of Digger communes were cleared by zealous landowners. The radicals ultimately made relatively little impact on the development of English society, despite the efforts of historians to recuperate them.

After Charles's execution, the abolition of the House of Lords and the establishment of a Commonwealth of England, one could have talked of a revolution. Parliament scored another victory on 3 September 1651 when it defeated the forces loyal to Charles's son. In 1653 Cromwell became Lord Protector for life – in practice, a dictator – and he subsequently purged Parliament several times. The Rump Parliament was abolished in a coup d'état, Cromwell famously telling MPs: 'You have sat too long for any good you have been doing lately. Depart, I say; and let us have done with you. In the name of God go!' He had the Chamber cleared by troops. 'It was all over: Parliament was extinguished, as lifeless as an old candle', writes Cromwell's biographer, Antonia Fraser, quoting Elias Ashmole, a royalist.[20] Cromwell led a parliamentary military offensive against Catholic Ireland. In Drogheda and Wexford thousands of soldiers and civilians were massacred. It was almost as if Cromwell had tried to follow the poet Edmund Spenser's suggestion of 1596, that the Irish should be starved into submission in order to erect a completely new polity.[21] There was also a mercenary element: Cromwell's soldiers had been promised Irish land.

Switching sides

Cromwell died in 1658. He was succeeded by his son Richard who, lacking any political or military base, lasted less than a year. A reconvened Parliament decided that a constitutional monarchy was better than anarchy and in 1660 welcomed back Charles's son, who accepted what his father had refused in the 1640s. A revolution had been necessary to obtain what the reformists had wanted all along. Again Hobbes, one of the most lucid minds of the seventeenth century, had seen this clearly:

> I have seen in this revolution a circular motion of the sovereign power through two usurpers, from the late King to this his son. For ... it moved from King Charles I to the Long Parliament; from thence to the Rump; from the Rump to Oliver Cromwell; and then back again from Richard Cromwell to the Rump; thence to the Long Parliament; and thence to King Charles II, where long may it remain.[22]

Hobbes's conclusion is understandable: *Behemoth* is about sudden political changes leading to a happy return to normalcy. Presumably the author wanted to endear himself to Charles II, to whom he served as tutor of mathematics in Paris in 1647–48. It worked. Charles welcomed Hobbes to his court, protected him against frequent accusations of atheism and blasphemy and even granted him a small pension, though he did not allow him to publish *Behemoth*. Previously Hobbes had been left unmolested by Oliver Cromwell's regime and was even praised by some of its supporters. In one of his earlier works, *Elements of Law* (1640), Hobbes had clearly been a royalist. As events changed, so did his allegiances, but he did not modify the essence of his political thought, enshrined in his masterpiece *Leviathan* (1651), which neither Cromwell nor Charles II challenged. (Behemoth was a biblical land monster, Leviathan was a biblical sea monster.) To exist at all, sovereignty must be absolute, Hobbes explained. Without an absolute sovereign there could be no civilization.

His doctrine could be used to justify any form of absolute government, which may explain why he was accused of subservience to Cromwell by royalists and of royalist sympathies by parliamentarians.[23] The Roman Catholic Church banned *Leviathan*, and after Hobbes's death Oxford University formally condemned and burned it.

During periods of great uncertainty, writers and intellectuals oscillated politically to survive. Edmund Waller, a royalist allowed to return to England in 1651, delivered a lengthy 'Panegyric to my Lord Protector' in praise of his rule over this sceptred isle. Waller observed how the oppressed could find redress in English courts, foreign pirates trembled at the thought of English retribution and that England, being an island, is protected from invasion:

> Angels and we have this prerogative,
> That none can at our happy seat arrive;
> While we descend at pleasure, to invade
> The bad with vengeance, and the good to aid.

As power changed hands, one changed one's approach. When Charles II was restored to the throne in 1660, Waller promptly delivered a poem, 'To the King, upon his Majesty's Happy Return'.

The more famous Andrew Marvell, author of 'To His Coy Mistress', wrote 'An Horatian Ode on Cromwell's Return from Ireland' (1650) after the massacres in Drogheda and the sack of Wexford. He must have hoped people had forgotten his earlier poems written in support of the royalist cause. When Cromwell died, Marvell wrote a lengthy poem (324 lines), 'Upon the Death of his Late Highness the Lord Protector', in which we read:

> Here ended all his mortal toils; he laid
> And slept in peace under the laurel shade.
> O Cromwell, Heaven's favourite!

Marvell was a survivor. Secretary to the Council of State with John Milton in 1657, elected to Parliament in 1659 when Cromwell was dead and the Protectorate dying, he continued to represent Hull until his death in 1678, having served under Charles II and his successor James II. At Cromwell's funeral, Marvell had participated in the procession with John Milton and John Dryden. When the monarchy was re-established, Dryden celebrated it with 'Astraea Redux, A Poem on the Happy Restoration and Return of His Second Majesty Charles II', which welcomes the new era of peace after the turmoil of the preceding decade. It begins: 'Now with a general peace the world was blest.' When the Catholic James II succeeded Charles II, Dryden converted to Catholicism and praised the birth of the new king's son with the lengthy poem 'Britannia Rediviva'. When the tide turned again with the ascension to the throne of William and Mary, however, Dryden refused to cooperate and left the court, forsaking its patronage (he had been poet laureate for twenty years).

John Milton was less circumspect. An enthusiastic supporter of Parliament in its struggle against Charles I, a few weeks after the execution of the king he published an influential pamphlet, *The Tenure of Kings and Magistrates: Proving that It Is Lawful, and Hath Been Held So Through the Ages, for Any, Who Has the Power, to Call to Account a Tyrant, or Wicked King, and After Due Conviction, to Depose, and Put Him to Death*.[24] In 1651 he wrote another pro-regicide text in Latin, *Pro Populo Anglicano Defensio*. Then, in 1654, came a *Second Defence* of the English people which praised the action of his fellow citizens in executing the monarch as 'the most heroic and exemplary achievements since the foundation of the world', because it 'freed the state from grievous tyranny'.[25] Impenitent and perhaps foolhardy, just as Charles II was about to return, Milton published *The Ready and Easy Way to Establish a Free Commonwealth, and the Excellence Thereof, Compared with the Inconveniencies and Dangers of Readmitting Kingship in This Nation* (1660). In it, he warned that monarchs might make some

> people wealthy indeed perhaps, and well fleeced, for their own shearing, ... but otherwise softest, basest, viciousest, servilest, easiest to be kept under: and not only in fleece, but in mind also sheepishest; and will have all the benches of judicature annexed to the throne, as a gift of royal grace.[26]

Less brilliant poets than Milton celebrated Cromwell in the hope of obtaining favours. Thus Payne Fisher, having fought with the royalists at the Battle of Marston Moor, penned a Latin poem to the winning side and celebrated Cromwell's war in Scotland with 'Veni, Vidi, Vici. The Triumphs of the Most Excellent & Illustrious Oliver Cromwell' (1652):

> Thus happy Cromwell, daring greatest things,
> Ads wounds to wounds, slaughters to slaughters brings;

> Leaving the road, his sword new wayes did hew
> Through that base people [the Scottish], till a conquest grew.

Fisher died in poverty at the age of seventy-seven, having spent a few years in prison, but he had at least survived Charles II. Milton too survived the Restoration, partly because his friend Marvell intervened on his behalf. As Marvell explained in *The Rehearsal Transpros'd* (1672–73), Milton was 'a man of great Learning and Sharpness of wit as any man. It was his misfortune, living in a tumultuous time, to be toss'd on the wrong side.'[27] Marvell was aware that most of the literature of his days depended on patronage. Milton, who had been blind since 1652, was able to finish his *Paradise Lost* a decade later. Nicholas McDowell's *Poet of Revolution: The Making of John Milton* draws out the irony that Milton's great English epic saw the light of day under the restored Stuart rule 'and thus under the very conditions of "inquisitorious and tyrannical duncery" that, in his polemical writings, he had repeatedly argued would prevent him from ever doing so'.[28]

Other less talented writers anticipated the advice given by William Whitehead, poet laureate under George III: avoid taking unbalanced positions.

> One rule remains. Nor shun nor court the great;
> Your truest centre is that middle state,
> From whence with ease th'observing eye may go
> To all which soars above, or sinks below.[29]

Whitehead, a minor poet, was writing from relative safety. Not so Samuel Pepys, the celebrated diarist, who saw not only the Civil War but also the Great Plague of London and the Great Fire of London. When a teenager, Pepys had probably bunked off school to witness the execution of Charles I. He strongly supported Cromwell but switched sides just in time, and managed to be on the ship that brought Charles II back to England.

In revolutionary times, almost by definition, it is not clear which side is *right*, and no one can really be trusted. The problem, in politics, is that most things are unpredictable, and yet, if one wants to shape events, one cannot but try to anticipate the future – hence the continuing good fortune of gurus, pseudo-prophets, pollsters and assorted forecasters.

One of the perennial uncertainties was that of popular opinion, the dreaded 'multitude'. Should one grant more power to the people? But what if they then demanded even more? Radicals too could be in danger: what if the people turned against them? Adam Ferguson, one of the most remarkable thinkers of the Scottish Enlightenment, put it succinctly in 1767:

> Every step and every movement of the multitude, even in what are termed enlightened ages, are made with equal blindness to the future; and nations stumble upon establishments, which are indeed the result of human action, but not the execution of any human design.[30]

Locke's most famous work, *Two Treatises of Government*, argues that should more power reside with the people, it is not the case that they will overthrow the government whenever they are discontented. Quite the contrary: 'People are not so easily got out of their old Forms', and 'this slowness and aversion of people to quit their old Constitutions' has meant that 'the many Revolutions' which the kingdom had seen 'still brought us back again to our old Legislative of King, Lords and Commons'. Revolutions only occur when the people have been made '*miserable*, and find themselves *exposed to the ill usage of Arbitrary Power*'. They do not occur because of minor matters ('every little mismanagement in publick affairs'), but because of a 'long train of Abuses, Prevarications and Artifices'.[31]

The *Two Treatises* was published in 1689. It was seen for a long time as justifying the Glorious Revolution of 1688, the ascension to the throne of William III of Orange and his wife Mary, as Locke indeed claims in his preface. The bulk of the text, however, as Peter Laslett demonstrated in a classic article, was written earlier, probably in 1679–80. It justified a revolution that had not yet occurred.[32]

'No Popish Prince'

Charles II refrained from persecuting those who had supported Cromwell's Commonwealth, but his reign marked only a temporary interlude in English upheavals. His brother and successor James II, crowned in 1685, faced a revolt supported by the Dutch Republic from one of Charles's illegitimate sons, the Duke of Monmouth, while also having to quell a rebellion in Scotland led by the Earl of Argyll. James II was a Catholic, probably because, like Charles, he had been in exile under the protection of the ultra-Catholic French King Louis XIV. Initially James

II accepted the division of power between monarch and Parliament, obtaining from MPs the sums necessary for his rule. Yet peace was not restored.

The religious element in these conflicts also contained a political one. Hostility to 'popery' entailed fear of the kind of despotic, absolutist and arbitrary government embodied in the person of the Louis XIV. The so-called Sun-King ruled, in the eyes of English Protestants and many French, over a bureaucratic, centralized, high-taxation state. By revoking the Edict of Nantes in 1685 and thus decreeing an end to official toleration of Protestants, provoking the exodus of so many skilled and talented Huguenots, Louis XIV had demonstrated an obscurantist Catholicism. Nevertheless, it is debatable that James II intended to re-establish absolute rule in England, let alone Catholic absolute rule.[33] When necessary, commercial and political considerations prevailed. Even the ultra-Protestant Cromwell had been prepared to ally himself with Catholic France against Spain and to wage war against the Protestant Dutch in 1652–54.

James II could have assuaged Protestant fears by defending his Catholicism from a liberal perspective, advocating for Catholics the same rights as for Protestants. But he did not. He increasingly favoured Catholics for positions of power in the army and the universities, stopped convening Parliament from November 1685, dismissed judges who disagreed with him and arrested dissenting bishops. It was obvious that the truce between monarch and Parliament was over. James II had attempted to bypass Parliament and rule by decree. The reforms accepted by Charles II as the price to be paid to return to the throne were, once again, in danger. The English Revolution was not yet over.

The Glorious Revolution had all the appearance of an invasion, but one solicited by the internal enemies of the existing dynasty. William of Orange, whose anti-Catholic credentials were impeccable, deployed a huge Dutch fleet and army to invade Great Britain. He had been invited by numerous English Protestants, including William Cavendish (later recompensed by being made duke of Devonshire) and Henry Compton, bishop of London (it was he, and not the archbishop of Canterbury, who eventually crowned William and Mary). William also received the support of officers from the English army. It was this coalition – the Dutch plus English Protestants – which ensured the deposition of James II and his exile. William of Orange, soon to be William III of England and William II of Scotland, having accepted the limitation of monarchical power, would rule conjointly with his wife Mary, the daughter of the ousted king. The statue of William of Orange erected in 1889 in Brixham, where he landed on 5 November 1688, bears his famous declaration: 'The liberties of England and the Protestant religion I WILL MAINTAIN.'

The decisive military confrontation occurred in mainly Catholic Ireland, where troops loyal to James II (the Jacobites) faced those loyal to William III. On 1 July 1690, the Jacobites were defeated in the Battle of the Boyne. The victory is still celebrated to this day by members of the Orange Order in Northern Ireland. James II escaped to France, to the anger of his followers who nicknamed him Séamus an Chaca (James the shit). Jacobite forces continued to fight for another year until their final defeat at the Battle of Aughrim, a bloodier confrontation which left more than 5,000 dead.

On 13 February 1689, Parliament had passed *An Act Declaring the Rights and Liberties of the Subject and Settling the Succession of the Crown*, generally known as the Bill of Rights, one of the most important documents of the famously unwritten British constitution. One of the central rules of the Bill of Rights was that 'no Popish prince' – no Catholic – could succeed to the throne. It gave Protestants some special rights and set limitations on the powers of the monarch. From then on, Parliament would be convened regularly, there would be free elections as decided by Parliament, free speech in Parliament could not be 'impeached or questioned' and, more importantly, taxation ('the levying of Money') would be entirely under parliamentary control. As he was crowned, William declared to MPs: 'We thankfully accept what you have offered us. And as I had no other intention in coming hither, than to preserve your Religion, Laws and Liberties, so you may be sure, that I shall endeavour to support them.'[34] By enthroning fervent Protestants, the Revolution ensured the removal of Catholicism from English politics for 140 years. Daniel Defoe could write with some satisfaction in his *An Enquiry into the Occasional Conformity of Dissenters in Cases of Preferment* (1698) that 'the Name of Protestant is now the common title of Englishman'.[35] A Toleration Act granted freedoms to Protestants outside the Church of England (6 per cent of the total population) but not to English Catholics or the even smaller number of English Jews.

The fundamental basis of the modern state is not just the legitimate use of force, as Max Weber had insisted, for this had existed for centuries, but fiscal powers. William and Mary waived any rights they might have had to collect customs duties, reducing their income and their power. The monarch was forced to call Parliament into session annually, and MPs obtained considerable leverage in military and hence in foreign affairs. The revolution settlement gave the Crown a powerful incentive to curry favour with MPs, who now controlled the annual military budget.[36]

By any standard, the Glorious Revolution was far less of a revolution than that conducted by Oliver Cromwell. Nevertheless, it established, once and for all, the supremacy of Parliament. Before 1688, its powers had been intermittent; afterwards, they became permanent.[37] The electorate, though small by contemporary standards, was not insignificant: entitled to vote were all those who owned the freehold of land that brought in an annual rent of at least 40 shillings (£2) – the sum had been fixed in 1429. In practice, at the time of the Long Parliament, it meant that the electorate consisted perhaps of between 27 per cent and 40 per cent of the adult male population, though such figures are unreliable.[38]

Catholic historians typically refer to the Glorious Revolution as the Revolution of 1688, while Whig historians prefer the Bloodless Revolution, forgetting the Battle of Aughrim. The term 'Glorious Revolution' was probably coined in 1689 by John Hampden, at a time when 'glorious' had a godly connotation.[39] Outside Britain the Glorious Revolution was often seen by liberals as another example of the national 'genius': how to reform the monarchy without trauma, without violence, without internal strife. It was interpreted as an alliance between a self-assured and forward-looking aristocracy and an intelligent and aspiring middle class. Many in Germany during the revolutions of 1848 hoped the same model could be applied there.[40] For Locke, the Glorious Revolution marked a definitive rejection of absolutism and the divine right of kings, although that right continued to be defended by conservative forces, particularly in the universities of Oxford and, to a lesser extent, Cambridge, bastions of royalist reaction. The pretence continued at large that whoever sat on the English throne had been somehow chosen by God.[41] Divine providence intervened at the right moment and, it appeared, always on the side of whoever was accepted as the sovereign.

The Glorious Revolution was perhaps, as Steven Pincus has written, the 'first modern revolution', since 'not only did the English *act* as a nation to promote a revolution in 1688–9, they also *understood* their actions as a national revolution' whose aim was to protect their liberties from absolute rule.[42] But it was certainly not a popular revolution, however one defines the word. It was a radical change brought about by the parliamentary elite with outside military help. On this both conservatives and radicals agreed: the former happy of the bloodless outcome, the second wishing for a different one.[43] For Christopher Hill, 1688 was 'a smudged compromise', not a revolutionary watershed.[44] For Marx, it 'brought into power, along with William of Orange, the landlord and capitalist appropriators of surplus-value. They inaugurated the new era by practicing on a colossal scale thefts of state lands, thefts that had been hitherto managed more modestly.'[45] The creation of the Bank of England in 1694 reinforced the attachment of property owners to the new regime. In 1698 the newly established Civil List made the Crown even more dependent on Parliament for its revenue. The civil service was expanded while taxation increased.[46] Interest rates dropped, to the advantage of investors and disadvantage of rentiers. The Glorious Revolution led to a 'financial revolution', including the establishment of a national debt with interest paid for by receipts from taxation and a growing stock market.[47]

The state which surfaced after the civil wars, Restoration and Glorious Revolution was significantly different from that which had originally crowned Charles I king of England. The country had not then been a power comparable to France, Spain or the Netherlands. England's population was probably around 5 million, double its size of the previous century. To this one could add the 3.5 million inhabitants of Scotland, Ireland and Wales, reaching a total of 8.5 million – similar to Spain, but fewer than the population of the territories which would eventually become Italy and Germany. France had by far the largest population in Western Europe, with 22 million people.

Successful revolutions do not necessarily bring peace but they do bring a clear victory for the new regime, which can defend itself from all and sundry from a position of strength since it 'owns' the state and with it the armed forces and the necessary financing.[48] For much of the seventeenth century, England was engaged in naval conflict with the Dutch Republic over trade and colonies. British naval power rested on a series of Navigation Acts, beginning in 1651 under Cromwell and followed by similar acts under Charles II and William and Mary. It was also under Cromwell, in 1655, that the so-called Western Design was launched, aimed at decreasing Spanish and Dutch power in the Atlantic. Unable to capture Hispaniola, the British colonized Jamaica, which became Britain's first colony in the Atlantic. The Navigation Acts established that trade with the new colonies such as Jamaica and North America should be a British monopoly under parliamentary control – something Adam Smith, usually a strong advocate of free trade, regarded as 'perhaps, the wisest of all commercial regulation of England'.[49] Britain had become the world's foremost trading nation, supplanting the Dutch.

In 1707, the kingdoms of Scotland and England (including Wales) were united, bringing a long dispute to an end. There was no return to anything ex ante, but some appearances of absolute rule lingered. Queen Anne was the last ruler to 'touch' her subjects to cure them of scrofula (including Samuel Johnson, to no effect). She was also the last to veto an act of Parliament. Subsequent monarchs tried to interfere with issues such as Catholic Emancipation, but their views did not prevail. David Hume, in a 1771 letter to his publisher William Strahan, listed with some anger the powers acquired by Parliament at the expense of the Crown:

> The right of displacing the Judges was given up; General Warrants are lost; the right of Expulsion the same; all the coercive Powers of the House of Commons abandon'd ... the Authority of the Government impair'd ... For God's sake, is there never to be stop put to the inundation of the Rabble?[50]

The fear was that there might be a return to the epoch of instability. Hume should not have been so worried.

First, though, there was a succession problem: William and Mary did not have heirs. William (Mary had predeceased him) was succeeded by Mary's sister Anne, who had no surviving children despite seventeen pregnancies. Pragmatism prevailed. An Act of Settlement was passed in 1701 thanks to the Whigs and some Tories, which reaffirmed, once again, that only a Protestant could ascend to the throne. As Anne was very ill, a successor had to be found. Fifty possible candidates were considered, and Parliament settled on Sophia, duchess of Hanover, a second cousin of Queen Mary and an unimpeachable Protestant. Sophia died in June 1714 at the age of eighty-three, however, two months before Queen Anne (who died at the age of forty-nine). Thus, the successor to the British Crown had to be Sophia's son George, who had no close connection with England and whose English was rudimentary.[51] He became a monarch with very limited powers, since Parliament was finally securely in charge of the destinies of the country under the hegemony of a Whig oligarchy that lasted for decades. By 1721 Robert Walpole had become the effective ruler of Great Britain, remaining in charge until 1742, a feat achieved not just by winning elections but by knowing how to obtain the approval of the House of Commons.[52] He is credited as the first and longest-serving prime minister, though the title had not yet been created.[53]

Jacobite attempts to depose the Hanoverian kings and return to a Stuart monarch failed. The last Stuart pretender, 'Bonnie' Prince Charlie, grandson of James II, saw his supporters engaged in the Jacobite rising of 1745 defeated at the famous Battle of Culloden by the duke of

Cumberland, a son of King George II, soon nicknamed 'Butcher Cumberland' by his Tory opponents. Handel's oratorio *Judas Maccabaeus*, to which he later added the famous 'See the Conquering Hero Comes', was composed especially for Cumberland.

The English Revolution which had started with the struggle against Charles I in 1642 was finally concluded in 1714, when all possible obstacles and threats to the supremacy of the British Parliament were eliminated. Hume recognized this with unmistakable lucidity. In an essay 'Of the Protestant Succession' – written two years after the definitive defeat of the Jacobite rising of 1745 but published only in 1752 when it was quite safe to do so – he weighed the relative advantages of sticking with the Stuarts, the linear descendants of the rightful heir to the throne, or accepting the permanency of the Hanoverian kings. He thought the Hanoverian succession preferable precisely because it 'violates hereditary right, and places on the throne a prince to whom birth gave no title to that dignity', while avoiding 'the inconveniences of elective monarchy'; or, to put it crudely, since the Hanoverians were upstarts and foreigners, they could make no grand 'claims and pretensions'. Under the Stuarts there had been constant turmoil and 'unnatural ferment and disorder' for nearly eighty years.[54] Now all this could be left behind: 'An uninterrupted harmony has been preserved between our princes and our Parliament.' In other words, since everyone finally knows their place, we can have peace and stability. The non-legitimate nature of the Hanover monarchy enabled their purely decorative role, which came with even fewer powers than today's figurehead presidents, such as those of Italy or Germany. What remained in their hands was a constantly declining power of patronage and favouritism. By the twentieth century, the monarch and the royal family had no influence at all on politics and gradually descended into real-life melodrama.

English ideas

The English Revolution had made no claims to universality. Unlike the French and the American Revolutions, let alone the Soviet and Chinese, it made no grand declaration about universal rights and had no messages to the world. The Civil War which led to Cromwell's Protectorate was not preceded by the kind of high-level theoretical or political disputation which came before the French Revolution (one thinks of Voltaire, Diderot, Rousseau and Montesquieu), or the American (Thomas Paine,

Benjamin Franklin and Alexander Hamilton) or, as in the case of Russia and China, by revolutionaries such as Lenin and Mao Zedong, who used theory and appealed to Marx. Only after the downfall of Charles I did England produce thinkers of immense importance such as Hobbes and Locke, and in the following century Scotland followed suit with David Hume, Adam Smith and Adam Ferguson.

But before the English Revolution, though there was great poetry (John Donne and Edmund Spenser) and great playwrights (Shakespeare, Christopher Marlowe, Ben Jonson), there was no real political theory: no Machiavelli or Erasmus of Rotterdam, only Thomas More. The English Reformation had no major theologians on a par with Luther and Calvin, only Richard Hooker. It is this that led Christopher Hill to write ironically in *The Intellectual Origins of the English Revolution Revisited*: 'One fact on which there is a wide agreement among historians is that the English Revolution had no intellectual origins.' While the French and Americans looked back to the English Civil War, the English themselves had nothing to look back to.[55] There was, however, one major guiding text: the Bible. In the reading of the time, it confirmed the superiority of Protestantism over Catholicism. Abroad there was much admiration if not for English thinkers then at least for English freedoms.[56] Previously the French had regarded England as a 'small, remote and uncivilized island where the climate was abominable and the language incomprehensible'.[57] As the English Revolution proceeded, and Parliament won its century-old battle with the monarchy, esteem grew.

The Enlightenment thinkers, especially Montesquieu, Diderot and Voltaire, celebrated the victory of Parliament and the resulting 'balanced' political system. Voltaire, who was in England in 1726–28, wrote: 'To be free means to depend only on laws. The English have loved the law, as fathers love their children, because they have made them, or they think they have made them.' In the House of Commons, 8 million citizens are 'really represented', and this 'makes Plato's republic look like a ridiculous dream'. English laws, he continued, somewhat overstating the powers of the House of Commons, return to each subject 'all the natural rights shattered by monarchies'. In England,

> you will not be snatched in the middle of the night from your wife and children and taken to a dungeon or a desert ... you will be able to publish what you want, and if you are accused of a crime, you will be judged by a jury made up of independent men.[58]

Voltaire did not mention that if you were Black you could be snatched from the west coast of Africa and sent by the English to a life of slavery in the Americas.

Montesquieu believed that the English system of government was far wiser than that of the Greeks or Romans because it constantly re-examined itself, as a free country should. He believed that 'in Europe the last gasp of liberty would come from an Englishman.'[59] Germaine de Staël in her history of the French Revolution was very clear:

> The revolution in England has lasted some fifty years ... and all efforts of these fifty years have had only a real and permanent aim: the establishment of the present constitution, that is to say, the most beautiful monument of justice and moral grandeur existing among Europeans.[60]

And Tocqueville, in his *L'Ancien Régime et la Révolution* (1856), could write that England in the seventeenth century was already a modern nation, though it preserved, like some relics, aspects of the Middle Ages.[61]

By then the English cult of moderation was in full swing, widely admired by all those, in France and elsewhere, who shunned revolutionary extremism. Here was a country which had been able to go beyond internal struggles and establish a free, moderate and 'balanced' society. As early as 1662, shortly after the return of Charles II, the Book of Common Prayer contained a preface declaring that it had been 'the wisdom of the Church of England ... to keep the mean between the two extremes', and that whenever 'a change hath been made of things advisedly established ... sundry inconveniences have thereupon ensued ... and greater than the evils that were intended to be remedied by such change'.[62]

As is often the case, intellectual opinion in Britain was divided over the professed virtues of English political life. Edmund Burke oozed self-satisfaction: while in France 'civil troubles' produced 'something ignoble and inglorious' (he meant the French Revolution), in England 'revolutions have been conducted by persons' (he was referring to Cromwell, the 'destroying angel') who 'sanctified their ambition by advancing the dignity of the people whose peace they troubled. They had long views. They aimed at the rule, not at the destruction of their country.' They had not, despite all the massacres, 'slain the *mind* in their country. A conscious dignity, a noble pride, a generous sense of glory and emulation, was not extinguished. On the contrary, it was kindled and inflamed.'[63]

Jonathan Swift was not so sure about dignity and pride. He was thinking of the conditions of the poor, especially the Irish poor, and he enshrined his thoughts in what became the most famous satirical essay in English literature: *A Modest Proposal for Preventing the Children of Poor People in Ireland, from Being a Burden on Their Parents or Country, and for Making Them Beneficial to the Publick* (1729). The premise was that a solution to the increasing poverty of the very young could be achieved by eating them: 'I have been assured ... that a young healthy child well nursed, is, at a year old, a most delicious nourishing and wholesome food, whether stewed, roasted, baked, or boiled', adding, 'I grant this food will be somewhat dear, and therefore very proper for landlords, who, as they have already devoured most of the parents, seem to have the best title to the children.' The immediate cause of Swift's indignation was the deep economic crisis affecting Ireland and the consequences of harvest failures, though his wider target was English oppression and the complicity of Irish landlords.[64] Another of Swift's targets was the growing school of political economy and the spread of facile solutions argued in pamphlets labelled 'A Humble Solution' or 'A Modest Proposal'. In his view these sought to reduce human beings to statistics and commodities.[65]

Freedom and slavery

Indignation stopped at home. The slave trade and slavery in the British colonies caused no protest until well after the arrival of the Hanover monarchs. In the period 1630–1750, observes Robin Blackburn, the British Empire promoted the 'uncontested exploitation of African bondage'.[66] In 1713, Daniel Defoe could write without any moral misgivings or ethical judgement, but with an understanding of the economic case:

> Those who know how far our Plantation Trade is Blended and Interwoven with the Trade to Africa, and that they no more be parted than the Child and the Nurse, need have no time spent to convince them of this; The Case is as plain as cause and Consequence: Mark the Climax. No African trade, no Negroes; no Negroes, no sugars, gingers, indicoes etc; no sugars, etc, no islands; no islands, no continent; no continent, no trade.[67]

Much of the slave trade was in the hands of the Company of Royal Adventurers Trading with Africa, established by Charles II as soon as he was restored to the throne. It became the Royal African Company, with, among others, John Locke and Samuel Pepys as shareholders (Locke was a shareholder because in 1672 he was paid for his services in shares; he sold them in 1675). The great composer George Frideric Handel was a shareholder too, from at least 1716.[68] The duke of York (the future James II) was both governor of the company and its largest shareholder. They were grim times for enslaved Africans but led to prosperity for Bristol and Liverpool.

The War of the Spanish Succession (1701–14) and Seven Years' War (1756–63), which ended with British acquisition of most of Canada and the West Indies, as well as Florida and further footholds in India, protected the growing British trading empire and, consequently, its finances and tax-gathering system. British freedoms depended on naval might, but so did British slavers. The famous patriotic song 'Rule, Britannia!' (1740), set to music by Thomas Arne from a poem by James Thomson, celebrated British sea power and the abolition of absolute monarchical rule. Britons would 'rule the waves' and never be slaves, unlike their many enslaved victims. As David Eltis has written: 'Countries that had developed the strongest antipathy to curtailment of liberty for their own people had the least inhibitions about creating an overseas labor system using non-European slaves.'[69] The slave trade, so far as England was concerned, was based on the acquisition of colonies in North America and what came to be called the West Indies (mainly islands in the Caribbean Sea). In the seventeenth and eighteenth centuries opposition to English colonialism rested not so much on humanitarian grounds but on the assumption that the colonies would depopulate England, eventually becoming independent and competing against her.[70] The colonialist lobby, though, was far stronger than its critics. One of its most articulate supporters was John Locke, who argued that America was the key to England's economic success.[71]

The connection between industrialization and the slave trade has been much discussed, particularly since the publication of Eric Williams's *Capitalism and Slavery* (1944). Many scholars have established that there was a major link.[72] There were, of course, other factors: without technological innovation, slave-trading nations such as Portugal, Spain or even France were late in industrializing. But a connection between colonialism and economic prosperity was recognized by many, including the poet and painter William Blake, who illustrated Europe's dependency in his 1796 engraving *Europe Supported by Africa and America*.[73]

Superior technology meant that England, and Lancashire in particular, could manufacture cotton cloth more efficiently than India. Raw

Europe Supported by Africa and America, print by William Blake,
1796, Victoria and Albert Museum, South Kensington

cotton was increasingly imported from the Americas, where it had been cultivated by enslaved Africans transported by British ships. Though the slave trade was a business, it obviously contained a strongly racist element since Europeans captured in wars were hardly ever sold as slaves. Huguenots, rebellious Irish, blasphemers, heathens and Jews accused of various crimes might be tortured, hanged, executed and imprisoned but not enslaved. Convicts could be condemned to forced labour instead of being executed, but they were not slaves and could not be bought and sold (nor could their children), and many had a fixed-term sentence. Europeans could be indentured servants, forced to work for free for a number of years to pay for their voyage. But again, they were not slaves.

There were few philosophical denunciations of the slave trade anywhere in Europe before the middle of the seventeenth century. Rare early exceptions were John Calvin and Jean Bodin.[74] Christian condemnation of the slave trade was unusual until the late eighteenth century, when it became important to the abolitionist cause. Religion, after all, can be used in various ways and some defenders of slavery reminded people of the curse of Ham – 'a servant of servants shall he be unto his brethren' – in Genesis (9:25), though the Bible does not mention Ham's skin colour. One of the main abolitionist texts of the eighteenth century was Montesquieu's satirical chapter in his *De l'esprit des lois* (1748), where he mocks the justifications offered for slavery.[75] Montesquieu's use of ridicule to show that the defence of slavery was not worth rebutting through an appeal to reason was particularly liked in Scottish Enlightenment circles.[76]

It was in England that the strongest anti-slavery movement occurred, probably because it also had the most important slave trade and the largest slave colonies – unlike the Netherlands which, despite its commitment to social freedoms at home, was among the last countries to take action against the slave trade.[77] The tide had been turning for a while. In 1760 in the British colony of Jamaica there was a large slave revolt (known as Tacky's Revolt, presumably named after its leader), the most important of the many slave wars until the Haitian Revolution of 1804.[78] The loss of America in 1783 was regarded by some as punishment for the immoral slave trade. As John Coffey has written: 'Many abolitionists thought that ending slavery would restore divine favour to Britain.'[79]

In 1769 Granville Sharp, influenced by Montesquieu, published *A Representation of the Injustice and Dangerous Tendency of Tolerating Slavery*, one of the first abolitionist tracts in England, and founded a Society for Effecting the Abolition of the Slave Trade.[80] In the same year William Wilberforce and other Evangelical Protestants also started lobbying for abolition. They were joined by Quakers and Methodists including John Wesley, as well as Olaudah Equiano, a former slave living in England and active in the abolitionist Sons of Africa group. His widely read autobiography, *The Interesting Narrative of the Life of Olaudah Equiano* (1789), which narrates his being kidnapped from Africa and enslaved, was translated into Dutch, German and Russian and reprinted several times.[81] Equiano quoted one of the earliest abolitionist poems, *The Dying Negro: A Poetical Epistle* (1773) by John Bicknell and Thomas Day, which includes the lines:

> Fall'n are my trophies, blasted is my fame,
> Myself become a thing without a name,
> The sport of haughty lords, and ev'n of slaves the shame.
> Curst be the winds, and curst the tides which bore
> These European robbers to our shore![82]

Even more popular was the poem *The Negro's Complaint* by William Cowper (1788) written from the point of view of the slave (and frequently quoted by Martin Luther King Jr during his civil rights campaign in the 1960s). Quobna Ottobah Cugoano, a friend of Olaudah Equiano, also a former slave and a committed Christian, published *Thoughts and Sentiments on the Evil and Wicked Traffic of the Slavery and Commerce of the Human Species* (1787), which went into three editions. In the appendix he described how he had been captured by other Africans and sold to the 'white-faced' people for *'gun, a piece of cloth, and some lead'*.[83] Robin Blackburn points to the importance to the abolitionist movement of the agitation of former slaves, 'invariably among the most popular speakers on abolitionist platforms'. By 1792 there were almost 400,000 signatures to abolitionist petitions, and some 51,000 abolitionist pamphlets and books were published.[84] Much discussed and read was the first account of a Black woman, Mary Prince, whose autobiographical *History of Mary Prince* was published in 1831, just two years before slavery itself was abolished in Britain and her colonies.

Josiah Wedgwood, the famous pottery entrepreneur, unitarian and friend of the abolitionist Thomas Clarkson (also grandfather of Charles

Josiah Wedgwood, *Antislavery Medallion* (c. 1787), Metropolitan Museum of Art, New York

Darwin) produced in 1787 a medallion for the abolitionist movement showing an enslaved Black inscribed: 'Am I Not a Man and a Brother?' This became the slogan of the abolitionists as well as a fashionable object to wear. In her *Rights of Men*, Mary Wollstonecraft (1790), in open polemic with Burke's writings on the French Revolution, took a stance against slavery. When, she demanded, had slavery been 'authorized by law to fasten her fangs on human flesh, and the iron eat into the very soul'?[85]

A new morality emerged out of the descriptions of sufferings and catastrophes, such as the decision in November 1781 of Captain Luke Collingwood to throw overboard more than 130 slaves he was carrying on the ship *Zong*. His plan was to obtain money from the insurance companies, claiming the vessel was running out of drinking water and that someone had to be sacrificed. Both Granville Sharp and Olaudah Equiano (who had informed Sharp of the event) were active in the legal campaign surrounding the *Zong*. The judge decided that throwing the slaves overboard was the same as throwing assets, but that the *Zong*'s owners could not claim insurance on the slaves because they had managed the ship badly. No one was punished for the massacre.

Years later the *Zong* incident still had the power to shock. J. M. W. Turner, having read Thomas Clarkson's *The History and Abolition of the Slave Trade* (1808), produced one of his masterpieces: *Slavers Throwing Overboard the Dead and the Dying*.

When the slave trade was abolished, William Wordsworth wrote a sonnet in praise of Clarkson: 'Sonnet, To Thomas Clarkson, on the Final Passing of the Bill for the Abolition of the Slave Trade, March 1807'.

> Clarkson! it was an obstinate Hill to climb:
> How toilsome, nay how dire it was, by Thee
> Is known ...
> The bloody Writing is for ever torn,
> And Thou henceforth shalt have a good Man's calm,
> A great Man's happiness; thy zeal shall find
> Repose at length, firm Friend of human kind!

At the same moment the engraver Henry Fuseli produced his illustration *The Negro Revenged*, which shows a slave ship being struck by lightning.

By then hardly anyone defended the trade. The House of Commons passed the Slave Trade Act by an overwhelming majority (282 to 16), more than 150 years after the beginning of the slave trade. Although the trade was abolished, slavery continued in the colonies. Almost at the same time,

J. M. W. Turner, *Slavers Throwing Overboard the Dead and the Dying – Typhoon Coming On* (1840), Museum of Fine Arts, Boston

the United States banned the importation of slaves, thus increasing the value of the slaves already there.[86] In 1823, in a speech in the House of Commons, the renowned economist David Ricardo had declared that he was 'inclined to blush with shame, to hide his face, when West Indian slavery was mentioned. It was a stain on the otherwise pure character of the country, which he ardently desired to see wiped away.'[87] It took another ten years for the 'stain' to be noticed by Parliament: the Slavery Abolition Act 1833 ended slavery in the colonies, in part thanks to the effort of Wilberforce's Society for the Mitigation and Gradual Abolition of Slavery Throughout the British Dominions, founded a decade earlier. William Gladstone, the son of a slave trader, opposed the Abolition Act, believing that slaves should have to achieve moral regeneration before becoming free. He was then a Tory MP and only twenty-four; he later repented.

The young Thomas Babington Macaulay, in an 1824 speech in favour of abolishing slavery in the British colonies, typically linked abolition to British magnanimity:

> She may boast of her ancient laws – of her magnificent literature – of her long list of maritime and military triumphs; – she may boast of the

vast extent and security of her empire; – but she has still higher praise; it is her peculiar glory, not that she has ruled so widely – not that she has conquered so splendidly – but that she has ruled only to bless, and conquered only to spare!'[88]

If Britain ruled only to bless, it also paid after 1833 very generous compensation to the slave owners of £20 million, roughly 40 per cent of annual state expenditure.[89] The 800,000 freed slaves got nothing and had to remain compulsorily apprenticed to their owners for another five years. Gladstone's father, John, received over £100,000 (more than £15 million in today's currency). Elizabeth Barrett Browning, wife of Robert Browning and a supporter of anti-slavery, also benefited, as did Thomas Babington Macaulay's sister Hannah because she had married Charles Trevelyan, a colonial administrator whose family owned 1,000 slaves. Even though Macaulay's father Zachary had made abolition his life's work, Macaulay never mentioned the trade in his multi-volume *History of England from the Accession of James II*.[90]

'Very proud of our constitution'

In the hundred years or so between the advent of the Hanover kings and slavery's abolition, Great Britain had become the world leading industrial power thanks in part to the slave trade; the world's leading financial centre thanks to the merchants of the city of London; and the world's largest empire thanks in part to the East India Company. The loss of the United States had been easily absorbed, as abolition would be. Britain continued to rule the waves well into the reign of Queen Victoria, empress of India.

Humanitarian abolitionism coexisted with the absolute certainty that the 'white race' was superior to all others: intellectually, ethically, economically and of course militarily. In 1849 Thomas Carlyle published anonymously his 'Occasional Discourse on the Negro Question' in *Fraser's Magazine*, later republished as 'Occasional Discourse on the Nigger Question'. Carlyle's view was that Blacks were born to be servants, just as women had to obey their husbands, while abolitionists were just 'windy sentimentalists'. At first Carlyle seemed to be isolated: John Stuart Mill was outraged, and the editor of *Fraser's Magazine* dissociated himself from the article. Soon, however, the Indian 'Mutiny' made his kind of racism more popular, and the n-word entered common parlance.[91] John

Stuart Mill had been outraged by Carlyle's overt racism but did not object to the colonial servitude of the 'backward' race, positing that 'despotism is a legitimate mode of government in dealing with barbarians, provided the end be their improvement and the means justified by actually effecting that end'.[92]

In his last completed novel *Our Mutual Friend* (1865–66), Dickens satirizes jingoistic middle-class pomposity, despite sharing some of the traits he mocks. One of his characters, Mr Podsnap, intones to a French gentleman:

> 'We Englishmen are Very Proud of our Constitution, Sir. It Was Bestowed Upon Us By Providence. No Other Country is so Favoured as This Country.' 'And OTHER countries,' said the foreign gentleman, 'They do how?' 'They do, Sir,' returned Mr Podsnap, gravely shaking his head, 'they do – I am sorry to be obliged to say it – AS they do … This Island was Blest, Sir, to the Direct Exclusion of such Other Countries … I would say … that there is in the Englishman a combination of qualities, a modesty, an independence, a responsibility, a repose, combined with an absence of everything calculated to call a blush into the cheek of a young person, which one would seek in vain among the Nations of the Earth.'

One can see Mr Podsnap's point. While Britain was at peace internally, the French had to absorb a bloody revolution, the Napoleonic dictatorship, two dynasties (Bourbon and Orléans), the revolution of 1848, and another Napoleonic empire, that of Louis Napoleon. A few years after Mr Podsnap's self-satisfied declaration, the French suffered a military defeat by Prussia in 1870 and faced the Paris Commune before finally giving birth to the Third Republic. The historian and politician François Guizot declared at the beginning of his *Discours sur l'histoire de la Révolution d'Angleterre* (1849) that the British constitutional monarchy and the *Amérique anglaise* (US) were successes that France and the rest of Europe had not been able to achieve.[93] He did not know at the time that the United States had yet to face its own civil war.

The English Revolution, bloody though it was during the seventeenth century, gave way to a lengthy social peace barely disturbed by riots and strife. The famous Peterloo massacre (1819) in St Peter's Field, Manchester, led to eighteen deaths. The Chartist demands (1838) aimed at making the Westminster system more democratic failed, but by 1918 most of their original demands had been fulfilled. In the same year women over the age of thirty who owned some property were also entitled to vote, though full equality would have to wait until 1928. Scotland, the original spark for the English Civil War, had been tamed and was an enthusiastic partner in the building up of the empire while maintaining elements of folkloristic national identity. Violence was exported: to Ireland, the Australian First Nations, India, Africa, the Caribbean and China. In England peace prevailed; elsewhere there was much blood. As Lord Palmerston as foreign affairs secretary famously declared in the House of Commons on 25 June 1850:

> As the Roman, in days of old, held himself free from indignity, when he could say *Civis Romanus sum*; so also a British subject, in whatever land he may be, shall feel confident that the watchful eye and the strong arm of England, will protect him against injustice and wrong.[94]

Gradually over the nineteenth century, barriers which prevented non-Anglicans – Nonconformists, Catholics and Jews – from voting, obtaining degrees, teaching in universities, standing for elections, being elected and so on were eliminated. The Roman Catholic Relief Act 1829 lifted most political restrictions on Catholics. Even now the monarch cannot be a Catholic because of being also the head of the Church of England, though since 2013 they have been free to marry a Catholic. Blasphemy – meaning blasphemy against Christian belief – was a crime until 2008, though the last time a person was sentenced to imprisonment for the offence in England was in 1883. Blasphemy laws remain in existence in Northern Ireland; in the Republic of Ireland they were removed only in 2020, after a referendum. The House of Lords was reformed, if you can call it that, at a snail's pace. The Church of England has remained the established Church but today counts for very little in the life of the nation. The absence of revolutionary upheavals led to the endurance of rules and habits well beyond the existence of any reason for their survival.

A remarkable lack of radicalism pervaded British politics. In British schools what has been glorified or studied with great emphasis includes Elizabeth I, Henry VIII and his wives, Victorian social reforms, the empire (but little about its victims) and, more recently, the British role in the wars of the twentieth century (with, of course, Winston Churchill). While the French, the Americans, the Russians and the Chinese have celebrated their revolutions, the British forgot theirs.

2

America: The Settlers' Rebellion

The American Revolution was *special*. Unlike the English Civil War, it was an anti-colonial revolt, the first of many, and unlike the English, the French, the Russian and the Chinese revolutions it did not have to destroy an ancient regime – no Stuart kings, no Bourbon kings, no tsars, no Qing dynasty, no aristocracy. And those Americans not in chains already enjoyed a standard of living that was among the highest in the world.

As Alexis de Tocqueville famously explained: 'The great advantage of the Americans is to have come to democracy without having to endure democratic revolution.'[1] Their revolution was meant to maintain the status quo once the ties to a distant mother-country had been broken. The example of anti-colonial revolt was followed across the Americas wherever there were a considerable number of European settlers. In Latin America, Spanish colonists threw off the yoke of Spain; and in Brazil their Portuguese counterparts cut their ties with Portugal. Dom Pedro, the first emperor (o Libertador) of Brazil, having left Portugal during the Napoleonic Wars, turned Brazil into an independent country and never went back. Outside the New World, the War of Independence had relatively little impact in comparison to the French or Russian Revolutions. America itself, of course, has had an enormous global impact, which might make the pronouncement of the historian Gordon Wood – 'it was one of the greatest revolutions the world has known, a momentous upheaval that not only fundamentally altered the character of American society but decisively affected the course of subsequent history' – less inflated than it appears at first.[2]

One consequence of settler colonialism was the elimination of many of the original inhabitants. They were massacred; they were expelled (what would now be called ethnic cleansing); they were confined to special areas (reserves); they were left to die of infectious diseases; they were individually assimilated, as with the Australian Aboriginal Protection Act 1869, which forcibly separated Aboriginal Australian children from their families.[3] Settlers remained colonialists, however anti-colonial their politics towards the metropole.

Empire-building was achieved by private enterprise with the encouragement of European states. At the time, few underestimated the importance of slavery and colonies. William Wood in his *A Survey of Trade* (1722) wrote: 'The *Labour of Negroes* is the principal Foundation of our *Riches* from the *Plantations*.' To underline the point, Marx wrote that capital comes 'dripping from head to foot, from every pore, with blood and dirt'.[4]

The British who colonized Australia, though they never seriously rebelled against British rule (apart from occasional outbursts of violence such as the so-called Rum Rebellion of 1808–10), attempted to eliminate Aboriginal Australians with ferocious cruelty, as in the Black War from the mid-1820s to 1832, which virtually wiped out the Aboriginal Tasmanians – an early form of genocide.[5] Their justification was that the Aboriginal Australians lacked a sovereign with whom they could negotiate, and so 'such lands fully belong to the discoverers and first occupiers'.[6]

Another type of anti-colonial revolt is where the original inhabitants – the indigenous who have been colonized – expel the colonial administration and any settlers and create an independent country, often within the borders established by the colonialists. In such cases they never return to the pre-colonial ancien régime. There was no return to the Mughal in India or to any of the displaced sovereigns in Africa, with minor exceptions. In Morocco there is a dynastic continuation, but Morocco was never strictly speaking a colony. Libya and Ethiopia reverted to monarchical rule, but these kings were later ousted by their subjects. The general rule is that settlers and the foreign administration are replaced by something new. This was the pattern in much of the Middle East (for instance in Algeria, Lebanon and Iraq), Asia (as in India and Vietnam), and in much of sub-Saharan Africa (as in Kenya and Nigeria).

There are variants. The Irish War of Independence led to the end of British rule in southern Ireland and the establishment, in 1922, of the Irish Free State. Constitutionally Ireland was not a colony but part of the United Kingdom. Independence for the islands of the West Indies, such as Jamaica and Trinidad, was granted not to the indigenous population, which had been almost exterminated, but to the descendants of the slaves (those forced to be settlers). The Boer Wars in Southern Africa were rebellions not by British colonists but by the descendants of Dutch settlers opposed to British rule. There are further variants. Jewish settlers in Palestine had no mother country, though some choose to believe that the land they occupy was given to them by God more than 3,000 years ago; they killed, expelled or subjugated the existing inhabitants, the Palestinians.

Locke and the Bible

The process alternately referred to as the American War of Independence, the Revolutionary War and the American Revolution should be considered in its two aspects: a war to free the colonies from their links with Britain (the War of Independence), and the establishment of, and struggle over, a new state (the revolution proper). As we have seen, the word 'revolution' was seldom used in pamphlets or articles in the years leading up to 4 July 1776.[7] Phase one concluded in 1781 with victory for the colonists, as enshrined in the 1783 Treaty of Paris. As for the revolution, matters are more complicated, since what emerged from the struggle against the British was a new state but not a new society, at least in the short term.

Taxation, as we know, lay at the heart of the original dispute: 'no taxation without representation', though the taxes were low. This was the central thread linking the American revolutionaries of the eighteenth century to the English parliamentarians of the seventeenth century. The privileged elite of American colonists wanted to be in control of their own affairs, particularly their finances, just as the English Parliament had wanted to wrest control over taxation from the monarch. Thomas Jefferson wondered why 160,000 British electors should rule over 'four million Americans'.[8] He did not wonder at the larger number of unenfranchised subjects in Britain itself.

The ideological justifications used by the rebels were largely based on the liberal principles defined by John Locke, an authority more quoted than read, buttressed by a Puritan reading of the Bible and various legal precedents.[9] These ultimately went hand in hand with Montesquieu's *The Spirit of Law* (1748) and its defence of the separation of powers between executive, legislative and judiciary, which Montesquieu erroneously considered a central feature of the British political system.

Resistance and revolution invite a variety of justifications not always consistent with each other. In the eyes of American revolutionaries there was no conflict between the Enlightenment and religion. The Declaration of Independence referred to the 'Laws of Nature and of Nature's God'. Human beings were endowed 'with certain unalienable Rights', not by nature but by 'their Creator'. Benjamin Franklin was to tell the 1787 Constitutional Convention: 'The longer I live the more convincing proofs I see of this Truth, that God governs the affairs of men.'[10] In the eighteenth century it was necessary to prove that God and the Bible were on your side.

James Otis's influential pamphlet of July 1764, *The Rights of the British Colonies Asserted and Proved*, quoted many passages from Locke's *Second Treatise* without mentioning him by name. Otis stressed that there was right of rebellion if one's property was in danger, pointed to the values of the Glorious Revolution, and endorsed Locke's declaration that

> slavery is so vile and miserable an estate of man, and so directly opposite to the generous temper and courage of our nation, that it is hard to be conceived that an Englishman, much less a gentleman, should plead for it.[11]

Though the famous dictum 'taxation without representation is tyranny' is often attributed to Otis, *The Rights of the British Colonies Asserted and Proved* was not revolutionary. It still assumed that once control of taxation was conceded to the colonists, the colonies could continue to be part of Great Britain. Otis repeatedly recognized the kingship of George III, 'whom may God long preserve and prosper', but insisted the settlers should have the same rights as his subjects in Britain: 'Every part has a right to be represented in the supreme or some subordinate legislature.' This did not prevent Otis from asserting a right to revolt: 'Whenever the administrators, in any of those forms, deviate from truth, justice and equity, they verge towards tyranny, and are to be opposed; and if they prove incorrigible, they will be deposed by the people, if the people are not rendered too abject.'[12]

The right to revolt had become an accepted truth. In his outstanding *Treatise on Human Nature* (1739–40), David Hume argued that 'in all our notions of morals we never entertain such an absurdity as that of passive obedience, but make allowances for resistance in the more flagrant instances of tyranny and oppression'.[13] Even Hobbes had accepted in *Leviathan* (1651), at the conclusion of the English Civil War: 'The Obligation of Subjects to the Sovereign, is understood to last as long and no longer, than the power lasteth, by which he is able to protect themselves.' If they cannot be protected, then the covenant – the contract of obedience – is null and void.[14] But the circumstances for overthrowing a sovereign, Hobbes warned, have to be extreme: 'Though of so unlimited a Power, men may fancy many evill consequences, yet the consequences of the want of it, which is perpetuall warre of every man against his neighbour, are much worse.'[15] Americans, consciously or not following Hobbes's advice, thought carefully about revolution.

They proceeded at first with moderate demands: not independence, but fiscal control. The famous duty on tea was not particularly burdensome; nor were the British Navigations Acts, which decreed that trade with the colonies should be a British monopoly. But these impositions were of symbolic and political significance.[16] The British Parliament appeared to compromise in 1766 when it abrogated an unpopular Stamp Act with the support of City of London merchants. At the same time, however, it passed a Declaratory Act which made it crystal clear to the American colonists that Westminster reserved the right to make any laws it wanted, and through the Townshend Acts laid down new tax measures.

In 1767–68, John Dickinson published a series of letters in the *Pennsylvania Chronicle* protesting the Townshend Acts. The letters were then collected in a book, *Letters from a Farmer in Pennsylvania to the Inhabitants of the British Colonies*. The first epistle opened with the assertion: 'My farm is small ... my servants are few ... I have a little money at interest.'[17] In fact, Dickinson was a prosperous lawyer and one of the richest men in the colonies; his father was a wealthy tobacco planter and slave owner. The *Letters* were in no way a call for independence. On the contrary, they asserted that the prosperity of the colonies was linked to 'their dependence on Great Britain'. Dickinson urged caution and praised both the English monarch ('we have an excellent prince') and England itself ('a generous, sensible and humane nation'). He urged Americans 'to behave like dutiful children, who have received unmerited blows from a beloved parent'.[18]

Dickinson quoted several times from the Whig politician William Pitt the Elder, who was British prime minister in 1766–68 and had, during a parliamentary debate on the Stamp Acts, dismissed the notion that colonies were somehow virtually represented in Parliament ('the most contemptible that ever entered into the head of a man'). Pitt argued that the 'Commons of America' had always had the power 'of giving and granting their own money. They would have been slaves if they had not enjoyed it.' Furthermore, 'taxation and representation are inseparable ... it is an eternal law of nature'.[19] In the same debate, on 14 January 1766, Pitt averred: 'This kingdom has no right to lay a tax upon the colonies ... the Americans are the sons not the bastards of England'.[20] Moderates on both sides of the Atlantic were thus joining hands. But moderation did not prevail for long. As Burke pondered: 'There is no more difficult subject for the understanding of men than to govern a Large Empire upon a plan of Liberty.'[21]

Most of the import duties introduced by the Townshend Acts were abolished by the government of Lord North in 1770, except for the duty on tea. When a shipment of tea from the East India Company arrived in Boston at the end of 1773, it was destroyed by a group of patriots who called themselves the Sons of Liberty. Letting the tea in, wrote John Adams in his diary, would have reduced Americans to the same lowly position as slaves in ancient Egypt, and subjected them to 'Ignominy, Reproach and Contempt, to Desolation and Oppression, to Poverty and Servitude'. George Washington refused to submit to an imposition which would 'make us as tame and abject Slaves, as the blacks we Rule over in such an arbitrary Sway'.[22] The following autumn, the so-called First Continental Congress convened to coordinate the resistance. The mood was still 'reformist', independence not yet on the table. Then came the failed British attempt to pacify Massachusetts and the fateful opening skirmishes at Lexington and Concord. In July 1775, a Second Continental Congress adopted *The Declaration of the Causes and Necessity of Taking Up Arms* drafted by John Dickinson and Thomas Jefferson: 'We have counted the cost of this contest, and find nothing so dreadful as voluntary Slavery.' By then, the original twelve United Colonies (Massachusetts, New Hampshire, Rhode Island, Connecticut, Pennsylvania, New York, New Jersey, Maryland, Delaware, Virginia, North Carolina and South Carolina, soon to be joined by Georgia) had organized an army and appointed a commander-in-chief. 'Our cause is just. Our union is perfect. Our internal resources are great, and, if necessary, foreign assistance is undoubtedly attainable.' Prudently the *Declaration* strove to reassure loyalists: 'We have not raised armies with ambitious designs of separating from Great Britain, and establishing independent states. We fight not for glory or for conquest.' This seemed, of course, to contradict every move being made, but suggested that the mood for compromise had not entirely vanished.[23]

In January the following year, Thomas Paine published his radical pamphlet *Common Sense*. Widely distributed and often read aloud, it contributed significantly to the spread of republicanism and boosted the case for separation from Great Britain. Here, common sense meant economic interest. Which was the most convenient arrangement for the settlers, dependence on Britain or independence from it?[24] The enormous popularity of the pamphlet contrasted with the intense dislike it provoked in quarters, where 'to be a Paine-hater was a badge of respectability'.[25] John Adams admired Paine's prose, its 'Strength and Brevity' and 'elegant Simplicity'.[26] But he thought *Common Sense* a 'Disastrous Meteor' and that his 'Arguments from the old Testament, were ridiculous, but whether they proceeded from honest Ignorance, and or foolish [Superstition] on one hand, or from willfull Sophistry and knavish Hypocricy on the other I know not [sic]'.[27]

Independence declared

As a young lawyer, Adams had successfully defended the British soldiers tried for firing on a crowd in March 1770, the famous Boston Massacre. At first, he held that there were advantages in remaining part of Great Britain. John Dickinson stood by this position, refusing to vote for the Declaration of Independence. Adams, having helped draft it, voted in its favour, but remained generally sceptical about revolution. When the French Revolution began, Adams, though accepting its ideals, was alarmed (as was Alexander Hamilton) by the radical turn it took, and denounced the revolutionaries for establishing a single legislature and for despising religion: 'I know not what to make of a republic of thirty million atheists.'[28]

Much of the Declaration, written in June 1776 by the Committee of Five – Thomas Jefferson was the main drafter, with help from Adams, Benjamin Franklin, Roger Sherman and Robert Livingston – was a well-rehearsed denunciation of George III. Then finally it arrived at the main business, departing from the professed loyalism of *The Declaration of the Causes and Necessity of Taking Up Arms* to state

> that these United Colonies are, and of Right ought to be Free and Independent States; that they are Absolved from all Allegiance to the British Crown, and that all political connection between them and the State of Great Britain, is and ought to be totally dissolved.

These were the fatal words Congress had inserted into Jefferson's draft.

It was the second paragraph that became famous, and not just in the US: 'We hold these truths to be self-evident, that all men are created equal, that they are endowed by their Creator with certain unalienable Rights, that among these are Life, Liberty and the Pursuit of Happiness.' Such words did not possess the quasi-sacred meaning they later acquired as part of the founding myth of the country.[29] The expression 'pursuit of happiness' was borrowed from Locke, who had argued that 'the highest perfection of intellectual nature lies in a careful and constant pursuit of true and solid happiness; so the care of ourselves, that we mistake not imaginary for real happiness, is the necessary foundation of our liberty'.[30]

There was, of course, a blatant contradiction between these lofty sentiments and the fact that slavery was widespread in the country. As Joseph Ellis wrote: 'It required herculean feats of denial not to notice that 20 percent of the American population, about 500,000 souls, were African Americans, and that fully 90 percent of them were slaves.'[31] Slave owners among the Founding Fathers included Jefferson, who owned 600, Benjamin Franklin (who was also, however, president of the Pennsylvania Abolition Society) and George Washington, who made sure his slaves could not be freed.[32] The contradiction was remarked upon even at the time, particularly in Britain, where anti-Americanism was influenced by a distaste for the institution of slavery; this position was shared by people as different as Samuel Johnson, John Wesley, Adam Smith and William Blake.[33]

In *The Theory of Moral Sentiments* (1759), Smith characterized slavery as the 'vilest of all states', with reference to ancient Greece; in *The Wealth of Nations* (1776) he argued it was not only wrong, but uneconomic.[34] Although Methodism concentrated on personal salvation, it was strongly anti-slavery. In his *Thoughts Upon Slavery* (1774), its founder, John Wesley, wondered 'how *Britons* can so readily admit of a change in their disposition and sentiments, as to practice in *America* what they abhor and detested in *Britain*?', adding:

> Better no trade, than trade procured by villany. It is far better to have no wealth, than to gain wealth, at the expense of virtue. Better is honest poverty, than all the riches brought by the tears, and sweat, and blood of our fellow-creatures.[35]

The writer and lexicographer Samuel Johnson, an anti-colonialist Tory, toasted to 'the next insurrection of the Negroes in the West Indies' and, discussing American slavery, asked scornfully why 'we hear the loudest yelps for liberty among the drivers of Negroes'.[36] At a dinner party, according to his biographer James Boswell, he declared: 'I am willing to love all mankind, EXCEPT AN AMERICAN.'[37] The abolitionist Thomas Day, author of the popular poem *The Dying Negro* (1773), was equally derisive: 'If there be an object truly ridiculous in nature it is an American patriot signing resolutions of independency with the one hand and with the other brandishing a whip over his affrighted slaves.'[38]

At the same time, many Britons supported the American revolutionaries because they agreed with their analysis that Britain was under the tyranny of an aristocratic ruling class. The great Whig orator Charles James Fox fearlessly supported them. Lord Rockingham, who as prime minister had passed the Declaratory Act which asserted the supremacy of the British Parliament over the colonists, changed tack once in opposition and became a supporter of the latter's rights. The pro-American position in some sectors of the British elite was a sign that there might be something to gain from American independence, if only because the war had turned out more costly than expected.[39] Had these leading politicians been listened to, the American colonies might have remained British for a little longer. A significant minority of white Americans wanted to remain loyal to Britain – the so-called loyalists or Tories – while many Native Americans, particularly the Cherokee, supported the British to block further colonial expansion into their territories. Encouraged by Britain's promise of freedom, 60,000 loyalist settlers exiled themselves to Canada, along with 15,000 black slaves.[40] Already in November 1775, Lord Dunmore, the British governor of Virginia, had offered freedom to all slaves who escaped from their masters and joined 'his Majesty's troops'.[41] Though no mass uprising of slaves occurred during the War of Independence (as in Haiti/Saint Domingue during the French Revolution), tens of thousands of slaves took advantage of the conflict to escape.[42] Meanwhile, of course, the British still promoted the slave trade.

In 1778, the North government sent the Carlisle Peace Commission to negotiate terms with the Continental Congress, offering some kind of representation within the empire akin to what later would be known as dominion status. It was too late. The rebels, by then aware that the British were about to withdraw from Philadelphia, wanted full independence. There was dismay in Britain. Edmund Burke blamed British misrule and thought it wrong to risk losing half an empire on account of an 'idle quarrel' over taxation; the colonists, he thought, had 'rustick' political tastes and primitive ideas of liberty, but they were still

Englishmen and could not be treated in the 'same manner' as 'the natives of *Hindostan* [sic]'.[43]

While the conventional American narrative is that the violence came mainly from the English, American patriots too launched a campaign of terror against loyalists who held by the British Crown.[44] Since the colonists were mainly of English descent, the War of Independence had all the hallmarks of a civil war. Of course, as in any war, all sides used violence and terror. The British won most of the important battles, such as those of Long Island, Manhattan, Brandywine and Germantown, but not the decisive battle of Yorktown, Virginia, where Americans had the crucial support of French troops. It was the fall of Yorktown on 19 October 1781 that forced Great Britain to concede defeat and accept the new independent state. 'The expense of it has been enormous,' William Pitt the Younger had complained in the House of Commons a few months earlier, when the writing was on the wall. 'And yet what has the British nation received in return? Nothing but a series of ineffective victories or severe defeats.' John Wilkes and his radical supporters in the City of London now begged the king to abandon the war in the American colonies: 'Your Majesty's fleets have lost their wonted superiority. Your armies have been captured. Your dominions have been lost.'[45]

Independence realized

Though the number of casualties was not particularly elevated, the grand total of Americans who died in the War of Independence is estimated at 1 per cent: 25,324 (including the thousands who died in camps) out of a population of 2,781,000.[46] Smallpox was a critical factor in American defeats, especially during the Canadian campaign and the siege of Boston in 1775–76.[47]

Britain's loss of the Thirteen Colonies had been largely due to its diplomatic isolation, since Spain and the Dutch Republic, following the French, sided with the colonies. The American Revolution might not have been successful or might not have concluded so relatively quickly without the help of the French monarchy – one which, unlike the British, was absolute. Peace negotiations took place in Paris, as if to underline France's role in the American victory.

For the British, the defeat by the colonists constituted a loss of morale and prestige, a wound to their belief that they were superior, more than a commercial damage, since from the trade point of view the

Caribbean colonies were far more profitable than the American ones.[48] In 1780 relatively little cotton originated from the southern states; the cotton imported into Britain and Europe came mainly from the West Indies, Brazil, India and the Ottoman Empire. Slave plantations in North America produced tobacco, rice, indigo and some sugar.[49] Sir John Seeley, in his famous 1883 lectures, described the American war as so 'ignominious' that it was quickly forgotten: 'We have tacitly agreed to mention [it] as seldom as we can.'[50] France, however, was left in great financial difficulty by its support for the Americans: support given in the hope of weakening Britain, whose banking and fiscal system was far more sophisticated. Instead, France emerged enfeebled and would soon have to face its own revolution, while Britain continued to industrialize at a faster pace and never lost a war again.

Having received help from absolutist France in its war against the British, George Washington refused to reciprocate when Revolutionary France fought Britain. Nor did he intervene to help Thomas Paine when he was imprisoned in France, causing Paine to write his public 1796 *Letter to George Washington*, in which he described Washington, by then president, as a hypocrite as well as an incompetent general. As Paine pointed out:

> Had it not been for the aid received from France in men, money and ships ... your cold and unmilitary conduct (as I shall shew in the course of this letter) would, in all probability, have lost America; at least she would not have been the independent nation she now is.[51]

Having achieved independence from Britain, the Americans had to decide what kind of state to construct. The Constitution ratified in 1788 was a contradiction of worthy rhetoric and political calculation. Its famous preamble to the Constitution read in altisonant tones:

> We the People of the United States, in Order to form a more perfect Union, establish Justice, insure domestic Tranquility, provide for the common defense, promote the general Welfare, and secure the Blessings of Liberty to ourselves and our Posterity do ordain and establish this Constitution for the United States of America.

Originally it had declared, more simply but less effectively, 'we the peoples of the states of New Hampshire, Massachusetts, Rhode Island [etc.]'. The United States of America was coming into being.

Since it was obvious that each colony – now a state – had to accept the final draft of the Constitution, how was power going to be shared between them and the central government within a federal structure? Senators, it was agreed, would represent each state, while the House of Representatives – the lower chamber – would be elected on a proportional basis. But larger states, since they contributed more to the nation's finances, thought they should have greater representation in the Senate as well. Benjamin Franklin suggested that each state should have an equal vote in the Senate in all matters except budgetary ones. Finally, on 16 July 1787, the Constitutional Convention adopted the Great Compromise (or Connecticut Compromise) by just one vote. Each state would have two senators, regardless of size. At the time, the most populous states (Pennsylvania, Virginia and Massachusetts) had roughly eight times the voters of those with the smallest population (Georgia and Rhode Island).[52] Today, the population of California (almost 40 million) is seventy times that of Wyoming (567,000), yet they return two senators each.

An equally serious, and equally infamous, distortion involved the electoral college. In almost all states, whichever presidential candidate wins the most votes gets all the electoral college votes for that state. The consequence is that it is perfectly possible to win the presidency with a losing share of the popular vote. It has happened, notably in 1888 when Benjamin Harrison was returned; in 2000 after George W. Bush was judged to have pipped Al Gore in Florida; and in 2016 when Hillary Clinton obtained almost 3 million votes more than Donald Trump but only 227 seats in the electoral college against Trump's 304.

The decision to have such an intermediate body derived from the Founding Fathers' suspicion of the 'multitude'. Originally it was believed that the electors of the electoral college would not be strictly mandated. Hamilton argued that the 'election should be made by men most capable of analysing the qualities adapted to the station' of president, and that 'a small number of persons ... will be most likely to possess the information and discernment requisite to such complicated investigations'. In this way one would avoid 'tumult and disorder', for the 'choice ... of an intermediate body of electors, will be much less apt to convulse the community with any extraordinary or violent movements, than the choice of ONE who was himself to be the final object of the public wishes'. He added, confidently: 'The process of election affords a moral certainty, that the office of President will never fall to the lot of any man who is not in an eminent degree endowed with the requisite qualifications.'[53] The results of some recent presidential elections must have sent Hamilton spinning in his grave. Since 1800 all efforts to reform the electoral college have failed.[54]

The Constitution was a compromise between those who wanted strong states and a weak central government and those who wanted the opposite. The result appeared to be an inefficient structure with a constitution that was extremely difficult to amend. Fear of strong government remained a feature of political discussion. Yet if one takes all its disparate institutions as a single whole, the US state is immensely powerful. As William Novak wrote in 2008:

> A primary reason that American state power remains so hidden is that it is so widely distributed among an exceedingly complex welter of institutions, jurisdictions, branches, offices, programs, rules, customs, laws, and regulations. There are more than 89,000 separate governmental units operating in the United States. Beneath the national government and 50 state governments, 3,033 counties, 19,492 municipal governments, 16,519 town or township governments, 37,381 special district governments, and 13,051 school districts all function with differing self-governing powers and further official subdivisions. Within the national government itself, the division, separation, and distribution of power can be overwhelming. The legislative branch includes 2 houses, 435 congressional districts, and more than 200 committees and subcommittees.[55]

The absence of a single powerful centre in a complex system of checks and balances feeds the myth of a weak state because no single person or group controls the whole. This is what makes Michael Mann's distinction between despotic power ('the range of actions which the elite is empowered to undertake without routine, institutionalized negotiation with civil society groups') and infrastructural power ('the capacity of the state actually to penetrate civil society' – that is, everywhere) so interesting and valid.[56] The US is an obvious example of infrastructural power.

The Constitution left suffrage to the states, and the criteria were mostly based on property and gender. Even though the dictum that all men, if not all people, are created equal was not really questioned, it is clear that elite opinion was almost identical to that in Britain and Continental Europe: the vote should be restricted. The revolutionaries believed that owning land made you a better citizen, more aware of your rights and obligations. So the solution was to increase the number of those owning land, thus increasing the power of competent people. It followed that, at the time and for much of the nineteenth century, American politicians and publicists believed that an ideal republic committed to political equality required an equitable distribution of wealth – unlike an aristocracy, which was based on privilege, nepotism, high taxes, a large bureaucracy, monopolies and an established church.[57]

The rule of the multitude, if unchecked, would lead to anarchy and disaster. As the conservative French writer Antoine de Rivarol ironically declared in 1789: 'There are two truths in this world one must never separate: 1. Sovereignty must reside in the people; 2. The people must never exercise it.'[58] The spirit of this ironic phrase was anticipated in *The Federalist Papers* written by Hamilton, James Madison and John Jay in 1787–88. While arguing in favour of the ratification of the Constitution, they were reluctant to give too many powers to the people. 'In all very numerous assemblies, of whatever character composed, passion never fails to wrest the sceptre from reason. Had every Athenian citizen been a Socrates, every Athenian assembly would still have been a mob.'[59] Hamilton thought only 'the discerning part of the community' should govern, while the 'ignorant and designing' should follow.[60] He was, deep down, more a Hobbesian than a Lockean.[61]

John Adams declared in a letter sent from Philadelphia on 26 May 1776, as the Declaration of Independence was being drafted: 'The only moral Foundation of Government is the Consent of the People.' But this did not actually mean 'that every Individual ... old and young, male and female, as well as rich and poor, must consent, expressly to every Act of Legislation'.[62] Trying to find a justification for the outcome he thought was preferable, he wondered: 'Whence arises the Right of the Men to govern Women, without their Consent? Whence the Right of the old to bind the Young, without theirs? ... But why exclude Women?' Some might argue that 'their Delicacy renders them unfit for Practice and Experience, in the great Business of Life, and the hardy Enterprizes of War, as well as the arduous Cares of State'. Besides, women had to look after the children, since 'Nature has made them fittest for domestic Cares'. Equally, destitute men 'are also too little acquainted with public Affairs to form a Right Judgment'. Adams doubted that one should change the existing system for fear that:

> New Claims will arise. Women will demand a Vote. Lads from 12 to 21 will think their Rights not enough attended to, and every Man, who has not a Farthing, will demand an equal Voice with any other in all Acts of State. It tends to confound and destroy all Distinctions, and prostrate all Ranks, to one common Levell.

So, in common with the enlightened opinion of the eighteenth century, women, children and the lower classes should not be entitled to vote.

In what her biographer described as 'the best-known proto-feminist statement of the Revolutionary era', Adams's wife Abigail urged her husband: 'Remember the Ladies, and be more generous and favourable to them than your ancestors.'

> Do not put such unlimited power into the hands of the Husbands. Remember all Men would be tyrants if they could. If perticuliar care and attention is not paid to the Laidies [sic] we are determined to foment a Rebelion [sic], and will not hold ourselves bound by any Laws in which we have no voice, or Representation. That your Sex are Naturally Tyrannical is a Truth so thoroughly established as to admit of no dispute, but such of you as wish to be happy willingly give up the harsh title of Master for the more tender and endearing one of Friend. Why then, not put it out of the power of the vicious and the Lawless to use us with cruelty and indignity with impunity. Men of Sense in all Ages abhor those customs which treat us only as the vassals of your Sex.[63]

John Adams responded as if it were a joke:

> I cannot but laugh ... Depend upon it, We know better than to repeal our Masculine systems. Altho they are in full Force, you know they are little more than Theory. We dare not exert our Power in its full Latitude. We are obliged to go fair, and softly, and in Practice you know We are the subjects.[64]

Abigail did not desist, and writing on 7 May 1776 she thundered and threatened:

> I can not say that I think you very generous to the Ladies, for whilst you are proclaiming peace and good will to Men, Emancipating all Nations, you insist upon retaining an absolute power over Wives. But you must remember that Arbitary power is like most other things which are very hard, very liable to be broken – and notwithstanding all your wise Laws and Maxims we have it in our power not only to free ourselves but to subdue our Masters, and without violence throw both your natural and legal authority at our feet.[65]

In subsequent correspondence she declared: 'If we mean to have Heroes, Statesmen and Philosophers, we should have learned women', because women are most responsible for educating their children and so should have the same educational advantages as men.[66] Abigail Adams was perfectly at home in politics while also running the farm in Braintree near Boston and raising four children. When John Adams became president, she handled his correspondence openly and voiced her criticism of political events such as the conduct of the inconclusive War of 1812 against Great Britain over naval rights.

The revolution did not do much for women, since America maintained much of the British legal tradition, including the idea that women had to be subjected in law to their husbands.[67] The English jurist William Blackstone was long popular in the US, his *Commentaries on the Common Law* (1765) a standard textbook. It argued that a married woman's legal existence was considered to be merged with that of her husband, so that she was not an independent being: 'Even the disabilities, which the wife lies under, are for the most part intended for her protection and benefit. So great a favourite is the female sex of the laws of England.'[68]

'Yours, not mine'

That the American Revolution was far from over was seen by some of the more percipient signers of the Declaration of Independence. Benjamin Rush, a physician from Pennsylvania who is far less celebrated than Jefferson, Washington, Hamilton and the like, declared:

> There is nothing more common than to confound the terms of the American revolution with those of the late American war. The American war is over: but this is far from being the case with the American revolution. On the contrary, nothing but the first act of the great drama is closed. It remains yet to establish and perfect our new forms of government; and to prepare the principles, morals, and manners of our citizens, for these forms of government, after they are established and brought to perfection.

Rush was an abolitionist and a proponent of women's education. His address concluded: 'The Revolution Is Not Over!'[69]

The revolution took a long time, particularly for enslaved African Americans. The Black abolitionist leader Frederick Douglass, in a famous oration delivered on 5 July 1852, proclaimed:

This Fourth July is *yours*, not *mine*. *You* may rejoice, I must mourn ... Whether we turn to the declarations of the past, or to the professions of the present, the conduct of the nation seems equally hideous and revolting. America is false to the past, false to the present, and solemnly binds herself to be false to the future ... What, to the American slave, is your 4th of July? I answer, a day that reveals to him, more than all other days in the year, the gross injustice and cruelty to which lie is the constant victim ... for revolting barbarity and shameless hypocrisy, America reigns without a rival.[70]

Though the Constitution did not mention slavery, what became known as the Fugitive Slave Clause established that a 'person held to service or labor' (a slave) who escapes to another state must be sent back to their master. Southern leaders were reassured that slavery was not in peril. Northerners regarded Southern slaveholders as a kind of aristocracy and slavery as repugnant, but they feared disunity more than slavery, and so tolerated it for decades. Some Southern delegates tried to enshrine slavery within the Constitution. Instead, there was a clause decreeing that members of the House of Representatives would be apportioned 'according to their respective Numbers, which shall be determined by adding to the whole Number of free Persons, and ... three fifths of all other Persons'. These other persons were obviously slaves who would count for three-fifths in congressional representation, thus increasing the political representation of slaveholders.

In *Notes on the State of Virginia* (1785), Thomas Jefferson, a slave owner, was ambivalent about slave ownership. He thought that it brought about 'the most unremitting despotism' by the masters and 'degrading submissions' by the slaves.[71] He had intended to denounce slavery in the Declaration of Independence but encountered considerable opposition.[72] Yet he certainly did not regard blacks as equal: *Notes on the State of Virginia* is shot through with virulent and deep-seated racism. He was not in favour of abolition, but wanted to prevent the introduction of more slaves. This is why, perhaps too generously, the historian David Brion Davis wrote: 'Jefferson's celebrated *Notes on Virginia* combined the antislavery ideals of the Enlightenment with a clinical diagnosis of Negro inferiority.'[73] His 'solution' for the gradual elimination of slavery in the US was one of child separation, where the children of slaves would be collected and 're-colonized' in Africa, dismissing the moral implications of separating children from their mothers.[74] Jefferson's ambivalence over slavery was manifest even later, during the Haitian Revolution when, as president, he cut off aid to the nascent republic and tried to isolate Haiti, fearing that its anti-slavery revolution would spread.[75]

The institution of slavery was extended, after 1812, to Louisiana, Mississippi, Alabama, Missouri, Arkansas, Florida and Texas, enabling cotton planters to grow even richer with slave labour. Cotton soon became the main export of the American South. On the eve of the Civil War, it comprised 61 per cent of American exports.[76] The same strip of land could not constantly be used for cotton, and so plantations moved south and west. The Treaty of Paris had set geographical limits to the new United States. It was not supposed to expand beyond the Appalachian Mountains, which stretch from Pennsylvania to Georgia and which today divide the Eastern Seaboard from the Midwest. It also excluded Florida, then in the hands of Spain, and Louisiana, then in the hands of France. The agreed limits were, of course, only the nucleus of what we know today as the US. The America that was born in 1776–83 could not have been more different from what it became. The original federation of thirteen states continued to grow over a century and a half: it grabbed most of the West from the indigenous inhabitants, the so-called Indians, whom Canadians call, more correctly, the First Nations.

The British banker Thomas Baring, one of the world's greatest cotton merchants, provided the necessary funds for the purchase of Louisiana in 1803 with the approval of the British government: it was considered good for America, good for Baring and good for British business.[77] What was then called Louisiana was far larger than today's Louisiana: it covered land from fifteen present-day states including Arkansas, Missouri, Kansas, Wyoming and Colorado. Spain sold Florida in 1819–21, its finances having suffered during the Peninsular War against Napoleon.

In 1845 came the annexation of Texas. The so-called Republic of Texas had declared independence from Mexico a decade earlier and soon favoured incorporation into the US. Migrants from the US had extended cotton cultivation and slavery in the territory. Slavery was illegal in Mexico, and planters felt they could not be safe unless Texas was assimilated into the US. Since the slavery question was divisive within Congress, two presidents in succession, Andrew Jackson and Martin Van Buren, hesitated over annexation. In the Senate there was an anti-slavery majority. This majority was strengthened by the outrage caused by a letter of April 1844 undiplomatically linking annexation to the defence of slavery; it had been sent to the British ambassador by Secretary of State John C. Calhoun, a Southern extremist. The Senate rejected annexation, but the House of Representatives accepted it out of fear that refusing the entry of Texas would lead to the secession of Southern states. So slavery was continually extended in the 'land of the free and the home of the brave', to use the words of the slave owner Francis Scott Key – words which in 1931 became part of the US national anthem, 'The Star-Spangled Banner'.

The massacre of Native Americans continued, and so did their removal from their land east of the Mississippi following the Indian Removal Act of 1830 introduced by President Andrew Jackson. Between 1830 and 1850, about 60,000 Native Americans were ethnically cleansed to make way for slave plantations. The removal, particularly pronounced in 1838–39 (the years of the so-called Cherokee Trail of Tears), was carried out by US troops and local militias – 'a lawless rabble' in the words of Senator Henry Clay, a strong opponent of the Indian Removal Act.[78]

Civil War

By the 1830s the US was governed as a liberal nineteenth-century republic, despite the fact that a significant part of its economy relied on slave labour – the kind of labour that had stopped existing in Europe centuries earlier. The young Alexis de Tocqueville, travelling the country while taking notes for his celebrated *De la démocratie en Amérique*, remarked: 'One thing ... incontrovertibly demonstrated by America ... is that the middle classes can govern a State ... In spite of their petty passions, their incomplete education, their vulgarity, they can demonstrably supply practical intelligence, and that is enough.'[79] From the end of the eighteenth century to the Civil War, property qualifications were increasingly eliminated and most adult white males were enfranchised. By 1855, all but six states had dropped their insistence that only taxpayers could vote.[80]

Slavery had become central to the economy of the South to an extent unimaginable outside the Americas. In China, India, the Middle East and elsewhere there was hardly any chattel slavery (meaning that the slave and his or her children are legally owned and can be sold); there were servants, slave girls, captured enemies forced into slave labour, indentured servants, workers kept in terrible conditions and serfs unable to leave the land, but no slave system central to the economy, as in the Americas. In 1790, there had been, according to the census, 697,897 slaves in the United States. By 1860, just as the Civil War was about to begin, there were nearly 4 million in an area which stretched halfway across the American continent into Texas. The American South, Brazil and Spanish Cuba and Puerto Rico were the slavery holdouts of the Western hemisphere.[81] Slavery had ended more or less gradually in the Northern states, beginning with Pennsylvania in 1784, then Connecticut and Rhode Island. In New York the last slaves were freed in 1827. But racism was pervasive even in those states which had abolished slavery. Gustave de Beaumont, who sojourned for ten months in the country with his friend de Tocqueville, writes of his shock at the colour segregation in a New York theatre in the foreword of his novel, *Marie or, Slavery in the United States: A Novel of Jacksonian America* (1840).

In a famous letter to *New York Tribune* editor Horace Greeley on 22 August 1862, Abraham Lincoln explained that the

> paramount object in this struggle *is* to save the Union, and is *not* either to save or to destroy slavery. If I could save the Union without freeing *any* slave I would do it, and if I could save it by freeing *all* the slaves I would do it; and if I could save it by freeing some and leaving others alone I would also do that.[82]

In fact, the four states that opted not to join the secession (Missouri, Delaware, Kentucky and Maryland) did not immediately free their slaves, while Lincoln's Emancipation Proclamation of 1863 only freed slaves in secessionist states.

The issue at stake in the Civil War was secession, but slavery was the major animating reason behind it.[83] Agitation against slavery had started well before the Civil War. The abolitionist paper the *Liberator*, read overwhelmingly by freed slaves, was founded in January 1831 by William Lloyd Garrison. Later that year Nat Turner, who was born in slavery, led a quickly suppressed rebellion in Virginia. He was hanged and his body then dismembered. The American Anti-Slavery Society was created two years later. Former slaves including Frederick Douglass, Sojourner Truth and Harriet Tubman joined the movement, often using the New Testament to argue against slavery.

John Brown, on the basis of deep religious conviction as well as his interpretation of the Declaration of Independence, incited a slave rebellion by attempting to take over a military arsenal at Harpers Ferry in Virginia in 1859. There were twenty-two participants in the rebellion, seven of whom were black. Brown was eventually captured and executed but, as the famous marching song intones, 'his soul is marching on'. In Europe there was widespread emotion. Victor Hugo wrote a letter to a London newspaper, widely reprinted on both sides of the Atlantic, including in the *Liberator*, imploring that Brown's life be spared, for 'one recoils' at the prospect of 'such a great crime committed by such a great people'.[84]

At first Lincoln, elected president in 1860 almost exclusively by Northern votes – his Republican Party was virtually non-existent in the South – had tried to reassure the South that his intention was not to end slavery but to stop its extension elsewhere. His main objective was the preservation of the Union. But Lincoln was determined that slavery should not be allowed in any new states. Southern states, especially South Carolina, feared that there would eventually be an anti-slavery majority in Congress and decided to secede.

On 21 March 1861, in Savannah, Georgia, Vice-President of the new Confederate States of America Alexander Stephens declared, in an unwitting paraphrase of the Declaration of Independence later known as the Cornerstone Speech, that the cornerstone of the new secessionist government 'rests upon the great truth, that the negro is not equal to the white man; that slavery – subordination to the superior race – is his natural and normal condition'. A great applause followed.[85] A statue of Stephens has resided in the National Statuary Hall Collection in the Capitol since 1927. Each state can nominate two statues, and there were no state-designated statues of African Americans until, in 2018, Florida replaced a statue of Confederate General Edmund Kirby Smith with one of African American civil rights feminist activist Mary McLeod Bethune.

When the Civil War began on 12 April 1861, European sympathies were, on balance, on the side of the Union. In 1862, Lancashire mill workers, though it was not at all in their personal interest since they depended on raw cotton picked by US slaves, boycotted American cotton (while, rather stupidly, many Southern cotton planters embargoed shipments of cotton to Europe). The mill workers' self-sacrifice was acknowledged by Lincoln himself in a letter sent in January 1863, 'to the working people of Manchester', in which he recognized their 'sufferings' and praised their unsurpassed 'sublime Christian heroism'. Extracts from the letter can be found on the pedestal of his statue in Lincoln Square, Manchester. Such self-sacrifice could not be found in the pages of *The Times* or the liberal daily *Manchester Guardian*, upholder of free trade. The *Guardian* sided with the slave-owning South, asserting that 'commercial considerations' should be examined since 'the bonds of the union have been as burdensome as the fetters to the negro'.[86] When Lincoln was assassinated it produced an editorial that included the line: 'Of his rule we can never speak except as a series of acts abhorrent to every true notion of constitutional right and human liberty.'[87] Gladstone, then the liberal chancellor of the Exchequer, was also on the side of the South, along with a significant section of the British elite. He accused those who sided with the North of being 'Negrophilist'.[88]

Unlike the *Spectator* – whose editor Meredith Townsend was full of praise for Lincoln – the other voice of liberalism, the *Economist*, was pro-Southern. Its editor Walter Bagehot was scathing about Lincoln, though he grudgingly became an admirer, particularly after Lincoln was dead. Bagehot had been sure the South would win and even managed to convince himself that a Southern victory would lead to the abolition of slavery, which 'we abhor'.[89] But on the whole European governments remained neutral, while progressive opinion – Karl Marx, John Stuart Mill, Victor Hugo, Giuseppe Garibaldi – sided clearly against the South and slavery.

Roughly 179,000 Black men served as soldiers in the Union Army, and 40,000 of them died. They were paid less than white soldiers and were usually commanded by white officers. When captured by the Confederate Army they were often executed, unlike white prisoners.[90]

The war that came to an end when Robert E. Lee and his Confederate troops surrendered to Ulysses S. Grant at Appomattox, Virginia, on 9 April 1865 could be seen as more of a revolution than the War of Independence. The abolition of slavery was 'an act of confiscation of revolutionary and virtually unprecedented proportions', observed the historian John Ashworth.[91] It seemed to indicate that the American Revolution might finally have culminated, at the cost of between 650,000 and 1 million casualties – more than American losses in all the numerous wars it fought since. Formal equality, at least for men, appeared within reach. The Civil War also marked the victory of the industrial-capitalist North against the slave-owning South. Charles and Mary Beard called it a second revolution: 'While the planting class was being trampled in the dust – stripped of its wealth and political power – the capitalist class was marching onward in seven league boots.' Northern industry was now assured 'an immense national market surrounded by a tariff wall', while the Southern gentry 'lay prostrate'.[92]

Reconstruction is seen off

A decisive intervention to repair the damage done by such a long period of slavery should have been undertaken. This is what Reconstruction was supposed to achieve. The Thirteenth Amendment introduced by Lincoln in 1865 ended slavery. The Fourteenth (1868) and Fifteenth Amendments (1870) made discrimination unlawful. Schooling for Blacks was introduced, and some Black men were elected to state and federal office. As Eric Foner put it, the Reconstruction Amendments 're-founded' the Constitution.[93] Had they been fully implanted, they would have concluded the American Revolution.

While the Founding Fathers of America are celebrated and remembered, the key framers of the Reconstruction Amendments – Senators Charles Sumner and Lyman Trumbull, along with congressmen James Ashley and Thaddeus Stevens, leader of the House of Representatives – have remained obscure. Stevens was depicted in John F. Kennedy's largely ghosted *Profiles in Courage* (1956), which won a Pulitzer, as a 'crippled, fanatical personification of the extremes of the Radical Republican movement'.[94] Stevens, who was born with a club foot, was committed to racial equality and advocated confiscating the land of Confederate planters and distributing it to the emancipated slaves to help them prosper in a largely agricultural society while breaking the economic power of its landed aristocracy.[95] Anyone writing a book of 'profiles in courage' should have had the courage to dedicate a chapter to Stevens, instead of a few snide remarks.

Also forgotten is the fact that the main pressure group behind the Thirteenth Amendment was the Women's Loyal National League organized by Elizabeth Cady Stanton and Susan B. Anthony, which in 1863 collected between 300,000 and 400,000 signatures for a petition to the Senate demanding the abolition of slavery by a constitutional amendment. In 1866, women's rights activists formed the American Equal Rights Association (AERA) to continue the antebellum solidarity between women's rights and abolition and to promote real universal suffrage for Blacks as well as for women.[96]

When Abraham Lincoln was assassinated in April 1865, his successor Andrew Johnson, a staunch racist and former slave owner from Tennessee, succeeded in diluting the gains of Reconstruction. As Engels wrote prophetically to Marx in July 1865:

His [Johnson's] hatred of Negroes comes out more and more violently ... If things go on like this, in six months all the old villains of secession will be sitting in Congress at Washington. Without coloured suffrage nothing can be done there.[97]

Johnson believed that Blacks possessed less 'capacity for government than any other race of people' and, if left to their own devices, would show 'a constant tendency to relapse into barbarism'. White men alone, he thought, should manage the South. According to Foner, this was probably the most blatantly racist pronouncement ever to appear in an official state paper of an American president.[98] Johnson made sure that the new administrations in the 'liberated' South were entirely controlled by whites; he indiscriminately pardoned rich Confederates, and restored land allocated to former slaves to its previous owners.[99] Johnson, who seemed 'to shrink, not grow, in the face of crisis', also vetoed a Civil Rights Act extending citizenship to Blacks, though Congress overrode him.[100]

A new system of economic exploitation came into being, achieving similar results as those obtained under slavery. As the *Economist*, that voice of British liberalism, intoned in December 1865: 'It is clear that the dark races must in some way or other be induced to obey white men willingly.'[101] The freedmen once free were forced by necessity to work for pitiful wages. W. E. B. Du Bois wrote that, following the Civil War: 'The slave went free; stood a brief moment in the sun; then moved back again toward slavery.'[102] As Robert Fogel and Stanley L. Engerman observed:

> Time on the cross did not come to an end for American blacks with the downfall of the peculiar institution. For they were held on the cross not just by the chains of slavery but also by the spikes of racism.[103]

In a normal civil war, once a side loses, it has lost forever: the Stuarts recovered the throne, but never their powers; the Bourbons, ousted in France after 1830, remained ousted; the tsars are gone forever, and so are the Chinese emperors. In the American case, by contrast, the losers retained most of their privileges. The leaders of the Confederacy were never prosecuted. The victorious Yankees imposed no mass executions or imprisonment on the vanquished rebels, who mounted a ferocious rearguard action against Black emancipation.[104] The era of Radical Reconstruction inaugurated by Congress was short-lived and quickly abandoned. The Fourteenth Amendment, supposed to protect the liberty and property of all people, did a better job protecting property than lives, especially Black lives. Congress tried to impeach President Andrew Johnson, but the Senate failed by a single vote to muster the two-thirds necessary for conviction. Reconstruction ended in 1877, when the last Southern state fell under the control of white supremacist Democrats and organizations such as the Ku Klux Klan. The Compromise of 1877 which settled a disputed presidential election removed Federal troops from the South, and with them what remained of protection for Black advances. On 4 July 1877 Daniel H. Chamberlain, South Carolina's Republican Governor in 1874-76, expressed his dismay. The removal of Federal troops meant

> the abandonment of Southern Republicans and especially the colored race, to the control and rule not only of the Democratic party, but of that class at the South which regarded slavery as a Divine institution, which waged four years of destructive war for its perpetuation, which steadily opposed citizenship and suffrage for the negro – in a word, a class whose traditions, principles and history are opposed to every step and feature of what Republicans call our national progress since 1860.[105]

Soon Chamberlain became a supporter of white rule, even as white vigilantes murdered thousands of Blacks, often around election time. Segregation was codified in several Southern states with Jim Crow laws (named for a pejorative expression for Blacks) and for decades maintained a terrifying, steady drumbeat of lynchings, whose annual total often surpassed 100. Few Southern Blacks could go to the polls again until Congress passed the Voting Rights Act in 1965. Voting rights were restricted in Southern states by violence, intimidation, literacy tests and various other techniques. Literacy tests also barred some poor white voters. In 1896 the Southern victory was given further strength when the Supreme Court reached its 'separate but equal' verdict in *Plessy v. Ferguson*, upholding the Louisiana Separate Car Act of 1890 which segregated passengers in train cars. The case originated when Homer Plessy, who was one-eighth Black (known at the time as an octoroon), boarded a train compartment in Louisiana reserved for whites.

In April 1873 in Colfax, Louisiana, a mob of former confederate soldiers killed an estimated sixty black militiamen serving in the US military.[106] Other massacres followed. On 2 July 1917 in the industrial city of East St Louis, Illinois, crowds of whites numbering thousands rampaged beating, shooting and hanging Black Americans, mainly workers who had migrated from the South. Of the forty-eight accounted dead, thirty-nine were Black.[107] In 1921, in Tulsa, Oklahoma, a white mob brutally attacked the Black community with the complicity of the authorities. There were no arrests, and the event was effaced from official history, although President Harding alluded to it a few days later in a speech at a Black university in Pennsylvania. In 1996 the Oklahoma state legislature announced a commission to study the Tulsa race riot; in 2001 the commission concluded it was 'probable that many people, likely numbering between 100–300, were killed during the massacre'.[108] The number of those killed was far greater than those killed in the famous Kishinev pogrom of 1903 in Tsarist Russia – yet officially the Tulsa massacre was a riot, not a pogrom. In June 2020, President Donald Trump held an election rally in Tulsa and failed to mention the massacre, instead criticizing demands to take down statues of Confederate soldiers.

The condition of Native Americans deteriorated further during the Civil War. Originally 'Indian Tribes' had been regarded as independent nations, but the Indian Appropriations Act (March 1871), decreed: 'No Indian nation or tribe within the territory of the United States shall be acknowledged or recognized as an independent nation, tribe, or power with whom the United States may contract by treaty.' This made it even easier for the federal government to seize lands previously controlled by Native Americans. In 1876 the Sioux and their Cheyenne allies defeated the American army at the battle of Little Big Horn (Custer's Last Stand) but were forced to surrender their land the following year. The Apache, led by the legendary Geronimo, surrendered in 1886. Geronimo spent the rest of his life being paraded as an attraction in various fairs and expositions, including in the ethnology section of the St Louis World's Fair in 1904. In December 1890 there occurred the Wounded Knee Massacre, where 300 Lakota (Sioux) were killed by American soldiers. Many of these events have been made famous in films and novels. Hostilities of varying intensity continued until 1924. The fate of Native Americans continued its downward trajectory, virtually forgotten by all, and barely mentioned until recently in numerous films and novels celebrating the 'conquest of the West' by white settlers.[109] Native Americans accused the Indian Health Service of sterilizing at least 25 per cent of Native American women between the ages of fifteen and forty-four during the 1970s. The justification used by the overwhelmingly white and male doctors was that they were helping the women to limit the size of their families (and simultaneously helping the government to cut funding for Medicaid and welfare programmes).[110]

The targets of American racism were not confined to African Americans or Native Americans. Henry George, the radical reformer and author of the bestselling *Progress and Poverty* (1879), railed against the Chinese, whose 'moral standard is as low as their standard of comfort'. They were, he said, 'incapable of understanding' America's political institutions.[111] In 1882 the Chinese Exclusion Act prohibited Chinese immigration and levied special taxes on the Chinese, who were also denied the right to own land. Anti-Chinese riots instigated by the trade unions (the Knights of Labor) broke out in Seattle. Samuel Gompers, leader of the American Federation of Labor, declared in 1901 that 'every incoming coolie ... means so much more vice and immorality injected into our social life'.[112]

In 1883 Emma Lazarus, a Jew of Sephardi extraction, penned her famous lines welcoming immigrants:

> Give me your tired, your poor,
> Your huddled masses yearning to breathe free,
> The wretched refuse of your teeming shore.
> Send these, the homeless, tempest-tost to me,
> I lift my lamp beside the golden door!

The poem was subsequently inscribed on the Statue of Liberty, a gift from the French. They should have added to the words welcoming the world's 'huddled masses' the qualifier 'as long as they are white'.

History and memory

Those who defended the 'Lost Cause of the Confederacy' maintained that its cause was just, since it had tried to shore up states' rights against an overbearing federal government. Historians of the Dunning School – named after William Dunning (1857–1922), professor of history at Columbia and president of both the American Historical Association and the American Political Science Association – presented Radical Reconstruction as a threat to white supremacy that had demanded in response a policy of segregation and discrimination. In an article in the *Atlantic* in October 1901, Dunning argued that 'the ultimate root of the trouble in the South had been, not the institution of slavery, but the coexistence in one society of two races so distinct in characteristics as to render coalescence impossible'. Slavery had been one way of resolving this 'problem', and its replacement had to 'express the same fact of racial inequality'. In *Reconstruction, Political and Economic* (1907), Dunning claimed: 'What animated the whites was pride of their race ... and a dread, partly instinctive, partly rational, lest their institutions, traditions, and ideals were to be appropriated or submerged.'[113]

Dunning's text was demolished by W. E. B. Du Bois in his *Black Reconstruction in America* (1935). But the Lost Cause myth persisted through decades of industrialization, urbanization, liberalization and modernization.[114] Southern whites have flown their flags, erected monuments to their leaders and heroes and celebrated the antebellum South as an idyllic society. Until recently statues to John C. Calhoun and Confederate Generals Thomas 'Stonewall' Jackson and Robert E. Lee graced squares and buildings near fluttering Confederate banners. Lee and Jackson have been commemorated on US postage stamps (the former as recently as 1995). It is almost as if present-day Germany had a Goebbels Institute of Cultural Studies and a Himmler School of Human Rights. At least ten military bases in the Southern states of the US have been named after Confederate generals: that is, in honour of officers who took up arms against the US army. Until 2017 Yale University had a residential undergraduate college named after the arch-racist John Calhoun, who had claimed in 1837 that the 'Central African race had never existed in so comfortable, so respectable, or so civilized a condition, as that which it now enjoyed in the Southern States', and that 'the defence of human liberty against the aggressions of despotic power had been always the most efficient in States where domestic slavery was found to prevail'.[115] Until 2020 there was a bust of Chief Justice Roger Taney in the Old Supreme Court Chamber in Washington. Taney had delivered the majority opinion in the infamous *Dred Scott* case (1857), which established that Blacks were 'an inferior order' who could not be considered US citizens.[116] It was only in 2021 that President Joe Biden made Juneteenth a federal holiday, marking the day (19 June) in 1865 when Gordon Granger, a Union general, rode into Galveston, Texas, two months after the end of the Civil War, to inform the last slaves that they were free.

On the fiftieth anniversary of the battle of Gettysburg in 1913, President Woodrow Wilson failed to mention slavery, what the Civil War had been about and which side had been in the right. Speaking to a segregated audience, and himself a Southern supporter of segregation, Wilson praised both sides of the Civil War, 'these gallant men in blue and gray [who] sit all about us here'. He exclaimed:

How wholesome and healing the peace has been! We have found one another again as brothers and comrades in arms, enemies no longer, generous friends rather, our battles long past, the quarrel forgotten – except that we shall not forget the splendid valor, the manly devotion of the men then arrayed against one another, now grasping hands and smiling into each other's eyes.[117]

It was as if the Civil War had been a terrible mistake, or a wholesome sporting event where both sides shake hands amicably at the end. Seen in Europe as an idealistic advocate of peace after the First World War and awarded a Nobel Prize for his efforts, Wilson was a racist even by the standard of the times. He enjoyed watching the first feature-length film to be shown at the White House, D. W. Griffith's *The Birth of a Nation* (1915), based on the novel *The Clansman: A Historical Romance of the Ku Klux Klan* by Thomas Dixon Jr.[118]

Commemorations of the War of Independence have grown by the year, almost exponentially, but a critical note is also increasingly struck. In 1984 a 'Memorial to the 56 Signers of the Declaration of Independence' was unveiled in Washington, DC. Most of the signatories owned slaves, a fact unmentioned on the monument. Arlen Parsa, a filmmaker, recently

Arlen Parsa's remake of John Trumbull's famous painting *Declaration of Independence* (@arlenparsa, 'This is one of the most famous paintings in American history', Twitter, 1 September 2019)

confronted the amnesia by putting red dots over the faces of slave owners in John Trumbull's famous painting *Declaration of Independence* (1819).[119]

It was a symbol of sorts for the fact that the struggle for equal rights was far from over. If the American Revolution was ultimately more than a revolt against British rule, it was also far less than the establishment of a society based on the idea that all are 'created equal'. The latter task was left incomplete even by the Civil War. Such failures have reverberated for more than one hundred and fifty years.

3
Debating the French Revolution

Debate over the causes and consequences of the French Revolution has never abated. Complex events always have complex interpretations, and if they also have a political and ideological dimension, as is the case here, the difficulties multiply. The historian Albert Soboul began his 1965 account of 1789 as follows: 'The Revolution marked the advent of bourgeois, capitalist society in the history of France' – adding that it was 'the classic model of the bourgeois revolution'.[1] Indeed in the West (and not only in the West), the start of the modern era is generally regarded as coinciding with the French Revolution.

Was it a bourgeois revolution, or a necessary factor in the development of capitalist society? France industrialized much later than Britain, the US, Belgium or even Germany, but earlier than most other countries. So, did the revolution make a difference? Was it inevitable? Did it accelerate change, removing obstacles to capitalism? If it had not occurred, would there not have been in any case an evolution towards a parliamentary republic – something like the Third Republic and its successors? Could the Orléans dynasty (1830–48) have evolved towards a relatively liberal parliamentary monarchy like the one in Britain?[2] Such speculations can be amusing and interesting but, like much counterfactual history, they cannot be tested.

One should note, in passim, that while the French Revolution has remained a bone of political contention, this is not the case with the English Civil War, where disagreement has largely been confined to historians. The overthrow of Charles I would widely be seen as a 'good thing' even if some might be a little perturbed by the execution of a king. But all ended well, with a monarch on the throne and everyone praying to God to save him or her. In the US, meanwhile, there has always been virtual unanimity on the benefits of independence. The American Civil War, as we have seen, has remained a greater source of controversy.

In France, the dispute began almost immediately on whether the French Revolution was a good or a bad thing, or whether it started well and ended poorly. Could it have been better if it had finished in 1791–92, prior to the beginning of the Terror, or in 1795 when the worst of the Terror was over? Germaine de Staël's *Considerations on the Principal Events of the French Revolution*, one of the earliest books on the French Revolution, praised 1789–91 but not what happened afterwards.[3] De Staël was the daughter of Jacques Necker, finance minister under Louis XVI.

The modern revisionist view of the French Revolution started in the 1970s. Under the mantle of the Cold War, some French intellectuals with little sense of history described the Revolution as the beginning of 'totalitarianism' – a term invented in Italy, first by anti-Fascists such as Giovanni Amendola (1923) and soon adopted, with positive connotations, by pro-Fascists such as the Italian philosopher Giovanni Gentile.[4] Hannah Arendt, in *The Origins of Totalitarianism* (1951), used it to describe both Nazi Germany and Stalin's Russia (but not Italian Fascism; nor does she mention Giovanni Gentile). Some historians drew parallels between Georges Danton and Benito Mussolini, or Maximilien Robespierre and Vladimir Lenin.[5] Totalitarianism was a trope for revisionist historians leading up to the bicentenary in 1989, which coincided with the fall of the Soviet Union and the massacre at Tiananmen Square in Beijing. Arno Mayer lamented in *The Furies* (2000) how 'ultraconservative' historians had

> argued that in addition to being an inexpiable sin, the French Revolution was the ultimate source of all the purgatorial fires of the twentieth century ... They read the Jacobin Terror by the light of the Bolshevik Terror ... and then went on to include the genocidal racism of the Third Reich.[6]

François Furet's *Penser la Révolution française* (1978) attempted to refute the Marxist presentation of the revolution as a bourgeois one. Furet had earlier co-produced a glossy two-volume study of the Revolution, *La Révolution française* (1965–66), described unkindly but not unjustly by Lynn Hunt as a coffee-table book.[7] Revisionism had been preceded by Alfred Cobban, whose 1954 inaugural lecture at University

College London was published as *The Myth of the French Revolution*. Cobban was barely acknowledged by Furet and his colleagues.[8] The main communist, socialist or *marxisant* historians against whom Furet wrote were Georges Lefebvre, author of *La Grande Peur de 1789* (1932) and *Quatre-vingt-neuf* (1939), and above all Albert Soboul, who had written *Les Sans-Culottes parisiens en l'An II* (1958) and *Histoire de la Révolution française* (1962). An earlier leftist position had been delineated by Jean Jaurès in *Histoire socialiste de la Révolution française (1901–07)*. Jaurès was a moderate socialist leader assassinated in 1914 for his opposition to the impending First World War.

Anti-revolutionary views of the French Revolution have a long lineage, including Chateaubriand's *Mémoires d'outre-tombe* (started in 1809 and published posthumously in 1850), and Hippolyte Taine's multi-volume *Origines de la France contemporaine* (1875–1893). Members of Chateaubriand's family had been executed in 1794. Right-wing thinkers denounced what they regarded as the mindless violence of the revolutionary crowd. Gustave Le Bon's *Psychologie des foules* (1895), largely based on the Italian Scipio Sighele's *La folla delinquente* (1891), described how crowds were characterized by *impulsivité* and an *absence de jugement et d'esprit critique* commonly noted in such 'inferior forms of evolution' as women, savages and children.[9] Pierre Gaxotte's reactionary *La Révolution française* (1928) was described by historian of revolution Crane Brinton in the *American Political Science Review* as 'not history'.[10] Gaxotte's extreme right-wing and anti-Semitic (but not pro-Nazi – he was a follower of the far-right Charles Maurras, founder of the Action Française) views did not prevent him writing regularly for *Le Figaro* and being elected in 1953 to the prestigious Académie française, where he fought against the election of women, panicking in 1980 that 'if we elected a woman we would end up electing a negro'.[11] In that year, the first woman to be elected, Marguerite Yourcenar, took her seat. Three years later, the Black poet and former president of Senegal Léopold Sédar Senghor was elected. By then Gaxotte was dead.

The long revolution

Louis XVI's decision to convene the États Généraux (8 August 1788) launched a century of extraordinary instability in France. The country moved from absolute monarchy, as was still the case in June 1789, to a constitutional monarchy later that year. It then became a republic following the attack on the Tuileries, the royal residence, by the people of Paris on 10 August 1792. This was the beginning of what some have called the Second French Revolution.[12] The radical republic was followed, in 1795, by the rule of the Directoire, a five-member committee. A new constitution was adopted which increased the powers of the more prosperous sectors of society. There was also a religious revival.

The economic history of the Directory, in the words of Denis Woronoff, is a 'history of crises', but as in all crises there were losers and winners. The losers, as always, were the poor. The winners came mainly from those already *riches*: landlords and wealthy farmers who had managed to accumulate some capital.[13] At first the new policies (liberal, in the economic sense) caused runaway inflation before the situation stabilized; by 1797, the economy was on the mend.[14] But calm was far from being restored: there were plots from both monarchists and Jacobins. In 1796 came the famous Conspiracy of the Equals led by François-Noël 'Gracchus' Babeuf, a proto-communist. It failed, and Babeuf was guillotined.

There were wars in Europe. By the end of 1798, Allied armies (British, Austrian and Russian) were marching once more against France. At first the French suffered defeats, discrediting the Directory. It was during this period of turmoil that the army, inevitably, became a political force. This was the key factor in the rise of its general, Napoleon Bonaparte, to power. On 9 November 1799 (18 Brumaire) the République bourgeoisie was overthrown in a military coup led by Napoleon, who made himself consul for life in 1802, and emperor in 1804. The republic hadn't been well entrenched, hence its weakness. An official report in April 1799 had concluded that only eight departments could be considered reliably republican: Creuse, Meurthe, Haute-Saone, Hautes-Pyrenees, Finistère, Jura, Haute-Garonne and Pyrenees-Orientales.[15] In mid-1793, writes Arno Mayer, 'some sixty of France's eighty-three departments were more or less out of control and a majority of the population in various degrees' was unfavourable to a republic.[16] The French Revolution, though centred on Paris, differed from region to region.

The period of almost continuous wars that had started in 1792 came to a close in 1815 at Waterloo, having been preceded by constant warfare for most of the eighteenth century. The restoration of the Bourbon dynasty in 1814 was followed by the so-called revolution of 1830, which put the Orléans dynasty in power with Louis-Philippe I, now more democratically known as king of the French, rather than king of France. He was to be the last French king.

Between 1799 and 1847 the French wrote six constitutions, none of which defined where political authority resided, unlike the previous three which had declared that power resided with the nation (1791), 'the people' (1793) and 'all citizens' (1795).[17] In 1848 another revolution established a short-lived Second Republic, which led to a coup d'état by Louis Napoleon, who had been elected president. In 1852, following in the footsteps of his uncle, he too became emperor, as Napoleon III. This Second Empire crumbled when it was defeated by the Prussians in the war of 1870. Out of this defeat the Third Republic was born, threatened by an attempt to establish a radical polity (the Paris Commune). The monarchists were still powerful, but by 1880 the new republic was well established. Only then could one say that the French Revolution was definitively over.

The constant change of regimes signalled that the French Revolution was not an event which could be encapsulated in the few years following the seizure of the Bastille. The best French minds had understood this clearly. In his recollection about 1848, Tocqueville wrote:

> The constitutional monarchy succeeded the Ancient Régime. The Republic succeeded the monarchy. The Empire succeeded the Republic. The Restoration succeeded the Empire. Then came the July Monarchy. After each of these successive transformations people said that the French Revolution, having completed what they presumptuously called its work, was over. They said it and believed it. Alas! I had myself hoped it was true during the Restoration and again after the government fell. And now the French Revolution has begun anew, for it remains the same revolution as before. The farther we go, the more obscure its end becomes.[18]

Albert Laponneraye, a proto-communist journalist and activist, editor of Robespierre's works, was not wrong when he wrote in the 1830s: 'The Revolution is still continuing and will only be concluded when the kings will have exterminated the people or the people will have exterminated the kings.'[19] Laponneraye died in 1849, just as Louis Napoleon was about to consolidate his power.

To write, as some do, that the French Revolution occurred between May 1789, when the king convened the États Généraux, and 27 July 1794 (9 Thermidor, Year II), when the moderates took over – or else ended on 9 November 1799 (18 Brumaire Year VIII), when Bonaparte seized power – is to disregard this century of strife.

'Let's do it'

At least until 1917, the French Revolution was *the* revolution. It had embraced universal values in a way that would have been unthinkable in seventeenth-century England, although the American War of Independence had anticipated it in this respect.[20] Thomas Paine wrote in *Common Sense* (1776): 'The cause of America is in a great measure the cause of all mankind.'[21] His letter to George Washington announced a present from 'Our very good Friend the Marquis de la Fayette', namely 'the Key of the Bastile [sic]', with a drawing 'representing the demolition of that detestible [sic] prison', and described such gifts as the 'first ripe fruits of American principles transplanted into Europe'.[22] The sentiments expressed in the Declaration of Independence were incorporated in the Declaration of the Rights of Man and of the Citizen of 1789. But it was the French Revolution that became the revolution *par excellence*. Much to her chagrin, and with some exaggeration, Hannah Arendt wrote: 'The sad truth of the matter is that the French Revolution, which ended in disaster, has made world history, while the American Revolution, so triumphantly successful, has remained an event of little more than local importance.'[23]

The French Revolution was, in Immanuel Wallerstein's words, 'a world-historical event'. For Eric Hobsbawm, it was 'a landmark' which set the pattern 'for all subsequent revolutionary movements', including socialist and communist ones.[24] It provided a pattern for modern politics more widely, as Lynn Hunt has noted, by creating 'parties, ideologies, dictators, mass movements'.[25] Engels, writing in 1847, took a different position. Objecting to a note of French exceptionalism in a speech by the socialist reformer and historian Louis Blanc, he contrarily observed: 'Without intending to deprecate in any manner the heroic efforts of the French Revolution, and the immense gratitude the world owes to the great men of the Republic', the English Industrial Revolution was far more cosmopolitan, since 'England invented the steam-engine; England erected the railway; two things which, we believe, are worth a good many ideas'. Furthermore, 'as far as ideas are concerned ... let us never forget Milton, the first defender of regicide, Algernon Sydney, Bolingbroke, and Shaftesbury, over their French more brilliant followers'.[26]

Yet there is no doubting the subsequent global popularity of the French Revolution symbolized by the reverence for the French flag in European progressive and nationalist circles. A tricolour was widely adopted, with changing colours, by nationalists in Italy and Germany, but also in Belgium, Hungary and even in distant Mexico. There were hardly any *national* flags previously. The first was what was later called the Stars and Stripes, created on 14 June 1777 at the Second Continental Congress. It consisted of thirteen stripes and thirteen stars representing the thirteen American colonies.

The French Revolution is celebrated in endless novels, plays and films, and not just in France. Songs connected to the revolution have had a global reach, above all with 'La Marseillaise', which was sang by anarchists accused of taking part in the Haymarket affair in Chicago in 1886 on their way to the gallows. It was later performed by military bands in Moscow and Petrograd to celebrate the downfall of the tsar.[27] There were other revolutionary songs even more blood-curdling, such as 'Ah ça ira' (It will be all right, or Let's do it).

> *Ah! ça ira, ça ira, ça ira*
> *les aristocrates à la lanterne!*
> *Ah! ça ira, ça ira, ça ira*
> *les aristocrates on les pendra!*
>
> *Si on n' les pend pas*
> *On les rompra*
> *Si on n' les rompt pas*
> *On les brûlera.*
>
> Ah! Let's do it, Let's do it, Let's do it,
> aristocrats to the lamp-post!
> Ah! Let's do it, Let's do it, Let's do it,
> the aristocrats, we'll hang them!
>
> If we don't hang them
> We'll break them
> If we don't break them
> We'll burn them.

'La Carmagnole' mocks Louis XVI (as Monsieur Veto) and Marie-Antoinette (Madame Veto):

> *Madame Veto avait promis, de faire égorger tout Paris,*
> *Mais son coup a manqué grâce à nos canonniers*
> *Dansons la Carmagnole, Vive le son du canon.*

> Madame Veto had promised to cut all the throats in Paris,
> But she failed thanks to our gunners.
> Let us dance the Carmagnole. Long live the sound of guns.

The English Civil War, by comparison, generated very little in terms of popular musical culture. There is 'Stand Up Now, Diggers All!' written by Gerrard Winstanley ('But the Gentry must come down, and the poor shall wear the crown'), but few know how to sing it. The best-known Scottish political song, 'The Skye Boat Song', is about the return of Charles Stuart (Bonnie Prince Charlie), the Jacobite rebellion of 1745 and the defeat at Culloden. It was written in the late nineteenth century by an Englishman and was far from revolutionary. Most of the best-known American political songs of the nineteenth century come from the Civil War, such as the famous 'Battle Hymn of the Republic' based on the music of the abolitionist song 'John Brown's Body'. Hardly any are connected to the War of Independence, except 'Yankee Doodle Dandy'. The lyrics of the best-known version of 'Yankee Doodle Dandy' are apolitical and were originally composed and sung by the English to make fun of dishevelled and disorganized colonials. The latter turned it into a song of defiance around 1781.

The English Revolution was not exported. English troops did not try to impose the new system on anyone, though they did undertake a bloody reconquest of Ireland. However, British ideas *were* exported, or rather imported, by reformers and revolutionaries. Locke was widely read by French intellectuals, such as Montesquieu and Diderot. Voltaire, in his bestselling *Letters on England* (1734), wrote admiringly about the British system and English 'freedoms'. In 1789 France, Adam Smith's *Wealth of Nations* (1776) was regarded as 'supportive of constitutional innovation'.[28]

English 'freedoms' and 'moderation' were often invoked during the debates of August and September 1789, when the rights of citizens were being discussed.[29] Bertrand Barère, president of the National Convention in November–December 1792, believed that the English model of a constitutional monarchy was suitable for France. But by 1794 he was denouncing the English, whom he had come to regard as under the thumbs of despots and bankers, declaring that French was the only republican language.[30]

The global renown of the French Revolution was also enhanced by the formidable role played by French culture and the French language throughout the nineteenth century. America, by contrast, was a distant prospect, which, in the European mind, had barely progressed from 'My America, my new-found-land', as John Donne had intoned in his poem 'To His Mistress Going to Bed' (1582). France made revolutions, but, after the failures of the Napoleonic Wars, never tried to export them; it became a *real* bourgeois country. Its aristocrats remained ensconced in the bureaucracy and the military, while Britain became a country of bankers and mill owners pretending to be aristocrats.

Lawyers, merchants, artisans

Marx and Engels, in the notes collected under the title *The German Ideology* (1845–6), had no doubt that the French bourgeoisie, 'by means of the most colossal revolution that history has ever known, was achieving domination and conquering the Continent of Europe', while the 'already politically emancipated English bourgeoisie was revolutionising industry and subjugating India politically'. As for 'the impotent German burghers', they 'did not get any further than "good will"'.[31] In his *Discours sur l'histoire de la Révolution d'Angleterre* (1849), François Guizot, a liberal-conservative politician and anglophile historian (he even translated Shakespeare), contrasted the successful English and American Revolutions with the failure of France to achieve a similar transition. He marvelled that the English, unlike the French, had succeeded in bringing about substantial change while preserving what was essential of their old regime.[32] But, like Marx, Guizot (who, as foreign minister, expelled Marx from France in 1845) was sure that both the English Civil War and the French Revolution had been bourgeois revolutions.[33] Marx, in an article in the *Neue Rheinische Zeitung* (15 December 1848) declared that the English Revolution of 1648 and the French Revolution constituted

> the *victory of the bourgeoisie as well as* the *victory of a new social order*, the victory of bourgeois property over feudal property, of nationality over provincialism, of competition over the guild, of the partition of estates over primogeniture, of the owner's mastery of the land over the land's mastery of its owner, of enlightenment over superstition, of the family over the family name, of industry over heroic laziness, of civil law over privileges of medieval origin.[34]

Tocqueville wrote in his *Souvenirs* (Recollections) that

By 1830 the triumph of the middle class was definitive, and so complete that all political power ... [was] confined and somehow squeezed within the narrow limits of the bourgeoisie, legally excluding everything below it and in fact all that had once stood above.[35]

But what was the French bourgeoise in 1789? It was certainly not a capitalist class in the sense of a class of entrepreneurs involved in manufacturing, though there were early signs of capitalism (but then there were some capitalist enterprises in ancient Babylon). A class of industrial capitalists had not even existed in England in 1648 or in the American colonies in 1776. The irony is that none of these bourgeois revolutions were led by what the Marx of *Das Kapital* and successive Marxist thinkers understood to be the bourgeoisie. Nineteenth-century historians of the French Revolution, people such as Guizot, Tocqueville and Taine, believed that it decreed the victory of an 'intermediate' commercial, landed or professional class in a country that was still overwhelmingly rural. Few merchants were elected to the État Généraux in 1789 or became prominent in revolutionary politics.[36]

Politically, the bourgeoisie was deeply divided, as it still is today. Some were still monarchists; others were moderate Girondins or radical Montagnards. Then there were the Thermidoreans of 1794 who opposed the Jacobins, and later the *régime directorial*.[37] The ever perceptive Tocqueville explained that the *classe moyenne*, the middle class,

> is never a compact subset of the nation of the nation or a distinct part of the whole; it always participates to some degree in the other classes and in some places merges with them. This lack of homogeneity and precise limits makes the government of the bourgeoisie weak and uncertain, but it makes the bourgeoisie itself impossible to grasp and in a sense invisible to those who would attack it when it ceases to govern.[38]

The French Revolution was led mostly by members of the professional classes (as was the American Revolution) – that is, by lawyers and journalists – while there had been a strong presence of London merchants in the English one. They were people of talent: lawyers, writers, merchants, bankers. As Lynn Hunt has pointed out, in France: 'The new political class was not socially homogeneous. Lawyers dominated national and regional politics; merchants, artisans, and shopkeepers were prominent in the cities; and a mixture of peasants, artisans, and small merchants ran the villages.'[39]

The leaders of the Soviet Revolution were not proletarians either; nor were those of the Chinese Revolution. Mao Zedong and Liu Shaoqi were the offspring of prosperous farmers, as was Trotsky. Qu Qiubai, general secretary of the Chinese Communist Party in 1927–28, wrote of his gentry family: 'We never washed our own clothes or cooked our own food; and of course we always wore long gowns.'[40] The fathers of Lenin and Zhou Enlai were civil servants. Nicolai Bukharin's parents were schoolteachers. Stalin was the son of a shoemaker who owned his own workshop, a petty bourgeois according to the classical Marxist definition. It is not the identity of leaders that define the class aspects of a revolution, but how these leaders define the classes and groups for whom they say they fight.

To say that the middle classes had triumphed can only mean that the subsequent political and economic set-up favoured their prosperity and ascent. They thrived in the nineteenth century, but so did members of the aristocracy. The aristocracy filled many of the important offices of state and the military, and in this sense only they continued to rule.[41] In an illuminating passage, Tocqueville pointed out the similarity of the classes 'above the people', apart from what he called the superficiality of good manners. Otherwise, 'all those ranked above the people were similar, they had the same ideas, the same habits, the same tastes, the same pleasures, they read the same books and spoke the same language. They differed only in their rights'.[42] Napoleon solidified his rule by distributing posts to all and sundry. Once emperor, he sold titles throughout his reign. Retailing titles of nobility became common practice everywhere in Europe. The Victorians did it with relish, as did the various rulers of statelets in pre-unification Italy and pre-unification Germany. Granting titles was a cheap way of enlarging one's support: those who became nobles were happy, and others worked harder out of aspiration. In the twentieth century, a significant portion of those with aristocratic titles could trace them back only to the nineteenth. The only ones who could object to the proliferation of titles were the members of the old aristocracy, and they counted less and less.

Among the French revolutionaries and reformers there were aristocrats such as Mirabeau, Talleyrand and the Marquis de Lafayette (all among the authors of the *Déclaration des droits de l'homme et du citoyen*), as well as Condorcet (who wanted equal rights to be extended to women and advocated the abolition of slavery) and François Christophe Kellermann (the general who, by defeating the Prussians at Valmy (1792), facilitated the abolition of the monarchy). There was also Louis-Philippe d'Orléans, who showed his commitment to the revolution by changing his name to Philippe Égalité and voted in favour of the execution of his cousin King Louis XVI. The Jacobin Louis Antoine de Saint-Just was a member of the minor nobility. Chateaubriand was not entirely wrong when he wrote in his *Mémoires d'outre-tombe*: 'The nobility started the revolution, the plebians concluded it.'[43]

Among those opposed to the ancien régime we also find members of the clergy, such as Henri Grégoire, a fighter for the emancipation of Jews and slaves (like Condorcet) and Emmanuel Joseph Sieyès, author of the famous pamphlet *Qu'est-ce que le tiers état?*, as well as Tayllerand, who was briefly Bishop of Autun (he quit as the revolution started). There were also writers, such as the proto-feminist and anti-slavery campaigner Olympe de Gouges, who in 1791 wrote a *Déclaration des droits de la femme et de la citoyenne* (Declaration of the Rights of Woman and of the Female Citizen). There was Etta Palm d'Aelders, who declared: 'Justice, sister of liberty, calls all individuals to the equality of rights, without discrimination of sex; the laws of a free people must be equal for all beings, like the air and the sun.'[44] There was the poet André Chenier; and there were, of course, Robespierre (a lawyer), Jean-Paul Marat (a Swiss doctor and journalist) and Danton (another lawyer). There were also a few members of the lower orders, such as Jacques Pierre Brissot, son of an illiterate (but not poor) innkeeper, who became a lawyer and journalist and leader of the moderate Girondin faction and a strong abolitionist.

Danton, Brissot, Robespierre, Philippe Égalité, Olympe de Gouges, André Chenier and Saint-Just ended up on the guillotine, along with many others. Marat was killed in his bath and Condorcet was probably murdered in his cell, but Mirabeau died of natural causes at the age of forty-two, while the Abbé Grégoire died at the age of eighty and the Abbé Sieyès at eighty-eight. Talleyrand became a celebrated diplomat also serving Napoleon and subsequent monarchs, and died peacefully at the age of eighty-four. The chief prosecutor, Antoine Fouquier-Tinville, scion of a prosperous bourgeois family who sent hundreds of people to the scaffold, was guillotined in his turn in May 1795. He is supposed to have said: 'I was the axe of the revolution. Should an axe be punished?' – a more poetic version of the well-known refrain 'I was only obeying orders'.[45]

To define the French Revolution as a bourgeois one, it would be necessary to show that the absolute monarchy and surviving vestiges of feudalism constituted an impediment to capitalist development. The view that they needed to be swept away if the bourgeoisie were to triumph relies on pronouncements by Marx and Engels, largely in the *Communist Manifesto*, though neither had made any serious study of the French Revolution.[46] This is not to deny that there was, at least in Paris, a very politically active bourgeoisie. The Sans-Culottes (those who wore trousers, unlike the aristocracy, who wore knee-breeches), are often characterized as proto-proletarians and labourers. They were in fact a heterogeneous group which included 'shop-keepers, retail merchants, traders, artisans, small manufacturers, hired labourers, porters, water-carriers, waiters in cafes, janitors in buildings, barbers, wig-makers, stonemasons, and makers of ladies' hats, they were the people of Paris'.[47] Some historians, on the basis of serious archival research, have even defined the 'sans-culotterie' as 'fundamentally a bourgeois movement'.[48]

If the Sans-Culottes were not purely proletarian, neither was the French monarchy 100 per cent absolute. It is true that in 1766, King Louis XV had declared that 'sovereign power resides in my person only … public order in its entirety emanates from me'.[49] In practice, he was not as absolute as he thought. Many of the monarch's political powers were in the hands of a powerful and entrenched aristocracy. Besides, like all absolute monarchs, he was bound by ancient rules and conventions. He was no dictator.

As the États Généraux were convened, the people were solicited to send what were called *cahiers de doléances*, documents in which the local assemblies electing deputies for the États Généraux would list their complaints (the practice had been not uncommon at least since the fourteenth century). These *cahiers* (some 30,000!) were often redacted by members of the legal profession who transmitted the complaints of the lower orders.[50] The complaints from the countryside were mainly about taxes and the perdurance of feudal rights. Those from towns, especially from members of the aristocracy and the bourgeois classes, were prevalently about ecclesiastical privileges and taxes, but they also included almost revolutionary demands, such as greater individual rights, habeas corpus and press freedom.[51] Some of these seemed inspired by the Enlightenment and the influence of what were seen as English freedoms.

Vestiges of feudalism – peasants having to pay dues such as the salt tax as well as the *taille* (the general tax), and in many cases being obliged to work on the landlord's land – were swept away on 4 August 1789 by the National Assembly. Economic power remained in the hands of the few, but the upper section of the nobility was weakened, as was the monarch. Meanwhile, with politics in constant ferment, social classes shifted imperceptibly. The nobles eventually kept their titles and status, though their legal advantages diminished considerably. This was only the first phase of the revolution. France was rocked by unrest, social strife and upheaval for at least a hundred years, and industrially it continued to lag behind countries that had experienced far less political commotion.

The royal coffers

Tocqueville argued that centralization of the French state was easily effected under Napoleon because the revolution had not destroyed it.[52] But like many other European states, the absolutist France of the ancien régime had coexisted with a diversity of rules and practices. The country was divided by internal barriers and different legal systems. Various tolls had to be paid to take goods from one region to another. Centralization was far more a result of the revolution and Napoleon than anything Colbert had managed to achieve under Louis XIV.[53]

Louis XIV and his successor (and great-grandson) Louis XV had left France's finances in a terrible state. Fortunes had been spent in the wars of the Spanish, Polish and Austrian succession, the Carnatic Wars with England over India (1746–63), the Seven Years' War (1756–63) as well as the War of American Independence. France's failure in the Seven Years' War led to the loss of much of its colonial empire in North America and India. Louis XV, known since 1744 as *le Bien-Aimé* (the well-beloved), died unlamented. The judgement of the famous literary critic Charles Sainte-Beuve, written in 1846, was ferocious:

> What was Louis XV? We have said it much, we have not said it enough: the most worthless, the basest, the most cowardly of all kings. During his long, agitated reign, he accumulated as it were his pleasure, all the misfortunes to bequeath them to his kind.[54]

France had suffered for much of the eighteenth century from inflation, partly due to the import of precious metals from the New World, partly from the increase in population. Overproduction of wine (1775–78) caused falling prices, and wine was an important sector of the economy. Nevertheless, the French economy had been fairly dynamic in terms of both agricultural and industrial growth. It was not a stagnant traditionalist society but an increasingly commercial one, sensitive to the market.[55]

The problem lay with the state finances. The wars had been costly, and military outlays were the main form of government spending.[56] Existing taxation had not been sufficient to fill the public coffers. More needed to be borrowed, or taxes had to be increased. And it is here that the fiscal origins of the French Revolution coincide with those of the English Civil War. It is one thing to believe in the divine right of kings, but does this right extend to taking my hard-earned money and spending it on wars about which I care little? The most hated exactions were not the feudal dues owed to landlords but the levies of the central government, since these were irregular and fell upon the peasantry as a bolt from the blue (*un coup de tonnerre*), something fatal and mysterious like wars or famines.[57] The tax on salt, 'the much-detested gabelle', was levied at six different levels in the various regions, producing a sense of social outrage and a propensity to smuggling and black-marketeering in equal measure.[58]

A state in debt because of wars was what the luckless Louis XVI had to face when he ascended the throne in May 1774 at the age of twenty. Fifteen years later he had to confront the revolution. He was not particularly intelligent; nor was his wife Marie Antoinette, who has been reviled, probably unjustly, ever since. She never said 'Qu'ils mangent de la brioche' (let them eat cake), just as Louis XV was never the first to say 'après moi le déluge'.[59] There is no reason why a royal family should be particularly clever or good at ruling: intelligence or expertise has nothing to do with their position.

Louis XVI's ministers, though, were both intelligent and competent. Jacques Turgot, the finance minister (1774–76), tried to free the economy from feudal restrictions and liberalize the grain trade; today he would be regarded as a neoliberal. But that was regarded as too progressive by the Court, and he was dismissed in 1776. His eventual successor, Jacques Necker, was a rich, adroit Protestant banker from Geneva, who decided to pay the debt the state had accumulated by borrowing even more. Today he would be regarded as a 'modern monetary theorist', someone who believes that one can increase the public debt almost indefinitely. This may be possible if the lenders believe that the state's finances are sound – one of the reasons why Necker took the novel step of making them public. But he had acquired many enemies, *and* he was a foreigner, *and* he was a Protestant. He was dismissed in 1781 (only to be recalled in 1788).

The difficult economic situation facing the country was, at least in part, due to France's financial and military contribution to the American War of Independence (the intention had been to damage Great Britain). It was a contribution which Necker had approved and Turgot opposed, the latter declaring that 'the first gunshot would drive the state to bankruptcy'.[60] The government had to borrow vast sums. It also had to find money to repay the interests on old debts such as those accrued during the Seven Years' War, but the compound interest made repayment increasingly difficult. The monarch could decide what to spend, but not how to raise revenue.[61] By 1786 it had become apparent that France was teetering on bankruptcy. Reluctantly, in 1788, the king called for the États Généraux to be convened the following year in the hope of convincing them to raise taxes. They had not met since 1614. This was a sign that the absolute monarch was not quite so absolute.

Those the king hoped to convince were not the members of the first two estates (the clergy and the nobility) but those of the Third Estate, the real taxpayers. But the elites were aware of the growing ferment and dissent. The British agriculturalist Arthur Young travelled in France and wrote in his diary of a dinner party in 1787 where the guests already feared to be on the

> eve of some great revolution in the government: ... everything points to it: the confusion in the finances great; with a deficit impossible to provide for without the states-general of the kingdom, yet no ideas formed of what would be the consequence of their meeting: no minister existing, or to be looked to in or out power, with such decisive talents as to promise any.

Meanwhile the court was

> buried in pleasure and dissipation; and adding to the distress ...a great ferment amongst all ranks of men, who are eager for some change, without knowing what to look to, or to hope for: and a strong leaven of liberty, increasing every hour since the American revolution.[62]

As Tocqueville wrote:

> The nobility had the cowardice to allow the Third Estate to be taxed as long as the nobility itself was not taxed; on that day were planted the germs for almost all the vices and abuses which troubled the old regime until the end, and finally led to its violent death.[63]

There were plenty of reasons for peasants and farmers to hate the nobility and their privileges. Tocqueville provided a heartfelt description of the dismal conditions of the peasantry under the ancien régime. Imagine an eighteenth-century peasant, he wrote, who is finally able to buy a piece of land using all the money he has saved. But he has to pay a fee to various neighbouring landlords, for whom he also has to work for free, and from whom he has to buy the right to sell his produce in the local market. He must pay off the toll keeper, mill owner and baker, not forgetting the Church. He accumulates hatred and envy.[64]

The streets of Paris were in turmoil well before the fourteenth of July.[65] The Marquis de Ferrières wrote to his wife that while he was at the Opera in Paris,

> blood was flowing in the faubourg Saint-Antoine. Five or six thousand workers assembled ... armed with sticks and furiously assaulted the home of a certain Réveillon, [Jean-Baptiste Réveillon] the director of the royal factory of the fine wallpapers of the Porte Saint-Antoine. They climbed the walls, broke the doors shouting that they intended to kill Réveillon, his wife and his children. They looted all they could find.

The Marquis noted, pessimistically, that the political situation was incandescent.[66] This became known as the *affaire Réveillon*, a riot which occurred over 26–28 April, caused by the fear that Réveillon was going to lower wages.

The États Généraux finally convened a week later. On 17 June, the Third Estate declared itself to be the French National Assembly (as the French parliament is still called today) before decamping to the Jeu de Paume (the old tennis court) three days later (20 June), where the famous oath was taken to draft a new constitution. This is one of the dates which could have been chosen to signal the beginning of the French Revolution. It was immortalized in the 1790s by Jacques-Louis David in a famous unfinished painting.

By 1791–92 the États Généraux had metamorphosed into a legislative assembly – a real parliament. It consisted of about 800–900 members, with about half from the Third Estate and the other half from the clergy and the nobility combined.[67] None of these estates were monolithic blocs. The French nobility may have numbered up to 350,000 people, though the numbers are probably closer to 100,000.[68] Very few of them (perhaps 4,000) lived at court in and around Versailles or owned impressive chateaux and plenty of land. Those whose rank was due to their possession of judicial or administrative posts were known as the *noblesse de robe* and were looked down upon by the real aristocrats, who themselves were

Jacques-Louis David, oil sketch for *Le Serment du Jeu de Paume* (1790s), Musée Carnavalet, Paris

nevertheless often just better-off farmers or officers who had acquired a title but little else. Taken as whole, this Second Estate owned one-fifth of the land.[69]

The clergy (the First Estate) consisted of some 120,000 people and included many poor priests, curates and monks who were far closer to the people than to the high clergy (bishops, abbots and so on). The latter, in turn, were closer to the nobility, but even in this group there were reformers. The Third Estate comprised everyone else: from the *haute bourgeoisie*, to professionals, functionaries and merchants, to the *petite bourgeoisie* of shopkeepers, employees, artisans, peasants and a variety of manual workers. But no peasant or worker was a delegate; they were overwhelmingly drawn from the upper echelons of the middle classes.[70] As Tocqueville explained in an article for the *Westminster Review* translated by John Stuart Mill:

> At the first glance it might be thought that in France the tiers-état was composed of the middle class, and stood between the aristocracy and the people. But this was not the case. The tiers-état included, it is true, the middle classes, but it also comprised elements which were naturally foreign to these classes. The richest merchant, the most opulent banker, the most skilful manufacturer, the man of letters, the man of science, might form part of the tiers-état, as well as the small farmer,

the shopkeeper, and the peasant who tilled the ground. Every man, in short, who was neither a priest nor a noble belonged to the tiers-état. It included rich and poor, the ignorant and the instructed. The tiers-état had thus within itself an aristocracy of its own.[71]

The Abbé Emmanuel Joseph Sieyès in his famous pamphlet of January 1789, *Qu'est-ce que le Tiers-État?*, posed three questions on the first page, answering each of them succinctly:

1. What is the Third Estate? Everything.
2. What has it counted so far politically? Nothing.
3. What does it demand? To become something.

He added that all the work that maintained society was performed by the Tiers-États, while the clergy and aristocracy occupied lucrative and prestigious positions but produced nothing.[72]

On 23 June 1789, Louis XVI, not yet realizing how serious the situation was, ordered the National Assembly to disperse. It refused, and since Louis could not crush it because the people of Paris had rioted, he began to give way. The problem was that since each estate had one vote, the Third Estate would always be outvoted by the combined forces of clergy and nobility, so Jacques Necker, who had been called back as minister of finance, proposed to double the voting weight of the Third Estate. He was now seen as a minister willing to serve the people, introducing measures to control the distribution of wheat to decrease the risk of famine. This was too radical for the king, who dismissed Necker once again on 11 July 1789, to the dismay of the National Assembly.[73] There was panic in financial circles, where the fear was state bankruptcy. The stock exchange was closed. Necker's sacking was one of the causes of the storming of the Bastille three days later; another was the threatening presence of foreign troops in the capital. The king again gave in. Alarmed at the news that the demonstrators had received the support of the French Guards, he withdrew the foreign troops, recalled Necker once more, and consented to double the voting weight of the Third Estate and work with the National Assembly. The king's brother, the Comte d'Artois (and future Charles X) opposed the move, complaining that this would only 'encourage the Third Estate to make new demands'.[74] But his advice fell on deaf ears. The people of Paris had scored a victory. At this stage few revolutionaries thought of a republic, but it was clear that there was a struggle for power between the monarchy and the National Assembly.

The events surrounding the storming of the Bastille constituted a major turning point. The Bastille itself was only of symbolic importance: it accommodated hardly any inmates.[75] The decision to demolish it, taken on 16 July, was equally symbolic.

Who are the citizens?

The scene was set for the most important statement of the Revolution, the *Déclaration des droits de l'homme et du citoyen* of 26 August 1789. As we noted earlier, much of this statement of principle relied on the American Declaration of Independence, though in the mythology of the French Revolution this is seldom acknowledged. Both the French and the American texts stressed equality, but the famous second sentence of the American Declaration – beginning 'we hold these truths to be self-evident, that all men are created equal' – acquired its present renown only during the Civil War. Before that, rights and taxation were regarded as far more important. Similarly, the English Bill of Rights signed into law in 1689, and a source of inspiration for the American Declaration, was about rights and parliamentary powers but did not even assert the principle of equality of all human beings. The French Declaration, which Fernand Braudel regarded as a landmark in the history of freedom and European civilization, was really aimed against feudal privileges.[76]

On 6 October 1789, deputies called for a contribution *patriotique*, a diplomatic way to get citizens to make a one-off payment of a quarter of their income to help the new regime to face the difficult economic circumstances. The state took over Church lands. The shrewd Mirabeau warned: 'In the final analysis the people will judge the Revolution by this fact alone: does it take more or less money?'[77]

Now the revolutionary process was in full swing, and the question arose: who are the citizens? Those concerned with women's rights and slavery, such as Condorcet and Olympe de Gouges, were quick to point out that not a word was spent on the conditions of women or of Black slaves in French plantations. By 1791 Olympe de Gouges had published her famous *Déclaration des droits de la femme et de la citoyenne*. Condorcet had advocated schemes for the gradual abolition of slavery since 1780 with his *Réflexions sur l'esclavage,* inspired by the English abolitionists, along with Brissot, Mirabeau, the Abbé Grégoire and the Marquis de Lafayette. The connection between the conditions of women and slavery was often made. Mary Wollstonecraft, in *A Vindication of the Rights of*

Woman (1792), frequently characterized women as slaves.[78] Even before then, proto-feminists such as Mary Astell, a High Church Tory loyalist, published anonymously her 1694 *Serious Proposal to the Ladies for the Advancement of their True and Greatest Interest*, signed 'by a lover of her sex', while in the 1706 edition her *Reflections upon Marriage* asked: 'If all Men are born Free, how is it that all Women are born Slaves?'[79] Throughout the following decades, whenever a revolution or a revolt threatened the established order, there were women who demanded that they too should be included in emancipation. Thus in 1849 the radical German feminist Louise Dittmar declared: 'The freedom of women is the greatest revolution, not just of our own day, but of all time, since it breaks fetters which are as old as the world.' Dittmar demanded that women should be liberated, 'otherwise women must pass on their slave-chains from generation to generation'.[80]

The status of women, which was barely modified by the English Civil War or the American War of Independence, changed, albeit only briefly, as a result of the French Revolution. Though these events certainly did not enfranchise women (here France was a latecomer) they at least produced organizations of women who explicitly demanded equal rights in property, divorce and politics.[81] On 5 October 1789, it was the women's March on Versailles, prompted by a severe shortage of bread in the capital, which compelled the king to abandon Versailles for Paris. On the whole, however, the conditions of women did not improve significantly during the revolution or afterwards. The revolution allowed divorce, but this was made illegal again during the Restoration, and was reinstated only in 1884 under the Third Republic. A law of 20 September 1792 gave women legal equality in marriage and replaced parish registers with civil records (*état civil*), to the displeasure of the Catholic Church. Needless to say, the application of the new laws lagged behind in the provinces.

Major constitutional changes had started on 6 October 1789, when the now almost powerless king, forced to reside in Paris, finally accepted the principles of the *Déclaration des droits de l'homme et du citoyen*. He was still formally in power but could not rule. He was merely, according to National Assembly, 'an agent of the sovereign nation'.[82] France was no longer an absolute monarchy. The revolution had abolished feudal privileges but also the right to form trade unions, with the Chapelier Law of 14 June 1791. This law forbade members of the same profession or trade or craft to join forces because it would be 'derogatory to liberty and the declaration of the rights of man'. It also banned as seditious assembly any movement aimed at refusing to pay rents, tithes or taxes.[83] Years later, Karl Marx was scathing. In *Das Kapital*, he wrote: 'During the very first storms of the revolution, the French bourgeoisie dared to take away from the workers the right of association just acquired', and 'confined the struggle between capital and labour within limits comfortable for capital'.[84] Anti-union legislation was confirmed by Napoleon in 1803 and 1810, and by the Second Republic in March 1849. Only under Napoleon III, in the 1860s, did it begin to be relaxed.

As revolutionary expectations increased, members of the nobility frightened for their lives, their status, and their future fled abroad, hoping that foreign powers would intervene. In the rest of Europe there was widespread anxiety among the ruling classes that the French Revolution would 'contaminate' their own populations. The Venetian diplomat Daniele Dolfin (aka Delfin) warned his government in 1793: 'The French Revolution is gradually bringing another equally dangerous revolution in the universal way of thinking.'[85]

In France many feared that a foreign invasion would crash the revolution. In the spring of 1792, anticipating an attack, France declared war on Prussia and Austria. The supposedly moderate Girondin faction led by Jacques-Pierre Brissot had argued that a preventive war was necessary to save the revolution ('we cannot be at peace until all Europe is in flames'). It was a key moment in the development of French nationalism. The famous opening couplets of 'La Marseillaise' written by Rouget de Lisle had as its original title 'Chant de guerre pour l'armée du Rhin' and was aimed against Austrians and Prussians. It was a military anthem before it became associated with the revolution. Many Jacobins opposed this pre-emptive war.[86] On 2 January 1792, at the Jacobin Club, Robespierre presciently opined that the idea that one could simply intervene in another country to change its regime was absurd:

> The most extravagant idea that can take root in the head of a politician is to believe that it is enough for one people to invade a foreign people to make it adopt its laws and constitution. No one likes armed missionaries.[87]

John Quincy Adams espoused similar views on 4 July 1821. America, he argued, 'goes not abroad in search of monsters to destroy' – a principle that today's 'liberal interventionists' fail to understand.[88] Robespierre's anti-war stance was particularly popular with women, who constituted one of his main bases of support.[89] Earlier in 1787, Robespierre had demonstrated his pro-feminism when he argued in favour of the admission of women to royal academies.[90] But some of the best-known proto-feminists of the time opposed Robespierre's Jacobin radicalism – women such as Olympe de Gouges, Charlotte Corday and Madame Roland were all guillotined.

France's initial unexpected victory against the Prussians at Valmy in September 1792 led to the unravelling of the European state system. By 1794 the French claimed to have liberated Belgium and then annexed it (from under Austrian rule) in the name of the revolution, while Russia and Prussia claimed to have liberated large parts of Poland, which they then annexed, to save them from revolutionary infection.[91] The internationalization of the revolution also precipitated the abolition of the monarchy and the advent of the republic. On 17 January 1793, by a tiny majority, the National Convention condemned Louis XVI to be executed in Place de la Révolution (today's Place de la Concorde). On 21 January he was beheaded before 20,000 spectators. Marie Antoinette followed him to the scaffold in October.

Robespierre, in a speech at the Constituent Assembly in May 1791, had asked for the death penalty to be repealed, as had Saint-Just, the other hard Jacobin, in his *L'Esprit de la Révolution et de la Constitution de France*. The main philosophers of the Enlightenment – Voltaire, Diderot and Montesquieu – had all been in favour of capital punishment. During the debate on the execution of Louis XVI (3 December 1792), Robespierre declared that he detested the death penalty and had for Louis 'neither love nor hatred. I only hate his crimes.' But, he went on, since the death penalty was extant, there was no reason not to treat the king as one would a common criminal.[92]

The Terror

During the whole of 1793, the government was mainly in the hands of the Jacobins (not a monolithic group) supported by the people of Paris.[93] This was the period which came to be known as the Terror, a process which gave the French Revolution an image of unparalleled cruelty. It was not, argues Marisa Linton, 'an inherent aspect of Jacobin ideology', but 'a contingent factor' due to the ferocity of an international war involving many European countries as well as a civil war.[94] It is often the case that the wars and the repression that come after a revolution are far more deadly than the revolution itself. This is certainly the case with the French and Russian Revolutions. It is not surprising that in these circumstances paranoia looms large, with fears of plots and counter-revolutionary conspiracies. It was believed that the king and aristocracy were conspiring to destroy the revolution, perhaps joined by the clergy, perhaps with foreign support, perhaps with help from unpatriotic peasants from the Vendée or the Chouannerie, perhaps with assistance from unreliable members of the Girondins or even the Jacobins. This paranoia, not entirely unjustifiable and prevalent in many countries even when not at war, increased the level of violence. As Timothy Tackett wrote, the alleged 'duplicity' of Louis XVI and others seemed to provide 'overwhelming evidence that even those whom one most trusted as supporters of the Revolution might actually be conspirators hiding behind a "mask of patriotism"'.[95]

The cruelty and violence of the French Revolution was not unusual, however. Even if one concentrates on events occurring in the same broad historical period, such as the Greek War of Independence, one is struck by how bloodthirsty they were.

> By the early summer of 1822 the Greek Revolution had cost the lives of upwards of 50,000 Turks, Greeks, Albanians, Jews, and others. Many more had been reduced to slavery or misery. Only a tiny minority had been killed in direct combat with the enemy. The Greek War of Independence hitherto was ... largely a series of massacres.[96]

The victims were guilty of belonging to the wrong community or religion.

One of the earliest uses of the word 'terror' was by Bertrand Barère who, on 5 September 1793, speaking at the Convention nationale, urged the revolutionaries to make terror the order of the day (*à l'ordre du jour*). In France, the actual Terror lasted just over two years (1792–94) with a number of repressive exceptional laws such as those of March 1793 and 10 June 1794 (*loi de la Grande Terreur*) which allowed the revolutionary authorities to seize a suspect and judge and execute him in less than twenty-four hours. Heads were chopped off, some paraded on pikes; people were drowned in the Loire near Nantes and prisoners were massacred in Paris out of fear that they would help foreign invading armies – massacres deplored by Robespierre.[97] The numbers of people executed have remained hotly disputed; strangely, there is very little reliable statistical work.

The main statistical text on the Terror is still that of the American historian Donald Greer.[98] The number of people guillotined was probably as high as 20,000 and only a minority (around 2,000) were aristocrats:

far fewer than the number of Communards summarily executed in 1871. Many more Parisians almost certainly died in prison. As Greer noted, while

> the impression of the Reign of Terror as a Reign of Blood almost unique in history is ineffaceable ... Americans at least should remember that our annual automobile accident death toll has passed the 35,000 mark before they conclude that France was a sea of blood in the Year II.

And that was in 1935.[99]

Far more died (possibly 200,000 or 300,000 people) in the subsequent civil war or resisting conscription, especially in the Vendée south of the Loire during what was a religious-royalist uprising, and in the revolt which took place in the area north of the Loire (mainly Brittany, Maine and Normandy) which became known as the Chouannerie (from the name of their leaders, the Chouan brothers).[100] This was the most violent moment of the revolution, and the war made it so. Marisa Linton distinguished between those executed who had been 'engaged in open rebellion against the Republic', those (the majority) who died in the Vendée 'in the midst of a full-scale civil war' and finally the terror used by revolutionaries against other revolutionaries.[101] Quite rightly, Colin Jones explains that in his book on the fall of Robespierre he avoided the term 'the Terror' as an 'unhelpful anachronism'.[102]

There was a White Terror following the fall of Robespierre which lasted over a year, or about as long as the Red Terror. Many of those involved were returnees, out for revenge.[103] Millions would die during the Napoleonic Wars. In the rebellious colony of Saint-Domingue, 100,000 died during the Napoleonic repression. In June 1848, the crushing of the working-class revolt in Paris by General Louis-Eugène Cavaignac, a staunch republican, led to some 10,000 casualties on both sides. This is barely remembered, though it was, according to Robert Tombs, 'the bloodiest fighting Paris had ever seen'.[104] It was remembered at the time by writers such as Delphine Gay de Girardin. She thundered against the men of the National Assembly who applauded the massacre:

> *Vous épouses, vous sœurs, vous mères éplorées.*
> *Cœurs brises, flancs meurtris, entrailles déchirées.*
> *Qui n'avez plus pour fils que de froids ossements.*
> *Avez-vous entendu ces applaudissements?*

> You inconsolable wives, sisters, mothers,
> With broken hearts, wounded flanks, torn guts,
> Who have nothing left of a son but cold bones.
> Have you heard this applause?[105]

The Semaine sanglante, as the crushing of the Paris Commune in 1871 became known, was even worse – according to Tombs, it was 'the worst civil bloodshed in Europe between the 1790s and the 1940s'.[106] Neither 1848 nor 1871 have ever been called 'the Terror', though the so-called revisionist school (Furet and others) blamed even these events on the revolution – unsurprisingly, since they blame twentieth-century communism and fascism on the revolution too.

The number of dead at the height of the Terror (1793–94) is probably in tune with the number who died during the English Civil War (including the dead in Ireland), and perhaps even with those who died in America during the War of Independence, though accounting for war-related casualties is extremely difficult.[107] The English crushing of the United Irishmen uprising of 1798 (partly inspired by the French Revolution, and watched with sympathy and a little military help from France) led to a death toll of at least 30,000 on both sides.[108] Outside Ireland, hardly anyone is aware of that. The Mexican Revolution of 1910 led to the deaths of around 1 million people out of a population then much smaller than that of France.[109] In the Spanish Civil War, according to Paul Preston, 200,000 people were probably killed in battle and a further 200,000 were murdered extra-judicially or executed during the conflict. Another 20,000 were executed after the war by the new regime of Francisco Franco. Many more died of disease and malnutrition in concentration camps. Half a million refugees were forced into exile.[110] Yet 'the Terror' has not habitually been used to describe the Spanish Civil War.

The much-loathed guillotine constituted, in fact, some kind of progress on the previous methods of executions. Death came quicker than by hanging or decapitation by the axe. As Colin Jones has written: 'The blade is as fast as lightning. This is very unlike the horrific mutilating tortures of *Ancien Régime* justice, where death came as a release after hours of excruciating physical torture.'[111] Besides, it was normal at the time to have public executions. The French spy François de La Motte in 1781 was hanged in Tyburn close to present-day Marble Arch in London for almost an hour, then his heart was cut out and burned while 80,000 turned out to witness the event. A year later, before a huge crowd, David

Tyrie, a Scottish spy, was hanged for twenty-two minutes, then beheaded; his heart was cut out and burned; he was then emasculated and quartered. In France, as elsewhere, the death penalty could be imposed for all sorts of crimes including illegally cutting down an oak tree, homosexual acts, theft and heresy. Altogether there were 150 crimes which merited capital punishments, though often such punishments were not applied.[112] The last public execution in France was in 1939; in the UK it was in 1868, and in the US it was in 1936, when a rapist was hanged (by a woman, the local sheriff) before a crowd of 20,000 people.[113]

Thoughts from abroad

One of the first thinkers to decry the violence of the French Revolution was Edmund Burke. His extremely successful *Reflections on the Revolution in France* published in 1790 was one of the main texts by a contemporary. As the historian Jacques Godechot wrote: 'It provided the counter-revolution with its doctrine.'[114] Burke had been a relatively liberal thinker (a Whig) who thought that popular consent was the basis of legitimate government. He had supported American independence. But he accused the French revolutionaries of wanting to cast learning 'into the mire, and trodden down under the hoofs of a swinish multitude … Their liberty is not liberal. Their science is presumptuous ignorance. Their humanity is savage and brutal.'[115] He then went on to lament that

> the age of chivalry is gone. That of sophisters, economists, and calculators, has succeeded; and the glory of Europe is extinguished for ever. Never, never more, shall we behold that generous loyalty to rank and sex, that proud submission, that dignified obedience, that subordination of the heart, which kept alive, even in servitude itself, the spirit of an exalted freedom.[116]

When Burke was writing these words, France was still a monarchy and the Terror had not started. His venom was directed as much against British sympathizers of the French Revolution who saw it as a continental version of the Glorious Revolution. His main purpose was to defend the British system and particularly the dominant position of the Anglican Church.[117] He regarded the French state as an absolutist one, though better than those in the rest of Europe. In denouncing the violence of the French Revolution, Burke seems to have been particularly alarmed at the women ('the vilest of women') who, as we mentioned above, successfully forced the royal family to move to Paris on 5 October 1789.

Burke's tone was distinctly hysterical and overdramatic. The king, the queen and their children, 'who once would have been the pride and hope of a great and generous people', were forced 'to abandon the sanctuary of the most splendid palace in the world', which was left 'swimming in blood, polluted by massacre, and strewed with scattered limbs and mutilated carcasses'.[118] A few years later his tone grew more frenzied still. In *Letters on a Regicide Peace* published in 1796, he referred to those who stormed Versailles as an 'allied army of Amazonian and male cannibal Parisians'.[119] After a diatribe against divorce, which had just been allowed by the French (in Britain it was virtually impossible until 1857), Burke declared:

> With the Jacobins of France, vague intercourse is without reproach; marriage is reduced to the vilest concubinage; children are encouraged to cut the throats of their parents; mothers are taught that tenderness is no part of their character; and to demonstrate their attachment to their party, that they ought to make no scruple to rake with their bloody hands in the bowels of those who came from their own. To all this let us join the practice of cannibalism, with which, in the proper terms, and with the greatest truth, their several factions accuse each other. By cannibalism, I mean their devouring, as a nutriment of their ferocity, some part of the bodies of those they have murdered; their drinking the blood of their victims.[120]

Similar misogynistic remarks contributed to the growing myth of the *tricoteuses*, women who sat quietly knitting while aristocratic heads were sliced off – though, perhaps, some did just that. Revolutionary women are often seen to be unfeminine, based on the stereotype of the malevolent witch. The myth was developed well after the French Revolution by writers such as Chateaubriand in his *Mémoires d'outre-tombe*, Dickens in *A Tale of Two Cities* (1859), where the 'ruthless' Thérèse Defarge knits throughout the novel, and Hippolyte Taine, author of the antirevolutionary *Origines de la France contemporaine* (1876). Taine repeats Burke's denunciation of 'the vilest of women', adding that 'no difficulty has been found in obtaining men and women among the prostitutes of the Palais-Royal', to which 'must be added washerwomen, beggars, bare-footed women, and fishwomen, enlisted several days before and paid accordingly'.[121] According to Taine, Burke had written 'a prophecy as well as a masterpiece', a book that showed that a military dictatorship was the inevitable end of the revolution. It would be the 'most absolute despotism' that has ever appeared.[122]

Among Burke's other French admirers were Joseph de Maistre, a Savoyard subject to the king of Sardinia, who wrote in a letter on 21 January 1791: 'I don't know how to tell you to what degree Burke has reinforced my anti-democratic and anti-Gallican ideas.'[123] In his *Considérations sur la France* (1797), de Maistre wrote: 'There is a *satanic* element in the French Revolution which distinguishes it from other revolutions known or perhaps that will be known', commenting a few pages later on the huge number of 'futile' laws passed by the National Assemblies. 'One sees only children killing each other to raise a house of cards.'[124]

Almost as celebrated, among those hostile to the revolution, was Jacques Mallet du Pan, a Swiss Protestant who settled in Paris after the Geneva Revolution of 1782. Du Pan coined the expression about the revolution 'devouring its children' (see the introduction). By then he had fled Paris. He eventually sought refuge in London, where he died in 1800. His key interventions during the French Revolution occurred when he was the political editor of the *Mercure de France*. But his *Considérations sur la France*, written in exile in Geneva, made him at the time almost as famous as Burke. Du Pan was distrustful of Catholics and of the masses, critical of the Declaration of the Rights of Man, and an upholder of landed property rights while admiring the British 'freedoms' that protected them.[125]

In England meanwhile, few endorsed Burke's rosy description of the ancien régime. According to Gareth Stedman Jones: 'The prevalent view – by the 1820s shared also by many Tories – was that Burke had exaggerated the evils of the Revolution and had temporarily lost his judgement.'[126] Overall, the sympathies of much of the British intelligentsia were with the French Revolution, particularly in its pre-Terror and pre-Napoleonic phases and particularly among the poets – William Blake, William Wordsworth, Samuel Taylor Coleridge, Byron, Percy Shelley and Robert Burns, to mention the best known.[127] Many liked the idea of a new era. Wordsworth wrote famously in *The Prelude*: 'Bliss was it in that dawn to be alive, / But to be young was very Heaven!'

But when the skies darken, as they often do, enthusiasm subsides and the simplistic trope of justice versus oppression, at first so attractive, becomes less so. The agriculturalist Arthur Young, in France during those years and sympathetic to the revolution in 1789, became hostile after 10 August 1792 when armed revolutionaries stormed the Tuileries

Palace, leading six weeks later to the abolition of the monarchy. In 1793 Young published *The Example of France: A Warning to Britain* which reflected his changed views. Even a progressive such as John Stuart Mill described the events of the revolution in *On Liberty* (1859) – a key text of nineteenth-century liberalism – as 'temporary aberrations ... the worst of which were the work of a usurping few, and which, in any case, belonged, not to the permanent working of popular institutions, but to a sudden and convulsive outbreak against monarchical and aristocratic despotism'. Eventually, he added, 'a democratic republic ... made itself felt as one of the most powerful members of the community of nations'.[128] Mill approved of the long-term consequences, not of the initial process.

In Germany reactions were equally mixed. The most illustrious German writer, Johann Wolfgang von Goethe, was perplexed at what he saw as the intolerance of the revolution. Friedrich Schiller was at first in favour, but became rapidly disenchanted. Without having requested it, Schiller was given honorary French citizenships in August 1792, though the decree spelt his name 'Giller'. Jeremy Bentham, Thomas Paine, William Wilberforce, George Washington and others were granted the same honour. Goethe and Schiller had very little faith in the wisdom of the masses – not an uncommon view in the late eighteenth century, or even today. Johann Gottfried Herder, a leading participant in the romantic *Sturm und Drang* (storm and stress) cultural movement in Germany, charted a similar itinerary: enthusiasm in 1789, followed by despair when the Terror began. Immanuel Kant, though disapproving of the Terror and the regicide, remained a staunch republican and a supporter of the revolution even in its Jacobin incarnation.[129] Hegel was appalled by the Terror and regarded the revolution as a 'historical mishap' which had unleashed a brand of 'malevolent energy'. The resulting fallout was not a model for imitation, but a lesson in what to avoid.[130]

In Italy, Vittorio Alfieri (1749–1803), then regarded as the main Italian dramatist (his plays have hardly been performed in the last fifty years, even in Italy), was at first enthusiastic for the revolution – he was in Paris in 1789. But he soon turned against the Terror, and by 1799 had published *Il Misogallo* (*misos*: hater of; *gallo*: the French). This was a bitter anti-French satire condemning Robespierre and defending Louis XVI.

After Robespierre was executed, an abundance of pamphlets demonized him. One by Le Blond de Neuveglise (a pseudonym for a priest who had taught Robespierre at the *lycée*) opened with these words: 'Finally he has fallen: drawn in the waves of blood he himself had spilled, he whom, Monsters, less monstrous than him, have called *The Tyrant*.'[131]

Until 1794 most Americans were supportive of the French Revolution, assuming that the French were simply emulating the American Revolution.[132] Then they parted ways. In his pamphlet *The Revolution in France Considered in Its Progress and Effects* (1794), the lexicographer Noah Webster, a conservative, denounced the 'crimes' of French revolutionaries and described the Jacobins as 'masters of blood', 'ferocious inhuman blood-hounds', and 'sanguinary demons'. France, wrote Webster, was a place of 'war and slaughter', 'anarchy and ferocity'.[133] Alexander Hamilton, always suspicious of democracy, opposed the revolution, while John Adams was upset by the anti-clericalism of the French, and above all for their excessive reliance on 'the people'. Men were created equal, thought Adams, but the rich were better than the poor: the 'distinction of wealth is the greatest and most influential distinction', he wrote. It should never be eradicated.[134] This remark can be found in one of the numerous marginal notes Adams appended to Mary Wollstonecraft's *Historical and Moral View of the Origin and Progress of the French Revolution and the Effect It Has Produced in Europe* (1794), one of the strongest of the numerous rebuttals to Burke's tirade against the French Revolution.

Wollstonecraft's text welcomed the revolution and the birth of a 'new spirit' of free thought. With a calm not exhibited by Burke, she pointed out that 'to mark the prominent features of this revolution, requires a mind, not only unsophisticated by old prejudices, and the inveterate habits of degeneracy; but an amelioration of temper, produced by the exercise of the most enlarged principles of humanity', and all 'in spite of the folly, selfishness, madness, treachery, and more fatal mock patriotism', while recognizing 'the violent, the base, and nefarious assassinations, which have clouded the vivid prospect that began to spread a ray of joy and gladness over the gloomy horizon of oppression'. Violence could not be understood outside the inheritance of the ancien régime's oppression.[135] John Adams's reaction to Wollstonecraft was quite in tune with his sexist response to his wife, who had asked him 'not to forget the ladies' (see Chapter 2). In one of his numerous marginal notes, he expostulated: 'Does this foolish Woman expect to get rid of an Aristocracy? God Almighty has decreed in the creation of human Nature an eternal Aristocracy among Men.'[136] One wonders what he made of Wollstonecraft's most famous work, *A Vindication of the Rights of Woman* (1792).

Thomas Paine's *Rights of Man* (1791), subtitled *Being an Answer to Mr. Burke's Attack on the French Revolution* and dedicated to George Washington, was another, even more forthright defence of republicanism:

All hereditary government is in its nature tyranny. An heritable crown, or an heritable throne, or by what other fanciful name such things may be called, have no other significant explanation than that mankind are heritable property. To inherit a government, is to inherit the people, as if they were flocks and herds.[137]

What turned many away from supporting the French Revolution was the violence, even though, from the point of view of centuries of history, the violence was far from exceptional. A peaceful transition would have attracted less interest. Scholars have privileged the role of violence for reasons not dissimilar to those of tabloid newspapers: violent conflict is more exciting than peaceful demonstrations. At the time, there was panic about the murderous proclivities of the out-of-control multitude. Carlyle's *The French Revolution* (1837), which influenced Dickens's *A Tale of Two Cities*, bathed Paris in blood:

Falling Bastilles, Insurrections of Women, thousands of smoking Manor houses, a country bristling with no crop but that of Sansculottic steel: … Of such may the Heavens have mercy; for the Earth, with her rigorous Necessity, will have none … O infatuated Sansculottes of France! Revolt against constituted Authorities; hunt out your rightful Seigneurs, who at bottom so loved you, and readily shed their blood for you … In confusion, famine, desolation, regret the days that are gone; rueful recall them, recall us with them. To repentant prayers we will not be deaf.[138]

But in 1789 there was, relatively speaking, little violence.[139] The number of political demonstrations had escalated in previous years, especially in the capital – a practice, as Micah Alpaugh has explained, which probably developed from religious processions.[140] In a subsequent study, Alpaugh demonstrates that violence, although present, was not the chief characteristic of protests in the key period of 1787–95.[141] There were some violent episodes and some gruesomeness, such as the parading of the severed head of the governor of the Bastille in retaliation for the dozen assailants killed. But the twenty-six demonstrations that took place between 14 July and 5 October, when the women's demonstration forced the king to leave Versailles, were relatively peaceful.[142] They were peaceful, but certainly neither quiet nor indifferent, at least in Paris – elsewhere, apathy might have been the norm. Activist popular groups were the leading protagonists throughout the years leading to 9 Thermidor (27 July 1794), the end of the Terror.[143] Then the 'incandescent phase' of the Revolution ended.[144] The possessing classes had won. The Terror paved the way for the rule of the bourgeoisie. In the words of Boissy d'Anglas, delegate to the Convention (23 June 1795):

> Finally we are able to guarantee the property of the rich, the survival of the poor, the jouissance of the entrepreneur ... We must be governed by our betters: our betters are more educated and more interested in the preservation of the laws; now, with very few exceptions, you will only find such men among those who possess property.[145]

Napoleon

The blood spilled in the 1790s meant that there are few recognized heroes of the revolution in a country which, unlike Britain, celebrates historical personalities. Vercingetorix, Clovis and Joan of Arc have no British equivalent (Boudicca or Boadicea, often mentioned in the nineteenth century, is hardly commemorated today). As already noted, the celebrations of the bicentenary of the revolution excluded the revolutionaries, especially Robespierre. The revolutionaries have been viewed as somewhat unpalatable by various presidents, including François Mitterrand and Emmanuel Macron – like most politicians, they regard history as a container from which here one can take whatever is convenient.[146]

Napoleon, however, has remained an exception. He is regarded as one of the great Frenchmen of all time, a real *Übermensch* even though, strictly speaking, he failed as an innovator, let alone as a revolutionary. It could be said that he tried to overturn the revolution, and he was responsible for far more deaths than all the Jacobins put together. At first, he claimed to speak on behalf of the French people and adopted revolutionary symbols, such as Marianne, before becoming himself the 'personification of the French nation'.[147] He achieved power in the equivalent of a military putsch on 9 November 1799 (18 Brumaire), after successfully repressing royalist insurrections such as those of 5 October 1795 (Vendémiaire) and 4 September 1797 (Fructidor). The turmoil and conflicts following his seizure of power have remained unparalleled in French history. Estimates of all the French military deaths of the Napoleonic Wars suggest a figure of around 1.8 million.[148]

During his occupation of Egypt, where he was defeated by the British at the Battle of the Nile (1–3 August 1798), Napoleon initially showed tolerance towards the Muslim population, realizing that he needed the support of the religious authorities if he was going to turn Egypt into a colony. Soon though, repression commenced: villages were seized and men shot or beaten with truncheons, their heads cut off and put on pikes; hostages were rounded up; camps razed to the ground; houses burned; flocks confiscated; people deported. As Bonaparte wrote in September 1798 to one of his generals (Charles Dugua):

> The Turks [the Egyptians] can be guided only with the greatest severity; every day I have five or six heads cut off in the streets of Cairo. We have had to treat them with consideration up to this point to destroy the reputation for terror that preceded us: now, on the contrary, we have to adopt the tone required to make these peoples obey; and for them, to obey is to fear.[149]

A revolt in Cairo was repressed in such a brutal way that, even on the basis of Napoleon's own figures, 'the loss of life in the two days of the revolt was far greater than that of Parisians throughout the Terror, in a city half the size of the French capital'. Other estimates, based on local sources, suggest that between 2,500 and 8,000 Cairenes were massacred – 'the largest single loss of civilian life during a decade of Revolutionary violence'.[150] The executioner of the repression was General Charles Dugua, who went on to try to repress the Haitian Revolution, in the course of which he died. His name is inscribed under the Arc de Triomphe along with other so-called military heroes.

The massacre in Egypt was the worst, but not the first Napoleonic massacre. The 1796 campaign in Italy was characterized by the systematic destruction of villages in Lombardy, such as Binasco, near Milan. Napoleon, in his *Proclamation aux habitants de la Lombardie* (25 May 1796) warned others: 'Those who, within twenty-four hours have not laid down their weapons and sworn their allegiance to the Republic will be regarded as rebels and their villages will be burnt. Let Binasco be a terrible example which will open their eyes.'[151] Neither the massacres in Cairo nor those in Italy were much remarked upon by nineteenth-century French historians, including those who were highly critical of Napoleon, such as Jules Michelet and Hippolyte Taine.[152] It should be said that little was known at the time of the Cairo revolt, so formidable was the propaganda machine of Napoleon and so oblivious were Europeans about the fate of non-Europeans.[153] Instead the Napoleonic expedition in Egypt is remembered for the large number of scientists who accompanied the French troops with the alleged purpose to bring enlightenment and rescue old treasures which could be better protected in Paris than in Cairo.[154]

Napoleon was often, at least at first, celebrated by progressives as the man who exported the French Revolution. But this is debatable. Much of this exporting consisted of the occupation of various territories; such conquests brought about important changes, or at least the desire for change, especially in still-divided Germany and Italy or occupied Poland. But Napoleon was the trigger, not, as so many considered him, the liberator. The revolution was exported not just in terms of ideas but also quite simply because the advancing Napoleonic forces destroyed, albeit often temporarily, the old regimes, and abolished elements of feudalism and clericalism. Thus the Cisalpine Republic in Northern Italy that Napoleon (who was twenty-eight at the time) created in 1797 lasted only a few years before becoming in 1802 part of the French-controlled Italian Republic, and eventually, in 1805, part of the Kingdom of Italy, with Napoleon himself as king. This was conquest in anything but name.

Finally, having conquered half of Europe – Napoleon *was* a brilliant general – and having had himself crowned emperor by the pope, the conquests rapidly began to unravel. Under his rule, nepotism reached uncommon heights. Relatives devoid of any talent were appointed to rule Naples, Spain, Holland and Westphalia. With the Concordat of 1801, Catholicism was re-established as the state religion. Napoleon's attempt to establish an outpost in the Middle East (the Egyptian campaign) ended in utter failure. His challenges to the British Navy failed at Aboukir on the Nile Delta (1798) and at Trafalgar (1805). His Spanish campaigns of 1807–14 (the Peninsular Wars) ended in disaster. His invasion of Russia was an absurd endeavour, which resulted in the annihilation of his Grande Armée of 650,000 soldiers, half of whom were not French. Many perished, were taken prisoner or deserted.[155] His rule left France shattered, yet his star shines to this day.

Napoleon, defeated in Russia, was forced to abdicate in 1814 and was exiled to the island of Elba, off the Tuscan coast. He subsequently returned, ruled for the Hundred Days with little popular support, and was finally defeated at Waterloo, 'the last great world-historical battle to be decided in the course of a day'.[156] Forced into his final exile at Saint Helena, Napoleon's conversations were turned into a text by Emmanuel de Las Cases, his confidant. This became known as *Le Mémorial de Sainte-Hélène* and added to the legend an aura of misfortune mixed with fortitude. In 1840, Napoleon's corpse was brought back from Saint Helena, where he died a prisoner of the British. The reigning monarch

Louis-Philippe hoped in vain that the Napoleonic legend would rub off on him; he agreed for the ashes, returned by the British as a sign of good will, would be kept in a monumental tomb in Les Invalides, where they still rest. An immense crowd accompanied the procession of the remains. Victor Hugo evoked this in a short poem, 'Le 15 décembre 1840. Écrit en revenant des Champs-Élysées', written with characteristic ebullience.

> Ciel glacé! soleil pur! Oh! brille dans l'histoire!
> Du funèbre triomphe, impérial flambeau!
> Que le peuple à jamais te garde en sa mémoire
> Jour beau comme la gloire,
> Froid comme le tombeau.
>
> O frozen sky! Pure sun! Shining in history!
> Funereal triumph, imperial torch!
> Let the people hold you forever in its memory
> The day was beautiful as the glory,
> And cold as the tomb.

Napoleon had also tried to suppress the one revolution which occurred in the wake of the French Revolution: the one in Saint-Domingue (Haiti). During the Terror, on 4 February 1794, the Convention nationale had abolished slavery in all French colonies and incorporated it in the new *Déclaration des droits et des devoirs de l'homme et du citoyen*. In England the House of Commons had proposed the abolition of the slave trade two years earlier, but it persisted until the House of Lords finally approved its abolition in 1807. In France, the colonies were no longer in 1794 colonies but an integral part of the republic. Freedom for the slaves did not last long. As first consul, Napoleon re-established slavery in the French colonies on 20 May 1802. It was finally abolished, once and for all, in 1848 by the Second Republic.

Earlier, in June 1791, the Jacobin Saint-Just (executed in 1794) looked forward in *L'Esprit de la Révolution* to a time where the 'Princes of Europe' would agree to enter into a general convention to abolish slavery and the slave trade everywhere – an early proposal for an international convention of human rights.[157] In October 1790 the Abbé Grégoire had already announced that the French Revolution would lead to a revolutionary process in the colonies. 'The volcano of freedom sparked in France will lead to a general explosion which will change the fate of humanity in both hemispheres'; he felt it would be a mistake to assume that those so long oppressed will not soon rise against the injustices of the white peoples.[158]

Grégoire was right: in Saint-Domingue, which was then by far France's richest colony, a revolution started in 1791, sparked by the ideals of *Liberté, egalité, fraternité*, a term coined by Robespierre the previous year. It was at first directed against the French settlers. The rebels wanted to abolish slavery and, at least initially, to remain part of France. The revolution continued for twelve years, during which time thousands of formerly enslaved Africans overcame the British, Spanish and Napoleonic French armies. Eventually, on 1 January 1804, the first independent Black republic in the Americas was established, led by Toussaint Louverture, Jean-Jacques Dessalines and Alexandre Pétion. Napoleon had sent a large fleet to Saint-Domingue; Louverture was captured and deported to France, where he died. But resistance and disease (yellow fever) forced the French to withdraw, and the colony became independent under its ancient name: Haiti.[159] Its subsequent history was most unhappy – it was torn by dictatorships and civil wars. In 1825, France, now under the Bourbon monarchy, threatened to invade Haiti again unless it paid a huge indemnity, which it did – with dire economic consequences.

While US President Thomas Jefferson offered assistance against Toussaint as part of a decade-long record of opposition to the slave revolt in Saint-Domingue, progressives celebrated Toussaint.[160] William Wordsworth wrote a poem in honour of the imprisoned and dying Louverture, 'the most unhappy of men!'

> Yet die not; do thou
> Wear rather in thy bonds a cheerful brow:
> Though fallen thyself, never to rise again,
> Live, and take comfort. Thou hast left behind
> Powers that will work for thee; air, earth, and skies;
> There's not a breathing of the common wind
> That will forget thee; thou hast great allies;
> Thy friends are exultations, agonies,
> And love, and man's unconquerable mind.

Alphonse Lamartine wrote a play, *Toussaint Louverture* (1848), which contained a *Marseillaise noire*: 'Enfants des noirs, proscrits du monde, / Pauvre chair changée en troupeau' (Children of the Blacks, outcasts of the world, / Poor flesh transformed into a herd). The historian Lynn Hunt, writing in 1995, remarked that slave revolts, including that of

Saint-Domingue (Haiti), had remained marginal to the study of the French Revolution, even though 'one in eight French people lived off colonial trade, and the single colony of Saint-Domingue had 500,000 slaves in 1789 whereas all the United States had 700,000'.[161] French foreign trade was then larger than that of Great Britain; it depended mainly on the Caribbean colonies and, above all, on Saint-Domingue.[162]

The issue of slavery was scarcely broached during the celebrations of the bicentenary of the revolution (another example of a country's constant rewriting of its own history). Recent scholarship has pointed out that it was during the Terror that an attempt was made to recognize that people of colour should have the same rights as others. But after 9 Thermidor and the purge of the Jacobins, the pro-colonial forces won the day.[163] As in the United States, people of colour (and women) would have had to wait for decades for the equal rights rhetoric of the founding days of the revolution to become reality.

The fascination with great personalities of history made Napoleon the best known of all Frenchmen, even though by an irony of history he was French only because his native Corsica had been ceded to France by the Republic of Genoa just a few months before his birth. His mother tongue was Corsican (far closer to mainstream Italian – Tuscan – than many Italian dialects) and he never lost a distinctive Italianate accent. Those who seek to defend him point to supposed achievements such as the Code Napoléon (1804), which was written by scholars of the ancien régime who understood how to fit in with the times. Much of it had been drafted before Napoleon had achieved power. The Code made no mention of enslaved people and reflected the prejudices of the time against women, regarded as 'perpetual minors'. Germaine de Staël, who in her epistolary novel *Delphine* (1802) had criticized such restrictions on women's liberty, was exiled from Paris by Napoleon. Restrictions on women continued. France was one of the last European countries (with Belgium, Italy and Switzerland) to grant women the vote. The administrative reorganization was the work of clever civil servants, who would have been clever, civil and servants under any regime or leader. Many members of the aristocracy – those who chose to remain in France instead of exiling themselves – continued to enjoy some of the power and privilege as before. Their numbers were increased by the titles Napoleon distributed liberally, though he did not necessarily obtain their everlasting loyalty – quite the contrary.[164]

Napoleon began to construct his own myth almost from his earliest military campaigns. He declared: 'The nation needs a leader, a leader decked in glory, and not in theories of government, phrases, speeches.' The nation followed, almost immediately. Even before he had taken over complete power in 1799, French theatres put on at least thirty plays that either mentioned Bonaparte or featured him as a character.[165] Others developed the legend, including great composers (Ludwig van Beethoven, Hector Berlioz, Robert Schumann), major poets (Heinrich Heine, Alexander Pushkin, Lord Byron), prominent painters (Jacques-Louis David, François Gerard, Horace Vernet) and, of course, historians. Walter Scott, the most successful novelist of his time, wrote one of the first biographies, *The Life of Napoleon*, in 1827. Alessandro Manzoni wrote a poem, 'Il cinque maggio', in honour of Napoleon's death on 5 May 1821, suggesting that the whole earth stands, stricken, astonished, mute (*percossa, attonita ... muta*) paying its respects to the 'Man of Destiny'. Alphonse de Lamartine followed Manzoni, writing in his poem 'Bonaparte' (1823) that 'no other mortal' left on the earth a greater mark (*une plus forte trace*).[166]

Goethe, in his *Conversations with Eckermann*, proclaimed:

Napoleon was the man! Always illuminated, always clear and decided ... His life was the stride of a demigod, from battle to battle, and from victory to victory ... His destiny was more brilliant than any the world had seen before him, or perhaps will ever see after him.[167]

Georg Hegel was equally in awe. On 13 October 1806, the French occupied Jenna, where Hegel was staying. In a letter to his friend, Friedrich Immanuel Niethammer, he exclaimed excitedly:

I saw the Emperor – this world-soul on horseback [*Weltseele zu Pferde*] – riding out of the city on reconnaissance. It is indeed a wonderful sensation to see such an individual, who, concentrated here at a single point, astride a horse, reaches out over the world and masters it.[168]

It was the zeitgeist on horseback.

There were always dissenting voices. One of these was François-René de Chateaubriand, one of the most distinguished writers of the period. Having dedicated to Napoleon the second edition of his masterpiece, *Génie du christianisme* (1803), he turned against the emperor with his ferocious pamphlet *De Buonaparte, des Bourbons* (1814), where the emperor is always referred to as Buonaparte, never the slightly more French *Bonaparte*, let alone *Napoléon*. Chateaubriand declared that Napoleon had done more to harm the human race in ten years than all the tyrants of ancient Rome; that he had caused the death of 5 million Frenchmen – an exaggeration; that he was a 'faux grand homme', born, above all, to destroy (*né surtout pour détruire*); and that, anyway, he was not French at all but Corsican and Italian. The pamphlet concluded with a celebration of the Bourbons – all of them, past and present.[169] Much later, in 1832, with Napoleon dead for over ten years, Wordsworth, in a sonnet, described Napoleon as 'the one Man that laboured to enslave The World'.[170]

Even Stendhal, though a supporter of the emperor, provided a famous account of the Battle of Waterloo in *La Chartreuse de Parme* (1838) seen entirely from the point of view of seventeen-year-old Fabrice, whose romantic dreams of fighting for the emperor evaporate before the harsh reality of a battle in which he understands nothing. Stendhal knew something about the absurdities and horrors of war, having been a soldier in the Napoleonic armies during the Russian campaign: there, like Fabrice, he had lost his last illusions.[171]

The Bourbon Restoration of 1815 should have subdued Napoleon's reputation considerably, but Louis-Philippe, having taken over in 1830, tried to associate his rule with the Napoleonic glory, and when Louis Bonaparte became emperor with the name of Napoleon III the myth took off – it has endured ever since.[172] Louis XVI was ridiculed; Danton, Robespierre and Marat were celebrated only by the left; the Bourbon kings (Louis XVIII and the more reactionary Charles X) were despised; the Orléans king (Louis-Philippe) was virtually forgotten – and yet the star of Napoleon continued to shine. Some historians, including Marxist ones such as Georges Lefebvre, regarded him as the heir of the French Revolution in the belief that a dictatorial force was essential to preserve its main gains.[173]

In August 1969, President Georges Pompidou travelled to Ajaccio to mark the bicentenary of Napoleon's birth, describing him, ludicrously, as a precursor of the European Union.[174] Since then, the praise has been toned down. By 2021, for the bicentenary of the emperor's death, Emmanuel Macron lay a wreath by his monumental tomb at the Hotel des Invalides at 17.49 hours, allegedly the exact moment of his death. This was preceded by a speech at the Institut de France in which he attempted, as usual, to strike a middle way between celebration and criticism so as not to offend anyone.[175] The Corsican ogre was a controversial figure, but, unlike Robespierre and other Jacobin leaders, he remains one of France's great mythologized national treasures, along with Joan of Arc, Vercingetorix and Charlemagne.

La Restauration

The regime that succeeded Napoleon is known as the Restoration, but it certainly did not restore the ancien régime. In history, matters seldom if ever return to their original point. The monarchy and the Bourbon dynasty, led by Louis XVI's younger brothers Louis XVIII and then Charles X, were fragile from the beginning. Louis XVIII had gained his throne thanks to foreign powers, lost it to Napoleon for the Hundred Days, and regained it again thanks to a German army led by Prince Blücher and a British one led by the Anglo-Irish Duke of Wellington – it was they who defeated Napoleon at Waterloo. An early verdict on the future Louis XVIII and Charles X by William Wickham, a senior British intelligence agent, was scathing: 'When one has observed them as closely and as often behind the scenes as I have', he wrote in 1796, 'one is tempted to believe that God Almighty has willed this appalling revolution, among other aims, for their personal correction.'[176]

Louis XVIII has been described as 'one of the most forgotten kings of France'.[177] Almost as forgotten has been the White Terror of 1815 (known as the Second White Terror to distinguish it from that of 1794–50). Lamartine was kinder, and described Louis XVIII as someone who bore with a brave face all the vicissitudes life threw at him.[178] Germaine de Staël thought he was 'un homme d'un esprit très-éclairé' (an enlightened man) whose ideas extends well beyond the court.[179]

Louis XVIII had to accept the Charte of 4 June 1814 (to call it a constitution would have been too daring), which gave him powers similar to those Louis XVI had been forced to grant in 1791. The Charte provided for a legislature composed of an upper house of nobles (Chambre des Paires) and an elected lower chamber of deputies. It also promulgated equality before the law, due process and relative freedom of the press.

The clergy made a comeback. This is not surprising, since the question of religion had never ceased to dominate French politics. Catholicism had been ferociously repressed during the first phase of the republic, part of the revolutionary campaign of dechristianization that started in 1793. A new calendar had been established beginning with Year One of the revolution (September 1792, when the monarchy was abolished), not with the birth of Christ. Churches were closed, and most of the clergy went into hiding. Priests and nuns were among the first victims of the *noyades de Nantes* – execution by drowning in the Loire. The victims, including anyone suspected of being a counter-revolutionary, numbered in the thousands. Then there was, in 1794, Robespierre's brief and useless attempt to introduce the *culte de l'Être supreme* as a state religion, possibly in an effort to contain the worst excesses of dechristianization. Robespierre's new God was distinctly revolutionary. As Robespierre declared in the inaugural speech at the Festival of the Supreme Being:

> The Supreme Being did not create kings to devour humanity. He did not create priests to harness us, like vile animals to the chariots of kings; and to give to the world examples of wickedness, pride, perfidy, avarice, debauchery, and deception. He created the universe to proclaim His power. He created men to help and love each other, and to attain happiness by following the path of virtue ...[180]

Catholicism was re-introduced after Napoleon, then resurrected on new foundations under the restored Bourbons and their successors. It was accepted with some misgivings by the Third Republic in 1870, until the 1905 law on *laïcité* which separated the state from the Church. The Charte of 1814, while proclaiming freedom of worship (Protestants and Jews had been emancipated in 1791), declared that Catholicism was the state religion. By 1830, with the advent of the Orléans dynasty, this was modified into the mere recognition that Catholicism was the religion of the majority. In 1850, under the Second Republic, the Falloux Laws – named after the staunchly Catholic minister Alfred de Falloux – strengthened the hold of the Catholic Church in French schools. Religion remained the ideological backbone of French conservatism for decades. But, with the intelligence of a movement that has managed to survive for centuries and thrive through endless change, the clergy now began a slow march towards modernization, despite the reactionary attempts by Pope Pius IX to hold everything back. Some even embraced republican opinions once they had ascertained that the era of monarchy had ended, at least in France.

Bureaucratic continuity marked not only the transition from the First Republic to Napoleon but also from Napoleon to the Restoration, since the Bourbons initially turned to the Napoleonic bureaucracy to find competent prefects and civil servants (Napoleon had likewise appointed personnel from the ancien régime). There was no thorough purge of imperial judges.[181] The great symbol of continuity was Charles de Talleyrand: minister of foreign affairs under Napoleon and Louis XVIII, one of the protagonists of the Congress of Vienna, briefly prime minister under Louis XVIII, then ambassador to London under Louis Philippe. Lamartine wrote of him that, though much criticized, 'he never tied himself to any government as a palace slave, but he had assessed them while serving them and abandoned them when these governments could no longer serve him'.[182] Known by his critics as the Diable boiteux (lame devil) because of his infirmity, he was mentioned by Gustave Flaubert in his dictionary of clichés (*Dictionnaire des idées reçues*): 'Talleyrand (Prince de): s'indigner contre' (to be indignant against). Yet de Staël, in her posthumously published *Considerations on the Principal Events of the French Revolution*, noted that M. de Talleyrand, 'when he wanted to, was the most amiable man produced by the ancien régime'.[183]

The Bourbon kings were imperilled from the beginning by a parliament deeply split between *ultraroyalistes*, who thought the Charte too liberal, and liberals, who thought it too monarchical. The ultras were, at first, the overwhelming majority (350 seats out of 398). They advocated a policy of retribution against former republicans and those who had supported Napoleon, but were grudgingly accepting of limits to the power of the monarch, as was even the arch-conservative Chateaubriand in his 1816 *De la monarchie selon la Charte*, where he advocated a British-style French constitutional monarchy.[184] The ultra-royalist journal *Le Conservateur*, founded in 1818 with Chateaubriand as one of its main contributors, ceased publication in 1820 as a protest against new laws restricting the press. So even the ultra-royalists had accepted some of the principles of liberalism.

The electoral reform of 1820 led to a further victory for the ultra-monarchists, to the dismay not only of the left and the liberals but also of moderate conservatives who accepted the revolution but not the republic. They did not oppose a constitutional system because they were frightened by the prospect of a return to anarchy and revolutionary violence: 'I think', wrote Guizot in 1820 about the moderate conservatives, 'this is a considerable and respectable force. They are my best allies.'[185]

The ultra-monarchists, however, further gained in power in 1824 when Charles X became king. They even tried to re-establish some elements of primogeniture – and failed. France had moved on: it could neither accept the kind of reactionary rule that further restricted press freedom, nor a new electoral system that favoured the ultras. By 25 July 1830, once again, barricades went up and the (banned) tricolour was flying everywhere in Paris. The Bourbon monarchy was so weak that it took only three revolutionary days – Les Trois Glorieuses, 27–29 July – to dispose of Charles X. Berlioz, who had just finished a cantata (*La Mort de Sardanapale*, which won the Prix de Rome) was desperate to join the Revolution. He wrote to his father on 2 August:

I was the first to come out of the Institut last Thursday [29 July] at 5 o'clock, at the moment when the capture of the Louvre was being completed ... As soon as I had written the last note you can imagine that my first thought was to run to where a mortal anxiety was calling me, traversing the last shots, the screams, the dead, the wounded, etc. ... The idea that so many brave people paid with their blood for the conquest of our liberties, while I am among those who were of no use, does not leave me a moment's rest ... Here everything is quiet, the wonderful order which has prevailed during this magical 3-day revolution continues and takes root; not a single robbery, no outrage of any kind. What a sublime people!'[186]

Victor Hugo, in a poem which praised the 1830 Revolution as well as his idol Napoleon, wrote 'three days sufficed to break your fetters' – adding:

> *Hier, vous n'étiez qu'une foule,*
> *Vous êtes un Peuple aujourd'hui.*

> Yesterday you were a mere crowd,
> Today you are a People.[187]

Charles X, true to the Bourbons' limited intelligence, had failed to understand that reaction could not pay. As Talleyrand is supposed to have said of the Bourbons: 'They have learnt nothing, forgotten nothing.' Charles X possessed, in the words of the journalist Hippolyte Castille, writing in 1858, 'the kind of lethal obstinacy that leads some men to shatter their skull on a hard surface'. Castille was almost as scathing about Charles's successor, Louis-Philippe (d'Orléans): he was 'much ado about nothing', (*beaucoup de bruit pour rien*), quoting Shakespeare.[188]

The House of Orléans

The Revolution of 1789, its gains and its legends, could not be completely erased, nor could the hopes raised by the Napoleonic interlude. Charles X had virtually no support in Paris, and only a little in the provinces. He was forced into exile and France faced yet another change of regime. The Bourbons disappeared from French history – quite unlamented – and the Orléans took over with Louis-Philippe, whose own father (known as Philippe Égalité) had embraced the republican cause and paid the price by ending up on the guillotine. This was the final attempt to establish a liberal monarchy. As we have seen, Louis-Philippe became not king of France, but king of *the French*. To emphasize rupture, he turned down the name of Philippe VII in favour of Louis-Philippe I. A new *charte* was proclaimed; the white flag of the Bourbon was lowered, and the tricolour went up.

It was in September–December 1830, shortly after Les Trois Glorieuses, that Eugène Delacroix painted his famous *Liberté guidant le peuple* (originally the subtitle, the title having been *Le 28 juillet*, the most crucial of the three days). A bare-breasted woman, representing Liberty, waves the tricolour with one hand, a rifle with the other. Wearing the revolutionary Phrygian cap, she guides the people, including a bourgeois in a top hat but otherwise in working clothes and a young boy brandishing two pistols (presumably the inspiration for the boy Gavroche in Victor Hugo's *Les Misérables*). Louis-Philippe, keen to demonstrate his revolutionary credentials, immediately bought the painting and allowed it to be exhibited. Heinrich Heine, writing in 1832, noted the substantial crowds who had come to admire it. He remarked with praise that Liberty had the appearance of a fishwife or even a prostitute, emancipating her from her goddess-like role and making her more part of the demos.[189]

More gestures towards *la révolution* occurred when the king agreed that Casimir Delavigne's song 'La Parisienne' (written in 1830) should be taken as the virtual national anthem of his reign. While the music was that of the German military march 'Ein Schifflein Sah Ich Fahren' (I saw a little ship go by), the words were unquestionably revolutionary (and French):

> *Peuple Français, peuple de braves,*
> *La Liberté rouvre ses bras;*
> *On nous disait: soyez esclaves!*
> *Nous avons dit: soyons soldats!*
>
> People of France, people of courage,
> Freedom opens her arms;
> We were told: be slaves!
> We shout: Let's be soldiers!

While everyone today would recognize the 'Marseillaise', hardly anyone remembers 'La Parisienne'.

Initially Orléans rule appeared liberal, seeming to espouse *le juste milieu* (middle way).[190] The press was freer and suffrage was a little less narrow, though even in 1847, a year before the regime collapsed, only 3 per cent of male adults could vote. It looked as if France had joined Britain as a liberal nation counterposed to reactionary Austria, Prussia and Russia, the Holy Alliance established in 1815.[191] For Marx, it marked the continuation of the bourgeois revolution, since it resulted 'in the transfer of government from the landlords to the capitalists, transferred it from the more remote to the more direct antagonists of the working men'.[192] For Albert Soboul it was a political compromise with the *grande bourgeoisie*.[193] Few doubted that the Orléanist was a bourgeois monarchy. François Guizot's famous injunction to 'enrich yourselves', uttered in a speech to the chamber on 1 March 1843, does not sound quite so insensitive when quoted in full: 'Strengthen your institutions, enlighten yourselves, enrich yourselves and you will improve the moral and material condition of our France.'[194]

The first challenge to the new regime came from the silk weavers in Lyon, *la révolte des Canuts*. Arguably one of the first workers' insurrections of modern times, it occurred in 1831 when the Canuts (about 8,000 master craftsmen and 30,000 apprentices) demanded a stable payment for the wares they were selling to the merchants (and who had been modifying prices at will). The merchants invoked the Chapelet Law of 1791, which prohibited associations, and the government tried to mediate. The protest turned into an uprising, which was duly repressed. A further revolt occurred in 1834. By then, emerging socialist organizations had added their weight, demanding the right to form trade unions. The army intervened and the uprising was crushed; there were many dead and many were deported to prisons abroad. It had ended in a bloodbath.[195]

The Orléans monarchy was doomed, like its predecessors, not just because of the Canuts but because of widespread corruption. It fell in 1848, the year of the 'Springtime of the Peoples'. That year has remained unparalleled in modern history, as revolutions, attempted revolutions, demonstrations and protest movements took place more or less at the same time in many European states. Christoper Clark calls it 'the only truly European revolution that there has ever been'.[196] The revolutionary movement started in Palermo, Sicily, in January 1848. Sicily was then part of the Kingdom of the Two Sicilies, with Naples as its capital. Initially the revolutionaries had considerable success. The king, who had started his rule as would-be liberal, granted a constitution but suspended it within a year, helped by the internal factionalism of the revolutionaries.

The demands, almost everywhere, were similar: liberal freedoms, constitutional rights, the end of absolute power, national liberation. In most countries, such as Moldavia and Wallachia, the movement was defeated, and the rights and constitutions granted were repealed. There were some victories. In Switzerland, after a short civil war (the Sonderbundskrieg), a federal constitution was granted; and in Austria and Hungary (both part of the Austrian Empire), serfdom was abolished. In Denmark, the absolute monarchy turned into a constitutional one, and in Poland landlords were killed by peasants in revolt. Initially, constitutions were granted in most Italian states, but only the Kingdom of Sardinia (Piedmont) under Carlo Alberto kept its new constitution (Statuto Albertino) when the movement had abated. In Austria and Germany liberal freedoms were revoked within a few years.

Some countries were spared. In tsarist Russia repression was such as to make protest almost impossible. In Great Britain, the Great Reform Act had already granted much of what liberals wanted (in Ireland, there was also the so-called Young Irelander Rebellion, a minor affair). Belgium had already had its own revolution in 1830 when it seceded from the Netherlands and became independent. Spain was in the middle of a civil war involving Catalonia (the Second Carlist War).

Whatever was haunting Europe in 1848 was not, as Marx and Engels famously wrote at the beginning of their *Communist Manifesto*, the spectre of communism (a movement then virtually unknown), but that of constitutional liberalism. This is the spectre that triumphed: by the end of the nineteenth century the only surviving absolute monarchies in Europe were the tsarist and Ottoman empires.

In France, 1848 was exceptional: it signalled the definitive end of the traditional monarchy in that country. In January of that year, before anything serious had started, Tocqueville, speaking in the Chamber of Deputies, warned: 'My deepest conviction, gentlemen, is this: I believe we are presently sleeping on a volcano.'[197] The causes for the downfall of the Orléans were multiple: an economic crisis stretching back to 1845, harvest failures, growing unemployment, the almost complete lack of reform under the conservative Guizot ministry after his victory in the 1846 elections, and the still very limited electorate – just under 250,000 electors in a population of 35 million. To this should be added that, when street violence erupted on 24 February 1848, the Paris National Guard was reluctant to intervene.[198] Tocqueville in his *Souvenirs* (drafted two years later) recollected that he had spent that afternoon walking around Paris:

Two things struck me above all others that day: the first was that the just-completed revolution had been not just primarily but solely and exclusively a popular uprising that had bestowed all power on 'the people' in the strict sense of the term, meaning the classes that work with their hands. The second was how little hatred, or for that matter any other keen passion, the lower classes thus suddenly invested with sole mastery displayed in the first flush of victory.[199]

The celebrated writer George Sand concurred, pointing out that the demonstrations, at least initially, were peaceful. It was the conservative bourgeoisie that was scared: 'It hides its money and its knees shake.'[200] What particularly dismayed contemporaries, however, was the extremely high level of corruption which implicated even Louis-Philippe, the so-called citizen-king, and his family. The open-air banquets held to bypass laws against demonstrations were sites where the corruption, nepotism and immorality of the ruling elite were denounced with vigour even by conservatives.[201]

Louis-Philippe tried to calm matters, sacking Guizot (then the most important politician in France) and recruiting as prime minister the popular moderate Adolphe Thiers, a leader of the July Revolution of 1830 (several times prime minister and eventually, in 1871, the man who would suppress the Paris Commune and inaugurate the Third Republic). But he also chose the wrong military man to repress the Parisian insurgents: the infamous Maréchal Thomas Bugeaud. His fame, or infamy, dates to 14 April 1834, when someone fired a shot against French soldiers from a house in rue Transnonain (now rue Beaubourg) in Paris, killing an officer. Under the orders of Bugeaud, soldiers entered the house and killed its twelve inhabitants, including women and children. Bugeaud was forever known as *l'homme de la rue Transnonain*, immortalized in a famous lithograph by Honoré Daumier representing the aftermath of the incident: one of the victims is shown in a night shirt, the body of a dead child underneath.

During the French occupation of Algeria in the 1840s Bugeaud had been a pioneer of what is now known as a scorched-earth policy, warning the Algerians that if they did not submit: 'I will enter your mountains, I will burn your villages and your crops, I will cut down your fruit trees.'[202] But he could not do this to Parisian workers in 1848 without serious consequences. The National Guards and even many in the army were reluctant to engage in another massacre, and so was Bugeaud, who probably started, a little late, to think of history's verdict.

Honoré Daumier, *Rue Transnonain, le 15 avril 1834*, lithograph printed by Delaunois July 1834

Taken by surprise by the events of February 1848, Louis-Philippe had to follow the path to exile his predecessor had taken, and the Second Republic was proclaimed. 'The February Revolution was unforeseen by everyone, but by him most of all', observed Tocqueville.[203] The king, at seventy-four, was no longer young. Tired of his apparently ungovernable country, he abdicated and exiled himself to England, where he died in 1850, at Claremont House near Esher.

From Second Republic to Second Empire

France was, again, without a king. A new revolution had started but the revolutionaries were divided, as they always are, between various factions ranging from left socialists such as Louis Auguste Blanqui, to moderate socialists such as Louis Blanc, radical republicans such as Alexandre Ledru-Rollin, and moderate republicans such as the poet Alphonse Lamartine. The new administration, known as the provisional government (24 February to 9 May 1848), abolished slavery and the slave trade, as well as capital punishment for political crimes. (France definitively abolished capital punishment only in 1981; it was the last European

Union country to do so.) Corporal punishment too was abolished, and the working day shortened to ten hours in Paris and eleven outside.

Universal manhood suffrage was introduced for the elections of 23 April 1848. The socialist Victor Considérant thought that women should be given the vote. He was not taken seriously. Even major women writers, such as Marie d'Agoult (author of a remarkable history of the 1848 revolution under the pseudonym of Daniel Stern), George Sand and Delphine Gay, thought women were not ready for it.[204] Tocqueville, the great liberal, thought Considérant must have been mad.[205] Conservative republicans won and abolished the state-run *ateliers nationaux* (national workshops) aimed at providing work or benefits for the unemployed of Paris. This led to another insurrection in Paris (22–26 June 1848), and another massacre with some 1,500 demonstrators shot straight away.[206] Marx thought this to be 'the most colossal event in the history of European civil wars'.[207] Marie d'Agoult, in her history of the 1848 events, aware of the class implications of the June events, noted that they signified the definitive separation of the two central facets of 1848: the political revolution and the social revolution. 'The proletariat,' she wrote, 'which twice challenged the principle of popular sovereignty, was severely punished and disappeared from the scene; from now on the movement belonged exclusively to the bourgeoisie.'[208]

Tocqueville thought this was 'necessary and awful'. The June days, he wrote, 'did not extinguish the revolutionary flame in France, but for a time at least they did put an end to what one might call the essential work of the February revolution'.[209] Victor Hugo too thought the workshops had encouraged the workers to be lazy.[210] The 'butcher of June' was General Cavaignac, then also minister of war. He believed that this exploit would ensure his election as president of the republic in December of that year, but the victory went to Louis Napoleon.

France was still overwhelmingly rural, and many electors did as their priests suggested, though some probably also wanted to register a protest against the elites represented by Cavaignac.[211] The election had taken place during an agricultural depression. Wheat prices, which had increased remarkably in 1845–47, crumbled the following year.[212] During his electoral campaign in March 1848, Tocqueville was 'pleasantly surprised' that in the countryside 'all landowners, regardless of background, ancestry, education, or means, had banded together into what seemed to be a single class'. They were all united by 'the universal hatred and terror that Paris inspired'.[213] And Paris had grown enormously, doubling its population to 1 million since the beginning of the century.

Peasants had been among the principal beneficiaries of the revolution of 1789. The Paris revolutionaries had forgotten that their predecessors had not only granted peasants the right to vote but had also abolished the tithe, eliminated compulsory labour and other feudal privileges and, above all, divided some of the land of the old nobility among the former serfs. Why should these beneficiaries now support Parisian workers in their demands? After all, in March 1848, the provisional government decided to increase by 45 per cent some of the existing taxes to resolve partially the public debt. This surtax affected the peasants particularly, and they did not forget it. The minister responsible for the surtax, Louis-Antoine Garnier-Pagès, defending his tax policies, lamented that everyone had turned against him, and no one was there to defend him: 'Everywhere in France there appeared a widespread clamour: I was the 45-centimes Man.'[214]

The new National Assembly had a conservative majority, which included many former monarchists ironically labelled *républicains du lendemain*. By now the revolutionaries were isolated; thus the great advances of French progressivism had brought to the fore a staunchly conservative force – one of the many instances of the so-called law of unintended consequences. Not for nothing had Marx and Engels, in their *Communist Manifesto*, praised the bourgeoisie for increasing the urban population, thus rescuing 'a considerable part of the population from the idiocy of rural life' – there was obviously a long way to go.

A new republican constitution, drafted by a commission which included Tocqueville, decreed that the president would be elected by universal male suffrage. In December 1848, in the first presidential elections ever, peasant proprietors, now the backbone of French conservatism, voted massively for a candidate whose name (Napoleon) seemed to them to guarantee the land gains they had achieved thanks to revolution.[215]

Louis Napoleon Bonaparte was one of the first politicians to realize the importance of branding and public relations, and was a pioneer of what would later be called the politics of the spectacle.[216] He obtained almost 5.5 million votes, trouncing General Cavaignac who got less than 1.5 million votes, the radical Ledru-Rollin with fewer than 400,000, and the poet Alphonse Lamartine with a paltry 18,000.[217] Many, of course, voted for Louis Napoleon to make sure Cavaignac would not win. Though not a good public speaker (not a requirement at the time), Louis Napoleon did what many politicians would in the years to come: appeal to all and sundry. He supported Catholicism and in 1849 sent troops to Rome to defend the pope against the republicans while urging him – in vain – to be more liberal. He also marketed himself as the champion of the family, private property, the old, the workers, the left and the right. His 'socialist' 1844 book *L'Extinction du paupérisme* provided him with 'left' credentials (one of the first uses of what would become a well-worn trope: 'neither left nor right'). Louis Napoleon followed Machiavelli's advice: the leader must know when to be a fox and when to be a wolf; when to use cunning and when to use force. The ambiguity worked: he won decisively.

The National Assembly, now in the hands of moderate conservatives, tried to restrict universal male suffrage (May 1850) against the wishes of Louis Napoleon (now seen as a champion of democracy). According to the legislation he was supposed to step down in 1852, at the end of his four-year mandate. Unable to change the law, he staged a coup d'état on 2 December 1851 – the anniversary of the Battle of Austerlitz, one of the most important victories of his uncle. It looked like a repeat of the Napoleonic coup of 18 Brumaire, so much so that Marx entitled his pamphlet *The Eighteenth Brumaire of Louis Bonaparte*. It began with the statement that if, as Hegel was alleged to have said, history repeats itself, 'he forgot to add: the first time as tragedy, the second time as farce'.[218]

But it was not a farce. Louis Napoleon buttressed his coup with a nationwide plebiscite that he won easily, with 78 per cent. As Alexander Herzen wrote in his memoirs: 'Louis-Napoleon, rubbing his sleepy eyes, stepped out of the gap and took everything into his hands – that is the petit bourgeois too, who fancied, from memory of old days, that he would reign and they would govern.'[219] A year later another plebiscite agreed he should become Emperor Napoleon III. Many of those who voted for him did so from fear of the socialists, by then a probable threat, and above all from a desire for peace and calm, especially in rural France. The birth of the Second Empire was unexpected. Ernest Renan, then a young up-and-coming scholar, wrote to his brother in June 1848, musing: 'Louis-Napoléon has become fashionable; but he is not a pretendant one should fear, in spite of his apparent popularity … they let him come up to show how incapable he is.' 'He'll be around for only a few days,' he added in another letter to his mother.[220] Tocqueville wrote that his supporters backed him for his mediocrity and his use of the spectacle: 'He owed his success more to folly than to reason, the theatre of the world being the very strange place it is: on its peculiar stage the worst plays sometimes enjoy the greatest success.'[221] The exemplary opportunist Adolphe Thiers backed Louis Napoleon, convinced that he could be easily manipulated, and is supposed to have added: 'This turkey who thinks he's an eagle, this cretin we will be able to handle.'[222]

The 'cretin' was around for twenty years, longer than any other French ruler since Louis XV. Mockery from many members of the intelligentsia caused him no harm. Marx's *Eighteenth Brumaire* had limited circulation, but even Victor Hugo's highly critical *Napoléon le Petit* (1852) failed to make a dent in the popularity of the new emperor. The savaging of Napoleon III continued through the years. According to the historian A. J. P. Taylor: 'Like most of those who study history, he learned from the mistakes of the past how to make new ones.'[223]

Yet the emperor presided over the modernization of France, something which neither Napoleon le Grand, nor the Bourbon kings, nor even Louis-Philippe d'Orléans had achieved. If the state was, in the words of the *Communist Manifesto*, 'the executive committee' of the bourgeoisie, then it had to take its distance from too close a connection with the bourgeoisie, since this class was fragmented and constantly evolving, which is why it needed a supervisory body to control and manage its anarchic tendencies. This is what the Second Empire was doing. Its detractors, of course, said that France was simply catching up with Great Britain and Belgium, but catching up can be a difficult enterprise. The formidable French banking system was created during the rule of Napoleon III, as was the railway network. Paris was quite transformed, and not just because Baron Hausmann built the famous *grands boulevards* but also because a vast sewer system was developed, significant public health measures were introduced and workers' houses were built. All this led to considerable economic growth. The Industrial Revolution was finally taking place in France too. The great French Revolution had not transformed France into a capitalist country; the Second Empire did.

The key economic policy was the signing of a free trade agreement with the United Kingdom in 1860, known as the Cobden–Chevalier Treaty, which reversed the previous protectionist policies. French trade did benefit (probably more than the treaty benefited Britain), and consumption increased.[224] Napoleon III's foreign policy was not so brilliant. At the beginning of his rule, just before he crowned himself emperor, he had famously announced in a speech in Bordeaux: 'L'Empire, c'est la paix!' (9 October 1852). Yet there were quite a few wars. There was the Crimean War (1854–56), in which France and Britain sided with the Ottoman Empire against Russia. It was a victory, but almost 100,000 French troops died.[225] Soon after, in July 1858, in concert with Camillo Cavour, the prime minister of the Kingdom of Piedmont-Sardinia, France agreed to fight Austria to help the unification of Northern Italy. However, the losses were such that Napoleon III had to come to terms with Austria. Cavour annexed Lombardy but not Venetia, while France obtained Nice and Savoy. Napoleon III's subsequent defence of Rome in 1861 delayed the complete unification of Italy and made him unpopular with Italian nationalists. France also enlarged its colonial empire, particularly in Indochina, having previously joined the British in the Second Opium War against China (1856–60).

Napoleon III's tragic and farcical adventure in Mexico, where he tried to instal as emperor the pro-French Austrian Archduke Maximillian, ended in disaster. The republican President Benito Juárez returned to power in 1867 and Maximillian, abandoned by Louis Napoleon, was executed. The emperor's defence of Rome and the pope might have endeared him to staunch Catholics but not to the growing anti-clerical Italian nationalist movement. French troops were removed from Rome only after Napoleon's defeat by Prussia in 1870, when the new Italian state could finally transfer its capital to Rome.

Napoleon III's end was tragic. In July 1870 he allowed himself to be dragged into a war with Bismarck's Prussia. Prussia was stronger and had recently won two wars: one against Denmark in 1864 over Schleswig-Holstein; the other against Austria in 1866, which ended with Prussia taking over most of Northern Germany. The Prussians defeated the French at Sedan, and Napoleon III, taken prisoner, was forced into exile in Chislehurst, England, where he died in 1873. With the emperor gone, the National Assembly declared France to be a republic (the third!). The Assembly still had a monarchist majority, which tried to continue the war but was soon forced to come to terms with the Prussians, who proclaimed the German Reich at Versailles on 18 January 1871. Germany was now united: it included not only the Southern German states, such as Bavaria and Württemberg, but also the French Alsace and most of Lorraine. The French would grieve the loss of their two provinces until 1914.

The Commune

In Paris, besieged by the Prussians, workers seized power, forcing the French government to flee to Versailles along with many frightened bourgeois. It was the birth of the Paris Commune, which, though it lasted only seventy days (18 March to 28 May 1871), left a significant mark in French and European history as one of the most celebrated failed revolutions.

The Commune also revealed that France was fundamentally split, between provincial rural France on the one hand, and a radical working-class and artisan Paris on the other. The domination of Paris over France had long been noted, but the Communards (as they were initially called by their opponents) may not have faced this issue.[226]

The inaugural programme of the Commune (19 April) boldly declared 'the end of the old political and clerical world, the world of militarism, bureaucracy, exploitation, speculation, monopolies and privileges which keeps the proletariat in bondage and caused the motherland to suffer misfortunes and disasters'.[227]

In its brief period of existence, the Commune was certainly revolutionary since it sought to overthrow the existing political system, though it lacked a coherent ideology – unsurprisingly, since it had been an improvised uprising. The Commune called for massive decentralization and the creation of self-governing communes. It decreed the separation of church and state, and proposed to extend the vote to women under the impulse of a new feminist movement which demanded full legal equality, including equal pay and women's right to organize in unions. Significantly, the Commune was the first French regime to put women in positions of responsibility, appointing them to administer welfare institutions, sending them on liaison missions to provincial cities, and including them on commissions to reform education and open new schools.[228] There were also more symbolic actions: the adoption of the flag and the destruction of the Colonne Vendôme with its statue of Napoleon (it was reconstructed a few years later).

Most of time, however, the Communards vainly attempted to repel the troops loyal to the new republican government led by the former monarchist Adolphe Thiers, that 'monstrous gnome' as Marx cruelly called him, who 'has charmed the French bourgeoisie for almost half a century, because he is the most consummate intellectual expression of their own class corruption'.[229] Guizot was barely kinder: for all his talent, Thiers remained a mere imitator – yet a cunning one, since he convinced Bismarck to free war prisoners so that the Commune could be defeated and order reestablished in Europe.[230]

The Commune ended in a bloodbath, the so-called Semaine sanglante (bloody week) of 21–28 May. The repression was massive. How many Communards were killed? The traditional estimate of between 20,000 and 30,000 deaths seems exaggerated; a more accurate figure is likely to be between 5,700 and 7,400.[231]

This figure which, if it errs, does so on the side of caution, would mean that the dead of the Commune (those executed or killed in combat, excluding those who died from lack of food or the spread of disease that accompanies all armed conflicts) matched those killed in Paris in 1793–94. Yet the assault on the Commune was never called the Terror. In the conclusion of *Civil War in France*, an 'instant' book published in 1871, Marx wrote:

> Working men's Paris, with its Commune, will be forever celebrated as the glorious harbinger of a new society. Its martyrs are enshrined in the great heart of the working class. Its exterminators, history has already nailed to that eternal pillory from which all the prayers of their priest will not redeem them.[232]

The Commune has been commemorated, but almost exclusively by socialists and anarchists. Victor Hugo, who was neither, did not fail to mourn those killed, however, and celebrated the heroism of the Communards in his poem 'Sur une barricade, au milieu des pavés', part of the collection *L'Année terrible* (1872). Other intellectuals were less kind, and condemned the Commune; these included George Sand, who had been on the left in 1848, and even Émile Zola and Théophile Gautier, as well as, unsurprisingly, Gustave Flaubert. The 150th anniversary of the Commune in 2021 was ignored by the Macron presidency. The Socialist mayor of Paris Anne Hidalgo did organize celebrations, despite opposition from the right.[233]

The subsequent decade of the Third Republic was characterized by political ambivalence. Though it *was* a republic, the majority of the deputies in the National Assembly elected in February 1871 were Catholic monarchists (396 out of 686 members). This majority was divided. The so-called *légitimistes* wanted another Bourbon king, the Orléanistes wanted an Orléans, and the small group of Bonapartistes wanted a strongman. The republicans too were divided between radicals and moderates. What the Commune did was scare the monarchists from insisting too soon for a return to the monarchy. The more they waited, the more the republic was consolidated. A set of constitutional laws (*not* a constitution) was finally promulgated in 1875. The first president was Patrice de Mac Mahon, a staunch monarchist who had led the French armies to defeat against Prussia and brutally crushed the Paris Commune the year after. He now found himself the elected president of the Third Republic, though with limited powers. Ironically, his family had fled Ireland with James Stuart as the Glorious Revolution was about to do away, once and for all, with any hint of Catholicism on the English throne. He and others like him assumed that the Third Republic would be a temporary construct. It has turned out to be, as of 2025, the longest-lasting republic in French history. In 1875, monarchist and clerical hopes were further strengthened, at least symbolically, when the first stone was laid for the Basilique du Sacré-Cœur at the top of the *butte* (hill) of Montmartre where many Communards had been executed. The project, warmly approved by the church authorities and by the ultra-conservative Pope Pius IX, was conceived as penance for the sins of the anti-clerical Commune but perhaps also for the defeat in the Franco-Prussian War, seen by many as a manifestation of divine wrath on a country in constant religious turmoil. The republicans somewhat reluctantly accepted the basilica, which still graces, if that is the word, the top of the Butte Montmartre, though few would regard it as an architectural masterpiece.[234]

The time of revolutions in France had passed. In the elections of 1876 and 1877 the monarchists were defeated, and in 1879 Jules Grévy became the first republican to be elected president. Most elected republicans were very conservative. They made sure that the president would have limited powers and that the elected assembly should be supreme. It was then that Léon Gambetta, once a fierce radical, renowned for his oratorical skills, having just been appointed president of the Chamber of Deputies, announced that France was finally a republic: 'Depuis hier, nous sommes en République.'[235] The previous year he had authored a pamphlet, *Le Cléricalisme, voila l'ennemi!* – making clear that the new republic would take a strong stand against Catholicism.

'The Marseillaise', which had been adopted as the national anthem in 1795 and was abolished by Napoleon in 1804, was reinstated. It was also decreed to make 14 July the national day: on 14 July 1790 there had been a Fête de la Fédération to celebrate Louis XVI's oath of allegiance to the French nation, made on the Champ-de-Mars in front of deputies from all the newly created *départements*. The National Assembly could have chosen another date, but its members were cautious: there was no question of commemorating 2 June 1793, the centenary of the Jacobin Republic and the Terror, or 21 January 1793 when Louis XVI was executed, even more insulting to the still powerful monarchists. For the same reason, neither 10 August 1792, when the royal residence (the Tuileries) was attacked, nor 21 September 1792, when the monarchy was abolished, could be adopted.

They could have chosen 26 August 1789, the anniversary of the Declaration of the Rights of Man and Citizens, or 21 February 1848, when demonstrations in Paris led to the abdication, a few days later, of the Citizen-King Louis Philippe and the final end of the monarchy. But 14 July was the safest date, precisely because its meaning was indeterminate: it did not mark the end of a regime, but only its weakening – the beginning of a long process; though, as Tocqueville wrote, 'La rage des historiens' (and, may I add, not only of historians) 'est de vouloir des évènements décisifs' (the historians' obsession is to seek turning points).[236] The seizure of the Bastille offered a suitable revolutionary moment, which, while not specifically republican, was still popular and heroic enough to satisfy radical feelings.[237] The French Revolution was finally over.

4
The 'National Revolutions' of the Nineteenth Century

Before their revolutions, England, the Thirteen Colonies and France were each ultimately ruled by a single authority: England by Charles I; the Thirteen Colonies by British Parliament; and France by Louis XVI. The revolutionary struggle was a struggle for political power. In the nineteenth century, however, revolutions – in the sense of the seizure of power within an existing state – failed. As we saw in the previous chapters, there were attempted liberal revolutions against absolutist-authoritarian regimes aimed at establishing a constitutional system, particularly in 1848. In most cases, what could be called the bourgeoisie took the lead. In most cases, the old regime survived, sometimes improved by reforms. In France, republican rule was definitively established in 1871, but this was not the result of yet another revolution but of the military defeat of the Second Empire by Prussia.

Far more frequently, the nineteenth century witnessed *national revolutions*, leading to the establishment of new states. These did not, in the main, come about through secession from a multinational state, as would become commonplace in the twentieth century – for instance, Ireland from the United Kingdom, Poland from Russia or Hungary from the Austrian Empire. The major nineteenth-century examples of secession arose from the gradual decline of the Ottoman Empire. This gave birth to new states (notably Greece, as we shall see below). The more common nineteenth-century route towards a nation-state, however, was through unifying existing states into a larger one. The most important cases were those of Italy and Germany, and it is these to which we shall devote much of this chapter. But there are others that should not be ignored.

Before Napoleon's invasion in 1798, Switzerland was a barely connected country of self-governing cantons. Napoleon centralized it, creating a French-dominated Helvetic Republic and a rising national self-awareness. Eventually, after Napoleon's defeat, Swiss autonomy was re-established and further sanctioned by the Congress of Vienna (1815), which recognized permanent Swiss neutrality. Calm was not immediately established since, in 1847, there was a civil war called the Sonderbundkrieg (for the separate alliance of cantons objecting to centralization). The Sonderbund was defeated, and Switzerland entered a long and still-enduring period of peace as a federal republic, free from foreign invasions or major civil disturbances.

Belgium too was a special case. The so-called Belgian Revolution was sparked by the desire of the Flemish and Walloon provinces of the Netherlands, separated by language but united by Catholicism, to acquire independence. In August 1830 there were riots in Brussels against Dutch rule, allegedly sparked by the first night of Daniel Auber's opera *La Muette de Portici*, which glorifies the Neapolitan revolution of 1647 led by Masaniello, a humble fisherman (see Introduction).[1] At the ensuing London Conference of 1830, the Great Powers recognized Belgian independence. The country's first king, Leopold I, had limited powers like the British monarch, and was a British protégé related to the British royal family. His first wife, Charlotte of Wales, was the daughter of the future George IV. A Dutch attempt to reverse Belgian independence was thwarted by the new liberal Orléans regime in France.

The Greek Revolution

The long decline of the Ottoman Empire led to the formation of several new states, each calling their struggle for independence a revolution. Many of these new states – Montenegro, Serbia, Bulgaria and Romania – first acquired a degree of autonomy from the Ottomans, occasionally after some armed unrest, but they obtained full independence only in 1878 at the Congress of Berlin, which was dominated by the Great Powers: Austria, Britain, France, Germany and Russia. None of the new states adopted a particularly liberal constitution.

In the 1820s there was considerable revolutionary turmoil in Southern Europe, particularly in Greece, Portugal, Piedmont, Naples and

Sicily, constitutional change being the main focus.² The violence and devastation in Greece, however, was far greater than anywhere else in Europe at the time.³ The so-called Greek Revolution was the earliest case of armed secession leading to an independent state in the nineteenth century. According to a four-volume history of the Greek rising rushed out in 1824 by François Pouqueville, French consul in Greece, the cause of national liberation belonged entirely to the Greeks called to rise by Georgios Yermanés, bishop of Patras.⁴ As we shall see, however, Greek independence was achieved mainly through the work of outsiders, including the French, the Russians and the British.

Greece had been part of the Ottoman Empire for centuries. When the struggle against the Sublime Porte (a metaphor for the Ottoman Empire) began in 1821, the odds were against Greek nationalists. It was not simply the obviously greater power of the Ottomans that told against them but the fact that most Greeks (the majority of whom were peasants) had little national feeling. Their main complaint was the burden of taxation, which they had to pay to Greek landlords who collected taxes on behalf of the Ottomans; so when they revolted, as they often did, it was against other Greeks, though some of the landlords were Muslims. Class prevailed over nation.⁵ The Greek revolutionaries tended to be educated Greeks influenced by the French Revolution and the Enlightenment. They often lived outside Greece itself. In fact, one of the most important Greek patriotic societies, the clandestine Filiki Eteria (Society of Friends), was founded in Odessa. Among its members was the great Russian poet Alexander Pushkin.

The first attempt at an insurrection was led by Alexander Ypsilantis, who had been a senior officer in the Russian army and an aide-de-camp to Tsar Alexander I. On 21 February 1821, he and his followers, wearing Russian uniforms, launched an attack from Russian soil; they aimed to liberate Greece and hoped to obtain the tsar's support. Alexander I ordered Ypsilantis to desist. The Orthodox patriarch, Gregorios V, faced the dilemma of whether to side with the revolutionaries and risk the anger of the sultan and the lives of the many Christians in the empire. Instead, he excommunicated Ypsilantis and issued an anathema against the Filiki Eteria.⁶ Ypsilantis was defeated, for which he blamed his cowardly troops.

A new, more successful Greek revolt occurred in the Peloponnese in March 1821 and led to a mass slaughter of Muslims. As the historian Willian St Clair wrote: 'Upwards of twenty thousand Turkish men, women, and children were murdered by their Greek neighbours in a few weeks of slaughter. They were killed deliberately, without qualm or scruple, and there were no regrets either then or later.'[7] The Greek forces included not only French and British sympathizers but also local Albanians, Vlachs and Slavs.[8] In retaliation, Turkish troops (including Albanians and Egyptians) massacred Greeks. The sultan stunned Europe by having the octogenarian Patriarch Gregorios V publicly hanged on Easter Day (22 April).[9] One of the worst massacres occurred the following year, when between 40,000 and 50,000 Greeks were killed by Turks and their allies on the island of Chios. This shocked European public opinion. Thomas Hughes, a Church of England clergyman, wrote pamphlets calling for the expulsion of the Turks from Europe, 'the most weak, contemptible, vice-stained tyrants that ever polluted the earth on which they trod, vilifying and degrading the fairest part of the creation'.[10] More balanced was Charles Brinsley Sheridan's *Thoughts on the Greek Revolution* (1822), which warned Hughes: 'It is no such easy task to root up an enormous population, and re-plant it in another quarter of the world.'[11] Meanwhile, massacres of 'barbarous' Turks by 'European' Greeks were generally ignored, though two Scottish philhellenes who fought with the Greeks later reported, with considerable integrity, large Muslim casualties at Greek hands.[12]

The Chios events received great prominence among Europe's intelligentsia. Eugène Delacroix painted his famous *Scène des massacres de Scio*, and Victor Hugo wrote 'L'Enfant', a poem about a blue-eyed, blond-haired boy left desolate on the island, dreaming of revenge: 'The Turks have been there. All is devastation and grief. / Chios, the isle of wines, is now a dreary reef.'

The Greek nationalists had two advantages. The first was the considerable strength of philhellenic sentiment in many European countries. The Germans, including Johann Wolfgang von Goethe, Friedrich Schiller, the poet Friedrich Hölderlin and the art historian Johann Joachim Winckelmann, were particularly obsessed with ancient Greece.[13] In Britain, poets such as Byron, Shelley and the Irish Thomas Moore supported the Greeks. Byron fought in Greece, dying in Missolonghi. In his poem 'The Isles of Greece', Byron wrote:

> The mountains look on Marathon—
> And Marathon looks on the sea;
> And musing there an hour alone,
> I dream'd that Greece might still be free.

Eugène Delacroix, *Scène des massacres de Scio* (1824), Louvre Museum, Paris

In Russia, Pushkin lent his support. In France, Hector Berlioz composed a cantata called *La Révolution grecque*, which opens: 'Lève-toi, fils de Sparte!' (Arise, son of Sparta!). Victor Hugo's 'Les Têtes du sérail', part of his series of *Orientales* (Eastern poems), demanded interventions to help Greece. In 1825, Chateaubriand wondered if 'hordes of savages [the Ottomans] will suffocate the resurgence of civilization in the tomb of the people who civilized the world'.[14] The idea that the Greeks were the direct descendants of the ancient Greeks (and Greece the cradle of civilization) was a well-established Enlightenment trope.[15] Moreover, unlike the Turks, the Greeks were Christians. William Wilberforce, who had long fought against the Atlantic slave trade, reflected a widespread British opinion when, in the House of Commons, he urged the government to drive back the Turks, 'a nation of barbarians, the ancient and inveterate enemies of Christianity and freedom, into Asia'.[16]

Thus, another Greek advantage was the anti-Turkish animosity of the Great Powers. Here geopolitics played a key role. Russia acted on behalf of Greece, not only out of Orthodox solidarity, but also for reasons of power politics. France and Great Britain wanted to contain Russian ambitions before the apparently inevitable collapse of the Ottoman strengthened the Tsarist Empire, and so they joined the anti-Ottoman mood. Greek nationalists could rely on the kind of foreign help that Polish nationalists or Hungarian nationalists could only dream of, since no one was going to fight the tsar to liberate Poland or the Austrian Empire to liberate Hungary.

By 1826, the Greeks themselves had been almost crushed. Egypt, acting for the Ottoman Empire of which it was part, occupied the Peloponnese. Ioannis Kapodistrias, who had been born into a noble family in Corfu and became a leading adviser to Tsar Alexander I (in practice, the foreign minister), successfully urged a Russian intervention, having originally counselled restraint. A turning point was the naval Battle of Navarino (20 October 1827), which saw Russians, British and French joining forces against the Turks and their Egyptian allies and decisively defeating them. This led to Greek autonomy, enshrined in the Treaty of Adrianople (1829). Kapodistrias found himself governor of Greece – self-governing, but still a tributary state under the Ottoman. The following year the London Protocol granted full independence to a Greek statelet within narrow borders. Epirus, Macedonia (and hence Thessaloniki, the second-largest Greek city), Crete, Samos and much else were excluded.

Kapodistrias was no liberal. He shared with many Enlightenment thinkers a distrust for the people, especially his own Greek people. He preferred 'enlightened despotism' and the 'moderation' of the English Glorious Revolution to the 'terror' of the French Revolution.[17] He thought that the Greeks were not ready for anything remotely resembling democracy and was wary of the constant political infighting. On the other hand, he was in favour of reforms from above to prevent revolution from below. In 1831, he was murdered by members of the prosperous Mavromichalis family, who had been alarmed at the possibility of land reform. The new Greek state needed revenue and had to raise taxes. In 1832 a new London conference established that Greece should become an independent kingdom, and a foreign monarch, Otto of Bavaria, was duly selected. Only seventeen years old, Otto knew no Greek and arrived in the new country with Bavarian troops and advisers. Plenty of cash was loaned to Greece to help the kingdom on its way.[18] At first, Otto ruled as an absolute monarch but was compelled to grant a constitution in 1843; he was finally deposed by a coup in 1862, and died in exile in his native Bavaria. Another foreign monarch then had to be found. The Greek National Assembly elected Prince William of Denmark, also aged seventeen, as king of the Hellenes (Otto had been king of Greece). He reigned for fifty years as George I, and was the grandfather of Prince Philip, Queen Elizabeth II's husband. In November 1912, during the First Balkan War, Greek forces took over Thessaloniki, thus expanding Greek boundaries. A year later, George I was murdered by an anarchist (or perhaps just a madman).

The events described above do not sound like a revolution, yet almost from the beginning the process leading to the formation a Greek state was called 'the Greek Revolution'.[19] The Greek experience looked more like an anti-colonial revolution, and so resonates with the American War of Independence. But the differences are remarkable. The American revolutionaries did not possess a national consciousness in 1776; they wanted to run their own affairs without British interference, but they were British (just as in Latin America the Spanish and Portuguese colonists wanted to get rid of the mother-country, Spain and Portugal, not alien oppressors). The Greek War of Independence, on the other hand, was fought not by settlers against the mother-country but by a people separated from their foreign ruler by religion and language. They were led by intellectuals and merchants, most of whom lived in places such as Smyrna, Constantinople, Alexandria and Thessaloniki – outside the borders of the new Greek statelet. This so-called revolution was largely determined by outsiders and above all by the geopolitical conflict between the Great Powers. Yet from these events sprang the Greek nation and Greek nationalism.

Who are the Germans? Who are the Italians?

The unification of Germany and of Italy, the most important new states of the nineteenth century, are not often regarded as revolutions in the history books. The main objective of German and Italian nationalists was to build a new state. Political reforms were, at most, a desirable outcome of unity. The revolutionary Giuseppe Mazzini, exiled from Genoa in 1831, wanted not just Italian unity but also a republic – but there was little support for this, and eventually even Mazzini had to accept the monarchy.

Some did talk of a German revolution at the time. Engels, in a letter to the socialist leader August Bebel (18 November 1884), called the victory of Prussia in 1866 a 'complete revolution', adding that Prussia had overthrown 'three thrones'. Presumably he meant Bavaria, Württemberg and Hesse. 'If that was not revolutionary, I do not know the meaning of the word.'[20] Bismarck too spoke of revolution. In a telegram to General

Edwin von Manteuffel (11 August 1866), alluding to the unification of Germany, he wrote: 'If revolution must be, then we would rather make it than suffer it.'[21] Even Disraeli, speaking in the House of Commons shortly after Germany's victory against the French in 1870, declared that the contest had been

> no common war, like the war between Prussia and Austria, or like the Italian war in which France was engaged some years ago; nor is it like the Crimean War. This war represents the German revolution, a greater political event than the French revolution of last century.[22]

Very few referred to Italian unification as a revolution, though it had a greater degree of popular participation. In 1861 the poet Theodosia Trollope, sister-in-law of the novelist Anthony Trollope, wrote letters from Florence where she lived, which were published as *Social Aspects of the Italian Revolution*. The preferred term, however, was Risorgimento: the Italian for 'rising again', conveying the sense of a return to past glories. It also contained a religious subtext, of resurrection.

Nationalists needed to define the nation. They assumed it had existed since time immemorial, but this was just part of the mythology. Nations had to be constructed. Who were the Germans? Who were the Italians? What should be the borders of the new nation? What was the national language? Germans did not speak the same German; Italians spoke a variety of dialects, not all mutually intelligible. Outside the literary classes there was little feeling of national identity. Besides, a feeling of identity does not inevitably lead to political identity: those who today regard themselves as Europeans or Sicilians do not necessarily wish to achieve a European or a Sicilian state.

Could one call German all those who spoke a Germanic language? This would have included not only all the inhabitants of present-day Germany, but also those of Austria, of large parts of Switzerland, of the Sudetenland in what was then Bohemia, Moravia and Czech Silesia (all then in the Austrian Empire). Germanic languages could also include Dutch, Danish, Norwegian and Swedish. Even English could be classified as a Germanic language and, far more so, Yiddish. The idea that there is a simple connection between language and nationality is as recent an invention as that of nation itself. As William Entwistle wrote in the 1920s: 'Its effect is practical: to insist that where there is a language there must be a nation, or where there is a nation there must be a national language.'[23] Some modern states, such as Switzerland and Belgium, do not fit this schema. Nor do some older ones, such as Spain. Although Castilian (modern-day Spanish) is dominant and spoken by all inhabitants, in Spain you will also hear Catalan, Galician and Basque.

Since there is a multiplicity of German dialects, what we call proper German is *Hochdeutsch* (High German). Before unification it was a literary language, used by Martin Luther in his translation of the Latin Bible. The inhabitants of what is now Germany spoke various forms of German, and someone from Lower Saxony could not understand someone from Bavaria, where there are various subdialects.

This lack of linguistic unity was far from being a peculiarity of Germany. Italian too was first and foremost a literary language of the elite. The inhabitants of the peninsula spoke their local languages, and if they were educated they could also speak Italian. To define a local language as a dialect often leads to the erroneous assumption that local languages were derived from a main language. In reality, the national language emerges out of a political or cultural struggle. Italian itself is in fact the variety of Tuscan spoken in Florence, as used by Dante *in La Divina Commedia*. In other words, Italian too is a dialect. It became a national language, in the sense of being used regularly by the vast majority of the population, only well after the establishment of the Italian state.

This seems to confirm the famous saying attributed to the Russian-Yiddish linguist Max Weinreich: 'A language is a dialect with an army and a navy.'[24] An Italian speaking the language of Bergamo (Bergamasque) cannot understand someone speaking Genoese (Ligurian) or Sicilian. In other words, the inhabitants of the Italian peninsula had no language in common, nor a history, since their land had always been divided between rival statelets. The nearest to unity reached by Italy before 1861 was during Napoleon's Italian campaign in the years 1796–99. Klemens von Metternich, the Austrian Empire's foreign minister at the time of the Congress of Vienna, was not entirely wrong when he said, famously, that Italy was 'only a geographical expression'.[25]

Only the Italian literary classes, a tiny percentage of the population in 1815, had some cultural unity. This gave them a historical dimension few others possessed. People who can read modern Italian can read today, with little difficulty, the poetry of Dante (1265–1321) or Francesco Petrarca (1304–74) and the tales of Giovanni Boccaccio (1313–75). Modern English speakers find it far more difficult to read the Middle English of Chaucer (1340–1400). Only with great effort can French speakers decipher the Middle French that François Rabelais used in his

Pantagruel (1532) and *Gargantua* (1534), more than two centuries after Dante's *Divina Commedia*.

The celebrated Italian writer Alessandro Manzoni, whose historical novel *I promessi sposi* (1840–42) was taught for years in all Italian schools, wrote the first draft in 1827 in an Italian full of what he regarded as foreign expressions (mostly French and local Milanese dialect, the languages he spoke at home). Then he went to Florence to re-write the novel using Florentine, the literary form of Tuscan. Italian became the real first language of most Italians only after the Second World War, principally because of radio and television. One could say that Italians learnt to speak their language not just thanks to Dante and Manzoni, or because of compulsory schooling, national military conscription, internal immigration and a unified bureaucracy, but above all through the diffusion of American films and TV shows dubbed into Italian, such as *I Love Lucy*, *Bonanza* and *Perry Mason*. The linguist Tullio De Mauro wrote that, when Italy was united, the number of Italians outside Tuscany and Rome who could speak Italian was perhaps 8 per cent.[26] Others put the numbers even lower.[27] If so, then Italians learnt to speak their language in less than a century, but they would not have done so had there not been an Italian state and a national TV broadcaster.

The state can elevate a dialect to the status of the national language. Thus in France in 1539, King Francis I established that French (what now we call Middle French) should be the language used in education and public administration. It was only the beginning of the struggle to impose French on the French. In 1794, the Abbé Grégoire, a major figure in the French Revolution, wrote *Why and How the Patois Must be Destroyed and French Made Universal*. He lamented that French was barely spoken in France. French citizens spoke, for example, Breton, Normand, Picard, Walloon, Flemish, Champenois, Catalan, Gascon or Languedocien. Nowadays some people still speak Occitan or Breton, but they all speak French: the language of education, of politics, of radio and television; the language used in law and in the bureaucracy. French is, quite simply, the variant of the dialect spoken in the Île-de-France, the region around Paris. France, however, had been unified well before Germany, and the state had been able to impose a standard language which tied it closer together. That was not the case with Italy or Germany. First came the state, then the national language.

Then there was the question of a national religion. Before unification, Italians (unlike Germans) may have appeared to be united by religion, since most were Catholic. But unity faced a difficult religious obstacle:

the pope was not only the spiritual leader of Catholics but also the direct temporal ruler of a considerable part of central Italy. It was impossible to unite Italy without challenging the pope. Pius IX denounced Italian unity and successive popes regarded themselves as prisoners of the Italian state (when Rome became the capital in 1870), until the Concordat between state and Church in 1929. Papal power did not depend at all on temporal power exercised in a few regions; it depended rather on the fact of the truth of an overwhelmingly Catholic country as well as the clerical power in the hands of an army of 130,000 priests and 20,000 parishes.[28]

Germans were not united by religion, since Protestantism was far from being the majority religion in the Rhineland, Bavaria or Austria (which were all largely Catholic). So religion could not unite Germany the way Catholicism could be a unifying force in Poland, faced with Protestant Germany to its west and Orthodox Russia to its east. Catholicism, by becoming a nationalist force in Ireland against Protestant England, could not unite all the Irish since there was an important and politically powerful Protestant minority in the North – hence the failure, so far, to unite the whole of Ireland.

German nationalism enthused about culture: not the culture of the elite, not that of ancient Rome and Greece, but that of the *Völk* (the word 'folklore' is one German word that has become almost universal). Johann Gottfried Herder (1744–1803), one of the first to use the term *nationalismus*, was a major exponent of cultural nationalism. He believed in the authenticity of the *Völk* as the essential unit of society: everyone, rich and poor, noble and commoner, was part of it. To promote his concept of the *Völk*, he collected folk songs published in his 1773 *Stimmen der Völker in ihren Liedern* (Voices of the Peoples in Their Songs). German literary nationalism invented a national narrative by using German heroic myths such as the *Nibelungenlied*, a medieval poem rediscovered in the eighteenth century which became popular only after it was translated into modern German in 1827 (and even more so after Wagner composed his *Der Ring des Nibelungen* cycle). In 1805–08, the poets Achim von Arnim and Clemens von Brentano, influenced by Herder's *Voices of the Peoples*, collected (and modified) folk poems and songs under the title of *Des Knaben Wunderhorn* (The Boy's Magic Horn). Many of these were set to music by notable German composers, including Schumann, Brahms and Mahler.

The same celebration of folk culture found its most important interpreters in the brothers Grimm, whose collection of fairy tales, duly sanitized, were published in various expanded editions between 1812 and

1857 and are still famous throughout the world, particularly 'Snow White' (Schneewittchen), 'Little Red Riding Hood' (Rotkäppchen), 'Cinderella' (Aschenputtel) and 'Hansel and Gretel' (Hänsel und Gretel). None of these contain any obvious pro-German nationalist element: the central idea is that of *Volkskultur*, though it was believed by many that the recovery of this *kultur* would be a condition for building the nation. In fact, many of these tales, including the famous ones such as 'Le Petit Chaperon rouge' and 'Cendrillon', had already been collected by Charles Perrault in the previous century. 'Cendrillon' (Cenerentola) already appears in the collection of Giambattista Basile (1566–1632), *Lo cunto de li cunti* (The tale of tales), written in Neapolitan. Similar tales existed also in antiquity, and in China.

Unlike the Germans, Italian intellectuals showed very little interest in the people, an elite attitude which still seems to exist today. The national narrative focused either on Italian victimhood – constantly invaded by barbarians and subsequently by the French, the Germans and the Spaniards – or on resistance to these foreign invaders, or a longing for the glories of Rome and, only occasionally, the celebration of the artistic culture of the Renaissance. Italian elites did their best to find expressions of Italian national identity in a variety of sources, such as the concluding section of Machiavelli's *Il Principe* (1513–14), where the prince is urged to unify Italy to protect her from foreigners. This, according to Francesco De Sanctis, the major Italian literary critic of the nineteenth century, was the moment when the concept of *patria* (fatherland) became not one's own village but the entire nation.[29] In the years following the French Revolution and the Napoleonic Wars, Italian literary nationalism intensified, far more than in Germany. It usually took the form of lamenting the dismal state of Italy compared to that of France or England (then the model countries to which others were supposed to aspire).

We have seen how Vittorio Alfieri (1749–1803), the main Italian dramatist of his time, turned against the French (see Chapter 3). He also turned on the 'plebs', the bourgeoisie, the Prussians, the Austrians, the Church and even the Italians, guilty of failing to rise against foreign despotism. He wrote in Piedmontese dialect the following insulting strophe:

> Già ch'ant cost mond l'un l'àutr bzògna ch'as rida,
> l'è un mè dubiet ch'i veui ben ben rumié:
> s'l'è mi ch'son 'd fer o j'italian 'd potìa.

(Giàcche in questo mondo bisogna che si rida l'uno dell'altro, io ho un piccolo dubbio che voglio ben bene rimasticare: se sono io che sono di ferro o gli italiani di fango.)

(Since in this world we should laugh at each other, I have a small doubt which I intend to chew over: whether I am made of iron or the Italians of dirt.)

Alfieri was regarded as one of the chief catalysts of Italian proto-nationalism by major poets such as Giacomo Leopardi, whose poem 'All'Italia' (1818) was full of regrets for the glories of the past. In his *Discorso sopra lo stato presente dei costumi degl'italiani*, written around 1824–26 but published only in 1906, Leopardi compares the character and mentality of Italians unfavourably to those of the French, Germans and English. 'The Italians,' he declared,

do enjoy conversation or they have none; they prefer have a stroll promenade [*passeggiata*], or go to shows, to mass, to hear a sermon. This sums up, he claimed, the entire life of the advantaged classes; they have habits, but not customs and the few they have are not national but provincial.[30]

This scorn towards other Italians would remain a feature of the Italian intelligentsia.

Also lamenting Italy's fate was the poet and novelist Ugo Foscolo, author of the epistolary novel *Le ultime lettere ultime lettere di Jacopo Ortis* (1802), where the protagonist commits suicide partly out of desperation for the miserable situation in which he finds Italy. Foscolo spent the last eleven years of his life in London, where he died in 1827. Even the painter Francesco Hayez was regarded as a proto-nationalist because of his immensely famous *Il bacio* (the kiss, 1859), a favourite of chocolate boxes everywhere. Hayez uses the colours of the French revolutionary flag, then seen as a pro-Italian nationalist gesture, though attention is inevitably focused on the passionate embrace of the two lovers.

Episodes from the past of resistance against invaders were usually transformed into prefigurations of the desire for unity. For instance, the Vespri Siciliani (the Sicilian Vespers), an insurrection in Sicily against French rule (1282) and certainly not a struggle for Italian unity, was the subject of a Hayez painting and an eponymous opera by Giuseppe Verdi, originally written for the Paris Opera. Even less national was the so-called Disfida di Barletta (Challenge of Barletta, 1503), set in a small town

Francesco Hayez, *Il bacio* (1859), Pinacoteca di Brera, Milan

in Southern Italy. A French knight insulted Italian mercenaries who were fighting in the Spanish army. The ensuing tournament was won by the Italians, led by Ettore Fieramosca. The event, entirely insignificant in terms of history, acquired a national connotation mainly after the Italian politician and novelist Massimo d'Azeglio, following in the footsteps of Walter Scott, wrote a historical novel about it in 1833 (*Ettore Fieramosca: Ossia, la disfida di Barletta*) and Fieramosca became a national hero. The aspiration towards a new Italy was increasingly common among the cultured classes, enhanced by works such as operas – Gioacchino Rossini's *Guglielmo Tell*, as well as the Hebrew slave chorus in Giuseppe Verdi's *Nabucco* – though neither deal with Italy. Such uses of the past, of course, were hardly peculiar to Italian nationalism. Virtually all national, religious and revolutionary movements have required some kind of historical validation.[31]

The intellectual input into German unification was less significant than in Italy (or Greece). There were relatively few intellectual nationalists. The German revolutionaries were officials, administrators, bureaucrats, businessmen, reformers – 'masters of the state machines of Prussia, Bavaria, Saxony': men such as Wilhelm von Humbolt, founder of the German educational system.[32] There was, of course, Johann Gottlieb Fichte, author of the *Address to the German Nation* (1808), who insisted on the importance of linguistic unity, and August Heinrich Hoffmann von Fallersleben whose poem 'Das Lied der Deutschen' (1841) provided some of the lines for Germany's national anthem. There was the movement Junges Deutschland (Young Germany), but like Mazzini's Giovane Italia it was quite ineffectual, and of its members only Heinrich Heine and George Büchner are remembered.

The great Goethe was not particularly concerned with German political unity. As he explained to his secretary Johann Peter Eckermann in the last years of his life, he welcomed the eventual elimination of internal customs barriers and different currencies, but did not want a 'very great empire having a single great capital'. German culture was what it was because it benefited from its various cities and universities: 'Their effect on the prosperity of Germany is incalculable.' All this would be lost if they lost their sovereignty and became mere provincial towns.[33]

Other leading German intellectuals, including Gotthold Ephraim Lessing and Friedrich Schiller, doubted Germany could be a nation.[34] The latter, in his *Das Deutsche Reich* (1795) wondered: 'Germany? But where is it? I cannot find it. Where the scholar begins, the political ends.'[35] Even more scathing (and alarmed) was Heinrich Heine in an essay written in Paris in 1833–34:

Watch out! … A drama will be performed in Germany compared with which the French Revolution will seem merely an innocent idyll … I advise you French, keep very quiet … I have your welfare at heart, and for this reason I tell you the bitter truth. You have more to fear from a liberated Germany than from the entire Holy Alliance together with its Croats and Cossacks.[36]

Jacob Grimm, one of the two brothers of fairy tales fame, worked at length on a massive German lexicon, but this was a cultural and linguistic project, not one aimed at contributing to national unity.[37] There is very little literature in modern German before the eighteenth century of the calibre of Shakespeare or Ronsard, let alone Dante or Machiavelli, though Jacob Christoffel von Grimmelshausen's 1669 picaresque *Simplicius Simplicissimus* may be regarded as the first major modern German novel.[38]

It took the Napoleonic invasion to provide a spark for the birth of German nationalism, though this was still very much a prerogative of members of the educated elite – writers such as Johann Gottlieb Fichte and Ernst Moritz Arndt, whose nationalist song 'Was ist des Deutschen Vaterland?' (1813) starts by asking: 'What is the German's fatherland?' It goes on to list the various German-speaking states, from Prussia and Swabia to Bavaria, Pomerania and Westphalia, and even Austria, Switzerland and the Tyrol. It answers, at the end of each strophe: 'Oh no! No! No! / His fatherland must be bigger!' It concludes:

> *Das ist des Deutschen Vaterland,*
> *Wo Zorn vertilgt den welschen Tand,*
> *Wo jeder Franzmann heißet Feind,*
> *Wo jeder Deutsche heißet Freund –*
> *Das soll es sein!*
> *Das ganze Deutschland soll es sein!*

> That is the German's fatherland,
> Where rage wipes out French trifle,
> Where every Frenchman is called enemy,
> Where every German is called friend.
> That's what it should be!
> The whole of Germany it should be!

Arndt's nationalism depended on culture, race and language. He was prepared to include the Flemish and Dutch, but (unlike Herder) not the Jews, for they did 'not fit' into his world, and the German tribe (*stamm*) must be kept free of these 'foreign elements'.[39] This stands in contrast to French revolutionary nationalism, where the racial element was not important.

The Italian Risorgimento

One of the unintended consequences of the Napoleonic Wars was to simplify the map of Europe in the sense of reducing the number of states which had survived since the Middle Ages. Napoleon could be seen by liberals as the man who would bring the ideals of the French Revolution to fruition domestically. They were disappointed, but such disenchantment often led to the birth of a national feeling of resistance against the foreign invader, who, it was felt, had betrayed the principles of the revolution. After the final defeat of Napoleon, much of Europe was reorganized by the victorious powers assembled at the Congress of Vienna between September 1814 and June 1815: Prussia, Russia, Austria and Great Britain. The coalition against Napoleon, Germaine de Staël noted, was the first time that four Great Powers (*quatre grandes puissances*) had entered into a coalition.[40] It was the birth of what came to be known the Concert of Europe, the first international order, though it was always unstable.[41] It is now known as 'the international community', meaning the West led by the US. As I write, it is insecure.

The final act of the Congress was signed on 9 June, nine days before Waterloo. Russia obtained Poland, and the Venetian Republic was incorporated into Austria, along with Lombardy. The pope recovered control over much of central Italy. The Duchy of Tuscany and that of Modena-Parma were ruled by members of the Habsburg dynasty, rulers of Austria. The Kingdom of the Two Sicilies (Southern Italy, with Naples as its capital) was ruled by the Bourbon dynasty. Thus, the only part of Italy in the hands of something approximating an Italian royal family was the so-called Kingdom of Sardinia (Piedmont), which also included the former Genoese Republic, the Liguria coastline and Savoy. In fact, some early nationalists (though the term may not be appropriate) such as the Milanese Francesco Melzi d'Eril, vice-president of the Napoleonic Italian Republic in 1802, advocated an independent kingdom of Northern Italy as early as 1798, while conscious that this could not happen without the consent of Napoleon.[42]

Revolutions need heroes. In Italy, Garibaldi was the obvious choice. Garibaldi had been Mazzini's most important follower until he was forced to escape to Latin America in 1836, where he led revolutionary uprisings in Brazil and Uruguay. Mazzini has long been regarded as one of the fathers of Italian unification, even though he failed in most of his endeavours. He wanted not just a republican Italy but also a federal Europe. Unlike Mazzini and the *mazziniani*, Garibaldi succeeded in most of his enterprises. Other *mazziniani* failed tragically. In 1844, the brothers Attilio and Emilio Bandiera arrived in Southern Italy assuming that the people would follow them in an uprising, but the local peasants, thinking they were Turkish marauders, denounced them to the authorities. The brothers were tried and executed. The so-called Spedizione di Sapri (1857), led by Carlo Pisacane, a left-wing *mazziniano*, was equally disastrous. Pisacane thought his expedition was the launching pad of a socialist revolution. His *Saggio sulla rivoluzione*, published posthumously in 1860, was influenced by the thoughts of Pierre-Joseph Proudhon. At the head of a few volunteers, Pisacane landed at the island of Ponza, then a penal colony, and freed some 300 prisoners, most of whom were not political prisoners but common criminals. He moved on to Sapri, south of Naples, where the locals and the authorities killed him and some of his followers, while the survivors were imprisoned for life.

The failures of Mazzini gave impetus to the rise of more moderate reformers, such as Vincenzo Gioberti, a priest whose *Del primato morale e civile degli italiani* (1843) advocated, quite unrealistically, an Italian confederation of states under the presidency of the pope. This fantasy was enhanced by the election in 1846 of Pius IX, who was at first regarded as a liberal. Pius released political prisoners and removed some curbs on the press and some anti-Semitic legislation, before turning into one of the most reactionary popes of the last two centuries. Gioberti, however, understood that the existence of the Italian people was more a wish than a fact. As he wrote, it was a 'presupposition and not a reality, a name and not a thing'.[43]

Meanwhile the real movement towards unification proceeded from above, though the intentions were more to strengthen the power of Piedmont than to unify the peninsula. Thus in 1847 King Carlo Alberto of Piedmont, having turned liberal, adopted a foreign policy aimed at the expulsion of Austria from north-eastern Italy, particularly Venetia. His Statuto Albertino (1848), prompted by unrest, transformed the Kingdom of Sardinia into a constitutional monarchy. He then led into a losing war with Austria, labelled by Italian nationalists as the First War of Independence, after anti-Austrian revolts in Milan, Padua and Venice. Various republican revolts in other parts of Italy, notably in Rome and Venice, were also repressed after initial successes. By then, Carlo Alberto had abdicated and been succeeded by his son Victor Emmanuel.

In 1852 Camillo Cavour became prime minister of the Kingdom of Sardinia (Piedmont). It would be during his period in office that an Italian state came into being. He modernized Piedmont considerably while the other Italian states lagged behind, which partly explains their rapid collapse. Unlike his predecessors, he understood that the expulsion of Austria from Italy could not be achieved without foreign support. A few troops sent to Crimea to help the French in the war against Russia facilitated a deal with Napoleon III (1858–59). It was agreed that if Piedmont was attacked by Austria, the French would intervene. The Austrian, duly provoked, fell into the trap. French and Italian troops, however, suffered heavy losses, as did the Austrians. French public opinion, particularly among Catholics (the pope had taken a stance against the war), forced Napoleon III to accept an armistice with Austria. Piedmont obtained most of Lombardy (but not Venetia), as well as Emilia-Romagna and Tuscany, but had to cede Nice and Savoy to France. That was the so-called Second War of Independence. Popular participation in the form of plebiscites in the newly acquired regions confirmed the Piedmontese takeover but could not disguise the fact that nothing had so far resembled a popular revolution.

Enter Garibaldi

Matters changed thanks to Garibaldi. He had realized that no national unity could possibly be achieved without Piedmont, even though Piedmont had played the patriotic card only to extend its power. But if one plays the same card for over a decade one ends up trapped by it: once a revolutionary movement had taken off, Piedmont could not turn its back.[44] On 11 May 1860, Garibaldi, with 1,000 volunteers, embarked near Genoa, and arrived, with British protection, in Sicily. Unlike previous failed expeditions, Garibaldi was welcomed when he landed there, his visit having been prepared for by remarkable politicians such as Francesco Crispi, a southerner and later prime minister, infamous for his authoritarianism but also one of the main creators of the legend of Garibaldi.[45]

Just across the Straits of Messina in the Basilicata region, at the extreme foot of the peninsula, a revolt arose against the authorities. Local grievances played a more important role than national feelings, but soon Garibaldi had obtained control of virtually the whole of the South. This was the decisive element which led to the unity of Italy, and the key part had been played by the South – against all expectations and the official northern view of the Risorgimento. Garibaldi was shrewd enough to declare his loyalty to King Victor Emmanuel, who, in turn, could not avoid sending his troops through the Vatican states. On 26 October 1860, Victor Emmanuel met Garibaldi in Teano, some sixty kilometres north of Naples, to stop him from marching on Rome and risking a war with France. Five months later, Victor Emmanuel became king of Italy. No one had expected that Italian unity would be achieved so quickly.[46]

Garibaldi had progressive European public opinion on his side. Sympathies for Italy pre-existed his expedition. Staying in Naples in 1850–51, Gladstone, not yet a fully fledged liberal, denounced the anti-liberal policies of the Bourbons in two pamphlets addressed to the Earl of Aberdeen, calling their regime 'the negation of God erected into a system of government'.[47] Just as the philhellene movement had contributed to the Greek War of Independence, Italophile public opinion (especially in Britain) helped the Risorgimento. Italophiles came from all sides: some were radicals, followers of Chartism; others were anti-Catholics who had cheered the anti-clericalism of Mazzini and Garibaldi. Dickens wrote an address in favour of the short-lived Roman Republic of 1848. Support came from workers, too: in 1856, workers in Newcastle organized a meeting attended by thousands of people to collect funds for the Italian struggle. Even more funds were collected to help the Garibaldi expedition. Garibaldi could unleash the kind of enthusiasm which Piedmontese moderates, including Cavour, could not. When Garibaldi visited England in 1864, he was feted by all and sundry – radical workers, intellectuals and aristocrats, as well as Liberal Prime Minister Palmerston, Gladstone, the Prince of Wales and the Conservative leader Lord Derby. He was welcomed at the Reform Club as well as Eton College. Some 30,000 people went to see him at Crystal Palace.[48] A biscuit consisting of currants baked between two thin layers of pastry was named after him, and in 1865 Nottingham Forest, a football team, chose for their colours the red uniform worn by Garibaldi and his followers. Queen Victoria, however, was among those who were relieved when Garibaldi left England.[49] The appreciation continued unabated in subsequent decades: George Macaulay Trevelyan's admiring Garibaldi biographical trilogy (1907–11) was the culmination of the British love affair.[50] Unsurprisingly Great Britain was the first to recognize formally the new Italian state.

Garibaldi also continues to be celebrated to this day because, once his missions were accomplished, he did not seek wealth or power but went into self-imposed exile in the island of Caprera, off the coast of Sardinia. An internationalist to the last, he supported Karl Marx's First International as well as the Paris Commune. As his erstwhile supporter Francesco Crispi wrote: 'God did not endow him either with Cromwell's mind or Napoleon's ambition ... his arena is not parliament but the public piazza and the field of battle.'[51]

Italian unification, however, had not been completely achieved. Rome remained under the control of the pope and was protected by French troops. Venetia was still in the hands of the Austrians, as was South Tyrol. Venetia was annexed only during the Third War of Independence (1866), more because the Austrians were defeated by the Germans at

Sadowa than for anything the Italians did (in fact they lost the most important battle, that of Custoza).

Rome was annexed in 1870 and became the country's capital after the withdrawal of French troops following Napoleon III's defeat at Sedan by the Germans. The pope responded by excommunicating King Victor Emmanuel, as well as the government and the entire parliament and anyone who voted in Italian elections. Trento and Trieste remained under Austrian control until after the First World War.

The heroes of the Italian Risorgimento should have been Cavour for his political intelligence, Garibaldi for his courage and military skills, and Bismarck for the wars he waged against Austria and France. Most Italians remained spectators of the process which led to Italian unity. Some, especially in the South, revolted against the new rulers with the same grievances as in the past, and were regarded as brigands. The northern dislike for southerners was pronounced: Cavour thought the South was rotten 'to the very marrow of the bones'. His envoy Luigi Carlo Farini, arriving in Naples to take up his post as viceroy, wrote to him from Naples:

> This is Africa: compared to these boors the Bedouins are the very flower of civilization … Even peasant women kill; and worse: they tie the gentlemen [galantuomi, the name they gave the liberals] by the testicles, and pull them into the street; then they ziff and zaff: unbelievable horrors.[52]

This explains why writer and politician Massimo d'Azeglio's famous comment became almost legendary: 'We have made Italy, now we have to make the Italians.'

The new Italian state was less liberal than Germany, Great Britain and France. Some of these illiberal features resulted from the fact that unification had disappointed many, especially in the South. The so-called *brigantaggio* – brigandage, as the northern establishment sought to characterize the unrest in Southern Italy – should be regarded as a prolonged civil war.[53] Instability came not only from the peasantry hoping for land reform, which Garibaldi had advocated, but also from important sectors of the southern middle classes who, having initially rallied round Garibaldi in the hope of enhancing their power, were soon disillusioned. They did not want to be ruled by the North, particularly as layers of the magistrature and bureaucracy were purged and substituted by northerners.[54] A folksong ('Garibaldi the Traitor') in Puglia expressed the disappointment of local peasants and their nostalgia for the Bourbon kings of Naples:

Ca amm'a fa de Garebbalde
ca iè mbame e tradetòre?
Nu velìme u rè Berbòne
ca respètte la religgione.

(Che facciamo di Garibaldi / Che è infame e traditore?/ Noi vogliamo il re Borbone che rispetta la religione.)

(What to do with Garibaldi / a disgraceful traitor? / We want the Bourbon king 'cos he respects religion).

Extending free trade to a South hitherto protected by tariffs damaged the shipbuilding and engineering sectors, as well rural domestic industries.[55] Unrest and discontent, though seldom as serious as that of the 1860s, continued. In 1893–94 a movement of Sicilian peasants called *fasci siciliani*, partly inspired by socialists and anarchists, led to land occupation and military intervention, including a state of emergency imposed by Prime Minister Francesco Crispi, himself a Sicilian – the first southerner to lead the government. There were summary executions, many people were deported, and basic freedoms were suspended. 'Making the Italians' seemed still a distant hope.

The Sicilian Garibaldino Crispi had become an authoritarian prime minister: he made it his mission in the 1870s and 1880s to complete the Risorgimento by 'educating' the Italians not to feel estranged from the new nation. His model, as was often the case among the Italian elites in the second half of the nineteenth century, appeared to be the England of gradual reforms rather than the France of constant unrest. The real point of reference was obviously Prussia: he proceeded to strengthen the central government at the expense of parliament; repressed social movements; and attempted (and failed) to reform landholding. Like almost all members of the elite he had nothing but contempt for the Italians. In a letter to a former Garibaldino, he lamented that the majority of Italians 'are listless and indifferent, as if politics were none of their business. Others are sceptical and mistrustful ... they think that nothing can be done.'[56] Yet Crispi advocated universal male suffrage. This would be granted, with considerable limitations, only in 1912.

If we consider the Risorgimento a revolution, it was an unfinished one. Gramsci described it as a 'failed revolution' (*rivoluzione fallita*), largely because it did not involve the rural population, particularly in the South, and failed to achieve agrarian reform. Landlords ruled before, and they ruled after. Southern Italian intellectuals were enthusiastically pro-unification, but the *mondo contadino* (the peasant world) was the great absent of the Risorgimento.[57] As Lucy Riall put it: 'Italian nationalist movements had no interest in rural life, and the peasantry had no interest in nationalism.'[58] What the Italian Risorgimento lacked, according to Gramsci, was the element of Jacobinism which, for him, entailed the alliance of the bourgeoisie with the peasantry.[59] In France, 'the Jacobins were able to drive the bourgeoisie forward with kicks in the backside' (*con calci nel sedere*).[60] In Italy, the followers of Mazzini had been completely outflanked by conservative forces: Cavour and Piedmont.

The gap between North and South endured for generations, compounded by the disdain and contempt the northern ruling classes exhibited towards the South. In Italy everyone was aware of the existence of this gap, though it was certainly exaggerated at the time.[61] This gap grew over the course of the twentieth century. Statistics used by Francesco Saverio Nitti, a southerner and later prime minister (1919–20), showed that the top regions in terms of individual wealth were in 1904 those of the North, with Piedmont highest, while all the southern regions were at the bottom, with Sicily and Sardinia coming last.[62]

Which Germany?

Germany was even more fragmented than Italy. If we call Deutschland all the territories where the main language was a form of German, we would find statelets – such as the territory ruled by the prince of Hohenlohe, squeezed between Stuttgart and Mannheim in what is today Baden-Württemberg – but also important states, such as Prussia, the dominant military power, and Bavaria. There were also free imperial cities such as Hamburg and Bremen, and others with differing types of autonomy. The German Confederation (Deutsche Bund) consisted of the forty-one German states that had survived the Napoleonic Wars or had been resurrected after 1815.[63] This was really just a union of sovereign states from which Prussia and Austria were excluded. Paradoxically, it included the king of England in his role as king of Hanover, the king of the Netherlands because he was also grand duke of Luxembourg, and the king of Denmark who was also the duke of Holstein and Lauenburg. Strictly speaking, the German-speaking parts of Switzerland and of the Austrian Empire were also part of Deutschland.

German nationalists were divided over whether to fight for Grossdeutschland or Kleindeutschland. The latter corresponds more or less to present-day Germany. The main obstacle against a Grossdeutschland was that it would have entailed the dismemberment of the Austrian Empire to incorporate Austria in the new Germany. Ernst Moritz Arndt, an early German nationalist, sided at first with the Grossdeutschland solution but changed his mind when he realized how difficult that would be. Even if this momentous unity had been achieved, there would no longer have been a clear Protestant majority in the new Germany since Austria was Catholic. Besides, few in Austria wanted to be absorbed into a German state; an exception was the pan-Germanist Georg Ritter von Schönerer, a staunch anti-Semite and anti-Catholic whose later influence on Hitler has been noted.[64] It was Hitler who achieved (albeit briefly) the Grossdeutschland project, thanks to the Anschluss of 1938.

In 1848, the year of the springtime of the peoples, German reformers (mainly academics and professionals) assembled in what was called the Frankfurt Parliament. Despite intense factionalism, they succeeded in drafting a constitution (which barely obtained a majority of the delegates). Some hoped that it would lead to Grossdeutschland.[65] At first the king of Prussia, Frederick William IV, sought to entice the liberals by declaring himself ready to unify Germany, but as the movement subsided so did his barely perceptible nationalist ardour. Just over a year after its creation the Frankfurt Parliament was forced to disband by troops from the state of Württemberg, to prevent a Prussian intervention. By 1859, when Austria and Piedmont were at war (with the French intervening in support of the Italians), even the Deutscher Nationalverein, newly founded in Frankfurt, sided with what was then the only possible solution: Kleindeutschland.

When it was finally achieved the new united *klein* Germany owed little to the national sentiments of the German bourgeoisie. They seemed relieved that a bloody revolution was not necessary to achieve a united Germany: Bismarck was going to do it for them. The process of German unification did not have heroes but it had a mastermind, or rather someone who could be construed as such. There is a long historiographical debate on whether Bismarck had intended to unify Germany, or that it was the unintended consequence of Prussian expansionism.[66] What is certain is that he wanted to expand Prussian power, and he could do that more easily if such expansion could be seen to be furthering the cause of German nationalism as well.[67] On 2 July 1859, in a letter to his wife, he expressed his circumspect and guarded views on nationalism:

'Nations and individuals, folly and wisdom, war and peace, they come and go like waves, and the sea remains.'[68] He was only too aware of the limits politicians had to face:

> The pathway a Prussian ministry is able to take is never very wide; the man from the far Left, when he becomes a minister, will have to move to his right, and the man from the far Right, when he become a minister, will have to move to his left, and there is no room on this narrow trail that the government of any large country is able to tread for the kind of sweeping divagations of doctrine that a man may unfold as an orator or a member of parliament.[69]

The 1864 war against Denmark extended Prussia's control over the duchies of Schleswig, Holstein and Lauenburg. Prussia then turned against Austria in a quick war which concluded with the defeat of Austria at Königgrätz (Sadowa) on 3 July 1866. At this stage Prussia took the lead among German states and annexed Schleswig-Holstein, Hanover, Hesse, Frankfurt and Nassau. Bismarck was clever enough to resist the temptation to disengage Austria from its empire, which would have made Grossdeutschland more likely.

Victory over France in 1870 led to Prussia hegemony over the remaining South German states: Baden, Württemberg, Bavaria and Hesse. In January 1871, the new German Reich or empire was born; it lasted until its defeat in 1918, at the end of the First World War. King Wilhelm of Prussia became the kaiser of the new Reich, in what was in effect a federal state. The various other rulers kept their titles, so the king of Bavaria retained his role, though of course with hardly any powers. The Reich had absorbed twenty-six states and extended in the east to areas that are now in Poland and in Russia, including the city of Königsberg (Kaliningrad since its annexation, along with Northern Prussia, to the Soviet Union), Bavaria to the south and Alsace to the west. The German middle classes just looked on.

Marx, in 1848, had been withering about the German bourgeoisie, who developed, he wrote,

> sluggishly, timidly and slowly ... it did not advance the interests of a new society against an old one, but represented refurbished interests within an obsolete society. It ... used phrases instead of ideas, ... it displayed no energy anywhere, ... without initiative, without faith in itself, without faith in the people, without a historic mission, an abominable

dotard – sans eyes, sans ears, sans teeth, sans everything – this was the Prussian bourgeoisie which found itself at the helm of the Prussian state after the March revolution.[70]

Earlier, in 'A Contribution to the Critique of Hegel's Philosophy of Right', he wrote: 'German history prides itself on having travelled a road which no other nation in the whole of history has ever travelled before … [yet] We have shared the restorations of modern nations without ever having shared their revolutions.' Other nations 'dared to make revolutions', but 'our masters were afraid': 'With our shepherds to the fore, we only once kept company with freedom, on the day of its internment.'[71]

Marx expected too much from the German bourgeoisie, which, after all, obtained what it wanted: the conditions for the development of a German-wide capitalism, without having to bother with revolution and political power. The timidity exhibited by German liberals was probably due to the lessons they had derived from the French experience: seeking popular support might unleash revolutionary feelings and expectations, with unpredictable consequences. There was another problem. In Italy, emergent capitalism was concentrated mainly in northern regions, such as Piedmont, which would dominate the unification process. In Germany, the militarily dominant region – Prussia, west of the Elbe – was economically backward and semi-feudal. The developed areas where the bourgeoisie was strong included the Rhineland, Hamburg, Bremen and Frankfurt. Besides, politically speaking, Piedmont was far more advanced than the other large Italian state, the Kingdom of the Two Sicilies. Piedmont was a constitutional monarchy; its southern counterpart was ruled by an ancien régime. The unification of Italy was also a revolution against old, absolutist rule, though there was considerable modernization in the southern kingdom.

One could say that the bourgeoise failed because it failed to live up to the expectations of those who believed it was a revolutionary class – a belief held by Marx as well as by many liberals. One of the problems is that, just as capitalism is not a cohesive force, the bourgeoisie, like the nobility, is made up of a variety of social groups, often in conflict with each other. This may explain why the bourgeoisie never led a revolution after 1800, though one can find, among the revolutionaries, plenty of bourgeois.

The process that had started with the formal establishment in 1833–34 of a Zollverein (customs union), an event that some thought might awaken national feelings, accelerated the economic unification of

Germany: free movement of goods, labour and capital; less bureaucracy for enterprises; a single currency; and single commercial law. So by the time of unification many of these national economic tendencies were already in place. This was certainly a bourgeois victory. In exchange, the bourgeoisie had to accept, which it did enthusiastically, the entire apparatus of aristocratic privileges. The landed gentry (the Junkers) continued to dominate land ownership, as well as the military and the state bureaucracy. By 1910 Germany had overtaken Britain in economic development.[72]

A lengthy historiographical debate attributes to the peculiarities of the unification of Germany the so-called Sonderweg, or special path – as if each country does not have its own special path towards various forms of democracy and of capitalism. According to this view, a supine bourgeoisie had allowed itself to be manipulated by an authoritarian ruling class, and this, according to some, may have contributed to the rise of Hitler.[73] This middle class probably was quite pleased to have a strong and stable state with a weak parliament and a strong executive ruling – as Bismarck famously put it, a country united through *Eisen und Blut* (iron and blood). This is what German capitalism needed.

Though German unification did not rely on overt popular support, since it was achieved by the might of the Prussian armies, once it was accomplished, the resulting state had far more democratic elements than the new Italian state, where Garibaldi's southern expedition had received not insignificant local support. While in Italy suffrage was severely restricted, in the new Reich there was virtual universal male suffrage. This also forms a contrast with Britain, the 'mother of democracy'. German elections were relatively fair, although many voters feared that the authorities would know how they voted, especially in the early years. Many Germans took part in the polls, starting with what was in 1871 a respectable turnout of 51 per cent, increasing to over 80 per cent by the beginning of the twentieth century – much higher than today's turnout in Britain or the US.[74] The Reichstag eventually gained powers over the annual budget and even over the military budget, albeit only every seven years. It was hamstrung, however, by two factors: the devolved powers to the various constituent states of the Reich and the power of the kaiser to appoint the government. The German people had universal manhood suffrage but little power.

It should not be thought that the wider the suffrage, the more progressive the state. The lessons from the expansion of the suffrage in France in 1848 was that it could play into the hands of conservatives. The lack of necessary connection between the extension of the suffrage and progressivism is evident if one looks at the percentage of men entitled to vote in most democratic European states towards the end of the nineteenth century. It shows how low-ranking is Britain as well as Sweden – the model of progressivism in the twentieth century – and how extensive was the suffrage in Greece and Spain. Expanding this to include non-European nations, we would note that universal manhood suffrage then existed in some Latin American countries, including Colombia, Argentina and Mexico, well before Europe.[75]

Soon the new German state was also building a welfare state – unlike the motherland of *liberté-egalité-fraternité*, where social reforms were in their infancy. Compared with Italy, social violence in Germany up to the First World War was minimal and contained, thanks to the existence of a strong and well-organized socialist party, strong trade unions and rapid economic advances. By 1914, Germany was ahead of the UK in industrial output. Yet the new Bismarckian state was also unmistakably

Table 4.1. Suffrage

	Percentage of male population with voting rights
France, 1893	84.9
Greece, 1881	83.7
Switzerland, 1890	83.5
German Reich, 1898	82.2
Spain, 1891	82.0
Belgium, 1896	79.4
Norway, 1898	77.2
Austria, 1897	75.6
Portugal, 1890	74.6
Serbia, 1890	68.0
Denmark, 1898	65.7
Great Britain and Ireland, 1897	64.7
Netherlands, 1897	45.1
Italy, 1897	24.2
Sweden, 1896	24.0

Source: Adapted from Erik Bengtsson, 'The Swedish *Sonderweg* in Question: Democratization and Inequality in Comparative Perspective, c.1750-1920', *Past and Present* 244, no. 1, August 2019, p. 139. See also Toke Aidt, Jayasri Dutta and Elena Loukoianova, 'Democracy Comes to Europe: Franchise Extension and Fiscal Outcomes 1830–1938', *European Economic Review* 50, no. 2, 2006, pp. 249–83.

authoritarian, persecuting the growing socialist party (the SPD) as well as the Zentrum, the Catholic party. This policy was a failure, and both the SPD and Zentrum became stronger than their equivalents elsewhere in Europe. At the first Reichstag elections (March 1871), the National Liberals emerged as the largest single party but without an absolute majority. They were, to all intents and purposes, the Protestant bourgeois party in the new Germany, opposing the Zentrum as well as the rising socialists and supporting Bismarck's anti-Catholic Kulturkampf in the 1870s thanks to the concessions Bismarck had granted them.[76] What the National Liberals could not stomach was the introduction of protectionism in July 1879, but this helped landowners, as well as many industrialists in the iron and steel sector, whose alliance, famously dubbed 'rye and steel', existed elsewhere as well.[77] Free-trading economic liberalism never recovered in imperial Germany.

Revolutions?

During unification neither Italians nor Germans endured major massacres, unlike the Irish in Cromwell's England or the inhabitants of the Vendée in Revolutionary France. No one was put in a reservation, as Native Americans were in the US. The losses in the unification struggles were not comparable to those of the American Civil War. Those conquered were not colonized, though many in the Italian South regarded the northerners as oppressors. In both states formal equal rights were extended to all, though Catholics in Bismarck's new Germany rightly resented the anti-Catholic Kulturkampf in 1872–78, and the suffrage in Italy remained very narrow. Whether or not the unification of Italy and Germany were *revolutions* rests, as always, on one's definition, and, since we are dealing with the nineteenth century, on whether they were *bourgeois* revolutions. In Germany, the desire for national unity had been strongest among the merchant classes and found a focus with the Zollverein, which to them was economically advantageous. In Italy, by contrast, the bourgeoisie was fractured and weak; it seldom expressed common economic aims. Those who hoped for a united Italy were mainly concentrated in the literary and professional classes, and their nationalism was far more political than economic.

In both cases, revolutionary national zeal had to don the clothes of a return to an idealistic past: the Holy Roman Empire in the case of Germany; and an invented Italy to which a resurgent nation could revive the glories of Rome and the achievements of the Renaissance. But one should not overemphasize this: among German nationalists the economic case was strong; it just needed some historico-ideological underlay. In the Italian case, the rationale was rather that only a united country could put an end to the foreign invasions which had plagued the peninsula since the fall of the Roman Empire and aspire to play the kind of role that Great Britain and France performed in Europe.

In both cases the strongest state, Prussia or Piedmont, was the main artificer of unity. In both cases, after the Napoleonic Wars, there was a stirring of nationalism among the educated classes. But the dissimilarities are more profound. The unification of Germany was essentially top-down, the work of Prussia under Bismarck. In Italy, Garibaldi's impact was bottom-up. By invading the South in 1860 and conquering it, he had forced Piedmontese intervention; but Cavour and Piedmont quickly recovered their position.

The aristocracy remained the dominant force in both countries, in control of the political, bureaucratic and military personnel, as almost everywhere else in Europe. The bourgeoisie was not, as a class, a major protagonist. The actual participants were a mixture of military men, politicians, intellectuals and professionals. The political system that emerged in unified Italy was not dissimilar to the Piedmontese system. In fact, one could easily show that the new Italy was a larger Piedmont. In Germany there were substantial reforms, but in practical terms much political power remained in the hands of the kaiser and the executive, as Bismarck had to discover to his cost. One of the political giants of the nineteenth century, he was easily forced to resign in 1890 by Wilhelm II.

Nevertheless, there is no question that in the decades following unification Germany became a fully fledged capitalist state, rivalling Great Britain. Italy remained a laggard, but a capitalist laggard, as she continued to be until after the Second World War. Then she became a fully fledged member of the advanced West, thanks to an economic development known as *il miracolo economico*. In the 1990s, her troubles – a stagnant economy and an unstable party-political system – re-emerged.

Germany too recovered very well from the war and from Nazism. It developed a sturdy economy, and a strong and stable political system. Its Nazi past, paradoxically, protected it from the kind of absurd foreign interventions in which the British and to a lesser extent the French indulged. Yet the verdict on unification has been ambivalent. Much German scholarship has suggested that the authoritarian manner of the country's unification was, if not *the* cause of the rise of Nazism, then at least one of its contributing factors (see the reference to the Sonderweg above). Much Italian scholarship (Benedetto Croce as well as Antonio Gramsci) has suggested that the problems of Italy could be attributed to the failure of Italian liberals to create a truly progressive liberal society – a *rivoluzione fallita*.

It is very likely, though impossible to determine, that German and Italian unification facilitated capitalist development. The expansion of a free trade area, the abolition of internal obstacles, and the free internal movement of labour (Italy) as well as immigration (Germany) contributed significantly to economic prosperity – though, in Italy, this aggravated the disparity between North and South. Could capitalism have developed without unification? This kind of counterfactual argument would not get us very far. Capitalism was developing in tsarist Russia and, a century later, would develop in Communist China. Capitalism develops under the most varied conditions.

5
The Rise and Fall of the Russian Revolution

The Russian Revolution, even more than the French Revolution, is a historical minefield. The regime it generated was politically contested or praised from the start, and the historical analysis of its vicissitudes could never be separated from the global perception of communism, the foundation ideology of both the Soviet Union and of the international communism movement.

Much scholarship on the Russian Revolution outside Russia has been dominated by Anglo-American scholars; the French, the Germans and the Italians have contributed much less. Many of these Anglo-Americans had Russian, Polish and German origins: Richard Pipes, Zbigniew Brzezinski, Leonard Schapiro, Adam Ulam, Walter Laqueur and Bertram Wolfe.[1] For the first decades after 1945, this traditional-Sovietology or totalitarian-model scholarship was influenced by the climate of the Cold War, often describing the authoritarian one-party state as the inevitable outcome of the events of 1917, or of the actions of Lenin or even of the works of Marx and Engels. Such views have become common among non-specialists and politicians in spite of considerable work by the subsequent revisionist school (Alexander Rabinowitch, Sheila Fitzpatrick, Archie Brown, Stephen F. Cohen, Steve A. Smith, J. Arch Getty and many others), which was preceded by the works of Isaac Deutscher and E. H. Carr (regarded by some as having been excessively soft on the USSR). After the fall of communism, matters calmed down. The Russian Revolution had become history – not quite like the Crusades, but history, nevertheless.

Paradoxically, the traditional totalitarian view, which today has little traction among scholars of the USSR, was not so far from the position of many Soviet historians. It was all down to the Bolsheviks. As Sheila Fitzpatrick explains, instead of being 'always right', as the official Soviet history had it, the Party was 'always wrong'.[2] Both Stalinists and Western anti-Stalinists regarded Stalin and his regime as the only possible outcome of Bolshevism. The official version of the revolution, embodied in the 1938 *History of the Communist Party of the Soviet Union (Bolsheviks)*, also known as the 'Short Course' and closely supervised by Stalin, explained that the victory of the revolution had been 'comparatively easy' since the enemy was weak and disorganized; the revolution was led by workers 'steeled in battle', who in turn followed the Bolsheviks, allied with the poor peasantry.[3]

Sometimes both Soviet and totalitarian views attributed post-1917 developments to the theories of Marx or the perspicacity of Lenin, even though Marx never theorized what a socialist society would look like and used the term 'dictatorship of the proletariat' less than half a dozen times in the fifty or so volumes of his work, and then only as a description of an exceptional and temporary state such as the Paris Commune. In a famous passage in the *Critique of the Gotha Programme* (1875), where he criticized the programme of the German Social Democratic Party, Marx suggested that the first phase of socialism would be governed by the principle 'to each according to the work performed', while the communist stage would follow that of 'to each according to their needs'. Neither formulation offered the minimal indication of what practical steps were needed for the organization of society. What socialism the Bolsheviks wanted was not clear: the definition changed with the passing of time, as do all definitions. Eventually, once they had achieved power, the commitment to central planning became the hallmark of what socialism should be about.

The actual Bolshevik takeover, which began in November 1917 and was completed around 1923, was seen as a major threat by Western political elites. This was not unreasonable. The success of the Bolsheviks led to attempted revolutions in many European countries, and even though these were all unsuccessful, they inevitably led to the Bolsheviks being seen not just as signalling the definitive end of the old regime in Russia but as a threat to the stability of the capitalist world. After all, the Bolsheviks themselves assumed that their victory would lead to revolutions in the rest of Europe. Not even the French had the serious ambition of exporting their revolution, except perhaps briefly under Napoleon before conquest prevailed over ideology.

The Russian revolutionaries, the Bolsheviks, wanted to establish a yet-to-be-defined socialist society; their liberal rivals wanted a democratic republic (as in the West), which seemed possible after the overthrow of the tsar. Both aspired to be more like the West. The Bolsheviks assumed that socialism was the inevitable future of the West; the liberals, led by Pavel Milyukov, wanted to catch up with existing democracies. Historical determinism prevailed on all sides.

To be like the West had been an enduring aim of Russian elites, from Peter the Great to Catherine the Great, to Alexander II. They believed that reforms such as the Emancipation of the Serfs in 1861 would lead to the industrialization of the country while keeping the autocracy more or less intact. The reforms were, at least in part, due to Russia's defeat in the Crimean War (1853–56), regarded as a humiliation caused by the country's backwardness. Further humiliations continued in 1904–05 with Russia's defeat by a non-Western power, Japan – a defeat which contributed to the attempted 1905 revolution. Russian political developments were thus always connected to international events in a way that none of the previous main revolutions – English, American or French – had been.

In 1919, two leading Bolsheviks, Nikolai Bukharin and Evgenii Preobrazhensky, wrote that the 'communist revolution can be victorious only as a world revolution'. If the revolution occurred in only one country, then 'the great robber States would crush the workers' State in the first country'.[4] The failures of the revolutions immediately after 1918 in Germany, Hungary and Austria, and the rise of Fascism in Italy, led to a change. Stalin's 1924 lectures on 'The Foundation of Leninism' at the University of Sverdlov were published in *Pravda* shortly after Lenin's death. They acknowledged that 'the victory of the revolution in one country' had been 'considered impossible, on the assumption that it would require the combined action of the proletarians of all or at least of a majority of the advanced countries to achieve victory'. But this view was set aside perforce, as it 'no longer fits in with the facts'. New conditions, such as 'the uneven and spasmodic character of the development of the various capitalist countries' and 'the development within imperialism of catastrophic contradictions' made imperative 'the victory of the proletariat in individual countries' – there was no alternative but to build socialism in one country.[5]

In April 1925, Nikolai Bukharin refined the position in *Can We Build Socialism in One Country in the Absence of the Victory of the West-European Proletariat?* All the Bolsheviks could do, at most, was to help communists in other countries. This had been accepted since 1919 when, as the civil war was raging, they founded the Third Communist International (the Comintern) with the aim of supporting communists all over the world – and not just in the advanced capitalist countries. Even before then, having just seized power, the Bolsheviks – until then quite Western-centric – issued an 'Appeal to the Moslems of Russia and the East' assuring them that their customs would be respected and extending their support to 'Moslems of the East, Persians, Turks, Arabs, and Hindus' against 'the greedy robbers of Europe'.[6] In 1920 an appeal was issued 'To the Enslaved Masses of Persia, Armenia and Turkey', inviting them to a congress to be held in Baku (Azerbaijan) in August, in which a manifesto to the Eastern peoples called for the 'liberation of mankind from the yoke of capitalist and imperialist slavery … In this holy war all the revolutionary workers and oppressed peasants of the West will be with you.'[7]

Unquestionably, there was an element of national pride: Russia, not the advanced countries of the West formerly praised by the intelligentsia, had turned out to be the first to break a path towards socialism. The October Revolution had changed Russia from a laggard to a pathbreaker: it had become, if not the centre of the world, then at least the repository of hopes for a better society and a new Third Rome.

At the Second Congress of the Comintern in 1920, Lenin issued the Twenty-One Conditions for parties wishing to join the new communist movement. The most important was that communists should form their own party and split from the 'reformist' socialist parties. But in its twenty-four years of existence the Comintern was unable to lead a single successful communist revolution or even to establish a major communist party in the West (in Germany in the 1920s and in France in the 1930s, the communist parties were smaller than the socialist parties). The Comintern was disbanded in 1943, in the middle of the Second World War, mainly to reassure the USSR's Western allies.

The end of communism in the USSR in 1989–91 signalled the end of a global communist threat, though an imagined Russian or Chinese threat continues to haunt leaders of the West, in perpetual need of an enemy. By the end of the twentieth century the few remaining communist states (Cuba, China, Vietnam, Laos and North Korea) did not display any ambition to export communism. China, Vietnam and Laos wanted to prosper economically using a market economy; Cuba wanted the US to end its sanctions; and North Korea wanted to maintain its seclusion despite its appalling poverty.

The novelty of 1917

Before 1917, major wars had not often caused revolutions. The Thirty Years' War (1618–48) was not a cause of the English Civil War; no war led to the American War of Independence or to the French Revolution; the unifications of Germany and Italy were not the result of external conflicts. But the First World War was the most direct cause of the Russian Revolution – despite of course the numerous pre-existing factors that led to the fall of the House of Romanov. Russia was on the brink of revolution before 1917, but a catalyst was needed to push the country over the brink. The war triggered the revolution.

Previous revolutions posed few threats elsewhere. Besides, the Russian Revolution, unlike the English, American and French revolutions, occurred in a multinational empire. It is true that the English Civil War had a major impact on Scotland and Ireland (and inspired reformers in other countries), but it remained within the confines of what became the United Kingdom. The French Revolution, it was feared, would lead to similar events in other countries, but its ideas had been circulating for some time; a far greater threat, from the point of view of Germans, Austrians and Spaniards, was represented by the Napoleonic armies. Such menace, the fear of invading forces, had more to do with traditional power politics than with ideology.

The American Revolution, at most, exported its ideas to the Spanish settlers in Central and Latin America, but no effort was exercised by the federal government to incite anyone to a revolution which would replicate their own. As we have seen, the US did not even support the French Revolution.

The unification of Italy and Germany and the independence of Greece could be seen as threatening the stability of multinational empires. But Austria, the main victim of German unification, was already facing internal threats, especially from Hungarian nationalism. The solution was the Austro-Hungarian compromise of 1867, which enabled the empire to survive almost unscathed until the end of the First World War. Nationalism presented a much bigger threat to the Ottoman Empire.

The Russian Revolution, unlike the French and the American, had few homegrown philosophical antecedents: no Rousseau, no Voltaire, no Diderot, not even a Hamilton or Jefferson. The Russian intelligentsia – overwhelmingly concentrated in Moscow and St Petersburg – took its theories from abroad. Even the word 'intelligentsia' comes from the German *die Intelligentz*. They borrowed from Rousseau, from Marx and from John Stuart Mill – even though, in the cultural field, Russia produced an astonishing and unrivalled array of poets, novelists and composers. Thinkers such as Herzen, Lenin or Plekhanov looked to the West and to Western thought, like most Russian intellectuals at the time. Even the Slavophiles, who longed for some mythical past society, borrowed their ideas from the West including from August von Haxthausen, a German whose idealized view of the Russian peasant had considerable influence in Russia itself during the 1840s.[8] Russia's desire to be European had marked its entire history, from Peter the Great to Putin. The Bolsheviks borrowed their symbolism from the West European radical tradition, especially the French: not only the American May Day and International Women's Day and the 1848 revolutions, but also the red flag, the 'Marseillaise', the 'Internationale', and the mythology surrounding the Paris Commune.[9]

The process of the Russian Revolution (from March 1917 to October 1917) was also distinct from all the others. It was never a matter of establishing the absolute power of an existing organ (as in the English Civil War and the French Revolution, which saw Parliament and the Third Estate respectively against the monarchy); neither was it an anti-colonial revolution, like the American. It had nothing to do with the unification of a state, as in Germany and Italy. Its civil war bears only superficial resemblance to the conflict in China between nationalists and communists. The kind of 'dual power' which existed for most of 1917 did not surface elsewhere.[10]

The Bolsheviks had to build a new regime from scratch. In Britain, Parliament had to establish its full power with respect to the monarchy, but Parliament already existed. In America, the Thirteen Colonies had to decide how to cooperate in a new state, but they already existed, while in France it took a century before the form of the new state (a republic) definitively emerged.[11] Here, Russia was exceptional. The Romanovs left nothing behind them except an unelected provisional government facing elected but powerless soviets. Having ruled Russia for three centuries, they departed, 'almost overnight, unlamented, there was no-one to defend it'.[12] As the poet Vladimir Mayakovsky put it in his 1924 *Ode to Lenin*, the 'two-headed, hook-beaked eagle' of the dynasty was 'spat out … like the chewed stump of a cigar'.[13] When, finally, an elected Constituent Assembly emerged in January 1918, it was dissolved by the Bolsheviks with supreme ease. The main objections, understandably enough, came from the Socialist Revolutionaries (SRs), since they had achieved a majority in what appears to have been a well-conducted election. For Lenin, there was now room for only one party: his.[14]

Communism also spoke a new internationalist idiom. It called, following Marx, for 'workers of all countries' to unite and overthrow capitalism. That the Bolshevik Revolution would lead to a classless society not just in Russia but everywhere was their founding myth. Every major political and economic move after the establishment of Bolshevik rule was justified in terms of this goal. Foundation myths have a complex itinerary: time is required for the construction of a narrative that is acceptable to the present and, hopefully, to posterity. As we noted earlier, the state which emerged from the English Civil War encountered the problem that it was difficult, though not impossible, to celebrate the regicide of Charles I in a monarchy. Eventually the Glorious Revolution of 1688 and its subsequent Bill of Rights were adopted and depicted as the birth of British freedoms along, quite improbably, with the Magna Carta (1215). This operation, however, had essentially been the work of nineteenth-century historians who also tried to find a positive role for Cromwell. By the twentieth century, however, few people, even in Britain, had heard of the Glorious Revolution. Britain's foundation myth did not require a particular event – only the generic assumption that it was the birthplace of freedom and democracy, an assumption sustained by a judicious selection of historical events.

In France, matters were far more controversial. It was not simple to find a way of holding together the end of absolute rule, the constitutional monarchy, the Jacobins, the Directoire, Napoleon and his empire, the Restoration, the revolution of 1848, and the advent of the Second Empire. It was only around 1880, when the Third Republic had become well established, that the revolution could be widely accepted, dissent being confined to the few remaining royalists and far-right organizations such as the Action Française.

In the US, the War of Independence became increasingly a part of national celebrations and was taught in schools as the birth of American democracy, ignoring, until recently, the issue of enduring slavery. Controversies on the liberalism of the American Revolution belong, broadly speaking, to the twentieth and twenty-first centuries, when the contradiction between the aspirations contained in the Declaration of Independence and the Constitution and the realities of racism and discrimination became increasingly obvious.

All revolutions are inevitably contested. Either they achieve what they set out to do, leaving some unhappy, or they don't and leave their followers disappointed – as the Russian Revolution did to the satisfaction of its detractors and the dismay of its supporters.

A question of dates

The date chosen for the celebration of the Russian Revolution was 7 November 1917 (or 25 October according to the Julian Calendar, hence the October Revolution). This was the day the Winter Palace of Petrograd was stormed by the Bolsheviks and their supporters. It was immediately regarded by the new revolutionary regime as *the* date to celebrate. Unlike the seizure of the Bastille on 14 July 1789, which had not brought about an immediate regime change, the seizure of the Winter Palace by Red Guard soldiers and sailors gave birth to a new Bolshevik government. Soviet historians, artists and filmmakers following the official line depicted the event in dramatic and heroic terms, just as novelists and later filmmakers portrayed the Fall of the Bastille as if the participants had been aware that they were writing a major chapter in the history of France and of the world. Just like the seizure of the Bastille, however, the storming of the Winter Palace encountered little opposition. It could be legitimately described as a coup d'état, but only if one regarded the Soviet Revolution as a one-day affair and only if one thought that coups d'état cannot have wide popular support.[15] Besides, you can have a coup d'état only if there is an *état*, and in Russia, in October 1917, there was none.[16] There was 'dual power', but as Lenin had explained six months earlier, this could not last long: 'Two powers cannot exist in a state.'[17] Or, as Shakespeare put it more poetically: 'When two authorities are up, / Neither supreme, how soon confusion may enter 'twixt the gap of both and take The one by th'other.'[18]

As Lenin explained, one of the two powers, the Provisional Government (under the control of the Liberals and the right Mensheviks) held 'in its hands all the organs of power' but had little support. The other, the Petrograd Soviet, where the Socialist Revolutionaries and the Bolsheviks had a majority, had little power, but enjoyed wide popular support.[19] The Soviets had a kind of democratic mandate, while the Provisional Government had not been elected. This has led some scholars to claim that 'the overthrow of the Provisional Government was one of the most democratic actions of the revolution', whereas 'the rise of Bolshevik power as a consequence was not'.[20]

The Winter Palace was not a prison, like the Bastille, nor was it the established seat of government or of the royal family; it was a monumental palace built by Peter the Great in 1711. It soon became the imperial residence of the tsar, but after the assassination of Alexander II in 1881 it was little used except for special occasions. Tsars chose as their normal residence the safer Alexander Palace, a few miles away. The Winter

Palace became the seat of the Provisional Government only in July 1917, with Alexander Kerensky as prime minister.

The celebration of the storming of the Winter Palace started while the ensuing civil war was still raging. A massive re-enactment staged on 8 November 1920 by Nikolai Yevreinov, a celebrated theatre director, deployed 6,000 participants and attracted 100,000 spectators. It was 'the most legendary of all mass spectacles during the Civil War'.[21] The liberal bourgeoisie is shown huddled in meetings while the oppressed masses organize. Finally, Red October arrives. Fifty windows in the Winter Palace are suddenly illuminated. The shots from the cruiser *Aurora* are heard, followed by the sound of guns and rifles. Then victory! And while a pathetic-looking Kerensky, dressed as a woman, is seen scuttling away, a large crowd sings the 'Internationale', and a fireworks display brings the spectacle to a close.[22]

In Moscow, Vsevelod Meyerhold celebrated the third anniversary of the revolution with a staging of the revolutionary drama *The Dawn* (*Les Aubes*, 1898) by Belgian symbolist Émile Verhaeren. At the end of the performance, a telegram was read to tumultuous applause announcing a major victory of the Red Army over the Whites.[23] Seldom had art been so intertwined with current events. The revolutions of 1917, February as well as October, became the Bolshevik revolutions: other protagonists were either losers or condemned to oblivion.

Sergei Eisenstein's *Battleship Potemkin* (1925) is widely regarded as a masterpiece. Three years later he directed *October: Ten Days that Shook the World*, which chronicled the revolution from the end of tsardom in February 1917 to Lenin mounting the podium to address the Congress of Soviets in October shortly before the storming of the Winter Palace.[24] Eisenstein's film depicted the common people desecrating the palace in rightful anger and showed how Lenin and the Bolsheviks gave this protest shape, coordination and discipline.[25] It was a representation of the connubium between populist revolt and organized revolution.

Following the revolution, 7 November became a public holiday; but 100 years later, in 2017, history had moved on. Communism was over and 7 November had almost returned to being an ordinary day – almost, since there was a perfunctory military parade in Red Square celebrating the moment during the Battle of Moscow in 1941 when troops had marched directly from Red Square to the eastern front to challenge the advancing German armies.[26] As Sheila Fitzpatrick put it, Vladimir Putin was aware that 'to celebrate meant offending one substantial public, while to refuse to celebrate or condemn meant offending another'. He suggested that the event might be downgraded from a revolution to an 'overturning' (*perevorot*).[27]

Americans celebrated the centenary of their revolution by installing the Statue of Liberty, a gift from France, while the French celebrated theirs by erecting the Eiffel Tower. But 'no global icon emerged in Russia in 2017' to mark its revolutionary centenary.[28]

Not having decided whether the revolution should be celebrated, the new post-Soviet authorities declared a public holiday on 4 November. It was to be National Unity Day, in remembrance of the defeat of Polish-Lithuanian forces by Russia in 1612. This battle ended the Polish–Muscovite Wars and the so-called Time of Troubles (a period of unrest, wars and famines spanning the period 1598 to 1613), and the beginning of the Romanov dynasty. In the twenty-first century, the date was of little significance to most Russians, but it was a nationalist date (or could be construed as such), and it was close to 7 November.

Other dates could have been chosen to celebrate the events of 1917, since the year of revolution was truly eventful. The most obvious would have been 8 March (23 February in the Julian calendar). On that fateful day, as the war continued with ever-increasing Russian losses, distressed women who had been queueing for bread in the cold took the opportunity of International Women's Day to stage a major demonstration in Petrograd, then the capital and a city of 2.5 million inhabitants. The lack of food, more than the serious military losses Russia had suffered so far, was the main immediate cause of the downfall of the Romanovs. Soon the protesting women, many of whom worked in the Vyborg cotton mills, were joined by as many as 150,000 workers, tired of deteriorating working conditions, falling real incomes, and inflation. The Imperial Guard was called in and, at first, obeyed orders to shoot. A few days later the soldiers started defecting, turning against their officers. Just over a week after the women's demonstration, there was growing dissent within the armed forces, the police and politicians. Mikhail Rodzianko, the conservative chairman of the Duma (parliament), who had been having second thoughts about Nicholas II since 1916, wrote in a message to General Nikolai Ruzsky, commander of the northern front: 'Hatred of the dynasty has reached its limit ... Everywhere troops have gone to the side of the Duma and the people, and the terrible demand for abdication ... has become definite.'[29] The tsar, who had been made aware of the gravity of the situation by a stream of letters from military and political authorities, reluctantly abdicated on 2 March. It had taken only a week to get rid of Nicholas, who, unable to designate his haemophiliac son as his successor, asked his brother, the Grand Duke Michael, to take over.[30] The grand duke decided that he would accept only if appointed by an elected Constituent Assembly, explicitly acknowledging that, while the autocracy could no longer continue, perhaps tsarism could survive as a constitutional monarchy. But events decided otherwise. The new (unelected) provisional government led by Prince Lvov had little power, while Petrograd was in the hands of the recently established Soviet of Workers' and Soldiers' Deputies, who refused to accept the continuation of the autarchy.

This signalled the end of the 300-year-old rule of the Romanovs, overthrown by a series of demonstrations which no single party had organized: neither the Liberals, nor the Mensheviks, nor the Socialist Revolutionaries, nor the Bolsheviks. The February Revolution had not been bloodless, but those killed were probably fewer than 2,000 – an insignificant number compared to the millions who were still dying in the war and those yet to die in the Russian Civil War. In fact, lives were probably spared since many soldiers deserted the eastern front, where losses had been enormous.

The First World War was the immediate cause of the Russian Revolution – not the class struggle between capitalists and workers, not the desire for a socialist society, not even a desire for a Western-style democracy. It had been preceded by signs of a major destabilization of the continent when Bulgaria, Greece, Montenegro and Serbia wrested most of the European territory of the Ottoman Empire in the course of the Balkan Wars (October 1912 to July 1913). Then the victorious Balkan states started quarrelling over the spoils, with Romania joining in against Bulgaria. These wars caused widespread ethnic cleansing and hundreds of thousands of casualties: Serbia alone lost 275,000 men, while Bulgaria suffered 300,000 casualties, of which 100,000 died.[31] The wars, however, were concentrated in the Balkans, thus sparing the big powers (which is why the Balkan Wars are barely discussed in the West).

The previous major European conflict, the Crimean War, had taken place some sixty years before. With the exclusion of the wars for the unification of Germany in the 1860s, the continent of Europe had been broadly at peace since the end of the Napoleonic Wars, unlike the United States which had to confront the great losses of its Civil War. China was also plagued by conflicts, particularly the 1899–1900 Boxer Rebellion (Yihetuan Movement) and the subsequent foreign intervention by an Eight-Nation Alliance, including troops from the US, Japan, Britain and Russia, culprits of officially sanctioned looting, rapes and mass killings.

The end of the First World War did not lead to peace and tranquillity. It was followed not only by the Russian Civil War but also by the end of the Austro-Hungarian and Ottoman Empires and the birth of new states. It led to the independence of Finland, Poland and the three Baltic republics. It also gave rise to Czechoslovakia, to the completion of Italian unification with the inclusion of the South Tyrol or Trentino–Alto Adige, and to the restoration of Alsace and Lorraine to France. The First World War was one of the preconditions for the rise of Italian Fascism. It led to failed revolutions in Germany, Hungary and Finland; widespread strikes in Italy in 1919–20 (the Biennio Rosso); the formation of Yugoslavia (first known as the Kingdom of the Serbs, Croats and Slovenes); the Greco-Turkish War (1919–22) resulting in the burning of Smyrna by Turkish troops; and the advent of the Atatürk military regime in Turkey under Mustafa Kemal. The end of the Ottoman Empire also led to the establishment of French and British protectorates throughout the Middle East. The First World War was also a factor in the birth of the Irish Free State in 1922 after the Irish War of Independence. Finally, the humiliation of Germany at Versailles contributed to its desire for revenge, facilitating the rise of Hitler and creating the conditions for the Second World War.

In Russia, meanwhile, the First World War caused more casualties than anywhere else: 3 million dead, almost half of these civilians. Among the Entente powers, France lost 1.7 million, Italy 1.2 million and the UK 1 million; the US, having joined the war in 1917, lost only 117,000. So Russian deaths amounted to one-third of all deaths of the Entente powers. Among the Central Powers, Germany lost 2.5 million, Austria-Hungary 1.5 million and the Ottoman Empire 3 million.[32]

The astonishingly perspicacious arch-conservative Russian politician, Pyotr N. Durnovo, who had been a particularly repressive interior minister (1905–06), warned the tsar in a memorandum written in February 1914, months before the war started, that should Russia enter a continental war with Germany, the country 'will be flung into hopeless anarchy', since 'the main burden of the war will fall on Russia' which was not prepared 'for so stubborn a war as the future war of the European nations will undoubtedly become'.[33] As Lenin would write, Russia was the 'weakest link'. Durnovo would have agreed, and his prophecy turned out to be accurate.

Even before the war started there had been an escalation of labour unrest in Russia. Lengthy strikes of metalworkers in St Petersburg waged during the spring and fall of 1913 were suppressed. Then just before the war, on 4 July 1914, there was a general strike in St Petersburg, which the

Bolsheviks were reluctant to back – which shows that the supposedly vanguard party was not always in the vanguard. The unrest continued once the war had started and, beginning in August 1915, there was a wave of political strikes particularly among the metalworkers of the Vyborg district of the capital.[34]

Of course, the anti-war feelings, such as they were, were not based on a political analysis; they seldom are. Rather, there were protests against the consequences of the war: scarcity of food, casualties, and, as is often the case, lack of understanding of what the war was about. It is probably true, as is commonly the case in wars, that most combatants were not aware of what they were fighting for; many of those in charge were not too sure either. The Russian general Aleksei Brusilov noted in his war memoirs that, at most, his soldiers knew that an archduke and his wife had been murdered in a country they had never heard of.[35] One should not generalize from anecdotes, however: the diary of A. A. Zamaraev, a peasant in a remote village in Vologda, reveals a surprising level of awareness about the course of the war and the generals leading it.[36] An examination of letters sent by workers to newspapers suggests that traditional economic demands, such as the eight-hour day, was more important than an end to the war.[37]

War can also be a teacher. In her poem 'In Memoriam, July 19, 1914', a reference to the day Russia declared war on Austria-Hungary, the great poet Anna Akhmatova wrote:

> We aged a hundred years, and this
> Happened in a single hour.[38]

The anniversary of the revolution should have been 8 March, since it kicked off the chain of events which led to October and the Bolshevik takeover. As the Russian revolutionary feminist Alexandra Kollontai declared, that was the day 'Russian women raised the torch of proletarian revolution and set the world on fire'. It was

> a historic and memorable day for the workers and peasants, for all the Russian workers and for the workers of the whole world. In 1917, on this day, the great February revolution broke out. It was the working women of Petersburg who began this revolution; it was they who first decided to raise the banner of opposition to the Tsar and his associates.[39]

Soon there was progress on this front: female suffrage was granted in many countries, with the notable exclusions (in Europe) of France, Belgium, Greece, Switzerland and Italy. But 8 March became Red Army Day, and 12 March was decreed the Day of the Overthrow of the Autocracy. By 1930, with Stalin well entrenched, only three official holidays remained: 1 January; 1 May (Labour Day); and, of course, 7 November.[40]

February to October

The obvious explanation for forgetting the February Revolution was that the Bolsheviks, though strong among the Petrograd workers, had played a minor role. The February Revolution had taken everyone by surprise, not just the Bolsheviks and the Socialist Revolutionaries (the party heir to the Narodniks enjoying remarkable support among the peasantry) but also the liberal-nationalist Kadets, whose official name was Narodnaia Svoboda or People's Freedom. Lev Kamenev and Stalin were in exile in Siberia and reached Petrograd in March. Lenin and Grigory Zinoviev were in exile in Switzerland and returned together in the special train, reaching Petrograd in April. Leon Trotsky, who was in New York and not yet a member of the Bolsheviks (he joined later that year), returned in May, as did Nikolai Bukharin who was also in New York.

Lenin, with German help, arrived at Finland Station, Petrograd, on 3 April (16 April) and announced his 'April Theses', a grand name for directives originally entitled *The Tasks of the Proletariat in the Present Revolution*.[41] Lenin's position was that the Bolsheviks should not support the Provisional Government, nor should they support continuing the war, nor should they think that the actual proletarian revolution should wait for the full development of a 'bourgeois' stage (as the February Revolution was regarded by many of them). It was not suggested then that Russia should make a separate peace with Germany. The 'immediate task', moreover, was not to 'introduce socialism', but to bring production and distribution under the control of the Soviet of Workers' Deputies, nationalizing the land and the banks. The Party should also change its name to communist and set up a revolutionary international organization.

It was quite clear to Lenin that the 'masses' were not ready for further revolution. He accepted that they had an 'unreasoning trust in the government of capitalists', and therefore it was necessary, with persistence and patience, to explain their error to them. He recognized that in the Soviets the Bolsheviks were still a minority facing 'a bloc of all the petty-bourgeois opportunist elements'.[42] 'It was owing to the immaturity, the backwardness, the ignorance of the poor peasants,' he wrote in 1918, 'that the leadership passed into the hands of the kulaks, the rich, the capitalists and the petty-bourgeois intellectuals. That was the period of the domination of the petty bourgeoisie, of the Mensheviks and Socialist Revolutionaries.'[43]

Lenin, who needed to convince the Bolsheviks, let alone the 'masses', suggested that the Party should deliberately position itself on the far left of the political spectrum. If subsequent events had led to a Russian withdrawal from the war in May or June, or a continuation of Russian involvement without the spectacular losses of the past, the April Theses would probably be confined to the dustbin of history along with Lenin, who was virtually unknown at the time. In fact, he initially failed to convince Kamenev, Stalin and a Bolshevik majority, who had instead favoured supporting the newly formed Provisional Government led by Prince Lvov and backed by the other parties, including the Mensheviks.

The Bolsheviks were not yet the centralized, monolithic party they became in the 1930s. This image of a highly disciplined party of professional revolutionaries, beloved by both Soviet and anti-communist historians in the West, depends more on Lenin's vision (as described in his 1902 pamphlet *What Is to Be Done?*) than on the realities of Bolshevism. The Bolsheviks were, of course, a secretive, almost conspiratorial party in the years leading up to 1917. This is hardly surprising: they could not run an open democratic party like the French or German Social Democrats. Tsarist Russia was a repressive autocratic system which restricted political participation and became more open only after the revolution of 1905. Nevertheless, by 1917 (and even before) there was real debate within the party. In fact, it would be accurate to note, as Mike Haynes has, that 'Bolshevik successes in 1917 reflected the fact that they were a substantially more democratic organization than their competitors'.[44]

Gradually and inevitably, positions changed during the eventful year of 1917. Kamenev soon fell into line and supported Lenin. The key factor was the war, and the attitude of soldiers and sailors who wanted the war to end. This is what helped the Bolsheviks to gain considerable ascendancy among the armed forces. Lenin had rightly guessed (or gambled?) that there would be a growing anti-war sentiment among the troops. That had not been the case before the overthrow of the tsar: an examination of petitions submitted showed that the main complaint was the harsh discipline enforced by the officers rather than the war itself. Having fought for three years, soldiers were not keen to declare that all had been in vain.[45] Most of the soldiers were peasants but the war fostered a feeling of reciprocal solidarity and a sense of organization. It also helped to develop some form of national identity. Peasants were no longer, as Karl Marx had described them, 'potatoes in a sack'.[46]

When Kerensky, vice president of the Petrograd Soviet and a leader of the moderate faction of the Socialist Revolutionary Party, was appointed minister for war, military operations appeared to become legitimate once again. This did not last, because Russia's war situation deteriorated further. As desertions and mutinies multiplied, those who were accused of fomenting them were called Bolsheviks by the authorities because they advocated immediate peace, all power to the Soviets and a social revolution, thus contributing to making Bolshevism and Lenin popular and more influential.[47]

In June, the Provisional Government with Kerensky as war minister, started an offensive on the eastern front. It failed and the General Staff blamed the defeat on the influence of the Bolsheviks.[48] The popularity of the Bolsheviks among the troops, both those at the front and those at the rear, grew even more since only the Bolsheviks had opposed the offensive. Nothing is more dangerous for the established order than disheartened and rebellious soldiers. It seemed to many, but not to Lenin, nor to the other Bolshevik leaders, and not even to the Petrograd Soviet, that the time was ripe for an insurrection. Working-class support for the Provisional Government was now at a low ebb. On 31 May the workers' section of the Petrograd Soviet voted for the Bolshevik resolution, calling for 'All Power to the Soviets'. Then on 18 June hundreds of thousands of workers marched, carrying anti-capitalist slogans.[49] These spontaneous demonstrations were repressed by troops loyal to the government. Prince Lvov resigned as prime minister (7 July), and the government, now under Kerensky, closed presses, arrested many Bolsheviks and tried to arrest Lenin, who went into hiding, first in Petrograd, then in the countryside and then in Finland, where he stayed for two months. He probably thought that the opportunity for a revolution had come and gone. There he found time to write *State and Revolution*, in which the revolution, counter-revolution and general turmoil devastating the country are barely mentioned. Instead, we have an extended discussion of the writings of Engels and Marx on the state, as well as ferocious polemics against assorted 'petty bourgeois' and 'opportunistic' writers, from Plekhanov to Kautsky. *State and Revolution* looks like the work not of someone who thinks that the revolution is round the corner, but rather who is preparing himself for the long haul.[50]

Lenin probably overestimated the strength of the Provisional Government.[51] At the end of July he wrote: 'During a revolution, millions and tens of millions of people learn in a week more than they do in a year of ordinary, somnolent life.' He added: 'It is clear that the first phase of our revolution has failed.'[52] But he was wrong – or perhaps that it was only a step back for, in 1904, he had written:

> One step forward, two steps back ... It happens in the lives of individuals, and it happens in the history of nations and in the development of parties. It would be the most criminal cowardice to doubt even for a moment the inevitable complete triumph of the principles of revolutionary Social-Democracy, of proletarian organisation and Party discipline.[53]

In revolutionary times nothing can be predicted or anticipated. Engels, prescient as he often was, wrote in a letter to Vera Zasulich:

> People who boasted that they had *made* a revolution have always seen the next day that they had no idea what they were doing, that the revolution *made* did not in the least resemble the one they would have liked to make. That is what Hegel calls the irony of history, an irony few historic personalities escape. Look at Bismarck, the revolutionary against his will.[54]

Turmoil continued. General Larv Kornilov, a Cossack whom Kerensky had appointed Supreme Commander in Chief (8 July), backed by both business circles and landowners as well as by the Allies (especially the British), demanded an enormous increase in the powers of the military, including the introduction of martial law in factories, as well as in Petrograd.[55] Kornilov had overreached himself. He was opposed by numerous workers and soldiers assembled by the Petrograd Soviet. His apparent grab for greater powers was an abysmal failure, and he was arrested.[56] Kerensky thought he had re-acquired control and even declared a republic on 15 September without waiting for a Constituent Assembly. He too had miscalculated. The events had led to a further increase in the popularity of the Bolsheviks, particularly in Petrograd, while the distrust against the Kerensky government intensified. As the historian Harvey Asher opined, echoing Kerensky himself: 'The Kornilov Affair was the prelude to Bolshevism.'[57]

Even in August 1917 when they were virtually banned, the Bolsheviks had been able to retain control of the Soviets in Ivanovo-Voznesensk (seat of a major textile industry), the Kronstadt naval base just outside Petrograd, and even of Yekaterinburg, where, a year later, the tsar and his family were executed. By September, they could rely on a majority in the Soviets of Moscow and Petrograd (where Trotsky became the chairman), as well as some 300,000 members.[58] And now they had allies: the Left Socialist Revolutionaries, having split, in the summer of 1917, from the main Socialist Revolutionaries, decided to support the Soviets over the Provisional Government.

As Kerensky's fortunes faded, Lenin, still in Finland, decided that it was now or never. History is often full of unexpected turns, and great leaders are those able to seize the day. In mid-September 1917, Lenin wrote to the Bolshevik Central Committee: 'The Bolsheviks, having obtained a majority in the Soviets of Workers' and Soldiers' Deputies of both capitals, can and *must* take state power into their own hands.'[59] Like Kerensky, he saw no point waiting for a Constituent Assembly. The Bolsheviks were relatively flexible, enough to be responsive to the prevailing mass mood, and this 'had at least as much to do with the ultimate Bolshevik victory as did revolutionary discipline, organizational unity, or obedience to Lenin'.[60] Lenin, by then, had the majority of the Bolshevik leadership on his side, but at first Zinoviev and Kamenev opposed taking power, publishing their disagreement in a non-party newspaper. A furious Lenin, perhaps suspecting that he would not be able to count on that majority for long, demanded their expulsion ('I will fight with all my might … to secure the expulsion of both of them from the Party').[61] Lenin's suggestion was disregarded by the Central Committee (which shows how far Lenin was from having complete control), but it ordered Kamenev and Zinoviev not to make public any future disagreements they had. They were expelled from the Central Committee but not from the Party and were soon back in the leadership. Zinoviev became head of the Petrograd Soviet and, in 1919, head of the Communist International, while Kamenev became acting head of the Soviet Union during Lenin's final years in 1923–24.

After four months in hiding, Lenin returned to Petrograd, revived the slogan 'All Power to the Soviets' that he had previously dropped and gave the signal for the seizure of power. It was 24 October. In the evening, a blank shot from the cruiser *Aurora* gave the signal for the assault on the virtually unprotected Winter Palace – the Red Guards vastly outnumbered the defenders. In any case, the revolutionaries were already in control of Petrograd before the fall of the Winter Palace. They took over the palace, raided the cellars and drank the tsar's wine. The poet Marina Tsvetaeva celebrated thus:

> Night. – Northeaster. – Roar of soldiers. – Roar of waves.
> Wine cellars raided. – Down every street,
> every gutter – a flood, a precious flood,
> and in it, dancing, a moon the colour of blood.
> …
> Barracks and harbour drink, drink.
> The world and its wine – ours!
> The town stamps about like a bull,
> swills from the turbid puddles.[62]

The day after the storming (7 November according to the new calendar), the Provisional Government was deposed. Alexander Blok celebrated the event too. His revolutionary and anti-clerical poem, 'Twelve', written in early 1918, has a dozen Red Guards (suggestive of the apostles) led by a Christ-like figure:

> Comrade, hold on to your gun, be brave!
> Let's put a bullet into Holy Russia
>   Into ancient, sturdy,
>   wood-hutted,
> Fat-assed Russia!
> Yeah, yeah, without the cross!
> …
> To the grief of all bourgeois
> We'll fan a worldwide conflagration,
> A conflagration drenched in blood –
> Give us Your blessing, O Lord![63]

Peasant opinion

The main appeal of the Bolsheviks, and what put them by the end of 1917 at the head of a genuinely popular movement, was their plan to withdraw from the war. The promise of land and bread was appealing, but peace was what might lead to land and bread. So the Bolsheviks, who always thought that a socialist revolution would almost certainly be a violent affair, seized power on what one might call a pacifist ticket. Lenin's great Bolshevik revolutionary slogan of 1917 – 'Peace, Bread, and Land' – made no mention of socialism and the overthrow of capitalism. The soldiers wanted peace, the peasants wanted land and the workers wanted bread.

All could be achieved under capitalism. A treaty could achieve peace (it did, at Brest-Litovsk). An agrarian reform would give peasants the land that they had not been able to obtain after the great tsarist reform of 1861. And capitalism, surely, could have provided bread to everyone, as it was gradually doing in the West. While historians are still debating whether the English Civil War or the French Revolution were bourgeois revolutions, most regard the Great October Revolution in Russia as a socialist anti-capitalist revolution – yet this communist revolution did not have communism as its immediate goal.

That the Russian people wanted peace above all else, something which escaped many Russian liberals, was obvious to people such as Samuel Hoare, head of the British Intelligence Mission to the Russian General Staff, who wrote to London at the end of 1916: 'Personally, I am convinced that Russia will never fight through another winter.'[64]

Those who had acquired power after the March Revolution, the liberal-nationalist Kadets led by Pavel Milyukov and the moderate socialists, thought that a democratic turn would make Russia better prepared to continue the war.[65] In May 1917, Milyukov even sent a telegram to the Allies in which he promised that Russia would continue the war with the same aims as the tsar, including the cession of Istanbul to Russia![66] Astonishingly, the Kadets did not seem to be aware that the people were weary of the war, part and parcel of the war-weariness sweeping the whole of Europe in 1917. The *Guardian* correspondent seemed better informed. Having travelled widely in the interior of Russia he wrote 'that if it were not for the revolutionary councils in the towns, villages and among the soldiers of the garrisons, the anarchy would be fifty times worse.'[67]

Petrograd was where the two Russian Revolutions of 1917 began, that of March and that of November. Of equal or even greater importance was what was occurring in Russia's huge countryside. Even there the war was a major factor (the Russian army was the peasantry in uniform), but so were older issues: land and food. The March Revolution and the fall of the tsar had raised the expectations of the peasants: the level of unrest in the countryside increased significantly during 1917.[68]

Contrary to a common belief, peasants were not (or were no longer) monarchists, and many welcomed the news of the tsar's abdication. 'Our village', wrote one peasant, 'burst into life with celebrations.'[69] The *muzhiks* (peasants) expected major changes from the new Provisional Government. This, however, was largely made up of liberals from the urban classes who had little understanding of peasant problems. The collapse of tsardom and the difficulty of the Provisional Government to set up new administrative organs in the countryside left the traditional village-based peasant bodies with considerable local powers.[70] The peasants took matters into their own hands, seizing land and refusing to pay rents, burning the estates of landowners and cutting wood illicitly.[71]

The divorce between the peasants and the tsarist regime had started far earlier, in the aftermath of the 1861 Emancipation of the Serfs Decree promulgated by Alexander II. This was soon followed by the establishment of locally elected assemblies, the *zemstvos*. It seemed that Russian autocracy was moving with the times, but the assassination of Alexander II in 1881 and the succession of Alexander III slowed down the process of reform. This was accompanied by the spread of terrorism responsible for the killing and maiming of some 17,000 people in the years preceding the Revolution.[72]

The 1861 Emancipation Decree delivered 20 million people from serfdom and from the arbitrary power of landowners. Nevertheless, many peasants felt themselves cheated: their burden of debt was heavier than ever, since now they owed the redemption payments, and the land retained by their former masters (*otrezki*) remained considerable.[73] Peasants, driven by hunger, rented some of it and so ended up working, once again, for landlords. For many *muzhiks* the emancipation brought little change. It is perhaps this that led Leo Tolstoy to write in his diary on 13 August 1865: 'The Russian revolution will not be against the Tsar and despotism, but against landed property. It will say: "Rob and steal from me – the man – anything you like, but leave us the land."'[74]

To add to peasant discontent there was the terrible famine of 1891, widely blamed on the authorities. This contributed to the peasant unrest of 1905–07, which was equally pronounced in non-Russian lands such as Poland, Finland, Estonia and Latvia. Attempts were made, notably by Pyotr Stolypin when prime minister (1906–11), to reorganize traditional patterns of land use and to encourage the development of capitalist farming.[75] The partial failure of the reforms contributed significantly to the further disenchantment of the peasantry with the tsar.[76] After the reform which followed the (failed) Revolution of 1905, the peasants acquired an increased share of the land either individually or as part of the peasant commune – the *mir* or 'the world', an institution which had already started its long decline.[77] By 1917 the structure of the autocracy was still intact, but reforms had established elections, parliaments and a far less restrictive censorship than in the past.

Russian peasant society, which had been relatively traditional until the early years of the twentieth century, was changing. Modernity was making its way in the countryside. Many of the more active peasants had experienced the world outside their villages as seasonal workers in agriculture and industry. Some returned to their villages to help with the harvest, or because of unemployment or strikes in the towns, where they helped to spread a general revolutionary mood. They were implementing Lenin's slogan about 'land to those who till it' before he had even returned to Russia and before the peasants had ever heard of him.

Lenin adapted his slogans to the situation (as one should), rather than deriving them from preconceived theory, though he always tried to find in Marx confirmation of what he had already decided. He regarded the 1905 unrest as an attempted bourgeois revolution, which the Bolsheviks should support:

> A *bourgeois* revolution is *in the highest degree advantageous to the proletariat*. A bourgeois revolution is *absolutely* necessary in the interests of the proletariat. The more complete and determined, the more consistent the bourgeois revolution, the more assured will be the proletarian struggle against the bourgeoisie for Socialism.[78]

In 1905 Lenin's attitude towards the peasantry was still confused. The peasants' ideology, he explained in 'The Attitude of Social Democracy to the Peasant Movement', was petty bourgeois. They were ignorant and conservative, and yet:

> We must help the peasant uprising in every way, up to and including confiscation of the land, *but certainly not including all sorts of petty-bourgeois schemes* ... At first we support the peasantry *en masse* against the landlords, support it to the hilt and with all means, including confiscation, and then (it would be better to say, at the same time) we support the proletariat against the peasantry *en masse*.[79]

Clearly the older Marxist view that only the urban proletariat could wage a revolution was being discarded. Now the peasants, in some circumstances and at a given time, could be part of the revolutionary forces. Meanwhile working-class organizations, mainly trade unions, were growing in all in urban centres – not only St Petersburg and Moscow but also Odessa and Kiev, where the Workers' Union of South Russia was inaugurated by Pavel Axelrod, a future Menshevik leader.[80]

The 1905 events in St Petersburg, starting with Bloody Sunday, were the antecedent of the 1917 Revolution. In a lecture in Zurich in January

1917, Lenin called it the 'beginning of the Russian revolution', while acknowledging that the demonstrators were not Social-Democrats but 'loyal God-fearing subjects', adding: 'In no capitalist country in the world, not even in the most advanced countries like England, the United States of America, or Germany, has there been anything to match the tremendous Russian strike movement of 1905.'[81]

Lenin was being realistic when he did not attribute a major role in 1905 to what was still his party, the Russian Social Democratic Labour Party. The party had been founded in Minsk (in today's Belarus) in March 1898. It was a tiny group representing various organizations, including the Jewish Bund. The manifesto was written by Peter Struve, then a Marxist, later a liberal and an anti-Bolshevik supporter of the Whites in the Civil War of 1918–21. The party's aim was a socialist society, but it was scathing (as Marx had been) about the potential of the Russian bourgeoisie to establish a bourgeois society.

This small party was split into various factions, of which the Bolsheviks were briefly in the majority after 1903. They acquired their name (derived from *bolshinstvo*, majority) during a congress held in London. One of the key votes took place at the Three Johns pub in Islington. Before 1898 the Russian revolutionaries were mainly Narodnik (populists) who believed in a peasant revolution, but they were unable to make much headway among the peasantry, and spent much of their time in terrorist activities. On 1 March 1881 they succeeded in assassinating the reformist Tsar Alexander II, but the only result was to enable the more reactionary Alexander III to succeed to the throne. The revolutionary storm some of terrorists expected did not take place.[82] More politically successful were the Narodniks' ideological heirs, the Socialist Revolutionaries, but they were weak in cities and did not play a major role in the 1905 Revolution in St Petersburg, though their influence in the countryside grew almost constantly.

A frustrating and unwinnable war was the immediate cause of what came to be known as the Revolution of 1905 – the war against Japan, which ended on 5 September with Russian defeat. In vain, the prescient Count Witte, the de facto prime minister, had earlier urged the tsar to implement reforms to avoid a revolution.[83] Like the events of 1917, the unrest originated in St Petersburg with the workers' strike at the armaments and shipbuilding Putilov plant. These workers, who had until recently been peasants, demanded workers' *soviets* (councils). This was the birth of soviet power. To back these demands, on 22 January 1905, a massive march with 50,000 participants (some say 100,000) took place, led by Georgy Gapon, a charismatic priest. The authorities reacted violently on Bloody Sunday, leaving a thousand dead, perhaps more.[84] That was, to quote a Chinese proverb famously used by Mao, the single spark that started a prairie fire. The fire would engulf Russia for decades to come.[85]

The domestic repercussions were considerable. The crew of the battleship *Potemkin* mutinied in Odessa. Socialist parties, including the Bolsheviks, grew in strength and influence. Nationalist parties emerged or became stronger in Finland, Poland, the Baltic provinces, Georgia and Ukraine.[86] Russia was in disarray, as demonstrations, counter-demonstrations, and random pogroms multiplied. The autocracy was scared; nothing like this had been seen at the time anywhere else in Europe. Concessions flowed, accompanied by further turmoil and strikes. The era of reforms, known as the Days of Freedom, was short-lived – less than two months (October to early December). The first Duma (parliament), elected in 1906, lasted only a month and a half. The elections were boycotted by most of the radical parties, which enabled the liberal Kadets to dominate the assembly, yet they were still too radical for the tsar and not radical enough for the revolutionary left. Nevertheless, in 1907 the former serfs' redemption payments were abolished.

The second Duma, elected in 1907, lasted just over a hundred days and was not boycotted by Mensheviks or Bolsheviks; the prime minister, Pyotr Stolypin, tried to exclude them. When he failed, the tsar dissolved the second Duma as well. The third Duma, far more compliant with the tsar's wishes thanks to a change in the electoral system engineered by Stolypin, and dominated by landed interests, lasted the full five years (1907–12). This Duma achieved little, and Stolypin was assassinated in Kyiv by Dmitry Bogrov, a Jewish member of the Socialist Revolutionaries who was probably also working for the Okhrana, the tsarist secret police.[87]

The countryside was in upheaval. The politicization of the peasantry led to the strengthening of the recently formed All-Russian Peasant Union. Village assemblies and peasant meetings adopted resolutions (*prigovory*), and sent declarations, appeals and telegrams to the state duma, and to political parties and newspapers.[88] This showed that peasants could be a revolutionary force, and Lenin, who had previously regarded them as inconsequential, learned the lesson. Until 1905, the Social Democrats (both Mensheviks and Bolsheviks) had regarded the peasantry as petty bourgeois, and consequently as a possible force for change in what they believed, following a rather deterministic view of

Marxist theory, would be the bourgeois-democratic stage of the revolution. Eventually a rural proletariat would emerge, fight against capitalist farmers, and join forces with the urban proletariat.

The significance of the revolution of 1905, as Maureen Perrie has written, was that it represented, for the first time in Russian history, a simultaneous attack on autocracy from all levels of society, 'from the middle classes, professional and commercial, to the urban workers, and the peasantry'.[89] Leaving aside revolts in Poland, there had been no seriously revolutionary attempt against the Romanov in the previous century. By 1910 strikes and demonstrations started anew, as did tsarist repression. In 1912 there was the Lena Goldfields massacre against striking workers, as well as increasingly bitter and violent confrontations between industrial workers in the years immediately preceding the war.[90]

What failed in 1905 succeeded in 1917.

The Bolsheviks in charge

If in March 1917, after the abdication of the tsar, expectations in the countryside were raised, they were soon dampened as the economic position of most peasants continued to deteriorate and as the privations and losses caused by the war accelerated. This explains, at least in part, why the October Revolution achieved considerable support in the countryside, though not necessarily to the advantage of the Bolsheviks.

As the Bolsheviks had promised, elections to the Constituent Assembly were held on 25 November, two weeks after the seizure of the Winter Palace. They were held under true universal suffrage, the like of which had not been seen in either the UK, the US or Germany, not to speak of France, Belgium or Italy. They were the fairest elections in Russian history until the fall of communism (and perhaps even after). In April, Lenin had declared that women should be 'on an equal footing with men, not merely nominally but in reality'.[91]

The results were a partial disappointment for the Bolsheviks since the peasants overwhelmingly supported the Socialist Revolutionaries, heirs to the populist (and terrorist) Narodnaya Volya. This might have been regarded as surprising since in July the SR-led government and Kerensky had refused to accede to the peasants' demands of 'land to the peasants'. The peasants were not sufficiently politically aware to be able to understand the complexities of the Petrograd political scene. The SRs were far from being a monolithic party: they were fragmented, weak and indecisive. Indeed, there was a clear breach between the policies of the SR Central Committee, which essentially offered support to the Provisional Government coalition, and the actions of its peasant supporters in the villages.[92] The slogan of 'land to the peasants' simply expressed something that was going on anyway: a surge in mass land seizure.

Well before the elections, the Socialist Revolutionaries were divided between a left faction close to the Bolsheviks and a more moderate one. The peasants' vote was itself problematic. In most cases, a secret ballot could not be held, so the villagers met in the square and cast a collective vote, usually, as they had done in the past, following the advice of those they trusted.[93] This effectively meant that interpretation of party policy was in the hands of local elder leaders, who did not necessarily promulgate policies acceptable to the party's central leadership.[94] The SRs were actually quite strong even among the working class and in urban centres, as they had been since the middle of 1917 (the working class was unstable, with many workers travelling back and forth from the countryside). Their lack of political acumen was shown by the refusals to accept the spontaneous land grab by the *muzhiks*. The SRs preferred to delay the matter until the convening of the Constituent Assembly.[95] Obviously the village poor had not seized the land to organize farms on socialist lines.[96]

The validity of the results of the elections to the Constituent Assembly have been contested ever since. What has remained undisputed, however, is that the Socialist Revolutionaries (taking both left and right factions together) emerged as the largest party, with 16.5 million votes (just over 37 per cent), according to the best available figures. The Bolsheviks were second with just over 10.5 million (almost 24 per cent), while the rest was divided between a multitude of parties. The Kadets and the Mensheviks were virtually wiped out. So socialist parties (which were consistently against the war) had a good two-thirds of the votes.[97]

Even Lenin, in 1919, accepted that the Socialist Revolutionaries and their allies had emerged as the strongest party. He pointed out that the majority of the electorate had voted for parties which were not only against the autocracy but also for some kind of socialist society.[98] In Moscow and Petrograd the Bolsheviks were the first party. The most scholarly assessment of the vote, that by Oliver Radkey, does not dispute contemporary views, including that of Lenin.[99]

Of the 707 elected members of the Constituent Assembly, the SR had a clear majority with 410 members and the Bolsheviks followed with 175. Then there were eighty-four members of various national groups, while the Kadets had only seventeen and the Mensheviks sixteen.[100] As explained above, however, the SRs were deeply divided, and only 40 out of the 410 members allied themselves with the Bolsheviks. Lenin thought this was almost certainly an underestimate of the real strength of the Left SRs in the country; he claimed that the results were invalid, giving him an excuse to dissolve the Constituent Assembly in January 1918. The dissolution of the Assembly (which met only once) caused few protests. Those who would have opposed it, the Kadets, had few seats in it and were soon outlawed. The Assembly had not had the time to develop any kind of popular following.[101]

This was the remarkable effect of the events of 1917: at the beginning of the year both the SRs and the Bolsheviks were barely known. By the end of the year, they were in charge. The poet Valeriu Marcu, author of the first biography of Lenin, could write, with perhaps some exaggeration, that in 1916: 'The whole Bolshevik Party ... consisted of a few friends who corresponded with [Lenin] from Stockholm, London, New York and Paris'.[102] Back then the SRs had been reduced to a skeletal organization, a passive constituency. Most of its leaders were in exile, weakened by repression.[103] In March, after the abdication of the tsar, the dominant parties seemed to be the Kadets and the Mensheviks. By October and November, matters had utterly changed. This is what revolutions do: the unthinkable and unlikely become thinkable and possible. The pivotal year of 1917 was over, but the Bolshevik Revolution had just started.

The February Revolution had been spontaneous, in the sense that it had not been prepared by a single organized force; hence the uncertainties that prevailed until October, when an organized force, the Bolsheviks, made a bid for power. Even after that there was a lengthy period of uncertainty – the Civil War – but what this proves is that the absolute requirement of all revolutions is a centrally organized force. Uprisings can weaken and even destroy a central force or dynasty, but to establish control you need a party or organization: in England the New Model Army; in France the National Assembly and then the Convention Nationale and the Committee of Public Safety; in America, Congress and the Continental Army; in Russia the Bolsheviks; in China, Mao's Red Army.

But organization is only half the trick; the rest demands the right circumstances. Lenin was aware of this. In March 1918 he explained at the Extraordinary Seventh Congress of the Bolshevik Party:

> The reason we achieved such an easy victory over Kerensky's gangs, the reason we so easily set up our government and without the slightest difficulty passed decrees on the socialisation of the land and on workers' control, the reason we achieved all this so easily was a fortunate combination of circumstances that protected us for a short time from international imperialism.[104]

The Bolsheviks, having achieved power, had to determine how to hold on to it and therefore how to end the war, or at least Russia's participation in it. Then later, they had to work out what policies were required to develop a socialist economy, their putative aim. These were far more complex tasks than those faced by the revolutionaries of the past. In the English case, there was an existing political structure (Parliament) and no compulsion to develop a new economy. In the American case, it was just a question of removing the links with Britain and deciding what rules should govern the common affairs of the now independent Thirteen Colonies. In the French case, what was not clear, for the following century, was the political architecture of the country; but, once again, the structure of the economy was not the major problem. The Bolsheviks' task was much harder than those which faced the English or American revolutionaries of the past. Like the French, they were facing armed enemies inside and outside the country, but these enemies were far more formidable than anything the French revolutionaries had to face.

The Bolsheviks were far from being a solid monolithic block. They obtained power because of divisions in the opposition as well as their own organizational abilities.[105] Back in March, Lenin had to convince the other comrades to adopt the slogan of 'all power to the Soviets' instead of simply supporting the new Provisional Government. Even on the eve of taking power, major leaders such as Kamenev and Zinoviev had second thoughts. Trotsky, who became a major Bolshevik protagonist, had joined the Bolsheviks only a few months before, and over the previous decades had often signalled his disagreements with Lenin. Even the power structures were unstable and untested. For instance, the first District of Petrograd, which had been in the hands of moderate socialists as recently as May 1917, having turned to the Bolsheviks and Left Socialist Revolutionaries in October 1917, remained, in the months after the seizure of power by the Bolsheviks, 'surprisingly independent'.[106] It would take over ten years for the strong centralized Soviet state to be constructed.

Buying time

The divisions inside the Bolsheviks, which in 1918 had become the Communist Party, were evident when the new revolutionary government led by Lenin had to confront its biggest immediate challenge: how to withdraw from the European war. The day after the seizure of power Lenin signed his Decree on Peace, which called on the governments of all the belligerent nations to initiate negotiations. By 15 December 1917 the Bolsheviks had agreed to an armistice with the Central Powers (Germany, Austro-Hungary and their Ottoman and Bulgarian allies). The negotiations, held at Brest-Litovsk in Belarus, lasted until March 1918, during which time the Bolsheviks had hoped to obtain a peace treaty which refrained from annexations, and which was based on the principle of national self-determination. This principle, recognized by US President Woodrow Wilson and eventually endorsed in 1919 at Versailles, had been developed by Lenin as early as 1903 and regularly advanced by the Bolsheviks ever since. In 1913, the Russian Social Democratic Labour Party defined 'self-determination' as 'the right to secede and form independent states', as Lenin had wished (against Rosa Luxemburg's view).[107]

It was obvious that the Bolsheviks had started the negotiation from a position of weakness, since their hold on power, recently achieved, was extremely unstable.[108] The Bolsheviks' hope was that Germany would not exact harsh terms because a rapid peace with Russia would enable her to concentrate on the Western front. Riots in Austria in January appeared to weaken the negotiating posture of Austro-Hungary and encourage the Bolsheviks' expectations of world revolution. Bukharin wanted to wage a revolutionary war against the advancing German armies.[109] Trotsky, then foreign minister, wanted to slow down the pace of negotiations, optimistically assuming that revolutions in Europe, above all in Germany, would benefit Russia. Lenin was less optimistic and more pragmatic, and urged him to make a deal as rapidly as possible. As he said in March 1918: 'One must know how to retreat.'[110]

The Bolsheviks needed breathing space. But there was turmoil even in their Petrograd stronghold. A study of the Assembly of Delegates from Petrograd Factories reveals the growing dissatisfaction in 1918 with conditions among the working class. There were complaints about growing unemployment due to the peace treaty, which had reduced labour demand in munition factories. Then, between May and June 1918, there were further protests against scarce food supplies. Protesting housewives and workers were shot in a Petrograd suburb. Some newspapers were closed.[111] Anti-Bolshevik unrest would continue in Moscow until 1921.[112]

The Civil War was a period of anarchy and carnage in which the most bloodthirsty forces were unleashed to fight for dominance in the former Russian Empire. One of the many problems facing the Bolsheviks was that, while they were ready to concede independence to Poland and Finland, Ukraine was a different matter. Ukraine, then virtually autonomous in the chaos of post-revolutionary Russia, was of great economic importance to the rest of Russia since it was the main supplier of grain, sugar, cast iron, coal and steel.[113] Ukraine was also home to a strong autonomist movement, but its elites regarded the country as a Russian region: Kyiv (Kiev) was the oldest Russian city. Russian, Jewish, and Polish culture prevailed in most urban centres; the identity of Ukrainian peasants was more religious (whether Orthodox or Catholic) than national. A quarter of Ukrainians lived in Austrian Galicia.[114] On one matter the Bolsheviks would have agreed with the counter-revolutionary general Anton Denikin: an independent Ukraine should not exist; it was simply one of the provinces of the Tsarist Empire. For the communists, Ukraine would be one of the constituent republics of the USSR.

The Central Powers held separate talks with the Ukrainian People's Republic, with which they signed a treaty on 10 February 1918. Ukraine had become a de facto protectorate of the Central Powers, obtaining independence in exchange for providing grain to Germany. During the war Russia had already lost control of Poland, Finland, Lithuania and most of Latvia. Germany was emboldened enough to resume military operations, which led Lenin to try to convince his comrades to accept whatever peace terms were demanded, however harsh. Trotsky and the Socialist Revolutionaries were against signing. Lenin assumed that not signing would have led to further military defeats and even harsher terms. His argument, backed by a threat of resignation, was supported by only six members of the Central Committee. Three voted against and four abstained, including Trotsky, who resigned as foreign minister.

At least there was a peace treaty, but it had been a very unsatisfactory one. In April–May 1920, Lenin compared Brest-Litovsk to highway robbery:

> Imagine that your car is held up by armed bandits. You hand them over your money, passport, revolver and car. In return you are rid of the pleasant company of the bandits. That is unquestionably a compromise … Our compromise with the bandits of German imperialism was just that kind of compromise.[115]

As a result of Brest-Litovsk, Russia lost Finland, Poland, the Baltic provinces, Ukraine and Crimea. In the Caucasus, Armenia and Azerbaijan declared independence, as did Georgia. The Brest-Litovsk Treaty was signed on 3 March. Russia had formally lost one-third of its population, but one should add that the territorial losses had preceded the signing of the treaty.

Lenin had accepted all this because he was convinced that there would be a successful revolution in the West – a view widely held throughout the Russian revolutionary movement before 1917 (although the majority of European socialists had been in favour of the war.) The idea that an anti-capitalist revolution would have to occur in several countries had long been an established view in the socialist movement. Engels, as early as 1847, in what was regarded as the first draft of the *Communist Manifesto*, had explained that it would not be possible for a revolution to take place in one country alone because by creating the world market, 'big industry has already brought all the peoples of the Earth, and especially the civilized peoples, into such close relation with one another that none is independent of what happens to the others'. It followed that 'the communist revolution will not merely be a national phenomenon but must take place simultaneously in all civilized countries – that is to say, at least in England, America, France, and Germany.' He added, only to be proved totally wrong, that the revolution would have 'the fewest difficulties in England'.[116]

In March 1918, Lenin was still convinced that,

> from the world-historical point of view, there would doubtlessly be no hope of the ultimate victory of our revolution if it were to remain alone, if there were no revolutionary movements in other countries. When the Bolshevik Party tackled the job alone, it did so in the firm conviction that the revolution was maturing in all countries and that in the end ... the world socialist revolution would come ... I repeat, our salvation from all these difficulties is an all-Europe revolution.[117]

But he also warned that

> the world socialist revolution cannot begin so easily in the advanced countries as the revolution began in Russia – in the land of Nicholas and Rasputin, the land in which an enormous part of the population was absolutely indifferent as to what peoples were living in the outlying regions, or what was happening there. In such a country it was quite easy to start a revolution, as easy as lifting a feather.[118]

There wasn't a successful revolution anywhere else, but the victory of the Entente Powers and the surrender of Germany later in 1918 meant that Brest-Litovsk would be a dead letter. The following three years of chaos enabled the Bolsheviks to re-acquire most of Ukraine, as well as Georgia, Armenia and Azerbaijan, while definitively losing control of Poland with the Treaty of Riga (1921). The Baltic provinces (Lithuania, Latvia and Estonia) became independent states until they were repossessed by the USSR in 1940, following the pact with Nazi Germany. By 1922 the Politburo proposed the creation of five nominally independent Soviet states linked in some kind of federation: Ukraine, Belorussia, Georgia, Armenia and Azerbaijan.[119] There were disputes: Stalin wanted as much centralization as possible; Lenin tended to be more tolerant towards national autonomy, presumably for pragmatic reasons. Eventually Lenin's proposal was accepted: there would be a union of Soviet Socialist Republics with the right of secession.[120] In a memo to the politburo (6 October 1922), Lenin set out his position:

> I declare war to the death on dominant nation chauvinism. I shall eat it with all my healthy teeth as soon as I get rid of this accursed bad tooth. It must be *absolutely* insisted that the Union Central Executive Committee should be *presided over* in turn by a: Russian, Ukrainian, Georgian, etc. Absolutely![121]

As a result, each Soviet republic was allowed to develop some cultural identity and, therefore, some form of limited national consciousness.

The Bolsheviks had managed to survive, and all thanks to the war, which had led to the March Revolution and the end of the Romanovs. It was the decision of all the other parties to continue the war, which led to the October Revolution, and the defeat of Germany by the Entente powers, which eliminated the worst consequences of the Brest-Litovsk Treaty. Even the emergence of the Bolsheviks as the sole party was, at least in part, due to the ambivalence of the Left Socialist Revolutionaries over Brest-Litovsk. Initially the Socialist Revolutionaries had been crucial for the consolidation of Bolshevik power. Then, dismayed at what they regarded as a capitulation to the Germans and worried about Bolshevik advances in their rural strongholds, they split from the Bolsheviks in July 1918, staging an uprising which failed, and which led to the arrest of most of their leaders. Those SRs who had opposed the uprising merged with the Russian Communist Party (Bolsheviks) in 1921. Those who refused to join the Bolsheviks supported the Whites in the Civil War, rather ineffectually.

Patterns of the Civil War

White reaction generated a long, bitter and terrible Civil War (1918–21), which caused far more casualties than the revolutions of 1917 or even Russian losses in the First World War. Some 10.5 million people lost their lives, including 6 million due to hunger and diseases, particularly in the Volga-Urals region, the North Caucasus and Ukraine. Another 2 million went into exile; millions more were maimed or orphaned.[122] Paradoxically, it was this Civil War that enshrined the Reds in power for decades to come – this was the true communist revolution. In October 1917, the Bolsheviks controlled a few urban centres including Petrograd and Moscow; ten years later, they were masters of the whole country.

At the start of the Civil War, what had been the Romanov Empire fractured into a mosaic of semi-independent statelets dominated by warlords who, unavoidably, ruled through terror. The Civil War was fought mainly between those on the right, though not united around a single project, and the Bolsheviks, who had emerged as the embodiment of the Revolution. The Civil War – or rather, wars – also involved nationalist movements from the Baltic to the Balkans, making the wars not merely Russian. Nationalism had not been a threat to the Tsarist Empire the way it had been to the Austro-Hungarian and Ottoman Empires. There were also peasant revolts, and acts of banditry by war veterans and deserters; but, as is often the case in a civil war, other forces emerged, mainly nationalist ones which hoped to break away from what had been the empire.

The broad ideology of the Whites was simple: these were people opposed to socialism in all its forms. They hoped for the restoration of the Russian Empire as it had existed before the revolutions of 1917, though not necessarily under an autocracy such as that of the Romanovs, since they occasionally paid lip service to the idea of restoring the dissolved Constituent Assembly. The disparate counter-revolutionary armies were led by an assortment of warlords unable to mount a unified response to Bolshevism. First there was Larv Kornilov, freed from prison in October 1917 by his supporters, who died while fighting in Yekaterinodar (Krasnodar since 1920) in southern Russia. Then there was General Mikhail Alekseyev, former chief of staff to Tsar Nicholas II and later commander under the Provisional Government, who died of a heart attack in 1918 in the Volga region. In Siberia and in the Urals, there was Admiral Alexander Kolchak, briefly regarded by his followers as the 'supreme ruler' of Russia but ignored by the peasants he hoped to rally. He was defeated in less than a year. Responsible for a massacre at Omsk after an SR-led uprising, he lacked the necessary political skills to hold his underlings together, and relied on the support of Alfred Knox, the leader of the British Mission to Siberia (where at state banquets 'God Save the King' inevitably followed the Russian anthem).[123] The British foreign office, barely competent in Russian affairs, thought that Kolchak had a real chance of success. They were soon disillusioned.[124]

Kolchak had the disadvantage of operating from Siberia, a vast area lacking transport facilities, and with little industry. In June 1919, defeated by the Red Fifth Army led by 'Red Napoleon' Mikhail Tukhachevsky who was twenty-six years old at the time, Kolchak tried to escape but was handed to the Red Army by the Czech Legion, his erstwhile allies, who in exchange were allowed to escape from Vladivostok. Kolchak was executed by a firing squad in February 1920 in Irkutsk. He remained reviled throughout the Soviet period but, like many others, his memory was resuscitated under Yeltsin and Putin. In 2008, the filmmaker Andrei Kravchuk provided an idealized portrait of Kolchak, and the woman he loved, in an openly anti-Bolshevik film, *Admiral*, which was followed by a television series.[125]

In southern Russia, Kornilov's successor General Anton Denikin was also defeated by Tukhachevsky. Denikin spent the rest of his life in exile, first in Europe, then in the US. His memoirs were later heavily edited in France to camouflage his anti-Semitic views.[126] His remains have been reburied in Moscow's Donskoy Monastery, where he lies near other warlords (and near Aleksandr Solzhenitsyn). In 2009 Putin laid flowers on Denikin's grave as well as on Solzhenitsyn's. Denikin's successor was Baron Peter N. Wrangel, who feigned to advance leftist policies while being one the architects of the White Terror. 'Thousands of ordinary peasants and workers were imprisoned, and hundreds shot, as suspected "spies"', recounts Orlando Figes. In the end, defeated, Wrangel admitted that the population had come to hate them.[127]

In the West, General Nikolai Yudenich established temporary control, hoping to take over Petrograd, well defended by troops organized by Trotsky, war commissar since March 1918, but Yudenich's incompetence and his virtual lack of popular support forced him to seek foreign help and, without much success, help from the national minorities of the Tsarist Empire.

It was also difficult for the Whites, mostly Great Russian chauvinists, to obtain the support of newly established nationalist regimes whose aim was to be freed of Russian tutelage, whether Red or White. They included Georgia, Azerbaijan and Armenia in the East, and in the West,

Poland, Finland, Latvia, Lithuania and Estonia. Those in the East were eventually reabsorbed into the new USSR. Those in the West succeeded in establishing themselves as independent states.

The nationalism of the White warlords became less credible because they had to rely on French and British troops (mainly undisciplined colonial troops who, of course, had no idea what they were fighting for), as well as by the so-called Czech Volunteers who had been fighting against the Central Powers in the First World War.[128] After Brest-Litovsk, many Czech Volunteers refused to disband, and joined forces in Russia with the Whites and the Allied forces that had landed in Murmansk, Arkhangelsk and Odessa, assuming that the Bolsheviks would not last.

At the beginning of 1918, Grigory Semenov (or Semyonov), a Cossack warlord, launched the counter-revolution in Transbaikalia and the Russian Far East. Largely financed by Japanese and Western money, having fled with his forces to China, he then consolidated his positions back in the Transbaikal region with the help of the Czech Volunteers. Hoping to establish a Mongol state under his dictatorship, his rule was closer to that of a bandit than a counter-revolutionary. Having succeeded Kolchak, his troops plundered, burned and murdered.[129] Forced out of Russia by the Red Army in 1921, he eventually took refuge in China, protected by the Japanese. He continued to plan to overthrow the Soviet Union until he was captured by the Russian forces during their invasion of Manchuria in 1945 and hanged.

General William Graves, the commander of the American Expeditionary forces in Siberia, wrote of his experiences in *America's Siberian Adventure*, a devastating indictment of the counter-revolutionary armies there. 'Kolchak Russians', Graves recalled, 'were not following the practice of civilized nations.' He was dismayed at the behaviour of the White forces he was meant to help. Semenov is constantly mentioned as a 'bandit' and a murderer. When his troops reached a village and the inhabitants tried to escape, Semenov's soldiers would shoot 'men, women, and children, as if they were hunting rabbits, and left their bodies where they were killed'. He reported that Sergey Rozanov (a White general) had instructed his troops that hostile villages 'should be burned down and all the full-grown male population should be shot; property, homes, carts, etc. should be taken for the use of the Army'. Later (7 August), Graves reported to his superiors in Washington that he had been 'unable to discover any enthusiasm for the Kolchak Government', whose army was disintegrating, and whose men treated the inhabitants worse than the Bolsheviks had ever done.[130]

Farther away in Mongolia there was the 'mad' Baron Roman von Ungern-Sternberg, friend of Semenov and even more brutal and anti-Semitic than Kornilov, rumoured to punish speculators, deserters, communists and Jews with a variety of imaginative deaths: feeding them to wolves, burning them at the stake, tearing them apart by wild horses or throwing them into burning locomotive furnaces 'to save ammunition'.[131] He was eventually turned over to the Bolsheviks by his own Mongolian troops. At his brief and perfunctory trial, Ungern-Sternberg was accused of mass murder of workers, peasants, Chinese and Jews in Mongolia, plotting to restore the Romanov and collaborating with the Japanese. He pleaded guilty to all charges except the last, and was executed.[132] He made it, along with General Custer (he of the 'Last Stand'), into the top fifteen worst military leaders in history in a book dedicated to military failures.[133]

Not all warlords fit the Reds-versus-Whites narrative. Between August 1920 and August 1921, a peasant revolt against the Bolsheviks occurred in the province of Tambov, some 300 miles from Moscow. It was led by Alexander Antonov, a former member of the Socialist Revolutionary Party who was eventually killed while fighting the Bolsheviks. Antonov opposed both the Reds and the Whites, claiming he was fighting for the kind of democratic regime embodied by the dissolved Constituent Assembly. The problem facing this and other similar rebellions was that while they were supposed to attract dissatisfied peasants, they also had to obtain food supplies from them, as well as able-bodied men. Inevitably, there was a 'practice of terror frequently ... detached from the larger political objectives'.[134]

In Ukraine, the Ataman (or Hetman in Ukrainian, meaning Cossack leader) Nestor Makhno led the Revolutionary Insurrectionary Army between 1917 and 1921. An anarchist revolutionary, his victories against troops of the Austro-Hungarian Empire had made him popular with local peasants, as he protected them from plunder. The same could not be said about Jews. Makhno and his anarchist army spent only twelve days in the *shtetl* (small town in Yiddish) of Kazatin (Koziatyn in Ukrainian) at the end of summer 1919, during which time his soldiers killed and tortured many Jews, and brutally raped at least forty Jewish women.[135] By November 1918, Makhno had joined the Bolsheviks in the fight against Denikin, then defected in 1919 while continuing to fight the Whites. He also fought against the independentist Ukrainian National Army. Trotsky was adamant: Makhno and his followers were no better than bandits. 'It is time to finish with this Anarcho-kulak debauchery, to finish with it firmly, once and for all, so that nobody will ever want to indulge in such conduct again', he wrote in June 1919.[136] After the final retreat of the Whites from Ukraine in 1920, Makhno was declared an outlaw by the Bolsheviks and sought refuge in Paris, where he worked as a carpenter and at the Renault car factory while continuing to write in the anarchist press.[137] He died there in 1934. He denied he had ever been anti-Semitic.[138]

During the Civil War, the epicentre of violence was in Poland.[139] The Poles were united in trying to regain the independence they had lost at the end of the eighteenth century, when the country had been partitioned between Russia, Prussia and Austria. In August 1920, the Poles, led by Józef Piłsudski, were able to stop Tukhachevsky just outside Warsaw in what became known (by Poles) as the Miracle of the Vistula (the river flowing through Warsaw). It was the only significant defeat of the so-called 'Red Napoleon'. The Treaty of Riga (March 1921) ended the Soviet–Polish conflict. The Poles gave up claims to Minsk in Belarus and Kyiv in Ukraine, but they achieved independence and expanded to the east, eventually annexing Vilnius (the main city in Lithuania) in 1922 and holding it until the Second World War.

Polish boundaries have shifted constantly. As Norman Davies remarked: 'Despite the Poles' own fervent belief in the *macierz* or "motherland", it is impossible to identify any fixed territorial base which has been permanently, exclusively, and inalienably, Polish.'[140]

Had the Red Army regained Warsaw, it could, in theory, have regrouped and marched to Berlin, Prague – even Budapest and Vienna – thus exporting the revolution. But that was never Lenin's intention, though he hoped that revolutions in the West, particularly in Germany, would come to Russia's rescue. The Soviet economy was in tatters, and the fighting in Central Asia, Siberia and the Far East was far from over.[141] So how did the Bolsheviks manage to triumph? One of their main advantages was the total disorganization, inefficiency and directionlessness of the Whites, whose only aim seemed to be a return to a sombre and miserable past. The Bolsheviks had the vision of a bright future. They had also inherited the centralized military bureaucracy of the old regime; they fought from the centre and not from the periphery, hence they had better communication lines, especially the railways.[142] Yet it does not follow that organization prevailed, even among the Bolsheviks. In Petrograd's First City Soviet, where the Bolsheviks were particularly powerful, matters were unplanned and there was little direction from top to bottom.[143] An intelligent appraisal by a historian writing in 1930 noted of the Bolsheviks:

Instead of a wonderfully organized revolutionary machine, moving majestically and irresistibly toward an assured victory, we see a much-divided party, kept together by the indomitable will of a single man, who himself was not completely sure of victory, but who was willing and able to stake everything on what he thought to be an excellent gambling chance. We now know also that to a very great extent he won by default.[144]

But the Bolsheviks had promised peace, land and bread, while the Whites' plan was never clear, except perhaps a return to the tsar or more wars. No peasant thought they would get land or bread from the Whites. Peace, bread and land had failed to materialize, but the Bolsheviks could argue that they wanted to withdraw from the war in Europe, that they had not started the civil wars, and land and bread would be obtainable once the fighting was over. The Reds lost some popularity during the Civil War. Lenin himself admitted 'that the proletariat saw no improvement of its position from Soviet Russia – if anything, it was often worse'. Workers were asking: 'What good has the Red Army done us, we are starving.'[145] Yet the Red Army managed to grow from 800,000 men in January 1919 to 3 million a year later.[146] By the end of the Civil War they claimed 5 million recruits, though it is unlikely that there could have been enough rifles, boots and food for all of them. They even succeeded in recruiting a considerable number of supporters in the countryside, as well as many officers and cadres from the existing army fighting in the West against the Entente powers.

There was also, of course, a Red Terror, whose casualties are difficult to calculate (as is the case for the White Terror). Richard Pipes mentions estimates of between 50,000 and 140,000, seeming to go for the higher figure without much justification.[147] Detachments of the Red Army perpetrated several massacres and brutalities throughout the Civil War in Ukraine.[148] However, the Bolshevik leadership often denounced anti-Jewish violence, punishing some perpetrators and instigators of pogroms.[149] Lenin was adamant in speaking against anti-Semitism. At the end of March 1919, he denounced anti-Jewish pogroms in no uncertain terms:

> Anti-Semitism means spreading enmity towards the Jews ... The landowners and capitalists tried to divert the hatred of the workers and peasants ... Only the most ignorant and downtrodden people can believe the lies and slander that are spread about the Jews. This is a survival of

ancient feudal times ... It is not the Jews who are the enemies of the working people. The enemies of the workers are the capitalists of all countries. Among the Jews there are working people, and they form the majority. They are our brothers, who, like us, are oppressed by capital; they are our comrades in the struggle for socialism.[150]

Earlier, the decree on anti-Semitism signed by Lenin on 27 July 1918 had been recorded on phonograph records and disseminated on trains, workers clubs and party meetings. 'In other words,' writes Elissa Bemporad, 'the Bolshevik condemnation of anti-Semitism was clear-cut, categorical and one of the most visible features of the new regime, maintained on the official level for all of Soviet history.' Thus, the Soviet Union became 'the only country in Europe in which holding antisemitic views was a crime no less than acting upon them'.[151] None of the White counter-revolutionaries pronounced themselves against anti-Semitism.

Red Terror was less pronounced than White Terror, largely because the Bolsheviks were more centrally organized, while their opponents consisted of disparate bands.[152] But slaughters can also be incited from above. In August 1918, Lenin prompted the Bolsheviks to enter a phase of Red Terror and, in blood-curdling tones, declared:

The kulaks are rabid foes of the Soviet government. Either the kulaks massacre vast numbers of workers, or the workers ruthlessly suppress the revolts of the predatory kulak minority of the people against the working people's government. There can be no middle course. Peace is out of the question ... The kulaks are the most brutal, callous and savage exploiters, who in the history of other countries have time and again restored the power of the landowners, tsars, priests and capitalists ... Ruthless war on the kulaks! Death to them! Hatred and contempt for the parties which defend them – the Right Socialist-Revolutionaries.[153]

When the circumstances changed, Lenin changed his views. Thus in February 1920 he declared that the proletarian revolution should 'create the new foundations of economic life side by side with petty peasant economy', and that the 'peasant, being dissatisfied, is demanding his legitimate rights – in exchange for grain he wants the industrial goods that we cannot give him until we have rehabilitated the economy'.[154] Once the Civil War was over, Lenin 'lost interest in the kulak objects of his hatred'.[155]

The White Terror was launched not just against the supporters of the Bolsheviks but on all sort of minorities, above all against the Jews. Most White military leaders were rabid anti-Semites and many were seriously convinced that the Bolshevik Revolution had been a Jewish conspiracy, a conviction sustained and buttressed by the fact that between a quarter and a third of the central committees of the Bolshevik and of the Socialist Revolutionary Parties were Jewish, and so were prominent Bolshevik leaders such as Trotsky, Kamenev and Zinoviev, not to speak of Rosa Luxemburg and Karl Radek in Poland, Karl Kautsky and Eduard Bernstein in Germany, Victor Adler and Otto Bauer in Austria, Béla Kun in Hungary, Emma Goldman in the United States – and of course Karl Marx, among many others.[156]

Thousands of Jews thronged to the Bolsheviks, whom they regarded as 'the most determined champions of the Revolution, and the most reliable internationalists'.[157] It is thus not surprising that the Civil War was marred by a larger number of pogroms than those which had taken place under the tsars. The infamous Kishinev pogrom of 1903, commemorated in Hayim Bialik's poignant Hebrew poem 'In the City of Slaughter', was a relatively minor affair in which only fifty people were killed and many more were injured. On a larger scale were the massacres, looting, humiliations and deportations of the Civil War, when 'Jews were killed on the roads, in the fields, on trains; sometimes whole families perished, and there was no one left to report on their fate'.[158] In Ukraine, some 1,500 anti-Jewish pogroms took place in which between 50,000 and 200,000 people perished.[159] In January 1919, near a *shtetl* in the Poltava province east of Kyiv, soldiers of the Ukrainian National Army forced Jewish men to undress and run naked in the snow. In order to exacerbate the gruesome entertainment, the victims were also ordered to sing, while the soldiers shot at them randomly: a 'carnival' of violence which was replicated all over Ukraine, home to a quarter of the Jews in the Tsarist Empire.[160] The perpetrators of the mass rape of Jewish women in the first half of 1919 (the Ukrainian *pogromschiki*) were largely soldiers of the Ukrainian National Army, as well as various apolitical gangs, but even Bolshevik troops participated in violence against women. It seems that public rapes created a 'bond' between the fighting men.[161]

It was the enormity of these pogroms more than the appeals of communism that sealed what Elissa Bemporad has called the Jewish–Bolshevik alliance.[162]

Many of these deeds were perpetrated by troops under the orders of Semen (or Symon) Petliura, who was president of the short-lived

Ukrainian People's Republic. I. S. Braude of the Russian Red Cross, who was also inspector of the Committee for Relief to Victims, reported after visiting the *shtetls* south of Kyiv that Petliura's army regiments perpetrated pogroms, and described in particular how on 10 July 1919, 'bandit packs, insurgents, groups, mobs, or simply peasants with pitchforks and scythes … beat, torture, and mutilate Jews'.[163] Defeated in the winter of 1919, Petliura withdrew to Poland and eventually lived in exile in Paris. In 1926, he was murdered by Samuel Schwarzbard, a Jewish anarchist (and Yiddish poet). After a famous trial, Schwarzbard was acquitted by a jury; his defence was that he was avenging the victims of Petliura's pogroms. In present-day Ukraine, Petliura is regarded by many as a national hero and is celebrated in many folk songs. There are monuments, statues and museums dedicated to him in Kyiv, the Ukrainian capital, and in Poltava where he was born.[164]

Though everyone can play the counterfactual game, it is not absurd to suggest that the more likely alternative to the Reds were not enlightened liberals or progressive social-democrats but odious strongmen comparable to Hitler and Mussolini.[165] After all, on the eve of the Second World War there was not a single liberal democracy in Eastern Europe: dictators ranged from King Boris in Bulgaria to King Zog in Albania, Antanas Smetona in Lithuania, King Alexander in Yugoslavia, Konstantin Päts in Estonia, Karlis Ulmanis in Latvia, King Carol in Romania and Admiral Miklos Horthy in Hungary, and there was a military regime in Poland. In the Ottoman Empire the massacre of the Armenians had already started during the First World War, and when the empire was dismembered, a dictator, Kemal Atatürk, emerged. In Western Europe, lest we forget, there was Mussolini in Italy, Hitler in Germany (with Austria annexed), Franco in Spain, Ioannis Metaxas in Greece, António de Oliveira Salazar in Portugal and Engelbert Dollfuss in Austria.

One does not need to refer to the Russian character or the backwardness of its past to explain the years of violence. Violence was intrinsic to European history. In the second half of the nineteenth century, violence was exported to the colonies, and here the main responsibility was with the two great civilized liberal democracies: France and Great Britain. In the first half of the twentieth century, violence, authoritarianism, murder and genocide plagued the whole of Europe – a historical dimension often forgotten by those who speak glibly of 'European values'.

Building socialism

By 1922, the communists had overcome all their political enemies: the Whites had been defeated, the liberals had emigrated and the Socialist Revolutionaries had been eliminated from political life – while Western countries were beginning to tolerate the new Soviet Union, at least at the diplomatic level. In 1922 Weimar Germany and Soviet Russia signed the Treaty of Rapallo renouncing territorial and financial claims on each other. Fear of internal Red subversion continued, but by 1924 the USSR had been recognized by the main European states, including Britain, France, Germany and Italy. The US waited until 1933. Lenin's Bolsheviks, almost irrelevant in the February Revolution, had won the day. They were helped by the war and the mistakes of their rivals and opponents. As Machiavelli would have said, Lenin had not only *Virtù* – the ability and genius to achieve one's goal – but also *Fortuna*, the circumstances individuals cannot control and without which no amount of *Virtù* could work its magic.[166]

However, the civil war, coming immediately after the three years of the First World War, had further aggravated the economic conditions of the country, bringing about destruction, harvest failures, fodder shortages and loss of cattle. The railways, essential for supplying food to the cities, were barely functioning. One of the few positive developments was that as the Bolsheviks regained territories such as Ukraine, they also regained food-producing land.

Lenin was fully aware that the Bolsheviks had no idea how to build a communist society. He declared in 1920:

> But if we are to build a communist society, let us frankly admit our complete inability to conduct affairs, to be organisers and administrators. We must approach the matter with the greatest caution, bearing in mind that only that proletarian is class-conscious who is able to prepare the bourgeois expert for the forthcoming navigation season and who does not waste his time and energy, more than enough of which is always wasted on corporate management.[167]

The rather utopian vision expressed in *State and Revolution*, written while he was underground, had morphed. Now the talk was of increasing production, discipline and control. Writing in 1923, as he approached death, Lenin noted: 'In times of revolution the utmost flexibility is demanded.'[168] Lenin's new slogans included rather mundane and obvious assignations:

> Keep regular and honest accounts of money, manage economically, do not be lazy, do not steal, observe the strictest labour discipline – it is these slogans, justly scorned by the revolutionary proletariat when the bourgeoisie used them to conceal its rule as an exploiting class, that are now, since the overthrow of the bourgeoisie, becoming the immediate and the principal slogans of the moment.[169]

During the Civil War, the main economic problem was relatively simple: how to obtain a surplus from the countryside to feed the soldiers and industrial workers without antagonizing the peasantry excessively – exactly the same problem facing the tsarist regime during the First World War. The answer adopted by the Bolsheviks was to militarize the economy further. The economic policies they adopted, known as War Communism, consisted in the forced requisition of the surplus produced by the peasantry, while taking over some industries as well as the banks. Which industries should be taken over was not clear. Bukharin and Preobrazhensky, in their popular and soon outdated *ABC of Communism* written in the middle of the Civil War, thought that only big firms should be nationalized.[170]

In fact, there was not much of a plan: no priorities were established as to which industry or firm should be taken over, and some of the nationalizations and expropriation of enterprises occurred because of initiatives from below.[171] The overall confusion was made evident when, in 1918, it was decided to nationalize the music-publishing industry, along with the confectionery industry in Moscow (now returned as the country's capital) and Petrograd – hardly central to the economy.[172]

The phrase 'War Communism' could be regarded as an attempt to justify the new policies in ideological terms, while also suggesting that such measures would be temporary, lasting only for the duration of the war. As Lenin recognized, War Communism 'was forced on us by extreme want, ruin and war', adding: 'It was the war and the ruin that forced us into War Communism. It was not, and could not be, a policy that corresponded to the economic tasks of the proletariat.'[173] War Communism was an emergency and improvised measure. Ideological justifications were provided by the Bolsheviks at the time, and later by Soviet historians who described it as the continuation of the revolution in its path towards socialism. Cold War historians have tended to adopt a similar position: ideology and Marxism remains the key explanatory factor.[174] Justifications should not have been necessary. Any economy, capitalist or socialist, would have had to take emergency measures during a major conflict, as indeed all did during the two world wars.[175]

In Russia the situation was particularly disastrous. In 1920–21, there was a major peasant revolt in the Tambov region (see above). In the naval base of Kronstadt, there was a rebellion by sailors in March 1921, just as the Civil War was abating and the Bolsheviks were moving away from War Communism. The uprising was particularly worrying because the sailors and soldiers in Kronstadt (known as the Fortress of the Revolution) had been key participants in both the February and the October Revolutions, when Trotsky hailed: 'Long live Red Kronstadt, the pride and glory of the revolution.'[176] The privations of War Communism had taken their toll, and the Kronstadt soldiers' anger was directed not against Soviet power as such, but against the Bolshevik government.[177]

The slogan 'Soviet power without the Bolsheviks' was derided by Lenin as a not-so-veiled attempt to undo the gains of the revolution. It was supported, he explained, by Mensheviks and Socialist Revolutionaries and hailed by émigré liberals and their leader, Pavel Milyukov, in exile in France, who realized that the slogan 'all power to the Soviets' was still popular but who hoped, vainly, to use it as an opportunity to overthrow the communists. His understanding of the local situation was minimal. Lenin, however, refrained from declaring that Kronstadt was a 'White conspiracy' (as many Soviet historians subsequently claimed), and referred instead to the 'Kronstadt events', conceding that there were economic factors involved, particularly the sharply deteriorating conditions of the peasantry.[178] What set Kronstadt off were the waves of peasant risings throughout the country and the working-class unrest in Petrograd.[179] The sailors, many of them of peasant extraction, exhibited a blend of anarchism and Slavic nationalism with a touch of traditional anti-Semitism, expressed in the slogan 'beat communists and Jews'.[180] The Bolsheviks feared that the mutiny (as they called it) would spread to the rest of the country.[181] The brutal suppression of Kronstadt was directed by Trotsky as commissar for war and implemented by Tukhachevsky, who had also crushed the Tambov rebellion. At the height of the Civil War, Trotsky was certain that the new state could 'but punish others – those who are clearly infringing labour solidarity, undermining the common work, and seriously impairing the Socialist renaissance of the country. Repression for the attainment of economic ends is a necessary weapon of the Socialist dictatorship.'[182]

Having suppressed the 'mutiny', the Bolsheviks, now in charge of vast areas (including the Caucasus, Ukraine, Georgia, Armenia and Siberia), had to make their peace with the peasants. The solution was the New Economic Policy (NEP), launched at the Tenth Party Congress in March 1921. The main concession was what Lenin called 'the Tax in Kind'. The peasant surplus was no longer going to be requisitioned. The peasants would pay a tax in kind (later changed to a money tax) and then decide what to do with their surplus, which is what would normally happen in a market economy. The objective, explained Lenin, was to take 'measures that will immediately increase the productive forces of peasant farming'. This 'putting the peasantry in the forefront', he added, presumably anticipating criticism, is not a 'renunciation of the dictatorship of the proletariat', though 'it is the revival of the petty bourgeoisie and of capitalism on the basis of some freedom of trade (if only local). That much is certain, and it is ridiculous to shut our eyes to it', adding that, faced with millions of small producers, 'to prohibit entirely, to put the lock on all development of private, non-state exchange, i.e., trade, i.e., capitalism ... would be foolish and suicidal'.[183]

Socialism was being redefined. It was no longer justified on the traditional ground that the more the means of production were collectively owned the nearer one was to the final objective: what mattered was who controlled the political system. In other words, one could have a partially capitalist economy (or state capitalist economy) and at the same time the 'dictatorship of the proletariat'. 'Can the Soviet state and the dictatorship of the proletariat be combined with state capitalism? Are they compatible?', Lenin asked rhetorically, replying: 'Of course they are.'[184] He added, disarmingly: 'Our bureaucratic practices prove that we are still doing a very bad job of it. We must not be afraid to admit that in this respect *we still have a great deal to learn from the capitalist.*'[185] This, of course, did not mean a total rebirth of market forces.[186]

The New Economic Policy lasted seven years (1921–28). Bukharin, who had earlier been one of the main spokesmen for the Left Opposition (fighting the Treaty of Brest-Litovsk and supporting War Communism), changed tack and became the chief champion of the NEP. Lenin was no longer around to use his prestige to keep the party united. Having been seriously ailing towards the end of 1921, he died on 21 January 1924. Five days later, Petrograd was renamed Leningrad. The central question remained: how to satisfy the peasants without alienating the workers. The USSR (as Soviet Russia had become in 1922), was now facing its worst famine since 1891. Estimates of the number of dead vary: 5 million is the figure most frequently quoted. Severe drought and failed harvests, continuous wars since 1914, but also the communist failure to admit openly the true gravity of the situation for fear of being blamed must account for the large number of deaths.[187] Eventually the authorities had to accept relief help from the American Relief Administration directed by Herbert Hoover, who became president of the US in 1929. With some justification they regarded the American aid as partly dictated by the hope of containing Bolshevism.

Having lost any hopes of a revolution in the West, the Bolsheviks had no choice but to continue attempting to construct a new society, hopefully with a prosperous peasantry and a growing working class. This was the basis of the NEP, or, as Bukharin put it in 1925, building socialism 'at a snail's pace'.[188] The NEP may just have been a tactical move, dictated by circumstances. Whether or not it was the proper framework for the construction of socialism was a matter of emphasis. Lenin and Trotsky tended towards the former. Bukharin had earlier thought that it was not a

> strategic retreat, but the solution to a large social, organizational problem ... We will say frankly: we tried to take on ourselves the organization of everything – even the organization of the peasants and the millions of small producers ... this is madness.[189]

The NEP period was also one of significant social advance. There were campaigns against anti-Semitism and illiteracy, mass education drives and various affirmative action movements. While in the West the feminist movement of 1920 was focused mainly on one issue, the suffrage, in the USSR there was a serious attempt to mobilize women around their overall social role through the Zhenotdel (the Communist Party's Women's Section) established in 1919 by the two leading revolutionary feminists, Alexandra Kollontai and Inessa Armand. This initiative encountered serious opposition from many men, particularly in Central Asia, where on each International Women's Day thousands of women would assemble in the marketplaces of eastern Soviet lands and defiantly tear off their veils.[190] Soon after the revolution, religious control over marriage was abolished, civil marriage was recognized, divorce was simplified and abortion was legalized. Some of these measures were partially repealed in the 1930s, but women had been granted separate earnings and complete legal and civic equality. The Zhenotdel, with the strong support of Lenin (other Bolsheviks were less keen) fought against domestic slavery and the double standard. It also directly intervened in family disputes on the side of beleaguered wives. While women started to achieve higher levels of industrial skill, Zhenotdel agents also enforced labour protection for women, as well as maternity care.[191] By 1930 the centralizing tendencies within the Communist Party were such than any semi-autonomous organization had become a cause for anxiety. The Party abolished Zhenotdel, without undoing its previous work.

During the NEP period, the peasants – or at least the prosperous ones, the kulaks, pejoratively called NEP men – became richer, while the workers and poorer peasants lagged behind. The kulaks were powerful not because they had a party or a strong lobbying organization – they had neither – but because of their position in the economy. As Anastas Mikoyan, an associate of Stalin, explained in 1928: 'The real bulk of the grain surplus was owned by the [middle peasants], who were often in no hurry to sell, if the appropriate quantities of consumers' goods which they needed to buy were not available.'[192] Poorer peasants, those without little livestock or food reserves, were forced to sell at a disadvantage. The kulaks, with their hard-earned money, would want to buy consumer goods, stimulating the growth of light industries and not the heavy industries which were supposed to provide the backbone of the new socialist society.[193] With the disappearance of aristocrats and capitalists, the NEP men were, as Lenin called them, the 'new bourgeoisie'.[194] Getting rid of aristocrats and capitalists was feasible: aristocrats were useless, and managers could be hired to replace capitalists. Getting rid of the peasants was impossible.[195] The NEP was, as Moshe Lewin put it, 'a pact with the devil'.[196] By 1928–29 it seemed to many that the NEP was not working satisfactorily, as unemployment was rising and peasants were not marketing an adequate quantity of grain.[197]

The new left opposition around Preobrazhensky, Trotsky, Kamenev and Zinoviev warned of the dangers ahead. The new class of kulaks would become an obstacle to socialism. Should peasants be allowed to get richer and richer? The so-called moderates (which then included Stalin!) thought that industrialization should proceed slowly. Vladimir Bazarov, the leading non-party economist on Gosplan, the State Planning Commission, believed that the problems of reconstruction and economic growth could be solved by maintaining elements of the market, as envisaged by the NEP, while the massive outlays of capital required for growth could come from the state.[198] In other words, you could have the NEP and socialism.

A period of internecine strife followed. Stalin and Bukharin joined forces to expel Trotsky, who had few supporters inside the Party. Only then did Stalin move to the left (one of his many turns) and adopted

Preobrazhensky's position, calling for rapid industrialization and forcing peasants to give up larger and larger parts of their surpluses.[199] Bukharin as well as Kamenev remained staunchly in favour of the NEP.[200]

Once Trotsky and his comrades were out of the way, Stalin dealt swiftly with Bukharin, who almost as swiftly recanted, declaring to the Central Committee of December 1930: 'It has become necessary, above all, to crush the kulaks.' In this way he approved Stalin's plan to give the poor peasants, as a collective, the land of the kulaks in the form of kolkhoz – what came to be known as collectivization.[201] What collectivization meant was still extremely vague: it was not even clear whether what was meant was voluntary or compulsory collectivization.[202] In fact, there had been few discussions of collectivization before 1930. The kolkhozes, then, were fairly primitive: they had neither schools nor hospitals nor newspapers; they lacked personnel or trained agronomists; and a majority of them were in backward regions such as the North Caucasus.[203] One thing was certain: the peasants did not want the kolkhozes. For many it was like returning to serfdom – all the more so when, in 1932, restrictions on mobility were introduced, as well as state control over procurements and prices on collective farms. What this meant was that the state was appropriating much of the produce while paying low prices for them.[204]

The idea behind the 'revolution from above', as it was called, was to achieve rapid industrialization – the aim not only of the Bolsheviks but also of virtually all Russian elites since the Emancipation Reforms of 1861. It would also increase the power of the party, which had been diminished by the NEP, which had relied on market forces to determine the pace of economic development.

Was the NEP compatible with rapid industrialization? Was the collectivization of agriculture necessary for industrial development? These questions have divided specialists of Soviet history.[205] E. H. Carr and R. W. Davies thought Bukharin's position was unrealistic or unworkable. They held that rapid industrialization could not have been achieved with the kind of market economy that prevailed in the 1920s; so did Theda Skocpol. Others, particularly Stephen Cohen, regarded Bukharin as the only real alternative to Stalin.[206] Moshe Lewin thought that a previously well-organized state collective sector might have made collectivization less disastrous. The major error was to have destroyed the NEP before any alternative structures had taken place.[207] Far from being a controlled experiment, the construction of socialism turned out to be a series of fumbles in the dark.

In any case, on the basis of data provided in the 1960s by the Soviet economic historian Alexander A. Barsov, some analysts have pointed out that, at best, collectivization's contribution to industrialization was modest.[208] The shift away from the NEP was probably also due to the communists' not unfounded perception that, faced with a hostile anti-communist world, it was necessary to build up one's defence industry.[209]

Stalin's position had now shifted decisively in favour of rapid industrialization. This appealed to a party formed largely during the years of revolution and civil war. Party cadres may have been brave revolutionaries, but they did not have the expertise required to build a state. Lenin had been forced to promote bourgeois experts, but Stalin went one step further and sought to form experts out of the new generation of workers. During the First Five-Year Plan (1928–32), he initiated a programme through which over 100,000 workers were sent to higher technical schools. The Great Purges, which took the form of expulsion from the Party from 1933 and a far more deadly form after 1936, accelerated the upward mobility of the newly enrolled technicians. Engineering, rather than Marxism–Leninism, became the required source of knowledge. Ideology consisted simply in doing what one was told.[210] As Stalin declared in 1931:

> We need commanding and engineering-technical cadres capable of understanding the policies of the working class ... and prepared to carry them out conscientiously. What does that mean? It means that our country has entered the phase of development when *the working class must create its own productive-technical intelligentsia*, capable of standing up for its own interests in production.[211]

Cadres were regarded by Stalin as the real backbone of the country. In a conversation with Georgi Dimitrov, the Bulgarian-born leader of the Comintern, Stalin remarked that though Trotsky was, after Lenin, the most popular man in the country in the 1920s – though not in the party – he, Stalin, was then 'little known' by the masses. But the middle cadres, whom Trotsky 'completely ignored', knew who he (Stalin) was and what he stood for:

> A great deal is said about great leaders ... But ... the main thing here is the middle cadres ... They are the ones who choose the leader, explain our positions to the masses, and ensure the success of our cause.[212]

Recruiting workers to the party meant that there were, for the first time in Russian history, some prospects for young workers to be upwardly mobile thanks to 'the party of the proletariat'.[213] The way to do away with bourgeois experts was to form proletarian ones, loyal to the communists. They would promote rapid industrialization, and hence 'socialism in one country' – a particularly appealing blend of socialism and nationalism. Trusting in expert engineers, rather than in Marxists, was the way forward. Stalin could be left to define the correct Marxist line. As a result, many subsequent communist leaders (Nikita Khrushchev, Lavrentiy Beria, Andrei Gromyko, Leonid Brezhnev, Alexei Kosygin, Yuri Andropov and many others) had technical qualifications, instead of being, as in many Western countries, lawyers or social scientists or former soldiers. And many Soviet leaders were not Russian: Stalin was from Georgia, as was Lavrentiy Beria; Felix Dzerzhinsky, founder of the secret police organizations Cheka and OGPU, was Polish. One of his successors, Genrikh Yagoda, head of the NKVD, was Jewish (then considered a nationality in the USSR); Anastas Mikoyan (deputy prime minister, 1955–64 and briefly head of state, 1964–5) was Armenian. Nikita Khrushchev was raised in Ukraine, Konstantin Chernenko was Ukrainian and Leonid Brezhnev was born in Ukraine to a Ukrainian mother. Yuri Andropov was half Jewish, while Andrei Gromyko was from Belarus.

Industrialization was a partial success, but the collectivization of agriculture was a catastrophe.[214] Between 1928 and 1932 half the country's livestock herd was lost, whether because the more prosperous peasants responded to forced collectivization by slaughtering their livestock or because food was redirected towards workers. There was late sowing, shoddy harvesting and poor maintenance of machinery. Mechanics left the villages for jobs in the cities, so that as many as 75 per cent of all tractors could not be repaired.[215] Between 1928 and 1935 some 17 million peasants settled in cities, thus doubling the urban population in an incredibly short time.[216] As Sheila Fitzpatrick has written: 'Malice, anger, and bitterness were rife in the village in the decade after collectivization' – and, though the state and its agents were the primary objects of peasant resentment, 'a great deal of peasant anger was directed against other peasants'.[217] It does not follow from any of this that keeping the NEP would have achieved a better or similar rate of industrialization.[218]

The Soviet state responded by toning down the tempo of collectivization. The peasants would be allowed to cultivate private plots and sell their produce at market prices. Stalin announced the changes with a famous article called 'Dizzy with Success' (2 March 1930), trying to make what was obviously a retreat appear as a necessary step back, and blaming local officials for implementing his policies too enthusiastically, while also reminding them: 'The collective-farm movement must rest on the active support of the main mass of the peasantry.'[219]

What *was* successful was industrialization. The first Five Year Plan (1928–32) was good for the workers, as production in steel, mining and chemicals went up, in contrast with the Great Depression in the West.[220] Against all expectations the industrial workforce more than doubled, and growth rates were high. Western estimates of industrial growth between 1928 and 1937 or 1940 range from 7.1 to 13.6 per cent, while official Soviet figures estimated growth at 16.8 per cent. Even the lowest estimate is substantial.[221] If collectivization helped at all in this achievement, it was only because the damages to agriculture contributed to the huge influx of labour from the countryside. This was particularly pronounced in Ukraine, where the dispossessed peasants moved into the coal and iron and steel industries. Between 1928 and 1932, about 12 million people, some voluntarily, some forcibly, moved from the countryside to the towns. Some peasants were deported from the villages in connection with dekulakization. Of these, about half ended up as industrial wage earners. If 39 per cent of peasants were still uncollectivized in 1932, by 1937 it was only 7 per cent.[222]

Fatalities

The price paid was tremendous. In 1933 the Soviet Union suffered a terrible famine which hit, in particular, Ukraine, the Volga region, the Caucasus, part of the Urals and Kazakhstan. Of course this was not reported in the USSR, while harvest failures in the rest of the world were.[223] The death toll may have amounted to 6 million people; Stephen Wheatcroft has suggested 4–5 million.[224] Stephen Kotkin goes for 'probably' 5–7 million, with 3.5 million in Ukraine alone (out of a population of 33 million), but 1.2–1.4 million in Kazakhstan (population of 6.5 million).[225] Others have estimated the losses in Ukraine alone to be in the region of 2.6 million, which would confirm the widely held view that, in proportion to population, the death toll in Kazakhstan was much higher.[226] As Kotkin wrote: 'There was no "Ukrainian" famine; the famine was Soviet.'[227] Davies and Wheatcroft, while acknowledging that Stalin was more concerned with the fate of industrialization than with the lives of the peasants, think it is 'inherently impossible to estimate the number of deaths from the numerous policy decisions approved by Stalin'.[228] 'In the end,' Catherine Merridale has written, 'historians will have to accept that a precise statistical balance sheet of the famine can never be drawn.'[229]

The bad harvest of 1932 may have been a major factor in the famine, as well as kulak resistance. The regime was still responsible for the deprivation and suffering of the population, but, contrary to what some Ukrainian nationalists and their sympathizers claim, the famine was the result of a failure of economic policy, of Stalin's 'revolution from above' and of a bad harvest, rather than of a deliberate genocidal policy against Ukrainians.[230] The same can be said about the tremendous losses due to the famine in Kazakhstan. The major cause for the famine there was, as in Ukraine, collectivization rather than any plan by Stalin to destroy all Kazakhs.[231] What is also undeniable is Stalin's negative attitude towards the peasantry and the assumption that difficulties were caused by enemy sabotage or by 'enemies of the people'. His disregard for peasant lives and use of violence against them has been well documented.[232]

It was obvious that the rich peasants, the kulaks, wanted to keep their land and that the poor peasants wanted more land for themselves, not to work in a collective farm. Violence during collectivization was widespread, and it was not just directed from on high; it was often the result of fear mixed with the breakdown of law and order. There was violence against Soviet officials by angry kulaks, violence against local peasants who were Soviet activists, violence against poor peasants (*bedniaks*) who had informed on other peasants. As Sheila Fitzpatrick has written, young Komsomol enthusiasts 'charged around in a state of wild excitement, unmasking Rightists and class enemies, intimidating bureaucrats, and destroying anything they could find of the old world'. Many peasants, not unjustifiably, regarded collectivization as a threat to a traditional way of life. This led to 'hysterical' rumours that all kolkhozniks 'be forced to dress like convicts; that wives would become common property', and so on.[233]

Then there were the purges and the deportations of 1937–38, mainly involving the Party and the state bureaucracy: managers rather than the intelligentsia, as is commonly believed, and more in towns than in the countryside.[234] The authority of managers was undermined, encouraging 'workers to break rules, ignore orders, and treat their bosses disrespectfully'.[235] It was a recipe for chaos. As the Great Purges were about to begin in 1936, the Party also launched a new Constitution which, at least on paper, appeared remarkably liberal and democratic, with free elections under the banner of universal suffrage. As Arch Getty has written, what probably occurred is not that 'Stalin planned all along only to stage a democratic farce', because if he had, 'he would not have proclaimed one thing for so long (contested elections), only to enact the opposite'. What happened, once again, was that the regime had not worked out fully the implication of contested democratic elections. Once it did, it opted to restrict the elections to single candidates and to allow only one party, though even the possibility of write-ins or crossed-out ballots worried the regime.[236] They did not need to be worried: most people simply put the ballot in the box; many potential dissidents refrained from running the risk of entering a booth, under the eyes of officials, to cross out names and write in the ones they wanted. The Constitution remained a fig leaf fooling some foreign admirers such as Beatrice and Sidney Webb, of Fabian fame, who wrote in 1942: 'It is clear that tested by the Constitution of the Soviet Union as revised and enacted in 1936, the USSR is the most inclusive and equalised democracy in the world.'[237] In 1936 an essay by Joseph R. Starr in the *American Political Science Review* treated the Constitution seriously. While conceding that it does not mean that 'the Communist dictatorship is relaxing its hold, nor that the dictatorship of the proletariat is to be replaced by conventional bourgeois democracy', Starr argued that 'the guaranties of rights, the electoral reforms, and the tendencies towards parliamentarism are not mere shams, designed to hoodwink the Russian people'.[238]

Though few dispute the existence of the purges (there do not seem to be purge deniers as there are some Holocaust deniers), scholars are divided on the death toll arising from them, on the causes of the purges and on the degree of Stalin's direct responsibility. Contrary to common belief, Stalin and his party were never organized enough to be in full control of everything that happened, even though this was the impression they wanted to convey. The country was far from being directed centrally from an all-knowing apparatus (as both Stalinists and many Cold War historians maintain).

The decision to accelerate industrialization in the heavy-industry sector, seen as necessary should the USSR be attacked from the outside – which is what happened in 1941 – meant that consumer goods would not be available for the citizenry. The new regime was therefore lacking what would have constituted an incentive to increase labour productivity. After all, in a capitalist society, workers do not work because they are ideologically supportive of capitalism (though some are) but because they need the work and think that the system will deliver consumer goods and a higher standard of living. Communism required a semi-religious ideological commitment: the prospect of a bright communist future – a new Jerusalem – or the fear that there would be a return to an unpleasant past. Since it was obvious that few would hold such views, suspicion of conspiracies, plots, sabotage, disloyalty, noncompliance, mutinies and counter-revolution were not just paranoid delusions lurking in Stalin's mind: they were intrinsic to the system. The idea of punishing 'the slightest violation of discipline … severely, sternly, ruthlessly' was frequently made early on by Lenin.[239]

The purges got out of hand, and the system became increasingly dysfunctional. People were recruited into the party at an increased rate.[240] Later many members were expelled, then they were reinstated. Perhaps 1.5 million had left the party between 1922 and 1935 by not renewing their membership and paying their dues.[241] In 1936 Stalin objected that too many had been expelled: he wrote a letter to regional party secretaries complaining that the rank and file was excessively repressed. Consequently, many expelled party members were reinstated, shortly before the purges.[242] Most members knew little about communism or Marxism, or even of their party's history. Some Bolsheviks admitted (in 1920) that many party members were politically semi-literate.[243]

The Party was unable to penetrate every corner. In some areas, such as Kazakhstan, the districts had no telephone links with their regional centres, let alone with its capital Akmolinsk (formerly Astana), or Moscow.[244] Short messages could be sent by telegraph, longer ones by courier. Corruption was rampant. Valuable party membership cards which gave access to resources were passed on from dead relatives.[245] Functionaries, faced with fanciful targets, reported fictitious statistics; peasants resisted passively; workers pretended to work. Party and state bureaucracy responded with procrastination and deception.[246] When something went wrong, the search for culprits, real or imaginary, was on. 'Enemies' were found, denounced as wreckers, kulaks and counter-revolutionaries, agitators and ex-oppositionists worming their way even into the Kremlin. Complaining or criticizing was risky.[247] As Moshe Lewin wrote: 'All this helped to spread a perception among the top ranks that their power was actually more fragile than it seemed.'[248]

A study of the archives of Novosibirsk in Western Siberia shows how important were regional leaders in the implementation of what they thought, or chose to think, were Stalin's policies, and how they tried to reconcile and fulfil the centre's contradictory directives.[249] According to the historian Arch Getty, 'like a psychotic mass killer who begins shooting in all directions', Stalin's centre 'opened fire on vague targets, giving local officials license to kill whomever they saw fit'. Stalin's regime 'resembled not so much a disciplined army as a poorly trained and irregular force ... and the aftermath resembled the chaos of a battlefield'.[250] Yevgenia Ginzburg, who spent years in the Gulag, refers in her memoirs (*Journey into the Whirlwind*, 1967) to a prisoner originally charged with Trotskyism, but when it was found 'they had exceeded the quota for Trotskyites'; she, being a Tartar, was charged with 'bourgeois nationalism'.[251] Local party leaders, afraid of being accused as 'enemies of the people', found it convenient to launch repressive campaigns against others to deflect accusations against themselves.[252] This might explain Stalin's increasing dissatisfaction with regional subordinates, who were either heavy-handed and ineffective or simply dragged their feet.[253] Among the so-called 'socially harmful elements' arrested and prosecuted were a variety of non-political 'transgressors', such as vagabonds, indigents, criminals, ex-convicts and gypsies.[254] Bandits were regarded as counter-revolutionaries and 'socially dangerous' elements; some of the gang leaders were former kulaks or members of non-Russian ethnic populations.[255]

The terror was unlikely to have been planned before 1936, or even planned at all. There were too many 'twists and turns of policy, crackdowns followed by real liberalization, inexplicable and contradictory changes ... personnel shuffles and reshuffles throughout the 1930s'. These do not suggest a plan for terror but rather constant indecision, false starts and short-term improvisation. It is thus simplistic to represent the complex political evolution of the country in the 1930s as the realization of a coherent and uniformly executed strategy led by an 'omnipotent' dictator totally in control of everything.[256] Stalin, of course, had real enemies, not only imaginary ones – from angry peasants to anxious or incompetent bureaucrats who in turn uncovered 'enemies', scapegoats, and 'counter-revolutionaries' among other bureaucrats.[257] Not all specialists would agree with this analysis: Oleg Khlevniuk, a Russian historian of Stalinism, for example, claims that the Great Terror was 'a series of centralized, planned mass operation that were conducted on the basis of Politburo decisions, that is, Stalin's decision'.[258]

Estimates of those who died in the Great Purges vary considerably. The number of those executed in the period 1937–38 is likely to be in the hundreds of thousands rather than the millions often assumed. Alec Nove estimated that the numbers shot in 1921–53 may have exceeded 800,000 but not 1 million.[259] J. Arch Getty estimated that 386,798 people were actually shot; Khlevniuk puts the number at 700,000.[260] But many also died in the Gulag because of the terrible conditions, pushing the numbers up to 1.5 million.[261] According to Stephen Wheatcroft, a specialist on the purges, the population detained in the Gulag system in the late 1930s was probably 4–5 million.[262] The controversy on numbers has been raging ever since, with the Western press, for obvious reasons, preferring the higher estimates of traditional Cold Warriors such as Robert Conquest. What has never been in dispute by either side is the enormity of the Red Terror in the USSR.[263]

Some, of course, were deported for criminal offences; but since some of these were categorized as counter-revolutionary, it is difficult to disentangle one from the other. When is a smuggler, a pilferer or an incompetent worker also a state saboteur or a counter-revolutionary? Ethnic Russians and Latvians were over-represented among the victims, probably because they were also over-represented in the state apparatus and in the party.[264] The deportations declined a little during the war but increased again in Stalin's final years (he died in 1953), though executions were much reduced.[265]

The fear of internal enemies was partly justified by the perceived threat from the West. As Geoffrey Roberts has pointed out: 'The fascist war threat was an all-pervasive theme of Soviet foreign and domestic policies in the 1930s.'[266] Stalin, like Lenin, felt that the USSR was taking part in an 'international civil war' against capitalist countries and that he needed to defend communism from 'the West'.[267] Fear of a Fifth Column which would be complicit with foreign powers in case of an invasion led to the persecution and deportation of national minorities in the USSR, such as Latvians, Estonians, Germans, Greeks, Finns and Koreans (massively deported from the Far East to Kazakhstan and Uzbekistan in September–October 1937).[268]

Fears of external intervention were not unfounded. Hitler had long made clear that the search for a living space or *Lebensraum* for Germans entailed the subjugation and enslavement of the Slavic people (all *Untermenschen* – subhuman) and establishing the Germans as a master race in western Russia. In March 1936 Hitler was allowed by Britain and France to remilitarize the Rhineland. Britain and France remained passive while, with help from Fascist Italy and Nazi Germany, democracy was suppressed in Spain. In 1936, Germany, Japan and Italy signed the anti-Comintern pact; then Japan invaded China; then France and Britain turned down Stalin's offer of an anti-fascist alliance while letting the Nazis proceed with the takeover of Austria and Czechoslovakia.[269] The threats from Japan, Germany and fascist Italy and Spain, and the deep anti-communism of France, Britain and the United States were used to justify rapid industrialization, as well as the purges required to get rid of traitors and spies.[270] No wonder Stalin was in constant fear that the West would not just fail to protect the USSR from Nazi Germany but would look on with satisfaction if Hitler launched an attack on it. This explains his last-minute decision to enter a pact with Hitler in 1939.[271]

Russians – who had experienced since the beginning of the century the war with Japan (1904–05), the Great War, two revolutions, a Civil War, two famines, Stalin's purges, rapid industrialization and the devastating collectivization of agriculture – may have come to believe that war and disasters were a natural part of everyday life. And everyday life was grim anyway: food and clothing were in short supply, bureaucratic red tape 'turned everyday life into a nightmare' and massive migration from the rural sector led to crowded apartments: 'The 1930s was a decade of enormous privation and hardship for the Soviet people, much worse than the 1920s.'[272]

The tone of impending doom had already been captured early on by Stalin himself in his famous 1931 speech to the First All-Union Conference of Leading Personnel of Socialist Industry:

> To slacken the tempo would mean falling behind. And those who fall behind get beaten. But we do not want to be beaten. No, we refuse to be beaten! One feature of the history of old Russia was the continual beatings she suffered because of her backwardness. She was beaten by the Mongol khans. She was beaten by the Turkish beys. She was beaten by the Swedish feudal lords. She was beaten by the Polish and Lithuanian gentry. She was beaten by the British and French capitalists. She was beaten by the Japanese barons. All beat her -because of her backwardness, because of her military backwardness, cultural backwardness, political backwardness, industrial backwardness, agricultural backwardness.[273]

He concluded: 'That is why we must no longer lag behind.'

Consciousness of its own backwardness was a well-established theme in Russia, ever since the days of Peter the Great, and was constantly aired by its intelligentsia. Such consciousness never really existed in England, France or the US, but it exists almost everywhere else. The price paid for catching up was enormous. In all countries the secret police and intelligence agencies always overestimate the perception of internal threats – partly to bolster their jobs, partly to cover their backs, just in case. But their Russian counterparts were also protecting their own lives: any failure would mean death or deportation – hence their full participation in the regime of terror. Many of these executioners were in turn executed. Executions reached upward, into the higher echelons of the party and of the state. Grigory Zinoviev and Lev Kamenev, who had opposed Stalin (and Lenin) were executed along with and senior generals and even with Mikhail Tukhachevsky, the Red Napoleon, hero of the Civil War, accused absurdly of collusion with Nazi Germany. Bukharin was tried and executed in 1938. Trotsky was exiled in 1929 and killed in Mexico in 1940 by a Spanish communist, presumably on Stalin's orders. Karl Radek died in a labour camp. Even Genrikh Yagoda, head of the NKVD (People's Commissariat for Internal Affairs, the main body in charge of the purges), was tried and executed, as was his successor Nikolai Yezhov, who was in turn succeeded by Lavrentiy Beria, shot in 1953 some months after Stalin's death.

Stalin was surrounded by people who feared him, and he feared them. The poet Osip Mandelstam, just released from internal exile, wrote the 'Stalin Epigram' in 1933, for which he was arrested, then released. In the poem he described the subservient clique around Stalin ('a riff-raff of scraggy-necked chiefs') in no uncertain terms:

> He plays with the lackeydoms of half-men
> [...]
> He forges decree after decree like horseshoes:
> In the groin, brain, forehead, eye.[274]

Mandelstam died in 1938 on his way to a labour camp in Siberia.

By 1939 it had become evident that mass terror was making the Party even more dysfunctional. So, at the Eighteenth Party Congress, Andrei Zhdanov, later notorious for his assault on the 'wrong kind of culture', admitted that the party's method of mass purging had produced 'excesses' and would not be used in the future.[275] Yet the years of the Great Purges saw a fall in mortality rates, while more people than ever before received an education. The numbers of university students grew from 169,000 in 1928–29 to 812,000 in 1940–41, and there was an impressive growth of students in secondary technical schools.[276] Whether such improvements would have happened anyway, as they did in the West under non-communist regimes, cannot be determined.

Yet by 1937 the Soviet economy had managed to recover industrially.[277] By 1939 the USSR was less backward than Stalin had lamented in 1931. It was ready to face a terrible enemy – Nazi Germany – but life for ordinary people was as far as one could have imagined from the socialist golden age envisaged in the days of the 'Great October Socialist Revolution'.

Barbarossa

On 22 June 1941 Germany launched its invasion of the USSR with more than 3 million soldiers, 'the most powerful military assault in human history'.[278] It was also a major strategic blunder. By attacking the USSR, Hitler 'ushered in his own destruction'.[279] It took Stalin by surprise, just as the Japanese attack on Pearl Harbor, less than six months later, took Roosevelt by surprise. Eventually, in February 1943 – well before the landing in Normandy by the Anglo-American Allies – the Red Army had defeated the German armies at Stalingrad after one of the longest battles in history (over five months). Stalingrad was unquestionably the turning point of the war and inevitably acquired the legendary aura of notable historic battles (Agincourt, Waterloo, Yorktown). As Vasily Grossman wrote, celebrating the beginning of the end for Nazism: 'For tens of millions of people the fire of Stalingrad was the fire of Prometheus.'[280] It was an unprecedented defeat for Nazi Germany. An entire German army was destroyed. The German General Hans Doerr, who had fought at Stalingrad and authored the first major German study of the battle, wrote that it was not just 'the turning point of the Second World War', but also the worst defeat in German history, 'and for Russia, its greatest victory'.[281]

The Red Army suffered for its triumph. The Stalingrad campaign cost the Soviet forces approximately 1.1 million casualties, 485,751 of them fatal. It was probably the bloodiest battle in history.[282] The whole war might have caused the death of 10 million Soviet soldiers and an untold number of civilians – probably 7 million (including 1.3 Soviet Jews).[283] The military historian John Erickson estimated that total German military losses – those killed, wounded, missing and made prisoners – amounted to 13.6 million, of which 10 million were on the eastern front.[284] This would not include the 350,000 German civilians who died during the Allied aerial bombing.[285]

Losses for Hitler's allies were also significant. In the Russian campaign 158,000 Romanians died, along with over 100,000 Italians and 80,000 Hungarians.[286] All these figures should be taken with caution; we will probably never know the extent of all Second World War deaths. If we were to include not just military deaths, but also the number of civilians killed in massacres, bombings, death camps and from disease and starvation, we might reach figures of around 70–85 million.

The Second World War in Europe was essentially a war between the USSR and Germany. The contribution of the Anglo-Americans was limited to North Africa and Italy until 6 June 1944, when they landed in Normandy. By then, however, the Red Army was in hot pursuit of the Wehrmacht, all the way from the bloody furnaces of Stalingrad and the salient of Kursk to the bunker in Berlin where the tragic itinerary of the Third Reich was completed. It is a strange irony of history that Western Europe was made free for liberal democracy by the relentless advance of Stalin's Red Armies. Stalin's rapid industrialization in the 1930s, at huge human cost, was one of the factors which enabled this victory.

The war transformed politicians such as Roosevelt, Churchill and de Gaulle into historical giants, but Stalin emerged stronger than any of them, and thanks to the war he remains admired by many Russians decades after his death, despite being denounced as a mass murderer by some of his successors. In 2012 almost half of the Russian population believed that 'Stalin was a wise leader who brought the Soviet Union to might and prosperity', and two-thirds agreed that 'for all Stalin's mistakes and misdeeds, the most important thing is that under his leadership the Soviet people won the Great Patriotic War'.[287] In February 2017, Moscow's independent Levada Center reported that 46 per cent of respondents viewed Stalin positively while only 21 per cent said that they hated or feared him.[288] Another Levada poll later in 2017 placed Stalin first among the most 'outstanding' figures in Russian history, ahead of Pushkin![289] Positive views have remained high (even among members of the younger generation): a 2019 survey showed that while only 4 per cent admired Stalin, 41 per cent had respect and 6 per cent affection; only 14 per cent felt enmity, fear or revulsion for him.[290]

Even in 2011 there was considerable nostalgia for what some regarded as the achievements of the Soviet Union, 'when people received salaries, education, and medicine', declared a seventy-two-year-old Tatar man interviewed in Kazan. 'The educational system was a grand achievement.' A fifty-five-year-old ethnic Russian woman interviewed in Samara lamented: 'Now, our parents have no safety net, so they are nostalgic. They have no money, only a pension, but no benefits … Today, we have to buy our apartments and pay for our children's education. Today, I feel economic uncertainty.' An opinion poll from the Levada Center in 2020 suggested that three out of four Russians think the Soviet era was the best time in their country's history.[291] A strong majority (60 per cent) view the victory in the Second World War as the greatest achievement of the Soviet Union.[292] The construction of socialism (as distinct from a welfare state, decaying in the post-Soviet era) does not loom large. The war does.

Even critics of Stalin, and those who were horrified by the purges and the executions, accepted that he was a great war leader. The cult, of course, had started before the war. A flavour of it can be gauged by the 'Poem about Stalin', written in 1937 at the height of the purges by Mirza Bayramov, one of the leading poets of Azerbaijan, and set to music by no less than Aram Khachaturian (of 'Sabre Dance' fame):

> I look at the people, there is spring in my soul,
> There is no poverty no sorrow.
> The country flourishes like a garden;
> In which the gardener is Comrade Stalin.[293]

The Stalin cult, undoubtedly 'necessary to the Soviet war effort', supported the pursuit of victory.[294] The obituaries which appeared in the Western press in 1953, when Stalin died, tended to be respectful, seldom describing him as a paranoid dictator. The great Chilean writer Pablo Neruda, winner of the 1971 Nobel prize for literature (and a communist), wrote on the occasion his 'Oda a Stalin':

> *Les enseñó la Paz*
> *y así detuvo*
> *con su pecho extendido*
> *los lobos de la guerra*
>
> He taught Peace
> and thus, he stopped
> with his outstretched chest
> the wolves of war

E. H. Carr, writing in 1953, in what amounts to an obituary, wrote:

> If we contrast the Russia of twenty-five years ago with the Russia of today, the outstanding and almost breath-taking contrast is the rise of Russia to become one of the two great world Powers; and this in turn is due to the astonishingly rapid expansion and modernization of the Russian economy.[295]

The Soviet Union had achieved, at great cost, what the Tsarist Empire never had: the status of a global power.

Most historians, including many who are far from indulgent with Stalin, agree that Russia was the country which really defeated Germany and won the Second World War. John Erickson, one of the major historians of the eastern front, has no doubt: his two-volume history is called *Stalin's War with Germany* – not Russia's War with Germany.[296] Geoffrey Roberts's contribution, *Stalin at War*, similarly recognized the leader's importance, as did David M. Glantz in his *Stalingrad Trilogy* and Richard Overy in *Russia's War*.[297]

In his war speeches Stalin appealed to nationalism far more than to communist or socialist ideals. Similarly, Germany was seldom described as a capitalist country (after all, Russia's western allies were capitalist too). Instead, Stalin declared, during the 1941 celebration for the anniversary of the October Revolution, that 'the Hitler regime is a copy of that reactionary regime which existed in Russia under tsardom', and that 'the Hitlerites suppress the rights of the workers, the rights of the intellectuals and the rights of nations as readily as the tsarist regime suppressed them'; furthermore, 'they organize mediaeval pogroms against the Jews as readily as the tsarist regime did'.[298] In his speeches at subsequent celebrations in 1943 and 1944 (after the victories of Stalingrad and Kursk) there is no mention of Marx, and barely a mention of Lenin or socialism. Instead, he praised the workers, the peasants and even the intelligentsia, along with the 'Socialist system engendered by the October Revolution' – not because it was constructing a classless society but because it had 'imbued our people and our Army with a great and invincible strength'.[299]

The military heroes of the past celebrated in one of his war speeches (1941) – 'our Russian forebears', as he called them – included Alexander Nevsky who had defeated the invading Teutonic forces at the Battle on the Ice in 1242, immortalized in Sergei Eisenstein's film of 1938; Dimitri Donskoi, who defeated the Mongols at the battle of Kulinovo in 1380; Kuzma Minin and Dimitri Pozharsky, who defeated the Poles in the early seventeenth century; Alexander Suvorov, who defeated the Turks and many others in the late eighteenth century; and Field-Marshal Mikhail Kutuzov, who stopped the advance of the Napoleonic armies. The Order of Suvorov, created in 1942, was awarded to senior army people for outstanding leadership in combat. There was obviously no mention of any Red generals, heroes of the 1917 Revolution and of the Civil War, since many of them, including Mikhail Tukhachevsky, had been executed on Stalin's orders.[300] Even the gold-braid epaulettes for officers, dating from tsarist days, were reinstituted. The revolutionary image of the USSR as the centre of world revolution was toned down, the Comintern was disbanded in 1943, and the national anthem, the 'Internationale', was dropped a in favour of a patriotic 'National Anthem of the Soviet Union'.

This nationalism, which would have been disdained by Lenin, could not be purely Russian, since there were so many nationalities in the Soviet Union. It was a new kind of nationalism: Soviet nationalism. Even Anna Akhmatova, the great Russian poet (born in Ukraine), who suffered persecution under Stalin, and whose husband Nikolai Gumilev had been executed in 1921 for alleged counter-revolutionary activity, celebrated Russianness during the war in her poem 'Courage' (23 February 1942):

> We will preserve you, Russian speech,
> from servitude in foreign chains[301]

Stalin's war was far from being a series of successes. In fact, for the first year or so, the defeats multiplied, and the Germans were able to advance to the gates of Moscow and Leningrad, where almost a million people died of hunger during a siege that lasted more than three years. Stalin was at least partly responsible for catastrophic Russian defeats in 1941 and 1942.[302] But the Red Army (and Stalin) learned from their mistakes and were able to rely on an increasing supply of goods from industries that had been relocated further east, as well as Lend-Lease aid from the US (though far more went to Britain). After Stalingrad and Kursk, the Red Army led by General Georgy Zhukov marched victoriously, with some setbacks, all the way to Berlin and beyond. It even advanced successfully in Manchuria, defeating the Japanese in the East. Without their intervention, the Japanese might not have surrendered after the dropping of atom bombs on Hiroshima and Nagasaki.[303]

When the war was over, the Red Army had 'liberated' most of Germany, as well as Bulgaria, Romania, Hungary, Czechoslovakia, Finland, Austria and Poland. Yugoslavia was liberated by its own largely communist partisan forces led by Josip Tito. Albania was liberated as early as November 1944 by local anti-fascist forces led by the recently created Communist Party of Albania under Enver Hoxha. Both Albania and Yugoslavia, having liberated themselves from Nazi rule with little help from the USSR, remained fiercely independent. Eventually the Soviets withdrew from Finland and Austria following guarantees that neither country would enter an anti-Soviet pact. They also withdrew from parts of Berlin in favour of the Allies. Lithuania, Latvia and Estonia had been annexed in 1940 to the USSR. This was the beginning of the division of Europe, division which survived until the collapse of communism and of the USSR in 1990–91.

What was once the dream of a world revolution was never fulfilled. Stalin himself had tried, unsuccessfully, to convince the Western Allies that he had no intention of spreading the revolution to the rest of the world. He even avoided helping the strongly pro-communist partisan forces of the Greek National Liberation Front during the civil war which raged in Greece between 1944 and 1949 – restraint which enabled the British to wipe out the communist-dominated resistance in favour of a pro-Western monarchy. Stalin's moderation did not pay. On the morrow of the Second World War, a new Cold War started with the Marshall Plan and NATO. Soviet economic development was hamstrung by the need to spend vast sums in military defence and to maintain control over what were in effect satellite states (East Germany, Bulgaria, Hungary, Romania, Czechoslovakia and Poland).

Future communist successes in the rest of the world (China, Vietnam, Laos, Cambodia, North Korea and Cuba) owed little to the USSR. None of them belonged to the kind of advanced capitalist countries where Lenin, in now-distant 1917, had thought the world revolution would continue. All the USSR was able to do was provide some ideological focus to emergent decolonized states, which, though they did not become (with few exceptions) socialist, were able to use their connection with the USSR to stand up to the West.

Much ink has been spent describing the various accords between the USSR and the Western Allies (Yalta and Potsdam) which allegedly carved up Europe. In fact, post-1945 Europe was shaped by the harsh realities of war far more than by diplomacy: communism stopped where the Red Army stopped. When the Red Army withdrew (as, for instance, in Finland and Austria), no communist regime was established. What the Comintern failed to do in almost twenty-five years of its existence, the Red Army achieved in the final years of the war, spreading the 'revolution' with little help from local communists – though in some cases, such as Czechoslovakia, the communists had considerable support (as they did in some Western countries, such as Italy, France and Finland). The Soviet goal was the establishment of a cordon sanitaire around the western flank of the USSR: realpolitik dressed up as ideology.

There were considerable differences within the so-called Communist Bloc. In Poland, land remained largely privately held. In Hungary, after the Soviet intervention in 1956, path-breaking economic reforms were introduced by János Kádár, well before the Gorbachev era. In Czechoslovakia, there were attempted reforms in 1968 under Alexander Dubček ('socialism with a human face'), followed by another Soviet intervention motivated by the fear that the so-called Prague Spring might lead to radical change in the other satellite countries and endanger the Warsaw Pact. Then the country reverted to a strong authoritarian regime under Gustáv Husák. Yugoslavia under Tito was relatively 'liberal'; Albania under Enver Hoxha was extremely illiberal – but neither country followed the Soviet path. Romania, under the highly repressive regime of Nicolae Ceaușescu, condemned the Warsaw Pact invasion of Czechoslovakia but never formally left the Pact itself – Ceaușescu's foreign policy was independent enough for him to be knighted by the British, as Mussolini had been before him and Mugabe was after him.

From the thaw to Perestroika

The USSR itself evolved. By the time of Stalin's death, the economy had recovered to pre-war levels, especially in agriculture.[304] Major reforms were discussed. It was agreed that consumer industries needed to increase their output, and it was recognized that the USSR faced grave agricultural problems.[305]

In 1956 Khrushchev denounced Stalin, had his remains removed from Lenin's mausoleum in the Red Square in 1961 and tried to debunk Stalin's role in the war. Millions were released from the Gulag. The economic reforms promulgated by Khrushchev improved the living standard of the Russian people without ever reaching that of advanced capitalist countries. Political executions virtually disappeared. Dissidents were sent to internal exile, expelled or incarcerated in mental hospitals, but not executed. The press became a little freer, culture less repressive. Intellectuals no longer had to toe the party line, as long as they did not openly challenge it. This expansion of cultural freedoms came to be known as 'the thaw'. Many in the Party, however, thought that reforms had gone too far and disapproved of Khrushchev's foreign policy, particularly after the Cuban debacle when the USSR appeared to buckle under American pressure.

Khrushchev was dismissed in 1964, and the speed of change abated; no further denunciations of Stalin followed. The thaw was followed by an 'era of stagnation' under Leonid Brezhnev, who unlike Khrushchev was a cautious operator, keen to consult everyone within the higher cadres.[306] His prime minister, Alexei Kosygin (in office for sixteen years), attempted to improve the efficiency of Soviet industry by introducing some market elements into the economy. As a result, there was a further improvement in the overall welfare and consumption of the Russian people. The number of those with higher education increased from 8.3 million in 1959 to 18.5 million in 1984. By 1979 there were 544 radios per 1,000 people, and by 1986 almost everyone had a television set.[307] Nevertheless, the Soviet consumer society paled in comparison to that of the West.

When Brezhnev died in 1982, following a brief interval under Yuri Andropov and then Konstantin Chernenko, Mikhail Gorbachev became leader. Andropov, a leading reformist, had wished him to be his successor. Gorbachev introduced a major programme of political reforms: Glasnost (transparency or openness) and Perestroika (reconstruction or transformation). Many leading cadres, such as Yegor Ligachev, who later became an opponent of Gorbachev, accepted at the time that reforms were needed. As Ligachev wrote in his memoirs, when Andropov became general secretary, like many other provincial Party secretaries, he was 'impatient for change, uncomfortably aware that the country was headed for social and economic disaster'.[308] A contributing factor to the demand for reform in the Soviet Union was the increasing alarm at the country's inability to make any progress in the war to defend the pro-Soviet government in Afghanistan against the Mujahideen – an alarm which led to protests and demonstrations.

Such alarm was then not recognized as a warning sign even by acute observers of the Soviet Union; most specialists assumed that the USSR could go on for a long time.[309] Richard Sakwa could write in 1988: 'The Bolshevik revolution appears to present a viable path of development and have an applicability far beyond the country of its birth.'[310] The CIA was equally certain that the USSR would survive, assuming as late as May 1988 that the USSR would intervene with force, if necessary, to preserve its rule in Eastern Europe: 'There is no reason to doubt his [Gorbachev's] willingness to intervene to preserve party rule and decisive Soviet influence in the region.'[311] As we know, he didn't.

It is difficult to resist making predictions, particularly when one is asked constantly to make them. Thus in 1993, after the fall of communism, Kenneth Waltz, a distinguished international relations theorist, assumed that the real challengers to American hegemony would be Japan and perhaps Germany, and that NATO's years were numbered.[312] Paul Kennedy in his *Rise and Fall of the Great Powers* (1987) suggested that expanding military expenditure ('imperial overstretch') would lead to the decline of *both* the USSR and of the US.

When Gorbachev took over, many observers of the USSR did not notice that major novelties were in the offing, though at the Twenty-Seventh Party Congress (1986), the first attended by Gorbachev as party secretary, some perceptible changes could be detected, particularly in foreign policy.[313] Change was obviously in the air. Archie Brown, writing in 1986, could already note that Gorbachev had made a 'dramatic impact' on the composition of the Politburo in only six weeks since becoming leader and that he clearly had political and economic changes in mind and that he 'will not be deterred by conservatism'.[314] Indeed, even before he became leader, visiting London in December 1984, Gorbachev impressed Margaret Thatcher, then prime minister, who declared (and was widely quoted): 'I like Mr Gorbachev. We can do business together' – an accolade shared by Denis Healey, then Labour shadow foreign secretary.

The reformers believed that everyone would rally round the reforms, because a disciplined Party had previously rallied round (or pretended to rally round) new initiatives. But that had been in the previous era of real or hard communism, when few dared to dissent. Once Gorbachev had started the process of dismantling the old system, resistance came from all quarters, from conservatives who thought matters were getting out of hand to radicals who thought the reforms did not go far enough. Most agreed that the system should be reformed and that it was reformable. They were divided on the key question of what was to be done.

Gorbachev tried to conciliate reformers and anti-reformers by democratizing the debate, but this could work only when, as in a real democracy, the two sides agree to submit themselves to the verdict of an electorate or of an arbitrator. Gorbachev toyed with the idea of a multi-party system but did not dare to go that far so soon. This would have amounted to dismantling the entire system; the main reformers wanted to reform to save the system, not to demolish it.[315] Instead, a small step was taken by introducing contested elections within the party, and by 1990 the Soviet press, unfettered by financial constraints or corporate ownership, became freer than its Western counterparts. Already, before such changes, foreign radio channels were infrequently jammed and in Central Europe (including East Germany) Western TV could be received. By 1985, most communist countries imported many TV entertainment programmes. In Hungary and Poland, TV carried advertising. In Hungary there were no controls over videos, and in 1988, some 200,000 were in use.[316] In Romania, hostility against the regime increased when the (quite non-political) BBC drama series *The Onedin Line*, highly popular in the 1970s and 1980s, was banned along with other shows.

Gorbachev's reforms encouraged the Polish authorities to allow free elections in 1989, which resulted in the victory of the previously banned Solidarity-led opposition. This was followed by the election in 1990 of Lech Wałęsa, the leader of Solidarity, as president – the first non-communist to be elected in a communist state. Hungary, while pursuing its reforms, allowed transit from East to West Germany, thus making the Berlin Wall redundant, which is why it was soon demolished with no opposition from the East German government. Gorbachev did not object to such developments. He even seemed to encourage them.[317]

Reforms require a robust central mechanism. But the centre of power in Russia had been inefficient and dysfunctional for a long time. The party had become a sprawling organization of nearly 20 million members, many of whom had joined for reasons of career and conformity. It was controlled, increasingly ineffectually, by a small apparatus at the top, while reformists and conservatives were fighting in the background.[318] In spite of legislation aimed at liberalizing the economy, such as the Law on the State Enterprise of 1987 and the Law on Co-operatives of 1988, there was no simple way to make the transition to a new economic system because the central machinery was losing power.[319] Reform in the Soviet Union might perhaps have needed to begin with a big purge of existing cadres using authoritarian methods and not liberalism.[320]

This is what was happening in China, where the economic reforms initiated by Deng Xiaoping were promulgated while the party retained power. Chinese developments were followed with interests by some of the Russian reformers such as Fedor Burlatsky (almost totally ignored by the Western media who preferred more vociferous dissidents). Burlatsky, who had been an adviser to Khrushchev and Andropov, saw Mao Zedong's successors as pragmatists who were intent on breaking with Mao's legacy, while asserting that everything they did was in accordance with Mao's thought. However, Gorbachev did not follow their example. His 'new political thinking' was meant to establish a clear line of demarcation with Russia's past. He thought that without political reforms he could not overcome the resistance of entrenched economic interests, particularly in the defence industry and in the vast network of collective farms.[321] As Archie Brown has written: 'Gorbachev's two major failures were in economic reform and in resolution of the "national question". But, as he adds, these were problems which could not be easily resolved.[322]

Though increasingly unpopular at home, Gorbachev was celebrated abroad for having ended the Cold War. When he died in August 2022, there was a marked contrast between muted commemorations in Russia disguising much resentment and the praise lavished in the West (a West which failed to support him when it should have, and expanded NATO instead). The former German Chancellor Angela Merkel, born in East Germany, declared: 'Mikhail Gorbachev wrote world history. He exemplified how a single statesman can change the world for the better.'[323]

The Cold War did not really end; it was transformed from a Cold War between two contrasting ideologies into one between rival geopolitical systems. The new Cold War was started in the West when Bill Clinton and then George W. Bush enlarged NATO, thus surrounding Russia. In June 1997 an open letter by American foreign policy experts including Sam Nunn (former chair of the Senate Armed Services Committee), Robert McNamara (former secretary of defense) and Paul Nitze (former deputy secretary of defense) warned that the expansion of NATO would be 'a policy error of historic proportion'.[324] In 1990, as the Soviet bloc was disintegrating, Gorbachev was given the Nobel Peace Prize.

In March 1991 Gorbachev had held a referendum on the question: 'Do you believe it essential to preserve the USSR as a renewed federation of equal sovereign republics in which the rights and freedoms of a person of any nationality will be fully guaranteed?' Estonia, Latvia, Lithuania, Armenia, Georgia and Moldova refused to conduct it. In the other nine republics, answers in the affirmative did not fall below 70 per cent (even in Ukraine), with a turnout of 80 per cent. As Archie Brown concluded: 'Independent statehood, combined with confederation, was not the choice of a majority of Soviet citizens.'[325]

In August 1991, a poorly organized military coup against Gorbachev failed. The consequence was that the Russian Republic under Boris Yeltsin, technically only one of the republics of the USSR, declared independence and banned the Communist Party. By then more than 4 million people had left the party; the remaining Soviet republics had little alternative but to go their own way, as the Baltic republics had done a little earlier. What had been the empire of the Romanovs, somewhat preserved by the communists under Lenin and Stalin, was no more.

The Gorbachev experiment had failed, but in less than seven years he had dismantled an authoritarian regime, reduced to shreds the so-called Iron Curtain and enabled Germany to be reunited. It was the first successful 'Velvet Revolution' of the East.[326] It also sparked a massive literature. By 1995 some 8,673 articles and books (excluding newspaper articles) on Gorbachev and Perestroika had been published in English alone.[327] 'Success', however, may not be the right word to describe what happened after the dissolution of the USSR. As Gorbachev declared in his resignation speech on 25 December 1991:

> The process of renovating the country and radical changes in the world community turned out to be far more complicated than could be expected. However, what has been done ought to be given its due. This society acquired freedom, liberated itself politically and spiritually, and this is the foremost achievement which we have not yet understood completely, because we have not learned to use freedom. And today I am worried by our people's loss of the citizenship of a great country. The consequences may turn out to be very hard for everyone.[328]

Post-communism: A Russian winter

Under Yeltsin, Russia became dominated by mafia-like plutocrats in what soon turned out to be one of the most unequal economies in the world, with the top 10 per cent owning 77 per cent of the wealth.[329] As Peter Nolan wrote: 'Many Russian "investment funds" were simply fronts for "mafia" activities, "cash rich from arbitrage activities", able to buy shares in companies in order to take over management control.'[330]

Those who appeared to have been 'exemplary communists' now turned into 'nationalist heralds'. As Branko Milanović observed, the communist Boris Yeltsin became a champion of free enterprise; in Kyiv, Leonid Kravchuk turned into a 'defender of the Ukrainian language (which he never spoke before)'; and Slobodan Milošević became a Serbian nationalist: 'The path is almost perfect: everybody follows the same playbook.'[331]

The so-called 'shock therapy' propounded by Yegor Gaidar, and massively encouraged by the West, ended in economic catastrophe (which was not the case in Poland). Its main advocates were sacked or forced to resign. The privatization of Russia's oil, gas and minerals was transformed into 'an orgy of looting by a well-placed cabal of insiders'.[332] Privatization occurred at too fast a pace while the state crumbled. Foreign investments never materialized. There was no major surge in exports.

The Chinese had shown that the process of privatization should have been supervised by a strong state. The project of radical reformers such as Abel Aganbegyan to steer the Soviet economy towards fulfilling the needs of the consumer failed to materialize.[333] The collapse of the Soviet

Union has been an 'unmitigated disaster for the population in terms of health'. Russia went through a period when what were called 'deaths of despair' increased enormously, due mainly to alcoholism, but also drug abuse, homicide and suicide.[334] During the period of Perestroika, in 1985–87, Gorbachev's anti-alcohol campaign had substantially reduced alcohol consumption, saving many lives. Then, with the collapse of the USSR, alcohol consumption resumed, increasing by 20 per cent between 1989 and 1994, with a consequent increase in mortality.[335]

Seventy years of Soviet history were challenged and condemned. Leningrad returned to its old name, St Petersburg (obviously Peter the Great was now more acceptable than Lenin). Statues erected in honour of the heroes of the October Revolution were destroyed, including that of Felix Dzerzhinsky, head of the secret police until his death in 1926. Many Moscow metro stations were renamed. On the seventy-fourth anniversary of the October Revolution in November 1991 Yeltsin declared that the revolution had had 'a wholly negative influence on the fate of Russia and the rest of the world'. In October 1993 the main Lenin Museum in Moscow was closed, and the traditional 7 November parade was cancelled.[336] The October Revolution was barely mentioned in popular culture, in favour of the Second World War and the Civil War. This trend had started under Brezhnev, as the Russian political scientist Maria Snegovaya has pointed out in an article called, appropriately, 'Where and Why Did the October Revolution Disappear from the Popular Memory?'[337] Before the fall of communism, in some of the films directed by Nikita Mikhalkov such as *At Home Among Strangers* (1974) and *The Slave of Love* (1976) the Bolsheviks were upstanding moral figures. By 2014, in Mikhalkov's *Sunstroke*, the Bolsheviks are moral freaks and the Whites innocent of all faults.[338] Mikhalkov had turned himself into a Slavophile nationalist, an upholder of Orthodox Christianity and an ardent supporter of Putin.

Paradoxically there was more internationally recognized Russian culture (including dissident culture) in the twenty-five years preceding the fall of communism than in the subsequent twenty-five years. Since 1990 there has been no Boris Pasternak (Nobel Prize 1958), no Mikhail Sholokhov (Nobel Prize 1965), no Aleksandr Solzhenitsyn (Nobel Prize 1970) and no Yury Trifonov (nominated for the Nobel Prize for his historical novel *The Impatient Ones*); no Yevgeny Yevtushenko (nominated for the Nobel Prize for his poem 'Babi Yar'), no Anna Akhmatova (the poet, known for *Requiem* and shortlisted for the Nobel Prize in 1965 and 1966) and no Vasily Grossman (author of the novels *Stalingrad* and *Life and Fate*, sometimes compared to Tolstoy's *War and Peace*).

What was once a global power was now treated with contempt by the West, above all by the US, for having failed to learn its new subordinate place in an American-dominated world. President Clinton's administration officials, such as Ambassador-at-Large to the USSR Strobe Talbott (1993–94), expected the Kremlin to accept the United States' own definition of Russia's national interest. This arrogant approach was referred by Talbott's adviser Victoria Nuland as the 'spinach treatment', comparing the process of telling the Russians what's good for them to trying to get children to eat healthy foods.[339] Putin, after his election to the presidency in 2000, hoped at first to see Russia integrated into what the West euphemistically calls 'the international community' by not protesting too much when the Baltic republics along with most former satellite states of the USSR joined NATO, or when the US established temporary military bases in Uzbekistan and Kyrgyzstan – all to no avail. As Perry Anderson put it: 'In condescension or contempt, the underlying American attitude speaks for itself: *vae victis*.'[340]

Vladimir Putin reined in the so-called oligarchs, most of whom owed their rise to his predecessor Yeltsin (an oligarch, in the West, would be called a tycoon or entrepreneur). Putin established a semi-authoritarian regime, though the press maintained some freedoms and some form of dissent was allowed. Election results were dubious under both Yeltsin and Putin. There is little doubt that both would have won anyway, although Gennady Zyuganov, the leader of the Russian Communist Party, obtained 32 per cent against Yeltsin's 35 per cent in the first round of the 1996 presidential elections. Yeltsin won by a strangely large margin the subsequent run-off.

Gas and oil, which account for most exports, once again came under some form of state control, as they are in most capitalist countries. Between 2000 and 2014, thanks to a rise in oil prices (but also to economic reforms), Russia experienced one of the greatest economic booms in its history. Living standards soared. Car sales doubled, travel abroad became more common, homeownership increased.[341] But when oil prices dropped, so did Putin's popularity. Nevertheless, in the partially rigged 2021 elections, Putin's United Russia Party obtained just under 50 per cent of the vote; the Communist Party (socially conservative and patriotic and Russia's main legal opposition force) obtained almost 19 per cent (up 6 per cent on the previous election, partly inflated by dissident votes); the far-right Liberal Democratic Party and the 'A Just Russia for Truth' Party (member of the Socialist International) each obtained just over 7 per cent of all votes. Russia could be regarded as a half-baked democracy but no longer a dictatorship. Meanwhile much of the Western press depicted Putin in the traditional way in which strong leaders are depicted: as someone who, with the support of a small clique, controls and decides everything in Russia; hence the frequency with which he is labelled a new tsar, as if such authoritarianism can be attributed almost exclusively to Putin and not, as Tony Wood puts it, 'to the cumulative outcome of Russia's post-Communist transformation'.[342]

There was no democratization in many of the former Soviet republics. Kyrgyzstan, ruled by a succession of strong men, remained deeply corrupt and marred by ethnic conflicts. Islam Karimov ruled Uzbekistan for twenty-seven years until his death, obtaining 80–90 per cent of the vote at each rigged election. In the absence of contested elections, Saparmurat Niyazov ruled Turkmenistan from 1985 until his own death in 2006, surrounded by a growing personality cult. Nursultan Nazarbayev held power in Kazakhstan for twenty-eight years before resigning in 2019 when the country's capital, following a *unanimous* vote in parliament, acquired a new name: Nur-Sultan. It reverted to its old name, Astana, in September 2022. Emomali Rahmon, regularly re-elected without any opposition, has been in power in Tajikistan since 1992. Finally, in Belarus, Alexander Lukashenko ('the last dictator in Europe') has ruled since 1994.[343] All of them – like Putin – were once members of the Communist Party.

Conflicts in the former USSR include Russia's brutal suppression of Chechen separatism and fighting between Armenia and Azerbaijan over the disputed territory of Nagorno-Karabakh. Georgia was in constant dispute with the pro-Russian separatisms of its own ethnic fringes in Abkhazia and South Ossetia. Ukraine, which saw its economy, once stronger than that of Russia's, collapse into civil war, lost some of its eastern territories in the Donbass area in 2014, where separatists enjoyed the support of Russia. Ukraine also lost Crimea to Russia, having gained it from Russia in 1954. Ukraine was eventually invaded by Russia in February 2022.

In the former satellite states of Central and Eastern Europe, matters were not so bad. Though their political system had collapsed, making a gradual transition to capitalism difficult, they were able to adopt a new institutional and economic framework thanks to the European Union, to which most acceded – though liberals could not rejoice at the illiberal (but democratically elected) governments in Hungary and Poland and the widespread corruption and personalistic politics extant in Romania, Bulgaria, Slovakia and the Czech Republic.

The balance sheet of the post-communist countries, in terms of their transition to capitalism, is not very good. In 2014 Branko Milanović sorted post-communist countries into 'clear failures' (those failing to reach in 2013 the real per capita income of 1990); 'relative failures' that grew more slowly than the average of rich OECD countries; those which kept up with the rich world; and 'success cases', which in the twenty-five years since the fall of communism had averaged better growth than the rich OECD countries. The 'clear failures' included Tajikistan, Moldova, Ukraine, Kyrgyz Republic, Georgia, Bosnia and Serbia; 'relative failures' included Russia, Macedonia, Croatia and Hungary; those that kept up with the West include the Czech Republic, Slovenia, Turkmenistan, Lithuania and Romania; and the success cases included Latvia, Bulgaria, Slovakia and Mongolia, but also three who did so thanks to their mineral resources: Azerbaijan, Kazakhstan and Uzbekistan. The greatest success stories in terms of economic growth were Albania, Poland, Armenia, Estonia and Belarus – the last a dictatorship which avoided large-scale privatizations and maintained an extensive welfare system as well as full employment.[344] Of course, this league-table approach takes no account of the growth in inequalities, which increased sharply even in some of the supposedly successful countries.

While Russia did not fare well, Ukraine fared even worse. According to the World Bank, Ukraine in 2021 was the poorest country in Europe, poorer also than Ecuador, Georgia, West Bank and Gaza, and Iraq.[345] Both Russia and Ukraine are plagued by corruption.[346] The Russian invasion of Ukraine will not improve the situation for either Russia or Ukraine. Vladimir Putin's 'historical' speech on the eve of the invasion contained a diatribe against Lenin, Stalin and all the Bolsheviks who had pandered to the nationalities of the Tsarist Empire.[347]-Devoid of ideology (except a rather predictable nationalism), present-day Russia, once a global power, is embittered by its lost status, surrounded by enemies (some real, some imaginary) and unable to regain the respect, fear and cultural and intellectual weight it had under the tsars and under the Bolsheviks. Revolutionary ambitions were now relegated to that 'great dust-heap called "history"'.[348]

The Great October Revolution had come to an end, and with it not only the Union of Soviet Socialist Republics but the empire of the Romanovs that the communists had territorially preserved almost entirely. Communism was abolished and, unexpectedly, those who did the elimination were the communists themselves, led by their secretary-general, Mikhail Gorbachev. The Soviets had not achieved socialism but had developed an industrial complex that made victory possible in the Second World War, thus paradoxically helping to save Western democracies. They had also attained virtual parity in education and health with the West and turned the country into one of the two superpowers. A country of semi-illiterate *mujiks* became a country overwhelmingly literate and urbanized. It was an achievement, but one which capitalist countries could claim too, and certainly not what was in Lenin's mind when his supporters stormed the Winter Palace in November 1917. After 1989, Russia, one might surmise, reverted to what it might have been had Lenin never guided the Bolsheviks: a capitalist state, much smaller than the Tsarist Empire, full of *nouveaux riches* created by the political elites and not by entrepreneurial genius, blatantly corrupt and unable to develop a healthy economy.

We shall never know what alternatives there were. But one thing is certain: the Great October Revolution failed and, at least so far, Russian capitalism has failed too.

6

The Chinese Revolution: Not a Dinner Party

A revolutionary era began in China with an uprising in Wuchang in 1911. This ended the 268-year reign of the Qing dynasty and more than 2,000 years of imperial rule. China had experienced foreign invasions, changes in dynasty, peasant rebellions – but all these led to the cyclical re-establishment of a dynastic order.[1] As the opening lines of Luo Guanzhong's fourteenth-century classic *A Romance of Three Kingdoms* proclaims: 'The empire, long divided, must unite; long united, must divide. Thus it has ever been.'[2]

What became known as the Chinese Revolution proceeded in a drastically different manner from revolutions in other countries. The Chinese Revolution began as a national revolution and continued through a long period of civil wars and foreign (Japanese) invasion, decades of strife and more casualties than all the bourgeois revolutions of the West combined. The Communist Party achieved a definitive victory in 1949. Eventually, after upheavals during the construction of socialism – the Great Leap Forward and the Great Proletarian Cultural Revolution – China became an exceptionally strong market economy, though one still ruled by the Communist Party.

Thus, the Wuchang uprising of 1911 was only one incident in a long and complex process; as Frederic Wakeman wrote, 'divorced from that larger context, the single moment loses ultimate significance.'[3]

Was it a capitalist-bourgeois revolution? Or a mere change of regime? The revolutionary process was initiated in 1911 with relatively little bloodshed. At first, it may have appeared as a change of regime, like the overthrow of dictatorships in Portugal, Spain and Greece in the 1970s.

These were not called revolutions – though briefly for media purposes, the one in Portugal was called the Carnation Revolution, just as the peaceful transition of power in Czechoslovakia in 1989 was called the Velvet Revolution.

No one would call the Chinese Revolution velvet or carnation, or any term suggesting a graceful transition. In 1927, paraphrasing the five 'constant virtues' of Confucius (Kong Qiu) – *ren* (benevolence), *yi* (righteousness), *li* (propriety), *zhi* (wisdom) and *xin* (trustworthiness) – Mao Zedong declared, in what became a famous quote:

> A revolution is not a dinner party, or writing an essay, or painting a picture, or doing embroidery; it cannot be so refined, so leisurely and gentle, so temperate, kind, courteous, restrained, and magnanimous. A revolution is an insurrection, an act of violence by which one class overthrows another.[4]

The great revolutions of the past began in major cities: London, Boston, New York, Philadelphia, Paris, St Petersburg and Moscow. The 1911 Revolution did not begin in any of the four major historical capitals of China, Xi'an, Luoyang, Nanjing or Beijing; nor did it begin in Shanghai or Guangzhou (Canton), or Hong Kong (then a British colony), though it did start in a major city – Wuchang. The communists fought their revolutionary war mainly in the countryside once they were forced to abandon their urban strongholds in 1927.

Eventually they led a peasant revolution while insisting that (as Marxist doctrine suggested) it was a proletarian revolution, thus demonstrating that peasants could after all be a revolutionary force. Yet, without the communists leading them, it is unlikely that peasant discontent would ever have been more than a spark – albeit a 'spark that starts a prairie fire', as Mao wrote (another famous quote). The peasants, on their own, would not have established a new state. Rebellious peasants do not seek power; they seek a better life and complain about taxes, about rent or about the poor harvest and natural disasters.[5]

The Communist Revolution was urban only in its final phase. The communist revolutionaries did not come from the main cities. Twelve out of thirteen founding members of the Chinese Communist Party (CCP) were from Hunan, Hubei, Jiangxi, Guizhou and Guangdong – all in South Central and southern China. Mao Zedong himself was born in Hunan, a region which produced a significant number of revolutionaries. In 1897 the British consul complained: 'Hunan, and Changsha [Hunan's capital] in particular, is the centre from which radiate all troubles in the Yangtze valley.'[6]

The first short-lived soviet was established by the CCP rebel forces (the Chinese Red Army) led by Mao in the Jinggang Mountains area on the Hunan–Jiangxi border, after the Kuomintang turned against them in 1927.[7] Mao's meagre troops were joined by a few others led by future Red Army leaders, such as Zhu De and Peng Dehuai. Eventually, in 1935, after being encircled by Kuomintang forces, Mao began the Long March to Yan'an (Yenan). The revolutionaries were away from the cities for more than ten years.

The 1911 uprising in Wuchang

The Chinese Revolution followed a far more complicated path than those in France or Russia. The immediate cause of the 1911 Revolution was a dispute over a railway building in Wuhan, the capital of Hubei province which now incorporates Wuchang. Local elites had invested in the railways and opposed the central-government attempt to take it over with the help of foreign banks – in effect a dispute between central government and provincial powers under the aegis of what was called the 'Railway Protection Movement'. Obviously, it was not a bourgeois revolution, but a reaction of local elites against the central state.[8] Anti-Qing activists took advantage of the railways protest to unleash widespread agitation, and the central authorities reacted by sending in troops. The response was the Wuchang Uprising of 10 October 1911 (remembered as 'Double Ten': the tenth day of the tenth month), which triggered an army mutiny. Other forces in the South soon participated in the revolt, to be joined by further uprisings in the rest of the country. What might at first have seemed a minor dispute led a few months later to the end of the Qing dynasty – just as a dispute over taxing tea led to the establishment of the United States of America.[9]

Calling the events of 1911 an 'accidental' revolution seems justified.[10] It was the collapse of an imperial regime, not a revolutionary takeover. Moreover, from the point of view of the Chinese economy, it was not a watershed: 'It did not mark a sharp break in policy, institutions or external relations', notes Loren Brandt.[11] The 1911 Revolution did not affect class relations, the rural–urban gap, foreign interference or local provincial power holders. Of course, it established new political principles, including a property-based male suffrage.[12]

The course of the communist conquest was extremely long. In Russia, February 1917 was the beginning of a relatively short process which enabled the Bolsheviks to establish control over the whole country after a few years of civil war; the events of 1911 in China were nothing like that. There was no organized party like the Bolsheviks; the Chinese Communist Party was formed ten years *after* the Wuchang Uprising. In Russia, 1917 was the first stage towards the establishment of absolute Bolshevik power; in China, 1911 was the first stage of the disintegration of the country. There would be no unity until the communist victory in 1949.

The Wuchang Uprising was far from being an isolated event. It had been preceded by an impressive series of failed revolts and disturbances, mainly involving supporters of Sun Yat-sen. In 1894 Sun had founded the Nationalist Kuomintang (KMT or National People's Party, originally known as the Revive China Society or Hsing Chung Hui), when in exile in Hawaii. He was subsequently regarded by Nationalists as the 'father of the nation' and by Communists as a forerunner of their revolution. Even Lenin celebrated the 1911 Revolution, praising Sun Yat-sen as a 'progressive Chinese democrat', a populist ('Narodnik') and the 'enlightened spokesman of militant and victorious Chinese democracy', though he disagreed with his ideas on economics.[13] Sun Yat-sen is still celebrated today, 150 years after his birth, both in the People's Republic of China and Taiwan.

In January 1903 there was the uprising of the 'Heavenly Kingdom of the Great Mingshun', which lasted three days. In December 1906, in Hunan, the Ping Liu Li Uprising took place; it involved local elites as well as miners and secret societies trying to keep foreign interests away from the local coal mines.[14] This was followed, in May 1907, by the Huanggang and the Huizhou Qinühu Uprisings. In the same year, in Anqing, a failed plot led by the feminist revolutionary and poet Qiu Jin (Jiu Jin) to assassinate the provincial governor was subsequently called an uprising. Qiu Jin paid with her life. The Qinzhou Uprising, also in 1907, was a tax revolt which failed, as did the Zhennanguan Uprising on the Vietnamese frontier on 1 December; this forced Sun Yat-sen, who was losing support among revolutionaries, to flee to Singapore. In March 1908, Huang Xing, Sun Yat-sen's second in command, launched a raid from a base in Vietnam. Later known as the Qin-lian Uprising, this was followed in April by the Hekou Uprising and, in November, by the Mapaoying Uprising. The anti-Qing movement continued unabated, despite recurrent failures – including, in April 1911, the Guangzhou (Canton) Uprising, now known as the Yellow Flower Mound Uprising, which was also led by Huang Xing, who survived what looked like a suicide mission.

So, the Wuchang Uprising was the one success story of the many failed struggles against the central authorities in the first decade or so of the twentieth century. Historically the Qing had benefited from the absence of a powerful caste of landed gentry of the kind seen in France before Louis XIV, or in Japan before the Meiji. It was also not a particularly demanding authority in terms of taxation.[15] In Imperial China, real state power was held by a bureaucracy whose posts were filled by competitive examinations based not on administrative competence but on knowledge of Confucian texts. This is what prompted Tocqueville to describe dynastic China as a model of 'democratic despotism', and it led the country into self-satisfied stagnation.[16] Regular invasion by 'barbarian' powers exposed its weakness. Defeat in the Opium War forced the Qing to increase military expenditure, which triggered a huge fiscal crisis. The problem was that the main tax was on landholdings, so while the population increased the tax exacted remained the same.[17] The proliferation of locally imposed surtaxes and sub-bureaucratic offices left the quotas remitted to the central government unchanged. The centre was poorer as a result. As in all revolutions, the issue of revenue-raising was of crucial importance.

The Qing also found it difficult to exploit the cause of nationalism and anti-imperialism, since the dynasty was seen by many as foreign, not just because it originated from Manchuria, but because it was increasingly seen to be in cahoots with the British and the Americans.[18] Sun Yat-sen himself exploited this idea of foreignness, claiming that he was restoring the Han 'ancestral land of four thousand years' from the 'filthy Manchu race' who had seized it by force 260 years before.[19]

The end of the dynasty was less dramatic than comparable events in England, France and Russia. No regal heads were chopped, and no royal family executed. There had been a dominant figure, the Empress Dowager Cixi, but she died before the fall of the dynasty. She had been consort-concubine of the Xianfeng Emperor and de facto ruler after his death in 1861. She maintained control of the government except when her nephew, the Guangxu Emperor, tried and failed to introduce modern reforms in the period known as the Hundred Days' Reform or Wuxu Reform (11 June to 22 September 1898). One of the main intellectual leaders of the Hundred Days movement was Kang Youwei, who advocated following the Japanese example – a constitutional monarchy, Western-style universities, business schools and capitalism – as in the so-called Meiji Restoration.[20] Conservatives who opposed the reformers managed to convince the Empress Dowager Cixi to crush the reform movement, in what amounted to a coup.[21] Cixi was back in control; the Guangxu Emperor was, to all intents and purposes, in detention. Kang Youwei fled abroad.

Eventually, Cixi too tried to pursue the path of reform, abolishing the traditional examination system, modernizing the military and proposing to write a new constitution. It was far too late. Every reform weakened the central government of the Qing while local provincial elites became stronger. The empress dowager died on 15 November 1908. Her nephew, the Guangxu Emperor, had died the day before, perhaps poisoned. So in 1911, there was no royal family of any significance left. The new emperor was the three-year-old Puyi. The regent and new empress dowager was Puyi's aunt Longyu, who was childless. On 12 February 1912, Longyu abdicated on behalf of the Qing dynasty. By then, the new Republic of China had been already proclaimed and presided over for a few brief weeks by Sun Yat-sen, who had returned from exile. The Qing's quiet disappearance paved the way for almost forty years of Civil War.

The end of the Qing was relatively quiet and bloodless. But it had been preceded by a century plagued by disasters far greater than anything that had occurred in France, England or the US before their revolutions. The religious-based White Lotus Rebellion (1794–1804) was followed by the First Opium War against the British (1839–42), whose aim was to force China to open its borders to the import of opium. This war ended with the Treaty of Nanjing, which compelled China to allow the opening of five treaty ports (including Shanghai and Canton, now Guangzhou), to cede Hong Kong to Britain and to pay a huge indemnity. In the Second Opium War (1856–60), the invading British and French troops looted and burnt the Yuanmingyuan, the imperial residence (Old Summer Palace). Then there was the Taiping Civil War (1850–64), known as the Taiping Rebellion in the West and as the Taiping Revolutionary Movement in present-day China.

The Taiping, a nationalist and religious movement led by Hong Xiuquan, who claimed to be the younger brother of Jesus, aimed at eliminating the Qing Dynasty and establishing the Taiping Heavenly Kingdom. It was welcomed by progressives in the West, particularly by Karl Marx, who could not have known much about Hong and his religious beliefs but thought it might lead to a revolution in Europe.[22] The rebellion was later praised by Sun Yat-sen and by Mao Zedong but denounced by Chiang Kai-shek's Nationalists. The Taiping rebels were able to gain control of most of central China and even started an agrarian reform before being definitively defeated by Qing forces in 1864, when Nanjing, the heavenly capital, was taken. The defeat of the Taiping rebels required the help of private militias, which in turn further weakened the Qing rulers.[23] Hong Xiuquan had just died, allegedly from eating weeds he believed to be biblical manna.[24] This was one of the bloodiest conflicts ever, with casualties estimated by some at 20–30 million.[25]

There followed the war with Japan (1894–95), which resulted in the humiliating Treaty of Shimonoseki, ceding control over Korea and the island of Taiwan. Previously China had regarded Japan as an inferior state. Now the ground had shifted: China was becoming almost a vassal state of Japan. Finally, there was the Boxer Rebellion of 1899–1901 ('Boxer' is a Western appellation for what was called the Society of the Righteous and Harmonious Fists, or Yihequan). This somewhat archaic movement with religious overtones was praised by subsequent revolutionaries because it had a popular base, especially among the peasantry. It rejected foreign imperialism and Christian missionaries, as well as the higher taxes imposed by the Qing dynasty to pay the indemnity imposed by the Shimonoseki Treaty. At first, however, the rebels declared they wanted to strengthen the Qing dynasty against foreigners. They intoned:

> When at last all the Foreign Devils
> Are expelled to the very last man
> The Great Qing, united, together
> Will bring peace to this our land.[26]

While the Qing imperial government remained hesitant on whether to suppress the Boxer rebels or join them (they eventually opted for the latter), an Eight-Nation Alliance (Britain, the United States, France, Germany, Italy, Japan, Russia and Austria-Hungary) intervened, manned largely by colonial troops. The forces seized Beijing, engaging in widespread looting and rape and forcing the empress dowager and the Guangxu Emperor to flee to Xi'an, allowing them to return only after signing another humiliating treaty.[27]

The Qing dynasty had succeeded in surviving all such cataclysms. It did not survive the Wuchang Uprising of 1911 – the final, critical stage of what had been a long and gradual decline.[28]

Sun's perplexity

Sun Yat-sen looms large in all the accounts of the 1911 Revolution, though his own direct role was minor. The general who led the Wuchang Uprising was Huang Xing, but even he failed to establish any degree of control over subsequent events. The strongman who emerged was General Yuan Shikai, who had forced the abdication of the child-emperor Puyi and his aunt, the empress dowager. Yuan, once a leading reformer, failed to quell the Wuchang Uprising as ordered by the Qing, and instead negotiated with the revolutionaries. He agreed to let Sun Yat-sen become the provisional president of the Republic of China for a few weeks, before becoming president himself in February 1912. He was probably behind the assassination of his main rival, Song Jiaoren, one of the leaders of the Kuomintang, who had won China's first elections.[29] A period of armed conflict followed, pitting the KMT led by Sun Yat-sen and Huang Xing against Yuan's forces. Eventually Yuan succeeded in forcing Sun and Huang Xing into exile: the former to Japan, the latter to the US. He then declared himself emperor in December 1915. His empire had little support though, lasting less than three months. Yuan died shortly after.

The weakness of China was now apparent to all. Yuan had failed to establish a central government, though in the few years he was in power he was able to continue some of the reforms already begun under the Qing.[30] He tried to reorganize the bureaucracy and to attract 'men of talent' educated in modern subjects.[31] All parties agreed that modernization required a strong central government more than democracy.

By 1916 China had entered the period of warlordism (*junfa*), in which a desire for local autonomy was backed by military force. At this stage the KMT attempted to assume a national role. With the help of the Comintern, it emerged as a centralized, authoritarian, Bolshevik-type semi-military party following the Leninist model, then the main example of what a revolutionary party should look like.[32] Instead of a communist ideology it embraced a social reformist agenda based on Sun Yat-sen's famous Three Principles of the People: *minzu*, or nationalism (independence from foreign domination); *minquan*, or democracy (the lack of which had contributed to Western superiority); and *minsheng*, or people's welfare.

What the 1911 Revolution had achieved, however, was to usher in a radical current in China's politics and among the intelligentsia, especially the students. Disillusioned with Confucianism, they were looking to the West as well as Japan for ideas and inspiration, despite their nationalist politics.[33] China – so proud of its history and self-sufficiency, which had never sought to project its strength in distant lands, which regarded itself as the centre of the world (the Middle Kingdom) – was forced, when it came to seek modernity, to rely for its ideas almost entirely on Western thinkers: on Locke, on Montesquieu, on Rousseau, on Adam Smith, on Karl Marx.

At the time of the Hundred Days' Reform of 1898, some had attempted to blend the Confucian notion of benevolence (*ren*) with Western ideas of liberty and equality. Others, such as Yan Fu (1854–1921), regarded by some as the 'father of Chinese liberalism', were more strongly anti-traditionalist. Yan Fu translated Adam Smith's *Wealth of Nations*, as well as John Stuart Mill's *On Liberty*, Thomas Henry Huxley's *Evolution and Ethics* and Montesquieu's *De l'esprit des lois* (all read by young radicals such as Mao Zedong before they had read any Marx or Engels). In 1949, Mao himself recognized that before the advent of communism and the Soviet Revolution, 'Chinese progressives went through untold hardships in their quest for truth from the Western countries'.[34] The opposite never occurred: Westerners translated some of the Chinese classics but not much in the way of works of history and philosophy.[35] Yan Fu believed that China had been damaged not only by foreign imperialism but by the attitude of Chinese intellectuals, who despised businessmen.[36] China, he explained, should turn her back on 'the way of the Sages' and the traditionalism that kept her people weak and ignorant.[37] By 1918, disillusioned with the West, Yan Fu had turned conservative and gone back to the teachings of Confucius.

Reformers were torn, as is often the case in what used to be called the Third World, between wishing to retain part of their heritage and realizing that they needed to adopt elements of Western culture. One of the most important reformers of the late Qing period, Zheng Guanying (or Cheng Kuan-ying), wrote that he had come to realize that

> the real source of Western success in government affairs as well as of Western wealth and power does not lie in battleships or guns, but in a parliamentary system which could bring about unanimous agreement between the ruler and the ruled.[38]

Before the Opium Wars of the mid-nineteenth century, China had regarded Westerners as barbarians. Those days were over. Now China needed to confront the West and modernity, and Westerners were to be admired as well as feared.

Sun Yat-sen himself did not disguise how inspired he was by the French Revolution, as well as by American federalism and the Meiji Restoration in Japan.[39] Nor did he hide his enormous admiration for Lenin and the Soviet Revolution.[40] He was a nationalist, but the term at the time did not necessarily signify an anti-Western attitude. He sought to make China strong by adopting and adapting aspects of foreign culture and technical expertise and even worked hard to attract foreign investment. This inevitably caused consternation, however, since anti-imperialism and foreign investment were widely seen as incompatible.[41] He seemed to realize the problem in 1924, when he wrote that China was becoming a semi-colony: 'We are being crushed by the economic strength of the Powers to a greater degree than if we were a full colony. China is not the colony of one nation but of all.'[42]

Sun argued that China's status was worse than 'semi-colonial', it was 'sub-colonial': in Shanghai, for instance, the Chinese were banned from many public places and from clubs; they were 'simply the slaves of all foreigners'.[43] In what were called 'treaty ports' but were not necessarily ports, foreign nationals – the British and French, and later the Americans, as well as Germans and Russians up to 1914 – enjoyed extraterritorial privileges almost as if they were residing in colonial outposts, though Chinese sovereignty was at least in theory preserved. These foreign tax-exempt enclaves, with their own food, sports, entertainment and clubs, could be found in almost every city of importance.[44]

Sun's perplexity was manifest. In his lecture on *minsheng* (welfare), he declared that state power should be used to build up the economy, otherwise a capitalist class, Chinese or foreign, would lead to more inequalities. In 1925, just before he died, he explained that some enterprises could be better conducted by the state, but others required competition: 'I have no hard and fast dogma. Much must be left to the lessons of experience.'[45] Like many revolutionaries, Sun Yat-sen was disappointed with the people he hoped to lead. The Chinese, he thought, do not have enough of a national sense; they were far too much connected to family and clan.[46]

The rise of Chinese Communism

The conjunction of nationalism and anti-imperialism – particularly evident among the educated classes, and almost absent among the Bolsheviks in 1917 – led to the next stage in the Chinese revolution: the May

Chinese protestors march against the Treaty of Versailles (4 May 1919)

Fourth Movement of 1919. This major event began as a student demonstration in Tiananmen Square, protesting the decision of the Great Powers convened at Versailles to grant the important coastal province of Shandong to Japan. (Both China and Japan had supported the Entente powers during the First World War.) Granting Shandong to Japan was seen as particularly insulting and humiliating, revealing once more the weakness of China in the face of foreign imperialism. The cultural and historical importance of Shandong could hardly be underestimated: it was a centre of Taoism, of Buddhism and of Confucianism (Confucius's hometown is in Shandong, as is Mencius's). Shandong had been the birthplace of the Boxer Rebellion. Once this had been defeated, control of the region had passed to Germany. When Germany lost the First World War, Shandong passed under Japanese control (until 1922 when the Washington Naval Conference restored possession of Shandong to China).

The Shanghai Student Union called for a boycott of Japanese goods, strikes and further demonstrations. Some of the emergent warlords supported the students out of hostility towards the Beijing government. The strange informal alliance between various warlords, Shanghai merchants and the 3,000 or so students who took part in the demonstrations enabled the May Fourth Movement to grow and spread to other parts of the country.[47] The entry of students into political, especially revolutionary, life was a novelty. Students had played hardly any role of importance in the Russian Revolution, and of course none in the previous major revolutions. They succeeded in forcing the Chinese delegates at Versailles to reject the Japanese demands. Eventually most of the warlords turned against the protesters, primarily out of concern for their powerbase.[48]

Mao, writing in 1939, pointed out that the May Fourth Movement, unlike the 1911 revolution, had been a mass event able to mobilize diverse social groups against Japanese imperialism and the warlords, and he stressed the importance of the intellectuals as leaders of the proletariat.[49] The May Fourth Movement was nationalist but also culturally pro-Western, attacking traditional Chinese customs such as arranged marriage, bound feet and above all the Confucian injunction that subjects must obey the ruler, the son must obey the father and the wife must obey the husband. The challenge to traditional Confucian values was a major part of the New Culture Movement: one of the slogans of the May Fourth Movement was 'Down with Confucius and Sons!'

For the Chinese Communists, but not just for them, the May Fourth Movement was the true beginning of 'their' revolution. Though he had little to do with its initial development, Sun Yat-sen too supported the May Fourth Movement, partly because he thought the increasingly ineffective KMT needed the support of youth. His soon-to-be successor, Chiang Kai-shek, a military man who was commandant of the Whampoa Military Academy, disapproved of the students' radical anti-traditionalism and remained committed to the promotion of China's cultural heritage and Confucian values, while also converting to Christianity.[50] For him, the 'real' Chinese Revolution was that of 1911.[51] He always regarded himself as a revolutionary who wanted to create a completely independent China. He regarded the communists as his main rivals in this project.

As in late-nineteenth-century Russia, and as in many so-called underdeveloped countries in the twentieth century, there was an ambivalence about the West and its culture: on the one hand, there was resentment of Western imperialism; on the other, it was necessary to fight it using not ancient cultural tools, but the very culture which the West propounded – liberalism, communism or socialism. It was as if one needed to be infatuated with the West to resist it. The May Fourth Movement contributed to the founding of the Chinese Communist Party (CCP) in 1921 in Shanghai, and to the reorganization of the Kuomintang in 1924. The CCP initially had virtually no popular roots. It was an association of mainly male students, teachers and intellectuals around the New Culture Movement at a time when the attraction of the Russian Revolution was being felt. The *Communist Manifesto* was fully translated into Chinese only in 1920. Though the number of workers in the party grew considerably during the 1920s (Shanghai by 1928 numbered around a quarter of a million factory workers), most early CCP members came from the gentry, from the merchant classes or from rich peasant families in parts of China where Western influence was strong.[52]

The CCP attracted into its orbit writers who have remained important in twentieth-century Chinese literature, such as Lu Xun, though he did not actually become a party member. Lu Xun was the celebrated author of *A Madman's Diary* (1918), a satire on Confucian culture inspired by Gogol's novella of the same title, while *The True Story of Ah Q* (1921) mocks revered Chinese traditions. Its protagonist, Ah Q, a mediocrity dismayed by his exclusion from the 1911 Revolution because of his low status, gets angrier and angrier 'until he was in a towering rage. "'So no rebellion for me, only for you, eh?" he exclaimed, nodding maliciously. "Curse you, you Imitation Foreign Devil – all right, be a rebel!"'[53]

Then there was Yu Dafu, whose novella *Chenlun* (Sinking, 1921), written while the author was in Japan, highlighted the humiliation felt by Chinese students when faced with the successes of Japan's Meiji Restoration. There were also Ding Ling, author of the feminist *Miss Sophia's Diary* (1927), where the protagonist's sexuality is described with remarkable frankness; and Mao Dun, later minister of culture (1949–65) in the People's Republic of China, whose novel *Midnight: A Romance of China* (1930) critically depicts Shanghai (the 'Paris of the East') under foreign rule, but cannot avoid casting admiring glances at the allure of its modernity.[54] Even in the nineteenth century, Shanghai was represented by traditionalists as a modern city which had renounced Confucian values in favour of the pursuit of money and the cult of novelty.[55] Later there was also an understandable resentment at the arrogance of foreigners in Shanghai: the public gardens on the Bund waterfront were closed to the Chinese (except those who served foreigners) until 1928.[56]

Many of the early communists had studied abroad, usually in Japan, Germany or France. Zhou Enlai, later prime minister, went to study in Paris (in 1920), as did the sixteen-year-old Deng Xiaoping. Zhu De, later the legendary commander of the Red Army, studied in Berlin and at the University of Göttingen.

In a letter to his cousin, Zhou wrote that there were only two paths out of China's crises: the gradual (or 'British') way, or violent revolution (the 'Soviet' way) – adding that he would prefer something in between.[57] Soon he was completely converted to the 'Soviet way'. At about the same time (December 1920), Mao Zedong too declared that he believed that the Russian-style revolution offered a solution where all else had failed. In January 1921, at a meeting of the New People's Study Society – the forerunner of the Chinese Communist Party – Mao listed four possible avenues: 'social policy', which he described as a 'stopgap measure'; social democracy (too parliamentarian); Bertrand Russell-type communism (too libertarian and leaving excessive room to capitalists); and anarchism, which denied political power. He opted for a fifth avenue – radical communism – because he thought it was the most practical way and the one most likely to deliver results.[58] At the time, Mao had read hardly any of the main texts of Marx and Engels.[59] Communism was the path a majority of the New People's Study Society found acceptable, and in July 1921 the Chinese Communist Party (CCP) came into being. Most Communists, including Mao, thought that the initial stage should be a national bourgeois revolution, hence their support for Sun Yat-sen. The peasants were not yet seen as possible leading protagonists of the Chinese Revolution. In 1922, Mao and other communists became very active in a major coal miners' strike in Anyuan, a locality which soon became known as 'Little Moscow'. By 1924, it was home to more than one-fifth of all party members.[60] The event was celebrated during the Cultural Revolution by the painter Liu Chunhua in his *Chairman Mao en Route to Anyuan* (1967), which appears to give most of the credit to Mao for the famous strike.

By June 1923, the CCP had decided to cooperate with the KMT in a united front against the warlords. In so doing, the Chinese communists were following the advice of the Comintern and their agent, Mikhail Borodin, who had also urged the newly formed party to join or infiltrate the well-established KMT. The CCP was a weak and tiny organization. It is true that in Russia, at the beginning of 1917, the Bolsheviks were not numerous – but they mattered, at least among workers in industrial centres. Besides, the Bolsheviks had been a major faction within the Social Democratic Party well before 1917. Most subsequent communist parties emerged out of splits from existing socialist parties of some significance – not the Chinese communists. Yet they grew from almost nothing to a considerable force during an exceptionally long revolutionary process.

The idea that the revolution is led by an existing strong revolutionary party waiting in the wings, ready to seize the right moment, has little historical substance. The norm is that there is first a revolutionary process, and during the process a revolutionary party emerges. Even in 1925 the CCP had, at most, a thousand members. Its association with the KMT and the Comintern played in its favour, and, by 1927, it had 57,000 members. Then it was seen as a threat and the KMT turned against it.[61]

However, as Lucien Bianco noted, membership figures tell only part of the story: the real strength of the party lay in its ability to mobilize the masses: 'During the summer of 1926 ... it was the CCP, which organized 1,200,000 workers and 800,000 peasants.'[62] This enabled the Communists to occupy the whole of Hunan province as well as nearby Wuhan, defeating the local warlords.

The death of Sun Yat-sen in 1925 was followed by a struggle within the KMT. Soon Chiang Kai-shek had gained overall control and launched a military campaign, the Northern Expedition, to establish a central authority in China. The successes of the Communists in Hunan accelerated the split with the KMT. Alarmed at the growing influence of the CCP, Chiang decided to crack down on them (though he still relied on financial help from the USSR). He was not only in dispute with the Communists but also with his own left-wingers. However, he needed to demonstrate his enduring radical credentials, so while he was breaking with the left he adopted some of their radical policies, particularly towards the peasants, emphasizing Sun Yat-sen's policy of 'land to the tillers'.[63] When, in September 1926, Chiang visited the Anyuan coal mine (like Mao), he called upon the workers to seize direct control of the mine.[64] This did little to disguise Chiang's shift to the right as warlords joined his forces, since what mattered to them was to be close to whoever was in control. Afterwards Chiang was unequivocally on the side of the landlords. As Lucien Bianco explains: 'To put the matter somewhat crudely, Chiang was interested in finding a solution to the agrarian problem only to deprive the Communists of their trump card.'[65]

China's woes continued. In the 1920s there were the two Zhili–Fengtian wars (1922 and 1924) for the control of Beijing (the Zhili faction was backed by Anglo-American business, the Fengtian by the Japanese). Soon Western powers virtually gave up interfering in Chinese affairs, leaving the field to the Japanese, against whom all Chinese anti-imperialist forces turned. Chiang's priority, however, was not just to contain the Japanese and the warlords but to eliminate the Communists. In April 1927, this policy culminated in a massacre of Communists with the help of the Shanghai mafia known as the Green Gang, the Qingbang. Thousands of trade unionists and activists were killed. Then Chiang Kai-shek established a Nationalist government in Nanjing and ceased his cooperation with the Soviets.[66] This was a major turning point in the history of the KMT and of modern China. It was the beginning of China's Civil War, which would last for over twenty years. Chiang had won the battle against the Communists but had lost the support of many progressives.[67]

Chiang's KMT did try to implement reforms, including a new civil code based on the German Civil Code of 1900 which had also been adopted in many other countries. The code acknowledged women as autonomous agents able to control their own marriage choices, inherit property and seek divorce.[68] The KMT still regarded itself as a revolutionary force inspired by Sun Yat-sen. It even welcomed Soviet advisers and adopted what might look like Leninist principles in the organization of the revolutionary party. Once it had established itself, however, the KMT opposed the idea of social revolution and class struggle.[69] By the 1930s, aroused by the successes of Mussolini and Hitler, Chiang even became attracted to fascism, declaring that was what China needed.[70] Beset by contradictory pressures and unable to establish a clear identity, the KMT continued to be riven by internal factional disputes. Many believed, quite reasonably, that the KMT had betrayed the revolution. In the longer term this helped the defeated Communists to regroup and recruit.[71]

A few months after the Shanghai massacre, in September 1927, Mao managed to lead the Autumn Harvest Uprising against the KMT and the landlords of Hunan and establish a Red Soviet base, the Hunan Soviet. It lasted only two months, and Mao was forced to retreat to the Jinggang Mountains. This led the Communists to create a military force, the Red Army. From then on, the revolution proceeded from the countryside to the towns. It still called itself a proletarian revolution, though there were few proletarians in the country and plenty of peasants. Mao was keen to recruit also those Marx would have defined as 'lumpenproletariat' or *declassés*. Rural workers who had lost employment had become *yumin* (rural vagrants). These, explained Mao, could be divided

> into soldiers, bandits, robbers, beggars and prostitutes. These five categories of people have different names, and they enjoy a somewhat different status in society. But they are all human beings, and they all have five senses and four limbs, and are therefore one. They each have a different way of making a living: the soldier fights, the bandit robs, the thief steals, the beggar begs, and the prostitute seduces ... They have secret organisations in various places ... To find a place for this group of people is the greatest and most difficult problem faced by China. China has two problems: poverty and unemployment. Hence, if the problem of unemployment can be solved, half of China's problems will be solved. The number of *yu-min* [rural vagrants] in China is fearfully large; it is roughly more than twenty million. These people are capable of fighting very bravely, and if properly led, can become a revolutionary force.[72]

The official Comintern line, less open-minded than Mao's, was that the only road was that of the proletarian insurrection. However, most Chinese Communists accepted that the revolution could begin not from urban centres but from the countryside, even if they assumed that an urban revolution would follow almost immediately after a major peasant uprising.[73] This is not what happened. Revolutionary processes are seldom established in advance and are hardly ever determined by the revolutionaries themselves but by circumstances. The Chinese Revolution became a peasant revolution because the Communists had lost power in the cities.

Mao, however, had stressed the importance of the peasant question as early as 1927, before the Shanghai massacre. He had visited Hunan (his birthplace) and investigated the conditions and aspirations of the peasantry there – all described in his famous 'Report on an Investigation of the Peasant Movement in Hunan' of March 1927. The peasant movement in Hunan was particularly strong. A few rich families owned much of the land, and demanded very high rents: 70–90 per cent of the crop in a poor harvest year.[74] Initially the KMT supported the peasants but, as the united front with the Communists collapsed, turned against the peasant movement until it subsided.[75] Mao criticized 'the wrong measures taken by the revolutionary authorities concerning the peasant movement' and was certain that 'the present upsurge of the peasant movement is a colossal event'. The peasants, he believed

> will rise like a mighty storm, like a hurricane, a force so swift and violent that no power, however great, will be able to hold it back … They will sweep all the imperialists, warlords, corrupt officials, local tyrants, and evil gentry into their graves. Every revolutionary party and every revolutionary comrade will be put to the test, to be accepted or rejected as they decide.[76]

The only way forward was for the Communists to 'march at their head and lead them'. This was the first of several reports Mao wrote on the peasantry, exhibiting increasing sophistication based on meticulous research.[77]

Mao and his supporters had to pay lip service to the Soviet Union, but Mao believed, even then, that one could not simply adapt the Soviet model to Chinese conditions. He proceeded to exclude those such as the so-called 'Twenty-Eight Bolsheviks' (mainly students just back from Moscow) who were committed to the Comintern line. His relationship with Stalin was always stormy.[78] This divergence became more manifest in January 1935 at the meeting of the Communist Politburo at Zunyi, in northern Guizhou, when Mao began to establish his supremacy within the CCP, though he did not formally become its leader until the early 1940s.[79]

A few months earlier, in October 1934, the Red Army had been forced to flee from Jiangxi to escape encirclement by the KMT forces. It was the beginning of the legendary Long March led by Mao. The details surrounding what was unquestionably a major event in modern Chinese history – it signalled the beginning of Communist ascendancy – have been much disputed. Legends aside, the Long March was a terrible retreat – though, with the passing of time, it assumed a mythical dimension almost on a par with *Washington Crossing the Delaware*, immortalized in the 1851 painting by Emanuel Leutze. The Communists had initially called the Long March the 'retreat', while the KMT referred to it as the 'Communist bandits escaping westward'.[80]

The ever-decreasing Communist forces marched for 6,000 miles, crossing rivers – and fighting the daring, and later somewhat mythologized, Battle of Luding Bridge over the Dadu River in Sichuan – and the high peaks of Jiajin in the Great Snowy Mountains of northern Sichuan. This took a heavy toll on the Red Army: many froze to death, fell into ravines, died of exhaustion or starved. By the time the Red Army reached Shaanxi in Northwest China in 1935, its forces were down to a mere 4,000 of the 86,859 who had begun the Long March.[81] At the sight of a heavy snowfall on his arrival in Shaanxi, Mao wrote one of his most famous poems, 'Snow', which established his standing as a classical poet.[82] It started with the romantic vision:

> The mountains, dancing silver snakes,
> The highlands, charging elephants,
> Triumphantly competing with the heavens' lofty height.
> And come a clear day,
> The land adorned with sunlight, draped in white,
> Seduces all who bear its sight.

Having mentioned some past 'heroes', the poem concludes:

> They are but history,
> For those who seek a greater figure yet
> Must look toward this age alone.

The Long March not only enabled the Communists to recover but also to recruit on the way, helped by growing peasant support – the result of their campaigns in favour of tax relief, rent reduction, land reform and defence against the Japanese.[83] Agrarian reforms were implemented by the Communists in the North even before their final victory, redistributing land and wealth to the peasants, battling against corruption and exploitation and encouraging peasants to organize.[84] By October 1936 Mao's troops had been joined in Shaanxi by two other Red armies.

Chiang Kai-shek's forces were far superior to those of the Communists, but he had to face the enmity and hostility of warlords and local power brokers who feared that Chiang, if too powerful, would turn against them and unify China under his control. Chiang had also to keep his own forces united and crack down on the rampant corruption of some of his supporters who misused public funds, imposed fiscal burdens on the people and failed to administer justice, while his government was unable to solve economic problems, including unemployment, poverty and inflation. The failures were due to Chiang's eagerness to wage war against the Communists to prevent them from mounting a counter-attack from their northern bases. His reluctance to try to control the economy was due to his fear of upsetting the business community. Afraid of antagonizing local landlords, he also refused to engage in a land reform, thus failing to achieve significant peasant support.[85] The huge inflation of 1937–49 was a major cause of the downfall of the KMT government and the success of the Communists, who quickly reduced the inflation rate.[86]

The war against Japan

The 1911 Revolution and its consequences had accelerated China's descent into chaos. Japan took advantage of this by beginning what would prove to be a fourteen-year war in China. In 1931 it invaded Manchuria and established a puppet state, Manchukuo. Japan's objectives seem to have been military and political rather than economic.[87] In its successful war against Russia in 1905–06, Japan had taken over Russian railway lines in Manchuria and built new ones. Many of the subsequent disputes between the Japanese and the Chinese were connected to the control, use and development of railway lines, important not only for the transfer of goods but, even more so, for the transportation of troops.[88] By then Japan had become the focus of Chinese nationalism, displacing the enmity against Western powers. The Japanese takeover of Manchuria met the almost complete indifference of what would today be called the 'international community'.[89] Behind the invasion was Japan's realization that China had become a failed state and that if Japan did not intervene, another power might. Japan's ambition was to replace the West (the British) as the dominant power in East Asia and to establish what it called a Greater Asia Co-Prosperity Sphere, which would include Southeast Asia.

The Kuomintang's weak response to the Japanese invasion of Northeast China contributed to its eventual downfall. Believing that the League of Nations would intervene, the KMT ordered its limited forces not to attack the powerful Japanese. In so doing, not only did it diminish its patriotic credentials but it also permitted the growth of volunteer militia which would be soon siding with the Communist forces, seen as the true patriots.[90] For Chiang, suppressing the Communists took precedence over resisting Japan. In 1932, after Japan's takeover of Manchuria, he was still arguing: 'Japan is not qualified to be our enemy; our present enemy is the red bandits.'[91] Even in November 1935, while the Japanese were advancing into China, Chiang Kai-shek indicated that he would continue to seek an accommodation through direct talks with Tokyo.[92] For this, Chiang was heavily criticized not just by the Communists and their supporters but by a large section of informed public opinion and the media.[93]

In Xi'an on 12 December 1936, one of Chiang's military commanders, Zhang Xueliang, kidnapped Chiang Kai-shek in what amounted to a coup d'état, and started negotiations with the Communists. This became known as the Xi'an Incident. Zhang ('the Young Marshal') was alarmed at Chiang's apparent stubborn insistence that the main enemy was the CCP and not Japan. The former had good reasons for prioritizing the struggle against the Japanese: his father, the warlord of Manchuria, had been murdered by the Japanese in 1928, forcing Zhang to evacuate Manchuria with his forces. Mao, pressed by the Comintern – then in favour of a broad anti-fascist front – sent Zhou Enlai to Xi'an to negotiate with the KMT. After only two weeks in captivity, Chiang Kai-shek agreed to give up his plans to destroy the Red Army.

This contributed to the CCP abandoning, at least temporarily, the goal of a revolution. In so doing it became more aligned with the turn of the Comintern, which had been urging Communists to form a united front against fascism since 1935. Georgi Dimitrov, general secretary of the Comintern, declared in 1937 that so far the Chinese Communist

Party had 'fought for the Soviets in China, for Soviet regions, created a Soviet government, created an army, [and] estranged a part of the army of Chiang Kai-shek from him in its aim of sovietisation'. But now the time had come to 'make the transition to the position of struggle not for the Sovietisation of China but for democracy, for unification on a democratic base of the forces of the Chinese people against Japanese imperialism, against Japanese aggression'.[94] Other factors supported a compromise with Chiang: the CCP needed military help from the USSR and Mao, described by John Garver as a 'genius of revolutionary strategy', could see the opportunities of tying the KMT into the war against Japan.[95]

The Xi'an Incident was an unexpected positive turn of fortune for the beleaguered Red Army stuck in northern Shaanxi. The Communists realized that this was their opportunity to recast themselves as the saviours of China from foreign invasion. They offered Chiang a deal he could not refuse: they would give up, for the time being, any ambitions to continue the 'class struggle'; they would rename the Red Army 'the National Revolutionary Army' and place it under the guidance of the Nanjing government (Chiang Kai-shek); and they would abandon the policy of land confiscation.[96] Chiang was under enormous pressure to accept the entreaties of the Communists, then not seen as a major threat since they were in distant Shaanxi. The Chinese people finally seemed united, at least against the Japanese. Fate was not so favourable to the Young Marshal. Zhang Xueliang, the hero of the whole Xi'an incident, was never forgiven by Chiang. To the resentment of many who had admired his action, he spent years in detention, first on the mainland, and then, when the KMT was defeated, in Taiwan. He was finally released on Chiang's death in 1975, and died in exile in Honolulu at the age of 100.

The war with Japan escalated. The KMT forces bore the brunt of the war effort, all to the longer-term advantage of the Communists. Following an incident on 7 July 1937 at the Lugou Bridge (known in the West as the Marco Polo Bridge) some ten miles south-west of Beijing, the Japanese decided to invade the rest of China. From a global perspective, this was the beginning of the Second World War. By August, the Japanese army was in reach of Shanghai; by early December it had occupied it after a protracted and bloody engagement. The incompetence of Chiang Kai-shek's forces was astonishing. They bombed inaccurately and ineffectively, hitting the city of Shanghai instead of the Japanese fleet and killing hundreds of civilians. Some 250,000 Chinese troops were killed or wounded, almost 60 per cent of the KMT's forces.[97] An eyewitness reported:

> Children in blood-drenched rags being carried through the streets in rickshaws, exhausted women enquiring directions to the nearest hospital, men, dazed and weak from loss of blood, with wounds untreated for several days. Such were the cases which wandered into Shanghai almost daily from the surrounding countryside.[98]

The Japanese moved towards Nanjing, then the capital. To preserve his forces Chiang fled west, first to Wuhan and then to Chongqing. Japanese soldiers then began the systematic plundering of Nanjing in the winter of 1937–38. They murdered 200,000 Chinese civilians and POWs and raped 20,000 women during a six-week period of astonishing brutality.[99] In a few weeks, more people were killed in Nanjing than in both Hiroshima and Nagasaki. This became known as the Rape of Nanjing:

> Not only did live burials, castration, the carving of organs, and the roasting of people become routine, but more diabolical tortures were practiced, such as hanging people by their tongues on iron hooks or burying people to their waist and watching them being torn apart by German shepherds [dogs].[100]

The Japanese poet Saeki Jinzaburo expressed his dismay at the deeds of his countrymen in a poem written shortly after the war:

> Seizing married women,
> Raping mothers in front of their children
> This is the Imperial Army.[101]

As the Japanese advanced towards Wuhan, an increasingly desperate Chiang Kai-shek ordered, in June 1938, that the dikes on the Yellow River should be destroyed to drown central Henan into a sea of mud in the hope of slowing down the Japanese advance. This mindless action led to the demolition of the houses and the destruction of the property of countless Chinese, causing some 500,000 deaths and creating about 3 million refugees.[102] In terms of casualties this was even worse than the Nanjing massacres. Chiang tried to cover his misdeed by blaming the Japanese, but all he had gained from his action was a little respite. Wuhan fell to the Japanese anyway.

Prior to the Japanese invasion, the Chinese industrial economy was doing relatively well in coastal areas despite warlords and internecine strife, growing at a rate of 6 per cent annually. Elements of modern industry had been developed, including railways, while China became less dependent on imports of rice, wheat and cotton.[103] The invasion put an end to hopes of prosperity. For the following three years, until Pearl Harbor, China stood alone against Japan. A much-weakened Chiang moved his capital again well to the west, to distant Chongqing, in Sichuan province. Chiang's loss of prestige was to the benefit of the Communists. Their newly organized Eighth Route Army soon consisted of 80,000 troops. Already in January 1937 the main army fighting against the Japanese in the Northeast was Communist-led.[104] Chiang's defeats strengthened Mao's belief that the right strategy against the Japanese would be the kind of guerrilla warfare he had proposed in 1930 when fighting Chiang Kai-shek: 'The enemy advances, we retreat; the enemy camps, we harass; the enemy tires, we attack; the enemy retreats, we pursue.'[105] The Japanese army advanced steadily but it was never in full control away from the cities and roads. It was overwhelmed by the immensity of China. Parts of the country were under Communist control (such as Yan'an), while others were under Japanese occupation or a Japanese puppet, or the KMT (such as Chongqing). Tibet had announced its independence, and other areas were under various warlords.

In his lecture 'On Protracted War' (May 1938), Mao pointed out that while Japan could not subjugate the whole of China, the war would be a long one: 'All the experience of the ten months of war proves the error both of the theory of China's inevitable subjugation and of the theory of China's quick victory.'[106] In answer to a question by the American journalist Edgar Snow, he explained that three conditions were required to win: an anti-Japanese united front, international support and the rise of revolutionary movement in Japan.[107] The first conditions held up somewhat; as for the second, Mao mistakenly thought that Britain and the US would help the Kuomintang. Real international intervention had to wait for the Second World War and above all for Japan's attack on Pearl Harbor. The third condition – revolution in Japan – never materialized.

Another of Mao's essays, on guerrilla warfare, is remarkable not only for its comprehensive military discussion but for the absence of ideological elements. There is hardly any mention of socialism or class struggle. There was only one goal – victory against the Japanese by exploiting China's home advantage:

The enemy forces, though strong (in arms, in certain qualities of their men, and certain other factors), are numerically small, whereas our forces, though weak (likewise, in arms, in certain qualities of our men, and certain other factors), are numerically very large. Added to the fact that the enemy is an alien nation invading our country while we are resisting his invasion on our own soil.[108]

This is not to say that ideology was discarded. Even in 'On Protracted War', there is a hint that the 'new China' would be a 'China of freedom and of equality'.[109] In his major essay 'On New Democracy' (1940), Mao presented himself as a national anti-imperialist (like Sun Yat-sen), and while paying lip service to the 'proletariat', he foregrounded the peasantry and the agrarian question. He assumed, as was not uncommon in Marxist thought, a two-stage revolution: a 'democratic' stage of a 'Chinese type', and then a socialist one. The difference with the traditional view was that even the first bourgeois stage would be led by the proletariat, and this because China was not a fully fledged capitalist state but a semi-colonial country. The outcome of the first stage would be a 'joint dictatorship of all revolutionary classes' that would usher in the new democratic China.[110] Private property would be maintained but the state would own the big banks and the big industrial and commercial enterprises.[111] It would be a development of Sun Yat-sen's 'Three Principles' and policies such as 'land to the tillers' and 'equalization of landlordship'.

This seems to be an attempt to justify in ideological terms the decision to form a united front with the 'bourgeois' KMT. Mao seemed to decide first on what to do and then justify his decision using Marxist ideas – not an uncommon practice: Lenin used it regularly. He was also deeply convinced that Soviet assistance was indispensable for China's victory against Japan.[112] This is why Mao defended the Non-aggression Pact between Germany and the USSR of August 1939 and why he did not fail to pay the required tribute to Stalin.[113] Later that year, on the occasion of Stalin's official birthday, Mao thanked him and the USSR for the help given during the war against Japan. 'His birthday will evoke warmth and affectionate congratulations from the hearts of all revolutionary people throughout the world', Mao declared, adding that 'Stalin is the true friend of the cause of liberation of the Chinese people'.[114] By the Seventh Party Congress in April 1945, Stalin was barely mentioned – an unusual slight in those days.[115] In 1956 Mao expressed to a Yugoslav delegation his feelings towards Stalin, for whom he supposedly felt only 'disgust' after their meetings in Moscow in 1949 and 1950. Of course, by then Stalin was dead and de-Stalinization was on the way.[116]

The war had become global with the German attack on the USSR in June 1941 and that by the Japanese on Pearl Harbor in December. Thanks to the so-called 'Rectification Campaign' of 1942, the Chinese Communist Party had become a formidable organizational weapon. Though still weaker than both the Japanese and the KMT, it enjoyed local support and was developing state structures.[117] Mao was now totally in charge of his party, having seen off his Moscow-trained rivals, while Chiang Kai-shek was beset with internal rivalries, defections, corruption, economic incompetence and a terrible famine in Henan, for which, as Rana Mitter wrote, 'Chiang's regime must be held responsible'.[118] The KMT conscripts were treated absurdly harshly: the recruits were frequently tied together with ropes around their necks and stripped of their clothing at night to prevent them from sneaking away. They were given tiny rations of rice and forced to drink from puddles by the road. Soon many of them (who came from poor families unable to bribe their way out of conscription) became weak and undernourished; probably more than a million perished during the eight years of the war because of food shortages, and many deserted.[119] The Sino-Japanese War led to the deaths of some 20 million Chinese and to 50 million displaced persons. Much of the industrial infrastructure was destroyed.[120] By comparison, the Second World War led to the deaths of 600,000 French people and fewer than 500,000 Americans and British, but left around 25 million Soviets dead.

Yet despite such devastation, Chiang still gave priority to containing the growing strength of the Communists, who had dealt with the famine problem in their Yan'an base in Shaanxi with great effectiveness, saving it from collapse.[121] Yan'an became, in practice, the embryonic matrix of the Chinese Revolution. It was from this Red base that Mao and the Chinese Communist Party launched their war against Japan and, once that was over, their struggle against the KMT in the following Civil War. Yan'an attracted revolutionaries from all over China, including many intellectuals and artists. This led Mao to devote time to stress the importance of revolutionary art and literature, something which was virtually unmentioned in the main phases of the American, French and Russian Revolutions (though celebratory art usually followed). The obvious explanation is that the Chinese Revolution was a lengthy process in which state building began well before power was achieved. Even cultural policy was developed during the revolution. Prompted by committed writers who had made the journey to the Red base, Mao delivered, in

May 1942 his 'Talks at the Yan'an Forum on Literature and Art', in which he stressed the importance of the cultural struggle in the revolution with the aim of reducing the importance of 'feudal' and 'comprador' (foreign) culture. There is little doubt that Mao wanted an art which was basically propagandistic, opposing the Japanese, supporting the Communist Party and eliminating petty-bourgeois ideas from the masses. The task of intellectuals was to learn the language of the masses and write for them. At the same time, Mao sought to preserve 'the legacies of the ancients and of foreigners'. One should not 'refuse to learn from them, even though they are the works of the feudal or bourgeois classes'.[122]

Paradoxically the advance of the Japanese into central and southern China was a major factor that favoured the Communists, since the Japanese destroyed KMT infrastructure while undermining the power of established elites and shattered the traditional world of the Chinese village.[123] The KMT was further weakened by having to deploy troops in Burma to help the Allies. The behaviour of Japanese troops – the looting and the raping, typical of a foreign force with no obvious long-term stake in the territory occupied – further contributed to the resentment of rural populations. Its 'three-all' policy – 'burn all, kill all, loot all' – made the Japanese army the 'greatest ally' of the CCP.[124] In addition, it should be recognized that Mao was a brilliant war leader. As David Apter has observed, Mao outwits the enemy, he improvises (like Lenin), fashions and reshapes events into general principles, and successfully erases the line between fantasy and fact – all indispensable elements in the mythologizing of the Communist revolution.[125]

The Communists had a further advantage. In the ten years before achieving power they ruled a large part of China, which included, by 1945, almost one-fifth of the whole population. Nothing like this occurred in the revolutions examined in other chapters so far. The Communists offered the peasantry a realistic prospective of some order after more than a century of disorder.[126] In Henan the local population could not forget the disaster which had ensued from Chiang's destruction of the dikes on the Yellow River, which is why they refrained from supporting him – to the delight of the Communists.[127]

A separate contributing factor to the eventual success of the Communists was the incompetence and poor judgement of Chiang Kai-shek and the KMT. Chiang wrongly assumed that he would receive significant military help from the US (he had received more from the USSR during the war against Japan). The reality was that the US always regarded China as a junior partner in the war against Japan. Insofar as the Americans,

British and Russians were concerned, they were the Big Three.[128] China was in the war but not one of the 'Big Three'. Chiang Kai-shek was hardly ever consulted on matters of strategy. Churchill had never disguised his scorn at China as one of the powers, declaring that the 'idea that China is going to have a say in the affairs of Europe … or that China should be rated for European purposes', not just at the same level as France or Poland 'or above even the smallest but ancient, historic and glorious States like Holland, Belgium, Greece and Yugoslavia – has only to be stated to be dismissed'.[129] The scorn was reciprocated. Zhou Enlai told American officers that the Chinese 'despise the British position'. This had followed the British loss of Singapore after only a day's fighting and their inability to hold on to Burma.[130]

General Stilwell, Roosevelt's adviser on China, had an extremely poor opinion of Chiang, believing, with some justification, that his was a 'rotten regime'. Chiang had an equally poor opinion of Stilwell, who, after more mishaps, was eventually recalled, but the Americans continued to regard China as a lost cause, and compared unfavourably the areas dominated by the KMT with those run by the Communists, where they found cohesion, discipline, lack of corruption and an absence of the desperate poverty so evident in KMT-held Chongqing. They were even impressed by the cultural shows Mao's supporters had managed to deploy for their benefit when they visited. Mao's talk at the Yan'an Forum had obviously paid off.[131]

Many foreign observers formed a favourable opinion of the Communists.[132] The best-known American sympathizer, the journalist Edgar Snow – author of the celebrated and influential *Red Star over China* (1937), written during his extended visit with the Communist forces and in the course of numerous interviews with Mao Zedong and Zhou Enlai – thought that Communist policies had established a solid bond between an impoverished peasantry, whose 'deepest concerns lay with land, food, and security' and the revolutionary party.[133] The agrarian reform implemented by the Communists in the North, even before their final victory, took the land away from the better-off landlords and gave it to the peasants.[134] As Lucien Bianco noted: 'The Communists paid attention to local problems and tried to satisfy the peasants' most pressing claims.'[135] It was a strategy that the KMT was never willing to adopt fully.

By July 1945, Japan had lost the war. The Chinese – both Communists and Nationalists – had played a secondary role in this. The Soviet Union was poised to attack Japanese forces in Manchuria and Korea, as agreed with the Allies at Yalta, but the *coup de grâce* was the atomic bomb detonated at Hiroshima on 6 August. The rapid Soviet invasion of Manchuria occurred on 9 August, the day the second atomic bomb hit Nagasaki. Japan had already been much weakened by the American bombing campaign on Japanese cities in 1944 and 1945, including the firebombing of Tokyo (using napalm), which caused almost 100,000 deaths and massive destruction in one night.[136]

China was finally free, but not at peace.

The return of the Civil War

After the Japanese withdrawal, Soviet and US troops occupied parts of the country while the CCP and the KMT half-heartedly continued their united front. Mao, in a circular dated 26 August 1945, explained that the CCP would recognize the status of the Kuomintang provided there was reciprocity:

> This would bring about a new stage of cooperation between the two parties and of peaceful development. In that event, our Party should strive to master all methods of legal struggle and intensify its work in the Kuomintang areas in the three main spheres, the cities, the villages, and the army (all weak points in our work there).

He then added:

> If the Kuomintang still wants to launch civil war after our Party has taken the above steps, it will put itself in the wrong in the eyes of the whole nation and the whole world, and our Party will be justified in waging a war of self-defence to crush its attacks.[137]

The Communists' initial reluctance to engage in a civil war was also due to the lukewarm support they were getting from Moscow. Throughout the war, all Soviet aid to China in the form of war materials was delivered to Chiang Kai-shek, and the Communists were very bitter about this.[138] At Yalta Stalin had promised Roosevelt that the Soviet Union would not support the CCP in the event of a civil war, probably having assumed that Mao would not be able to defeat the KMT.[139] To add to Mao's dismay at Stalin's behaviour there was also the Sino-Soviet Treaty of Friendship signed with Chiang on 14 August 1945, a day before Japan's formal surrender.[140]

Chiang Kai-shek did not want a lasting truce with the Communists. He was determined to control the whole of China, confident he would get significant American help. This he did, though it did not help much, since one of the most serious problems he faced was the corruption spreading through his administration. In October 1945 he had noted:

> The military, political and party officials in Nanking [Nanjing], Shanghai, Peiping [Beijing] and Tientsin have been leading extravagant lives, indulging in prostitution and gambling, have forcibly occupied the people's larger buildings as offices ... They have resorted to every perverse act, even including blackmailing ... To be corrupted to this extent without any self-respect in the recovered areas is a disgrace to the local people, a sin committed against our heroic martyrs who have been sacrificed in the war.[141]

Yet nothing was done. In an astonishing reflection in January 1948, when it was becoming clear that the KMT was losing the war, Chiang Kai-shek declared: 'Never, in China or abroad, has there been a revolutionary Party as decrepit and degenerate as we are today; nor one as lacking spirit, lacking discipline, and even more, lacking standards of right and wrong as we are today.'[142] He acknowledged the KMT's superiority in terms of troops and equipment, but also that its officers were 'unprofessional' and 'do not use their brains', while expressing his unabashed admiration for the Communists, who had everything the Nationalist regime lacked: organization, discipline and morality. He even praised the egalitarian ethos of Communist troops while disparaging those of the KMT.[143]

The Communists were able to exploit the many economic grievances which emerged once the Japanese had left, from the massive inflation that followed the Japanese withdrawal to the growing unemployment and strikes in Shanghai and Canton.[144] The KMT had lost the support of liberals and intellectuals, who were dismayed at the censorship imposed, the banning of newspapers, at dissident journalists being forced to 'confess' that they supported the Communists, and at the corruption.[145] The KMT's popularity continued to plummet as its behaviour seemed to parallel that of the Japanese: brutality, torture and looting. When the KMT recaptured an area, the punishment meted out to peasants who had supported the Communists could be extremely ferocious. In one case the expropriated landlord killed someone in each family in the village.[146]

To add to anti-Western feelings, there was the behaviour of American troops in China. They were there to supervise the truce of 13 January 1946 between the CCP and the KMT, but their brutality, which included rapes, drunkenness, gambling, looting and arrogant violence (the accusation came also from all sources, not just Communist ones), added to the popularity of the Communists.[147] Harry Truman, who became president after Roosevelt's death in April 1945, had been advised not to support Chiang. US intelligence confirmed that the USSR was refraining from giving important material aid to the Communists. But the Cold War had just broken out, and Truman did not want to be seen as soft on communism, so some aid was extended to Chiang. This took the form of the 1948 China Aid Act – much too late to have any effect, as some of those in Washington would have been only too aware.[148] This was one of the many foreign policy miscalculations that have characterized US policy towards China since 1945.

In December 1948, Admiral John Inglis, chief of US Naval Intelligence, discussing the Communist advance with Roscoe H. Hillenkoetter, the first director of the CIA, and Stafford LeRoy Irwin, director of the Military Intelligence Division, revealed his ignorance and prejudices about Chinese matters as well as his distrust of Chiang Kai-shek, who was preparing to evacuate to Taiwan:

> One thing that puzzles us is the superiority and the strategic direction of the Chinese Communists and their ability to support themselves logistically and in communications. It just doesn't seem Chinese ... And another thing, turning our attention to the situation in Formosa [Taiwan]. Does anyone know a strong man in Formosa who we would do well to back instead of carpetbaggers from China or Chiang Kai-shek?[149]

Victory for the PLA

The Americans, though aware of the incompetence of the KMT, failed to see the superior competence of the Communists.[150] The Red Army had grown from just over 90,000 in 1937 to just under a million in 1945, attracting an increasing number of defectors from the KMT enticed by the offer of being integrated into the Red Army with the same rank.[151] In September 1948 Lin Biao launched a major attack in Manchuria, and the entire region fell to the Communists. By then Mao could claim that 1.6 million peasants who had obtained land had joined the People's

Liberation Army (as the Communist forces had been renamed in July 1946).[152] Chiang's forces numbered 2.5 million, yet he kept losing for a number of reasons, including his military incompetence. By 1948 Truman, having been re-elected with a small majority on a very low turnout (51 per cent), had virtually abandoned Chiang.[153]

The decisive battle between the CCP and the KMT was the two-month Huaihai campaign (or Battle of Hsupeng) north of the Yangzi River. Fought between November 1948 and January 1949, it was 'the largest military engagement fought after World War II', involving more than 1.8 million soldiers across 200 kilometres. It ended with a clear Communist victory despite the KMT's numerical superiority.[154]

As the People's Liberation Army (PLA) approached Beijing in January 1949, the KMT general, Fu Zuoyi, realizing his forces were isolated, decided to surrender (he later became a minister in the Communist government). On 31 January 1949, the PLA entered Beijing. Derk Bodde, an American sinologist who was present at the victory parade in February 1949, wrote:

> What made it especially memorable to Americans was the fact that it was primarily a display of American military equipment, virtually all of it captured or obtained by bribe from Kuomintang forces in the short space of two and half years.[155]

On 25 March, Mao arrived in Peiping (Beijing), symbolizing the reincarnation of the party as an urban one.

The PLA advanced everywhere, entering Nanjing, the KMT capital, in April 1949 and encountering no resistance – an event duly celebrated by Mao in a poem:

> Our mighty army, a million strong, has crossed the Great River.
> The City, a tiger crouching, a dragon curling, outshines its ancient glories;
> In heroic triumph heaven and earth have been overturned.[156]

Shanghai was liberated on 25 May 1949, though it was more a handover than a takeover. Randall Chase Gould, an American journalist who had worked for the English-language *Shanghai Evening Post* since 1931, eventually becoming its editor, wrote that the foreign community was not dismayed when the Communists took over because 'we had suffered increasingly from maladministration by most of the dominant figures of the Nationalist regime'. He added that no one had 'the slightest confidence' in the capacity of the KMT, contrasting the 'superb' behaviour of the Communist troops who 'insisted on paying for whatever they took' to the lack of discipline of the Nationalists.[157] In September 1949, when forced to resume publication on Communist terms (they demanded that the paper should be operated by its trade unions), Gould left China.

By August 1949, the People's Liberation Army controlled most of mainland China. Its victory was extraordinary. A country the size of a continent was conquered by an army of peasants, and at a pace that dumbfounded military experts.[158] By December, Chiang Kai-shek's Nationalists had been forced to retreat to Taiwan with some 2 million soldiers and supporters. Earlier, in February 1947, they had massacred between 18,000 and 28,000 of Taiwan's inhabitants (the 28 February or 228 Incident), including many members of the island's elite, alienating the local population. Proportionately speaking, this was a higher death toll than for the Great Cultural Revolution.[159] Taiwan, previously known in the West with its Portuguese name of Formosa ('beautiful'), had been a Japanese colony between 1895 and 1945, so its links with the mainland had been loosened. The island remained under martial law until 1987, during which period over 100,000 people were imprisoned for political reasons. An official public holiday now takes place on 28 February and Chiang Kai-shek is held responsible for ordering the massacre.[160]

The Civil War between the KMT and the CCP had not been one between communism and liberal democracy as some surmised during the Cold War. Rather, it was a struggle between a Communist Party reluctant to fight another war and an authoritarian KMT determined to destroy the Communists. The success of the Communists was not just due to the incompetence and corruption of the KMT. The key had been their ability to introduce elements of agrarian reform and rent reduction in the areas they occupied.[161] One schoolteacher, interviewed shortly after he left the Communist area, explained that 'after the farmer receives his share of land', the only way of preserving it from the return of the landlords was to support the CCP.[162] The efficacy of land reform depended on the distribution of land tenure in the various areas. In Communist-held Hopei and Shantung, a substantial proportion of rural farm families did not own sufficient land to be self-supporting, and in the Northeast where the CCP carried out land reform, poor peasants were half the population.[163] Mao was quite clear that the land problem was closely connected to the war effort.[164]

The Communists also had to take account of the class division in the rural sectors: there were the landlords who lived entirely off the labour of others; the rich peasants, who farmed their land and hired labourers; the middle peasants, who owned their land but did not hire anyone; the poor peasants, who owned little or no land and had also to work for others; and, finally, hired farm labourers who owned no land at all. Clearly an agrarian reform would be largely in the interests of the poor peasants and landless labourers, and it was obviously towards these that the CCP directed its main appeal, but even rich peasants had to be enticed onto the side of the revolution.[165]

During the war against the Japanese and even during the Civil War, the CCP maintained that socialism could be only a distant goal. After all, China was more backward than Russia had been in 1917. Even in 1940, in his 'On New Democracy' (see above), Mao wrote that the goal was not the dictatorship of the proletariat but 'a dictatorship of all the revolutionary classes', a 'transitional form of state to be adopted in … colonial and semi-colonial countries'. There was virtually no discussion of what a socialist society should look like and plenty of rhetoric about the working people and their enemies: the feudal lords, the reactionaries and the 'running dogs' of imperialism. The reluctance to make socialism the immediate next step was standard among the East European states created by the advance of the Soviet Red Army: these should be people's democracies, and not yet socialist states. Indeed, in Poland, most of the land remained in private hands throughout the communist period. All the countries, however, became one-party dictatorships.

The Chinese Communists sought to appeal to virtually all social groups. On May Day 1946, an editorial in the *Liberation Daily* in Yan'an declared: 'Private capital is an indispensable force in the reconstruction of the liberated areas' and trade unions must also 'persuade the workers not to demand overmuch from the capitalists'.[166] This was quite unlike the Bolsheviks' period of War Communism during the Russian Civil War, which deployed radical left policies (see previous chapter). The moderate line of the Chinese Communists was upheld even when they finally began to conquer major cities. Since the Red Army was still largely a peasant army, efforts were made to contain the almost inevitable violence that an occupying army displays. Instructions included: 'Do not eat in the streets. Do not walk arm-in-arm in the streets. Urinate and defecate in latrines only.'[167]

By 27 February 1947, an internal directive drafted by Mao for the party's Central Committee warned: 'Precautions should be taken against the mistake of applying in the cities the measures used in rural areas for struggling against landlords and rich peasants and for destroying the feudal forces.' A 'sharp distinction' should be made between 'the feudal exploitation practiced by landlords and rich peasants, which must be abolished, and industrial and commercial enterprises run by landlords and rich peasants, which must be protected.' One should not pursue a 'one-sided and narrow-minded policy of "relief", which purports to uphold the workers' welfare but in fact damages industry and commerce and impairs the cause of the people's revolution'.[168]

On 18 January 1948, Mao, in another directive ('On Some Important Problems of the Party's Present Policy') argued that those who claimed that 'the poor peasants and farm labourers … should rule the country' were wrong. The rulers of the country, he claimed, should include even the 'enlightened gentry' and the 'new rich peasants', middle and small capitalists, ordinary intellectuals ('students, teachers, professors, scientific workers, art workers') and professionals. The policy adopted in Communist areas, of encouraging private industry and commerce, 'was correct and should be continued in the future'. Even landlords who 'engaged in physical labour for five years or more … may now have their class status changed in accordance with their present condition, provided their behaviour has been good'.[169]

Mao continued to urge moderation: 'Reactionaries must be suppressed but killing without discrimination is strictly forbidden; the fewer killings, the better. Death sentences should be reviewed and approved by a committee formed at the county level.'[170] The aim was clear: to reassure all and sundry that the Communists were not against private property or enterprise and that all that was required of people was not to side with the Kuomintang. But the workers were not forgotten. As the Communists returned to their original urban bases, they organized unions and increased wages. In 1948, the Communists, having captured the city of Harbin in Manchuria, held the Sixth All-China Labour Congress with delegates also from KMT-controlled areas. This established the eight-hour day, as well as equal pay for equal work for men and women and paid maternity leave for women.[171]

By then the impending Cold War meant that the US would no longer hold a balanced position between the Communists and the Nationalists. A Communist victory, or so the Americans thought, would mean a victory for the Soviet bloc. But Asian matters were of secondary importance to both the USSR and the US: Europe was what mattered. In the end this was more to the advantage of the Chinese Communists than of the Chinese Nationalists. The Cold War also turned out to be to the advantage of the defeated Japanese. Their country was quickly integrated into the West, just as West Germany would be. Yesterday's mortal enemies became the friends of tomorrow. Yesterday's allies (the USSR) became mortal enemies.

The revolutionary process which had started with the fall of the Qing dynasty in 1911 seemed about to enter a new phase. The warlords had been defeated. The Japanese invaders had been forced to withdraw by a combination of American advances, atomic bombing and the threats of Soviet armies. The subsequent stage was the Communist victory celebrated in Tiananmen Square, when, on 1 October, Mao Zedong, atop the Gate of Heavenly Peace, proclaimed the founding of the People's Republic of China with its capital at Beiping, which was returned to the former name of Beijing. The 'Mandate of Heaven' had now been conferred to Mao Zedong.

Mao was now the unchallenged Great Leader, his standing sanctioned by the war. A victorious war always immeasurably enhances the prestige of leaders, as was the case with Stalin in Russia, Churchill in Britain, Roosevelt in the US and de Gaulle in France. The seizure of power by the Bolsheviks towards the end of 1917 was followed by several years of civil war. In China, on the other hand, the Civil War had preceded the seizure of power. After that no real threat emerged against Communist rule: the unrest that followed (such as the Cultural Revolution) was all their own work.

The New Democracy

China, now Xinhua, the New China, was finally under a stable central authority governing a vast and populous country whose boundaries approximated those of the late Qing Empire. The great Communist achievement was that China was finally at peace, united under a strong government whose aim was to reconcile all those not actively opposed to the new regime.[172] It had taken more than a century to achieve such stability – and it was soon to be disrupted by the Great Leap Forward and the Cultural Revolution.

Revolutions often end up with a strong centre, as was obviously the case in France after a century of turmoil. The US adopted a federal structure but the dispute between states' rights and the federal government has been a constant theme of its history. The UK has always been a highly centralized state, despite recent devolution to the Celtic fringe. The Russian Revolution eventually settled on a federal model: at the time of its dissolution, fifteen republics coexisted under the aegis of the Union of Soviet Socialist Republics. The centre, however, was always dominant; the Soviet republics were never autonomous in any meaningful sense.

China too conceded autonomy to five regions where a significant proportion of the population belonged to one or more of the fifty-five ethnic-minority groups which are not Han (Chinese). The Han comprise over 90 per cent of the population of China, though the Han themselves are divided by language, habits and even food.[173] The process of establishing the autonomous regions was realized gradually, and followed the spirit of post-1911 revolutionaries that China should be a republic of 'five races': Han, Manchu, Mongol, Uyghur and Tibetan.[174] Inner Mongolia was established in 1947. Tibet, which had acquired independence after the fall of the Qing, was virtually annexed in 1951, as an autonomous region. This was followed by largely Muslim Xinjiang in 1955, and then in 1958 by Ningxia (also containing many Muslims) and Guangxi. As in the US, and unlike in the USSR, secession was not permitted in law. Serious ethnic separatist challenges came mainly from the Xinjiang Uyghur Autonomous Region and the Tibetan Autonomous Region.[175]

The period following the 'Liberation' of October 1949 was seen by the Communists as signifying the defeat of imperialism, feudalism and bureaucratic-capitalism (the KMT). But the British were allowed to keep Hong Kong, and while large landlords lost much of their land, capitalists were tolerated if they were deemed patriotic – that is, if they accepted the regime. It was the era of New Democracy, a term used to distinguish China from the previous era without suggesting that it had become socialist – a time of consensus and collaboration between the Communists and ill-defined 'progressive forces', including some members of the bourgeoisie. Those actively opposed were severely repressed.

On the morrow of their great victory, the situation facing the Communists was dire. The economy had been severely damaged by the war: prices had increased and unemployment was high. The Communists were not fully in control of every part of the country and obviously not of Taiwan where the KMT had sought refuge, taking the national Treasury.[176] The Communist victory was, as Mao put it,

> only the first step in a long march of ten thousand li ... After several decades, the victory of the Chinese people's democratic revolution, viewed in retrospect, will seem like only a brief prologue to a long drama.

A drama begins with a prologue, but the prologue is not the climax. The Chinese revolution is great, but the road after the revolution will be longer, the work greater and more arduous.[177]

The 'prologue' proved relatively successful. The overall judgement on the CCP's first years in power tends to be positive.[178] At first, moderation seemed to prevail. On 30 June 1949, a few months before the founding of the People's Republic and on the anniversary of the founding of the Communist Party, Mao had declared that the present policy 'was to regulate capitalism, not destroy it', but to do so under 'the leadership of the working class'.[179] The 'Common Programme' adopted in September 1949, and which served as China's constitution until 1954, did not mention the word socialism, while private enterprises were encouraged.[180] There was a sharp decline in inequalities in the countryside, the currency was stabilized, there was a fall in mortality rates, an improvement in nutrition levels and landlord holdings were considerably reduced, while preserving 'the essence of the rich peasant economy'.[181] There were considerable improvements in public health, safety at work, transportation systems and mortality rates.

In some parts of China, peasants seized the land – at times violently. It was a revolution conducted as much from below as from above. Soon, however, land reform was carried out by administrative means. It was, in the words of Jack Gray, 'the greatest act of expropriation in human history'.[182] The human losses were not insignificant: during the agrarian reform of 1949–53 the number of landlords and so-called counter-revolutionaries executed (usually by locals) is likely to have been between 200,000 and 800,000, perhaps more.[183] In spite of his sympathies for Mao's revolution, William Hinton in his account of the land reform in the village of Zhangzhuangcun (Long Bow) in North China accepts that the sudden destruction of landed privileges, though it led to rapid social advances, was often accompanied by 'excesses and tragedies'. People were beaten to death by angry crowds, some were wrongly dispossessed and revolutionary leaders 'rode roughshod over their followers'.[184] The campaign against counter-revolutionaries targeted not only supporters of the KMT and those who had collaborated with the Japanese, but also members of secret societies as well as ordinary criminals.

There were successes in foreign policy: China, at great cost in terms of casualties, forced the US to a standstill in Korea while establishing itself as a leading non-aligned country at Bandung in 1955.[185] China managed to withstand the embargo and the sanctions placed by the US in 1951 – a 'strategic embargo' which turned into a transparent euphemism for economic warfare.[186] China even survived, with difficulty, the sudden withdrawal of Soviet aid and technicians in 1960, as the dispute with the USSR developed.[187] In fact, relative economic isolation developed China's self-reliance. The economy improved, the private sector was under control and some forms of limited collectivization in agriculture were achieved without the kind of trauma afflicting the USSR.

The liberation of women had been one of the priorities of the Chinese Communist Party from its foundation, inspired by the May Fourth Movement.[188] In fact, women participated in the many uprisings preceding the 1911 Revolution. In 1909, when 'a young woman in a village in remote Kansu killed herself because her husband's parents opposed her plans to unbind her feet and to enter school, her farewell letter was widely circulated in the press'.[189] Towards the end of the nineteenth century, Yan Fu, a Westernizing Chinese scholar (see above), had written that of all the 'noxious practices' plaguing China, two stood out: one the addiction to opium; the other the practice of binding women's feet.[190] Foot binding had been formally abolished by imperial edict in 1902, but it persisted.

The 'feminine ferment', to use Marx's words, was not a Western prerogative. In the late nineteenth and early twentieth centuries, female poets such as the revolutionary Qiu Jin raged against foot binding and the denial of education to girls in her manifesto, *A Respectful Proclamation to China's 200 Million Women Comrades*. In one of her poems, she wrote:

> Unbinding my feet, I clean out a thousand years of poison
> With heated heart arouse all women's spirits.[191]

In his 'Report on an Investigation of the Peasant Movement' (1927), Mao had added the subjection of women by their husbands as one of the four 'systems of authority' to be overthrown, along with the state system, the clan and religious orders.[192] Now in power, the Communists declared in their 'Common Programme' (Article 6):

> The People's Republic of China shall abolish the feudal system which holds women in bondage. Women shall enjoy equal rights with men in political, economic, cultural, educational and social life. Freedom of marriage for men and women shall be put into effect.[193]

Divorces rapidly increased, often initiated by the woman. In 1950, the Communists introduced the New Marriage Law, which ended legal concubinage and forced marriage – though, of course, there is often a substantial gap between the promulgation of a law and its implementation. A few years later the CCP backtracked: it toned down its challenge of the urban and rural patriarchy and made divorce more difficult.[194]

Nevertheless, some sort of female emancipation – embodied in Mao's much quoted saying, 'women hold up half the sky' and in successful ballets such as *Red Detachment of Women* (1964) – progressed, even through the turmoil of the Cultural Revolution, albeit at a snail's pace. In the late 1980s women accounted for only 20 per cent of students at the prestigious Peking (Beijing) University.[195] By 2023, 56 per cent of women had a degree, as against 34 per cent of men, though China had dropped to 102 out of 146 countries in the World Economic Forum's gender-equality league table. China had seventy-eight 'self-made' women billionaires – more than double the rest of the world combined (India had three). Even so, women have remained seriously under-represented at the higher level of politics: there was not a single woman in the twenty-four-member Politburo (there had been some previously), nor in the seven-member Politburo Standing Committee.[196]

The Great Leap Forward

By the early to mid-1950s, Mao was beginning to discard his moderate approach (just as the Soviet Union had abandoned the NEP a decade after its adoption). On 31 July 1955 he warned:

> An upsurge in the new, socialist mass movement is imminent throughout the countryside. But some of our comrades, tottering along like a woman with bound feet, are complaining all the time, 'You're going too fast, much too fast.' Too much carping, unwarranted complaints, boundless anxiety and countless taboos – all this they take as the right policy to guide the socialist mass movement in the rural areas. No, this is not the right policy, it is the wrong one.[197]

The following May, Mao launched the Hundred Flowers Campaign, in which he urged intellectuals to express their opinions openly. Perhaps he thought it could weaken his opponents in the party bureaucracy, where the move encountered some opposition; perhaps he thought he could attract non-party intellectuals. The campaign failed because the criticisms exceeded expectations. Mao 'had not imagined that he would unleash such hostility'.[198] Naïve intellectuals who had believed the slogans were duly punished during the subsequent repressive Anti-Rightist Campaign.

In 1958, a rapid transition to socialism was called forth under the banner of the Great Leap Forward. This was an attempt to resolve the problem that no substantial growth could be achieved in a country with the size and population of China by dividing the land into numerous separate parcels. China had a particularly unfavourable man:land ratio, leading to a massive surplus of rural labour and little capital.[199] China was facing the same problem as Russia: how to produce a surplus in the countryside to fund industrialization.[200] At first China tried to follow the Soviet model but it soon changed tack. Agricultural production lagged behind industrial output, and agrarian reform had redistributed almost half of cultivated land, creating a very large number of small unproductive farms. This was regarded as unsustainable in the long run, so it was decided to increase the size of collectives and further decentralize industrial development. The alternative to collectivization would have required the ideologically unpalatable alternative of moving towards some kind of capitalist farming.

The objective of the Great Leap Forward was no different from that of virtually all underdeveloped countries: industrialization. Mao's absolute priority (and here he joins Stalin) was industrialization even at the expense of the countryside. A revolution made by peasants had turned into a nightmare for them. Workers would be fed first, peasants last. Even Zhou Enlai, a moderate who managed to ship relief grain to hard-hit Sichuan and Anhui, declared in 1961, 'we must tighten the countryside to protect the cities'.[201] China was technologically backward and had scarce capital. It was one of the poorest countries in the world, with a life expectancy lower than most African countries. It could not afford to import machinery.[202] Therefore it would use the large surplus of rural labour in a variety of industrial projects while speeding up the rate of transfer of agricultural surplus to the towns.

Collectivization proceeded at a slower pace and with less brutality than in the USSR. However, the consequences were equally dire. Also disastrous was the attempt to develop 'backyard steel furnaces': the steel produced was of low quality and the resources used meant that the local communes, hoping to please the central authorities, neglected their crops.[203] The Great Leap Forward coincided with a massive famine, one of the worst in Chinese history. In absolute terms it was probably the worst famine ever: the death toll was enormous, with estimates ranging from 12 million to 16.5 million, to 23 million, 30 million, and 45 million.[204] The official Chinese estimate puts the figure at 'only' 15 million, 2.5 per cent of the Chinese population at the time, and more than the victims of the drought in northern China (1928–30). In some regions, such as Henan in central China and Wuwei in the North, the death toll was much higher than the average.[205] Yet the overall excess death rate was far lower, in relative terms, than that of the Irish famine of the 1840s which killed a million people (a quarter of the population), or the Finnish famine of 1867–68.[206] Famines had plagued China for a very long time.

Much of the famine during the Great Leap Forward was manmade, but causation is difficult to establish. Carl Riskin mentions

> output collapse, irrational methods of cultivation, destruction of work incentives, wasteful consumption of available foodgrain, ignorance of the planning authorities, over-procurement of grain by the government, increased exports in the midst of the crisis, failure to initiate imports in time, bad weather, etc.[207]

Of these, the 'inflexibility of the centrally planned procurement system was an important contributing factor probably explaining between 32 and 43 per cent of the total mortality'.[208] Feeding the cities at the expense of the countryside accounted for the far greater proportion of deaths in the rural sector.[209] Mao saw himself as the representative of the poorer peasants, the uneducated, the labourers; yet these were the groups most heavily hit by the Great Leap Forward. His utopianism, characterized by 'ever greater pressures to outstrip impossible targets', was instrumental in 'precipitating the famine that devastated the countryside', writes Mark Selden.[210]

Mao chose to disregard some of the information he received and to believe in what he wanted, an only too common characteristic of those in power. He was probably sent many misleading reports by officials who were afraid of being accused of being 'rightist'. Though he occasionally recognized that 'excesses' were being committed, and sporadically doubted the optimism of reports, he was unwilling to abandon the Great Leap Forward until October 1960 – when, realizing the enormity of what had happened, he started to depart from it.[211]

The Great Leap Forward went through various phases. It started with a not unsuccessful early utopian radicalism late in 1957, which gave way to a period of relative moderation from autumn 1958 to July 1959. This was followed by a renewed radicalism, and finally a retreat in October 1960 when the full dimensions of the catastrophe had become evident.[212] At the Lushan Conference in July 1959, convened to discuss the Great Leap Forward, Mao accepted, in a somewhat bizarre and rambling speech, that things were not going well:

> Gentlemen, all of you have ears, so listen. They all say we are in a mess. Even if it is hard to listen to it, we must listen to it and welcome it. As soon as you think in this way, it ceases to be unpleasant to the ears ...
>
> Many things have happened which we could not possibly predict beforehand ...
>
> But comrades, in 1958 and 1959 the main responsibility was mine, and you should take me to task ...
>
> If you don't agree with me then argue back. I don't agree with the idea that the Chairman cannot be contradicted. Anyway, the fact is that you have been contradicting me one after the other, though not by name ...
>
> I have committed two crimes, one of which is calling for 10,700,000 tons of steel and the mass smelting of steel. If you agreed with this, you should share some of the blame ... I cannot pass on the blame: the main responsibility is mine ...
>
> Marx also made many mistakes. Every day he hoped that a European revolution would arrive, but it did not arrive ... Have we failed this time? All the comrades present say there have been gains; it is not a complete failure. Is it mainly a failure? No, it's only a partial failure. We have paid a high price. A lot of 'communist wind' has blown past, but the people of the whole country have learned a lesson ...
>
> The chaos caused was on a grand scale and I take responsibility. Comrades, you must all analyse your own responsibility. If you have to shit, shit! If you have to fart, fart! You will feel much better for it.[213]

Earlier, Marshal Peng Dehuai, a veteran of the revolutionary wars and now defence minister, had warned Mao, in a letter that Mao made public, that there was considerable starvation in many areas and implored him to change tack. Mao at first hesitated then rejected the warning, labelling Peng a leader of the 'anti-party clique'.[214] Peng thought that by embedding his criticism in a private letter, he would help Mao to save face, but the criticisms had been amply discussed and an open confrontation between Mao and Peng was inevitable. Those who had rallied round Peng now turned against him, such was the loyalty towards Mao. In the autumn of

1958, Peng composed a poem highlighting his dissent with Mao and the Great Leap Forward:

> Grain scattered on the ground, potato leaves withered;
> Strong young people have left to make steel;
> Only children and old women reap the crops;
> How can they pass the coming year?
> Allow me to raise my voice for the people![215]

Soon Peng was sacked from his ministerial post, but not expelled from the party. Mao partially rehabilitated him in 1966, but Peng soon became one of the main victims of the Cultural Revolution when Red Guards humiliated and tortured him despite interventions by Zhou Enlai. He died in jail in 1974.[216] Peng was posthumously rehabilitated by the reformist administration of Deng Xiaoping. In 2016, he was the subject of a successful historical drama television series.

The Great Leap Forward was certainly not imposed by Mao on a recalcitrant party. It was supported by a significant number of the leadership (including, by his own admission, Deng Xiaoping) and many cadres, probably because Mao was also venerated by a significant proportion of the population.[217] The extent to which the famine was aggravated by government policy remained a matter of debate.[218] In a speech at the famous Seven Thousand Cadres Central Work Conference in January 1962, Mao again took responsibility for the failure of the Great Leap.[219] Blame was also attributed to 'leftist' mistakes, to the departure of Soviet technicians following the break with Moscow in 1960 and to the disorganization of local party members.[220] For instance, some cadres in Wuwei, one of the most affected areas, 'drastically exaggerated the grain output and thus increased the amount of out-transferred grain'. A better estimate might have averted the huge death toll in the region.[221] Communal dining halls contributed to the disaster, as private kitchens were demolished to melt steel and metal: 'A new kind of tyranny emerged that took on aspects of the prison camp. How well one ate, or whether one ate at all, was in the hands of the cadres who controlled the food.'[222]

Despite the disaster of the Great Leap Forward, if one takes the whole period of China under Mao, growth rates increased – though not as much as those of other East Asian countries. Even though food consumption per head was lower in the 1970s than in the 1930s, China was able to raise life expectancy at birth higher than India and to spread literacy even in the poorer regions.[223] As Lucien Bianco, far from being an unconditional admirer of the Maoist experiment, pointed out: 'The industrial infrastructure built in haste during the Great Leap Forward bore fruit some years after the disaster ... China did not stagnate during the Maoist era but advanced less rapidly than the capitalist world.'[224] Despite the damage inflicted on the rural economy, the mobilization in the communes achieved a remarkable expansion in irrigation and multiple cropping, as well as some degree of rural industrialization.[225] The deployment of rural and city workers for giant irrigation and construction projects brought prosperity to previously infertile regions.[226]

It is important not to minimize the scale of the failure of the Great Leap Forward. Life expectancy and literacy might have been even better without it. Chinese history books refer to the years 1958–61 with anodyne terms such as 'three difficult years', often blaming the weather and the withdrawal of Soviet help. In 2012 a regional editor of the *People's Daily* in Gansu used Weibo, one of the main social media platforms in China, to deny there had been a famine. Weibo was overwhelmed by a storm of messages by relatives of those who had died, and the editor promptly apologized.[227]

The Cultural Revolution

The consequences of the disaster of the Great Leap Forward were an internal struggle between the more anarchistic followers of Mao who insisted on mass mobilization and those such as Liu Shaoqi who advocated a top-down development strategy which would privilege the most efficient producers. This dispute was the basis for the subsequent Great Proletarian Cultural Revolution. Mao always had a distrust for highly institutionalized decision-making. There were precedents. In 1951 there was the Three-Anti Campaign: against corruption, waste and a stifling bureaucracy. A year later the Five-Anti Campaign was more clearly anti-capitalist since the vices to be expunged were 'bribery, tax evasion, theft of state property, cheating on government contracts and stealing state economic information.'[228] At the beginning of the Cultural Revolution, Mao promulgated anti-establishment slogans such as 'bombard the headquarters' and 'to rebel is justified'. The practical application of such vague calls to arms could not appeal to bureaucrats who, understandably enough, would have preferred precise and predictable orders.[229]

The Cultural Revolution, still much under-researched in China, can be divided into two periods. The first (1966–67) was characterized by a high level of popular turmoil in which student activism prevailed and the level of casualties was relatively low. The second (1968–76) was far more politically repressive, particularly by local authorities, and amounted to an armed conflict.[230] As Theda Skocpol has written, nothing like the Cultural Revolution could have happened in Soviet Russia under Stalin or his successors.[231] It was relatively unplanned, as Mao admitted in October 1966; so was the development of the Red Guards movement, though of course both were inspired by Mao's call to create a 'great disorder under heaven' in order to achieve, ultimately, 'great order under heaven'.[232]

The initial phase (August 1966) was launched in Beijing and led mainly by students and intellectuals, as had been the case in the May Fourth Movement of 1919. These actions were often motivated by a desire to reject old traditions and so-called feudal culture. Militants waved the famous Little Red Book made up of quotations from the writings of Mao Zedong.

The aim of the Cultural Revolution was to destroy the Four Olds – ideas, culture, habits and customs – and replace them with the Four News: new ideas, new culture, new habits and new customs. The Central Committee of the CCP endorsed it but warned that it was bound to encounter resistance from 'those in authority who have wormed their way into the Party and are taking the capitalist road'.[233] In 1969 Mao declared the campaign to be over. But the turmoil continued, paving the way for the second, far more murderous phase, which was largely rural and 'tied to the consolidation of power by new established local government'.[234] Mass killings were the result of local representatives of the state engaging in a reign of terror, despite half-hearted attempts by the centre to tone down excessive violence.[235]

The Cultural Revolution took various forms. It was a mass insurgency that targeted party officials, intellectuals, school officials and members of supposedly reactionary households. Many were subjected to humiliating public beatings, even torture. A considerable number of the Red Guards who started the process were high-school students facing difficulties in being admitted to university and confronting difficult career prospects, while children of the old, educated elites appeared to be favoured.[236] Many were angry, and perhaps did not require urging from on high to rise up against parents, teachers and party cadres.[237] There were armed battles between factions amounting to a virtual civil war, especially in 1968. And there was a nationwide campaign of organized terror by the authorities targeting those with the wrong class origins or political histories. A massacre of 169 students occupying the premises of a local newspaper in Xining, the capital city of Qinghai province, on 23 February 1967 was conducted by the local army, perhaps on its own initiative.[238]

Ji Xianlin, a famed specialist of the culture of ancient India, wrote in the preface to his memoirs: 'Anyone who knows anything about the Cultural Revolution knows that just about every school, government institution, factory, production unit, and even some army divisions at the time were divided into opposing factions', and each faction considered itself to be the true revolutionary.'[239] Ji was himself victim to considerable persecution. The unrest included much looting as well as the destruction of national treasures, Confucian relics and Buddhist statues.[240] Many of the deaths were due not only to the activities of young Red Guards but resulted from local initiatives, vendettas, clan rivalries and the inevitable cruelties which occur when all authority is suspended: a kind of Hobbesian war of all against all. Yang Su tells of one episode of many, in which various male descendants of local landlords were bludgeoned to death because of their 'class belonging': 'There was no army, Red Guards, or systematic bureaucratic machinery of genocide; rather neighbours killed neighbours.'[241] It was this that caused the greatest number of deaths.[242]

The estimate of deaths, as usual, varies: from 750,000 to 1.5 million.[243] This is a very large toll, but in per capita terms, death rates were higher in Stalin's Russia and Pol Pot's Cambodia.[244] While Stalin's purges were started from the top and carried out by communist cadres, the Cultural Revolution was a far more decentred and anarchic experiment – though resulting in a high number of victims. The Red Guards were encouraged by Mao, but the Cultural Revolution could not be described as a totalitarian terror operation since it mobilized a variety of groups, including 'students from politically stigmatized households, demobilized soldiers, and other groups organized to press their interests and make demands against Party authorities'.[245] It was not a mere power struggle among the ruling elites but a wider social conflict.[246] Stalin had tried to concentrate all power in the party. Mao, by contrast, deeply influenced by anarchist ideas in his youth, attempted to dismantle both party and state structures.[247]

The anarchic element could be seen in the proliferation of peculiar campaigns such as that of the Revolutionary Workers of the Hairdressing Trade in Guangzhou, who demanded not only that 'all old ideas, culture, customs, and habits' be 'demolished' but even that what they called 'bizarre bourgeois hairstyles ... should vigorously and speedily' be eradicated in favour of 'new proletarian hairdos', or the campaign of

'Middle School Red Guards' that 'public baths' should 'consistently desist from serving'

> bourgeois sons of bitches. Don't give them massage baths, foot rubs, backrubs; don't let them bow our heads again, or abuse and ride roughshod over us. We order those under thirty-five to quit drinking and smoking immediately. Bad habits of this sort absolutely may not be cultivated.[248]

Elsewhere Red Guards issued commands forbidding the wearing of pointed shoes and jeans.[249] In her autobiographical account, *Spider Eaters*, Rae Yang recalls:

> When we went out, however, we always put on the complete outfit of a Red Guard ... But we would not wear skirts, blouses, and sandals. Anything that would make girls look like girls was bourgeois. We covered up our bodies so completely that I almost forgot I was a girl. I was a Red Guard. Others were Red Guards too. And that was it.[250]

Once the campaign had entered its more violent phase, neither Mao nor the centre were able or willing to stop local authorities. It was a failure of a weak state, unable to control what it had unleashed, rather than the expression of a strong totalitarian regime. During this time, student turmoil was occurring in many other quite different countries, though never elsewhere reaching the heights of the Cultural Revolution: France in May 1968, and then in Italy, Germany, Japan, Mexico, Brazil and Mexico; in the US against the war in Vietnam; and in Czechoslovakia against the Soviet-inspired regime. In all these cases the existing authorities were the target of dissenters. In China, however, the students were urged to rebel from the top, encouraged to establish independent organizations and permitted to travel between cities free of charge, often receiving financial and material support. At least initially, the state's repressive machinery was immobilized by central directives that forbade public security organs to interfere in the activities of the Red Guards.[251] Because of the divisions within the central leadership and the ambiguity of Mao's directives, Red Guards, local cadres and ordinary citizens were often forced to think and act on their own.[252] The result was three years of chaos during which the Chinese state came to a standstill.[253]

Mao's project was to continue the revolution, hoping to generate an entirely new collectivist spirit based on what he thought was the creativity of the people and not simply the industrialization of China and its prosperity (which is what his successors tried, with significant results). After the failures of the Great Leap Forward, Mao probably thought his control of the party was slipping away. In launching the Cultural Revolution, he aimed to combat bureaucracy, transform human nature and build a new society.[254] The justification behind the Cultural Revolution was that the CCP was becoming a set of entrenched bureaucratic interests separate from the workers and peasants.[255] The party was becoming a new class, as was happening in the other communist countries. Every society, however new, inherits the inequalities of the previous one. Those born in prosperous families, equipped with cultural capital, have an unavoidable advantage over those of working-class background, even if the prosperity has been lost. As Stuart Schram has written:

> Mao's belief in the decisive importance of ... subjective forces engendered a utopian vision in which the Chinese people ... could lift themselves by their own heroic efforts to the economic level of the most advanced Western countries ... it was in large measure these illusions which led Mao, and China, to disaster.[256]

By 1969 the Cultural Revolution was almost over, and many of the 17 million young people who had gone to the countryside went back home, unlamented. The backlash was not particularly brutal. It had just been another mistake. Coded language was used as when Zhou Enlai criticized 'anarchism' at various conferences in 1971 and 1972.[257] In present-day China the Great Cultural Revolution, almost universally regarded as a failure, is barely discussed – a major episode of history conveniently forgotten. As one of the many critics of Maoism, Lucian Pye, has written: 'The most astonishing aftermath of the Cultural Revolution was the speed with which institutional chaos was replaced by orderly hierarchies and regularized bureaucracies once the "left" had been defeated.'[258] One unintended consequence of the Cultural Revolution was that an entire generation of educated youth learned much about politics and the diversity in China, including how hard life was in the countryside. Some even read the classics of Marxism for the first time, which paradoxically widened their consciousness.[259] The decade of the Cultural Revolution also contributed to the formation of a distinctive youth identity and youth popular culture, as in the West.[260] At the same time, the Cultural Revolution damaged the myth of an invincible party and ideology.[261]

The old elites, humiliated during the Cultural Revolution, crawled back into power. While Liu Shaoqi, rival and possible successor to Mao, died under house arrest in 1969 (he was rehabilitated in 1980), many of those purged survived. Deng Xiaoping, who had always been careful not to antagonize Mao, was purged during the Cultural Revolution, denounced as a 'capitalist roader', and taken with his family to Jiangxi province to engage in physical labour and be 're-educated'. He was not expelled from the party, however, as Jiang Qing, Mao's wife and one of the (in)famous Gang of Four, had demanded. In 1973, at the important Tenth Party Congress, Deng and other 'capitalist roaders' were reinstated to the Central Committee. The see-saw continued: Deng was dismissed again shortly before Mao's death in 1976, only to become de facto leader soon afterwards. Hu Yaobang, a relatively liberal voice in the 1980s who was party chairman (1981–82), general secretary (1982–87) and once a close ally of Deng's, had been repeatedly purged during the Cultural Revolution. Xi Jinping, general secretary of the CCP since 2012 and president since 2013, saw his father Xi Zhongxun, a senior official, purged and imprisoned during the Cultural Revolution, then later rehabilitated. Xi himself was sent to work in the countryside for seven years.

The cult of Confucius easily survived the onslaught of the Red Guards who, in November 1966, smashed statues of the sage in his native Qufu. A few years later Confucius was honoured again and taught in schools; since 1984 an official ceremony has been held each year on his birthday at Qufu, while the numerous Chinese cultural centres throughout the world are named for Confucius and not for Mao. In November 2013 President Xi visited Qufu and praised Confucian culture while criticizing the Cultural Revolution.[262]

However strong the institutions had proved to be post-Mao, Chinese leaders remained alert to the dangers of conceding too much freedom lest another eruption would come; hence the brutal repression of the demonstrations in Tiananmen Square in 1989.

Nixon in China

As the Cultural Revolution was entering its final phase, a major turning point occurred in foreign policy. Richard Nixon was trying to disengage from Vietnam while China was thinking of reconstructing the country after the Cultural Revolution.[263] In February 1972, Nixon, invited by Mao Zedong and Zhou Enlai (presumably as part of an anti-Soviet initiative), visited China with Henry Kissinger, then his national security adviser, in what he called, echoing Zhou Enlai, 'the week that changed the world'.[264] Kissinger, who had visited China earlier in July 1971 to prepare the ground, was so impressed with Zhou Enlai that he wrote later that Zhou was one of the greatest leaders he had ever met.

> In some sixty years of public life, I have encountered no more compelling figure than Zhou Enlai. Short, elegant, with an expressive face framing luminous eyes, he dominated by exceptional intelligence and capacity to intuit the intangibles of the psychology of his opposite number.

Kissinger expressed plenty of admiration for Mao too, as well as for Mao's de facto successor Deng Xiaoping.[265] Zhou's popularity in China was also remarkable: when he died in 1976 some 2 million people paid tribute to him.

The Nixon visit may not have changed the world, as it was claimed, but it did signal a major turning point in Sino-American relations. Already in 1971, the People's Republic of China, with American support, had resumed the China seat at the United Nations, ousting Taiwan. Full diplomatic relations were established with the US under President Carter. The US's erstwhile ally Taiwan was almost dumped, although, to the displeasure of Beijing, Congress passed the Taiwan Relations Act which allowed for the continuation of arms sales to the island. Unsurprisingly, China felt that the US was reneging on the spirit of the agreements entered: that 'there was only one China', that Taiwan was a part of it and that the solution of the Taiwan problem was China's alone.[266] The Shanghai Communiqué agreed in February 1972 made this abundantly clear: 'The United States acknowledges that all Chinese on either side of the Taiwan Strait maintain there is but one China and that Taiwan is a part of China.'[267]

The Nixon visit also signalled a new shift in Chinese foreign policy. In the 1950s, particularly since the Bandung Conference, China had been intent on being among the main proponents of the policy of non-alignment, thus already departing from a strictly pro-Moscow line and moving closer to India, Indonesia and other Asian and African nations. After the 1970s such goals were far less visible. Third World solidarity was jettisoned, all the easier since it barely existed except in rhetoric. In early 1979 China even invaded Vietnam, partly to protect its Cambodian ally Pol Pot (supported by the West and removed by the Vietnamese), partly to resolve a border dispute, partly 'to teach Vietnam a lesson'. The war lasted less than a month. Despite Beijing's victory claim, it is generally agreed that the Chinese had performed poorly in the conflict.[268] It was China that was taught a lesson, and this was China's last foreign intervention. China would no longer seek to be the centre of the world revolution. Indeed, it no longer sought world revolution: the new goal was to play a full part in the global economy.

Leaving Mao behind?

On 27 June 1981, five years after Mao's death, an important resolution adopted by the Sixth Plenum of the Central Committee included a critique of the Cultural Revolution:

> Comrade Mao Zedong began to get arrogant at the very time when the Party was confronted with the new task of shifting the focus of its work to socialist construction, a task for which the utmost caution was required. He gradually divorced himself from practice and from the masses, acted more and more arbitrarily and subjectively, and increasingly put himself above the Central Committee of the Party.[269]

It added that 'Comrade Mao Zedong had become arrogant and self-satisfied' about his successes, and as a result, in the decade 1955–65, 'his personal arbitrariness gradually undermined democratic centralism in party life, and the personality cult grew graver and graver'. In reality, the cult had started much earlier. The party's Seventh National Congress (April–June 1945) established 'Mao Zedong Thought' as the guideline for all its work. But views change, and in 1981 the party declared that during the Cultural Revolution Mao's leadership was characterized by 'left' errors while the Mao cult 'was frenziedly pushed to an extreme'. The CCP decided that the Cultural Revolution was a 'ten-year disaster resulting in a national chaos'.

In order not to relegate Mao to the dustbin of history (as Khrushchev had attempted to do with Stalin in 1956), the resolution added:

> Comrade Mao Zedong was a great Marxist and a great proletarian revolutionary, strategist, and theorist. It is true that he made gross mistakes during the Cultural Revolution, but, if we judge his activities as a whole, his contributions to the Chinese revolution far outweigh his mistakes. His merits are primary and his errors secondary.[270]

It was safer and simpler to put most of the blame onto Lin Biao – once Mao's unofficial successor – and his main supporters, the so-called Gang of Four who were arrested after Mao's death.[271] Lin Biao died in a plane crash in 1971, having allegedly plotted to stage a coup against Mao. By the summer of 1979, many former senior party officials were reinstated. The radicals were booted out; militant Maoism was now on the way down.

The 1981 resolution, unexcitingly called 'Resolution on Certain Questions in the History of Our Party since the Founding of the People's Republic of China', amounted to directives to future historians of the CCP. Ideologically speaking, it relied more on Mao's 1940 'On New Democracy' than on anything he had written or done since the 1950s. It was thought better to admit that the party made 'mistakes', rather than blame Mao or indulge in de-Maoization.[272] Mao's embalmed corpse is still in the memorial hall in Tiananmen Square, contrary to predictions such as the one made by Nicholas Kristof, a Pulitzer Prize–winning *New York Times* columnist and co-author of books on China.[273] By contrast, statues of Chiang Kai-shek, once a ubiquitous feature of Taiwan's streets and parks, have been removed since the island embraced democratic rule.[274]

On 25 October 1980, Mao's de facto successor Deng Xiaoping noted that 'Comrade Mao Zedong was not an isolated individual, he was the leader of our Party until the moment of his death', and warned: 'When we write about his mistakes, we should not exaggerate, for otherwise we shall be discrediting Comrade Mao Zedong, and this would mean discrediting our Party and State.'[275] Later histories highlighted the claim that Mao had considerable support for the mistakes he made – which is why 'Mao Zedong Thought' was regularly recruited to back various aspects of Deng's reforms, a little like using the Bible to justify whatever one intends to do.

The Deng experiment of going beyond Mao while harnessing the support of 'Mao Zedong Thought' suggests that it would have been difficult to ditch Mao altogether. Mao's decisions during the Civil War and the unification of the country had so often proved correct that his popularity survived the disastrous policies of the Great Leap Forward and the Cultural Revolution. It is also possible that the turmoil of the Mao years made the subsequent reforms more viable, something akin to creative destruction. By the time of Mao's death in 1976, per capita grain production was lower than it had been in 1957. Many of the bigger factories were still operating with technology imported from the Soviet Union in the 1950s, and the equipment was in a state of disrepair. Universities had been virtually closed for almost a decade.[276] But the Maoist years were not only a time of untrammelled disasters, since considerable human capital was developed.[277] A recovery had started as soon as the more extreme phase of the Cultural Revolution ended. China grew faster than India, though far less than South Korea or Taiwan. By the late 1960s, most urban households owned radios and could watch movies, while elementary schools had grown rapidly in number. By 1976, some 80 per cent of young adults were literate.[278] The Mao era saw an industrial revolution that established the foundation for China's economic development: in 1949 China's industrial sector was smaller than Belgium's; in twenty-five years, despite the turmoil, China had become a major industrial power.[279] Moreover, during the Maoist period, rudimentary healthcare had been successfully extended into the countryside, thanks to what was called the Cooperative Medical System. This provided basic medical security for most rural residents, though the system was considerably reduced after 1978.[280] There were improvements in health, literacy and infrastructure that laid the basis for the subsequent economic growth.[281] The overall progress explains the continuing popularity of the regime. In fact, it is probably because of the improvements in health and education in the Mao years, as well as the capacity for modern management, that China has proved so attractive for foreign capital, with considerable help from the Chinese diaspora.[282]

In 1977, the Eleventh Party Congress ratified a new policy of 'reform and opening' and made Deng the de facto 'paramount' leader. Deng was by then seventy-two years old. He did not seek formal titles: he was only the *deputy* chairman of the CCP and the *deputy* prime minister. There was no personality cult of Deng, nor were statues or pictures of him erected in public buildings. At the Central Economic Work Conference in 1978, Deng triggered decades of reforms that would help China to become the second-largest economy in the world. He called on citizens: 'Emancipate the mind, seek the truth from facts and unite as one in looking to the future.'[283] No doubt the tremendous advances of other Asian economies – Japan, South Korea and Taiwan – influenced the Chinese leadership. As Perry Anderson has written: 'The task of making good the lag between communism in China and capitalism in East Asia was a formidable agenda for any programme of reforms' – but Deng and his comrades 'tackled it with a vigour born not just from the momentum, still active, of the Revolution they had made, but from a millennial self-confidence, battered for a century, but ultimately unbroken, of the oldest continuous civilization in the world'.[284]

As Deng was about to depart in practice from Maoism, he tried to maintain continuity, announcing four cardinal principles: no-one should challenge the socialist path, nor the dictatorship of the proletariat, nor the leadership of the Communist Party, nor 'Mao Zedong Thought'. This did not prevent Deng from listing the problems facing the country. In August 1980 he deplored the enduring power of the bureaucracy, its abuses of power, its inertia, its inefficiency, its corruption, its arbitrariness, how it shifted responsibility to others, how it suppressed democracy and how it practised favouritism.[285]

Deng, the chief promoter of reforms, did not advance concrete economic policies. Like many of Confucius's *Analects*, Deng's pronouncements were vague and cryptic, though the politically pragmatic intentions behind his famous use of the Sichuanese proverb were clear: 'It doesn't matter if the cat is white or black, so long as it catches mice.'[286] Deng never expressed any original economic ideas; yet this was his strong point, because without a vision of his own he showed his willingness to let economic developments unfold without constant political interference.[287] That said, no major policies went ahead without his assent. He allowed rural reforms to go forward, and the lack of a general reform plan enabled the process to proceed gradually and experimentally.[288] The process worked: by 1984, eight years after Mao's death – thanks to a partial decollectivization, the relaxation of controls over agricultural prices and greater freedom conceded to peasants to grow what they wanted – agricultural production had trebled.[289] While Russia's path towards industrialization was largely autarkic, specific examples of economic development were mentioned by Deng Xiaoping in his talks after his 1992 tour of southern China.[290] It was reported that peasants were saying: 'Mao led us to stand up; but Deng allowed us to fill our bellies.'[291] The peasants saw their purchasing powers increase, which contributed hugely to the Chinese 'economic miracle'. It was a practical application of Deng's remark in 1978 when the economic reforms were launched: 'We talked too much about politics and too little about economics.'[292]

In the hope of attracting foreign investment, special economic zones (SEZs) were established in areas such as Guangdong and Fujian which then had little industry. At first most of this investment came from Hong Kong and Taiwan, and in the decade after 1978 it contributed less to the economy than the newly emerging rural industry.[293] However, the requirements of industrialization demanded some movement of people away from the land. This is why the people's communes were dismantled in 1982, and land transferred to households.

Millions of peasants lost their land and were compelled (some with compensation) to move to the towns – an unprecedented urbanization.[294] The communes had some positive aspects but it was clear they would eventually have had to be reformed or abolished. They were abolished.[295] The policy was initiated from above, but soon many peasants took matters into their own hands and did much of the dismantling themselves.[296]

Rural industry was given a crucial impetus by the semi-spontaneous development and expansion of the so-called Township and Village Enterprises (TVE), which was independent of government but supervised by local party officials. The Communist authorities allowed local areas to experiment in this way, publicizing any successes and allowing other areas to follow suit. The land was not privatized, and the ownership of the TVE was never regulated or even made clear. In many cases these were companies owned by the locality; in others they were de facto private enterprises. This assuaged fears that this was a road to capitalism because it maintained the image of collective property. In practice, local party officials behaved differently in different areas: some followed what they believed were the wishes of the central leadership; others were open to local pressures; and others still followed their own personal interests. The result was that the Chinese state was not always in control of these institutions.[297] Private TVEs (meaning those recognized as private by the authorities) outperformed the ones that were collectively owned.[298] The TVEs created many jobs and improved the living conditions of millions of locals, not just those who worked in the enterprises. It has been estimated that between 1978 and 1988 China's poverty headcount declined by 154 million, and that much of this could be attributed to the TVEs.[299] Their share of China's total industrial output rose from 22 per cent in 1978 to 37 per cent in 1995.[300] Only in the 1990s, after the TVEs had reached their peak did Chinese growth become increasingly driven by state-controlled investments and, since 2000, by exports.[301]

Many of the reforms associated with Deng built on strategies the Communists had deployed during the Chinese Civil War and the first years of the People's Republic of China, when they consciously exploited market mechanisms.[302] Instead of prioritizing heavy industry, as in Stalin's Russia, there was a focus on light industry. Even so, thanks to imported technology from Japan – now China's main 'friend' in spite (or because) of its past – China's steel production leapt from 37.2 million tons in 1982 to 61.2 million tons in 1989, to 101 million tons in 1996, when China became the world's largest steel producer.[303] In December

2001 China, now ruled by the pragmatic Jiang Zemin, Deng's successor, acceded to the World Trade Organization.

In the thirty years after 1980, Chinese success became even more evident: exports had multiplied over a hundred times and Guangdong had become home to modern factories, skyscrapers, large industrial sites, world-class hotels, superhighways and traffic jams. The country was 'the factory of the world', making 90 per cent of the world's personal computers and mobile phones, 80 per cent of its air conditioners and most of its toys, solar panels, shoes and so on.[304] From 1978 onwards, there was also a huge and consistent increase in the number of Chinese students studying in the West (whereas the USSR and East European countries had always feared that their students would never return home).[305] When communism fell apart in the Soviet Union in 1989–91, China could boast of having achieved an average annual growth of 10 per cent since 1978.[306] There were of course major problems, such as inflation following the lifting of price controls in 1988, which led to pressure for more conservative policies under Chen Yun while Deng continued to fight for further opening and faster growth.

The success of China, as against Russian failures, was not only due to the combination of intelligent economic policies and the maintenance of the one-party rule, but also to objective factors, such as the long coastline that made transport less expensive at a time when a new globalization was developing, the existence of millions of overseas Chinese émigrés throughout Southeast Asia, and a large domestic market. India, by comparison, although enjoying similar advantages as well as a linguistic connection to the English-speaking world and a democratic system, did not fare so well.[307] Ironically China, though usually labelled as totalitarian, was devoid of many of the rules and regulations of advanced capitalist countries: there were no (or few) rules for food and drugs, product and workplace safety or working conditions. There was no minimum wage and no law against anyone filling a bottle with a liquid and labelling it 'wine'.[308] Deng also abolished the idea that class should be considered when selecting officials. In fact, entrepreneurs were soon allowed to join the Communist Party.

The Soviet events served as a counter-example of what would happen if China went too fast or too slow. It was seen as a justification for the kind of reforms pursued in China and the maintenance of an ideological commitment to communism. As Kerry Brown pointed out, the spectre of the Soviet Union's failure cast a long shadow.[309] While only a very few privileged citizens from the USSR could study or travel abroad or buy foreign goods, Communist China sent tourists abroad, and they almost all returned.

Some scholars, such as Peter Nolan, think that the radically different nature of the *anciens régimes* in China and in Russia may explain the survival and prosperity of the Communist Party of China and the disintegration of the Communist Party of the Soviet Union.[310] Others point out that while one of the problems in the USSR was an ossified bureaucracy, in China it was the opposite: the Cultural Revolution had weakened the bureaucracy, and senior-level bureaucrats sent to work in farms and factories returned to positions of authority having learned a thing of two about the needs of the lower strata of society.[311] Whatever the origin of the differing paths taken by the USSR and China, the negative example of the downfall of the USSR had been regularly used by the Chinese to justify caution. The Chinese view is that Gorbachev's mistake was to have assumed that one needed to democratize the country before proceeding with economic reforms. This is not how other successful Asian economies progressed. South Korea and Taiwan were dictatorships for decades while improving their economy, before proceeding to democratic presidential elections in 1987 and 1996 respectively. For reforms to work, a strong state was required – something which the Russians had failed to achieve, democratizing first and hoping for the best.

In 1979, Deng had warned:

> Talk about democracy in the abstract will inevitably lead to the unchecked spread of ultra-democracy and anarchism, to the complete disruption of political stability and unity, and to the total failure of our modernisation programme. If this happens ... China will once again be plunged into chaos, division, retrogression and darkness, and the Chinese people will be deprived of all hope.[312]

The Chinese authorities advanced cautiously. There was no big bang or shock therapy, as some, particularly in the West, had advocated for Eastern Europe and the former USSR. The Chinese, quite rightly (and unlike the Russians), took no notice of Western advice, whether from the IMF or the World Bank.[313] Reform did not involve rapid and widespread privatization. Pragmatism and experimentation characterized the way the Chinese tackled the reform process. As Deng declared in 1992:

> We should be bolder than before in conducting reform and opening to the outside and have the courage to experiment. We must not act like

women with bound feet. Once we are sure that something should be done, we should dare to experiment and break a new path.[314]

This gradual approach, known as 'crossing the river by feeling the stones', consisted in implementing partial reforms experimentally, starting in some localities and moving to others if the initial experiment had been successful. As Bert Hofman has explained, it helped to circumvent political resistance to reform and enabled problems to be identified early, giving the authorities a chance to modify the reforms or discard them altogether, thus also avoiding loss of face.[315] It was particularly significant that, in the relation between central and local authorities on welfare schemes, the centre generally restrained its urge to interfere.[316] Decentralization has been a major trend since (and even before) the People's Congress, often justly described as a rubber stamp, acquired a greater role.[317]

In 1992, Deng, by then physically weak, started his famous trip to South China (the *nanxun*). Deng probably chose to go to the South because, with its special economic zones (SEZs), it was already ahead of the North in terms of economic reform and opening up to international capitalism.[318] Having praised the Shenzhen Stock Exchange as an example of a 'socialist market' (many of the firms listed were part-owned by the state), Deng tried to assuage fears that the advancing economic reforms constituted an abandonment of socialism: 'The proportion of planning to market forces is not the essential difference between socialism and capitalism,' Deng explained. 'A planned economy is not equivalent to socialism, because there is planning under capitalism too; a market economy is not capitalism, because there are markets under socialism too.' Unable, like all of us, to define socialism, he explained that its essence 'is liberation and development of the productive forces, elimination of exploitation and polarization, and the ultimate achievement of prosperity for all'.[319] Zhu Rongji, close to Deng and soon to be prime minister, more pragmatically declared that one should not worry 'whether things are "socialist" or "capitalist"'.[320] In the English-language collection of Zhu's writings and speeches, *On the Record*, Mao is barely mentioned.

Tiananmen

Young people had previously demonstrated at Tiananmen Square in 1976, against the Gang of Four. Then in 1989 hundreds of thousands of mainly young people filled the square once again, demanding greater political openness and a clampdown on corruption and excessive bureaucracy. This was the biggest challenge faced by Deng. At their peak it is estimated that more than a million people gathered there. The massive demonstrations encountered some support at first among the Communist leadership: the general secretary, Zhao Ziyang, told the protesters that they had a right to criticize the party. Soon, however, Deng, perhaps fearing a renewal of the Cultural Revolution, decided that the movement had to be crushed. Martial law was declared on 20 May, though it remained unenforceable for two weeks. On 3–4 June there was a crackdown on the remaining demonstrators, estimated at 100,000. Perhaps as many as 700 were killed, few if any in the actual square and not all students.[321] The event caused worldwide consternation, far more than when South Korean President Chun Doo Hwan (who had just come to power in a military coup) led a similar crackdown against demonstrators in the city of Kwangju in May 1980, resulting in hundreds of deaths, proportionately more than in China. Neither the US nor the main European countries allowed the events of Tiananmen to modify their relations with China, though they expressed, as expected, some disapproval. The recently installed Japanese Prime Minister Uno Sōsuke refused to condemn the massacre.[322] Realism prevailed.

Existing scholarly work on the events leading to the Tiananmen massacre (or 'incident', as it is officially known) has not been able to explain how such huge demonstrations could have occurred without some organizational help within the Communist Party. It is unlikely that so many could have marched behind banners without some cooperation or help; and the subsequent armed repression was badly organized and initially half-hearted.[323] It can be assumed that the protesters were encouraged by circles close to Hu Yaobang, the CCP leader who had been forced to resign in 1987 and whose liberal attitudes had been popular with students and intellectuals. Hu had died in April 1989, and thousands of students gathered for the memorial service in his honour. The Tiananmen protesters did not demand an end to the Communist regime. They were not revolutionaries; their aims were moderate. They wanted more freedom and less corruption.[324] While the original official verdict that the event was 'counter-revolutionary' was never reversed, the country accelerated its shift towards a market economy, privatization and deregulation. This led some to see Tiananmen Square as a form of popular resistance against marketization.[325]

One of the reasons why the Tiananmen movement failed is the same as why the Arab Spring and May 1968 in France were unsuccessful. It was essentially an urban movement which had little to say to the rural population. Whatever discontent there might have been in the countryside had mainly to do with quite different issues, such as the lack of proper payment for grain requisition or the failure to deliver chemical fertilizer.[326] In the case of China, it is likely, as Deng explained during his 1992 tour in the South of the country, that the regime survived the Tiananmen Square unrest because the country was becoming far more prosperous:

> I can say that without the economic results of reform and opening, we would not have survived through June 4 [1989]; then there would have been chaos and civil war. Why did our country remain very stable after June 4? This was because the reform and opening promoted economic development and improved our people's lives ... The key to reform and opening at the moment lies in the development of the economy.[327]

Though we cannot possibly know what would have happened if a different course of action had been taken, China enjoyed, in the decades following Tiananmen, relative stability and rapid economic growth, and hundreds of millions of Chinese were living far more comfortable lives, materially at least, than in 1989.[328] The authorities seemed to acknowledge the underlying economic and social causes of the protests by trying to tackle economic and social instability. Intellectual life was repressed, but no more than before. In fact, thanks to the internet and to the ease with which Chinese citizens could travel and study abroad, the space for learning and debate increased.[329] But liberalization, to say nothing of democratization in the sense of free and fair elections, seems a long way off.

Deng died a few months before the Fifteenth Congress in 1997 at the age of ninety-two, having officially retired in November 1989 after the Tiananmen massacre. It was the end of an era, since Deng had been on the Long March and had survived all his comrades from those revolutionary times. The path he had started continued, and since nothing succeeds like success, in 2004 private property rights were included in the Chinese constitution, thus heralding another major step in the market-building phase.[330] Planning as a system which allocates resources – the communist ideal type – had been abandoned in the 1980s. It was turned into a set of guidelines and policies seeking to obtain specific outcomes. Under Deng and his successors, the bureaucracy (already weakened by the Cultural Revolution, see above) was decentralized and expanded by giving more power to local officials. The government followed Mao in this: when political dominance was threatened by other leaders or by ministry officials, it turned to provincial leaders for support. As provincial leaders developed power, they resisted change from the top.[331] China thus became far less totalitarian than many Western experts believed, even though the promotion of the market has coexisted with a Communist regime and a Communist ideology. China did not become capitalist, nor did it advance towards socialism. Maoism remains a major ideological force in today's China, and, like all ideologies, it is constantly reinterpreted and is becoming increasingly nationalistic.[332] The vague term 'socialism with Chinese characteristics' suggested an unknown terrain upon which China's economy developed. China's astonishing growth was due only in part to cheap labour: India has cheap labour, but its growth has not matched China's. The key factor has been the huge public investment promoted by a state which still controls the private sector to a far greater extent than the state in any rich countries, including Japan.

Contrary to uninformed predictions such as Gordon G. Chang's *Coming Collapse of China* (2001), neither China nor its party have collapsed.[333] David Shambaugh was equally pessimistic about the CCP's chances of survival in his more recent *China's Future*.[334] Predictions can be tricky, and one should probably hedge one's bets, perhaps remembering the saying attributed to the semi-legendary Lao Tzu: 'Those who have knowledge don't predict. Those who predict don't have knowledge.'

Shrewd observers such as John Gittings have honestly admitted that outsiders regularly fail to predict what will happen in China. They did not think Mao would win the Civil War, and did not foresee the break with the USSR in the late 1950s, nor the Great Leap Forward, nor the Cultural Revolution (nor how quickly it would be officially repudiated). They were taken by surprise by the détente between China and the US; nor did many imagine that China would enter a long period of spectacular and unparalleled economic growth.[335] In terms of purchasing-power parity, China's GDP overtook that of the US in 2017, though of course it is still a long way behind in per capita terms.[336] Yet, in per capita terms, China is better off than Argentina, Malaysia and Mexico, and a long way ahead of India, having been, in 1950, one of the poorest countries in the world.[337] In a way, China has recovered the primacy it held in 1750, when its share of global manufacturing output was 32.8 per cent, more than the whole of Europe put together.[338]

Serious problems remain. Inequality has increased, as has environmental degradation and corruption. The old Communist system of social welfare and working conditions have deteriorated, and prostitution has become more widespread. The gap between rural China and urban China has increased so much that, in the opening years of the century, the percentage of illiterates in the countryside actually increased.[339] This was probably because many peasant families kept children at home to assist in farm work once the communes were dismantled, and many teachers abandoned teaching to till the fields.[340] Beijing, one of the world's most magnificent cities in 1949, became one of the ugliest and most polluted, through a combination of Maoist planning and the market economy.[341] Rampant corruption continued to be a problem: between 2012 and 2017, the Communist Party's Central Commission for Disciplinary Inspection took action against 1.4 million party members in order to contain the corruption within the party, which had spread thanks to the growth of the market economy.[342] It was often necessary to pay bribes just to get into a good school or access good healthcare, though by the 2020s corruption had been somewhat curtailed.[343]

Many Muslim Uyghurs became the object of repression and extrajudicial incarceration because of the terrorist activities of a few. Hundreds of thousands of Uyghurs have been detained in so-called re-education camps. There was also considerable social and working-class unrest in other parts of the country. The number of recorded labour disputes increased from nearly 20,000 in 1994 to almost 270,000 ten years later.[344] A migrant worker interviewed in December 2000 in Shenzhen (known as the thriving Silicon Valley of China) complained:

> There is no fixed work schedule. A twelve-hour workday is minimum. With rush orders, we have to work continuously for thirty hours or more … It's very exhausting, because we have to stand all the time … The shop floor is filled with thick dust. Our bodies become black inside working day and night. When I get off from work and spit, it's all black … In the factory, your entire body is under his [the employer's] control. You lose control over yourself. You have to do whatever he wants you to. It's like you're sold to him.[345]

Already in 2003 it had become apparent that among the primary causes of urban dissent were the widening gap between rich and poor and the prospect of unemployment, while minorities – mainly religious ones including the Falun Gong, the Muslim Uyghurs and the Tibetan Buddhists – became more vociferous.[346] When Xi Jinping, at the 2018 National People's Congress, denounced 'separatism', he meant Xinjiang, Tibet and Hong Kong, as well as, presumably, Taiwan. Like the Chinese emperors of the past, he seemed not to have any imperial or colonial ambitions beyond the boundaries of what he regards to be the confines of China proper.

It should be said that the central government has tried, not unsuccessfully, to promote economic growth in areas with minority populations. In 1988, it contributed more than 60 per cent of the budget of the Xinjian Uyghur Autonomous Region and in the Ningxia Hui Autonomous Region as well as considerable financial support to Tibet.[347]

By 2014 China was home not only to the largest middle class in the world but also to a class of dollar millionaires; the country has become almost as unequal as the US. By 2021, according to Credit Suisse estimates, the number of dollar millionaires had gone up to 5.3 million individuals, ranking second after the United States in the world.[348] In her 2013 novel *Dinner for Six*, Lu Min describes the thoughts of the striving and ambitious Marina, somewhat dismayed by the rise of a new class which seemed to be feasting

> at a banquet of desires, oozing wealth and good cheer, staged in a blaze of lights and flowers, the tables covered lights, glasses, ice cubes, saucers filled with condiments, bottles of wine, dishes of beautiful food ... while elsewhere, in dim rooms with flickering light bulbs, the potato-eater families sat together, silently chewing on the defeat and their hunger, tolerating each other's self-loathing and trying to keep each other warm.[349]

Yet 770 million have been raised out of poverty, and extreme poverty has been eliminated, transforming China into a high-tech powerhouse 'that is on course to eclipse America's in size'.[350] The 'Made in China' label is now a global one and the country manufactures everything from microchips to motor vehicles. China is now the world's largest manufacturer and trader, and a high-tech powerhouse: of the nineteen firms created in the past twenty-five years that are now worth over US$100 billion, nine are in America and eight in China. Europe has none.[351]

When China was Communist, it was accused of wanting to conquer the world; when it became more of a market economy, it was accused of seeking global hegemony. The 'yellow peril' has been redefined. It is as if Lord Palmerston's famous aphorism – 'we have no eternal allies, and we have no perpetual enemies. Our interests are eternal and perpetual' – had been transmogrified by the West, particularly by the United States, into something new: 'We have no perpetual enemies, but we require enemies perpetually.' An alarmist tone pervades American think-tanks:

'One of the most pressing challenges the Biden administration will face', intoned Jude Blanchette of the Center for Strategic and International Studies in 2021, 'is how to compete with, and push back against, China's increasingly powerful and disruptive state capitalist system, which not only threatens U.S. economic and strategic interests, but also undermines the regulatory and legal architecture that underpins the global economy.' Presumably it was safer when they were Communists. But, as Blanchette went on: 'China now has more companies on the Fortune Global 500 list than does the United States (124 versus 121), with nearly 75 percent of these being state-owned enterprises (SOEs).'[352] China's life expectancy rate is on a par with that of the US.[353]

One of the main problems looming ahead, however, is a demographic crisis caused in part by China's one-child policy, now abandoned. Its population is rapidly ageing and its labour force declining, though its less-than-generous welfare system may contain the huge cost of age-related spending.[354] One of the obvious ways of compensating for a falling population is to increase the productivity of the workforce.

The Communist Party which rules China is remote from the centralized and tightly knit organization of professional revolutionaries envisaged by Lenin. It consists of over 95 million members, open not so much to ideologically pure men and women (though they should know a thing or two about Marxism–Leninism) as to those who have intellectual and practical skills, including entrepreneurs. Contrary to the image of the party abroad, it is far from being a monolithic structure. In fact, there is a vast range of internal positions, particularly in the higher echelons of the party. The problem is the lack of transparency: internal debates rarely surface. A personality cult has grown around the 'paramount' leader Xi Jinping, the sort of cult which Deng had eschewed. China has prospered without making any concessions to transparency or democracy. While many Western commentators are pessimistic about China's future, 'the Chinese economy indifferently trudges on'.[355]

What became the ultimate goal of the Communist Party was not so much building socialism and advancing towards communism as re-emerging as a strong and respected nation. National pride coexisted with communist ideology. Love of country, of its history and the current state of its wealth seem to suggest that, 'for the first time in modern history', China is winning.[356] As Xi Jinping declared in 2014:

> Since the Opium War of the 1840s the Chinese people have long cherished a dream of realising a great national rejuvenation. China used to

be a world economic power. However, it missed its chance in the wake of the Industrial Revolution and the consequent dramatic changes, and was thus left behind and suffered humiliation under foreign invasion... we must not let this tragic history repeat itself... China has stood up. It will never again tolerate being bullied by any nation.[357]

Those Western observers who thought that China's acceptance of elements of the so-called free market was the first step towards the construction of capitalism in China assumed a simplistic binary world in which markets are either free or unfree. The real world is far more complex. It is a world in which state intervention can take many forms, which can in turn favour some enterprises and not others. These cannot be foreseen. The rule of capital does not exist; what exists is the rule of the unpredictable. The task of politics is to attempt to rule the unpredictable. As Deng declared at a major Communist meeting in 1981: '*Bu zhenglun*' (let's dispense with theory). That was remarkable, coming from the leader of a party committed to Marxism and what was then called Mao Zedong Thought.[358] Under Xi Jinping, the drive towards stronger markets abated. If there is capitalism in China, it is capitalism 'with Chinese characteristics'.

The Chinese Revolution has taken the strangest course. It was inspired by the Russian Revolution – first with Sun Yat-sen, then with the Communists – but soon went its own way. While the Russian Revolution achieved a remarkable industrialization, it failed to achieve a consumer society. The Chinese, while not abandoning the association with communism or the Communist Party's one-party rule, have provided the majority of its population with unparalleled consumption for what was a so-called Third World country, and have turned the People's Republic into a world economic power. 'As the 21st century advances,' writes Stephen Smith, 'it may come to seem that the Chinese Revolution was the great revolution of the 20th century.'[359]

Capitalism in any form was certainly not what Mao Zedong thought would happen when, in Tiananmen Square, on 1 October 1949, he announced the birth of the People's Republic of China. It may have been in the minds of some who, in 1911, celebrated the uprising which abolished the Qing dynasty. The dreams of many reformers and revolutionaries during and after the Qing Empire, and maintained through the civil wars, the struggle against the Japanese invaders and the communist revolution, was to make China rich and powerful once again.

Conclusion

So what is special about a revolution? The introduction noted that, since the French Revolution, the term has been deployed in a huge variety of circumstances. Today, it can simply mean momentous change. Endless attempts have been made to pin the word down, as if arriving at a satisfactory definition would solve any historical problem. The distinguished historian Charles Tilly hazarded one of the best definitions:

> Consider a revolution to be a forcible transfer of power over a state in the course of which at least two distinct blocs of contenders make incompatible claims to control the state, and some significant portion of the population subject to the state's jurisdiction acquiesces in the claims of each bloc. The blocs may be single actors, such as the class of great landlords, but they often consist of coalitions among rulers, members and/ or challengers.[1]

This is still unavoidably vague, as Tilly himself seems to recognize on the following page: 'Under such a definition, unsuccessful rebellions, bloodless coups and top-down social transformations do not quite qualify as revolutions but remain their close kin.'[2] Earlier he had disarmingly admitted: 'I ended up sceptical about all efforts to formulate single models of revolution.'[3]

To provide an example of the complexities of defining such contested processes, allow me a brief excursus on the military takeover of Chile by General Augusto Pinochet in 1973, an event which hardly anyone called a revolution. In 1964 Eduardo Frei, a centrist Christian Democrat backed by the US, won the Chilean presidential elections with 56 per cent of the popular vote under the slogan 'revolución en libertad' (revolution in liberty). His reforms did not satisfy the left, while the right found them too radical. The subsequent presidential election in 1970 saw the victory of Salvador Allende, the candidate of Popular Unity, a coalition of socialists, communists and social democrats. It was a fragile victory. Allende had obtained only 36 per cent of the vote – just one point ahead of Jorge Alessandri, his main conservative opponent. The Christian Democratic vote had collapsed. Undaunted by his limited support, Allende proposed significant reforms, including nationalization of copper mines – copper, much of which was owned by American companies, was the country's main export – and the haulage industry, the main form of transport in Chile. There was substantial opposition from the armed forces, considerable dismay in Washington and some popular dissent, especially among lorry drivers who went on strike in October 1972. Yet at the congressional election of March 1973, Popular Unity increased its vote to 43 per cent. Clearly there were what Tilly would have called two blocs of contenders: Allende's bloc had on its side the political and moral authority of being the legally constituted government; the other bloc, based on the armed forces, had some popular sympathy and the support (backed by considerable financial assistance) of the Nixon administration.[4]

The army coup took place on 11 September 1973. Allende himself was one of its victims.[5] On 27 June 1974 Pinochet, who had not been among the initial conspirators, assumed the title of supreme chief of the nation. After a massive repression of the left and of the trade unions, he proceeded to liberalize and privatize the economy with the assistance of the so-called Chicago Boys, Chilean economists who had studied at the University of Chicago under the neoliberal Milton Friedman. A period of remarkable economic growth ensued, accompanied by an increase in inequality and corruption. Pinochet remained in power until the late 1980s, when he lost a referendum he had expected to win. The margin of his defeat (56 per cent against 44 per cent) shows that the dictatorship still enjoyed considerable support. Pinochet's attempt to stage another coup failed. He remained commander-in-chief of the army until March 1998, and was then a senator for life with an immunity that lasted until 2000. He died in 2006 while under house arrest.

The Chilean events are commonly referred to as a coup d'état, since they followed a well-established pattern of military intervention against an elected left-wing government. Yet the Chilean events had many of the revolutionary characteristics outlined by Tilly. They certainly constituted a forcible transfer of power (and led to significant changes in the economy), and some significant portion of the population acquiesced to the claims of each bloc. But this revolution was engineered by the right, and by and large the right does not like revolutions.

Since 1789, revolution has acquired, in almost all cases, a progressive ideological connotation. Even the detractors of the French Revolution in the nineteenth century (such as Chateaubriand, Burke and Taine) or in the twentieth century (Furet and others) accepted that it was a revolution; they just did not approve of it. A revolution is usually seen as left-wing, or at least as liberal. It describes an uprising against an authoritarian regime. Even what might constitute the most obvious exception to this rule – the Islamic Revolution in Iran in 1979 which gave rise to a regime no one would call liberal – originally had a progressive aspect since it toppled a US-backed monarchical dictatorship and was supported by many liberals, reformists and leftists in the West.

In her important *States and Social Revolutions* (1979), Theda Skocpol recognizes that what she calls social revolutions are not only relatively rare in history, but also quite distinct from one another, 'occurr[ing] in a particular way in a unique set of socio-structural and international circumstances'.[6] In fact she is unable to find too many similarities linking the three revolutions she examines in depth (the French, Russian and Chinese). Monocausal explanations simply highlight what some revolutions have in common; they do not define them. War or the threat of war loomed large in some more than in others. Financial problems were an important element in the English, French and American revolutions but quite tangential in Russia and China. Monarchical oppression on its own hardly explains the revolutions of 1648 or 1789 – the English and French had suffered in previous reigns without revolting.

Nationalism has often been a major element in revolutions. It was integral to the anti-Catholic aspect of the English Civil War, and important for the French Revolution, at least during the Napoleonic Wars. It was obviously the major element of the American War of Independence and, even more so, the unification of Italy and Germany. It played a key role in the Chinese Revolution, but it was not at the centre of the Russian Revolution, since what emerged from the October Revolution was a Soviet state encompassing various nationalities, whose identities were enhanced by the Soviet regime and which later took advantage of its collapse. An overarching Soviet nationalism was boosted in the long interval by a sense of being encircled by the anti-communist capitalist world, above all during the struggle against Nazi Germany in the Second World War, known as the Great Patriotic War.

The question of success

How successful were the revolutions? Here we face another major problem. Regimes come and go. Getting rid of a regime is the easy part of the revolutionary process; consolidating one's position is more difficult. The real problem, however, is how to accomplish the objectives of the revolution, since there are often contrasting aims and aspirations which constantly change.

If a revolution is simply about the overthrow of the ancien régime, all those I have included in this book could be deemed successful. The French and the English got rid of an absolute monarchy, the Americans got rid of the English, the Bolsheviks got rid not so much of the Romanovs (they had gone by March 1917) but of any other possible successors (the liberals as well as the right-wing leaders of the Civil War). The Chinese Communists eliminated their Nationalist rivals, the Imperial Qing dynasty having already departed in 1911.

The national revolutions of the nineteenth century were successful too. Germany remained united throughout the Deutsches Kaiserreich (Second Reich), the Weimar Republic and the Nazi dictatorship (and was even temporarily enlarged through the Anschluss with Austria in 1938). It even survived the Second World War and Cold War, though for just over forty-five years it was divided by outside forces between West and East. Italian unity was not imperilled by the twenty years of Fascist dictatorship, the experience of the Second World War or the transition to a relatively stable republic; independentist movements cannot be regarded as serious threats (they are certainly far less significant than Scottish or Catalan nationalism). In Sicily an independentist party managed 8.8 per cent of the vote in the first regional elections of 1947 before sinking into oblivion; and the so-called Lega Nord, which wants the North to split from the rest of the peninsula, has dropped 'Nord' from its election leaflets to curry favour in the South.

No doubt the nature of bourgeois revolution will continue to be debated but one thing is certain: the Puritan revolutionaries in England in the seventeenth century, the Patriots in the American Revolutionary War (1775–83) and the French Revolutionaries in the 1790s could not even imagine they were fighting for a capitalist society. Capitalism, of course, did emerge, but few would dispute that it would have emerged anyway. When those revolutions started there was no real industrial bourgeoisie, though there were forms of agrarian and mercantile capitalism, especially in England. Charles I and Louis XVI could have survived, after concessions, and ruled over a developing capitalism (as was the case under Charles II and his successors, and Louis XVIII and his). Great Britain wanted to maintain its rule over the American settlers, not impede the development of its economy. The struggle, in all cases, was about political power and control.

In the end the French, American and English Revolutions accomplished their initial aim. They constructed a state which was called upon to do things that the states of old could not have dreamt of. The new states waged wars, regulated markets, educated people and developed welfare systems. Today the state appears weak in those three countries because it is not under the absolute control of a single force, but it is far more pervasive in the life of its citizens than any previous regime.

In Republican France (post-1870), power was at first confined to a deeply divided parliament, hence the constant succession of governments. The post-1958 Gaullist reforms established a president (elected by universal suffrage after 1962) who was powerful only if he or she could rely on a majority in parliament. In Britain, where the prime minister is unbound by a constitution (there isn't one), matters are not that different: the prime minister is powerful only as long as he or she has a Commons majority. When the French president could not rely on a majority in parliament, he too was almost powerless. This was called *la cohabitation*, as when the Socialist President François Mitterrand had to cohabit with Gaullist Prime Ministers Jacques Chirac (1986) and Édouard Balladur (1993), and when President Chirac was forced, in turn, to accept the Socialist Lionel Jospin as prime minister in 1997.

The American president is even weaker than the British prime minister or the French president because he or she must face a Congress divided into two chambers, elected at different times and in different ways. Being able to control a majority is thus difficult if not impossible, also because the party system is not as strong as in Europe. Moreover, there is a written Constitution that is difficult to amend and whose interpretation is in the hands of the nine judges of the Supreme Court (Franklin D. Roosevelt failed in his attempt to expand the numbers in 1937). The Supreme Court can invalidate the decisions of Congress and of the president. It is true that the president appoints the judges of the Supreme Court, but not without the approval of the Senate; besides, he or she must face judges appointed by previous presidents. The president, though generally regarded as an extremely powerful figure, cannot do much without the Senate and the House of Representatives. The importance of the president has nothing to do with the American political system and everything to do with the global power of the US.

There is a powerful Congress in Washington, divided into two chambers. The House of Representatives, though rife with gerrymandering, is in principle relatively proportional. The Senate, as we have seen, is not. As if this were not sufficient, there are also fifty states with distinctive powers – over, for instance, police and some taxation – each a replica of the central government, with a governor, senate and house of representatives. By comparison the British prime minister is more powerful, since she or he has usually a majority in the House of Commons, does not face a constitution and can appoint anyone to the House of Lords. But Britain is a middle-sized power quite unlike the US, and so it does not matter much, to the rest of the world, how powerful the British prime minister is.

In Britain, as in the US, the electoral system ensures that, in practice, there are only two parties vying for power. This should make for greater strength and stability than in countries where the electoral system makes it almost impossible for a single party to have a majority (Germany and Italy, for instance). Yet in Britain, each party is a de facto coalition between a hard right (or hard left) and a more moderate centre right (or centre left), so that in practice it is difficult for the prime minister to rule from a position of great strength. In the years 2015–23, five prime ministers from the same party succeeded each other in Britain, all constrained by opposition from inside their party: David Cameron, Theresa May, Boris Johnson, Liz Truss and Rishi Sunak. The general election of 2024 revealed the absurdities of the electoral system. In terms of votes, the third-strongest party (the right-wing Reform Party) ended up with just five members of Parliament. The fourth party, the Liberals, gained seventy-two. The Labour Party, with fewer votes than in 2017 and 2019, won with a massive majority. What matters in British elections is not the number of votes but how they are distributed.

In France, Emmanuel Macron – elected president in 2017 and re-elected in 2022 – faced strikes and turmoil and lost his parliamentary majority in the legislative elections of 2022. The far right, led by Marine Le Pen, obtained its best results ever in the presidential elections of 2022. The snap parliamentary elections of 2024 left the country even more unstable, since no obvious parliamentary majority emerged. In the US, the first Trump presidency was seen by some as a neurotic aberration and by others as an exhilarating phase. It changed very little in practice, save for Trump's appointment of three relatively young conservative judges to the Supreme Court. His non-acceptance of defeat and the subsequent so-called insurrection of 6 January 2022 (a demonstration which got out of hand because of the inability or the unwillingness of the police to control it) have passed into history. Trump returned in 2025, and the Republican Party has emerged as more right-wing than ever (but politics in Italy, France and Britain have also shifted to the right). These developments may have weakened the vainglorious claims of American liberalism, but so far they have not seriously threatened its existence.

None of this, however, seems to imperil the overall political system of these countries. Any threat to their economies comes from the inevitable changes in global capitalism, such as the economic rise of China. The revolutions in England, France and the US, and the unifications of Italy and Germany, have given rise to political systems whose great stability is due to their capacity to withstand change: the coming and going of political parties; the lies and corruption of politicians; the changing mood of the electorate; the vicissitudes of the international economy. Their strength – what made these old revolutions successful – lies in the success of what would be later known with the generic and undefinable term of liberalism. The main characteristic of this liberalism is precisely that it is flawed. The flaws are evident, as a survey of our three main examples of revolution can attest. In England, the perdurance of the ideological weight of the monarchy (though the monarch has no power); the presence of an anachronistic unelected chamber, the House of Lords, which is periodically reformed without any significant changes being made; and the enduring class system. Elite public schools (Eton, Winchester, Harrow) have no parallel in the rest of the West, which could be taken to indicate their redundancy. In 2019 income inequality (the Gini coefficient) in the UK was lower than in the US but higher than in all other West European countries.[7] British liberalism was dented by blasphemy laws directed exclusively against those who blasphemed against Christianity: there was a successful prosecution in 1977 against *Gay News* for a poem depicting Jesus as gay. Blasphemy as an offence was finally abolished in 2008. Until the Race Relations Act of 1965 it was not illegal in Britain to prevent someone to enter a restaurant or pub on grounds of race, and even then one could discriminate on employment and housing until 1968.

British politicians of both left and right constantly refer to 'Global Britain', boasting of its past, present and future achievements. Much of this reveals a fear of losing British identity – all the more so since it may well be the case that Ireland will be reunited and Scotland will become independent, thus undoing what was achieved during the seventeenth and eighteenth centuries. No other country insists so much on its global weight – except, of course, the US, which is, after all, a real global power, though a declining one. Britain's flaws are numerous and constantly debated. Yet the British political system barely changed even while the country lost its pre-eminent international economic position as well as its colonies.

In France, the systemic flaws are of a different order. For all the bluster about equal rights celebrated in the slogan *Liberté, égalité, fraternité*, France was never in the forefront of any of these three aspirations. It was, after Britain, the main colonialist country in the late nineteenth century, and it held on to colonies such as Indochina and Algeria with all the violence it could muster. It was one of the last countries in Europe to grant the suffrage to women and one of the last to abolish capital punishment. It maintained a system of political censorship far more severe than that of Britain or the United States. Pacifist songs such as 'Quand un soldat' (written in 1952 by Francis Lemarque and sung by the popular Yves Montand) and 'Le Déserteur' by Boris Vian (written in 1954, as the Indochina War gave way to the Algerian War) were soon banned by the state broadcaster; the latter was unbanned only in 1962. Anti-war songs were not banned in the United States during the Vietnam War. Much of the political censorship in France was directed against anti-militarism; this included banning the daily *Libération* and the satirical journal *Charlie Hebdo* from military barracks.

The so-called *laïcité*, based on the separation of Church and state established in 1905, acquired Islamophobic connotations with the ban on the wearing of headscarves in many public places in April 2011 (a measure also adopted in Belgium), strengthening the prohibition of religious symbols in France.[8] The *patrie des droits de l'homme* (land of human rights) was becoming the *pays de la pensée unique*. By contrast, (Conservative) British Prime Minister Theresa May backed the right of Muslim women to wear a headscarf or hijab, adding, 'what a woman wears is a woman's choice', though she had also presided at the Home Office over a 'hostile environment' for undocumented migrants.[9]

Some people, of course, are offended by the wearing of headscarves, but then some people are also offended by women wearing mini-skirts. Religious symbols are seldom banned in other countries. By 2004, the wearing of visible religious signs in schools was banned in France; such signs included hijabs (head coverings), Jewish yarmulkes and large Christian crosses. But the *laïcité* is lifted when it is convenient: almost

20 per cent of all students in France attend private schools, almost all of which are Catholic and largely funded by the state.[10] When Pope John Paul died in April 2005, an executive order requested flags to be lowered to half-mast in all public buildings and President Jacques Chirac and other top officials attended a memorial service at Notre Dame Cathedral. While citizens of Arab origin comprise 8 per cent of the population, there were only nine people of Arab heritage in the French parliament as of 2022. Discrimination and racism are common in the land of the revolution. The so-called *mission civilisatrice* has failed utterly to export liberalism anywhere in the French Empire, though of course, that was an ideological slogan aimed to cover imperial conquest.

In the United States, where the key sentence of the Declaration of Independence avers that 'all men are created equal' and have 'unalienable Rights', including to 'life, liberty and the pursuit of happiness', racism has remained a major problem. The extension of civil rights to people of colour in the 1960s failed to end de facto discrimination. Black Americans are imprisoned at a rate that is roughly five times the rate of white Americans. In twelve states (including non-southern states, such as Delaware, Illinois, Michigan and New Jersey), more than half the prison population is Black.[11] People of colour are poorer, and so is their health: in 2021 new cases of tuberculosis per 100,000 reached 5.85 for Hawaiians, 3.72 for Native Americans and 2.03 for Black people, but only 0.35 for whites.[12] Black Americans are at higher risk of heart disease, stroke, cancer, asthma, influenza and pneumonia, diabetes and HIV/AIDS; their life expectancy at birth (2020 figures) is 72.8 years, while for white people it is 77.5 years.[13]

The incarceration rate in the US is one of the highest in the world (2025), with 541 per 100,000 inhabitants – below only those of El Salvador, Cuba, Rwanda and Turkmenistan, and much higher than the rates in France (117), Italy (106) and Germany (68).[14] In 2020 the American police killed over a thousand people. Black people, who comprise roughly 14 per cent of the population, are killed by the police at more than twice the rate of white Americans.[15] The rate of intentional homicide in the US in 2020 was 6.52 per 100,000. This is lower than Russia (7.33) but far, far higher than other leading Western nations. In China, intentional homicide is 0.5 per 100,000, better than virtually anywhere in the West.[16] In the US, more than 107,000 people died from drug-related overdose in 2022, including illicit drugs and prescription opioids.[17] According to the CDC, over the two decades before 2023 around 806,000 people died from an opioid overdose in the US.[18]

Meanwhile the US spends vast sums of money policing the world, with hundreds of overseas military bases, while struggling to win wars: Korea, Vietnam, Iraq and Afghanistan were not military successes. Nation-building in foreign lands has remained a chimera.[19] In the Guantánamo detention camp, an American military prison on the island of Cuba, hundreds of people have been detained without trial since the 9/11 attack on the Twin Towers. By 2023 there were still more than thirty prisoners, most of whom have been held for nearly twenty years. Many have been subjected to various forms of torture and humiliation, including sexual humiliation. The American Civil Liberty Union stated in January 2023:

> We can never forget or accept the horrors of torture, indefinite detention, and unfair trials that have defined Guantánamo for over two decades. The iconic images of the first prisoners remain shamefully and globally indelible: orange jumpsuits on brown bodies, hands tied together, eyes and ears masked.[20]

Yet in spite of all these flaws, the US remains a liberal democracy, and it is obviously more liberal and more democratic than it was in 1776.

In the US, Britain and France, xenophobia and distrust of outsiders and immigrants is not confined to the fringes. In the UK, the anti-immigrant and Eurosceptic UKIP party was the largest in the 2014 elections to the European Parliament (a poll where voters felt freer to vote for the party they liked, since the electoral system was more proportional). The Brexit Party repeated this feat in 2019. As mentioned above, it came third in the 2024 general election under its new name, Reform. In France, in the second round of the 2022 presidential elections, the far-right candidate Marine Le Pen obtained 41 per cent of the electorate; in 2024 her party led in the first round. In the US, Donald Trump, whose dislike of immigrants was made manifest in the 2016 election (which he won), famously declared that Mexicans are 'bringing drugs. They're bringing crime. They're rapists. And some, I assume, are good people.' Four years later he was still able to obtain 74 million votes, though he lost to Joe Biden. In 2024 when he won for a second time, he promised voters to implement mass deportations.

Defining liberal democracy usually entails providing a shopping list of features without explaining how they interrelate. The list includes the separation of powers – particularly a relatively independent judiciary – and, above all, free and fair elections. Yet a remarkable number of electors do not exercise their vote, whether out of disdain, laziness, despair, voter suppression or simply because of bad weather. France, which used to have a high rate of electoral participation, had a turnout in 2022 of 72 per cent, the lowest since 1969. In the immediately following legislative elections, turnout was a dismal 46–7 per cent. In 2022 the US had the highest turnout since 1900 in a presidential election: 66 per cent. A similar turnout was achieved in Britain in 2019.

So no one is elected by a majority of the electorate, but only, if at all, by a majority of voters. That between a third and a fourth of the electorate do not use their right to vote, is difficult to interpret. Increasingly, voters vote for parties or people who used to be outside normal politics. In France, the politics of the Fifth Republic (post-1958) for decades turned on a choice between the left (communist and socialist) and the Gaullist centre right. The 2017 and 2022 elections showed that the electorate preferred an unknown and relatively inexperienced centrist (or centre rightist) – Emmanuel Macron – and the leader of the radical right (Marine Le Pen), while the socialist and Gaullist candidates were humiliated. In the 2024 assembly elections it was Macron's turn to be humbled, while the left and particularly the radical left (Jean-Luc Mélenchon) performed strongly.

In the end, in all three countries, as in virtually all democratic countries, the wealthy few exercise far greater power over politics than the average voter. It is almost as if it had been decreed that universal suffrage could be granted once there was an underlying understanding that those with money would be able, in practice, to buy votes. Yet in spite of all this – in spite of the regular announcements that democracy is in danger; in spite of the disenchantment with politicians, who are constantly reviled; in spite of the low turnout in elections; in spite of the anger at inequality, the worries about global warming while private consumption is at its height, the rampant anti-capitalist ideology in fiction, the widespread dislike for the rich while so many want to get rich – in spite of all this, the system remains firm and solid: not just in France, Britain, the US, Germany and Italy, but also in other well-established liberal democracies (such as Scandinavia, Belgium, Holland and Ireland), as well as in countries which a couple of generations ago were under military rule (Spain, Portugal and Greece).

Given the stability of the political system in Britain, France and the US – despite all the flaws I have listed (and there are plenty more) – one might conclude that their revolutions have been successful, surviving the momentous changes of the last few centuries. Even in Italy and Germany, the political system is well entrenched. Italy had an exceptionally stable party system until the early 1990s and does not seem to be threatened by the rise of its far-right parties. German institutions have so far parried the rising popularity of the far-right AfD. Matters might change, as they do in history, but as I write, few are able to envisage a realistic alternative to existing liberal democratic systems.

So success may be the wrong word, but the system is likely to endure without achieving what its most enthusiastic supporters claim on its behalf. In history, a process either continues and evolves, or continues and degenerates, or it collapses – but it never reaches its goal. Great Britain, France and the United States were regarded as liberal democracies even in the nineteenth century, when they waged wars of colonial annexation or upheld slavery and exterminated indigenous peoples; when they restricted the suffrage, when they had laws against homosexuality, when they had capital punishment (as the United States still does). Self-satisfaction is a constant and inevitable obstacle to reform; yet to live without reform, without change, is utopian.

The appeals of communism

The Soviet and Chinese revolutions were a quite different endeavour from those of England, America and France. Their avowed aim was not just to get rid of a regime and its political system but to establish a new economic order that had never before existed. The victorious protagonists defined their revolutions as the first step towards the construction of a socialist society.

These revolutions, especially the Russian, inspired massive international enmity – as had, among some, the French Revolution (an enmity which did not arise for the English Civil War or American War of Independence). This hostility lasted throughout the existence of the Soviet Union, with a pause during the Second World War, and it continued towards Russia even after the end of communism, escalating after the 2022 invasion of Ukraine. But there was also an undercurrent of friendship and solidarity with Russian communism, not only among newly formed communist parties in the West and elsewhere, but also within in the anti-colonial movement. Unlike Fascism and Nazism, the Russian Revolution received considerable backing from non-state actors abroad, including significant support from intellectuals. Many of the latter abandoned the Soviet path after 1956, when the extent of Stalin's crimes was revealed by the Russians themselves. The height of the intelligentsia's involvement with the Soviet Union occurred during the 1930s.

Intellectuals from all parts of the left embraced what James Billington described as a 'visionary-futurist' view of the Russian Revolution: ready to ignore its worst aspects in the hope that a coming millennium would validate the original aims – just as many had previously accepted the French Revolution regardless of the Terror.[21]

In the 1930s, at the height of Stalin's purges, renowned intellectuals, especially in France, defended the USSR. These included avant-garde writers and artists who joined the French Communist Party, such as Louis Aragon, Andre Breton, Tristan Tzara and Paul Eluard, as well as sympathizers such as Robert Desnos, Raymond Queneau, Jean-Paul Sartre, Simone de Beauvoir, the German artist Max Ernst and the Swiss sculptor Alberto Giacometti. In Britain, left-wing publishers such as Gollancz reissued Fabian Sidney and Beatrice Webbs' *Soviet Communism: A New Civilization* without the original question mark, as well as numerous writings by Marx, Engels, Lenin and Stalin. Gollancz also published John Strachey's influential *The Coming Struggle for Power* (1933). Strachey became a Labour politician but never disguised his sympathies for Soviet communism. Two of Britain's foremost scientists, Professors J. D. Bernal and J. B. S. Haldane, joined the British Communist Party (CPGB) alongside major historians such as Eric Hobsbawm (who never left it), Christopher Hill and distinguished poets such as Stephen Spender. In reality, they were not joining the CPGB, a tiny and irrelevant party; they were joining the international communist movement, then led by Joseph Stalin.[22] Even the Right Reverend Hewlett Johnson, the so-called Red Dean of Canterbury, was an unwavering supporter of Stalin, of communism and of the USSR. Though he never joined the party he was, unquestioningly, a fellow traveller – a term which has a pejorative undertone, especially in the US, but its origin was in the Russian term *poputchik*: one who travels the same path.

The attraction towards communism was essentially based on an optimistic vision of a future non-capitalist society, while accepting and, at times, disregarding the horrors of the Soviet purges and the accompanying deportations. Emblematic was Romain Rolland's 1935 exhortation, typical of the 'visionary-futurist' view:

> I see in Russia a people trying, despite unfathomable suffering, to give birth to a new order. This new order is bloody, filthy just like the human baby just prized from the womb of the mother. In spite of the disgust,

in spite of the horror of terrible mistakes and crimes, I go towards the newly-born and embrace him: he is the hope, the miserable hope of the human future.[23]

Bertolt Brecht's 1940 poem 'To Those Born Later' includes the lines:

> I came among men in a time of revolt
> And I rebelled with them.
> So passed my time
> Which had been given me to on earth.

It concludes:

> But you, when the time comes at last
> When man is helper to man
> Think of us
> With forbearance.[24]

Of course, the far right too had its intellectuals, but one of the many differences between the far right and the communist left was that the left shared with liberalism a universal language and hence a universal appeal. It did not address itself specifically to a race, a colour or a nation but to a world of workers (proletarians of all countries) in which almost everyone could recognize themselves, regardless of creed or national identity. This is why a list of prominent pro-fascist or protofascist intellectuals is inevitably short: Julius Evola; Ezra Pound; Charles Maurras; Martin Heidegger; Carl Schmitt; and the quite forgotten (except in Italy) Giovanni Gentile and Ugo Spirito. Many of these expressed their views under Fascism and did not face the problems of those who sympathized with Soviet communism in capitalist countries.

Some of those distinguished thinkers who signed or supported the 1925 Manifesto of Fascist Intellectuals (the philosopher Giovanni Gentile, the writer Curzio Malaparte, the Futurist Filippo Tommaso Marinetti, the playwright Luigi Pirandello, the composer Ildebrando Pizzetti and the poet Giuseppe Ungaretti) broke with fascism – sometimes, as in the case of Marinetti, during Fascism. The appeal of white racism, pro-colonialism and anti-Semitism was inevitably wider. In places such as Britain and even more so in France there were many who sympathized with fascism and many more who were anti-Semitic, but hardly any had any intellectual significance.

There had always been, of course, right-wing intellectuals, especially in France, who voiced racist and illiberal views, often buttressed by an appeal to pseudo-science – but there was no fascist regime for them to support. I am thinking of the French naturalist Georges Cuvier, the German philosopher Arthur Schopenhauer, the French writer Arthur de Gobineau, the American author Madison Grant (who wrote *The Passing of the Great Race*, 1916), the eugenicist Francis Galton and, more recently, far-right commentators such as Alain de Benoist and many others. Some, mainly before 1945, thought they could prove the inferiority of non-whites by measuring the shape or size of people's skulls. More recently, some claim that there is an unbridgeable cultural gap between 'real' Europeans and Muslim immigrants. These right-wing intellectuals cannot hold a candle to the achievements or commitments of pro-Soviet intellectuals.

Even in popular songs, there is a scarcity of pro-fascist or pro-Nazi songs. Italian Fascism produced hardly any songs of note despite the country's musical tradition. The best known are 'Faccetta Nera' about the conquest of Abyssinia (disliked by the Mussolini regime, for whom it conjured the spectre of miscegenation) and 'Giovinezza' (Youth), the official Fascist anthem:

> 'Faccetta Nera'
> *Faccetta nera, bell'abissina*
> *Aspetta e spera che già l'ora si avvicina!*
> *quando saremo insieme a te*
> *noi ti daremo un'altra legge e un altro*
> *Re.*
>
> Pretty black face, beautiful Abyssinian
> Wait in hope, for the hour is coming!
> When we'll be with you
> We'll give you another law, another
> King.
>
> 'Giovinezza'
> *Giovinezza, giovinezza, primavera di bellezza,*
> *nel fascismo è la salvezza della nostra libertà.*
>
> Youth, youth, springtime of beauty,
> In fascism is the salvation of our liberty.

Left-wing partisan songs, on the other hand, are abundant in France and in Italy, many, of course, diffused after the end of the Second World War, often having borrowed the music from Russian and Ukrainian songs. Communist and Soviet culture was always far more appealing than Fascist or Nazi culture. I am thinking of the Italian 'Fischia il vento' (originally 'Katyusha' composed by the Jewish-Ukrainian Matvey Isaakovich Blanter in 1938), the globally renowned partisan song 'Ciao bella ciao' and the French 'Le Chant des partisans' (the hymn of the Resistance written in 1941 by Anna Marly, a composer born in Russia).

The peak of pro-Sovietism coincided with the height of Stalin's purges in the 1930s because it also coincided with the rise of the far right throughout much of Europe. In Italy there was an established Fascist regime since 1922; in Germany Nazism had taken over in 1933. Then there was Franco's successful armed attempt to supress the Popular Front government in Spain (1936–39). Far-right regimes existed throughout much of Europe, from Greece, Portugal and Albania, to Poland, the Baltic republics, Romania and Hungary.

The Russian Revolution had raised enormous hopes, but as we know, they were dashed. The USSR failed because it was never able to establish an economic system even remotely superior to capitalism, though it made remarkable progress in resolving the problem that had been central to tsarist Russia: the creation of an industrial society. But Japan had achieved something similar after the Meiji Restoration without the mayhem suffered by the peoples of the Soviet Union. Yet it would be wrong to see liberal democracy as a realistic choice in the years following either the Russian or the Chinese Revolution. The struggle was between communism and the kind of right-wing authoritarian dictatorship that prevailed in Eastern Europe in the 1920s and 1930s, or in Taiwan after 1949. Even after the fall of communism, Russia was unable to find a liberal path.

In some (lucky) countries, a flawed liberalism prospered with an ever-growing consumer society. In the USSR the gap between hopes and realities was enormous, even though, after Stalin's death, the regime became far less repressive and considerable economic progress was achieved. Then, just as the 1917 Revolution had not been planned by anyone, the collapse of 1989–91 was equally unintentional. In the downfall of the USSR there were, of course, contingent factors, such as the lengthy and costly war in Afghanistan, the Chernobyl nuclear disaster of April 1986 (which the regime tried at first to keep under wraps) and the turmoil in the satellite states of Eastern Europe – above all in Poland, where, in June 1989, the first free elections since 1947 saw the victory of the anti-Soviet party known as Solidarność (Solidarity).

The wider causes of the downfall were connected to the creation of a planned economy. This, in the imagination of the revolutionaries and their successors, was supposed to be far more efficient than the capitalist market economies. The planning mechanism turned out to be reasonably efficient in industrializing the country and avoiding the business cycles of capitalism. But business cycles are capitalism's way of advancing towards new patterns of consumption and economic organization. The Soviet planned economies had none of these mechanisms. Aspects of planning which certainly enjoyed popular support, such as full employment and job certainty, did not offer the flexibility that a market economy could provide. The lack of so many goods, at a time when Russians became increasingly aware of the consumer choices available in capitalist societies, meant that there was a widespread sense that somehow communism had failed, and consumer capitalism was better. But as we have seen, capitalism in post-communist Russia was not a success either, even before the disastrous invasion of Ukraine (whose economy was seriously underperforming even before the invasion, with a lower per capita GDP than Egypt).[25]

That the Russian Revolution, all things considered, was a failure was also the opinion of the successors to the communists, especially Vladimir Putin (a former KGB agent). In his address of 21 February 2022, a few days before the invasion of Ukraine, Putin denounced the Bolsheviks (Lenin, Stalin and others) for pandering to nationalisms, especially Ukrainian nationalism.[26]

What of China?

As we have seen, the Chinese Communists took far longer to achieve power than revolutionaries in the other four cases we analysed, not counting the national revolutions. The Chinese Revolution did not give rise to a specific start date on a par with 1642 (or 1688) in England, 1776 in America, 1789 in France and 1917 in Russia. It is celebrated on 1 October, when the CCP's conquest of power was proclaimed. The Chinese Revolution was also, unlike the others, a genuine peasant revolution because the Communists were forced to leave their urban stronghold and seek refuge in the countryside. In China the revolutionaries started to change the social and economic framework of the areas they had conquered before the definitive seizure of central power. This the Bolsheviks could not do.

In China, the semi-utopian communism of the Great Leap Forward and the Cultural Revolution gave way to a new, and so far successful, market economy controlled by the same Communist Party which was supposed to construct a socialist society. It did so without upholding basic liberal values – just as the Western revolutions disregarded them for decades – and has shown no sign of embracing them. The remarkable material benefits of socialism with Chinese characteristics have been such that, should they continue, there may not be a serious challenge to the existing regime. As we pointed out, China's economic success lies in the unusual combination of a strong authoritarian state and the gradual development of a market economy. Whether the state will be able to control the market, allowing it the necessary flexibility, is a matter for speculation. At present the growth of inequalities is tolerated because increased prosperity has not been confined to the top of society.

China has become the strongest manufacturing country in the world. Its exports have been so successful that many in the West, especially in the US, have advocated a return to protectionist measures. China's rise has transformed the international economic system to an extent not remotely paralleled by the USSR. In fact, its rise was concomitant to Russia's stagnation. An analysis by the Australian Strategic Policy Institute (a think-tank definitely not friendly towards China) suggested that China's global technological lead extends to thirty-seven out of forty-four technologies tracked, including defence, space, robotics, energy, the environment, biotechnology and artificial intelligence, as well as key quantum technology areas.[27]

China's largest export markets are countries as varied as the US, Japan, Germany, South Korea, Vietnam, Australia and Indonesia. Its exports are not primary products but broadcasting equipment, computers, integrated circuits and office-machine parts.[28] This means that damaging China – one of the apparent aims of American foreign policy – will also damage many other countries, including the US. By contrast, Russia (population 143 million), whose GDP is smaller than that of Canada (population 39 million) exports very few manufactured products.[29] In Russia it is not only communism that has failed but also capitalism.

Communist revolutions have been rare. Mongolia became communist in the early 1920s as a direct consequence of the Bolshevik intervention. When Soviet Communism collapsed, so did Mongolian communism. In Vietnam the communist revolution was part of an anti-colonial uprising.

Communist North Korea was a consequence of the post-1945 partition of the country between the USSR, which occupied the North, and the US, which occupied the South.

Communist military interventions have also been rare. The USSR intervened militarily in 1939 (when Hitler invaded Poland), occupying the Baltic republics, Finland and parts of Poland. The USSR also intervened in Hungary (1956) and in Czechoslovakia (1968) to reassert control over these satellite countries; then it intervened in Afghanistan (1979) to buttress a friendly government under threat. Beijing, leaving aside areas such as Tibet, which was regarded by most countries as part of China, has refrained from intervening outside its borders. The exceptions have been the border dispute with India (October–November 1962) – the so-called Sino-Indian War, more a skirmish than a war, though the border dispute continues – and the equally short war with Vietnam in 1979. China refrained from forcibly taking over Hong Kong and Macau; the two regions were returned to China, in 1997 and 1999 respectively, according to the terms of the nineteenth-century treaties. China has not yet shown any sign of intervening militarily in Taiwan.

Looking forward

At the end of the twentieth century, after the collapse of communism, only a few intellectuals discussed the genuine possibility of post-capitalism, and no significant political party aimed at ending capitalism, even though the disenchantment with it was undimmed. Fredric Jameson observed that the failure of the utopian imagination was 'the same ... as that of the political revolutions designed to achieve the same transition in real life: the absence of a third term between the two systems, the absence of a mechanism'.[30] In the classical utopian literature, a revolutionary process had not usually been envisaged. Thomas More's famous *Utopia* (1516) is a political satire about the present describing a fictional island where there is no private property (though each household can have two slaves if the slaves are foreign!) and there is tolerance of diverse religions. Tommaso Campanella in his *La città del Sole* (The City of the Sun, 1602) described an imaginary classless communist society where everyone works with equal dignity. Neither Campanella nor More explain how the state of affairs comes about: the actual revolution is missing. Later utopias, such as Edward Bellamy's *Looking Backward* (1888) and William Morris's *News from Nowhere* (1890) – where the narrator falls into a mysterious sleep and awakes a century later in Utopia – also fail to spell out how matters proceeded from A to Z. Today, a quarter of the way through the twenty-first century, the many prognoses of capitalism's demise usually argue that the capitalist system is mutating (or regressing) into 'something worse'.[31]

Nowhere in the non-communist world are there communist parties of any importance. The surviving main communist states (China, Cuba and Vietnam) are unlikely to be willing to risk their prosperity to export the revolution – something not even the USSR had really tried. There will be uprisings aimed at regime change, such as the failed Arab Spring of 2011 (partially successful only in Tunisia, where it started), but what about revolutions aimed at establishing an entirely new economic and political order?[32] There are hardly any universalistic movements. Reformist demands are largely to do with identities and human rights, namely that there should be greater representation for under-represented groups. Demands for fairer representation do not alter the foundations of the system: even if half the CEOs were women or 20 per cent were Black, the system would go on the same way as before – which is not to deny the legitimacy of such demands. The same goes for inequality: the reduction of inequality would not require revolution since liberal capitalism does not require inequality, though it certainly produces it. Other reforms deal with the threat to the environment and whether such a threat would require a limitation of consumption via the markets (by making some goods more expensive, thus contributing to inequality) or by prohibiting some goods.

Is this the end of the revolutionary era? Some left-wing thinkers such as Göran Therborn tend to think so. Therborn writes that although there are challenges aplenty for new lefts to contest, the two great dialectics of the twentieth century – industrial capitalism and capitalist colonialism – appear to have stalled.[33] Of course, since there are many authoritarian regimes, there is ample space for revolutions on the pattern of the classical liberal democratic revolutions, but they would amount to a catch-up with the West rather than the kind of innovative political change heralded by the French or Russian Revolutions. Social democracy itself – never a worldwide movement, being confined to Western Europe and Western outposts such as Australia and New Zealand – is in serious decline. Alternative visions – recent leftist social movements such as Occupy and Indignados; leftist trends within the organized left (Jeremy Corbyn in the Labour Party, Bernie Sanders in the US, Syriza in Greece); the Latin American left epitomized by Lula in Brazil, Rafael Correa in Ecuador,

Evo Morales in Bolivia and Hugo Chávez in Venezuela – have ended at best with some important reforms, or else in failure.

Does it mean that capitalism is immovable? Not at all, since the chief characteristic of capitalism is that it changes constantly. As George Lawson points out: 'The world's largest taxi company owns no taxis (Uber); the largest accommodation provider owns no real estate (Airbnb); the world's largest global phone companies own no infrastructure (Skype, WeChat).'[34] Karl Marx himself insisted: 'The present society is no solid crystal, but an organism capable of change, and is constantly changing.'[35] This was a position he had held since the days of the *Communist Manifesto*: 'The bourgeoisie cannot exist without constantly revolutionizing the instruments of production, and thereby the relations of production, and with them the whole relations of society.' He did not see revolution in a deterministic way, as the result of an inevitable process, as did so many of his followers and his opponents.[36] Marx did not provide a Marxist theory of revolution.

The process of systemic evolution is a constant in human history. To turn this evolution into a revolution requires an accumulation of problems – some political, some economic, some ideological. Then, at an unforeseeable moment, fate (there is no other word) strikes. A war, an incident, a demonstration, an economic crisis, a foreign intervention – and then the revolution occurs – and then, when it's over, history continues its course. As Diderot put it: 'Nous croyons conduire le destin, mais c'est toujours lui qui nous mène' (We think we are in control of destiny, but it is destiny that is always in control).[37]

Acknowledgements

THANKS to:

Lauro Martines, Paul Auerbach, Marina Lewycka, John Gittings, Stella Tillyard, Ivo Galante, Vassilis Fouskas.

Notes

Introduction

1 As reported in *Le Monde*, 11 January 1989, quoted in Eric Hobsbawm, *Echoes of the Marseillaise: Two Centuries Look Back on the French Revolution*, Verso, 1990, p. x; also quoted in Steven Laurence Kaplan, *Farewell, Revolution: Disputed Legacies, France, 1789–1989*, Cornell University Press, 2018, pp. 61, 152.
2 'Déclaration de M. Michel Rocard, premier ministre, sur la célébration du bicentenaire de la Révolution française et de la liberté de culte et la naissance du premier culte réformé à Paris, Paris le 7 juin 1989', Vie publique, vie-publique.fr.
3 Theda Skocpol, *States and Social Revolutions: A Comparative Analysis of France, Russia, and China*, Cambridge University Press, 1979, p. 4. On the problems encountered by social scientists who attempt to define revolution, see Eric Hobsbawm, 'Revolution', in Roy Porter and Mikuláš Teich, eds, *Revolution in History*, Cambridge University Press, 1987, esp. pp. 8–9.
4 William Henry Drayton, *A Charge on the Rise of the American Empire*, in Reiner Smolinski, ed., *The Kingdom, the Power, and the Glory: The Millennial Impulse in Early American Literature*, Kendall Hunt, 1998, available as Electronic Texts in American Studies 39, digitalcommons.unl.edu/etas, p. 13. John Hannigan's blog, which led me to Drayton, was formerly available at blogs.brandeis.edu.
5 'From Thomas Paine to Benjamin Franklin, 20 June 1777', Founders Online, founders.archives.gov; Thomas Paine, 'The American Crisis: Philadelphia, April 19, 1783', US History, ushistory.org/Paine.
6 'John Adams to Thomas Jefferson, 24 August 1815', Founders Online, founders.archives.gov.
7 Howard Zinn, *A People's History of the United States: 1492 – Present*, 3rd edn, Routledge, 2013 (1980), p. 59.
8 Eric Foner, *Reconstruction: America's Unfinished Revolution, 1863–1877*, Harper Perennial, 2014.
9 'Not Letting the Facts Ruin a Good Story', *South China Morning Post*, 15 June 2011; Fiona Macdonald, 'The Greatest Mistranslations Ever', BBC Online, 2 February 2015. This is not a new problem. The celebrated historian and political activist, Liang Qichao (1873–1929), author of biographies of European nation-builders including Cavour, Cromwell and Bismarck, attempted to clarify the conceptual implications of translating Western and Japanese concepts of revolution into Chinese. He explained that

the Chinese character (hanzi) used for 'revolution' combined both the meanings of reform and revolution, and therefore did not lend itself to easy translation. Revolution in China came to embody visions of future change, ranging from the overthrow of Manchu rule to broader definitions addressing questions of social inequalities. Daniel Leese, '"Revolution": Conceptualizing Political and Social Change in the Late Qing Dynasty', *Oriens Extremus* 51, 2012, pp. 25–61, esp. p. 41.
10 Perry Anderson, 'The Notion of Bourgeois Revolution', in *English Questions*, Verso, 1992, pp. 106–10.
11 Texts in Karl Marx, *Selected Writings*, ed. David McLellan, Oxford University Press, 2000, pp. 642–3; see also Gareth Stedman Jones, 'Karl Marx's Changing Picture of the End of Capitalism', *Journal of the British Academy* 6, 2018, pp. 187–206.
12 Karl Marx, *Theories of Surplus Value*, Part II, Progress Publishers, 1968, p. 580.
13 See Donald Sassoon, *Mussolini and the Rise of Fascism*, HarperCollins, 2008.
14 The Fascist takeover, however, left the monarchy in place: 'I do not think that the monarchy has really any interest in opposing what must now be called the Fascist revolution', Mussolini pointed out to a mass rally of Fascists assembled in Udine, a few weeks before the March on Rome. Benito Mussolini, 'Discorso di Udine, 20 settembre 1922' / 'Speech in Udine, September 20, 1922', Biblioteca Fascista, bibliotecafascista.blogspot.com.
15 See Winston Churchill, 'Zionism versus Bolshevism', *Illustrated Sunday Herald*, 8 February 1920.
16 Hermann Rauschning, *The Revolution of Nihilism: Warning to the West*, Longmans, Green & Co., 1939 (originally *Die Revolution des Nihilismus*, 1938).
17 Christopher Hitchens, *Love, Poverty and War: Journeys and Essays*, Nation Books, 2004, p. 469, originally in *Vanity Fair*, October 2003.
18 For instance: Mario Einaudi, *The Roosevelt Revolution*, Harcourt Brace, 1959; Paul Craig Roberts, *The Supply-Side Revolution*, Harvard University Press, 1984; Murray Friedman, *The Neoconservative Revolution: Jewish Intellectuals and the Shaping of Public Policy*, Cambridge University Press, 2006.
19 Robert Owen, *The Revolution in the Mind and Practice of the Human Race, or, The Coming Change from Irrationality to Rationality*, Effingham Wilson, 1850, p. 30.
20 Arno Mayer, *The Furies: Violence and Terror in the French and Russian Revolutions*, Princeton University Press, 2000, p. 24.
21 Virginia Blackburn, *Theresa May. The Downing Street Revolution*, John Blake, 2016.
22 'How Nespresso's Coffee Revolution Got Ground Down', *Guardian*, 14 July 2020.
23 Jason Beattie, 'Quiet Revolutionary Keir Starmer Genuinely Believes Victory Is Within His Grasp', *Daily Mirror*, 27 September 2022.
24 Dale Yoder, 'Current Definitions of Revolution', *American Journal of Sociology* 32, no. 3, November 1926, p. 433.
25 Jacques Mallet du Pan, *Considérations sur la nature de la Révolution de France, et sur les causes qui en prolongent la durée*, Emm. Flon, 1793, p. 80. Other attributions include Pierre Vergniaud's speech to the Convention on 12 March 1793; see François-Alphonse Aulard, ed., *Les Grands Orateurs de la Révolution*, F. Rieder, 1914. Alexander Herzen was one of the many writers who used this formula in his *From the Other Shore*, Weidenfeld and Nicolson, 1956 (1850), p. 50.
26 Marisa Linton, 'Ten Myths About the French Revolution', blog.oup.com, 26 July 2015.
27 Mark R. Beissinger, *The Revolutionary City: Urbanization and the Global Transformation of Rebellion*, Princeton University Press, 2022, pp. 19, 25.
28 Crane Brinton, *The Anatomy of Revolution*, revised and expanded edn, Vintage Books, 1965 (1938), p. 16. China and Mao Zedong are barely mentioned even in the expanded edition of 1965.

29 Brinton, *The Anatomy of Revolution*, p. 205.
30 Barrington Moore Jr, *Social Origins of Dictatorship and Democracy: Lord and Peasant in the Making of the Modern World*, Beacon Press, 1966, esp. chs 7 and 8.
31 Skocpol, *States and Social Revolutions*, p. 286.
32 Jonathan Israel, *Democratic Enlightenment: Philosophy, Revolution, and Human Rights 1750–1790*, Oxford University Press, 2011, pp. 869–71.
33 Richard Whitmore and James Livesey, 'Etienne Clavière, Jacques-Pierre Brissot et les fondations intellectuelles de la politique des Girondins', *Annales historiques de la Révolution française* 321, 2000, pp. 4–5.
34 See the discussion of the concept in Moses I. Finley, 'Revolution in Antiquity', in Porter and Teich, *Revolution in History*; also in Henning Börm, 'Stasis in Post-Classical Greece: The Discourse of Civil Strife in the Hellenistic World', in H. Börm and N. Luraghi, eds, *The Polis in the Hellenistic World*, Franz Steiner Verlag, 2018, pp. 53ff.
35 Aristotle, *The Politics*, trans. T. A. Sinclair, Penguin, 1967, Book II, ch. 7, p. 74.
36 Ibid., p. 76.
37 Ibid., p. 200.
38 Josiah Ober, 'Aristotle's Natural Democracy', in Richard Kraut and Steven Skultety, eds, *Aristotle's Politics: Critical Essays*, Rowman & Littlefield, 2005, p. 229.
39 Mogens Herman Hansen, *The Athenian Democracy in the Age of Demosthenes: Structure, Principles, and Ideology*, University of Oklahoma Press, 1999, pp. 86–94. To calculate the number of slaves in Athens is not a simple matter: see William L. Westermann, *The Slave Systems of Greek and Roman Antiquity*, American Philosophical Society, 1955, pp. 5–12.
40 Josiah Ober, *The Athenian Revolution: Essays on Ancient Greek Democracy and Political Theory*, Princeton University Press, 1996, ch. 4, 'Athenian Revolution', pp. 32–52.
41 Aldo Schiavone, *Spartacus*, Harvard University Press, 2013, p. 117.
42 Marcus Aurelius Cicero, *Letters to Friends*, vol. 2, ed. and transl. D. R. Shackleton Bailey, Harvard University Press, p. 312.
43 In his introduction Syme stated that his book would attempt to discover 'the resources and devices by which a revolutionary leader arose in civil strife, usurped power for himself and his faction, transformed a faction into a national party, and a torn and distracted land into a nation, with a stable and enduring government. Ronald Syme, *The Roman Revolution*, Clarendon Press, 1939, p. 4.
44 Jean Froissart, *Chronique de France, d'Angleterre et de Bretagne*, Desclée, De Brouwer, n.d., p. 12: 'Écrasé d'impôts, las de payer et de souffrir, le peuple se soulève, comme il se soulève toujours, sans savoir ce qu'il fait ni ce qu'il veut, absurde, abominable ... Jacques Bonhomme s'en va comme une brute en délire ... Il pille, il brûle ... il tue, et de telle fureur, que les cruautés des gens d'armes ne sont rien auprès de ses boucheries.'
45 On the stories behind the 1381 Peasant Revolt, including the story of the rape, see Lister M. Matheson, 'The Peasants' Revolt Through Five Centuries of Rumor and Reporting: Richard Fox, John Stow, and Their Successors', *Studies in Philology* 95, no. 2, Spring 1998, pp. 121–51.
46 The decolonization of India, a largely but not entirely peaceful movement, was not called the Indian Revolution. The British labelled the earlier rebellion of 1857 the Sepoy or Indian Mutiny; some later Indians called it the First War of Independence, though even this was contested. Marx described it as 'the Indian Revolt': *New York Daily Tribune*, 16 September 1857.
47 Aléxis de Tocqueville, *L'Ancien Régime et la Révolution*, Michel Lévy Frères, 1856, p. 159.
48 M. A. Shaban, *The 'Abbāsid Revolution*, Cambridge University Press, 1970.
49 Dénes Harai, 'Couronne ardente et danse anthropophage: le décryptage de la

symbolique de l'exécution de György Dózsa, chef révolté en Hongrie (1514)', *Histoire, économie et société* 38, no. 1, 2019.
50 Yuhua Wang, *The Rise and Fall of Imperial China: The Social Origins of State Development*, Princeton University Press, 2022, p. 34.
51 Samuel Cohn, *Laboring Classes in Renaissance Florence*, Academic Press, 1980, pp. 9–11, 69. See also Alessandro Stella, *La Révolte des ciompi. Les Hommes, les lieux, le travail*, Éditions de l'École des Hautes Études en Sciences Sociales, 1993.
52 James H. Billington, 'Six Views of the Russian Revolution', *World Politics* 18, no. 3, April 1966, p. 453.
53 J. W. Smit, 'The Netherlands Revolution', in R. Foster and J. P. Greene, eds, *Preconditions of Revolution in Early Modern Europe*, Johns Hopkins University Press, 1970, p. 52.
54 Lauro Martines, *Furies: War in Europe 1450–1700*, Bloomsbury Press, 2013, p. 65.
55 Christopher Hill offers examples of the limited use of the word 'revolution' in England before 1688: Christopher Hill, *A Nation of Change and Novelty: Radical Politics, Religion and Literature in Seventeenth-Century England*, Routledge, 1990, pp. 82–101.
56 'Revoluzione', in Lessicografia della Crusca in Rete, lessicografia.it.
57 See Machiavelli, *The Prince*, ch. 26.
58 For a useful overview of how the term was used at the time, see Ilan Rachum, 'Italian Historians and the Emergence of the Term "Revolution", 1644–1659', *History* 80, no. 259, June 1995, pp. 191–206; Ilan Rachum, 'The Meaning of "Revolution" in the English Revolution (1648–1660)', *Journal of the History of Ideas* 56, no. 2, April 1995, pp. 195–215. Much of this work found its way into Ilan Rachum, *Revolution: The Entrance of a New Word into Western Political Discourse*, University Press of America, 1999.
59 *Le rivolvtioni di Napoli descritte dal Signor Alessandro Giraffi*, Filippo Alberto, 1648.
60 See Rosario Villari, *La rivolta antispagnola a Napoli: Le origini (1585–1647)*, Laterza, 1967.
61 Robert Mentet de Salmonet, *Histoire des troubles de la Grand' Bretagne*, Antoine Vitré, 1649 (published in English 1785): 'Entre toutes les reuolutions qui font arriuées en ce fiecle, celle de la Grand' Bretagne eft la plus confiderable, la plus eftrange e la funefte dans toutes les circonftances.' Not much is known about Monteith, but see Marc-André Béra, 'Montet de Salmonet, historien des Troubles et écrivain inconnu', *Annales* 8, no. 2, 1953, pp. 184–91.
62 Gabriel Naudé, *Science des princes, ou Considérations politiques sur les coups d'état*, n.p., 1673 (1639), p. 342.
63 Ibid., pp. 590–1.
64 Cited in Royce MacGillivray, *Restoration Historians and the English Civil War*, Martinus Nijhoff, 1974, pp. 19–20.
65 Quoted in Rachum, 'The Meaning of "Revolution"', p. 206.
66 See Eric Hobsbawm, 'The General Crisis of the European Economy in the 17th Century', *Past and Present* 5, no. 1, May 1954, pp. 33–53, and Eric Hobsbawm, 'The Crisis of the 17th Century II', *Past and Present* 6, no. 1, November 1954, pp. 44–65; H. R. Trevor-Roper, 'The General Crisis of the 17th Century', *Past and Present* 16, no. 1, November 1959, pp. 31–64. The contributions were eventually collected in T. H. Aston, ed., *Crisis in Europe, 1560–1660*, Routledge, 1965.
67 There were some rare exceptions; see Ilan Rachum, 'The Entrance of the Word "Revolution" into French Political Discourse (1648–1653)', *Historical Reflections / Réflexions Historiques* 23, no. 2, Spring 1997, pp. 229–49.
68 Vernon F. Snow, 'The Concept of Revolution in Seventeenth-Century England', *Historical Journal* 5, no. 2, 1962, p. 169.
69 I. Bernard Cohen, *The Revolution in Science*, Belknap Press, 2001, pp. 477–8.

70 Christopher Hill, *The World Turned Upside Down: Radical Ideas in the English Revolution*, Viking Press, 1972, p. 12.
71 Michael Drayton, 'To My Noble Friend Master William Browne, of the Euill Time'.
72 'The World is turned upside down. To the tune of, When the King enjoys his own again', listed in *Thomason Tracts*, vol. 1, 669, f. 10 (47).
73 Acts 17:1–6 (Revised Standard Edition).
74 Montesquieu, *Esprit des Lois*, Firmin Didot Frères, 1860, pp. 87–1.
75 Maupeon entitled his book *Journal historique de la révolution opérée dans la constitution de la monarchie françoise par M. de Maupéou, Chancelier de France*. When Louis XV died, Maupeou was forced into exile and the reforms were abandoned by Louis XVI. See also for the background Keith Michael Baker, *Inventing the French Revolution: Essays on French Political Culture in the Eighteenth Century*, Cambridge University Press, 1990, pp. 41–58.
76 H. Arnold Barton, 'Gustav III of Sweden and the Enlightenment', *Eighteenth-Century Studies* 6, no. 1, Autumn 1972, p. 8; see also Montesquieu, *Esprit des Lois*, p. 230.
77 Barton, 'Gustav III of Sweden and the Enlightenment', p. 11. See also Michael Roberts, *The Age of Liberty: Sweden 1719–1772*, Cambridge University Press, 2003, who describes the events of 1719 and 1772 as revolutions, p. 1.
78 Vincenzo Cuoco, *Saggio storico sulla rivoluzione napoletana del 1799*, Laterza, 1913, pp. 90, 109, 114, 163; see also Bruce Haddock, 'Between Revolution and Reaction: Vincenzo Cuoco's Saggio storico', *European Journal of Political Theory* 5, no. 1, January 2006, pp. 22–33. For a different take on the wider context informing Cuoco's views, see John A. Davis, *Naples and Napoleon: Southern Italy and the European Revolutions 1780–1860*, Oxford University Press, 2006, pp. 95–8.
79 See Marx, *Selected Writings*, p. 361.
80 Andrew Archibald Paton, *A History of the Egyptian Revolution, from the Period of the Mamelukes to the Death of Mohammed Ali; from Arab and European Memoirs, Oral Tradition, and Local Research*, Trübner & Co., 1863, vol. 1, p. v.
81 Note, however, that Ferriter described it as a revolution; see Diarmaid Ferriter, *A Nation and Not a Rabble: The Irish Revolution 1913–1923*, Profile Books, 2015.
82 Bulent Gokay, 'Kinross on Ataturk: A Note', *Middle Eastern Studies* 27, no. 4, October 1991, p. 694.
83 Ibid., p. 697.
84 Dankwart A. Rustow, 'Atatürk as Founder of a State', *Daedalus* 97, no. 3, Summer 1968, pp. 809, 814.
85 Hale Yilmaz, *Becoming Turkish: Nationalist Reforms and Cultural Negotiations in Early Republican Turkey 1923–1945*, Syracuse University Press, 2013, pp. 92–8.
86 Walter F. Weiker, 'Atatürk as a National Symbol', *Turkish Studies Association Bulletin* 6, no. 2, September 1982, pp. 3–4.
87 Alistair D. Swale, *The Meiji Restoration: Monarchism, Mass Communication and Conservative Revolution*, Palgrave Macmillan, 2009, p. 1.
88 Mark Ravina, *To Stand with the Nations of the World: Japan's Meiji Restoration in World History*, Oxford University Press, 2017, pp. 5–7.
89 Timothy B. Weston, 'The Founding of the Imperial University and the Emergence of Chinese Modernity', in Rebecca E. Karl and Peter Gue Zarrow, eds, *Rethinking the 1898 Reform Period: Political and Cultural Change in Late Qing China*, Harvard University Asia Center, 2002, pp. 102–3.
90 Ayşe Kadioğlu, 'The Paradox of Turkish Nationalism and the Construction of Official Identity', *Middle Eastern Studies* 32, no. 2, April 1996, p. 177.
91 Malise Ruthven, *Fundamentalism: The Search for Meaning*, Oxford University Press, 2005, p. 148.

92 Arang Keshavarzian, *Bazaar and State in Iran: The Politics of the Tehran Marketplace*, Cambridge University Press, 2007, p. 1.
93 Ibid., p. 273.
94 Nikki R. Keddie, *Modern Iran Roots and Results of Revolution*, Yale University Press, 2003, see esp. pp. 135, 234 ff., 302; this is an expanded version of Keddie's *Roots of Revolution* (1981). See also Robin Wright, *The Last Revolution*, Knopf, 2000; Robin Wright, *In the Name of God: The Khomeini Decade*, Bloomsbury, 1991. On women's education, see Mitra K. Shavarini, 'The Feminisation of Iranian Higher Education', *International Review of Education* 51, no. 4, July 2005, pp. 329–47.
95 Hobsbawm, *Echoes of the Marseillaise*, p. x.
96 Hannah Arendt, *On Revolution*, Penguin, 1973, p. 115.
97 See the discussion on the contrasting views between violence in wars and in revolutions in Mayer, *The Furies*, p. 5.
98 Antoine Boulay de la Meurthe, *Essai sur les causes qui, en 1649, amenèrent en Angleterre l'établissement de la république, sur celles qui devaient l'y consolider, sur celles qui l'y firent périr*, François-Jean Baudouin, Year VII (1799), p. 122.
99 Thomas Babington Macaulay, 'Parliamentary Reform (March 2, 1831). A Speech Delivered in the House of Commons on the 2d of March, 1831', in *The Miscellaneous Writings and Speeches of Lord Macaulay*, vol. 4, Project Gutenberg, gutenberg.org.
100 Earl Grey, debate on the Reform Bill [Reform Act 1832], House of Lords, 22 November 1831, *Hansard Parliamentary Debates*, 3d series, vol. 1, col. 613.
101 Martin Sklar, *The Corporate Reconstruction of American Capitalism, 1890–1916: The Market, the Law, and Politics*, Cambridge University Press, 1988, pp. 109–10.
102 Tang Xiaoyan and Zhang Chi, 'Crise en période de prospérité l'ancien régime et la révolution dans la Chine d'aujourd'hui', *Annales historiques de la Révolution française* 387, January–March 2017, p. 144. See also Marianne Bastid, 'L'Ouverture aux idées d'occident: quelle influence de la révolution française sur la révolution républicaine de 1911?', *Extrême-Orient Extrême-Occident* 2, 3e trimestre 1983, pp. 21–39, esp. pp. 22–3. This, however, is controversial: substantial research suggests that the uses of the French Revolution by Kang occurred later in 1906; on this, see Chen Jianhua, 'World Revolution Knocking at the Heavenly Gate: Kang Youwei and His Use of *Geming* in 1898', *Journal of Modern Chinese History* 5, no. 1, June 2011, pp. 89–108, esp. p. 97.
103 Bastid, 'L'Ouverture aux idées d'occident', p. 28.
104 Hung-Chao Tai, *Land Reform and Politics: A Comparative Analysis*, University of California Press, 1974, p. 9.
105 Cristóbal Kay, 'Why East Asia Overtook Latin America: Agrarian Reform, Industrialisation and Development', *Third World Quarterly* 23, no. 6, December 2002, see esp. pp. 1074, 1076–7, 1079, 1085.
106 Anna Plassart and Hugo Bonin, 'Democratic Struggle or National Uprising? The Canadian Rebellions in British Political Thought, 1835–1840', *Global Intellectual History* 7, no. 1, 2022, pp. 28–46.
107 Tocqueville, *L'Ancien Régime et la Révolution*, pp. 191–2. 'Ce n'est pas toujours en allant de mal en pis que l'on tombe en révolution. Il arrive le plus souvent qu'un peuple qui avait supporté sans se plaindre, et comme s'il ne les sentait pas, les lois les plus accablantes, les rejette violemment dès que le poids s'en allège. Le régime qu'une révolution détruit vaut presque toujours mieux que celui qui l'avait immédiatement précédé, et l'expérience apprend que le moment le plus dangereux pour un mauvais gouvernement est d'ordinaire celui où il commence à se réformer … Le Mal qu'on souffrait patiemment comme inévitable semble insupportable dès qu'on conçoit l'idée de s'y soustraire.' Translation from Alexis de Tocqueville, *The Ancien Régime and the French Revolution*, trans. Arthur Goldhammer, Cambridge University Press, 2011, p. 157.

108 Otto Pflanze, 'Bismarck and German Nationalism', *American Historical Review* 60, no. 3, April 1955, p. 552. He wrote the same thing in a telegram on 11 August 1866, after defeating Austria: Heinrich August Winkler, *Germany: The Long Road West 1789–1933*, Oxford University Press, 2006, p. 165.
109 Federico De Roberto, *I Viceré*, Casa editrice Galli, 1894, p. 669.
110 See Arno Mayer, *The Persistence of the Old Regime: Europe to the Great War*, Pantheon Books, 1981, where the final downfall of the old regime is attributed not to a revolution but to the Second World War.
111 Wendell Phillips, 'Woman's Rights', in *Speeches, Lectures, and Letters*, James Redpath, 1863, p. 36. Skocpol quotes Phillips – 'revolutions are not made, they come' – ignoring the wider context; see her *States and Social Revolutions*, p. 17.
112 Karl Marx, *The Eighteenth Brumaire of Louis Bonaparte*, Progress Publishers, 1967, p. 10.
113 Mikhail Sholokhov, *And Quiet Flows the Don*, Penguin, 1980, p. 281.
114 David Hume, *A Treatise of Human Nature*, vol. 2, Fontana Collins, 1972, p. 264 (Book III pt 2, sec. 7).
115 Aléxis de Tocqueville, *Recollections: The French Revolution of 1848 and Its Aftermath*, ed. Olivier Zunz, transl. Arthur Goldhammer, University of Virginia Press, 2016, p. 4.
116 Fernand Braudel, 'Histoire et Sciences sociales: La Longue Durée', *Annales. Économies, Sociétés, Civilisations* 13, no. 4, 1958, p. 728.
117 Fernand Braudel, *Grammaire des civilisations*, Flammarion, 1993 (1963), p. 67.
118 Montesquieu, 'De la politique', in *Mélanges inédits*, G. Gounouilhou and J. Rouam, 1892, p. 157.
119 François Guizot, *Histoire parlementaire de France*, vol. 1, Michel Lévy Frères, 1863, Project Gutenberg, gutenberg.org: 'Les révolutions, messieurs, emploient presque autant d'années à se terminer qu'à se préparer; et de même que longtemps avant le jour où elles ont éclaté, la société se sentait travaillée d'une lutte sourde et douloureuse, de même, longtemps après qu'elles paraissent accomplies, elles agitent et tourmentent les gouvernements et les peuples.'

1. The English Civil War

1 But not by Jonathan North. See Jonathan North, *Nelson at Naples: Revolution and Retribution in 1799*, Amberley, 2018.
2 Lord Wellington, *London Gazette*, 22 June 1815, no. 17028, p. 1215, reporting the dispatch sent to the War Department dated 19 June 1815.
3 Quentin Skinner, 'Rethinking Political Liberty', *History Workshop Journal* 61, Spring 2006, p. 156.
4 John Morrill, *The Nature of the English Revolution*, Routledge, 2014, p. 6.
5 Thomas Hobbes, *The English Works of Thomas Hobbes*, vol. 6, *Behemoth: The History of the Causes of the Civil Wars in England*, John Bohn, 1840, p. 166.
6 Ibid., p. 168.
7 Christopher Hill, *The English Revolution 1640: Three Essays*, Lawrence and Wishart, 1949 (1940), pp. 9, 13.
8 Brian Manning, *The English People and the English Revolution*, Heinemann, 1976, p. v. See also Manning's *Aristocrats, Plebeians and Revolution in England 1640–1660*, Pluto Press, 1996; Jonathan Barry, introduction to Jonathan Barry and Christopher Brooks, eds, *The Middling Sort of People: Culture, Society and Politics in England, 1550–1800*, Palgrave, 1994, p. 2.
9 Christopher Hill, *A Nation of Change and Novelty: Radical Politics, Religion, and Literature in Seventeenth Century England*, Routledge, 1990, p. 100.

10 David Cressy, 'Revolutionary England 1640–1642', *Past and Present* 181, November 2003, pp. 41, 58, 64.
11 The text of the Grand Remonstrance is in Samuel Rawson Gardiner, ed., *The Constitutional Documents of the Puritan Revolution 1625–1660*, 3rd edn, Clarendon Press, 1906, pp. 202–32 (quoted passages pp. 202–6).
12 Bishops were removed from the Lords by the Clergy Act of 1640, repealed in 1661 when the monarchy was restored.
13 Niccolò Machiavelli, *Discorsi sopra la prima deca di Titio Livio* in *Opere scelte*, Editori Riuniti, 1973, p. 202 (book I, ch. 25).
14 Karl Marx, *The Eighteenth Brumaire of Louis Bonaparte*, Progress Publishers, 1967, p. 10.
15 Gardiner, *The Constitutional Documents of the Puritan Revolution*, pp. 233–6.
16 Lawrence Stone, *The Causes of the English Revolution, 1529–1642*, Routledge, 2002, p. 116.
17 Ian Gentles, *The New Model Army: Agent of Revolution*, Yale University Press, 2022, pp. 18, 46, 54, 62.
18 Quoted in Christopher Hill, 'Gerrard Winstanley: 17th Century Communist at Kingston', lecture, Kingston University, 24 January 1996, available at libcom.org.
19 James Holstun, *Ehud's Dagger: Class Struggle in the English Revolution*, Verso, 2000, p. 393.
20 Antonia Fraser, *Cromwell, the Lord Protector*, Knopf, 1973, p. 421.
21 See Edmund Spenser, *A View of the Present State of Ireland*, 1633 (written 1596); Nicholas Canny, 'Reviewing *A View of the Present State of Ireland*', *Irish University Review* 26, no. 2, Autumn–Winter 1996, pp. 252–67.
22 Hobbes, *The English Works*, vol. 6, p. 418. See also Mark Hartman, 'Hobbes's Concept of Political Revolution', *Journal of the History of Ideas* 47, no. 3, pp. 487–95.
23 R. S. Peters, *Hobbes*, Greenwood Press, 1979, p. 33; Jon Parkin, 'The Reception of Hobbes's Leviathan', in Patricia Springborg, ed., *The Cambridge Companion to Hobbes's Leviathan*, Cambridge University Press, 2007, p. 452.
24 The extent of Milton's commitment to Cromwell is controversial and has been amply discussed by scholars; see, among others, Go Togashi, 'Contextualizing Milton's *Second Defence of the English People*: Cromwell and the English Republic, 1649–1654', *Milton Quarterly* 45, no. 4, December 2011, pp. 217–44.
25 See text in John Milton, *Prose: Major Writings on Liberty, Politics, Religion and Education*, ed. David Loewenstein, Blackwell, 2013, p. 321.
26 John Milton, *The Readie and Easie Way to Establish a Free Commonwealth*, n.p., 1660, available from Renascence Editions, based on the British Museum copy, scholarsbank.uoregon.edu.
27 John McWilliams, 'Marvell and Milton's Literary Friendship Reconsidered', *Studies in English Literature, 1500–1900* 46, no. 1, Winter 2006, p. 162.
28 Nicholas McDowell, *Poet of Revolution: The Making of John Milton*, Princeton University Press, 2020, p. 418.
29 Quoted in Robert Howell Griffiths, 'Modération et centrisme politique en Angleterre de 1660 à 1800', *Annales historique de la Révolution Française* 357, July–September 2009, p. 133.
30 Adam Ferguson, *An Essay on the History of Civil Society*, A. Finley, 1819, p. 222.
31 John Locke, *Two Treatises of Government*, ed. Peter Laslett, Cambridge University Press, 1988, pp. 414–15, paras 223, 227, 228.
32 See Peter Laslett, 'The English Revolution and Locke's Two Treatises of Government', *Cambridge Historical Journal* 12, no. 1, 1956, pp. 40–55; and introduction to John Locke, *Two Treatises of Government*, ed. Peter Laslett, Cambridge University Press, 1988, esp.

pp. 46 ff. See also Vernon F. Snow, 'The Concept of Revolution in Seventeenth-Century England', *Historical Journal* 5, no. 2, 1962, p. 174.
33 See John Miller, *James II*, Yale University Press, 2000, pp. 64–6.
34 *The Parliamentary Debates: Official Reports*, vol. 5, p. 111.
35 Cited in Peter Marshall, 'The Naming of Protestant England', *Past and Present* 214, 2012, p. 87.
36 Steven C. A. Pincus and James A. Robinson, 'What Really Happened During the Glorious Revolution?', in Sebastian Galiani and Itai Sened, eds, *Institutions, Property Rights, and Economic Growth: The Legacy of Douglass North*, Cambridge University Press, 2014, p. 209; Gary W. Cox, 'British State Development After the Glorious Revolution', *European Review of Economic History* 24, no. 1, February 2020, pp. 26 ff.
37 Julian Hoppit, *A Land of Liberty? England 1689–1727*, Oxford University Press, 2000, p. 26.
38 Derek Hirst, *The Representative of the People? Voters and Voting in England Under the Early Stuarts*, Cambridge University Press, 2005, pp. 104–5.
39 Ulrich Niggemann, 'Some Remarks on the Origins of the Term "Glorious Revolution"', *Seventeenth Century* 27, no. 4, 2012, pp. 477–87.
40 Lothar Gall, *Bismarck: The White Revolutionary*, vol. 1, *1815–1871*, Unwin Hyman, 1986, p. 38.
41 H. T. Dickinson, *Liberty and Property: Political Ideology in Eighteenth Century Britain*, Methuen, 1977, pp. 20, 34–5.
42 Steven Pincus, *1688: The First Modern Revolution*, Yale University Press, 2009, p. 31; '"To Protect English Liberties": The English Nationalist Revolution of 1688–1689', in Tony Claydon and Ian McBride, eds, *Protestantism and National Identity: Britain and Ireland, c.1650–c.1850*, Cambridge University Press, 2007, p. 87.
43 Edward Vallance, *The Glorious Revolution: 1688 – Britain's Fight for Liberty*, Pegasus, 2008, pp. 10–11.
44 Hill, *A Nation of Change and Novelty*, p. 101.
45 Karl Marx, *Capital*, vol. 1, Progress Publishers, 1965, p. 723.
46 John Brewer, *The Sinews of Power: War, Money, and the English State, 1688–1783*, Harvard University Press, 1990, pp. 64–70.
47 As Timothy H. Breen explained, 'unlike their continental adversaries, the British had learned how to pay for large-scale war without bankrupting its citizens and, thereby, without sparking the kind of internal unrest that frequently destabilized other ancien regime monarchies'. Timothy H. Breen, 'Ideology and Nationalism on the Eve of the American Revolution: Revisions *Once More* in Need of Revising', *Journal of American History* 84, no. 1, June 1997, p. 16.
48 Mark Knights, 'The Long-Term Consequences of the English Revolution: Politics, Political Thought and the Constitution', in Michael Braddick, ed., *The Oxford Handbook of the English Revolution*, Oxford University Press, 2015, pp. 518–34.
49 Adam Smith, *An Inquiry into the Nature and Causes of the Wealth of Nations*, book 4, ch. 2, adamsmithworks.org.
50 James A. Harris, 'Hume', in Mark Garnett, ed., *Conservative Moments: Reading Conservative Texts*, Bloomsbury, 2018, p. 32.
51 See Ragnhild Hatton, *George I*, Yale University Press, 2001, esp. pp. 130–1.
52 J. H. Plumb, *England in the Eighteenth Century (1714–1815)*, Pelican, 1961, p. 73.
53 Walpole was First Lord of the Treasury, a title even present-day prime ministers keep.
54 David Hume, 'Of the Protestant Succession', in *Selected Essays*, Oxford University Press, 2008, pp. 294–7.
55 Christopher Hill, *The Intellectual Origins of the English Revolution: Revisited*, Clarendon Press, 1997, pp. 3, 6.

56 Edouard Tillet, *La Constitution anglaise, un modèle politique et institutionnel dans la France des lumières*, Presses universitaires d'Aix-Marseille, 2001, esp. pp. 71–109.
57 C. P. Courtney, 'Montesquieu and English Liberty', in David W. Carrithers, Michael A. Mosher and Paul A. Rahe, eds, *Montesquieu's Science of Politics*, Rowman & Littlefield, 2001, p. 273.
58 Voltaire, *Dictionnaire philosophique*, vol. 5, in *Oeuvres complètes de Voltaire*, vol. 40, Dupont Libraire, 1824, pp. 112–4.
59 Montesquieu, *Considérations sur les causes de la grandeur des romains et de leur décadence*, Poussielgue, 1907 (1734), p. 76; see also Courtney, 'Montesquieu and English Liberty', p. 287.
60 Germaine de Staël, *Considérations sur les principaux événements de la Révolution Française, depuis son origine jusques et compris le 8 Juillet 1815*, in *Œuvres complètes de Mme de Staël*, book 1, vol. 1, Dambray Fils, 1820, pp. 17–18.
61 Aléxis de Tocqueville, *L'Ancien Régime et la Révolution*, Michel Lévy Frères, 1856, p. 51.
62 See comments in Howell Griffiths, 'Modération et centrisme politique en Angleterre', p. 124.
63 Edmund Burke, *Reflections on the Revolution in France*, James Dodley, 1790, pp. 70–1.
64 Ian McBride, 'The Politics of *A Modest Proposal*: Swift and the Irish Crisis of the Late 1720s', *Past and Present* 244, no. 1, August 2019, p. 90.
65 George Wittkowsky, 'Swift's Modest Proposal: The Biography of an Early Georgian Pamphlet', *Journal of the History of Ideas* 4, no. 1, January 1943, esp. pp. 89–94.
66 Robin Blackburn, *The Overthrow of Colonial Slavery, 1776–1848*, Verso, 2011, p. 42. This is still the best book on this subject.
67 Quoted in Evan R. Davis, introduction to Daniel Defoe, *Robinson Crusoe*, Broadview Press, 26 April 2010, p. 26 (originally in Daniel Defoe, *Defoe's Review*, vol. 9, p. 89).
68 See Holly Brewer's brilliant and scholarly 'Slavery, Sovereignty, and "Inheritable Blood": Reconsidering John Locke and the Origins of American Slavery', *American Historical Review* 122, no. 4, October 2017, pp. 1052–4; see also David Hunter, 'Critical Exchanges: Handel and Slave-Trading Companies: Handel, an Investor in Slave-Trading Companies: A Response to Ellen Harris', *Music and Letters* 103, no. 3, August 2022, pp. 532–40.
69 See the interesting discussion in David Eltis, 'Europeans and the Rise and Fall of African Slavery in the Americas: An Interpretation', *American Historical Review* 98, no. 5, December 1993, pp. 1399–423.
70 Barbara Arneil, 'Trade, Plantations, and Property: John Locke and the Economic Defense of Colonialism', *Journal of the History of Ideas* 55, no. 4, October 1994, p. 594.
71 Ibid., p. 596.
72 Robin Blackburn, *The American Crucible: Slavery, Emancipation and Human Rights*, Verso, 2011, pp. 102 ff. See also Robin Blackburn, *The Making of New World Slavery, 1776–1848*, Verso, 1988; Maxine Berg and Pat Hudson, *Slavery, Capitalism and the Industrial Revolution*, Polity, 2023.
73 William Blake, *Europe Supported by Africa and America*, 1796, engraving, illustration from John Gabriel Stedman, *Narrative of a Five Years' Expedition Against the Revolted Negroes of Surinam in Guiana on the Wild Coast of South America* (1796). Stedman's volume contains numerous illustrations by Blake illustrating the plight of slaves.
74 See Jean Bodin, *Les Six Livres de la République*; Henry Heller, 'Bodin on Slavery and Primitive Accumulation', *Sixteenth Century Journal* 25, no. 1, Spring 1994.
75 Charles de Secondat Montesquieu, *De l'esprit des lois*, book 15, ch. 5, 'De l'esclavage des nègres'.
76 Ross Carroll, *Uncivil Mirth: Ridicule in Enlightenment Britain*, Princeton University Press, 2021, pp. 154–60.

77 Eltis, 'Europeans and the Rise and Fall', p. 1421.
78 Vincent Brown, *Tacky's Revolt: The Story of an Atlantic Slave War*, Belknap–Harvard University Press, 2020, pp. 4–6, 14, 228. The author points out that it was more a fully fledged war than a revolt.
79 John Coffey, '"Tremble, Britannia!" Fear, Providence and the Abolition of the Slave Trade, 1758–1807', *English Historical Review* 127, no. 527, August 2012, p. 849; see also pp. 845–7.
80 David Brion Davis, *The Problem of Slavery in Western Culture*, Oxford University Press, 1966, p. 487.
81 James Walvin, *African's Life, The Life and Times of Olaudah Equiano 1745–1797*, Continuum, 2000, pp. 161–4.
82 John Bicknell and Thomas Day, *The Dying Negro: A Poem*, 3rd edn, W. Flexney, 1775, p. 9.
83 Ottobah Cugoano, 'Narrative of the Enslavement of Ottobah Cugoano, a Native of Africa; Published by Himself, in the Year 1787', in Abolitionist, *The Negro's Memorial, or, Abolitionist's Catechism*, Hatchard and Co., J. and A. Arch, 1825, p.124, available at Documenting the American South, docsouth.unc.edu.
84 Blackburn, *The American Crucible*, p. 366, and *The Overthrow of Colonial Slavery*, pp. 100, 140–1, 144; James Walvin, *The Zong: A Massacre, the Law and the End of Slavery*, Yale University Press, 2011, p. 175.
85 Mary Wollstonecraft, *A Vindication of the Rights of Men*, 2nd edn, Joseph Johnson, 1790, p. 74.
86 Paul Starr, *Entrenchment: Wealth, Power, and the Constitution of Democratic Societies*, Yale University Press, 2019, p. 74.
87 David Ricardo, *The Works and Correspondence of David Ricardo*, ed. Piero Sraffa, vol. 5, *Speeches and Evidence*, Cambridge University Press, 1952, p. 483.
88 Thomas Babington Macaulay, speech read at the General Meeting of the Society for the Mitigation and Gradual Abolition of Slavery throughout the British Dominions, 25 June 1824, Richard Taylor, 1824, p. 76.
89 Catherine Hall, 'Troubling Memories: Nineteenth-Century Histories of the Slave Trade and Slavery', *Transactions of the Royal Historical Society*, Sixth Series, vol. 21, 2011, p. 148.
90 Ibid., pp. 153, 157–9, 162, 169. On Trevelyan, see Laura Trevelyan, 'Grenada: Confronting My Family's Slave-Owning Past', BBC News, 11 May 2022.
91 Catherine Hall, 'The Economy of Intellectual Prestige: Thomas Carlyle, John Stuart Mill, and the Case of Governor Eyre', *Cultural Critique* 12, Spring 1989, pp. 167–96, esp. pp. 178–82. On the use of the word 'nigger', see Victor G. Kiernan, *The Lord of Humankind*, Little, Brown and Co., 1969, p. 48. Carlyle's article was virtually unmentioned in Harold Bloom's edition of essays *Thomas Carlyle*, Chelsea House Publishers, 1986. See also Jude V. Nixon, 'Racialism and the Politics of Emancipation in Carlyle's "Occasional Discourse on the Nigger Question"', in 'Carlyle at 200 Lectures II', special issue, *Carlyle Studies Annual* 16, 1996, pp. 89–108.
92 John Stuart Mill, *On Liberty*, Penguin, 1974, p. 69.
93 Laurent Theis, *Guizot. La Traversée d'un siècle*, CNRS Éditions, 2014, pp. 71–2.
94 This is Lord Palmerston's so-called Don Pacifico speech about intervention in Greece.

2. America: The Settlers' Rebellion

1 Alexis de Tocqueville, *De la démocratie en Amérique*, Michel Lévy Frères, 1864, p. 167, or in English, Alexis de Tocqueville, *Democracy in America*, trans. Arthur Goldhammer, Library of America, 2004, p. 589 (passage also used by Louis Hartz in

the introduction to his *The Liberal Tradition in America*, Harcourt, Brace & World, 1955).
2 Gordon Wood, *The Radicalism of the American Revolution*, Vintage Books, 1993, p. 5.
3 Patrick Wolfe, 'Settler Colonialism and the Elimination of the Native', *Journal of Genocide Research* 8, no. 4, 2006, pp. 387–409.
4 William Wood, *A Survey of Trade*, Walthoe, 1722, p. 179, cited in Julian Hoppit, *A Land of Liberty? England 1689–1727*, Oxford University Press, 2000, p. 267; Karl Marx, *Capital*, vol. 1, Progress Publishers, 1965, p. 760.
5 See Lyndall Ryan, *Tasmanian Aborigines. A History Since 1803*, Allen and Unwin, 2012; see also the map of massacres in Australia devised by Ryan and her team: 'Colonial Frontier Massacres in Australia, 1788–1930', Centre for 21st Century Humanities, c21ch.newcastle.edu.au.
6 Frank Welsh, *Great Southern Land. A New History of Australia*, Allen Lane, 2004, p. 24.
7 Ilan Rachum, 'From "American Independence" to the "American Revolution"', *Journal of American Studies* 27, no. 1, April 1993, pp. 74–5, 80–1.
8 John Ferling, *Jefferson and Hamilton: The Rivalry That Forged a Nation*, Bloomsbury, 2014, p. 36.
9 Alex Tuckness, 'Discourses of Resistance in the American Revolution', *Journal of the History of Ideas* 64, no. 4, October 2003, pp. 547–9; see also Donald Lutz, 'The Relative Influence of European Writers on Late Eighteenth Century American Political Thought', *American Political Science Review* 78, 1984, p. 189; see also Hartz, *The Liberal Tradition in America*, pp. 59–61.
10 John Coffey, '"Tremble, Britannia!": Fear, Providence and the Abolition of the Slave Trade, 1758–1807', *English Historical Review* 127, no. 527, August 2012, p. 854; J. C. D. Clark, 'Providence, Predestination and Progress: Or, Did the Enlightenment Fail?', *Albion* 35, no. 4, Winter 2003, p. 582.
11 John Locke, *Two Treatises of Government*, ed. Peter Laslett, Cambridge University Press, 1988, p. 366; James Otis, *The Rights of the British Colonies Asserted and Proved*, in Max Beloff, ed., *The Debate on the American Revolution, 1761–1783*, Nicholas Kaye, 1949, p. 55. For an examination of the uses of Locke by James Otis, see Lee Ward, 'James Otis and the Americanization of John Locke', *American Political Thought* 4, no. 2, Spring 2015, pp. 181–202.
12 Otis, *The Rights of the British Colonies Asserted and Proved*, pp. 51, 69, 59.
13 Hume, *A Treatise of Human Nature*, p. 276 (book 3, pt 2, sec. 9).
14 Thomas Hobbes, *Leviathan*, ed. C. B. Macpherson, Penguin, 1968, p. 272 (pt 2, ch. 21).
15 Ibid., p. 260 (pt 2, ch. 20).
16 Robert Whaples, 'Where Is There Consensus Among American Economic Historians? The Results of a Survey on Forty Propositions', *Journal of Economic History* 55, no. 1, March 1995, p. 145.
17 John Dickinson, *Letters from a Farmer in Pennsylvania to the Inhabitants of the British Colonies*, J. Almon, 1774, p. 5.
18 Ibid., p. 33.
19 Ibid., pp. 32, 42, 74.
20 For the text, see Edward St Germain, 'William Pitt's Stamp Act Speech', americanrevolution.org.
21 Richard Bourke, *Empire and Revolution: The Political Life of Edmund Burke*, Princeton University Press, 2015, p. 297.
22 John Adams, '1773. Decr. 17th [from the Diary of John Adams]', Founders Online, founders.archives.gov; George Washington letter to Bryan Fairfax 24 August 1774, quoted in Don Herzog, *Sovereignty R.I.P.*, Yale University Press, 2020, pp. 107–8; see also Bailyn's argument that this was not 'simply lurid rhetoric', in Bernard Bailyn, *The*

Ideological Origins of the American Revolution, Belknap–Harvard University Press, 1977 (1967), p. 233.
23 'IV. The Declaration as Adopted by Congress, [6 July 1775]', Founders Online, founders.archives.gov.
24 Vernon L. Parrington, *The Colonial Mind, 1620–1800*, vol. 1, *Main Currents in American Thought*, Harvest Books, 1954 (1927), p. 335.
25 Ibid., p. 334.
26 Joseph J. Ellis, *Revolutionary Summer: The Birth of American Independence*, Random House, 2013, p. 20.
27 John Adams, *Diary and Autobiography of John Adams*, ed. L. H. Butterfield, vol. 3, Harvard University Press, 1961.
28 David G. McCullough, *John Adams*, Simon and Schuster, 2001, pp. 417–18.
29 Pauline Maier, *American Scripture: Making the Declaration of Independence*, Vintage, 1998, pp. 134, 136, 146, 214.
30 John Locke, *Essay Concerning Human Understanding*, book 2, ch. 21, sec. 52: 'The Necessity of pursuing true Happiness the Foundation of Liberty.' On the study of Locke at the time, see Bailyn, *The Ideological Origins of the American Revolution*, pp. 27–30.
31 Ellis, *Revolutionary Summer*, p. 33.
32 Erica Armstrong Dunbar, *Never Caught: The Washingtons' Relentless Pursuit of Their Runaway Slave, Ona Judge*, Simon and Schuster, 2017, pp. 66–7.
33 Linda Colley, *Britons: Forging the Nation, 1707–1837*, Yale University Press, 2005, p. 352; on Blake, see David Bindman, 'Blake's Vision of Slavery Revisited', *Huntington Library Quarterly* 58, no. 3/4.
34 Adam Smith, *The Wealth of Nations*, Penguin, 1986, pp. 184, 488. The view that slavery was uneconomic was contradicted in Robert William Fogel and Stanley L. Engerman, *Time on the Cross: The Economics of American Negro Slavery*, Norton, 1995 (see below).
35 John Wesley, *Thoughts upon Slavery*, 1st US edn, Philadelphia, 1778, pp. 16, 45–6.
36 Samuel Johnson, *Taxation No Tyranny, an Answer to the Resolutions and Address of the American Congress*, T. Cadell in the Strand, 1775, p. 89; see also the same words cited in James Boswell, *The Life of Samuel Johnson* (1791), entry for 23 September 1877. On Johnson's anti-colonialism, see Donald Greene, *The Politics of Samuel Johnson*, 2nd edn, University of Georgia Press, 1990, p. 270.
37 Boswell, *The Life of Samuel Johnson*, entry for 15 April 1778.
38 Thomas Day, *Fragment of an Original Letter on the Slavery of the Negroes: Written in the Year 1776*, John Stockdale, 1784, and Garrison and Knapp, 1831, p. 10.
39 Stephen Conway, 'Britain and the Impact of the American War, 1775–1783', *War in History* 2, no. 2, July 1995, pp. 127–50.
40 Maya Jasanoff, *Liberty's Exiles: The Loss of America and the Remaking of the British Empire*, Harper Press, 2011, pp. 6–8.
41 David Brion Davis, *The Problem of Slavery in Western Culture*, Oxford University Press, 1966, pp. 9–10.
42 Peter Kolchin, *American Slavery: 1619–1877*, Hill and Wang, 2003, p. 72.
43 Bourke, *Empire and Revolution*, pp. 461, 698–9, 504.
44 Holger Hoock, *Scars of Independence: America's Violent Birth*, Crown, 2017, p. 12.
45 John Sainsbury, *Disaffected Patriots: London Supporters of Revolutionary America, 1769–1782*, McGill-Queen's University Press, 1987, p. 160; the author of the actual text was John Jebb.
46 Data in Howard Peckham, *The Toll of Independence: Engagements and Battle Casualties of the American Revolution*, University of Chicago Press, 1974, p. 131; the author rightly warns that the estimates must be taken with considerable caution.

47 Ann M. Becker, 'The Smallpox in Washington's Army: Strategic Implications of the Disease During the American Revolutionary War', *Journal of Military History* 68, no. 2, April 2004, p. 383.
48 This had been just as true early in the century; see Hoppit, *A Land of Liberty?*, pp. 265–6, 319–20.
49 Sven Beckert, *Empire of Cotton: A Global History*, Alfred A. Knopf, 2014, p. 100.
50 John Seeley, *The Expansion of England: Two Courses of Lectures*, Macmillan, 1914, pp. 26–7.
51 'To George Washington from Thomas Paine, 30 July 1796', Founders Online, founders.archives.gov.
52 See US Census Bureau, *1790 Census: Return of the Whole Number of Persons within the Several Districts of the United States*, available at census.gov.
53 Alexander Hamilton, *Federalist* no. 68, 'The Mode of Electing the President: From the Independent Journal. Wednesday, March 12, 1788', in Alexander Hamilton, John Jay and James Madison, *The Federalist Papers*, Project Gutenberg ebook, gutenberg.org.
54 See Alexander Keyssar, *Why Do We Still Have the Electoral College?*, Harvard University Press, 2020.
55 William J. Novak, 'The Myth of the "Weak" American State', *American Historical Review* 113, no. 3, June 2008, p. 765; see also the important debate that followed in the pages of the *American Historical Review* 115, no. 3, June 2010, esp.: Julia Adams, 'The Puzzle of the American State … and Its Historians'; John Fabian Witt, 'Law and War in American History'; Gary Gerstle, 'A State Both Strong and Weak'; Novak, 'Long Live the Myth of the Weak State? A Response to Adams, Gerstle, and Witt'.
56 Michael Mann, 'The Autonomous Power of the State: Its Origins, Mechanisms, and Results', in John A. Hall, ed., *States in History*, Blackwell, 1986, pp. 109–36 (citations p. 113).
57 James L. Huston, 'The American Revolutionaries, the Political Economy of Aristocracy, and the American Concept of the Distribution of Wealth, 1765–1900', *American Historical Review* 98, no. 4, October 1993, p. 1089.
58 Antoine Rivarol, *Journal politique national des États généraux et de la Révolution de 1789*, vol. 1, Sabatier, 1790, p. 129.
59 James Madison, *Federalist* no. 55, 'The Total Number of the House of Representatives: For the Independent Journal. Wednesday, February 13, 1788', in Hamilton, Jay and Madison, *The Federalist Papers*, gutenberg.org.
60 Ferling, *Jefferson and Hamilton*, pp. 5, 181, 186.
61 Parrington, *The Colonial Mind*, pp. 301, 305.
62 'From John Adams to James Sullivan, 26 May 1776', Founders Online, founders.archives.gov.
63 'Abigail Adams to John Adams, 31 March 1776', Founders Online, founders.archives.gov (original source *The Adams Papers*, Adams Family Correspondence, vol. 1, December 1761–May 1776, ed. Lyman H. Butterfield, Harvard University Press, 1963, pp. 369–71). See also Woody Holton, *Abigail Adams*, Simon and Schuster, 2020, p. 39, which describes Abigail as a 'protofeminist'.
64 'John Adams to Abigail Adams, 14 April 1776', Founders Online, founders.archives.gov.
65 'Abigail Adams to John Adams, 7 May 1776', Founders Online, founders.archives.gov.
66 Joseph J. Ellis, *First Family: Abigail and John*, Knopf, 2010, p. 50.
67 Linda K. Kerber, *Women of the Republic: Intellect and Ideology in Revolutionary America*, University of North Carolina Press, 1980, pp. 82–3, 119.
68 Quoted in ibid., p. 140; also in Mary Beard, *Woman as a Force in History: A Study in Traditions and Realities*, Macmillan, 1946, p. 79.
69 Benjamin Rush, 'An Address to the People of the United States … on the Defects of

the Confederation' (1787), in Colleen A. Sheehan and Gary L. McDowell, eds, *Friends of the Constitution: Writings of the 'Other' Federalists, 1787–1788*, Liberty Fund, 1998.

70 Frederick Douglass, 'Oration, Delivered in Corinthian Hall, Rochester, July 5, 1852', in Fred Lee Hord and Jonathan Scott Lee, eds, *I Am Because We Are: Readings in Black Philosophy*, University of Massachusetts Press, 2016.

71 Thomas Jefferson, *Notes on the State of Virginia*, John Stockdale, 1787, p. 270.

72 Ferling, *Jefferson and Hamilton*, p. 49.

73 Davis, *The Problem of Slavery*, p. 177.

74 Eric Foner, *The Fiery Trial: Abraham Lincoln and American Slavery*, W. W. Norton & Co., 2011, pp. 17–18.

75 Jonathan Israel, *The Expanding Blaze: How the American Revolution Ignited the World, 1775–1848*, Princeton University Press, 2017, p. 382.

76 Paul Starr, *Entrenchment: Wealth, Power, and the Constitution of Democratic Societies*, Yale University Press, 2019, p. 57.

77 Beckert, *Empire of Cotton*, pp. 106–7.

78 Wolfe, 'Settler Colonialism and the Elimination of the Native', pp. 391–2, 399; John P. Bowes, 'American Indian Removal Beyond the Removal Act', *Native American and Indigenous Studies* 1, no. 1, Spring 2014, p. 81.

79 Hugh Brogan, *Alexis de Tocqueville: Prophet of Democracy in the Age of Revolution*, Profile, 2006, p. 201.

80 Alexander Keyssar, *The Right to Vote. The Contested History of Democracy in the United States*, Basic Books, 2000, p. 29.

81 Kolchin, *American Slavery*, p. 93.

82 Abraham Lincoln, 'Letter to Horace Greeley', 22 August 1862, abrahamlincolnonline.org.

83 Robin Blackburn, *The Reckoning: From the Second Slavery to Abolition, 1776–1888*, Verso, 2024, ch. 7.

84 Victor Hugo, *Œuvres complètes*, vol. 37, *Actes et paroles*, vol. 2, *Pendant l'exil, 1852–1870*, Albin Michel, 1938, pp. 142–4.

85 The text of the speech can be found in Alexander H. Stephens, 'Cornerstone Speech', American Battlefield Trust, battlefields.org.

86 See *Manchester Guardian*, 13 May 1861.

87 Widely quoted, including by *Guardian* columnist Martin Kettle, in what can only be described as a pathetic attempt to excuse it, by asserting that 'it was of its era' – ignoring that others of the same era took quite different positions. See Martin Kettle, 'Lincoln, Evil? Our Certainties of 1865 Give Us Pause Today', *Guardian*, 24 February 2011.

88 Georgios Varouxakis, '"Negrophilist" Crusader: John Stuart Mill on the American Civil War and Reconstruction', *History of European Ideas* 39, no. 5, p. 730. On Gladstone's lack of interest in the slavery question, see Roland Quinault, 'Gladstone and Slavery', *Historical Journal* 52, no. 2, June 2009, pp. 363–83.

89 Alexander Zevin, *Liberalism at Large: The World According to the Economist*, Verso, 2019, pp. 99–103.

90 'Black Soldiers in the U.S. Military During the Civil War', US National Archives, Educator Resources, archives.gov.

91 John Ashworth, 'The American Civil War: A Reply to Critics', *Historical Materialism* 21, no. 3, 2013, pp. 102–3.

92 Charles A. Beard and Mary R. Beard, *The Rise of American Civilization*, new edn, Macmillan, 1947, vol. 2, pp. 105–6, 256.

93 See the preface to Eric Foner, *The Second Founding: How the Civil War and Reconstruction Remade the Constitution*, W. W. Norton, 2019; see also Randall Kennedy, 'Racist Litter' (review of Eric Foner), *London Review of Books* 15, 30 July 2020.

94 John F. Kennedy, *Profiles in Courage*, memorial edn, Hamish Hamilton, 1964, p. 151.
95 Kolchin, *American Slavery*, p. 212.
96 Kathryn Kish Sklar, *Women's Rights Emerges within the Antislavery Movement 1830–1870*, Bedford / St Martin Press, 2000, p. 71.
97 Quoted in Blackburn, *The American Crucible*, p. 420.
98 Eric Foner, *Reconstruction: America's Unfinished Revolution, 1863–1877*, Harper Perennial, 2014, p. 180.
99 Foner, *The Fiery Trial*, p. 322.
100 Ibid., p. xx.
101 Beckert, *Empire of Cotton*, p. 271.
102 W. E. B. Du Bois, *Black Reconstruction in America*, Albert Saifer, 1935, p. 30.
103 Fogel and Engerman, *Time on the Cross*, pp. 261, 133, 263. For a more recent reappraisal, see Thomas Weiss, review of *Time on the Cross*, Economic History Association, Project 2001: Significant Works in Economic History, 15 November 2001, eh.net.
104 Peter Kolchin, 'Comparative Perspectives on Emancipation in the U.S. South: Reconstruction, Radicalism, and Russia', *Journal of the Civil War Era* 2, no. 2, June 2012, p. 205.
105 Wilton B. Fowler, 'A Carpetbagger's Conversion to White Supremacy', *North Carolina Historical Review* 43, no. 3, July 1966, p. 292.
106 Foner, *Reconstruction: America's Unfinished Revolution*, p. 437. See also Joel M. Sipress, 'From the Barrel of a Gun: The Politics of Murder in Grant Parish', *Louisiana History* 42, no. 3, Summer 2001, pp. 303–21.
107 Malcolm McLaughlin, 'Reconsidering the East St Louis Race Riot of 1917', *International Review of Social History* 47, no. 2, August 2002, p. 187.
108 Tulsa Historical Society and Museum, 'The Attack on Greenwood', tulsahistory.org.
109 Shirley Rombough and Diane C. Keithly, 'Native Americans, the Feudal System, and the Protestant Work Ethic: A Unique View of the Reservation', *Race, Gender and Class* 12, no. 2, 2005, p. 106. See also Robert F. Berkhofer, *The White Man's Indian: Images of the American Indian from Columbus to the Present*, Knopf Doubleday, 1979.
110 Jane Lawrence, 'The Indian Health Service and the Sterilization of Native American Women', *American Indian Quarterly* 24, no. 3, Summer 2000, p. 410.
111 Henry George, 'The Chinese in California', *New York Daily Tribune*, 1 May 1869.
112 Alexander Saxton, *The Indispensable Enemy: Labor and the Anti-Chinese Movement in California*, University of California Press, 1971, p. 271.
113 William A. Dunning, *Reconstruction, Political and Economic, 1865–1877*, Harper & Brothers, 1907, pp. 213–14.
114 Rollin G. Osterweis, *The Myth of the Lost Cause, 1865–1900*, Shoe String Press, 1973, p. 7.
115 John C. Calhoun, 'Speech on the Reception of Abolition Petitions', 6 February 1837, in *Union and Liberty: The Political Philosophy of John C. Calhoun*, ed. Ross M. Lence, Liberty Fund, 1992, available at the Online Library of Liberty, oll.libertyfund.org.
116 For background, see Thomas Laqueur, 'While Statues Sleep', *London Review of Books* 42, no. 12, 18 June 2020.
117 Woodrow Wilson, 'Address at Gettysburg', 4 July 1913, American Presidency Project, presidency.ucsb.edu.
118 Eric Steven Yellin, *Racism in the Nation's Service: Government Workers and the Color Line in Woodrow Wilson's America*, University of North Carolina Press, 2013, p. 104.
119 The large painting depicts the presentation of the draft of the Declaration, but it shows only forty-two signers, and some of those depicted, such as John Dickinson, did not sign.

3. Debating the French Revolution

1. Albert Soboul, *La Révolution française*, Presses Universitaires de France, 1965, p. 5.
2. François Furet, *Penser la Révolution française*, Gallimard, 1978; Eric Hobsbawm, *Echoes of the Marseillaise: Two Centuries Look Back on the French Revolution*, Verso, 1990; Lynn Hunt, 'Forgetting and Remembering: The French Revolution Then and Now', *American Historical Review* 100, no. 4, October 1995, pp. 1119–35. A balanced view of the debate can be found in Julien Louvrier, 'Penser la controverse: la réception du livre de François Furet et Denis Richet, La Révolution française', *Annales historiques de la Révolution française* 351, January–March 2008, pp. 151–78; see also Michael Scott Christofferson, *French Intellectuals Against the Left: The Antitotalitarian Moment of the 1970s*, Berghahn Books, 2004. For a *marxisant* review of the debate, see George C. Comninel, *Rethinking the French Revolution: Marxism and the Revisionist Challenge*, Verso, 1987.
3. Germaine de Staël, *Considérations sur les principaux événements de la Révolution Française, depuis son origine jusques et compris le 8 Juillet 1815*, in *Œuvres complètes de Mme de Staël*, vol. 1, tome 1, Dambray Fils, 1820, pp. 312–17.
4. Gentile used the term in 1928 in an article, 'The Philosophical Basis of Fascism', and then again, in 1932, in the entry for 'Fascismo' in the *Enciclopedia Italiana* – though the entry was attributed to Mussolini. For thorough review of the term 'totalitarianism', see Bruno Bongiovanni, 'Totalitarianism: The Word and the Thing', *Journal of Modern European History* 3, no. 1, 2005, pp. 5–17.
5. See the critique by Peter Gay in his 'Rhetoric and Politics in the French Revolution', *American Historical Review* 66, no. 3, April 1961, pp. 664–76, especially the last paragraph.
6. Arno Mayer, *The Furies: Violence and Terror in the French and Russian Revolutions*, Princeton University Press, 2000, pp. xiv–xv.
7. Lynn Hunt, review of Furet's *Penser la Révolution française*, *History and Theory* 20, no. 3, October 1981, p. 313, in Lynn Hunt, *Politics, Culture, and Class in the French Revolution*, University of California Press, 1986, p. 11. She found Furet's discussion of revolutionary politics to be 'entirely abstract'.
8. In Furet, *Penser la Révolution français*, Cobban is mentioned three times: pp. 88, 153, 193. For a polemical take on the 'totalitarian' school, see Maurice Agulhon, 'La Révolution française au banc des accusés', *Vingtième Siècle*, January–March 1985, pp. 7–18.
9. Gustave Le Bon, *Psychologie des foules*, Félix Alcan, 1895, pp. 24–7. For a recent treatment of the concept of 'crowd', see the introduction by Enzo Traverso and the essay by David Bidussa ('Le folle come oggetto di indagine storica'), in Georges Lefebvre, *Folle Rivoluzionarie*, Fondazione Giangiacomo Feltrinelli, digital edn, May 2021. The classic text on crowds and the French Revolution still is George Rudé, *The Crowd in the French Revolution*, Oxford University Press, 1973, pp. 32–43; see particularly pt III, 'The Anatomy of the Revolutionary Crowd', pp. 178–239.
10. Crane Brinton, review of Gaxotte's *The French Revolution*, *American Political Science Review* 26, no. 6, December 1932, p. 1122.
11. Michel Feltin-Palas, 'L'Académie française se résout à la féminisation', *L'Express*, 19 February 2019. Other distinguished intellectuals, such as Claude Lévi-Strauss and Georges Dumézil, were also hostile to accepting women in the Academy.
12. R. R. Palmer, *The Age of the Democratic Revolution: A Political History of Europe and America, 1760–1800*, Princeton University Press, 1964, p. 3.
13. Denis Woronoff, *La République bourgeoise de Thermidor á Brumaire 1794–1799*, Éditions du Seuil, 1972, pp. 132–7.
14. Jeremy D. Popkin, *A Short History of the French Revolution*, Prentice Hall, 1998, p. 107.

15 Hunt, *Politics, Culture, and Class in the French Revolution*, p. 141.
16 Mayer, *The Furies*, p. 49.
17 Lucia Rubinelli, 'Taming Sovereignty: Constituent Power in Nineteenth-Century French Political Thought', *History of European Ideas* 44, no. 1, 2018, p. 62.
18 Aléxis de Tocqueville, *Recollections: The French Revolution of 1848 and Its Aftermath*, ed. Olivier Zunz, trans. Arthur Goldhammer, University of Virginia Press, 2016, pp. 47–8.
19 Cited in Sudhir Hazareesingh and Karma Nabulsi, 'Entre Robespierre et Napoléon: les paradoxes de la mémoire républicaine sous la monarchie de Juillet', *Annales. Histoire, Sciences Sociales* 65, no. 5, September–October 2010, p. 1236. The article thoroughly discusses Laponneraye's concurrent commitment to Jacobinism *and* Napoleon.
20 For a study of the 'globalization' of the Declaration of Independence, see David Armitage, *The Declaration of Independence: A Global History*, Harvard University Press, 2007, pp. 108 ff.
21 Thomas Paine, *Common Sense*, Penguin, 1976, p. 63.
22 'To George Washington from Thomas Paine, 1 May 1790', Founders Online, founders.archives.gov.
23 Hannah Arendt, *On Revolution*, Penguin, 1973, p. 56.
24 Immanuel Wallerstein, 'The French Revolution as a World-Historical Event', *Social Research* 56, no. 1, Spring 1989, pp. 33–52; Eric Hobsbawm, *The Age of Revolution 1789–1848*, Mentor, 1962, p. 76.
25 Hunt, *Politics, Culture, and Class in the French Revolution*, p. 3.
26 Friedrich Engels, 'Reform Movement in France. Banquet of Dijon', *Northern Star*, 18 December 1947, available in Karl Marx and Frederick Engels, *Collected Works*, vol. 6, Progress Publishers, 1976, p. 397.
27 On the Marseillaise in 1917 Russia, see Orlando Figes, *A People's Tragedy: The Russian Revolution 1891–1924*, Pimlico, 1997, pp. 346, 357.
28 Richard Whatmore, 'Adam Smith's Role in the French Revolution', *Past and Present* 175, May 2002, p. 82.
29 Robert Howell Griffiths, 'Modération et centrisme politique en Angleterre de 1660 à 1800', *Annales historique de la Révolution française* 357, July–September 2009, p. 120.
30 Bertrand Barère de Vieuzac, 'Rapport du Comité de salut public sur les idiomes', 27 January 1794 (8 pluviôse, year II), L'Aménagement linguistique dans le monde, axl.cefan.ulaval.ca. See also David Bell, 'Lingua Populi, Lingua Dei: Language, Religion, and the Origins of French Revolutionary Nationalism', *American Historical Review* 100, no. 5, December 1995.
31 Karl Marx and Frederick Engels, *The German Ideology*, Progress Publishers, 1976, p. 208.
32 Laurent Theis, *Guizot. La Traversée d'un siècle*, CNRS Éditions, 2014, pp. 71–2, 168.
33 Douglas Johnson, *Guizot: Aspects of French History, 1787–1874*, Greenwood Press, 1963, pp. 75, 359.
34 Karl Marx, *The Revolutions of 1848: Political Writings*, vol. 1, Penguin, 1973, pp. 192–3.
35 Tocqueville, *Recollections*, p. 4.
36 Among these were the Monneron brothers; see Oliver Cussen, 'The Lives of Merchant Capital: The Frères Monneron and the Legacy of Old Regime Empire', *French History* 34, no. 3, September 2020, pp. 294–316.
37 Donald Sutherland, 'The Revolution in the Provinces: Class or Counterrevolution?', in Stephen G. Reinhardt and Elizabeth A. Cawthorn, eds, *Essays on the French Revolution: Paris and the Provinces*, Texas A & M University Press, 1992, p. 116.
38 Tocqueville, *Recollections*, p. 53.
39 Hunt, *Politics, Culture, and Class in the French Revolution*, pp. 151, 167.

40 Steve A. Smith, 'Workers, the Intelligentsia and Marxist Parties: St Petersburg, 1895–1917 and Shanghai, 1921–1927', *International Review of Social History* 41, no. 1, April 1996, p. 29.
41 Arno Mayer, *The Persistence of the Old Regime: Europe to the Great War*, Pantheon Books, 1981.
42 Aléxis de Tocqueville, *L'Ancien régime et la révolution*, Michel Lévy Frères, 1856, p. 147.
43 Chateaubriand, *Mémoires d'outre-tombe*, Kraus Reprint, 1975, vol. 5, ch. 10, p. 279, available at Project Gutenberg, gutenberg.org.
44 Popkin, *A Short History of the French Revolution*, p. 88.
45 According to the historian and activist Albert Laponneraye, *Histoire de la Révolution française*, F. Didot, Père et Fils, 1838, p. 158.
46 See for instance Albert Soboul, *Histoire de la Révolution française*, vol. 1, *De la Bastille à la Gironde*, Gallimard, 1962, p. 8.
47 The key text is still Albert Soboul, *Les Sans-culottes parisiens en l'an II*, Éditions Librairie Clavreuil, 1958, esp. pp. 439–55. See also Palmer, *The Age of the Democratic Revolution*, p. 47.
48 Richard Mowery Andrews, 'Social Structures, Political Elites and Ideology in Revolutionary Paris, 1792–94: A Critical Evaluation of Albert Soboul's "Les Sans-culottes parisiens en l'an II"', *Journal of Social History* 19, no. 1, Autumn, 1985, pp. 71–112, see p. 100.
49 David A. Bell, *Men on Horseback: The Power of Charisma in the Age of Revolution*, Farrar, Straus and Giroux, 2020, p. 95.
50 Roger Chartier, 'Cultures, lumières, doléances: Les Cahiers de 1789', *Revue d'histoire moderne et contemporaine* 28, no. 1, January–March 1981, pp. 69–70.
51 Ibid., pp. 86–9.
52 Tocqueville, *L'Ancien régime et la révolution*, p. 132.
53 Philippe Minard, 'Economie de marché et Etat en France: mythes et légendes du colbertisme', *L'Économie politique* 37, 2008/1, pp. 77–94.
54 Charles-Augustin Sainte-Beuve, 'Relation inédite de la dernière maladie de Louis XV', 15 February 1846, in *Portraits Littéraires*, vol. 3, Garnier, 1862, available at Project Gutenberg, gutenberg.org.
55 Colin Jones, 'Bourgeois Revolution Revivified: 1789 and Social Change', in Gary Kates, ed., *The French Revolution: Recent Debates and New Controversies*, 2nd edn, Routledge, 1998, pp. 92–3, 105.
56 The issue of state finance before the revolution is ably discussed in Michael Sonenscher, *Before the Deluge: Public Debt, Inequality, and the Intellectual Origins of the French Revolution*, Princeton University Press, 2009, pp. 4–9.
57 Francois Hincker, *Les Français devant l'impôt sous l'ancien régime*, Flammarion, 1971, p. 18.
58 Colin Jones, *The Great Nation: France from Louis XV to Napoleon 1715–99*, Penguin, 2002, p. 144.
59 Véronique Campion-Vincent and Christine Shojaei Kawan, 'Marie-Antoinette et son célèbre dire', *Annales historiques de la Révolution française* 327, 2002, pp. 29–56; Sonenscher, *Before the Deluge*, p. 1 – though it may have been the king's mistress, the author of the deluge phrase or the father of the moderate revolutionary Honoré Gabriel Riqueti, comte de Mirabeau.
60 Quoted in Jones, *The Great Nation*, p. 299.
61 For an examination of the debt situation see François R. Velde and David R. Weir, 'The Financial Market and Government Debt Policy in France, 1746–1793', *Journal of Economic History* 52, no. 1, March 1992, pp. 3, 6, 10; see also David R. Weir, 'Les Crises

économiques et les origines de la Révolution française', *Annales, Economies, sociétés, civilisations* 44, no. 1, 1989, pp. 923 ff.
62 Arthur Young, *Travels During the Years 1787, 1788, and 1789: Undertaken More Particularly with a View of Ascertaining the Cultivation, Wealth, Resources, and National Prosperity of the Kingdom of France, 1792*, 3rd edn, George Bell and Sons, 1890, p. 97. It became an immediate literary success on its original publication, with a French translation appearing in 1793. Young claims he had not altered anything from the conversation, note p. 98.
63 Tocqueville, *L'Ancien régime et la révolution*, p. 175.
64 Ibid., pp. 70–1.
65 Robert Darbnton, *The Revolutionary Temper: Paris, 1748–1789*, Allen Lane, 2023.
66 Charles Élie, marquis de Ferrières, *Correspondance inédite* (1789, 1790, 1791) Armand Colin, 1932, pp. 37–40.
67 Bell, *Men on Horseback*, p. 95.
68 Soboul, *Histoire de la Révolution française*, vol. 1, pp. 144–5, who claims 350,000; Guy Chaussinand-Nogaret, *La Noblesse au XVIIIe siècle*, Editions Complexe, 2000 (1976). The latter source estimates the number as nearer to 100,000, but admits it could be more, pp. 11, 39–50.
69 Soboul, *Histoire de la Révolution française*, vol. 1, p. 25.
70 Jones, *The Great Nation*, p. 408.
71 Aléxis de Tocqueville, *Memoir, Letters, and Remains of Alexis de Tocqueville*, vol. 1, Macmillan, 1861, p. 225.
72 Emmanuel-Joseph Sieyès, *Qu'est-ce que le Tiers-Etat*, n.p., 1789, pp. 1, 3.
73 Soboul, *Histoire de la Révolution française*, vol. 1, p. 156.
74 Vincent W. Beach, 'The Count of Artois and the Coming of the French Revolution', *Journal of Modern History* 30, no. 4, December 1958, p. 320.
75 William H. Sewell Jr, 'Historical Events as Transformations of Structures: Inventing Revolution at the Bastille', *Theory and Society* 25, no. 6, December 1996, pp. 851–4.
76 Fernand Braudel, *A History of Civilization*, Allen Lane, 1994, p. 329.
77 Jones, *The Great Nation*, pp. 432–5.
78 Moira Ferguson, 'Mary Wollstonecraft and the Problematic of Slavery', *Feminist Review* 42, Autumn 1992, pp. 82–102.
79 The apparent inconsistency, to modern eyes, between Astell's Toryism and feminism is carefully explained in Patricia Springborg, *Mary Astell: Theorist of Freedom from Domination*, Cambridge University Press, 2005, esp. p. 3.
80 Bonnie S. Anderson, '*Frauenemancipation* and Beyond: The Use of the Concept of Emancipation by Early European Feminists', in Kathryn Kish Sklar and James Brewer Stuart, eds, *Women's Rights and Transatlantic Antislavery in the Era of Emancipation*, Yale University Press, 2007, p. 88.
81 Hunt, 'Forgetting and Remembering', p. 1131.
82 Ambrogio A. Caiani, *Louis XVI and the French Revolution 1789–1792*, Cambridge University Press, 2012, p. 11.
83 Florence Gauthier, 'The French Revolution: Revolution of the Rights of Man and the Citizen', in Mike Haynes and Jim Wolfreys, eds, *History and Revolution: Refuting Revisionism*, Verso, 2007, p. 78.
84 Marx, *Capital*, vol. 1, p. 741.
85 Palmer, *The Age of the Democratic Revolution*, p. 34.
86 Brissot, quoted in R. R. Palmer, 'The World Revolution of the West: 1763–1801', *Political Science Quarterly* 69, no. 1, March 1954, p. 11.
87 Maximilien Robespierre, in 'Glanes et documents', *Annales historiques de la Révolution française* 57, no. 259, January–March 1985, p. 105. For Robespierre's position

on defensive and offensive wars, see also Georges Michon, *Robespierre et la guerre révolutionnaire 1791–1792*, M. Rivière et Cie, 1937, p. 52; also Thibaut Poirot, 'Robespierre et la guerre, une question posée dès 1789?', *Annales historiques de la Révolution française* 371, January–March 2013, pp. 115–35.

88   John Quincy Adams, *An Address Delivered at the Request of a Commission at the Citizens of Washington; On the Occasion of Reading the Declaration of Independence, on the Fourth of July 1821*, Davis and Force, 1821, p. 29.

89   Noah C. Shusterman, 'All of His Power Lies in the Distaff: Robespierre, Women and the French Revolution', *Past and Present* 223, 2014, esp. p. 141.

90   Alyssa Goldstein Sepinwall, 'Robespierre, Old Regime Feminist? Gender, the Late Eighteenth Century, and the French Revolution Revisited', *Journal of Modern History* 82, no. 1, March 2010, p. 2. Far more sceptical of Robespierre's pro-women attitude is Claude Guillon (*Robespierre, les femmes et la Révolution*, Éditions Imho, 2021), who goes as far as saying that Robespierre contributed to the political defeat of women in the early revolutionary period.

91   Palmer, *The Age of the Democratic Revolution*, p. 86.

92   Jacques Goulet, 'Robespierre la peine de mort et la Terreur (II)', *Annales historiques de la Révolution française* 55, no. 251, January–March 1983, p. 49.

93   Albert Soboul, *Les Sans-culottes parisiens en l'an II*, 1958. Shortened English translation, *The Parisian Sans-Culottes and the French Revolution 1793–4*, Clarendon, 1964. All page references hereafter are to this English translation.

94   Marisa Linton, *Choosing Terror: Virtue, Friendship and Authenticity in the French Revolution*, Oxford University Press, 2013, p. 10.

95   Timothy Tackett, *The Coming of the Terror in the French Revolution*, Harvard University Press, 2015, p. 346. This deals at great length with the growing obsession with conspiracies and attributes much of the Terror to this paranoia.

96   William St Clair, *That Greece Might Still Be Free: The Philhellenes in the War of Independence*, OpenBook, 2008, p. 92.

97   Mayer, *The Furies*, p. 183.

98   See Donald Greer, *The Incidence of the Terror During the French Revolution: A Statistical Interpretation*, Harvard University Press, 1935; for a critical observation on the interpretation of the data see also Richard Louie, 'The Incidence of the Terror: A Critique of a Statistical Interpretation', *French Historical Studies* 3, no. 3, Spring 1964, pp. 379–99.

99   Greer, *The Incidence of the Terror*, p. 127.

100   Ibid., p. 109.

101   Linton, *Choosing Terror*, pp. 11–12.

102   Colin Jones, *The Fall of Robespierre: 24 Hours in Revolutionary Paris*, Oxford University Press, 2011, p. 434; on the use of 'la Terreur', see also Michel Biard and Marisa Linton, *La Révolution française face à ses demons*, Armand Colin, 2020.

103   Donald Greer, *The Incidence of the Emigration During the French Revolution*, Harvard University Press, 1951, pp. 99–100; Olwen Hufton, 'The Reconstruction of a Church 1796–1801', in Gwynne Lewis and Colin Lucas, eds, *Beyond the Terror: Essays in French Regional and Social History, 1794–1815*, Cambridge University Press, 1983, p. 36; Mayer, *The Furies*, p. 210.

104   Robert Tombs, *France 1814–1914*, Longman, 1996, p. 383.

105   Whitney Walton, 'Writing the 1848 Revolution: Politics, Gender, and Feminism in the Works of French Women of Letters', *French Historical Studies* 18, no. 4, Autumn 1994, p. 1011; the poem '24 Juin 24 Novembre' can be found in *Poésies complètes de Madame Émile de Girardin (Delphine Gay)*, Michel Lévy Frères, 1865, pp. 351–2.

106   Tombs, *France 1814–1914*, p. 430.

107 See data in Howard Peckham, *The Toll of Independence: Engagements and Battle Casualties of the American Revolution*, University of Chicago Press, 1974, p. 131.
108 R. F. Foster, *Modern Ireland 1600–1972*, Penguin, 1989, p. 280.
109 On the death toll of the Mexican Revolution, see the careful article by Robert McCaa, 'Missing Millions: The Demographic Costs of the Mexican Revolution', *Mexican Studies / Estudios Mexicanos* 19, no. 2, Summer 2003, pp. 367–400, esp. pp. 387–96.
110 Paul Preston, *The Spanish Holocaust. Inquisition and Extermination in Twentieth-Century Spain*, Harper Press, 2012, p. i.
111 Jones, *The Fall of Robespierre*, p. 17.
112 Jacques Goulet, 'Robespierre la peine de mort et la Terreur' (I), *Annales historiques de la Révolution française* 53, no. 244, April–June 1981, pp. 220–1.
113 William R. Wood, 'Capital Punishment / Death Penalty', in William J. Chambliss, ed., *Corrections*, SAGE, 2011, p. 5.
114 Jacques Godechot, *The Counter-revolution: Doctrine and Action 1789–1804*, Princeton University Press, 1971, p. 66.
115 Edmund Burke, *Select Works of Edmund Burke*, vol. 2, *Reflections on the Revolution in France*, Liberty Fund, 1999 (1790), pp. 117–18 or pp. 94–5, available at Online Library of Liberty, oll.libertyfund.org.
116 Ibid., p. 107.
117 Richard Bourke, *Empire and Revolution: The Political Life of Edmund Burke*, Princeton University Press, 2015, p. 677.
118 Burke, *Reflections on the Revolution in France*, p. 105.
119 Edmund Burke, *Select Works of Edmund Burke*, vol. 3, *Letters on a Regicide Peace*, Liberty Fund, 1999 (1874–78), p. 122.
120 Ibid., p. 130.
121 Hippolyte Taine, *The French Revolution*, trans. John Durand, vol. 1, Henry Holt & Co., 1878, pp. 97–8 (English translation of *Les Origines de la France contemporaine*).
122 Hippolyte Taine, *Origines de la France contemporaine*, vol. 3, *La Révolution, l'anarchie*, Librairie Hachette et Cie, 1909, p. 188.
123 Godechot, *The Counter-revolution*, p. 88.
124 Joseph Marie Maistre, *The Works of Joseph de Maistre*, ed. and trans. Jack Lively, Allen and Unwin, 1965, pp. 71, 81.
125 Godechot, *The Counter-revolution*, pp. 71–4.
126 Gareth Stedman Jones, 'The Redemptive Power of Violence? Carlyle, Marx and Dickens', *History Workshop Journal* 65, no. 1, Spring 2008, p. 3.
127 For a review of the extensive literature on British writers and the French Revolution, see M. O. Grenby, 'Writing Revolution: British Literature and the French Revolution Crisis, a Review of Recent Scholarship', *Literature Compass* 3/6, 2006, pp. 1351–85.
128 John Stuart Mill, *On Liberty*, Penguin, 1974, p. 62.
129 This is well explained in Sidney Axinn, 'Kant, Authority, and the French Revolution', *Journal of the History of Ideas* 32, no. 3, July–September 1971, pp. 423–32.
130 Richard Bourke, *Hegel's World Revolution*, Princeton University Press, 2023, pp. xiii, 189.
131 Le Blond de Neuveglise / Liévin-Bonaventure Proyart, *La Vie et les crimes de Robespierre, surnommé Le Tyran, depuis sa naissance jusqu'à sa mort*, Chez Tous les Libraires, 1795, p. 1.
132 Jonathan Israel, *Democratic Enlightenment: Philosophy, Revolution, and Human Rights 1750–1790*, Oxford University Press, 2011, p. 479.
133 Rachel Hope Cleves, 'On Writing the History of Violence', *Journal of the Early Republic* 24, no. 4, Winter 2004, p. 652.

134 Daniel I. O'Neill, 'John Adams versus Mary Wollstonecraft on the French Revolution and Democracy', *Journal of the History of Ideas* 68, no. 3, July 2007, p. 463.
135 Mary Wollstonecraft, *An Historical and Moral View of the Origin and Progress of the French Revolution and the Effect It Has Produced in Europe*, J. Johnson, 1795, pp. v–vii. See also Barbara Taylor, *Mary Wollstonecraft and the Feminist Imagination*, Cambridge University Press, 2003, p. 54.
136 Quoted in O'Neill, 'John Adams versus Mary Wollstonecraft', p. 467; the Wollstonecraft text with John Adams's annotation in the John Adams Library (Boston Public Library) is available at Internet Archive, archive.org.
137 Thomas Paine, *The Rights of Man*, Penguin, 1984, p. 172.
138 Thomas Carlyle, *The French Revolution: A History*, ch. 2.1.II, p. 266, available at Project Gutenberg, gutenberg.org; on Carlyle's influence on *A Tale of Two Cities*, see the introduction by the editors and the essays by Mark Philp and Gareth Stedman Jones in Colin Jones, Josephine McDonagh and Jon Mee, eds, *Charles Dickens,* A Tale of Two Cities *and the French Revolution*, Palgrave Macmillan, 2009; see also David R. Sorensen, '"The Unseen Heart of the Whole": Carlyle, Dickens, and the Sources of "The French Revolution" in "A Tale of Two Cities"', *Dickens Quarterly* 30, no. 1, March 2013, pp. 5–25.
139 Micah Alpaugh, 'The Politics of Escalation in French Revolutionary Protest: Political Demonstrations, Non-violence and Violence in the *Grandes Journées* of 1789', *French History* 23, no. 3, September 2009, pp. 336–59. Alpaugh developed this theme in his *Non-violence and the French Revolution: Political Demonstrations in Paris, 1787–1795*, Cambridge University Press, 2015.
140 Alpaugh, 'The Politics of Escalation in French Revolutionary Protest', p. 340.
141 Alpaugh, *Non-violence and the French Revolution*.
142 Alpaugh, 'The Politics of Escalation in French Revolutionary Protest', p. 553.
143 Colin Jones, 'The Overthrow of Maximilien Robespierre and the "Indifference" of the People', *American Historical Review* 119, no. 3, June 2014, p. 692.
144 To use the concluding words of Eric Hazan, *A People's History of the French Revolution*, Verso, 2014, p. 416.
145 Soboul, *La Révolution française*, p. 92.
146 On the more absurd pseudo-psychoanalytical treatment of Robespierre as well as more serious historical works, see the amusing survey by Marc Belissa and Julien Louvrier, 'Robespierre dans les publications françaises et anglophones depuis l'an 2000', *Annales historiques de la Révolution française* 371, January–March 2013, pp. 73–93.
147 Hunt, *Politics, Culture, and Class in the French Revolution*, p. 229.
148 Matthew White, 'Statistics of Wars, Oppressions and Atrocities of the Nineteenth Century (the 1800s)', Necrometrics (Part of the Historical Atlas of the 20th Century), necrometrics.com.
149 Patrice Gueniffey, *Bonaparte 1769–1802*, Belknap–Harvard University Press, 2015, pp. 456–9.
150 Joseph Clarke, 'A "Theatre of Bloody Carnage": The Revolt of Cairo and Revolutionary Violence', in Erica Charters, Marie Houllemare and Peter H. Wilson, eds, *A Global History of Early Modern Violence*, Manchester University Press, 2020, p. 222; see also Gueniffey, *Bonaparte 1769–1802*, p. 465.
151 '1796. La Première Campagne d'Italie', Napoléon & Empire, napoleon-empire.net.
152 Pieter Geyl, *Napoleon: For or Against*, Peregrine Books, 1965; this is a discussion of the French historiography on Napoleon originally published in Dutch (1946).
153 Jean-Paul Bertaud, 'L'Expédition d'Egypte et la construction du mythe napoléonien', in 'Bonaparte, les îles méditerranéennes et l'appel de l'Orient (Actes du Colloque

d'Ajaccio 29–30 Mai 1998)', special issue, *Cahiers de la Méditerranée* 57, 1998, pp. 281–8. This special issue has almost nothing on the Cairo revolt. There is no mention of the Cairo revolt either in Palmer's global view on the French Revolution and its Napoleonic aftermath (*The Age of the Democratic Revolution*). Even the book on Napoleon by the Marxist historian Georges Lefebvre (*Napoléon*, 1935) ignores the massacres in Egypt and in Italy. Andrew Roberts appears to excuse both in his apologetic biography of Napoleon, *Napoleon the Great*, Allen Lane, 2014, pp. 98–9, 181–2.
154 Clarke, 'A "Theatre of Bloody Carnage"', p. 223.
155 Pierre Goubert, *The Course of French History*, Routledge, 1991, p. 228.
156 Marco D'Eramo, 'After Waterloo', *New Left Review* 94, July–August 2015, p. 79.
157 Daniel Piquet, *L'Émancipation des noirs dans la Révolution française, 1789–1795*, Karthala, 2002, p. 34.
158 Quoted in Florence Gauthier, *L'Aristocratie de l'épiderme: Le Combat de la Société des Citoyens de Couleur, 1789–1791*, CNRS Éditions, 2007, ch. 3, 'La Naissance du côté gauche sur le problème colonial, octobre 1790', available at books.openedition.org.
159 On Toussaint, see the classic C. L. R. James, *The Black Jacobins: Toussaint L'Ouverture and the San Domingo Revolution*, Secker & Warburg, 1938; also the more recent Sudhir Hazareesingh, *Black Spartacus: The Epic Life of Toussaint Louverture*, Allen Lane, 2020.
160 On Jefferson's position, see Tim Matthewson, 'Jefferson and Haiti', *Journal of Southern History* 61, no. 2, May 1995, pp. 209–48, esp. p. 216.
161 Hunt, 'Forgetting and Remembering', p. 1129; Robin Blackburn, *The Overthrow of Colonial Slavery, 1776–1848*, Verso, 2011, p. 163. For a history of the uprising against Napoleon, see also Philippe R. Girard, *The Slaves Who Defeated Napoléon, Toussaint Louverture and the Haitian War of Independence, 1801–1804*, University of Alabama Press, 2011.
162 David Geggus, 'Racial Equality, Slavery, and Colonial Secession During the Constituent Assembly', *American Historical Review* 94, no. 5, December 1989, p. 1291.
163 Florence Gauthier, *Triomphe et mort du droit naturel en Révolution 1789–1795–1802*, PUF, 1992; see also Yves Benot, whose main texts on slavery and colonization are collected in *Les Lumières, l'esclavage, la colonisation*, ed. Roland Desné and Marcel Dorigny, Éditions la Découverte, 2005.
164 Natalie Petiteau, 'Lecture socio-politique de l'empire: bilan et perspectives', *Annales historiques de la Révolution française* 359, January–March 2010, pp. 185–6.
165 Bell, *Men on Horseback*, pp. 117–18.
166 See H. Gaston Hall, 'New Light on Manzoni's "Ei fu" in Relation to French Literature', *Modern Language Review* 66, no. 3, July 1971, pp. 568–79; see also Kenneth Cornell, 'May 5, 1821 and the Poets', *Yale French Studies* 26, 1960, pp. 50–4.
167 Johann Wolfgang von Goethe and Johann Peter Eckermann, *Conversations of Goethe with Johann Peter Eckermann*, Da Capo Press, 1998, pp. 245–6, 11 March 1828.
168 G. W. F. Hegel, *Hegel: The Letters*, trans. Clark Butler and Christine Seiler, Indiana University Press, 1984, p. 114.
169 François-René de Chateaubriand, *De Buonaparte, des Bourbons*, in *Œuvres. Mélanges politique*, vol. 15, Boulanger et Legrand, n.d. (probably 1850), pp. 10, 14, 22, 27, 24–9.
170 William Wordsworth, 'To B. R. Haydon, on Seeing His Picture of Napoleon Buonaparte on the Island of St. Helena', in response to Benjamin Haydon's painting *Napoleon Musing After Sunset* (1829), showing Napoleon from the back, perched on a rock at St Helena looking on the sea.
171 Cécile Meynard, 'Stendhal et les campagnes napoléoniennes', *Revue italienne d'études françaises* 9, 2019.
172 Frédéric Bluche, *Le Bonapartisme. Aux origines de la droite autoritaire (1800–1850)*,

Nouvelles Éditions Latines, 1980, p. 12; see also Robert and Isabelle Tombs, *That Sweet Enemy: The French and the British from the Sun King to the Present*, Heinemann, 2006, p. 304.

173 Georges Lefebvre, *Napoleon*, Taylor & Francis, 2011, pp. 54, 58 ff.
174 Laura O'Brien, 'Napoléon n'est plus? Reflections on a Bicentenary', *French History* 35, no. 4, 2021, p. 539.
175 See text of Emmanuel Macron's speech 'Commémoration du bicentenaire de la mort de Napoléon Ier', 5 May 2021, elysee.fr.
176 Palmer, *The Age of the Democratic Revolution*, p. 222.
177 Martin Wrede, 'Louix XVIII. Le Portrait du roi restauré, ou la fabrication de Louis XVIII', *Revue d'histoire moderne et contemporaine* 53, no. 2, April–June 2006, p. 112.
178 Alphonse de Lamartine, *Œuvres complètes de Lamartine*, vol. 19, *Histoire de la Restauration*, n.p., 1861, p. 27.
179 de Staël, *Considérations sur les principaux événements*, p. 52.
180 Cited in Hazareesingh and Nabulsi, 'Entre Robespierre et Napoléon', p. 1228.
181 James K. Kieswetter, 'The Imperial Restoration: Continuity in Personnel and Policy Under Napoleon I and Louis XVIII', *Historian* 45, no. 1, November 1982, pp. 34, 37.
182 Lamartine, *Histoire de la Restauration*, p. 27.
183 de Staël, *Considérations sur les principaux événements*, p. 43.
184 Chateaubriand, *De la monarchie selon la Charte*, in *Œuvres. Mélanges politique*, vol. 15, esp. pp. 135–41.
185 François Guizot, *Du gouvernement de la France depuis la Restauration et du ministère actuel*, Éd. Ladvocat, 1820, p. 190.
186 'Berlioz to His Father Louis Berlioz (*CG* no. 170; 2 August [1830])', 'Berlioz in Paris: Institut de France', at Hector Berlioz, hberlioz.com.
187 'Yesterday you were a mere crowd, Today you are a People.' Victor Hugo, 'Dicté après Juillet 1830', *Les Chants du crépuscule*.
188 Hippolyte Castille, *Les Journaux et les journalistes sous l'Empire et la Restauration*, F. Sartorius, 1858, pp. 46–7.
189 Heinrich Heine, *De la France*, Michel Lévy Frères, 1872, pp. 339–40; originally *Französische Zustände*, 1832; see also Nicos Hadjinicolaou, '"La Liberté guidant le peuple" de Delacroix devant son premier public', *Actes de la recherche en sciences sociales* 28, June 1979, pp. 3–26.
190 Tombs, *France 1814–1914*, p. 356.
191 Heinrich August Winkler, *Germany: The Long Road West 1789–1933*, Oxford University Press, 2006, p. 71.
192 Karl Marx, *The Civil War in France*, Foreign Language Press, 1966, p. 65 (Third Address, May 1871).
193 Soboul, *La Révolution française*, p. 55.
194 Speech to the Chamber (1 March 1843), in François Guizot, *Histoire parlementaire de France. Recueil complet des discours de M. Guizot dans les Chambres, de 1819 à 1848*, vol. 4, Michel Lévy Frères, 1864, p. 68.
195 Fernand Rude, *Les Révoltes des canuts 1831–1834*, Maspero, 1982.
196 Christopher Clark, introduction to *Revolutionary Spring: Fighting for a New World 1848–1849*, Penguin, 2023.
197 Tocqueville, *Recollections*, p. 12.
198 William Fortescue, 'Morality and Monarchy: Corruption and the Fall of the Regime of Louis-Philippe in 1848', *French History* 6, no. 1, March 2002, p. 84.
199 Tocqueville, *Recollections*, p. 51.
200 George Sand, *Souvenirs de 1848*, Calmann Lévy, 1880, p. 3.
201 Fortescue, 'Morality and Monarchy', p. 90.

202 Henry D'Ideville, *Le Maréchal Bugeaud d'après sa correspondance intime, 1784–1849*, vol. 2, Firmin-Didot, 1881, p. 486.
203 Tocqueville, *Recollections*, p. 46.
204 Walton, 'Writing the 1848 Revolution', pp. 1012–16.
205 Hugh Brogan, *Alexis de Tocqueville: Prophet of Democracy in the Age of Revolution*, Profile, 2006, p. 452.
206 Jean Sigmann, *1848: The Romantic and Democratic Revolution in Europe*, Allen & Unwin, 1973, p. 228; Brogan writes that 3,000 would be a 'gross underestimate' in *Alexis de Tocqueville*, p. 458.
207 Karl Marx, *The Eighteenth Brumaire of Louis Bonaparte*, Progress Publishers, 1967, p. 17. He had written something similar about the actual French Revolution a few years earlier in *The German Ideology* (see above).
208 Daniel Stern (pseudonym of Marie d'Agoult), *Histoire de la révolution de 1848*, vol. 2, Charpentier, 1862, p. 471.
209 Tocqueville, *Recollections*, p. 118.
210 Brogan, *Alexis de Tocqueville*, p. 460.
211 Sigmann, *1848*, p. 226; note, however, that Jean-Luc Maynaud warns, on the basis of regional research, against regarding the peasants as a politically homogeneous class, see his 'Les Paysanneries françaises face à la Seconde République', in 'Le XIXe Siècle en question', special issue, *1848. Révolutions et mutations au XIXe siècle* 6, 1990, pp. 55–64, esp. pp. 56–8; see also Maurice Agulhon, *The Republican Experiment 1848–1852*, Cambridge University Press, 1983, p. 72.
212 Agulhon, *The Republican Experiment*, p. 84.
213 Tocqueville, *Recollections*, pp. 62–3, 70–1.
214 Louis-Antoine Garnier-Pagès, *Un épisode de la Révolution de 1848. L'Impôt des 45 centimes*, Pagnerre, 1850, p. vi; see also George Fasel, 'The Wrong Revolution: French Republicanism in 1848', *French Historical Studies* 8, no. 4, Autumn 1974, pp. 669–70.
215 Brogan, *Alexis de Tocqueville*, p. 472.
216 The term was developed by Guy Debord in his 1967 book *La Société du spectacle*, where he suggests that the phenomenon had come about in the 1920s. On Napoleon III and 'spectacle politics', see Matthew Norman Truesdell, *Spectacular Politics: Louis-Napoleon Bonaparte and the Fête Impériale, 1849–70*, University of California Press, 1992.
217 Bluche, *Le Bonapartisme*, p. 265.
218 Marx, *The Eighteenth Brumaire of Louis Bonaparte*, p. 10.
219 Alexander Herzen, *My Past and Thoughts: The Memoirs of Alexander Herzen*, University of California Press, 1982, p. 396.
220 Jean Balcou, 'Ernest Renan et Napoléon III', *Études Renaniennes* 115, 2014, p. 15.
221 Tocqueville, *Recollections*, pp. 144–5, 159.
222 Michel Winock, 'Un Bonaparte à l'Élysée', *L'Histoire* 258, October 2001.
223 A. J. P. Taylor, 'Mistaken Lessons from the Past', *Listener*, 6 June 1963.
224 Gabrielle Cadier, 'Les Conséquences du traité de 1860 sur le commerce franco-britannique', *Histoire, économie et société* 7, no. 3, 1988, pp. 355–80, esp. pp. 359–61.
225 Orlando Figes, *The Crimean War: A History*, Picador, 2012, p. 480.
226 It was noted by Montesquieu, by Mirabeau, by the English traveller Arthur Young and by Tocqueville, among others; see Tocqueville, *L'Ancien régime et la révolution*, pp. 134, 136, 140.
227 'Déclaration de la Commune de Paris au Peuple Français', in *Le Cri du Peuple*, 21 Avril 1871.
228 Eugene Schulkind, 'Socialist Women During the 1871 Paris Commune', *Past and Present* 106, February 1985, p. 136.

229 Marx, *The Civil War in France*, p. 46. Thiers was 155 centimetres tall.
230 Johnson, *Guizot: Aspects of French History*, p. 192.
231 Robert Tombs, 'How Bloody Was *La Semaine Sanglante* of 1871? A Revision', *Historical Journal* 55, no. 3, 2012, pp. 679–97, esp. figures on pp. 693–5; of course, this has been questioned by other scholars. See Michèle Audin, *La Semaine sanglante. Mai 1871, Légendes et comptes*, Libertalia, 2021 (Audin, a mathematician, estimates the dead at 15,000, with 10,000 just during the Semaine sanglante). See also Jacques Rougerie, *La Commune de 1871*, Que Sais-Je?, 2021, and *Paris insurgé: La Commune de 1871*, Gallimard, 1995 (Rougerie suggests that 10,000 dead is a plausible figure).
232 Marx, *The Civil War in France*, p. 99.
233 On the centenary see Jacques Rougerie, 'Le Centenaire de la Commune, Moisson, problèmes, ouvertures', *Revue Historique* 2, October–December 1971, pp. 409–22; on the 150th, see Denis Cosnard, '"Légende noire" contre "légende rouge": la difficile commémoration des 150 ans de la Commune de Paris', *Le Monde*, 19 February 2021.
234 For an analysis, see David Harvey, 'Monument and Myth', *Annals of the Association of American Geographers* 69, no. 3, September 1979, pp. 362–81, esp. p. 377.
235 Georges and Janine Hémeret, *Les Présidents, République française chronologie et recherches iconographiques*, Prodifu, 1981, p. 44.
236 Alexandre de Tocqueville, 'Réflexions sur l'histoire de l'Angleterre', in *Voyages en Angleterre et en Irlande*, ed. Jean Pierre Mayer, Gallimard, 1967, p. 36. On the issue of choosing dates to celebrate, see Mona Ozouf, 'De thermidor à brumaire: le discours de la Révolution sur elle-même', *Revue historique* 243, January–March 1970, pp. 31–66, esp. pp. 41–2.
237 For a reflection on the first centenary of 1789, see Hobsbawm, *Echoes of the Marseillaise*, ch. 3. On the decision leading to the adoption of 14 July, see Pascal Ory, 'La République en fête: Les 14 Juillet', *Annales historiques de la Révolution française* 52, no. 241, July–September 1980, pp. 445–6; Charles Rearick, 'Festivals in Modern France: The Experience of the Third Republic', *Journal of Contemporary History* 12, no. 3, July 1977, pp. 443–5.

4. The 'National Revolutions' of the Nineteenth Century

1 The riots had been planned in advance; they were not caused by the opera itself. See Sonia Slatin, 'Opera and Revolution: *La Muette de Portici* and the Belgian Revolution of 1830 Revisited', *Journal of Musicological Research* 3, nos 1–2, 1979, pp. 45–62.
2 See Maurizio Isabella, *Southern Europe in the Age of Revolution*, Princeton University Press, 1923, particularly the section on constitutional order, pp. 27–32.
3 Ibid., p. 209.
4 David Brewer, *The Greek War of Independence: The Struggle for Freedom from Ottoman Oppression and the Birth of the Modern Greek Nation*, Overlook Press, 2001, pp. 1–3.
5 I thank Vassilis Fouskas for his considerable help over the section on the Greek War of Independence. On taxation, see ibid., pp. 8–12.
6 Emmanouil Chalkiadakis, 'Reconsidering the Past: Ecumenical Patriarch Gregory V and the Greek Revolution of 1821', *Synthesis* 6, no. 1, p. 186, ejournals.lib.auth.gr.
7 William St Clair, *That Greece Might Still Be Free: The Philhellenes in the War of Independence*, Oxford University Press, 1972, p. 1.
8 Constantine Tsoukalas, 'European Modernity and Greek National Identity', *Journal of Southern Europe and the Balkans* 1, no. 1, May 1999, p. 9.
9 Alexis Heraclides and Ada Dialla, *Humanitarian Intervention in the Long Nineteenth Century: Setting the Precedent*, Manchester University Press, 2015, pp. 107–9.

10 St Clair, *That Greece Might Still Be Free*, p. 59.
11 Charles Brinsley Sheridan, *Thoughts on the Greek Revolution*, John Murray, 1822, p. 2.
12 Georges Finlay, *History of the Greek Revolution*, vol. 1, Blackwood and Sons, 1861, p. 172, who estimated that some 20,000 Muslims were killed in April 1821. See also Thomas Gordon, *History of the Greek Revolution*, published in 1832.
13 Eliza May Butler, *The Tyranny of Greece over Germany*, Cambridge University Press, 1935, p. 333 (republished in 2012). For a modern scholarly study, see Suzanne L. Marchand, *Down from Olympus: Archaeology and Philhellenism in Germany, 1750–1970*, Princeton University Press, 1996; see also Stephen Gaukroger, 'Ancestors and Aliens: Classical Antiquity, the Orient, and the Construction of a European Cultural Identity, 1500–1914', ch. 6, unpublished manuscript.
14 Chateaubriand (François-René de), *Note sur la Grèce*, Le Normant Père Libraire, 1825, p. 8.
15 Tsoukalas, 'European Modernity and Greek National Identity', p. 8.
16 Cited in Davide Rodogno, *Against Massacre: Humanitarian Interventions in the Ottoman Empire, 1815–1914*, Princeton University Press, 2012, p. 70.
17 Patricia Kennedy Grimsted, 'Capodistrias and a "New Order" for Restoration Europe: The "Liberal Ideas" of a Russian Foreign Minister, 1814–1822', *Journal of Modern History* 40, no. 2, June 1968, p. 179.
18 Brewer, *The Greek War of Independence*, p. 350.
19 Maxime Raybaud, a French philhellene officer who took part in the Greek War of Independence, calls it a revolution though it had just started when he was writing it; see Maxime Raybaud, *Mémoires sur la Grèce pour servir à l'histoire de la guerre de l'Indépendance*, Tournachon-Molin, 1824, p. 5. See also Sheridan, *Thoughts on the Greek Revolution*; Samuel Gridley Howe, *An Historical Sketch of the Greek Revolution* (1828); Thomas Gordon, *History of the Greek Revolution* (1832); Finlay, *History of the Greek Revolution*.
20 'Engels to August Bebel: In Plauen Near Dresden', 18 November 1884, in *Gesamtausgabe*, International Publishers, 1942, available at 'Marx–Engels Correspondence 1884', marxists.org.
21 Heinrich August Winkler, *Germany: The Long Road West 1789–1933*, Oxford University Press, 2006, p. 165.
22 Benjamin Disraeli, 'Address to Her Majesty on Her Most Gracioius Speech', 9 February 1871, *Hansard Parliamentary Debates*, 3d series, vol. 204, pp. 81–2.
23 William J. Entwistle, *Aspects of Language*, Faber & Faber, 1923, p. 27.
24 Weinreich explained that the phrase was used by a member of his audience after a lecture in New York in 1943 or 1944.
25 First used by Metternich in his *Memorandum to the Great Powers*, 2 August 1814, then in a letter to the Austrian diplomat Anton Prokesch-Osten, 19 November 1819, and also in a letter to Lord Palmerston (1847). See 'Italy', in J. K. Hoyt and K. L. Roberts, *Hoyt's New Cyclopedia of Practical Quotations*, Bartleby, 2009 (1922), available at bartleby.com.
26 Tullio De Mauro, *Storia linguistica dell'Italia unita*, vol. 1, Laterza, 1963, p. 43.
27 Ernesto Ragionieri, *Storia d'Italia. Dall'unità a oggi*, vol. 4, pt 3, Einaudi, 1976, p. 1714.
28 Ibid., p. 1726.
29 Francesco De Sanctis, *Storia della letteratura italiana*, vol. 2, Feltrinelli, 1960, p. 106.
30 Giacomo Leopardi, *Discorso sopra lo stato presente dei costumi degl'italiani*, Marsilio, 1989, p. 132.
31 On the Italian Risorgimento, with an emphasis on it being a cultural phenomenon, see Alberto Mario Banti, *Il Risorgimento Italiano*, Laterza, 2008.
32 Nicholas Boyle, *Goethe: The Poet and the Age*, vol. 1, *The Poetry of Desire*, Clarendon Press, 1991, p. 5.

33 Johann Wolfgang von Goethe and Johann Peter Eckermann, *Conversations of Goethe with Johann Peter Eckermann*, Da Capo Press, 1998, pp. 280–1.
34 Winkler, *Germany*, pp. 33–4.
35 Hinrich C. Seeba, '"Germany: A Literary Concept": The Myth of National Literature', *German Studies Review* 17, no. 2, May 1994, p. 358.
36 Heinrich Heine, 'Concerning the History of Religion and Philosophy in Germany', in *The Romantic School and Other Essays*, ed. Jost Hermans and Robert C. Holub, Continuum, 1985, pp. 243–4.
37 Seeba, '"Germany: A Literary Concept"', pp. 356–8.
38 Steven Moore, *The Novel: An Alternative History, 1600–1800*, Bloomsbury, 2013, pp. 61 ff.
39 Winkler, *Germany*, p. 60, where *stamm* is translated as race.
40 Germaine de Staël, *Considérations sur les principaux évenemens [sic] de la Révolution française, depuis son origine jusques et compris le 8 Juillet 1815*, in *Œuvres complètes de Mme de Staël*, vol. 3, Dambray Fils, 1820, p. 31.
41 See Glenda Sluga, *The Invention of International Order: Remaking Europe After Napoleon*, Princeton University Press, 2021.
42 Giulio Bollati, *L'italiano. Il carattere nazionale come storia e come invenzione*, Einaudi, 1983, p. 23.
43 Vincenzo Gioberti, *Del primato morale e civile degli italiani*, vol. 2, S. Bonamici e compagnia, 1846, pp. 104–5.
44 Christopher Duggan, *Francesco Crispi: From Nation to Nationalism*, Oxford University Press, 2002, p. 163.
45 Ibid., pp.175 ff; Lucy Riall, *Garibaldi: Invention of a Hero*, Yale University Press, 2007, pp. 3–4, 237, 365.
46 Francesco Barbagallo, *La questione italiana. Il Nord e il Sud dal 1860 a oggi*, Laterza, 2013, p. 7.
47 William Gladstone, *Two Letters to the Earl of Aberdeen, on the State Prosecutions of the Neapolitan Government*, John Murray, 1851, p. 9.
48 Elena Bacchin, *Italofilia. Opinione pubblica britannica e risorgimento italiano 1847–1864*, Carocci, 2014, pp. 51, 63, 66, 231, 241.
49 On Garibaldi's reception in England and the subsequent cult, as well as opposition to it, see Riall, *Garibaldi*, pp. 334–42.
50 George Macaulay Trevelyan, *Garibaldi's Defence of the Roman Republic* (1907); *Garibaldi and the Thousand* (1909); and *Garibaldi and the Making of Italy* (1911).
51 Riall, *Garibaldi*, p. 322.
52 Nelson Moe, '"Altro che Italia!" Il Sud dei piemontesi (1860–61)', *Meridiana* 15, September 1992, pp. 86–7.
53 John A. Davies, *Conflict and Control: Law and Order in Nineteenth-Century Italy*, Macmillan, 1988, p. 160.
54 Ibid., p. 171.
55 Ibid., p. 188.
56 Duggan, *Francesco Crispi*, pp. 1, 241, 426–7.
57 Ermanno Rea, *La fabbrica dell'obbedienza. Il lato oscuro e complice degli italiani*, Feltrinelli, 2011, pp. 97, 162–4.
58 Lucy Riall, *The Italian Risorgimento: State, Society and National Unification*, Routledge, 1994, p. 73.
59 Antonio Gramsci, 'Il problema della direzione politica nella formazione e nello sviluppo della nazione e dello Stato moderno in Italia', in *Quaderni del Carcere*, quaderno 19, §24, available at quadernidelcarcere.wordpress.com.
60 Antonio Gramsci, 'Machiavelli', in *Quaderni del Carcere*, quaderno 15, §11, available at quadernidelcarcere.wordpress.com.

61 Barbagallo, *La questione italiana*, pp. 48–9.
62 Francesco Saverio Nitti, 'La ricchezza dell'Italia', in Lucio Villari, ed., *Il capitalismo Italiano del Novecento*, vol. 1, Laterza, 1975, pp. 40–1.
63 Winkler, *Germany*, p. 64.
64 Brigitte Hamann, *Hitler's Vienna: A Dictator's Apprenticeship*, Oxford University Press, 1999, p. 405.
65 Winkler, *Germany*, p. 91.
66 Taylor was the chief proponent of this view. See A. J. P. Taylor, *Bismarck: The Man and the Statesman*, Hamish Hamilton, 1955.
67 William Carr, *A History of Germany, 1815–1985*, Edward Arnold, 1987, p. 83; for an early discussion of this unsolvable debate, see Otto Pflanz, 'Bismarck and German Nationalism', *American Historical Review* 60, no. 3, April 1955, pp. 548–66.
68 Lothar Gall, *Bismarck: The White Revolutionary*, vol. 1, *1815–1871*, Unwin Hyman, 1986, p. 29.
69 Speech on 29 January 1863, quoted in ibid., p. 226.
70 Karl Marx, 'The Bourgeoisie and the Counter-revolution', *Neue Rheinische Zeitung* 169, December 1848, available at marxists.org.
71 Karl Marx, 'A Contribution to the Critique of Hegel's Philosophy of Right', first published in *Deutsch-Französische Jahrbücher*, February 1844, available at marxists.org.
72 Paul Bairoch, 'Niveaux de développement économique de 1810 à 1910', *Annales* 20, no. 6, November–December 1965, p. 1096.
73 The debate is endless. See Ralf Dahrendorf, *Society and Democracy in Germany*, W. W. Norton, 1967; Gordon A. Craig, *Germany 1866–1945*, Oxford University Press, 1978; Jürgen Kocka, 'German History Before Hitler: The Debate About the German Snderweg', *Journal of Contemporary History* 23, no. 1, January 1988, pp. 3–16; George. L. Mosse, *The Crisis of German Ideology: Intellectual Origins of the Third Reich*, Grosset & Dunlap, 1964; David Blackbourn and Geoff Eley, *The Peculiarities of German History: Bourgeois Society and Politics in 19th-Century Germany*, Oxford University Press, 1984.
74 Margaret Lavinia Anderson, 'Voter, Junker, Landrat, Priest: The Old Authorities and the New Franchise in Imperial Germany', *American Historical Review* 98, no. 5, December 1993, p. 1450.
75 José Antonio Aguilar Rivera, Eduardo Posada-Carbó and Eduardo Zimmermann, 'Democracy in Spanish America: The Early Adoption of Universal Male Suffrage, 1810–1853', *Past and Present* 256, no. 1, August 2022, pp. 165–202.
76 David Blackbourn, *Populists and Patricians: Essays in Modern German History*, Routledge, 2014, p. 160.
77 Carr, *A History of Germany*, p. 134.

5 The Rise and Fall of the Russian Revolution

1 David Shearer, 'From Divided Consensus to Creative Disorder: Soviet History in Britain and North America', *Cahiers du monde russe* 39, no. 4, October–December 1998, p. 560.
2 Sheila Fitzpatrick, 'Revisionism in Soviet History', *History and Theory* 46, no. 4, December 2007, p. 80.
3 Central Committee of the CPSU, *History of the Communist Party of the Soviet Union (Bolsheviks)*, International Publishers, 1939, pp. 212–14.
4 Nikolai Bukharin and Evgenii Preobrazhensky, *The ABC of Communism*, ed. E. H. Carr, Pelican, 1969, p. 186.
5 Stalin, *The Foundation of Leninism*, in *Works*, vol. 6, Foreign Languages Publishing, 1953, pp. 71–196, available at marxists.org.

6 Originally in *Izvestiia* 232, 7 December 1917, pp. 1–2, available at Seventeen Moments in Soviet History, soviethistory.msu.edu.
7 Cited in Stephen White, 'Communism and the East: The Baku Congress, 1920', *Slavic Review* 33, no. 3, September 1974, p. 500.
8 See August von Haxthausen, *The Russian Empire: Its People, Institutions and Resources*, vol. 2, Chapman and Hall, 1856, pp. 229–30; this is a shortened translation of the original.
9 On the impact of outside ideas and themes on the Russian Revolution, see Matthew Rendle, 'Making Sense of 1917: Towards a Global History of the Russian Revolution', *Slavic Review* 76, no. 3, Fall 2017.
10 See the comments in Steven Smith, 'Writing the History of the Russian Revolution After the Fall of Communism', *Europe-Asia Studies* 46, no. 4, 1994, p. 576.
11 The uncertainties concerning the form of the new state in October 1917 are ably discussed by Richard Sakwa in 'The Commune State in Moscow in 1918', *Slavic Review* 46, no. 3, Autumn–Winter 1987, pp. 429–49.
12 Dominic Lieven, *Towards the Flame: Empire, War and the End of Tsarist Russia*, Allen Lane, 2015, p. 351.
13 Vladimir Mayakovsky, *Vladimir Ilyich Lenin. A Poem*, Progress Publishers, 1970, pp. 108–10.
14 *The Debate on Soviet Power: Minutes of the All-Russian Central Executive Committee of Soviets*, ed. John L. H. Keep, Clarendon Press, 1979, p. 355.
15 Richard Pipes, 'Did the Russian Revolution Have to Happen?', *American Scholar* 63, no. 2, Spring 1994, p. 224; this idea is constantly repeated throughout Pipes's works on 1917, as for instance in the chapter 'The October Coup', in *The Russian Revolution, 1899–1919* (1990).
16 This point is made in Stephen A. Smith, *The Russian Revolution: A Very Short Introduction*, Oxford University Press, 2002, p. 38.
17 V. I. Lenin, 'The Tasks of the Proletariat in Our Revolution', in *Collected Works*, vol. 24, Progress Publishers, 1964, p. 61.
18 Shakespeare, *Coriolanus*, III, i.
19 Lenin, 'The Tasks of the Proletariat', p. 60.
20 Christopher Read, 'Ten Months that No Longer Shake the World? The Centenary of the Russian Revolution and Beyond', *Revolutionary Russia* 34, no. 1, 2021, p. 126; this article provides fascinating and detailed account of the state of scholarship one hundred years after the revolution.
21 Lars Kleberg, *Theatre as Action: Soviet Russian Avant-Garde Aesthetics*, Macmillan, 1993, p. 64.
22 Katerina Clark, *Petersburg, Crucible of Cultural Revolution*, Harvard University Press, 1996, pp. 122–3.
23 Kleberg, *Theatre as Action*, pp. 65–6; presumably the forced evacuation of the White Army from Crimea.
24 Elizabeth Henderson, 'Majakovskij and Eisenstein Celebrate the Tenth Anniversary', *Slavic and East European Journal* 22, no. 2, Summer 1978, p. 158; see also Lola Lorant, review of *Nikolai Evreinov and Others: 'The Storming of the Winter Palace'*, in Inke Arns, Sylvia Sasse and Igor Chubarov, eds, *Critique d'art*, 25 May 2019.
25 Kleberg, *Theatre as Action*, pp. 2–3.
26 Christopher Read, 'Centennial Thoughts on an Exhausted (?) Revolution', *Revolutionary Russia* 3, no. 2, 2018, p. 194.
27 Sheila Fitzpatrick, 'Celebrating (or Not) the Russian Revolution', *Journal of Contemporary History* 52, no. 4, October 2017, pp. 285–6.
28 Read, 'Ten Months That No Longer Shake the World?', p. 91.

29 Mark D. Steinberg, *The Fall of the Romanovs: Political Dreams and Personal Struggles in a Time of Revolution*, Yale University Press, 1995, pp. 42, 60.
30 See letters to the tsar from General Brusilov and General Alekseev, in ibid., pp. 90–1.
31 Barbara Jelavich, *History of the Balkans*, vol. 2, Cambridge University Press, 1983, p. 136.
32 Figures from Nadège Mougel, *World War I Casualties*, trans. Julie Gratz, Centre Virtuel de la Connaissance sur l'Europe, 2011 (includes list of sources; figures have been rounded up or down).
33 The text of the Durnovo memorandum is in Frank A. Golder, ed., *Documents of Russian History, 1914–1917*, Century Co., 1927, pp. 3–23; for a contextualization of the memorandum, see David M. McDonald, 'The Durnovo Memorandum in Context: Official Conservatism and the Crisis of Autocracy', *Jahrbücher für Geschichte Osteuropas* 44, no. 4, 1996, pp. 481–502.
34 Leopold H. Haimson, 'The Problem of Political and Social Stability in Urban Russia on the Eve of War and Revolution Revisited', *Slavic Review* 59, no. 4, Winter 2000, pp. 850, 851, 864.
35 Alekseï Alekseevich Brusilov, *A Soldier's Note-book, 1914–1918*, Greenwood Press, 1971, p. 37.
36 S. A. Smith, 'Citizenship and the Russian Nation During World War I: A Comment', *Slavic Review* 59, no. 2, Summer 2000, p. 324.
37 Marc Ferro, 'The Aspirations of Russian Society', in Richard Pipies, ed., *Revolutionary Russia*, Harvard University Press, 1968, pp. 143–8.
38 Anna Akhmatova, 'In Memoriam, July 19, 1914', in *The Complete Poems of Anna Akhmatova*, 2nd ed., ed. Roberta Reeder, trans. Judith Hemschemeyer, Zephyr Press 1992, p. 210.
39 Alexandra Kollontai, 'International Women's Day', 1920, marxists.org. See also Elizabeth A. Wood, 'February 23 and March 8: Two Holidays That Upstaged the February Revolution', *Slavic Review* 76, no. 3, Fall 2017, p. 732.
40 Wood, 'February 23 and March 8', p. 733.
41 See Lenin, 'The Tasks of the Proletariat', pp. 19–26.
42 Ibid., p. 62.
43 V. I. Lenin, 'The Proletarian Revolution and the Renegade Kautsky', in *Collected Works*, vol. 28, Progress Publishers, 1965, p. 301.
44 Mike Haynes, 'Liberals, Jacobins and Grey Masses in 1917', in Mike Haynes and Jim Wolfreys, eds, *History and Revolution: Refuting Revisionism*, Verso, 2007, p. 110.
45 Marc Ferro, 'The Russian Soldier in 1917: Undisciplined, Patriotic, and Revolutionary', *Slavic Review* 30, no. 3, September 1971, pp. 484, 490.
46 Karl Marx, *The Eighteenth Brumaire of Louis Bonaparte*, Progress Publishers, 1967, p. 106.
47 Ferro, 'The Russian Soldier', pp. 504–6.
48 Ibid., p. 500.
49 Ronald Grigor Suny, 'Toward a Social History of the October Revolution', *American Historical Review* 88, no. 1, February 1983, p. 38.
50 V. I. Lenin, *State and Revolution*, in *Collected Works*, vol. 25, Progress Publishers, 1964, pp. 381–492.
51 Norman E. Saul, 'Lenin's Decision to Seize Power: The Influence of Events in Finland', *Soviet Studies* 24, no. 4, April 1973, p. 493.
52 V. I. Lenin, 'Lessons of the Revolution', in *Collected Works*, vol. 25, p. 227.
53 V. I. Lenin, *One Step Forward, Two Steps Back*, in *Collected Works*, vol. 7, Progress Publishers, 1961, p. 412.
54 Friedrich Engels, letter to Vera Zasulich, 23 April 1885, in Karl Marx and Friedrich

Engels, *The Selected Correspondence of Marx and Engels*, Martin Lawrence, 1934, pp. 437–8.
55 James D. White, 'The Kornilov Affair: A Study in Counter-revolution', *Soviet Studies* 20, no. 2, October 1968, pp. 187–90, 199, 203, 205.
56 Katkov doubted Kornilov had planned anything resembling a coup; see George Katkov, *The Kornilov Affair: Kerensky and the Break-up of the Russian Army*, Longman, 1980; Kornilov himself, claimed Katkov, was the victim of a Kerensky-inspired conspiracy.
57 Harvey Asher, 'The Kornilov Affair: A Reinterpretation', *Russian Review* 29, no. 3, July 1970, pp. 289, 299, 300. Kerensky called his 1919 book *The Prelude to Bolshevism: The Kornilov Rising*.
58 S. A. Smith, review of *October 1917: A Social History of the Russian Revolution* by Marc Ferro, *Soviet Studies* 33, no. 3, July 1981, p. 458.
59 V. I. Lenin, 'The Bolsheviks Must Assume Power: A Letter to the Central Committee and the Petrograd and Moscow Committees of The R.S.D.L.P.(B.)', 12–14 September 1917, in *Collected Works*, vol. 26, Progress Publishers, 1964, p. 19; Saul, 'Lenin's Decision to Seize Power', p. 500.
60 Alexander Rabinowitch, *The Bolsheviks Come to Power*, Pluto Press, 2004, p. xxi.
61 V. I. Lenin, 'Letter to Bolshevik Party Members', 18 October 1917, in *Collected Works*, vol. 26, pp. 217.
62 Marina Tsvetaeva (1892–1941) 'Night. Northeaster', in *1917: Stories and Poems from the Russian Revolution*, ed. and trans. Boris Dralyuk, Pushkin Press, 2016.
63 Alexander Blok, 'Twelve', trans. Maria Carlson, Russian Poetry in Translations, ruverses.com.
64 Quoted in Catherine Merridale, *Lenin on the Train*, Allen Lane, 2016, p. 43.
65 Lieven, *Towards the Flame*, p. 354.
66 Richard Sakwa, 'Russia's Identity: Between the "Domestic" and the "International"', *Europe-Asia Studies* 63, no. 6, August 2011, p. 958.
67 Quoted in Haynes, 'Liberals, Jacobins and Grey Masses in 1917', p. 116.
68 Graeme J. Gill, 'The Mainsprings of Peasant Action in 1917', *Soviet Studies* 30, no. 1, January 1978, pp. 65, 67, 76; for a quantitative analysis of peasant unrest in this period, see Evgeny Finkel, Scott Gehlbach and Dmitrii Kofanov, '(Good) Land and Freedom (for Former Serfs): Determinants of Peasant Unrest in European Russia, March–October 1917', *Slavic Review* 76, no. 3, Fall 2017, pp. 710–21.
69 Orlando Figes, 'The Russian Revolution of 1917 and Its Language in the Villages', *Russian Review* 56, no. 3, July 1997, pp. 331–2.
70 Gill, 'The Mainsprings of Peasant Action in 1917', p. 80.
71 Maureen Perrie, 'The Russian Peasant Movement of 1905–1907: Its Social Composition and Revolutionary Significance', *Past and Present* 57, November 1972, p. 128.
72 Anna Geifman, *Thou Shalt Kill: Revolutionary Terrorism in Russia, 1894–1917*, Princeton University Press, 1993, pp. 12–13, 21.
73 Hans Rogger, *Russia in the Age of Modernization and Revolution 1881–1917*, Longman, 1983, p. 76.
74 Leo Tolstoy, *Diaries*, vol. 1, *1847–1894*, ed. Reginald F. Christian, Faber & Faber, 1985, p. 184.
75 David Macey, 'Reflections on Peasant Adaptation in Rural Russia at the Beginning of the Twentieth Century: The Stolypin Agrarian Reforms', *Journal of Peasant Studies* 31, nos 3–4, 2004, p. 407.
76 For a more nuanced view, see Macey, 'Reflections on Peasant Adaptation', pp. 400–26.
77 Lieven, *Towards the Flame*, p. 65.
78 V. I. Lenin, 'Two Tactics of Social-Democracy in the Democratic Revolution', in *Collected Works*, vol. 9, Progress Publishers, 1962, p. 50.

79 V. I. Lenin, 'The Attitude of Social Democracy to the Peasant Movement', in *Collected Works*, vol. 9, p. 237.
80 Franco Venturi, *Roots of Revolution: A History of the Populist and Socialist Movements in Nineteenth Century Russia*, Grosset & Dunlap, 1966, p. 518.
81 V. I. Lenin, 'Lecture on the 1905 Revolution', delivered in Zurich on 22 January 1917, in *Collected Works*, vol. 23, Progress Publishers, 1964, pp. 236, 239.
82 A riveting account of the assassination can be found in Venturi, *Roots of Revolution*, pp. 709–20.
83 David A. Macey, *Government and Peasant in Russia, 1861–1906: The Prehistory of the Stolypin Reforms*, Northern Illinois University Press, 1987, p. 63.
84 Jonathan D. Smele, *The 'Russian' Civil Wars 1916–1926: Ten Years That Shook the World*, Oxford University Press, 2015, p. 10.
85 Abraham Ascher, *The Revolution of 1905: Russia in Disarray*, Stanford University Press, 1988, pp. 87–9.
86 Hugh Seton-Watson, *The Russian Empire, 1801–1917*, Clarendon Press, 1967, p. 608.
87 Charles A. Ruud and Sergei A. Stepanov, *Fontanka 16: The Tsars' Secret Police*, McGill-Queen's University Press, 1999, pp. 174–9.
88 O. G. Bukhovets, 'The Political Consciousness of the Russian Peasantry in the Revolution of 1905–1907: Sources, Methods, and Some Results', *Russian Review* 47, no. 4, October 1988, p. 358.
89 Perrie, 'The Russian Peasant Movement of 1905–1907', p. 123.
90 Leopold Haimson and Eric Brian, 'Labor Unrest in Imperial Russia During the First World War. A Quantitative Analysis and Interpretation', in Leopold Haimson and Giulio Sapelli, eds, *Strikes, Social Conflict and the First World War: An International Perspective*, Feltrinelli, 1992, pp. 390–1.
91 Lenin, 'The Tasks of the Proletariat', p. 71.
92 Sarah Badcock, '"We're for the Muzhiks' Party!" Peasant Support for the Socialist Revolutionary Party During 1917', *Europe-Asia Studies* 53, no. 1, January 2001, p. 133.
93 Antonello Venturi, 'L'impossibile sconfitta dei socialisti-rivoluzionari russi', *Meridiana* 88, 2017, p. 114.
94 Badcock, '"We're for the Muzhiks' Party!"', p. 140.
95 Venturi, 'L'impossibile sconfitta dei socialisti-rivoluzionari russi', p. 118.
96 Moshe Lewin, *Russian Peasants and Soviet Power: A Study of Collectivization*, Northwestern University Press, 1968, p. 133.
97 Oliver Henry Radkey, *Russia Goes to the Polls: The Election to the All-Russian Constituent Assembly, 1917*, Cornell University Press, 1989, pp. 150–1. This is the best available source (Radkey revises the data from his previous 1950 study).
98 V. I. Lenin, 'The Constituent Assembly Elections and The Dictatorship of the Proletariat', in *Collected Works*, vol. 30, Progress Publishers, 1965, p. 256.
99 Radkey, *Russia Goes to the Polls*, pp. 150–1.
100 E. H. Carr, *The Bolshevik Revolution 1917–23*, vol. 1, Penguin, 1983, p. 120.
101 Ibid., pp. 127–30.
102 Quoted in Merridale, *Lenin on the Train*, p. 89.
103 Carr, *The Bolshevik Revolution*, p. 7.
104 V. I. Lenin, 'Political Report of the Central Committee, Extraordinary Seventh Congress of the R.C.P.(B)', 7 March, 1918, *Collected Works*, vol. 27, Progress Publishers, 1965, p. 92.
105 Alexander Rabinowitch, *The Bolsheviks Come to Power*, Norton, 1976, p. 294.
106 Alexander Rabinowitch, 'The Evolution of Local Soviets in Petrograd, November 1917–June 1918: The Case of the First City District Soviet', *Slavic Review* 46, no. 1, Spring 1987, pp. 21–3.

107 Rita Augestad Knudsen, 'Moments of Self-Determination: The Concept of "Self-Determination" and the Idea of Freedom in 20th- and 21st-Century International Discourse', PhD thesis, London School of Economics and Political Science, October 2013, pp. 59 ff, 68. That Lenin had been the pioneer in this field was recognized in the *American Political Science Review* as early as 1918; see Charles G. Fenwick, 'The Russian Peace Treaties', *American Political Science Review* 12, no. 4, November 1918, pp. 706–11.

108 The next paragraphs rely on Borislav Chernev, *Twilight of Empire: The Brest-Litovsk Conference and the Re-making of East-Central Europe, 1917–1918*, University of Toronto Press, 2017.

109 Stephen F. Cohen, *Bukharin and the Bolshevik Revolution: A Political Biography, 1888–1938*, Oxford University Press, 1980, pp. 62–3.

110 Lenin, 'Political Report of the Central Committee, Extraordinary Seventh Congress', p. 101.

111 Alexander Rabinowitch, 'Early Disenchantment with Bolshevik Rule: New Data from the Archives of the Extraordinary Assembly of Delegates from Petrograd Factories', in Kevin McDermott and John Morison, eds, *Politics and Society Under the Bolsheviks*, Macmillan, 1999, p. 41.

112 Richard Sakwa, *Soviet Communists in Power: A Study of Moscow During the Civil War, 1918–21*, St Martin's Press, 1988, pp. 94–5, 240–4.

113 Lieven, *Towards the Flame*, p. 52.

114 Ibid., pp. 53–6.

115 Lenin, '"Left-Wing" Communism: An Infantile Disorder', in *Collected Works*, vol. 31, Progress Publishers, 1966, p. 37.

116 Frederick Engels, *The Principles of Communism*, Pluto Press/Monthly Review, n.d., p. 14.

117 Lenin, 'Political Report of the Central Committee, Extraordinary Seventh Congress', p. 95.

118 Ibid., pp. 98–9.

119 Moshe Lewin, *The Soviet Century*, Verso, 2005, p. 20.

120 Ibid., pp. 22–3.

121 V. I. Lenin, 'Memo to the Political Bureau on Combating Dominant Nation Chauvinism', 6 October 1922, in *Collected Works*, vol. 33, Progress Publishers, 1965, p. 372; see also Lewin, *The Soviet Century*, p. 25.

122 Jonathan D. Smele, *Historical Dictionary of the Russian Civil Wars, 1916–1926*, Rowman & Littlefield, 2015, pp. 2, 253 (citing Russian sources Vadim V. Erlikhman and Iurii. A. Poliakov). See also Jochen Böhler, 'Enduring Violence: The Postwar Struggles in East-Central Europe, 1917–21', *Journal of Contemporary History* 50, no. 1, January 2015, p. 63, who reports similar figures.

123 Jonathan D. Smele, *Civil War in Siberia: The Anti-Bolshevik Government of Admiral Kolchak 1918–20*, Cambridge University Press, 1996, p. 120. This and the next paragraph rely on what is *the* book on Kolchak.

124 Charlotte Alston, 'The Suggested Basis for a Russian Federal Republic: Britain, Anti-Bolshevik Russia and the Border States at the Paris Peace Conference, 1919', *History* 91, no. 1, January 2006, pp. 28–30.

125 Mark Lipovetsky, 'Screening the Revolution: Transformations of the Revolutionary Narrative in Russian Film since the 1960s', in Megan Swift, ed., *Revolutionary Aftereffects: Material, Social, and Cultural Legacies of 1917 in Russia Today*, University of Toronto Press, 2022, p. 235.

126 Irina Astashkevich, *Gendered Violence: Jewish Women in the Pogroms of 1917 to 1921*, Academic Studies Press, 2018, p. 66.

127 Orlando Figes, *A People's Tragedy: The Russian Revolution 1891–1924*, Pimlico, 1997, pp. 717, 666.
128 Böhler, 'Enduring Violence', p. 70.
129 See Jamie Bisher, *White Terror: Cossack Warlords of the Trans-Siberian*, Routledge, 2009, pp. 59–60; Richard Pipes, *Russia Under the Bolshevik Regime*, Knopf, 1994, p. 46.
130 William S. Graves, *America's Siberian Adventure, 1918–1920*, Jonathan Cape and Harrison Smith, 1931, see in particular ch. 7, 'Kolchak and Recognition'.
131 Paul Du Quenoy, 'Warlordism à la russe: Baron von Ungern-Sternberg's anti-Bolshevik crusade, 1917–21', *Revolutionary Russia* 16, no. 2, 2003, p. 8, quoting *Asian Odyssey*, (1940), an autobiographical account of Dmitri Alioshin who served in Siberia and Mongolia under General Kolchak and Baron von Ungern-Sternberg.
132 Du Quenoy, 'Warlordism à la russe', p. 2.
133 John Jennings and Chuck Steele, eds, *The Worst Military Leaders in History*, Reaktion Books, 2022, entry by John Jennings who put him under the rubric 'criminal'.
134 Erik C. Landis, 'Waiting for Makhno: Legitimacy and Context in a Russian Peasant War', *Past and Present* 183, May 2004, pp. 209, 218.
135 Astashkevich, *Gendered Violence*, p. 60. Matters improved once the communists were in control: according to the Yad Vashem website: 'In the late 1920s and early 1930s Kazatin had a Jewish council that held its deliberations in Yiddish [and] there were Yiddish-language schools in the town.' See 'Kazatin', Yad Vashem, yadvashem.org.
136 Leon Trotsky, 'The Southern Front: II. Denikin's Offensive (May 15–August 1919): The Makhno Movement', in *The Military Writings of Leon Trotsky*, vol. 2, *1919*, available at marxists.org.
137 Smele, *Historical Dictionary of the Russian Civil Wars*, p. 51.
138 See his 1927 appeal, 'To the Jews of All Countries', in Nestor Makhno Archive, nestormakhno.info.
139 Böhler, 'Enduring Violence', p. 66.
140 Norman Davies, *God's Playground: A History of Poland*, vol. 1, *The Origins to 1795*, Clarendon Press, 1981, p. 24.
141 Smele, *Historical Dictionary of the Russian Civil Wars*, p. 52.
142 Peter Holquist, 'The Russian Revolution as Continuum and Context and Yes – as Revolution', *Cahiers du Monde russe* 58, nos 1–2, January–June 2017, p. 94.
143 Rabinowitch, 'The Evolution of Local Soviets in Petrograd', p. 36.
144 Michael Karpovich, 'The Russian Revolution of 1917', *Journal of Modern History* 2, no. 2, June 1930, p. 227.
145 V. I. Lenin, 'The Ninth All-Russia Conference of the R.C.P. (B): Speech on the Immediate Tasks of Party Development', 24 September 1920, in *Collected Works*, vol. 42, Progress Publishers, 1969, pp. 207, 212.
146 Smele, *Historical Dictionary of the Russian Civil Wars*, pp. 38–40, 45–6, 61.
147 Richard Pipes, *The Russian Revolution, 1899–1919*, Knopf Doubleday, 2011 (1990), p. 838. The estimates are based on a projection from the official number of those executed in Ukraine in 1920 (fewer than 4,000). For a critical review of this text, see Israel Getzler, 'Richard Pipes's "Revisionist" *History of the Russian Revolution*', *Slavonic and East European Review* 70, no.1, January 1992, pp. 111–26.
148 Arno Mayer, *The Furies: Violence and Terror in the French and Russian Revolutions*, Princeton University Press, 2000, p. 295.
149 Astashkevich, *Gendered Violence*, p. 59.
150 V. I. Lenin, 'Anti-Jewish Pogroms', in *Collected Works*, vol. 29, Progress Publishers, 1965, pp. 252–3.
151 Elissa Bemporad, *Legacy of Blood: Jews, Pogroms, and Ritual Murder in the Lands of the Soviets*, Oxford University Press, 2019, pp. 10–14.

152 Orlando Figes, 'The Red Army and Mass Mobilization During the Russian Civil War 1918–1920', *Past and Present* 129, November 1990, pp. 195–6.
153 V. I. Lenin, 'Comrade Workers, Forward to the Last, Decisive Fight!', in *Collected Works*, vol. 28, pp. 55–6.
154 V. I. Lenin, 'Speech at the Third All-Russia Conference of Directors of Adult Education', 25 February 1920, in *Collected Works*, vol. 30, p. 374.
155 Getzler, 'Richard Pipes's "Revisionist" *History*', p. 122.
156 See Oleg Budnitskii, 'The Jews and Revolution: Russian Perspectives, 1881–1918', *East European Jewish Affairs* 38, no. 3, 2008, p. 329.
157 Leonard Schapiro, 'The Role of the Jews in the Russian Revolutionary Movement', *Slavonic and East European Review* 11, December 1961, p. 164.
158 Joshua Sanborn, 'The Genesis of Russian Warlordism: Violence and Governance During the First World War and the Civil War', *Contemporary European History* 19, no. 3, August 2010, pp. 201, 209, quoting the 2006 Russian edition of Oleg Budnitskii's text – now translated as *Russian Jews Between the Reds and the Whites, 1917–1920*, University of Pennsylvania Press, 2012.
159 Böhler, 'Enduring Violence', p. 72.
160 Astashkevich, *Gendered Violence*, p. 27.
161 Ibid., p. 55.
162 Bemporad, *Legacy of Blood*, pp. 17 ff.
163 Astashkevich, *Gendered Violence*, p. 55.
164 An attempted defence of Petliura can be found here: Taras Hunczak, 'A Reappraisal of Symon Petliura and Ukrainian-Jewish Relations, 1917–1921', *Jewish Social Studies* 31, no. 3, July 1969, pp. 163–83. It is followed, in the same journal, by a refutation: Zosa Szajkowski, 'A Reappraisal of Symon Petliura and Ukrainian-Jewish Relations, 1917–1921: A Rebuttal', *Jewish Social Studies* 31, no. 3, July 1969, pp. 184–213.
165 On Russian history and counter-factualism see Georgi M. Derluguian, 'Alternative Pasts, Future Alternatives?', *Slavic Review* 63, no. 3, Autumn 2004, pp. 535–52, esp. p. 541; see also Jonathan D. Smele, '"If Grandma Had Whiskers ..." Could the Anti-Bolsheviks Have Won the Russian Revolutions and Civil Wars? Or, the Constraints and Conceits of Counterfactual History', *Revolutionary Russia* 33, no. 1, pp. 6–37; see also the rejoinder by Laura Engelstein, '"A Single Civilian Whore": Reflections on the Might-Have-Beens of the Russian Civil War', *Revolutionary Russia* 33, no. 1, pp. 50–63.
166 These concepts are central to Machiavelli's *The Prince*, but see esp. chs 6, 7, 8, 9 and 11; for an examination of these concepts, see Nicola Badaloni, 'Natura e società in Machiavelli', *Studi Storici* 10, no. 4, October–November 1969, pp. 675–708.
167 V. I. Lenin, 'Speech Delivered at the Third All-Russian Congress of Water Transport Workers', 15 March 1920, in *Collected Works*, vol. 30, p. 431.
168 V. I. Lenin, 'Our Revolution (Apropos of N. Sukhanov's Notes)', 16 January 1923, in *Collected Works*, vol. 33, p. 476.
169 V. I. Lenin, 'The Immediate Tasks of the Soviet Government', 28 April 1918, in *Collected Works*, vol. 27, pp. 243–4.
170 Bukharin and Preobrazhensky, *The ABC of Communism*, pp. 311–15; Cohen, *Bukharin and the Bolshevik Revolution*, pp. 83–4.
171 Silvana Malle, *The Economic Organization of War Communism, 1918–1921*, Cambridge University Press, 2002, pp. 50–2.
172 Confectionary was regarded as the food of the rich and had long been pilloried in tsarist Russia. See Ronald D. LeBlanc, 'Bonbons and Bolsheviks: The Stigmatization of Chocolate in Revolutionary Russia', *Languages, Literatures, and Cultures Scholarship* 452, 2018.

173 V. I. Lenin, 'The Tax in Kind', April 1921, in *Collected Works*, vol. 32, Progress Publishers, 1965, p. 342.
174 For a useful review of the differing positions, see Malle, *The Economic Organization of War Communism*, esp. pp. 3–28, and her discussion of Bukharin's initial position on War Communism. See also Paul Craig Roberts, '"War Communism": A Re-Examination', *Slavic Review* 29, no. 2, June 1970, pp. 238–61.
175 For a useful discussion on War Communism poised between ideology and war requirements, see Sakwa, *Soviet Communists in Power*, pp. 23–38; see also Antonella Salomoni, '"War Communism": A Reassessment', in Silvio Pons and Andrea Romano, eds, *Russia in the Age of Wars, 1914–1945*, Fondazione Feltrinelli, 2000, for whom the term was a 'rhetorical device invented in 1921' to underline the passage to the NEP, p. 55.
176 Bertram D. Wolfe, 'Leon Trotsky as Historian', *Slavic Review* 20, no. 3, October 1961, p. 497; on Kronstadt in 1917, see Israel Getzler, *Kronstadt 1917–1921: The Fate of a Soviet Democracy*, Cambridge University Press, 2002, pp. 19 ff.
177 Neil Croll, 'The Role of M. N. Tukhachevskii in the Suppression of the Kronstadt Rebellion', *Revolutionary Russia* 17, no. 2, 2004, p. 18.
178 Lenin, 'Speech Delivered at The All-Russia Congress of Transport Workers', 27 March 1921, in *Collected Works*, vol. 32, pp. 278–81.
179 Paul Avrich, *Kronstadt, 1921*, Princeton University Press, 1970, p. 112.
180 Ibid., pp. 52 ff.
181 Ibid., see the introduction, esp. p. 6.
182 Leon Trotsky, *Terrorism and Communism (Dictatorship versus Democracy): A Reply to Karl Kautsky*, 1920, ch. 8, available at marxists.org.
183 Lenin, 'The Tax in Kind', pp. 341–4.
184 Ibid., p. 345.
185 Ibid., p. 353.
186 Vincent Barnett, 'Soviet Commodity Markets During NEP', *Economic History Review* 48, no. 2, May 1995, p. 346.
187 Charles M. Edmondson, 'The Politics of Hunger: The Soviet Response to Famine, 1921', *Soviet Studies* 29, no. 4, October 1977, p. 508.
188 Cohen, *Bukharin and the Bolshevik Revolution*, p. 183.
189 Ibid., p. 146.
190 Richard Stites, 'Zhenotdel: Bolshevism and Russian Women, 1917–1930', *Russian History* 3, no. 2, 1976, p. 188.
191 Ibid., pp. 174, 180, 187–9, 192.
192 Simon Johnson and Peter Temin, 'The Macroeconomics of NEP', *Economic History Review* 46, no. 4, November 1993, p. 764.
193 E. H. Carr, *Socialism in One Country, 1924–1926*, vol. 1, Pelican Books, 1970, p. 353.
194 Ibid., p. 102.
195 E. H. Carr, *The Bolshevik Revolution, 1917–1923*, vol. 2, Penguin, 1972, p. 278.
196 Moshe Lewin, *Lenin's Last Struggle*, University of Michigan, 2005, p. 22.
197 J. Arch Getty and Oleg V. Naumov, *The Road to Terror: Stalin and the Self-Destruction of the Bolsheviks, 1932–1939*, Yale University Press, 1999, pp. 40–1.
198 William G. Rosenberg, 'Beheading the Revolution: Arno Mayer's "Furies"', *Journal of Modern History* 73, no. 4, December 2001, p. 925.
199 Theda Skocpol, 'Old Regime Legacies and Communist Revolutions in Russia and China', *Social Forces* 55, no. 2, December 1976, particularly p. 306.
200 Lars T. Lih makes a strong case that Bukharin did not see War Communism and the NEP as intrinsically contradictory: Lars T. Lih, 'Bukharin's "Illusion": War Communism and the Meaning of NEP', *Russian History* 27, no. 4, Winter 2000, pp. 417–59;

on Kamenev's position, see Alexis Pogorelskin, 'Kamenev and the Peasant Question: The Turn to Opposition, 1924–1925', *Russian History* 27, no. 4, Winter 2000, pp. 381–3; on Bukharin, see Cohen, *Bukharin and the Bolshevik Revolution*.

201 For Bukharin's speech, see Getty and Naumov, *The Road to Terror*, p. 46.
202 Sheila Fitzpatrick, *Stalin's Peasants: Resistance and Survival in the Russian Village After Collectivization*, Oxford University Press, 1994, p. 39.
203 Lewin, *Russian Peasants and Soviet Power*, pp. 273–4.
204 Fitzpatrick, *Stalin's Peasants*, p. 129.
205 A lucid discussion of the issue can be found in Mark Harrison, 'Why Was NEP Abandoned?', in Robert C. Stuart, ed., *The Soviet Rural Economy*, Rowman & Allanheld, 1984, pp. 63–78, and 'The Peasantry and Industrialisation', in R. W. Davies, ed., *From Tsarism to the New Economic Policy: Continuity and Change in the Economy of the USSR*, Macmillan Palgrave, 1990, pp. 104–26. See also Robert C. Allen, *Farm to Factory: A Reinterpretation of the Soviet Industrial Revolution*, Princeton University Press, 2004.
206 See R. W. Davies, *The Soviet Economy in Turmoil, 1929–1930*, Harvard University Press, 1989; Carr, *Socialism in One Country*, 3 vols; Skocpol, *States and Social Revolutions*, p. 225; Cohen, *Bukharin and the Bolshevik Revolution*; see also many of the contributors to Davies, *From Tsarism to the New Economic Policy*; see also William G. Rosenberg, 'The Problem of Market Relations and the State in Revolutionary Russia', *Comparative Studies in Society and History* 36, no. 2, April 1994, pp. 356–96.
207 Moshe Lewin, *The Making of the Soviet System: Essays in the Social History of Interwar Russia*, Pantheon Books, 1985, pp. 91, 116.
208 See Alexander A. Barsov, 'Balans stoimostnych obmenov mezdu gorodom i derevnei', Nauka, 1969, whose data were used by James Millar in his landmark 'Soviet Rapid Development and the Agricultural Surplus Hypothesis', *Soviet Studies* 22, no. 1, July 1970, pp. 77–93. My remarks are based on Paul Gregory, 'The Soviet Agricultural Surplus: A Retrospective', *Europe-Asia Studies* 61, no. 4, June 2009, pp. 669–83. See also Michael Ellman, 'Did the Agricultural Surplus Provide the Resources for the Increase in Investment in the USSR During the First Five Year Plan?', *Economic Journal* 85, no. 340, December 1975, pp. 844–63.
209 Davies, *From Tsarism to the New Economic Policy*, p. 26.
210 Sheila Fitzpatrick, 'Stalin and the Making of a New Elite, 1928–1939', *Slavic Review* 38, no. 3, September 1979, pp. 377–402, esp. pp. 399–401.
211 Ibid., p. 381.
212 Georgi Dimitrov, *The Diary of Georgi Dimitrov, 1933–1949*, Yale University Press, 2003, p. 66.
213 Sheila Fitzpatrick, *The Russian Revolution, 1917–1932*, Oxford University Press, 2008, p. 11.
214 James R. Millar, 'Mass Collectivization and the Contribution of Soviet Agriculture to the First Five-Year Plan: A Review Article', *Slavic Review* 33, no. 4, December 1974, p. 764.
215 Daniel Stone, 'The Economic Origins of the Soviet Famine of 1932–1933: Some Views from Poland', *Polish Review* 37, no. 2, 1992, p. 177.
216 Lewin, *The Making of the Soviet System*, p. 303.
217 Fitzpatrick, *Stalin's Peasants*, p. 233.
218 Mark Harrison, 'Why Did NEP Fail?', Department of Economics, University of Warwick, pp. 6–8; subsequently published in *Economics of Planning* 16, no. 2, January 1980, pp. 57–67.
219 J. V. Stalin, 'Dizzy with Success: *Concerning Questions of the Collective-Farm*

Movement', *Pravda*, 2 March 1930, and in Stalin, *Works*, vol. 12, Foreign Languages Publishing, 1955, available at marxists.org.
220 Getty and Naumov, *The Road to Terror*, pp. 43–4.
221 R. W. Davies, 'Industry', in R. W. Davies, Mark Harrison and Stephen G. Wheatcroft, eds, *The Economic Transformation of the Soviet Union, 1913–1945*, Cambridge University Press, 1994, p. 140.
222 Fitzpatrick, *Stalin's Peasants*, pp. 80, 153.
223 Ibid., p. 74.
224 Stephen G. Wheatcroft, 'More Light on the Scale of Repression and Excess Mortality in the Soviet Union in the 1930s', *Soviet Studies* 42, no. 2, April 1990, p. 358.
225 Stephen Kotkin, *Stalin*, vol. 2, *Waiting for Hitler, 1928–1941*, Penguin, 2017, p. 127.
226 Jacques Vallin, France Meslé, Serguei Adamets and Serhii Pyrozhkov, 'A New Estimate of Ukrainian Population Losses During the Crises of the 1930s and 1940s', *Population Studies* 56, no. 3, November 2002, p. 262; see also Alec Nove, 'How Many Victims in the 1930s? II', *Soviet Studies* 42, no. 4, October 1990, p. 812.
227 Kotkin, *Stalin*, vol. 2, p. 129.
228 R. W. Davies and Stephen G. Wheatcroft, 'Stalin and the Soviet Famine of 1932–33: A Reply to Ellman', *Europe-Asia Studies* 58, no. 4, June 2006, p. 632.
229 Catherine Merridale, 'The 1937 Census and the Limits of Stalinist Rule', *Historical Journal* 39, no. 1, March 1996, p. 239.
230 Mark B. Tauger, 'The 1932 Harvest and the Famine of 1933', *Slavic Review* 50, no. 1, Spring 1991, p. 89. Graziosi, however, thinks the famine in Ukraine was directed against nationalist aspirations; see Andrea Graziosi, 'The Soviet 1931–1933 Famines and the Ukrainian Holodomor: Is a New Interpretation Possible, and What Would Its Consequences Be?', *Harvard Ukrainian Studies* 27, no. 1/4, 2004–2005, pp. 97–115, esp. p. 106.
231 Sarah Cameron, *The Hungry Steppe: Famine, Violence, and the Making of Soviet Kazakhstan*, Cornell University Press, 2018; see also Niccolò Pianciola, 'The Collectivization Famine in Kazakhstan, 1931–1933', *Harvard Ukrainian Studies* 25, nos 3–4, Fall 2001, pp. 237–51. On the debate of whether the famine and its consequences could be described as 'genocidal', see the contributions to Norman Naimark, *Stalin's Genocides*: 'Perspectives on Norman Naimark's *Stalin's Genocides*' by Mark Kramer, Joshua Rubenstein, Paul Hollander, Andrea Graziosi, Jeffrey S. Hardy, Michael Ellman, Roman Szporluk, Jeffrey J. Rossman and Norman Naimark, *Journal of Cold War Studies* 14, no. 3, Summer 2012, pp. 149–89.
232 Michael Ellman, 'Stalin and the Soviet Famine of 1932–33 Revisited', *Europe-Asia Studies* 59, no. 4, June 2007, pp. 674, 677.
233 Fitzpatrick, *Stalin's Peasants*, pp. 42–3, 47.
234 J. Arch Getty and William Chase, 'Patterns of Repression Among the Soviet Elite in the Late 1930s: A Biographical Approach', in J. Arch Getty and Roberta T. Manning, eds, *Stalinist Terror: New Perspectives*, Cambridge University Press, 1993, p. 229.
235 Sheila Fitzpatrick, 'Workers Against Bosses: The Impact of the Great Purges on Labor-Management Relations', in Lewis H. Siegelbaum and Ronald Grigor Suny, eds, *Making Workers Soviet: Power, Class, and Identity*, Cornell University Press, 1994, p. 338.
236 J. Arch Getty, 'State and Society Under Stalin: Constitutions and Elections in the 1930s', *Slavic Review* 50, no. 1, Spring 1991, pp. 18–35, esp. pp. 28–32.
237 Sidney and Beatrice Webb, *The Truth About Soviet Russia*, Longmans, Green & Co., 1942, p. 19; their admiration for Stalin's Russia was made clear in their 1935 book *Soviet Communism: A New Civilisation?*.

238 Joseph R. Starr, 'The New Constitution of the Soviet Union', *American Political Science Review* 30, no. 6, December 1936, p. 1151.
239 For instance, at the Eleventh Congress of the Communist Party (March 1922), when he discussed the New Economic Policy as a necessary and 'incredibly difficult' retreat. Lenin, *Collected Works*, vol. 33, p. 282.
240 E. H. Carr, 'Stalin', *Soviet Studies* 5, no. 1, July 1953, p. 5.
241 Lewin, *The Soviet Century*, p. 45.
242 J. Arch Getty, 'The Politics of Repression Revisited', in Getty and Manning, *Stalinist Terror*, p. 51.
243 Sakwa, *Soviet Communists in Power*, p. 152.
244 Gábor Tamás Rittersporn, 'Rethinking Stalinism', *Russian History* 11, no. 4, Winter 1984, p. 345.
245 J. Arch Getty, *Origins of the Great Purges: The Soviet Communist Party Reconsidered, 1933–1938*, Cambridge University Press, 1987, pp. 31–4.
246 James Harris, 'Was Stalin a Weak Dictator?', *Journal of Modern History* 75, no. 2, June 2003, p. 376.
247 Ibid., p. 382.
248 Lewin, *The Soviet Century*, p. 82.
249 James Hughes, *Stalinism in a Russian Province: Collectivization and Dekulakization in Siberia*, Macmillan, 1996, esp. pp. 33–43, 173 ff.
250 J. Arch Getty, '"Excesses Are Not Permitted": Mass Terror and Stalinist Governance in the Late 1930s', *Russian Review* 61, no. 1, January 2002, p. 135.
251 Quoted in Alec Nove, 'Stalinism: Revisionism Reconsidered', *Russian Review* 46, no. 4, October 1987, p. 413.
252 Getty, '"Excesses Are Not Permitted"', p. 119.
253 See Sarah Davies and James Harris, *Stalin's World: Dictating the Soviet Order*, Yale University Press, 2014, pp. 29–33.
254 David R. Shearer, *Policing Stalin's Socialism: Repression and Social Order in the Soviet Union, 1924–1953*, Yale University Press, 2009, p. 3.
255 David Shearer, 'Crime and Social Disorder in Stalin's Russia: A Reassessment of the Great Retreat and the Origins of Mass Repression', *Cahiers du Monde russe* 39, nos 1–2, January–June 1998, pp. 121, 127.
256 J. Arch Getty and Oleg V. Naumov, *Yezhov, The Rise of Stalin's 'Iron Fist'*, Yale University Press, 2008, p. 212, and *The Road to Terror*, p. xiii. See also, making these points, the pioneering work of Gábor Tamás Rittersporn summed up in his 'Rethinking Stalinism'.
257 Gábor Tamás Rittersporn, *Stalinist Simplifications and Soviet Complications: Social Tensions and Political Conflicts in the USSR, 1933–1953*, Harwood Academic Publishers University of California, 1991, see esp. pp. 153 ff and 252 ff.
258 Oleg V. Khlevniuk, *Master of the House: Stalin and His Inner Circle*, Yale University Press, 2008, p. xx.
259 Alec Nove, 'Terror Victims. Is the Evidence Complete?', *Europe-Asia Studies* 46, no. 3, 1994, p. 537.
260 Getty, '"Excesses Are Not Permitted"', p. 132; Khlevniuk, *Master of the House*, p. xx.
261 J. Arch Getty, Gábor T. Rittersporn and Viktor N. Zemskov, 'Victims of the Soviet Penal System in the Pre-War Years: A First Approach on the Basis of Archival Evidence', *American Historical Review* 98, no. 4, October 1993, pp. 1022–4.
262 Wheatcroft, 'More Light on the Scale of Repression', p. 366.
263 For a flavour of the dispute, see, among others, Stephen Wheatcroft's articles over a period of twenty years: 'On Assessing the Size of Forced Concentration Camp Labour in the Soviet Union, 1929–56', *Soviet Studies* 33, no. 2, April 1981, pp. 265–95;

'Towards a Thorough Analysis of Soviet Forced Labour Statistics', *Soviet Studies* 35, no. 2, April 1983, pp. 223–37; 'The Scale and Nature of German and Soviet Repression and Mass Killings, 1930–45', *Europe-Asia Studies* 48, no. 8, December 1996, pp. 1319–53; 'Victims of Stalinism and the Soviet Secret Police: The Comparability and Reliability of the Archival Data. Not the Last Word', *Europe-Asia Studies* 51, no. 2, 1999, pp. 315–45; see also, in a response to Wheatcroft, Robert Conquest, 'Victims of Stalinism: A Comment', *Europe-Asia Studies* 49, no. 7, November 1997, pp. 1317–19.

264 Getty et al., 'Victims of the Soviet Penal System', pp. 1028–9.
265 Ibid., p. 1039.
266 Geoffrey Roberts, 'The Fascist War Threat and Soviet Politics in the 1930s', in Pons and Romano, *Russia in the Age of Wars*, p. 147.
267 Silvio Pons, *The Global Revolution: A History of International Communism, 1917–1991*, Oxford University Press, 2014, pp. 65–74.
268 Oleg Khlevniuk, 'The Reasons for the "Great Terror": The Foreign-Political Aspect', in Pons and Romano, *Russia in the Age of Wars*, pp. 162–3.
269 Getty, *Origins of the Great Purges*, p. 95; Hiroaki Kuromiya, 'Accounting for the Great Terror', *Jahrbücher für Geschichte Osteuropas*, 2005, Neue Folge, Bd. 53, H. 1, 2005, pp. 86–101, esp. p. 88; Aaron Hale-Dorrell, Angelina Lucento and Oleg Khlevniuk, 'Top Down vs. Bottom-up: Regarding the Potential of Contemporary "Revisionism"', *Cahiers du monde russe* 56, no. 4, 2015, p. 848.
270 Sheila Fitzpatrick, *Everyday Stalinism: Ordinary Life in Extraordinary Times: Soviet Russia in the 1930s*, Oxford University Press, 1999, pp. 2–3, 10–11, 41.
271 See Geoffrey Roberts, *The Unholy Alliance: Stalin's Pact with Hitler*, I. B. Tauris, 1989, as well as *Stalin's Wars: From World War to Cold War, 1939–1953*, Yale University Press, 2006.
272 Fitzpatrick, *Everyday Stalinism*, p. 41.
273 Stalin, 'The Tasks of Business Executives: Speech Delivered at the First All-Union Conference of Leading Personnel of Socialist Industry', 4 February 1931, available at marxists.org.
274 Osip Mandelshtam, 'We exist, without sensing our country beneath us', in *Selected Poems*, trans. James Greene, Penguin Classics, 1991.
275 Sheila Fitzpatrick, 'Stalin and the Making of a New Elite, 1928–1939', *Slavic Review* 38, no. 3, September 1979, p. 398.
276 Stephen G. Wheatcroft, 'The Great Leap Upwards: Anthropometric Data and Indicators of Crises and Secular Change in Soviet Welfare Levels, 1880–1960', *Slavic Review* 58, no. 1, Spring 1999, p. 60; Lewin, *The Making of the Soviet System*, p. 234.
277 Andrei Markevich and Mark Harrison, 'Great War, Civil War, and Recovery: Russia's National Income, 1913 to 1928', *Journal of Economic History* 71, no. 3, September 2011, pp. 696–7.
278 Jochen Hellbeck, 'Operation Barbarossa Was a War of Racial Annihilation', *Jacobin*, 22 June 2021.
279 Adam Tooze, *The Wages of Destruction: The Making and Breaking of the Nazi Economy*, Penguin, 2007, p. 429.
280 Vasily Grossman, *Stalingrad*, trans. Robert and Elizabeth Chandler, Harvill Secker, 2019, p. 876.
281 Michael K. Jones, *Stalingrad: How the Red Army Triumphed*, Pen & Sword Books, 2011, p. 5.
282 'The 5 Bloodiest Battles in History', *Military History Matters*, 2 November 2010.
283 United States Holocaust Memorial Museum, 'Introduction to the Holocaust', *Holocaust Encyclopedia*, encyclopedia.ushmm.org.

284 John Erickson, *Stalin's War with Germany: The Road to Berlin*, vol. 2, Yale University Press, 1999, p. ix.
285 Richard Overy, *The Bombing War: Europe, 1939–1945*, Penguin, 2013, p. 401; Richard Evans estimates the number of those who died during the Allied bombing at between 400,000 and 500,000; see Richard Evans, *The Third Reich at War: How the Nazis Led Germany from Conquest to Disaster*, Penguin, 2009, p. 462.
286 Stephen Walsh, *Stalingrad, the Infernal Cauldron 1942–1943*, Simon and Schuster, 2000, pp. 169–74.
287 Maria Lipman, 'Stalin Is Not Dead: A Legacy That Holds Back Russia', in Maria Lipman, Lev Gudkov and Lasha Bakradze, *The Stalin Puzzle: Deciphering Post-Soviet Public Opinion*, ed. Thomas De Waal, Carnegie Moscow Center, 2013, p. 16.
288 *Moscow Times*, 15 February 2017.
289 *Newsweek*, 26 June 2017; see also Smele, 'If Grandma Had Whiskers', p. 26, n. 39.
290 'Stalin's Perception', Levada-Center, survey press release, 19 April 2019, levada.ru.
291 '75% of Russians Say Soviet Era Was "Greatest Time" in Country's History – Poll', *Moscow Times*, 24 March 2020.
292 Charles J. Sullivan, 'Breaking Down the Man of Steel: Stalin in Russia Today', *Canadian Slavonic Papers / Revue Canadienne des Slavistes* 55, nos 3–4, September–December 2013, pp. 474–5.
293 Mirza Bayramov, 'Poem about Stalin', trans. Terry Metheringham, Lewes U3A, 2021.
294 Richard Overy, *Why the Allies Won*, Random House, 2012, p. 318.
295 E. H. Carr, 'Stalin', *Soviet Studies* 5, no. 1, July 1953, p. 7.
296 John Erickson, *Stalin's War with Germany*, vol. 1, *The Road to Stalingrad*, and vol. 2, *The Road to Berlin*, Weidenfeld & Nicolson, 1983.
297 Geoffrey Roberts, *Stalin's Wars: From World War to Cold War, 1939–1953*, Yale University Press, 2006; David M. Glantz's Stalingrad trilogy written with Jonathan House: vol. 1, *To the Gates of Stalingrad*; vol. 2, *Armageddon in Stalingrad*; vol. 3, *Endgame at Stalingrad* (2 books) – all published by the University of Kansas Press, 2009–2014; Richard Overy, *Russia's War 1941–1945*, Penguin, 2010.
298 Stalin, *On the Great Patriotic War of the Soviet Union*, Foreign Language Publishing, 1946, p. 29, https://www.ibiblio.org/.
299 Ibid., p. 163.
300 Ibid., p. 41.
301 Anna Akhmatova, 'Courage', in *Poems of Akhmatova*, ed. and trans. Stanley Kunitz with Max Hayward, Mariner Books, 1973, p. 125.
302 David M. Glantz, 'Soviet Military Strategy During the Second Period of War (November 1942–December 1943): A Reappraisal', *Journal of Military History* 60, no. 1, January 1996, p. 115.
303 Tsuyoshi Hasegawa, *Racing the Enemy: Stalin, Truman, and the Surrender of Japan*, Belknap–Harvard University Press, 2005, p. 298.
304 Lewin, *The Soviet Century*, p. 127.
305 Robert J. Service, 'The Road to the Twentieth Party Congress: An Analysis of the Events Surrounding the Central Committee Plenum of July 1953', *Soviet Studies* 33, no. 2, April 1981, p. 232.
306 Archie Brown, *The Gorbachev Factor*, Oxford University Press, 1997, p. 3.
307 Ibid., p. 18.
308 Yegor Ligachev, *Inside Gorbachev's Kremlin: The Memoirs of Yegor Ligachev*, Routledge, 2018. p. 16.
309 Dominic Lieven, 'Western Scholarship on the Rise and Fall of the Soviet Regime: The View from 1993', *Journal of Contemporary History* 29, no. 2, April 1994, pp. 195–227;

310 Sakwa, *Soviet Communists in Power*, p. xvii.
311 Director of Central Intelligence, NIE 11/12-9-88, May 1988, *Soviet Policy Towards Eastern Europe Under Gorbachev*, p. 155, reiterated on p. 158.
312 Kenneth Waltz, 'The Emerging Structure of International Politics', *International Security* 18, no. 2, Fall 1993, pp. 44–79, esp. p. 76.
313 Mary Dejevsky, 'The Gorbachev Era Begins', *World Today* 42, no. 4, April 1986, pp. 55–7.
314 Archie Brown, 'Gorbachev: New Man in the Kremlin', *Problems of Communism* 34, no. 3, May–June 1985, pp. 4, 21.
315 Stephen Cohen, introduction to Ligachev, *Inside Gorbachev's Kremlin*, p. xxii.
316 David Lane, 'From State Socialism to Capitalism', *Communist and Post-Communist Studies* 39, no. 2, June 2006, p. 148.
317 Mark Kramer, 'The Collapse of East European Communism and the Repercussions Within the Soviet Union (Part 1)', *Journal of Cold War Studies* 5, no. 4, Fall 2003, p. 194.
318 Stephen F. Cohen, 'Was the Soviet System Reformable?', *Slavic Review* 63, no. 3, Autumn 2004, p. 472.
319 Archie Brown, 'The Soviet Union: Reform of the System or Systemic Transformation?', *Slavic Review* 63, no. 3, Autumn 2004, p. 494.
320 Derluguian, 'Alternative Pasts, Future Alternatives?', p. 549.
321 This is the argument in Chris Miller, *The Struggle to Save the Soviet Economy: Mikhail Gorbachev and the Collapse of the USSR*, University of North Carolina Press, 2016, see particularly ch. 3, 'Gorbachev's Gamble: Interest Group Politics and Perestroika'.
322 Brown, *The Gorbachev Factor*, p. 130.
323 See also Jonathan Steele's balanced obituary: 'Mikhail Gorbachev Obituary', *Guardian*, 31 August 2022; as well as Archie Brown, 'A Peaceful Yet Radical Social Transformer: Mikhail Gorbachev Leaves a Blazing Legacy', in the same issue.
324 Zoltan Barany, *The Future of NATO Expansion: Four Case Studies*, Cambridge University Press, 2003, p. 17.
325 Brown, *The Gorbachev Factor*, p. 256.
326 Andrei Grachev, 'Gorbachev and the "New Political Thinking"', in Wolfgang Mueller, Michael Gehler and Arnold Suppan, eds, *The Revolutions of 1989: A Handbook*, Austrian Academy of Sciences Press, 2015, p. 46.
327 Joseph L. Wieczynski, ed., *The Gorbachev Bibliography, 1985–1991: A Listing of Books and Articles in English on Perestroika in the USSR*, Norman Ross Publishing, 1995.
328 'Mikhail Gorbachev's Resignation Speech', 26 December 1991, transl. Associated Press, World History Commons, worldhistorycommons.org.
329 *Global Wealth Report*, Credit Suisse Research Institute, November 2017, p. 55.
330 Peter Nolan, *China's Rise, Russia's Fall: Politics, Economics and Planning in the Transition from Stalinism*, Macmillan, 1995, p. 280.
331 Branko Milanovic, 'Three Steps to Freedom. Secessionism and the Collapse of Communist Federations', *Global Inequality and More 3.0* (blog), 15 February 2024, branko2f7.substack.com.
332 Stefan Hedlund, 'Such a Beautiful Dream: How Russia Did Not Become a Market Economy', *Russian Review* 67, no. 2, April 2008, p. 191.
333 Lane, 'From State Socialism to Capitalism', p. 148.
334 Mikko A. Vienonen and Ilkka J. Vohlonen, 'Integrated Health Care in Russia: To Be or Not to Be?', *International Journal of Integrated Care* 1, March 2001.
335 Lincoln C. Chen, Friederike Wittgenstein and Elizabeth McKeon, 'The Upsurge of

Mortality in Russia: Causes and Policy Implications', *Population and Development Review* 22, no. 3, September 1996, p. 521.
336   R. W. Davies, *Soviet History in the Yeltsin Era*, Macmillan, 1997, pp. 38–40, 59.
337   Lipovetsky, 'Screening the Revolution', p. 214.
338   Ibid., p. 238.
339   Nikolas K. Gvosdev and Christopher Marsh, *Russian Foreign Policy: Interests, Vectors, and Sectors*, CQ Press, 2013, p. 81; see also Dimitri K. Simes, 'Losing Russia: The Costs of Renewed Confrontation', *Foreign Affairs* 86, no. 6, November–December 2007, p. 40.
340   Perry Anderson, 'Incommensurate Russia', *New Left Review* 94, July–August 2015, p. 41.
341   Timothy Frye, *Weak Strongman: The Limits of Power in Putin's Russia*, Princeton University Press, 2021, pp. 88–9.
342   Tony Wood, *Russia Without Putin: Money, Power and the Myths of the New Cold War*, Verso, 2018, see particularly pp. 7–9.
343   Frye, *Weak Strongman*, p. 23.
344   Branko Milanovic, 'After the Wall Fell: The Poor Balance Sheet of the Transition to Capitalism', *Challenge* 58, no. 2, 2015, pp. 135–8; on Belarus, see Viachaslau Yarashevich, 'Political Economy of Modern Belarus: Going Against Mainstream?', *Europe-Asia Studies* 66, no. 10, December 2014, pp. 1703–34.
345   'GNI per Capita, Atlas Method (Current US$)', World Bank Open Data, data.worldbank.org.
346   According to the Corruption Perceptions Index established by Transparency International – not a highly reliable index since it is based on 'perceptions', in 2021, Russia ranked 136th and Ukraine 122nd, above Malawi (110th position); transparency.org.
347   Vladimir Putin, 'Address by the President of the Russian Federation', President of Russia, 21 February 2022, en.kremlin.ru.
348   The phrase was first coined by the British Liberal Party politician Augustine Birrell, in 1884, referring to Carlyle; see his *Obiter Dicta*, Elliot Stock, 1886, p. 10.

6. The Chinese Revolution: Not a Dinner Party

1   Joseph Needham, 'Social Devolution and Revolution: Ta Thung and Thai Phing', in Roy Porter and Mikuláš Teich, eds, *Revolution in History*, Cambridge University Press, 1987, p. 61.
2   I am using the translation by Moss Roberts (abridged version): Luo Guanzhong, *Three Kingdoms: A Historical Novel*, University of California Press and Foreign Languages Press, 1991.
3   Frederic Wakeman, *The Fall of Imperial China*, Free Press, 1975, p. 225.
4   Mao Zedong, 'Report on an Investigation of the Peasant Movement in Hunan', March 1927, in *Selected Works of Mao Tse-tung*, vol. 1, Foreign Language Press, 1965, p. 28.
5   Lucien Bianco, 'Peasant Movements', in *Cambridge History of China*, vol. 13, part 2, pp. 273–87, 288–94.
6   Quoted in Luke S. K. Kwong, 'What's in a Name: Zhongguo (Or "Middle Kingdom")', *Historical Journal* 58, no. 3, September 2015, p. 795.
7   Zheng Yangwen, 'Hunan: Laboratory of Reform and Land of Revolution: Hunanese in the Making of Modern China', *Modern Asian Studies* 42, no. 6, November 2008, pp. 1133, 1117, 1135.
8   See Mary Wright, introduction to Mary Wright, ed., *China in Revolution: The First*

Phase 1900–1913, Yale University Press, 1968, p. 50; see also Wakeman, *The Fall of Imperial China*, p. 234.
9 Wright, *China in Revolution*, p. 49.
10 Rana Mitter, '1911: The Unanchored Chinese Revolution', *China Quarterly* 208, December 2011, p. 1012.
11 Loren Brandt, 'Reflections on China's Late 19th and Early 20th-Century Economy', *China Quarterly* 150, June 1997, p. 284.
12 Peter Zarrow, 'Felling a Dynasty, Founding a Republic', in Jeffrey N. Wasserstrom, ed., *The Oxford History of Modern China*, Oxford University Press, 2022, p. 126.
13 V. I. Lenin, 'Democracy and Narodism in China', *Nevskaya Zvezda*, 15 July 1912, in *Collected Works*, vol. 18, Progress Publishers, 1963, pp. 163, 167.
14 Marisela Connelly, 'The Ping Liu Li Uprising', in David N. Lorenzen, ed., *Studies on Asia and Africa from Latin America*, El Colegio de Mexico, 1990, pp. 36–58.
15 Joseph W. Esherick, 'Ten Theses on the Chinese Revolution', *Modern China* 21, no. 1, January 1995, p. 57.
16 Hiroshi Watanabe, 'Alexis de Tocqueville and Three Revolutions: France (1789–), Japan (1867–), China (1911–)', *International Journal of Asian Studies* 17, no. 2, 2020, pp. 166–7.
17 Yuhua Wang, *The Rise and Fall of Imperial China: The Social Origins of State Development*, Princeton University Press, 2022, pp. 178, 186.
18 On anti-Manchu racism, see Richard L. Mumford, 'Crane Brinton's Pattern and the Chinese Revolution of 1911', *Journal of the History of Ideas* 42, no. 4, October–December 1981, p. 711.
19 Luke S. K. Kwong, 'The Rise of the Linear Perspective on History and Time in Late Qing China c. 1860–1911', *Past and Present* 173, November 2001, pp. 179, 186.
20 See Marianne Bastid, 'L'Ouverture aux idées d'occident: quelle influence de la révolution française sur la révolution républicaine de 1911?', *Extrême-Orient Extrême-Occident* 2, 3e trimestre 1983, p. 23; Daniel Leese, '"Revolution": Conceptualizing Political and Social Change in the Late Qing Dynasty', *Oriens Extremus* 51, 2012, p. 35. The position of Kang Youwei, reformer of revolutionary, has been the object of controversies; see Young-Tsu Wong, 'Revisionism Reconsidered: Kang Youwei and the Reform Movement of 1898', *Journal of Asian Studies* 51, no. 3, August 1992, pp. 513–44.
21 Wong, 'Revisionism Reconsidered', pp. 533–7.
22 Karl Marx, 'Revolution in China and in Europe', *New York Daily Tribune*, 14 June 1853.
23 Yuhua Wang, *The Rise and Fall of Imperial China*, p. 31.
24 Jonathan Spence, *God's Chinese Son: The Taiping Heavenly Kingdom of Hong Xiuquan*, HarperCollins, 1996, p. 325.
25 Ibid., p. xi; Tobie Meyer-Fong, *What Remains: Coming to Terms with Civil War in 19th Century China*, Stanford University Press, 2013, see esp. pp. 1, 11; see also Tobie Meyer-Fong, 'Where the War Ended: Violence, Community, and Commemoration in China's Nineteenth-Century Civil War', *American Historical Review* 120, no. 5, December 2015, pp. 1724–38.
26 Jonathan D. Spence, *The Search for Modern China*, W. W. Norton, 1991, p. 232.
27 See Hans van de Ven, 'Robert Hart and Gustav Detring During the Boxer Rebellion', *Modern Asian Studies* 40, no. 3, July 2006, pp. 631–62, esp. pp. 635 ff; Robert Hart was the Inspector-General of China's Imperial Maritime Custom Service from 1863 to 1911. See also Sabine Dabringhaus, 'An Army on Vacation?: The German War in China, 1900–1901', in Manfred F. Boemeke, Roger Chickering and Stig Förster, eds, *Anticipating Total War: The German and American Experiences, 1871–1914*, Cambridge University Press, 1999; on the looting and massacres by Western troops, see Robert Bickers, *The Scramble for China: Foreign Devils in the Qing Empire, 1832–1914*, Allen

Lane, 2011, pp. 346–52; Christopher Hibbert, *The Dragon Wakes: China and the West 1793–1911*, Penguin, 1984, pp. 350–2.
28 Julia C. Strauss, 'The Evolution of Republican Government', *China Quarterly* 150, June 1997, p. 333; see also Yeh-Chien Wang, *Land Taxation in Imperial China, 1750–1911*, Harvard University Press, 2013.
29 Jack Gray, *Rebellions and Revolutions: China from the 1800s to the 1980s*, Oxford University Press, 1990, p. 148.
30 Mary Backus Rankin, 'State and Society in Early Republican Politics, 1912–18', *China Quarterly* 150, June 1997, pp. 260–3.
31 Strauss, 'The Evolution of Republican Government', p. 336.
32 Esherick, 'Ten Theses on the Chinese Revolution', pp. 64–5.
33 Edmund S. K. Fung, 'Were Chinese Liberals Liberal? Reflections on the Understanding of Liberalism in Modern China', *Pacific Affairs* 81, no. 4, Winter 2008/2009, pp. 557–6.
34 Mao Zedong, 'On the People's Democratic Dictatorship', 30 June 1949, in *Selected Works of Mao Tse-tung*, vol. 4, Foreign Languages Press, 1961, p. 412.
35 Wang Chaohua, introduction to Wang Chaohua, ed., *One China, Many Paths*, Verso, 2003, p. 9.
36 Cheng-chung Lai, 'Adam Smith and Yen Fu: Western Economics in Chinese Perspective', *Journal of European Economic History* 18, no. 2, Fall 1989, pp. 373–5.
37 Yan Fu (Yen Fou), *Les Manifestes de Yen Fou*, ed. François Houang, Fayard, 1977, p. 126; see also Immanuel C. Y. Hsü, *The Rise of Modern China*, Oxford University Press, 1990, pp. 422–3.
38 Key Ray Chong, 'Cheng Kuan-ying (1841–1920): A Source of Sun Yat-sen's Nationalist Ideology?', *Journal of Asian Studies* 28, no. 2, February 1969, p. 251.
39 Bastid, 'L'Ouverture aux idées d'occident', p. 22.
40 Andrea Graziosi, 'A Century of 1917s', *Harvard Ukrainian Studies* 36, nos 1/2, 2019, p. 17.
41 Michael R. Godley, 'Socialism with Chinese Characteristics: Sun Yatsen and the International Development of China', *Australian Journal of Chinese Affairs* 18, July 1987, pp. 111–12.
42 Ibid., p. 117.
43 Jeffrey N. Wasserstrom, *Global Shanghai, 1850–2010: A History in Fragments*, Routledge, 2009, p. 68.
44 Albert Feuerwerker, 'The Foreign Presence in China', in *The Cambridge History of China*, vol. 12, *Republican China 1912–1949, Part 1*, ed. John K. Fairbank, Cambridge University Press, 2008, esp. pp. 128–54.
45 Godley, 'Socialism with Chinese Characteristics', p. 121.
46 John Fitzgerald, 'The Misconceived Revolution: State and Society in China's Nationalist Revolution, 1923–26', *Journal of Asian Studies* 49, no. 2, May 1990, p. 326.
47 Zhongping Chen, 'The May Fourth Movement and Provincial Warlords: A Reexamination', *Modern China* 37, no. 2, March 2011, p. 141.
48 Ibid., pp. 153–4.
49 Mao Zedong, 'The May 4th Movement', May 1939, in *Selected Works of Mao Tse-tung*, vol. 3, Foreign Languages Press, 1965, pp. 237–9.
50 Joseph T. Chen, 'The May Fourth Movement Redefined', *Modern Asian Studies* 4, no. 1, 1970, p. 68.
51 Wang Gungwu, 'Outside the Chinese Revolution', *Australian Journal of Chinese Affairs* 23, January 1990, p. 34.
52 Steve A. Smith, 'Workers, the Intelligentsia and Marxist Parties: St Petersburg, 1895–1917 and Shanghai, 1921–1927', *International Review of Social History* 41, no. 1, April 1996, pp. 35, 39–40.

53 Lu Xun, *Selected Stories of Lu Hsun: The True Story of Ah Q and Other Tales*, trans. Yang Hsien-yi and Gladys Yang, Warbler Classics, 2021, Kindle edn, p. 101.
54 Leo Ou-fan Lee, 'Shanghai Modern: Reflections on Urban Culture in China in the 1930s', in Dilip Parameshwar Gaonkar, ed., *Alternative Modernities*, Duke University Press, 2001, p. 87.
55 S. A. Smith, *Revolution and the People in Russia and China: A Comparative History*, Cambridge University Press, 2008, p. 31.
56 Rana Mitter, *A Bitter Revolution: China's Struggle with the Modern World*, Oxford University Press, 2004, p. 51.
57 Barbara Barnouin and Changgen Yu, *Zhou Enlai: A Political Life*, Chinese University Press, 2006, p. 26.
58 Hans J. van de Ven, *From Friend to Comrade: The Founding of the Chinese Communist Party, 1920–1927*, University of California Press, 1992, pp. 25, 45; see also Stuart Schram, 'Mao Tse-tung's Thought to 1949', in *The Cambridge History of China*, vol. 13, *Republican China 1912–1949, Part 2*, ed. John K. Fairbank and Albert Feuerwerker, Cambridge University Press, 1986, p. 805.
59 Gray, *Rebellions and Revolutions*, p. 206.
60 Elizabeth J. Perry, 'Reclaiming the Chinese Revolution', *Journal of Asian Studies* 67, no. 4, November 2008, pp. 1150–2.
61 Van de Ven, *From Friend to Comrade*, p. 149.
62 Lucien Bianco, *Origins of the Chinese Revolution 1915–1949*, Stanford University Press, 1971, p. 56.
63 Tien-wei Wu, 'A Review of the Wuhan Debacle: The Kuomintang-Communist Split of 1927', *Journal of Asian Studies* 29, no. 1, November 1969, pp. 126, 129–31.
64 Perry, 'Reclaiming the Chinese Revolution', p. 1157.
65 Bianco, *Origins of the Chinese Revolution*, p. 124.
66 Barnouin and Yu, *Zhou Enlai: A Political Life*, p. 35.
67 Bradley Kent Geisert, 'From Conflict to Quiescence: The Kuomintang, Party Factionalism and Local Elites in Jiangsu, 1927–31', *China Quarterly* 108, December 1986, p. 685.
68 Gail Hershatter, 'State of the Field: Women in China's Long Twentieth Century', *Journal of Asian Studies* 63, no. 4, November 2004, pp. 991–1065. For a wider discussion and a comparison with the Qing code, see Philip C. C. Huang, 'Women's Choices Under the Law: Marriage, Divorce, and Illicit Sex in the Qing and the Republic', *Modern China* 27, no. 1, 2001. Huang points out that the Qing legal formulation also afforded women some important protections, which the Guomindang reformulation took away (pp. 13–14).
69 Strauss, 'The Evolution of Republican Government', pp. 341–3.
70 Lloyd E. Eastman, 'Nationalist China During the Nanking Decade 1927–1937', in *The Cambridge History of China*, vol. 13, p. 143; see also Spence, *The Search for Modern China*, p. 417.
71 Esherick, 'Ten Theses on the Chinese Revolution', p. 51.
72 Quoted in Stuart R. Schram, 'Mao Tse-tung and Secret Societies', *China Quarterly* 27, July–September 1966, p. 4.
73 Hsiao Tso-Liang, 'The Dispute over a Wuhan Insurrection in 1927', *China Quarterly* 33, January–March 1968, pp. 121–2.
74 Yokoyama Suguru, 'The Peasant Movement in Hunan', *Modern China* 1, no. 2, April 1975, pp. 206–7.
75 Ibid., pp. 222, 236.
76 Mao, 'Report on an Investigation of the Peasant Movement in Hunan', pp. 23–4.
77 Spence, *The Search for Modern China*, pp. 373–4.
78 Esherick, 'Ten Theses on the Chinese Revolution', p. 50.

79 Thomas Kampen, *Mao Zedong, Zhou Enlai and the Evolution of the Chinese Communist Leadership*, Nordic Institute of Asian Studies Press, 2000, pp. 10 ff, 66; John W. Garver, *Chinese-Soviet Relations, 1937–1945*, Oxford University Press, 1988; see also John W. Garver, 'The Origins of the Second United Front: The Comintern and the Chinese Communist Party', *China Quarterly* 113, March 1988, pp. 29–59. The relationship between Stalin and Mao has been a source of dispute among historians for quite a while. See Michael M. Sheng, 'Mao, Stalin, and the Formation of the Anti-Japanese United Front: 1935–37', *China Quarterly* 129, March 1992, pp. 149–70; in the same issue, see Garver's response: 'Mao, the Comintern and the Second United Front', pp. 171–9.

80 Enhua Zhang, 'The Long March', in Wang Ban, ed., *Words and Their Stories: Essays on the Language of the Chinese Revolution*, Brill, 2011, pp. 34–5.

81 Harrison E. Salisbury, *The Long March: The Untold Story*, Harper & Row, 1985, pp. 2, 31, 236–9; see also Jack Gray, *Rebellions and Revolutions*, p. 270 (which provides similar numbers). Mitter, in *A Bitter Revolution*, says 8,000 (p. 161); other authors mention 10,000.

82 C. N. Tay, 'From Snow to Plum Blossoms: A Commentary on Some Poems by Mao Tse-Tung', *Journal of Asian Studies* 25, no. 2, February 1966, p. 287.

83 Salisbury, *The Long March*, pp. 34, 62.

84 Lucien Bianco, 'Les Politiques agraires de la Révolution chinoise', *Revue d'histoire moderne et contemporaine* 63-4/4 bis, October–December 2016, pp. 138–9; Hongyi Harry Lai, 'The Life Span of Unified Regimes in China', *China Review* 2, no. 2, Fall 2002, pp. 93–124; Theda Skocpol, 'Old Regime Legacies and Communist Revolutions in Russia and China', *Social Forces* 55, no. 2, December 1976, pp. 284–315.

85 Lai, 'The Life Span of Unified Regimes in China', p. 114.

86 Isabella M. Weber, *How China Escaped Shock Therapy: The Market Reform Debate*, Routledge, 2021, pp. 69, 83.

87 Akira Iriye, 'Chinese-Japanese Relations, 1945–90', *China Quarterly* 124, December 1990, p. 624.

88 Ian Nish, 'An Overview of Relations Between China and Japan, 1895–1945', *China Quarterly* 124, December 1990, pp. 603–4.

89 Jonathan Haslam, *The Spectre of War: International Communism and the Origins of World War II*, Princeton University Press, 2021, pp. 92–4.

90 Anthony Coogan, 'Northeast China and the Origins of the Anti-Japanese United Front', *Modern China* 20, no. 3, July 1994, p. 285.

91 So Wai Chor, 'The Making of the Guomindang's Japan Policy, 1932–1937: The Roles of Chiang Kai-Shek and Wang Jingwei', *Modern China* 28, no. 2, April 2002, p. 231; Parks M. Coble Jr, 'Chiang Kai-shek and the Anti-Japanese Movement in China: Zou Tao-fen and the National Salvation Association, 1931–1937', *Journal of Asian Studies* 44, no. 2, February 1985, p. 293.

92 So, 'The Making of the Guomindang's Japan Policy', p. 240.

93 Coble, 'Chiang Kai-shek and the Anti-Japanese Movement', pp. 294–5.

94 Georgi Dimitrov, 'Speech on the Chinese Question: Delivered 10 August 1937 at the Meeting of the Secretariat of the ECCI', available at marxists.org.

95 John W. Garver, 'The Soviet Union and the Xi'an Incident', *Australian Journal of Chinese Affairs* 26, July 1991, pp. 145–75, esp. pp. 158–9, 170.

96 Wu Tien-wei, *The Sian Incident: A Pivotal Point in Modern Chinese History*, Center for Chinese Studies, University of Michigan, 1976, pp. 101, 182–4; this is one of the most detailed works on the Xi'an Incident.

97 Spence, *The Search for Modern China*, p. 447.

98 Quoted in Christian Henriot, 'Shanghai and the Experience of War: The Fate of Refugees', *European Journal of East Asian Studies* 5, no. 2, 2006, p. 221.

99 The figures were established by the 1946–48 Tokyo War Crimes Trial (International Military Tribunal for the Far East), the equivalent of the Nuremberg Trials. Of course, inevitably, such figures have been disputed; see the balanced overview in Daqing Yang, 'Convergence or Divergence Recent Historical Writings on the Rape of Nanjing', *American Historical Review* 104, no. 3, June 1999, pp. 842–65, esp. p. 844. The massacre was first described in the West by Edgar Snow in his 1941 book *Scorched Earth*.
100 Iris Chang, *The Rape of Nanking: The Forgotten Holocaust of World War II*, BasicBooks, 1997, p. 6.
101 Quoted in Franz-Stefan Gady, 'Japan at Peace: The Improbable Military Resurgence', *Foreign Affairs*, 16 September 2015.
102 Diana Lary, 'Drowned Earth: The Strategic Breaching of the Yellow River Dyke, 1938', *War in History* 8, no. 2, April 2001, p. 206. See also slightly different figures in Rana Mitter, *China's War with Japan 1937–1945: The Struggle for Survival*, Allen Lane, 2013, pp. 158–60.
103 Gray, *Rebellions and Revolutions*, pp. 152–4, 244–5.
104 Coogan, 'Northeast China and the Origins', p. 308.
105 Mao Zedong, 'A Single Spark Can Start a Prairie Fire', 5 January 1930, in *Selected Works of Mao Tse-tung*, vol. 1, p. 124.
106 Mao Zedong, 'On Protracted War', in *Selected Works of Mao Tse-tung*, vol. 2, Foreign Languages Press, 1965, p. 114.
107 Ibid., p. 117.
108 Mao Zedong, 'Problems of Strategy in Guerrilla War Against Japan', *May 1938*, in *Selected Works of Mao Tse-tung*, vol. 2, p. 83.
109 Mao, 'On Protracted War', p. 150.
110 Mao Zedong, 'On New Democracy', in *Selected Works of Mao Tse-tung*, vol. 2, pp. 343, 344–7, 350.
111 Ibid., p. 353.
112 Ibid., p. 355.
113 Mao Zedong, 'The Identity of Interests Between the Soviet Union and All Mankind', in *Selected Works of Mao Tse-tung*, vol. 2, pp. 275–83.
114 Mao Zedong, 'Stalin, Friend of the Chinese People', in *Selected Works of Mao Tse-tung*, vol. 2, pp. 335–6.
115 Lyman P. Van Slyke, 'The Chinese Communist Movement During the Sino-Japanese War, 1937–1945', in *The Cambridge History of China*, vol. 13, p. 722.
116 Hua-yu Li, 'Reactions of Chinese Citizens to the Death of Stalin', *Journal of Cold War Studies* 11, no. 2, Spring 2009, p. 75.
117 Esherick, 'Ten Theses on the Chinese Revolution', pp. 67–8.
118 Mitter, *China's War with Japan*, p. 273.
119 Lloyd E. Eastman, 'Nationalist China During the Sino-Japanese War 1937–1945', in *The Cambridge History of China*, vol. 13, pp. 572–5.
120 Kerry Brown, *China's Dream: The Culture of Chinese Communism and the Secret Sources of Its Power*, Polity, 2018, p. 27.
121 Mitter, *China's War with Japan*, pp. 223–4, 269–73, 278–80.
122 Mao Zedong, 'Talks at the Yan'an Forum On Literature and Art', May 1942, in *Selected Works of Mao Tse-tung*, vol. 3, p. 81; see also Ellen R. Judd, 'Prelude to the "Yan'an Talks": Problems in Transforming a Literary Intelligentsia', *Modern China* 11, no. 3, July 1985, pp. 377–408; Timothy Cheek, 'The Fading of Wild Lilies: Wang Shiwei and Mao Zedong's Yan'an Talks in the First CPC Rectification Movement', *Australian Journal of Chinese Affairs* 11, January 1984, pp. 25–58.
123 Pavel Osinsky and Jari Eloranta, 'Why Did the Communists Win or Lose? A

Comparative Analysis of the Revolutionary Civil Wars in Russia, Finland, Spain, and China', *Sociological Forum* 29, no. 2, June 2014, p. 334.
124 Bianco, *Origins of the Chinese Revolution*, p. 152.
125 David E. Apter, 'Mao's Republic', *Social Research* 54, no. 4, Winter 1987, p. 708; see also David E. Apter, 'Yan'an and the Narrative Reconstruction of Reality', *Daedalus* 122, no. 2, Spring 1993, pp. 207–32.
126 Chalmer A. Johnson, *Peasant Nationalism and Communist Power: The Emergence of Revolutionary China 1937–1945*, Stanford University Press, 1962, p. 7; see also his later defence of his position on peasant nationalism: 'Peasant Nationalism Revisited: The Biography of a Book', *China Quarterly* 72, December 1977, pp. 766–85.
127 Mitter, *China's War with Japan*, p. 323.
128 This was also the impression of Owen Lattimore, appointed by Roosevelt as adviser to Chiang Kai-shek; see Owen Lattimore, *China Memoirs: Chiang Kai-shek and the War Against Japan*, ed. Fujiko Isono, University of Tokyo Press, 1990, p. 86.
129 Akira Iriye, 'Japanese Aggression and China's International Position 1931–1949', *The Cambridge History of China*, vol. 13, pp. 532–3, and more on Churchill's Sinophobia on p. 537.
130 Spence, *The Search for Modern China*, p. 470.
131 Mitter, *China's War with Japan*, pp. 300–2, 329–32; see also Lattimore, *China Memoirs*, p. 216.
132 Iriye, 'Japanese Aggression and China's International', p. 335.
133 Mark Selden, 'Yan'an Communism Reconsidered', *Modern China* 21, no. 1, January 1995, pp. 11–12.
134 Bianco, 'Les Politiques agraires de la Révolution chinoise', pp. 138–9.
135 Bianco, 'Peasant Movements', p. 323.
136 David Fedman and Cary Karacas, 'A Cartographic Fade to Black: Mapping the Destruction of Urban Japan During World War II', *Journal of Historical Geography* 38, no. 3, July 2012, p. 319; Masahiko Yamabe, 'Thinking Now About the Great Tokyo Air Raid', *Asia-Pacific Journal* 9, issue 3, no. 5, January 2011, p. 4. Yamabe points out that currently 105,400 are recorded in the Tokyo Memorial Hall.
137 Mao Zedong, 'On Peace Negotiations with the Kuomintang: Circular of the Central Committee of the Communist Party of China', in *Selected Works of Mao Tse-tung*, vol. 4, pp. 48–9.
138 Lattimore, *China Memoirs*, p. 213.
139 Jian Chen, *Mao's China and the Cold War*, University of North Carolina Press, 2001, pp. 24–5.
140 George W. Atkinson, 'The Sino-Soviet Treaty of Friendship and Alliance', *International Affairs* 23, no. 3, July 1947, pp. 357–66.
141 Suzanne Pepper, *Civil War in China: The Political Struggle, 1945–1949*, Rowman & Littlefield, 1999, p. 20.
142 Lloyd E. Eastman, 'Who Lost China? Chiang Kai-shek Testifies', *China Quarterly* 88, December 1981, pp. 658.
143 Ibid., pp. 659–61; see also p. 668, quoting similar comments made by Chiang in his 1956 book *Soviet Russia in China*.
144 Pepper, *Civil War in China*, pp. 99, 109, 118.
145 Ibid., pp. 132 ff.
146 Ibid., p. 303.
147 Robert Shaffer, 'A Rape in Beijing, December 1946: GIs, Nationalist Protests, and U.S. Foreign Policy', *Pacific Historical Review* 69, no. 1, February 2000, pp. 31–64, esp. p. 36. On the rape case, see Jeffrey N. Wasserstrom, *Student Protests in Twentieth*

Century China: The View from Shanghai, Stanford University Press, 1991, pp. 240 ff; see also Pepper, *Civil War in China*, pp. 52–4, 74.
148 John H. Feaver, 'The China Aid Bill of 1948: Limited Assistance as a Cold War Strategy', *Diplomatic History* 5, no. 2, Spring 1981, pp. 107–9, 112.
149 Odd Westad, *Decisive Encounters: The Chinese Civil War 1946–50*, Stanford University Press, 2003, p. 238.
150 Suzanne Pepper, 'The KMT–CCP Conflict 1945–1949', in *The Cambridge History of China*, vol. 13, p. 787.
151 Van Slyke, 'The Chinese Communist Movement', p. 621.
152 Pepper, 'The KMT–CCP Conflict', p. 757.
153 Westad, *Decisive Encounters*, p. 197.
154 Ibid., p. 199.
155 Derk Bodde, *Peking Diary: A Year of Revolution*, Henry Schuman, 1950, pp. 103–4; this was confirmed by Owen Lattimore, in his *China Memoirs*, p. 215.
156 Mao Zedong, 'The People's Liberation Army Captures Nanking', April 1949, available at marxists.org.
157 Randall Gould, 'Shanghai During the Takeover, 1949', *Annals of the American Academy of Political and Social Science* 277, September 1951, pp. 182–4, 186.
158 Bianco, *Origins of the Chinese Revolution*, p. 180.
159 See table in Andrew G. Walder, 'Rebellion and Repression in China, 1966–1971', *Social Science History* 38, nos 3–4, Fall/Winter 2014, p. 534.
160 Thomas J. Shattuck, 'Taiwan's White Terror: Remembering the 228 Incident', Foreign Policy Research Institute, 27 February 2017, fpri.org; see also Allan J. Shackleton, *Formosa Calling: An Eyewitness Account of the February 28th, 1947 Incident*, Taiwan Publishing Co. and Taiwan Communiqué, 1998.
161 Mark Selden, *China in Revolution: The Yenan Way Revisited*, M. E. Sharpe, 1995, p. xi.
162 Pepper, *Civil War in China*, p. 207.
163 Ibid., pp. 232–42.
164 Mao Zedong, 'A Three Months' Summary', 1 October 1946, in *Selected Works of Mao Tse-tung*, vol. 4, p. 116.
165 Pepper, *Civil War in China*, p. 243; see also Mao Zedong on how to treat rich peasants in *Selected Works of Mao Tse-tung*, vol. 4: 'Smash Chiang Kai-shek's Offensive by a War of Self-Defence', 20 July 1946, pp. 89–90; 'Greet the New High Tide of the Chinese Revolution', 1 February 1947, p. 124; 'The Present Situation and Our Tasks', 25 December 1947, pp. 164–7; 'On Some Important Problems of the Party's Present Strategy', 18 January 1948, pp. 182–5; 'Different Tactics for Carrying Out the Land Law in Different Areas', 3 February 1948, p. 194; 'Essential Points in Land Reform in the New Liberated Areas', 15 February 1948, pp. 201–3; 'On the Question of the National Bourgeoisie and the Enlightened Gentry', 1 March 1948, p. 209; 'A Circular on the Situation', 20 March 1948, p. 219; 'Speech at a Conference of Cadres in the Shansi-Suiyuan Liberated Area', 1 April 1948, p. 229.
166 Quoted in Pepper, *Civil War in China*, p. 349.
167 Pepper, *Civil War in China*, pp. 385–8.
168 Mao Zedong, 'On the Policy Concerning Industry and Commerce', 27 February 1948, in *Selected Works of Mao Tse-tung*, vol. 4, p. 203.
169 Mao Zedong, 'On Some Important Problems of the Party's Present Policy', 18 January 1948, in *Selected Works of Mao Tse-tung*, vol. 4, pp. 182, 183, 185.
170 Mao, 'Essential Points in Land Reform in the New Liberated Areas', p. 202.
171 Pepper, *Civil War in China*, p. 363; Israel Epstein, 'Main Directions in Chinese Labor', *Science and Society* 13, no. 4, Fall 1949, pp. 313–26; Klaus H. Rringsheim, 'Trade

Unions and the Chinese Communists', *Southwestern Social Science Quarterly* 46, no. 2, September 1965, p. 116.
172 Roderick MacFarquhar, 'On "Liberation"', *China Quarterly* 200, December 2009, p. 891.
173 Kam Louis, ed., *The Cambridge Companion to Modern Chinese Culture*, Cambridge University Press, 2008, p. 138.
174 Zarrow, 'Felling a Dynasty, Founding a Republic', p. 127.
175 Michael Clarke, 'Ethnic Separatism in the People's Republic of China History, Causes and Contemporary Challenges', *European Journal of East Asian Studies* 12, no. 1, 2013, p. 110, the issue is dealt with in the entire essay, pp. 109–33.
176 S. A. Smith, 'The Early Years of the People's Republic, 1950–1964', in Wasserstrom *Oxford History of Modern China*, p. 207.
177 Mao Zedong, 'Report to the Second Plenary Session of the Seventh Central Committee of the Communist Party of China', 5 March 1949, in *Selected Works of Mao Tse-tung*, vol. 4, p. 374.
178 Julia Strauss, 'Morality, Coercion and State Building by Campaign in the Early PRC: Regime Consolidation and After, 1949–1956', *China Quarterly* 188, December 2006.
179 Mao, 'On the People's Democratic Dictatorship', p. 421.
180 John Gittings, *The Changing Face of China: From Mao to Market*, Oxford University Press, 2005, pp. 23 ff.
181 Chris Bramall, *Chinese Economic Development*, Routledge, 2009, pp. 105–7.
182 Gray, *Rebellions and Revolutions*, pp. 290–1.
183 See Frederick C. Teiwes, 'Establishment and Consolidation of the New Regime', in *The Cambridge History of China*, vol. 14, *The People's Republic, Part 1: The Emergence of Revolutionary China, 1949–1965*, ed. Roderick MacFarquhar and John K. Fairbanks, Cambridge University Press, 1987, p. 87; see also Benedict Stavis, *The Politics of Agricultural Mechanization in China*, Cornell University Press, 1978, pp. 25–30; and also A. Doak Barnett, *Cadres, Bureaucracy and Political Power in Communist China*, Columbia University Press, 1967.
184 William Hinton, *Fanshen: A Documentary of Revolution in a Chinese Village*, Vintage, 1966, p. xi.
185 Strauss, 'Morality, Coercion and State Building', pp. 891–2.
186 Alan P. Dobson, 'The Kennedy Administration and Economic Warfare Against Communism', *International Affairs* 64, no. 4, Autumn 1988, pp. 600–1.
187 Shu Guang Zhang, *Beijing's Economic Statecraft During the Cold War, 1949–1991*, Johns Hopkins University Press, 2014, pp. 7, 21–58, 59 ff. For an eyewitness account of a Soviet specialist reluctantly forced to leave China see Mikhail Klochko, 'The Sino-Soviet Split: The Withdrawal of the Specialists', *International Journal* 26, no. 3, Summer 1971, pp. 556–66.
188 Elizabeth Croll, *Feminism and Socialism in China*, Routledge and Kegan Paul, 1978, chs 6 and 7.
189 Wright, introduction to *China in Revolution*, p. 34.
190 Yan Fu (Yen Fou), *Les Manifestes de Yen Fou*, pp. 86–8.
191 Cited in Jonathan D. Spence, *The Gate of Heavenly Peace: The Chinese and Their Revolution, 1895–1980*, Faber & Faber, 1982, p. 52.
192 Mao, 'Report on an Investigation of the Peasant Movement in Hunan', p. 44.
193 Croll, *Feminism and Socialism in China*, p. 223.
194 Yuhui Li, 'Women's Movement and Change of Women's Status in China', *Journal of International Women's Studies* 1, no. 1, 2000, p. 32.
195 Ibid., pp. 31–2, 36; the educational data are from Beverley Hooper, 'Gender and

Education', in Irving Epstein, ed., *Chinese Education: Problems, Policies, and Prospects*, Garland Publishing, 1991, pp. 352–74.

196 Data in Cissy Zhou and Echo Wong, 'Behind the Women Billionaires: China Receding on Gender Equality', *Financial Times*, 28 December 2022.
197 Mao Zedong, 'On the Co-operative Transformation of Agriculture', 31 July 1955, in *Selected Works of Mao Tse-tung*, vol. 5, Foreign Languages Press, 1977, p. 184.
198 Richard Kraus, 'Let a Hundred Flowers Blossom', in Wang Ban, *Words and Their Stories*, p. 254.
199 Jack Gray, 'Mao in Perspective', *China Quarterly* 187, September 2006, pp. 661.
200 Bianco, 'Les Politiques agraires de la Révolution chinoise', pp. 142–4.
201 Zhou Enlai, 'On Addressing the Problems of the Great Leap Forward', quoted in Jeremy Wallace, *Cities and Stability: Urbanization, Redistribution, and Regime Survival in China*, Oxford University Press, 2014, p. 71.
202 Figures in Cormac Ó Gráda, 'The Ripple That Drowns? Twentieth-Century Famines in China and India as Economic History', *Economic History Review* 61, no. S1, August 2008, pp. 10–11.
203 James Kai-sing Kung and Justin Yifu Lin, 'The Causes of China's Great Leap Famine, 1959–1961', *Economic Development and Cultural Change* 52, no. 1, October 2003, pp. 53–4; a partial defence of the backyard steel furnaces can be found in Gray, 'Mao in Perspective', p. 664.
204 Carl Riskin, 'Seven Questions About the Chinese Famine of 1959–61', *China Economic Review* 9, no. 2, 1998, p. 113; see also Ezra F. Vogel, *Deng Xiaoping and the Transformation of China*, Harvard University Press, 2011, pp. 41–2; and Dingping Guo, 'The Changing Nature of Chinese Socialism Comparative Perspectives', *European Journal of East Asian Studies* 8, no. 1, 2009, p. 5. Becker and Dikötter go for the highest number: Jasper Becker, *Hungry Ghosts: Mao's Secret Famine*, John Murray, 1996; and Frank Dikötter, *Mao's Great Famine: The History of China's Most Devastating Catastrophe, 1958–62*, Bloomsbury, 2011; Yang Jisheng, *Tombstone: The Untold Story of Mao's Great Famine*, Allen Lane, 2012, which first came out in Hong Kong in 2008 and which puts the number of deaths at 36 million. For a critical review of Dikötter, see Cormac Ó Gráda, 'Great Leap into Famine: A Review Essay', *Mao's Great Famine: Population and Development Review* 37, no. 1, March 2011, pp. 191–202.
205 On Wuwei, see Shuji Cao and Bin Yang, 'Grain, Local Politics, and the Making of Mao's Famine in Wuwei, 1958–1961', *Modern Asian Studies* 49, no. 6, November 2015, pp. 1675–1703.
206 Ó Gráda, 'The Ripple That Drowns?', p. 10, and Cormac Ó Gráda, 'Making Famine History', *Journal of Economic Literature* 45, no. 1, March 2007, p. 19.
207 Riskin, 'Seven Questions About the Chinese Famine', p. 115.
208 Xin Meng, Nancy Qian and Pierre Yared, 'The Institutional Causes of China's Great Famine, 1959–1961', *Review of Economic Studies* 82, no. 4 (293), October 2015, pp. 1569–70.
209 Kung and Lin, 'The Causes of China's Great Leap Famine', p. 52.
210 Mark Selden, 'Jack Gray, Mao Zedong and the Political Economy of Chinese Development', *China Quarterly* 187, September 2006, p. 684.
211 Thomas P. Bernstein, 'Mao Zedong and the Famine of 1959–1960: A Study in Wilfulness', *China Quarterly* 186, June 2006, pp. 427, 440–1; see also Gray, *Rebellions and Revolutions*, p. 314.
212 Bernstein, 'Mao Zedong and the Famine of 1959–1960', p. 421.
213 Mao Zedong, 'Speech at the Lushan Conference', 23 July 1959, in *Selected Works of Mao Tse-tung*, vol. 8, Kranti Publications, 1994.

214 Lucien Bianco, 'Les Paysans et la Révolution chinoise: avant la victoire et après la défaite communistes', *Revue d'histoire moderne et contemporaine* 46, no. 3, July–September 1999, p. 594.
215 Jürgen Domes, *Peng Te-huai: The Man and the Image*, C. Hurst & Co., 1985, p. 83.
216 Ibid., pp. 120–2.
217 Stuart R. Schram, 'To Utopia and Back: A Cycle in the History of the Chinese Communist Party', *China Quarterly* 87, September 1981, p. 424.
218 Bianco, 'Les Politiques agraires de la Révolution chinoise', pp. 133, 148; see also Yang Jisheng, *Tombstone*, and his book on the cultural revolution: Yang Jisheng, *The World Turned Upside Down: A History of the Chinese Cultural Revolution*, Swift Press, 2021.
219 Bianco, 'Les Politiques agraires de la Révolution chinoise', p. 134.
220 Felix Wemheuer, 'Dealing with Responsibility for the Great Leap Famine in the People's Republic of China', *China Quarterly* 201, March 2010, pp. 179–81.
221 Cao and Yang, 'Grain, Local Politics, and the Making of Mao's Famine', p. 1700.
222 James C. Scott, 'Tyranny of the Ladle', *London Review of Books* 34, no. 23, 6 December 2012. This is a review of various books on the famine including Yang Jisheng's *Tombstone*.
223 Chris Bramall, 'The Last of the Romantics? Maoist Economic Development in Retrospect', *China Quarterly* 187, September 2006, pp. 687–9.
224 Lucien Bianco, *Stalin and Mao: A Comparison of the Russian and Chinese Revolutions*, Chinese University Press, 2018, p. 34.
225 Weber, *How China Escaped Shock Therapy*, p. 94.
226 Spence, *The Search for Modern China*, p. 580.
227 Hui Zhao, Jun Liu and Raphaël Jacquet, 'Réseaux sociaux et mémoire collective en Chine: Le Débat à propos de la Grande Famine sur Weibo', *Perspectives Chinoises* 1, 2015, pp. 44 ff.
228 Spence, *The Search for Modern China*, p. 536.
229 Michel C. Oksenberg, 'Policy Making Under Mao Tse-Tung, 1949–1968', *Comparative Politics* 3, no. 3, April 1971, pp. 326–7.
230 Jonathan Unger, 'The Cultural Revolution at the Grass Roots', *China Journal* 57, January 2007, pp. 109–14.
231 Skocpol, 'Old Regime Legacies and Communist Revolutions', p. 309.
232 Mao Zedong, 'Just a Few Words' (text of October 1966), in Michael Schoenhals, ed., *China's Cultural Revolution, 1966–1969: Not a Dinner Party*, M. E. Sharpe, 1996, pp. 4–6; see also Roderick MacFarquhar and Michael Schoenhals, *Mao's Last Revolution*, Belknap–Harvard University Press, 2006, p. 53.
233 Schoenhals, *China's Cultural Revolution*, p. 34.
234 Yang Su, 'Mass Killings in the Cultural Revolution: A Study of Three Provinces', in Joseph W. Esherick, Paul G. Pickowicz and Andrew G. Walder, eds, *The Chinese Cultural Revolution as History*, Stanford University Press, 2006, p. 113; this is treated more extensively in Yang Su, *Collective Killings in Rural China During the Cultural Revolution*, Cambridge University Press, 2011.
235 Yang Su, 'Mass Killings in the Cultural Revolution', pp. 97, 119, 121; see also Andrew G. Walder and Yang Su, 'The Cultural Revolution in the Countryside: Scope, Timing and Human Impact', *China Quarterly* 173, March 2003, p. 98.
236 Unger, 'The Cultural Revolution at the Grass Roots', pp. 118–19.
237 Spence, *The Search for Modern China*, p. 606.
238 Schoenhals, *China's Cultural Revolution*, p. 137.
239 Ji Xianlin, *The Cowshed Memories of the Chinese Cultural Revolution*, New York Review Books, 2016 (originally written in 1992 and published in China in 1998).
240 MacFarquhar and Schoenhals, *Mao's Last Revolution*, pp. 118–21.

241 Yang Su, *Collective Killings in Rural China*, p. 2.
242 Walder, 'Rebellion and Repression in China', pp. 513–39.
243 Walder and Yang Su, 'The Cultural Revolution in the Countryside', p. 96.
244 See tables in Walder, 'Rebellion and Repression in China', p. 534.
245 Andrew G. Walder, 'Rebellion of the Cadres: The 1967 Implosion of the Chinese Party-State', *China Journal* 75, January 2016, p. 102.
246 Anita Chan, 'Dispelling Misconceptions About the Red Guard Movement: The Necessity to Re-examine Cultural Revolution Factionalism and Periodization', *Journal of Contemporary China* 1, no. 1, September 1992, pp. 61–85.
247 Gray, *Rebellions and Revolutions*, p. 200.
248 Schoenhals, *China's Cultural Revolution*, pp. 210–11, 214–16.
249 Yan Jiaqi and Gao Gao, *Turbulent Decade: A History of the Cultural Revolution*, University of Hawai'i Press, 1996, p. 75.
250 Rae Yang, *Spider Eaters: A Memoir*, University of California Press, 1997, p. 135.
251 Walder, 'Rebellion of the Cadres', p. 103.
252 See Joseph W. Esherick's contribution to 'Mao and the Cultural Revolution in China', *Journal of Cold War Studies* 10, no. 2, Spring 2008, p. 118.
253 Walder, 'Rebellion of the Cadres', p. 120.
254 Stuart R. Schram, 'The Limits of Cataclysmic Change: Reflections on the Place of the "Great Proletarian Cultural Revolution" in the Political Development of the People's Republic of China', *China Quarterly* 108, December 1986, p. 619.
255 A sturdy defence of the Cultural Revolution can be found in Xing Li, 'The Chinese Cultural Revolution Revisited', *China Review* 1, no. 1, Fall 2001, pp. 137–65.
256 Stuart R. Schram, 'Mao Zedong a Hundred Years On: The Legacy of a Ruler', *China Quarterly* 137, March 1994, p. 132.
257 Yan and Gao, *Turbulent Decade*, p. 409.
258 Lucian W. Pye, 'Reassessing the Cultural Revolution', *China Quarterly* 108, December 1986, p. 607.
259 Gittings, *The Changing Face of China*, pp. 141, 150.
260 Paul Clark, *Youth Culture in China: From Red Guards to Netizens*, Cambridge University Press, 2012, pp. 10 ff.
261 See preface to Yang Jisheng, *The World Turned Upside Down*.
262 Daniel A. Bell, *The Dean of Shandong: Confessions of a Minor Bureaucrat at a Chinese University*, Princeton University Press, 2023, p. 10.
263 An exhaustive account can be found in Margaret Macmillan, *Nixon and Mao: The Week That Changed the World*, Random House, 2008.
264 Henry Kissinger, *On China*, Penguin, 2012, p. 530.
265 Ibid., p. 241; on Deng, see pp. 321 ff.
266 John W. Garver, *China's Quest: The History of the Foreign Relations of the People's Republic of China*, Oxford University Press, 2016, pp. 419–24.
267 The full text can be found at '203. Joint Statement Following Discussions with Leaders of the People's Republic of China', Office of the Historian, history.state.gov.
268 Xiaoming Zhang, 'China's 1979 War with Vietnam: A Reassessment', *China Quarterly* 184, December 2005, p. 855.
269 *Resolution on Certain Questions in the History of Our Party Since the Founding of the People's Republic of China (Adopted by the Sixth Plenary Session of the Eleventh Central Committee of the Communist Party of China on June 27, 1981)*, para. 24.2, marxists.org.
270 Ibid., para. 27. For a discussion of continuity with the Mao era, see Arif Dirlik, 'Mao Zedong in Contemporary Chinese Official Discourse and History', *China Perspectives* 2, 2012, pp. 17–27.

271 Thomas Heberer and Feng-Mei Heberer, 'Fifty Years On: The "Great Proletarian Cultural Revolution" in the Age of the Internet – Still Haunting China', *European Journal of East Asian Studies* 15, no. 2, 2016, p. 210.
272 Brown, *China's Dream*, pp. 37–9.
273 See Nicholas Kristof, 'Looking for a Jump-Start in China', *New York Times*, 5 January 2013 – also predicting that forthcoming rule of Xi Jinping would be 'liberal' and that Liu Xiaobo, the Nobel Peace Prize-winning writer, would be released from prison. He wasn't. He was released on medical grounds (after being diagnosed with terminal liver cancer) only in late May 2017 and died shortly after.
274 'Editorial: Good Riddance to a Tyrant', *Taipei Times*, 7 February 2007.
275 Deng Xiaoping, 'Remarks on Successive Drafts of the "Resolution on Certain Questions in the History of Our Party Since the Founding of the People's Republic of China"', in *Selected Works of Deng Xiaoping*, vol. 2, Foreign Languages Press, 1995, available at dengxiaopingworks.wordpress.com.
276 Vogel, *Deng Xiaoping and the Transformation of China*, pp. 1–2.
277 See Lin Chun, *The Transformation of Chinese Socialism*, Duke University Press, p. 2.
278 Vogel, *Deng Xiaoping and the Transformation of China*, p. 704
279 Maurice J. Meisner, *The Deng Xiaoping Era: An Inquiry into the Fate of Chinese Socialism, 1978–1994*, Hill and Wang, 1996, pp. 189–90.
280 Shaoguang Wang, 'Adapting by Learning: The Evolution of China's Rural Health Care Financing', *Modern China* 35, no. 4, July 2009, p. 381.
281 Richard Curt Kraus, 'The Cultural Revolution Era, 1964–1976', in Wasserstrom, *The Oxford History of Modern China*, pp. 253–4; see also Richard Curt Kraus, *The Cultural Revolution: A Very Short Introduction*, Oxford University Press, 2012, pp. 13–20, 63–5, 82.
282 Giovani Arrighi, *Adam Smith in Beijing: Lineages of the Twenty-First Century*, Verso, 2007, p. 351; see also Wang Hui, *The End of the Revolution: China and the Limits of Modernity*, Verso, 2009, preface to the English edition, pp. xvii–xxxiii.
283 Bert Hofman, 'Reflections on 40 Years of China's Reforms', in Ross Garnaut, Ligang Song and Cai Fang, eds, *China's 40 Years of Reform and Development 1978–2018*, Australian National University Press, 2018, p. 53.
284 Perry Anderson, 'Two Revolutions: Rough Notes', *New Left Review* 61, January–February 2010, p. 79.
285 Deng Xiaoping, 'On the Reform of the System of Party and State Leadership', 18 August 1980, in *Selected Works of Deng Xiaoping*, vol. 2, dengxiaopingworks.wordpress.com.
286 Jean-François Huchet, 'The Economic Legacy of Deng Xiaoping', *China Perspectives* 11, May–June 1997, p. 9; Huchet points out that the cat was in fact ginger in the original saying.
287 Barry Naughton, 'Deng Xiaoping: The Economist', *China Quarterly* 135, September 1993, p. 491.
288 Ibid., pp. 500, 508, 510.
289 Bianco, 'Les Politiques agraires de la Révolution chinoise', p. 151.
290 Deng Xiaoping, 'Excerpts from Talks Given in Wuchang, Shenzhen, Zhuhai and Shanghai', 18 January–21 February 1992, in *Selected Works of Deng Xiaoping*, vol. 3, Foreign Languages Press, 1994, available at dengxiaopingworks.wordpress.com.
291 Naughton, 'Deng Xiaoping: The Economist', p. 507.
292 Quoted in Wu Guoguang, 'The Return of Ideology?', in John Wong and Zheng Yongnian, eds, *The Nanxun Legacy and China's Development in the Post-Deng Era*, Singapore University Press, 2001, p. 226.
293 Huchet, 'The Economic Legacy of Deng Xiaoping', p. 11.

294 You-tien Hsing, *The Great Urban Transformation: Politics of Land and Property in China*, Oxford University Press, 2012, p. 17 and ch. 7.
295 Gittings, *The Changing Face of China*, pp. 136–7.
296 Minxin Pei, *From Reform to Revolution: The Demise of Communism in China and the Soviet Union*, Harvard University Press, 1994, pp. 96–7.
297 Sally Sargeson and Jian Zhang, 'Reassessing the Role of the Local State: A Case Study of Local Government Interventions in Property Rights Reform in a Hangzhou District', *China Journal* 42, July 1999, pp. 79, 99.
298 Yasheng Huang, *Capitalism with Chinese Characteristics*, Cambridge University Press, 2008, p. 80.
299 Yasheng Huang, 'How Did China Take Off?', *Journal of Economic Perspectives* 26, no. 4, Fall 2012, pp. 147–9.
300 Wing Thye Woo, 'The Real Reasons for China's Growth', *China Journal* 41, January 1999, p. 129.
301 Huang, 'How Did China Take Off?', pp. 165–6; Hofman, 'Reflections on 40 Years of China's Reforms', p. 56.
302 Weber, *How China Escaped Shock Therapy*, pp. 84, 91.
303 Vogel, *Deng Xiaoping and the Transformation of China*, p. 114. On the improvement of economic ties with Japan, see Zhang, *Beijing's Economic Statecraft*, p. 135–69.
304 William A. Callaghan, 'China Rising, 2000–2010', in Wasserstrom, *Oxford History of Modern China*, p. 334.
305 All data in Vogel, *Deng Xiaoping and the Transformation of China*, pp. 394–422, 444, 455–6.
306 Ibid., p. 473.
307 On China's advantages, see ibid., pp. 473–4.
308 Ibid., p. 706.
309 Brown, *China's Dream*, p. 127.
310 Peter Nolan, 'The CPC and the Ancient Régime', *New Left Review* 115, January–February 2019, p. 26.
311 Wang Hui, *The End of the Revolution*, p. xviii.
312 Quoted in Peter Nolan, *China's Rise, Russia's Fall: Politics, Economics and Planning in the Transition from Stalinism*, Macmillan, 1995, p. 164.
313 Weber, *How China Escaped Shock Therapy*, pp. 1–2.
314 Deng, 'Excerpts from Talks Given'.
315 Hofman, 'Reflections on 40 Years of China's Reforms', p. 58.
316 For an analysis, see Tom Cliff, 'Face Funds: Political Manoeuvres Around Nonstate Welfare in Rural China', *China Review* 17, no. 2, June 2017, pp. 151–78, particularly p. 172.
317 Dingping Guo, 'The Changing Patterns of Communist Party-State Relations in China: Comparative Perspective', *Journal of East Asian Affairs* 31, no. 1, Spring/Summer 2017, pp. 83, 91.
318 John Wong, 'The Economics of the *Nanxun*', in Wong and Zheng, *The Nanxun Legacy*, p. 40.
319 Deng, 'Excerpts from Talks Given'. See also Richard Baum, *Burying Mao: Chinese Politics in the Age of Deng Xiaoping*, Princeton University Press, 1994, p. 359.
320 Zhu Rongji, *On the Record: The Road to Reform 1991–1997*, Brookings Institution, 2013, p. 110.
321 Jeffrey N. Wasserstrom and Kate Merkel-Hess, 'Tiananmen and Its Aftermath, 1989–1999', in Wasserstrom, *Oxford History of Modern China*, p. 305, a remarkably interesting account of the Tiananmen incident. The number of those killed, as usual, cannot be reliably estimated, some claim 'between 2,000 and 7,000', while the government claimed only 300 deaths; see Meisner, *The Deng Xiaoping Era*, p. 405.

322 June Teufel Dreyer, *Middle Kingdom and the Empire of the Rising Sun: Sino-Japanese Relations, Past and Present*, Oxford University Press, 2016, p. 183.
323 Gittings, *The Changing Face of China*, pp. 237–46.
324 Meisner, *The Deng Xiaoping Era*, p. 403.
325 Lin, *The Transformation of Chinese Socialism*, p. 213.
326 Joseph W. Esherick and Jeffrey N. Wasserstrom, 'Acting Out Democracy: Political Theatre in China', *Journal of Asian Studies* 49, no. 4, November 1990, p. 858.
327 Quoted in Pei, *From Reform to Revolution*, p. 47.
328 Vogel, *Deng Xiaoping and the Transformation of China*, p. 638.
329 Wang Chaohua, *One China, Many Paths*, p. 13.
330 Hofman, 'Reflections on 40 Years of China's Reforms', pp. 62–3.
331 Susan L. Shirk, '"Playing to the Provinces:" Deng Xiaoping's Political Strategy of Economic Reform', *Studies in Comparative Communism* 23, no. 314, Autumn/Winter 1990, pp. 227–8, 230–1, 234–6.
332 See Christopher Marquis and Kunyuan Qiao, *Mao and Markets: The Communist Roots of Chinese Enterprise*, Yale University Press, 2022, esp. pp. 90 ff.
333 For another example of someone who was pessimistic – and wrong – about China's prospects, see Will Hutton, *The Writing on the Wall: China and the West in the 21st Century*, Little Brown, 2007. For an exceedingly optimistic interpretation, see Martin Jacques, *When China Rules the World*, Penguin, 2009.
334 David Shambaugh, *China's Future*, Polity Press, 2016, p. 136.
335 Gittings, *The Changing Face of China*, p. 326.
336 World Bank data as reported in the article 'Richard Nixon in China: 50 Years On', *Financial Times*, 20 February 2022.
337 'GNI per Capita, Atlas Method (Current US$)', World Bank Open Data, data.worldbank.org.
338 Paul Bairoch, 'International Industrialization Levels from 1750 to 1980', *Journal of European Economic History* 11, no. 2, Fall 1982, p. 296. In 1750 China and India produced more than half the world's manufacturing output.
339 Huang, *Capitalism with Chinese Characteristics*, p. 43.
340 Meisner, *The Deng Xiaoping Era*, p. 247.
341 Peter Nolan, *China at the Crossroad*, Polity, 2004, p. 121, and on the environment, see also pp. 27–30.
342 Nolan, 'The CPC and the Ancient Régime', p. 2; see also He Qinglian, 'A Listing Social Structure', in Wang Chaohua, *One China, Many Paths*, pp. 164–5.
343 Bell, *The Dean of Shandong*, p. 66.
344 Ching Kwan Lee, *Against the Law: Labor Protests in China's Rustbelt and Sunbelt*, University of California Press, 2007, p. 44.
345 Ibid., p. 197.
346 John W. Lewis and Xue Litai, 'Social Change and Political Reform in China: Meeting the Challenge of Success', *China Quarterly* 176, December 2003, p. 931.
347 Zang Xiaowei, 'Income Inequality by Ethnicity in Urban China', in Wong and Zheng, *The Nanxun Legacy*, p. 123.
348 Christian Henriot, 'The Great Spoliation: The Socialist Transformation of Industry in 1950s China', *European Journal of East Asian Studies* 13, no. 2, 2014, p. 155; for the Credit Suisse estimate, see 'Chinese Millionaires – Statistics and Facts', statista.com.
349 Lu Min, *Dinner for Six*, Balestier Press, 2022, p. 320.
350 'Success and Danger for China's Communists at 100', *Financial Times*, 30 June 2021.
351 'The New Geopolitics of Global Business', 'Leaders', *Economist*, 5 June 2021.
352 Jude Blanchette, 'Confronting the Challenge of Chinese State Capitalism', Center for Strategic and International Studies, 22 January 2021, csis.org.

353 'Life Expectancy at Birth, Total (Years) – China', World Bank Open Data, data.worldbank.org.
354 George Magnus, *Red Flags: Why Xi's China Is in Jeopardy*, Yale University Press, 2018, p. 197.
355 Nathan Sperber, 'Forecasting China?', *NLR–Sidecar*, 8 September 2023.
356 Brown, *China's Dream*, p. 164.
357 Quoted in James Kynge, 'What Will Xi's China Do Next?', *Financial Times*, 20 October 2020.
358 Kevin Rudd, 'The World According to Xi Jinping: What China's Ideologue in Chief Really Believes', *Foreign Affairs* 101, no. 6, November/December 2022.
359 S. A. Smith, *Russia in Revolution: An Empire in Crisis, 1890 to 1928*, Oxford University Press, 2017, p. 391.

Conclusion

1 Charles Tilly, *European Revolutions, 1492–1992*, Blackwell, 1995, pp. xiii, 8.
2 Ibid., p. 9.
3 Ibid., p. xiii.
4 Peter Kornbluh, *The Pinochet File*, New Press, 2003, see esp. pp. 79 ff.
5 Hugh O'Shaughnessy, *Pinochet, the Politics of Torture*, New York University Press, 2000, p. 56. O'Shaughnessy was then the correspondent for the *Observer* in Chile.
6 Theda Skocpol, *States and Social Revolutions: A Comparative Analysis of France, Russia, and China*, Cambridge University Press, 1979, p. 33.
7 Mike Brewer and Thomas Wernham, 'Income and Wealth Inequality Explained in 5 Charts', Institute of Fiscal Studies, 9 November 2022, ifs.org.uk.
8 Myriam Hunter-Henin, 'Why the French Don't Like the Burqa: Laïcité, National Identity and Religious Freedom', *International and Comparative Law Quarterly* 61, no. 3, July 2012, p. 614.
9 Theresa May, Prime Minister's Questions, House of Commons, 1 February 2017, parliament.uk.
10 Ahmet T. Kuru, 'Secularism, State Policies, and Muslims in Europe: Analyzing French Exceptionalism', *Comparative Politics* 41, no. 1, October 2008, p. 7.
11 Ashley Nellis, *The Color of Justice: Racial and Ethnic Disparity in State Prisons*, Sentencing Project, 2021.
12 See John Elflein, 'New Cases of Tuberculosis per 100,000 Population in the U.S. in 2023, by Race/Ethnicity', Statista, 25 April 2024, statista.com.
13 'Black/African American Health', Population Profile, Office of Minority Health, US Department of Health and Human Services, 16 January 2025, minorityhealth.hhs.gov.
14 'Incarceration Rates by Country 2025', World Population Review, at worldpopulationreview.com.
15 '10,429 People Have Been Shot and Killed by Police from 2015 to 2024', *Washington Post*, washingtonpost.com.
16 'Intentional Homicide', United Nations Office on Drugs and Crime, dataunodc.un.org.
17 'Drug Overdose Deaths: Facts and Figures', National Institute on Drug Abuse, nida.nih.gov.
18 'Understanding the Opioid Overdose Epidemic', CDC, 9 June 2025.
19 See Fintan O'Toole, 'The Lie of Nation Building', *New York Review of Books*, 7 October 2021.
20 'ACLU Statement on the 21st Anniversary of Guantánamo', ACLU press release, 10 January 2023, aclu.org.

21. On the 'visionary-futurist' view of the Russian Revolution, see James H. Billington, 'Six Views of the Russian Revolution', *World Politics* 18, no. 3, April 1966, p. 464.
22. See Bill Jones, *The Russia Complex: The British Labour Party and the Soviet Union*, Manchester University Press, 1977, pp. 14–16.
23. Romain Rolland, *Quinze ans de combat 1919–1934*, Édition Rieder, 1935, p. 88.
24. Bertolt Brecht, *Poems 1913–1956*, ed. John Willett and Ralph Manheim, Minerva, 1994, pp. 319–20.
25. IMF data: World Economic Outlook Database, October 2022, imf.org; World Bank data: 'GDP per capita, PPP (Current International $)', World Bank Open Data, data.worldbank.org.
26. Vladimir Putin, 'Address by the President of the Russian Federation', 21 February 2022, President of Russa, en.kremlin.ru.
27. Jamie Gaida, Jennifer Wong-Leung, Stephan Robin and Danielle Cave, 'ASPI's Critical Technology Tracker', Australian Strategic Policy Institute, 1 March 2023, aspi.org.au.
28. 'China', profile, Observatory of Economic Complexity, oec.world.
29. 'GDP (Current US$)', World Bank Open Data, data.worldbank.org.
30. Fredric Jameson, 'In Hyperspace', *London Review of Books* 37, no. 17, 10 September 2015.
31. See, for instance, McKenzie Wark, *Capital Is Dead: Is This Something Worse?*, Verso, 2019; Jodi Dean, *Capital's Grave: Neofeudalism and the New Class Struggle*, Verso, 2025.
32. Hugh Roberts, *Loved Egyptian Night: The Meaning of the Arab Spring*, Verso, 2024, p. xi. Roberts is in 'no doubt that what had occurred in Tunisia was a revolution' because it was a change of regime.
33. Göran Therborn, 'The World and the Left', *New Left Review* 137, September–October 2022, p. 23; (this is essential reading).
34. George Lawson, *Anatomies of Revolution*, Cambridge University Press, 2019, p. 242.
35. Karl Marx, preface to the first German edition of 1867, *Capital*, vol. 1, Progress Publishers, 1965, p. 10.
36. Gareth Stedman Jones, 'Karl Marx's Changing Picture of the End of Capitalism', *Journal of the British Academy* 6, 2018, pp. 187–206.
37. Denis Diderot, *Jacques le fataliste et son maître*, Folio Gallimard, 1973, p. 65.

Index

'A Just Russia for Truth' Party, 255
Abbasid Revolution, 13
Aberdeen, Earl of, 172
Argyll, Earl of, 46
Abkhazia, 256
Aboriginal Protection Act (1869), 66
Aboukir, 129
Abyssinia, 338
Accademia della Crusca, 15
Act of Settlement (1701), 51
Act of Union (1840), 30
Action Française, 97, 190
Adams, Abigail, 79, 80
Adams, John, 2–3, 70–1, 78–80, 116, 125
Adler, Victor, 223
Afghanistan, 249, 333, 339, 342
Africa, 8, 54, 55–7, 58, 64, 66, 67, 81, 173, 243, 298, 308
African Americans, 72, 80, 85, 91
Aganbegyan, Abel, 253
Age of Liberty, 21
Agincourt, 242
AIDS/HIV, 332
Ajaccio, 134
Akhmatova, Anna, 196, 246, 254
Akmolinsk, 237
Albania, 118, 156, 224, 246, 248, 257, 339
Albania, Communist Party of 246
Alberto, Carlo (king), 141, 170
Alekseyev, Mikhail, 216
Alessandri, Jorge, 325
Alexander I (king), 155, 158
Alexander II (king), 186, 191, 204, 206
Alexander III (king), 204, 20
Alexander Palace, 191
Alexandria, 159
Alfieri, Vittorio, 124, 164, 165

Algeria, 1, 66, 142, 331
All-China Labour Congress, Sixth, 292
Allende, Salvador, 325
All-Russian Peasant Union, 207
All-Union Conference of Leading Personnel of Socialist Industry, First, 240
Alpaugh, Micah, 126
Alsace, 148, 177, 195
Alternative für Deutschland (AfD), 335
Amendment, Fifteenth, 87
Amendment, Fourteenth, 87, 88
Amendments, Reconstruction 87
Amendment, Thirteenth, 87
Amendola, Giovanni, 96
American Anti-Slavery Society, 84
American Civil Liberty Union, 333
American Civil War (1861–65), 1, 4, 9, 27–8, 34, 82, 83–6, 88, 90, 92–4, 96, 114, 181
American Equal Rights Association (AERA), 87
American Federation of Labor, 91
American Relief Administration, 229
American War of Independence (1775–83), 1, 2, 3, 16, 65, 67, 73, 74, 86, 93, 100, 102, 109, 115, 120, 159, 188, 190, 326, 335
Amsterdam, 4
Anderson, Perry, 4, 255, 311
Andropov, Yuri, 233, 249, 251
Anne, Queen, 51
Anschluss (1938), 176
Anthony, Susan B., 87
Antonov, Alexander, 219
Anyuan (China), 272, 273
Apache, 90
Appomattox (Virginia), 86
Apter, David, 284
Arab Spring, 32, 318, 343

Arabic script, 24
Aragon, Louis, 336
Arc de Triomphe, 128
Arendt, Hannah, 27, 96, 100
Argentina, 180, 319
Aristotle, 10
Arkhangelsk (Russia), 218
Armand, Inessa, 229
Armenia, 187, 214, 215, 217, 224, 228, 233, 252, 256, 257
Arnoldo da Brescia, 12
Arndt, Ernst Moritz, 168, 176
Arne, Thomas, 56
Arnim, Achim von, 163
Artois, Comte d'. *See* Charles X (king)
Asher, Harvey, 200
Ashley, James, 87
Ashmole, Elias, 41
Ashworth, John, 86
Assarino, Luca, 15
Astana, 237, 256
Astell, Mary, 115
Atatürk, Mustafa Kemal, 24, 195, 224
Athens, 11
Attica (ancient Greece), 11
Auber, Daniel, 16, 154
Aughrim, Battle of (1691), 48, 49
Augustus, Gaius Julius Caesar (Octavian), 11
Aurora (ship), 192, 201
Austerlitz, Battle of (1805), 146
Australia, 64, 66, 341, 343
Australian Strategic Policy Institute, 341
Austria, 98, 108, 116, 117, 140, 147, 148, 153, 154, 158, 160, 161, 163, 164, 168, 169, 170, 171, 172, 175, 176, 177, 180, 186, 188, 195, 212, 220, 223, 224, 239, 246, 247, 265, 327
Austro-Hungarian Empire, 2, 188, 195, 216, 219
Autumn Harvest Uprising, 274
Avogadro, Giovanni Battista Birago, 15
Axelrod, Pavel, 205
Azerbaijan, 187, 214, 215, 217, 244, 256, 257

Babeuf, François-Noël, 98
Babylon, 104
Bagehot, Walter, 86
Bakunin, Mikhail, 9
Balkan Wars (1912–13), 159, 194
Balladur, Édouard, 328
Bandiera, Attilio, 169
Bandiera, Emilio, 169
Bandung Conference, 295, 308
Bank of England, 50
Barère, Bertrand, 102, 118
Baring, Thomas, 82
Barsov, Alexander A., 232
Basile, Giambattista, 164

Basilique du Sacré-Coeur, 151
Bastille, 33, 99, 113–14, 126, 152, 191
Battle on the Ice (1242), 245
Bauer, Otto, 223
Bavaria, 148, 158, 159, 161, 163, 167, 168, 175, 177
Bayramov, Mirza, 244
Bazarov, Vladimir, 230
Beard, Charles, 86
Beard, May, 86
Beatles, 5
Beaumont, Gustave de, 84
Beauvoir, Simone de, 336
Bebel, August, 159
Beethoven, Ludwig van, 133
Beijing (Peiping), 7, 96, 260, 265, 269, 273, 279, 287, 289, 293, 297, 303, 308, 309, 320, 342
Beijing (Peking) University, 297
Beissinger, Mark, 8
Belarus, 206, 212, 220, 233, 256, 257
Belgian Revolution, 16
Belgium, 95, 101, 117, 132, 141, 147, 154, 160, 180, 197, 208, 285, 311, 331, 334
Bellamy, Edward, 342
Belorussia, 215
Bemporad, Elissa, 222, 223
Benoist, Alain de, 338
Bentham, Jeremy, 124
Bergamo (Italy), 161
Beria, Lavrentiy, 233, 241
Berlin Wall, 251
Berlioz, Hector, 133, 137
Bernal, J. D., 336
Bernstein, Edward, 30, 223
Bethune, Mary McLeod, 85
Bialik, Hayim, 223
Bianco, Lucien, 273, 285, 301–2
Bicknell, John, 58
Biden, Joe, 92, 322, 333
Biennio Rosso, 195
Bill of Rights, 48, 114, 190
Billington, James, 336
Binasco (Italy), 128
Bishop of Autun, 106
Bismarck, Otto von, 31, 148, 149, 159, 173, 176, 177, 179, 180, 181, 182, 200
Black War (1820s–32), 66
Blackburn, Robin, 55, 59
Blackburn, Virginia, 6
Blackstone, William, 80
Blake, William, 56, 57, 72, 123
Blanc, Louis, 100, 143
Blanchette, Jude, 322
Blanqui, Louis Auguste, 143
Blanter, Matvey Isaakovich, 339
Blok, Alexander, 202

Bloodless Revolution, 49
Bloody Sunday, 205, 207
Blücher, Gebhard von, 37, 135
Boadicea (Boudicca, queen), 127
Boccaccio, Giovanni, 161
Bodde, Derk, 289
Bodin, Jean, 57
Boer Wars, 67
Bogrov, Dmitry, 207
Bohemia, 160
Bolivia, 15, 344
Bolshevik Central Committee, 201
Bolsheviks, 4, 8, 23, 34, 36, 41, 96, 185–7, 189–90, 191–2, 194, 196, 197–201, 202, 205–12, 213–16, 218, 219–24, 225, 226–9, 231, 237, 249, 254, 257, 258, 262, 268, 272, 275, 291, 293, 327, 341
Bolshevism, 185, 198, 199, 200, 216, 229
Bonaparte, Napoleon. *See* Napoleon I
Bonaparte, Louis Napoleon. *See* Napoleon III
'Bonaparte' (Lamartine), 133
Bonhomme, Jacques, 12, 13
Bordeaux, 147
Boris, King, 224
Borodin, Mikhail, 272
Bosnia, 257
Boston, 21, 70, 74, 80, 260
Boston Massacre (1770), 71
Boswell, James, 73
Bottai, Giuseppe, 4
Boudicca (Boadicea, queen), 127
Boulay de la Meurthe, Antoine, 28
Bourbon dynasty, 27, 63, 65, 88, 98, 131, 133, 134, 135, 136, 137, 138, 139, 147, 150, 169, 172, 173, 174
Boxer Rebellion, 194, 265, 269
Bradshaw, John, 36
Braganza, House of, 16
Brahms, Johannes, 163
Brandt, Loren, 261
Brandywine, Battle of, 74
Braude, I. S., 224
Braudel, Fernand, 35, 114
Brazil, 65, 75, 84, 169, 305, 343
Brecht, Bertolt, 337
Bremen, 175, 178
Brentano, Clemens von, 163
Brest-Litovsk, 203, 212, 213, 214, 215, 218, 228
Brest-Litovsk Treaty (1918), 214, 215
Breton (language), 162
Breton, Andre, 336
Brexit Party, 333
Brezhnev, Leonid, 233, 248, 249, 254
Brinton, Crane, 8–9, 97
Brissot, Jacques Pierre, 106, 114, 116
Bristol (England), 55
British Intelligence Mission, 203

Brittany, 13, 119
Brixham (England) 47
Brown, Archie, 184, 250, 251, 252
Brown, John, 84
Brown, Kerry, 314
Browning, Elizabeth Barrett, 62
Browning, Robert, 62
Brusilov, Aleksei (general), 196
Brussels, 16, 154
Brzezinski, Zbigniew, 184
Büchner, George, 167
Budapest, 220
Bugeaud, Maréchal Thomas, 142
Bukharin, Nikolai, 105, 186, 197, 212, 226, 228–31, 241
Bulgaria, 154, 194, 212, 224, 246, 247, 256, 257
Burke, Edmund, 54, 60, 70, 73, 121–2, 123, 125, 326
Burlatsky, Fedor, 251
Burma, 284, 285
Burns, Robert, 123
Bush, George W., 76, 252
Butte Montmartre (Paris), 151
Byron, Lord, 123, 133, 156

Caesar, Julius, 11
Cairo, 23, 128–9
Calhoun, John C., 82, 92
Calvin, John, 53, 57
Calvinism, 38
Cambodia, 28
Cambridge, University of, 49
Camden, William, 18
Cameron, David, 329
Campanella, Tommaso, 342
Canada, 30, 56, 73, 341
Canton (Guangzhou), 260, 262, 264, 287, 304
Canuts, 140
Caprera (Italy), 172
Caribbean colonies, 56, 64, 75, 132
Carlisle Peace Commission, 73
Carlyle, Thomas, 62–3, 126
Carnatic Wars (1746–63), 108
Carnation Revolution, 260
Carr, E. H., 184, 231, 244
Catalan, 161, 162, 327
Catalonia, 18, 141
Catherine the Great, 14, 186
Catholic Gunpowder Plot (1605), 37
Catholicism, 44, 47, 48, 53, 129, 135, 136, 145, 151, 154, 163. *See also* Church, Roman Catholic
Catholics, 1, 15, 16, 21, 23, 28, 37, 42, 43, 46, 47–8, 49, 64, 123, 129, 148, 163, 171, 181, 332
Caucasus, 214, 216, 228, 231, 234
Cavaignac, Louis-Eugène, 119, 144–5

Cavendish, William, 47
Cavour, Camillo, 147, 148, 170, 172, 173, 175, 182
Ceaușescu, Nicolae, 24
Center for Strategic and International Studies, 322
Centers for Disease Control and Prevention (CDC), 332
Central Economic Work Conference (1978), 311
Central Powers, 195, 212, 213, 218
Centre Pompidou, 7
Chamber of Deputies (France), 135, 141, 151
Chamberlain, Daniel H., 89
Chambre des Paires, 135
Champ-de-Mars (Paris), 151
Champenois (language), 162
Chang, Gordon G., 319
Chapelet Law (1791), 115, 140
Charlemagne, 134
Charles I (king), 7, 17, 27, 33, 36, 37–8, 42, 44–5, 50, 52–3, 95, 153, 190, 327
Charles II (king), 36, 37, 42–7, 50, 54–5, 328
Charles V (emperor), 12
Charles IX (king), 16
Charles X (king), 113, 134, 135, 137, 138
Charlotte of Wales, 154
Chartist demands (1838), 63
Chateaubriand, François-René de, 97, 106, 122, 133, 137, 157, 326
Chávez, Hugo, 344
Chen Yun, 314
Chenier, André, 106
Chernenko, Konstantin, 233, 249
Chernobyl, 339
Cherokee, 73
Cheyenne, 89
Chiang Kai-shek, 265, 270, 273, 277–8, 279–81, 283, 284–8, 290, 310
Chicago, 101
Chicago Boys, 325
Chicken War, 14
Chile, 324, 325
China, People's Republic of, 7, 8–9, 14, 18, 20, 25, 29, 34–6, 53, 64, 83, 148, 164, 183, 187, 189, 194, 210, 213, 218, 224, 239, 247, 251, 259–60, 262–99, 301–2, 305–23, 330–2, 340–2, 343
China Aid Act (1948), 288
Chinese Civil War (1927–49), 264, 273, 283, 286, 290, 291, 310, 313, 319
Chinese Communist Party (CCP), 105, 260, 261, 262, 270, 271, 272–3, 276, 278, 279, 283, 284, 286, 288, 289, 290, 291, 295, 296, 297, 303, 306, 307, 309, 310, 311, 317, 319, 340
Chinese Exclusion Act (1882), 91

Chios (Greece), 156
Chirac, Jacques, 328, 332
Chislehurst (England), 148
Chongqing, 280, 281, 285
Chouan brothers, 119
Chouannerie, 118, 119
Christ, Jesus, 20
Christianity, 20
Chun Doo Hwan, 317
Churchill, Henry, 5
Churchill, Winston, 5, 37, 64, 243, 285, 293
Church of Byzantium, 12
Church of England, 38, 48, 54, 64, 121, 156
Church of Rome, 12
Church of Russia, Eastern Orthodox, 12
Church of Scotland, Presbyterian, 38
Church, Roman Catholic, 12, 43, 115, 136. *See also* Catholicism; Catholics
Cicero, 11
Cisalpine Republic, 129
City of London, 38, 62, 69, 74
Civil List, 50
Civil Rights Act (1964), 88
Cixi, Empress Dowager, 263, 264
Claremont House, 143
Clark, Christopher, 140
Clarkson, Thomas, 59, 60
Clay, Henry, 83
Cleomenes, King, 11
Clinton, Bill, 252, 255
Clinton, Hillary, 76
Cobban, Alfred, 96–7
Cobden–Chevalier Treaty (1860), 147
Code Napoléon (1804), 132
Coffey, John, 58
Cohen, Stephen F., 184, 231
Colbert, Jean-Baptiste, 108
Cold War, 96, 184, 226, 236, 239, 247, 252, 290, 292, 293, 327
Coleridge, Samuel Taylor, 123
Colfax (Louisiana), 89
Collingwood, Luke (captain), 60
Colombia, 180
Colombo, Cristoforo, 37
Colonne Vendôme, 149
Columbus, Christopher, 37
Comintern, 187, 232, 239, 246, 247, 266, 272, 275, 278
Committee for Relief to Victims, 224
Committee of Five, 71
Committee of Public Safety, 210
'Common Programme', 295, 296
Commonwealth of England, 17, 41, 46
Communist Party, British (CPGB), 336
Communist Party, French, 336
Communist Party of Albania, 246
Communist Party, Russian, 215, 255

Communist Party's Central Commission for Disciplinary Inspection, 320
Company of Royal Adventurers Trading with Africa, 55
Compromise of 1877, 89
Compton, Henry, 47
Concert of Europe, 169
Condorcet, Marquis de, 105, 106, 114
Confucius, 260, 267, 269, 270, 307, 312
Congress of Berlin, 22, 154
Congress of the Comintern, Second (1920), 187
Congress of Vienna (1815), 136, 154, 161, 169
Congress of the Bolshevik Party, Extraordinary Seventh, 210
Connecticut, 70, 76, 84
Connecticut Compromise, 76
Conquest, Robert, 239
Considérant, Victor, 144
Conspiracy of the Equals (1796), 98
Constantinople, 12, 159
Continental Army, 210
Continental Congress, First, 70, 73
Continental Congress, Second, 70, 101
Convention Nationale, 118, 130, 210
Cooperative Medical System, 311
Copernicus, 18
Corbyn, Jeremy, 343
Corday, Charlotte, 117
Corfu, 158
Corn Laws, 21
Cornerstone Speech, 85
Correa, Rafael, 344
Corsica, 132
COVID-19, 6
Cowper, William, 59
Cressy, David, 39
Crete, 158
Creuse (France), 98
Crimean War (1853–56), 147, 160, 186, 194
Crispi, Francesco, 171, 172, 174
Crispi, Garibaldino, 174
Croce, Benedetto, 183
Cromwell, Oliver, 7, 17, 33, 36–7, 40–5, 46–7, 49, 50, 52, 54, 172, 181, 190
Cromwell, Richard, 42
Crystal Palace, 172
Cuba, 84, 187, 247, 248, 332, 333, 343
Cuban Revolution (1959), 29
Cugoano, Quobna Ottobah, 59
Culloden, Battle of (1745), 51, 102
Cultural Revolution, Great Proletarian (1966–76), 4, 7, 28, 34, 259, 272, 290, 293, 297, 301, 302–11, 315, 317–19, 341
Cumberland, Duke of, 51–2
Cuoco, Vincenzo, 21
Custer, General, 90, 219

Cuvier, Georges, 338
Czechoslovakia, 8, 195, 239, 246, 247–48, 260, 305, 342
Czech Republic, 8, 256, 257
Czech Silesia, 160

Dadu River, 276
d'Agoult, Marie, 144
d'Anglas, Boissy, 127
Dante Alighieri, 161, 162, 167
Danton, Georges Jacques, 7, 96, 106, 134
Darwin, Charles, 59–60
Daumier, Honoré, 142
David, Jacques-Louis, 111, 112, 133
Davies, Norman, 220
Davies, R. W., 231
Da Vinci, Leonardo, 37
Davis, David Brion, 81
Day, Thomas, 58, 73
Day of the Overthrow of the Autocracy, 197
Days of Freedom, 207
d'Azeglio, Massimo, 166, 173
Declaration of Independence, 2, 36, 68, 71, 78, 80, 81, 84, 85, 93, 100, 114, 190, 332
Declaration of the Rights of Man and of the Citizen (*Déclaration des droits de l'homme et du citoyen*), 1, 100, 106, 114, 115, 123, 151
Declaratory Act (1766), 69, 73
Decree on Peace, 212
Defarge, Thérèse, 122
Defoe, Daniel, 48, 55
de Gaulle, Charles, 37, 243, 293
Delacroix, Eugène, 129, 156, 157
Delavigne, Casimir, 139
Delaware, 70, 84, 332
De Mauro, Tullio, 162
Deng Xiaoping, 34, 251, 271, 301, 307–8, 310, 312
Denikin, Anton, 213, 217, 219
Denmark, 141, 148, 158, 175, 177, 180
Derby, Lord, 172
De Roberto, Federico, 32
De Sanctis, Francesco, 164
Desnos, Robert, 336
Dessalines, Jean-Jacques, 131
de Staël, Germaine, 54, 96, 132, 135, 137, 169
de Valera, Éamon de, 23
Deutscher, Isaac, 184
Deutscher Nationalverein, 176
Dickens, Charles, 63, 122, 126, 172
Dickinson, John, 69, 70, 71
Diderot, 52, 53, 102, 117, 188, 344
Diggers (True Levellers), 18, 41
Dimitrov, Georgi, 232, 278
Ding Ling, 271
Disraeli, Benjamin, 160
Dittmar, Louise, 115

Dixon, Thomas, Jr, 93
Doerr, Hans, 242
Dolfin, Daniele, 116
Dollfuss, Engelbert, 224
Donbass (Ukraine), 256
Donne, John, 53, 103
Donskoi, Dimitri, 245
Donskoy Monastery, 217
Douglass, Frederick, 80–1, 84
Dowager Cixi, 263, 264
Dózsa, György, 13
Drayton, Michael, 19
Drayton, William Henry, 2
Dred Scott case, 92
Drogheda (Ireland), 42, 43
Dryden, John, 43–4
Dubček, Alexander, 248
Du Bois, W. E. B., 88, 92
Dugua, Charles, 128
Duma, 193, 207
Dunmore, John Murray, 4th Earl of, 73
Dunning, William, 91–2
Durham, Lord, 30
Durnovo, Pyotr N., 195
Dutch Republic, 9, 15, 38, 46, 50, 74
Dutch Revolt (1566–1648), 14–15
Dzerzhinsky, Felix, 233, 254

East Germany (German Democratic Republic), 247, 250, 252
East India Company, 62, 70
East St Louis (Illinois), 89
Easter Rising, 23
Eastern Orthodox Church of Russia, 12
Eckermann, Johann Peter, 167
Ecuador, 257, 343
Edgehill (Warwickshire), Battle of (1642), 37
Edict of Nantes (1685), 47
Edo period, 14
Edward Hyde (Lord Clarendon), 17
Égalité, Philippe, 106
Egypt, 23, 70, 127–8, 129, 156, 158, 340
Eiffel Tower, 193
Eighth Route Army, 281
Eight-Nation Alliance, 194, 265
Eisenstein, Sergei, 192, 245
El Salvador, 332
Elba (Italy), 129
Elbe (river), 178
Elizabeth I (queen), 15, 38, 64
Elizabeth II (queen), 159
Elliott, J. H., 17
Ellis, Joseph, 72
Eltis, David, 56
Eluard, Paul, 336
Emancipation of the Serfs (1861), 186, 204
Emancipation Proclamation (1863), 84

Emilia-Romagna (Italy), 171
Emmanuel, Victor (king), 170, 171, 173
Engels, Friedrich, 4, 87, 100, 103, 107, 141, 145, 159, 184, 199, 200, 214, 267, 272, 336
Engerman, Stanley L., 88
England, 2, 4, 9, 15, 17, 18, 21, 36–9, 41, 43, 45, 47–8, 50–1, 53–4, 56, 58, 62, 64, 69–70, 80, 100, 102, 104, 108, 123, 130, 143, 148, 153, 156, 164, 172, 174, 175, 181, 206, 210, 214, 240, 263–4, 327, 330, 335, 340
English Civil War (1642–51), 1, 15, 16–19, 36–9, 45, 52, 53, 64, 65, 69, 95, 102, 103, 109, 115, 120, 188, 189, 190, 203, 326, 335
English Peasants' Revolt, 13
English Revolution, 4, 18, 34, 38, 39, 47, 52–3, 63, 102, 103
Entente Powers, 195, 215, 221, 269
Entwistle, William, 160
Epirus (Greece), 158
Equiano, Olaudah, 58, 59, 60
Erickson, John, 242, 245
Ernst, Max, 336
Esher, 143
Estonia, 204, 215, 218, 224, 239, 246, 252, 257
États Généraux, 34, 97, 99, 104, 107, 110, 111
Ethiopia, 66
Eton College, 172, 330
Europe, Eastern, 8
European Parliament, 333
European Union, 134, 256
Evola, Julius, 337

Fabians, 30
Fairfax, Thomas, 40
Falloux Laws (1850), 136
Falloux, Alfred de, 136
Falun Gong, 320
Farini, Luigi Carlo, 173
Farouk, King, 23
Faure, Félix, 7
Fawkes, Guy, 37
February Revolution, 143, 144, 194, 196, 197, 210, 225
Fengtian faction, 273
Ferguson, Adam, 46, 53
Ferrières, Marquis de, 111
Festival of the Supreme Being, 136
Fête de la Fédération, 151
Fichte, Johann Gottlieb, 167, 168
Fieramosca, Ettore, 166
Fifth Republic (post-1958), 334
Figes, Orlando, 217
Filiki Eteria (Society of Friends), 155
Finistère (France), 98
Finland, 195, 197, 199, 201, 204, 207, 213–14, 218, 246–7, 342
Finnish famine of 1867–68, 299

First estate, 112
First Five-Year Plan (1928–32), 232
First Nations, 64, 82
First Reichstag elections (March 1871), 181
Fisher, Payne, 44–5
Fitzpatrick, Sheila, 184, 185, 192, 233, 235
Five-Anti Campaign, 302
Flaubert, Gustave, 137, 150
Flemish provinces, 162
Florence, 14, 160, 161, 162
Florida, 56, 76, 82, 85
Fogel, Robert, 88
Foner, Eric, 3, 87, 88
Ford, Henry, 5
Fortress of the Revolution, 227
Foscolo, Ugo, 165
Fouquier-Tinville, Antoine, 106
Fourteenth of July (France), 35
Fourth of July (US), 35
Fox, Charles James, 73
France, 1, 4, 7, 9, 13, 15, 16, 18, 22, 27, 28, 30, 33, 35, 37, 47, 48, 50, 54, 56, 63, 74–5, 82, 88, 95–9, 101–4, 108–10, 112, 115–26, 129–32, 134–50, 153–4, 157, 160, 162, 164, 171, 173, 174, 175, 177, 179, 180, 181, 182, 187, 189–91, 193, 195, 197, 201, 214, 217, 224, 225, 227, 239–40, 247, 261, 263–5, 285, 293, 305, 318, 328, 329, 331–6, 337, 338, 339, 340
Francis I (king), 162
Franco, Francisco, 11, 120
Frankfurt, 176, 177, 178
Frankfurt Parliament, 76
Franklin, Benjamin, 53, 68, 71, 72, 76
Fraser, Antonia, 41
Frederick William IV (king), 176
Freeman, Chas, 3
Frei, Eduardo, 324
French Declaration, 114
French Revolution, 1, 3, 4, 7, 9, 13, 15, 22, 26, 29, 34, 35, 52, 54, 60, 71, 73, 95–107, 109, 111, 114–26, 129–30, 132, 134, 147, 152, 155, 158, 160, 162, 164, 167, 168, 184, 188, 189, 203, 268, 324, 326, 335, 336
French Revolution, Second, 98
Friedman, Milton, 325
Froissart, Jean, 12
Fructidor coup, 127
Fu Zuoyi, 289
Fugitive Slave Clause, 81
Fujian (China), 312
Furet, François, 96–7, 120, 326
Fuseli, Henri, 60

Gaidar, Yegor, 253
Galicia (Austrian), 213
Galilei, Galileo, 37
Galton, Francis, 338

Galveston, Texas, 92
Gambetta, Léon, 151
Gandhi, Mahatma, 13
Gang of Four, 307, 310, 316
Gansu (China), 302
Gapon, Georgy, 207
Garibaldi, Giuseppe, 22, 31, 36, 86, 169, 171–4, 179, 182
Garnier-Pagès, Louis-Antoine, 145
Garrison, William Lloyd, 84
Gascon (language), 162
Gate of Heavenly Peace, 293
Gaullism, 328, 334
Gautier, Théophile, 150
Gaxotte, Pierre, 97
Gay, Delphine, 119, 144
Gaza, 257
Geneva, 6, 9
Geneva Accords (1954), 23
Geneva Revolution (1782), 123
Genoa, Republic of, 37, 132, 159, 169, 171
Genoese (language), 161
Gentile, Giovanni, 96, 337
George, Henry, 91
George I (king), 34, 159
George II (king), 52
George III (king), 45, 68, 71
George IV (king), 154
Georgia (country), 5
Gerard, François, 133
German Civil Code (1900), 274
German Confederation (Deutsche Bund), 175
German Peasants' War, 13–14
Germantown, 74
Germany, 2, 4, 8, 22, 49, 50, 52, 59, 92, 95, 100, 105, 124, 129, 141, 148, 153, 154, 159–61, 162–64, 167–68, 173, 175–76, 178–79, 180–83, 186–89, 194–95, 197, 206, 208, 212–15, 220, 223, 224–25, 239, 242, 243, 245, 246, 247, 249, 252, 265, 269, 271, 282, 305, 326, 327, 329, 330, 332, 334, 339, 341
Germany, East (German Democratic Republic), 247, 250, 252
Germany, West (Federal Republic of Germany), 251, 293
Geronimo, 90
Getty, J. Arch, 184, 235, 237, 238
Gettysburg, Battle of (1863), 92
Giacometti, Alberto, 336
Ginzburg, Yevgenia, 238
Gioberti, Vincenzo, 170
Giraffi, Alessandro, 16
Girardin, Delphine Gay de, 119–20
Girondins, 104, 106, 116, 118
Gittings, John, 319
Gladstone, William Ewart, 37, 61–2, 86, 171, 172
Glantz, David M., 245

Glorious Revolution (1688), 2, 4, 17, 46, 47, 49–50, 68, 121, 150, 158, 190
Gobineau, Arthur de, 338
Godechot, Jacques, 121
Goebbels, Joseph, 4
Goethe, Johann Wolfgang von, 124, 133, 156, 167
Gogol, Nikolai Vasilievich, 271
Goldman, Emma, 223
Gollancz (publisher), 336
Gompers, Samuel, 91
Goodfellow, Jack, 12
Gorbachev, Mikhail Sergeyevich, 248–53, 254, 257, 315
Gore, Al, 76
Gouges, Olympe de, 106, 114, 117
Gould, Randall Chase, 289, 290
Gracchi brothers, 11
Gramsci, Antonio, 21, 174, 175, 183
Grand Bazaar of Tehran, 26
Grand Remonstrance, 22 November 1641, 39–40
Granger, Gordon, 92
Grant, Madison, 338
Grant, Ulysses S., 86
Graves, William (general), 218
Gray, Jack, 295
Great Compromise, 76
Great Depression, 234
Greater Asia Co-Prosperity Sphere, 278
Great Fire of London, 45
Great Leap Forward (1958–62), 34, 259, 293, 297–302, 306, 310, 319, 341
Great October Revolution (7 November, Russia), 35, 187, 191, 192, 203, 208, 215, 227, 245, 254, 258, 326
Great Patriotic War, 244, 326
Great Plague of London, 45
Great Powers, 22, 154, 157, 159, 169, 269
Great Purges, 232, 235, 238, 241
Great Reform Act (1832), 141
Greco-Turkish War (1919–22), 195
Greece, 2, 22, 28, 72, 153–8, 163, 166, 180, 188, 194, 197, 224, 247, 259, 285, 334, 339, 343
Greek National Assembly, 158
Greek National Liberation Front, 247
Greek War of Independence, 118, 159, 172
Greeley, Horace, 84
Green Gang (Qingbang), 273
Greer, Donald, 118, 119
Grégoire, Abbé, 106, 114, 130–1, 162
Gregorios V, 155, 156
Gregory VII, Pope, 11
Grey, Lord, 29
Grévy, Jules, 151
Griffith, D. W., 93
Grimm, Jacob, 163, 167

Grimmelshausen, Jacob Christoffel von, 167
Gromyko, Andrei, 233
Grossdeutschland, 176, 177
Grossman, Vasily, 242, 254
Gualdo Priorato, Galeazzo, 16
Guangdong (China), 260, 312, 314
Guangxi (China), 294
Guangxu Emperor, 29, 263, 264, 265
Guangzhou (Canton), 260, 262, 264, 287, 304
Guantánamo (Cuba), 333
Guanzhong, Luo, 259
Guise, Duc de, 16
Guizhou (China), 260, 276
Guizot, François, 35, 63, 103, 104, 137, 140, 141, 142, 149
Gulag, 238, 239, 248
Gumilev, Nikolai, 246
Gustav III (king), 20–1

Habsburg Empire, 24, 169
Haiti, 73, 81–2, 128, 131, 132. *See also* Saint-Domingue
Haitian Revolution (1804), 58, 81, 128
Haldane, J. B. S., 336
Hamburg, 175, 178
Hamilton, Alexander, 53, 71, 76, 78, 80, 125, 188
Hampden, John, 49
Han Chinese, 263, 294
Handel, George Frideric, 52, 56
Hanoi, 7
Hanover, 51, 52, 55, 175, 177
Hanoverian Succession, 39
Harding, Warren G., 90
Harpers Ferry, 84
Harrison, Benjamin, 76
Harrow School, 330
Hausmann, Baron, 147
Haute-Garonne (France), 98
Haute-Saône (France), 98
Hautes-Pyrénées (France), 98
Haxthausen, August von, 189
Hayez, Francesco, 165, 166
Haymarket affair (1886), 101
Haynes, Mike, 198
Healey, Denis, 250
Hegel, Georg Wilhelm Friedrich, 124, 133, 146, 200
Heidegger, Martin, 337
Heine, Heinrich, 133, 139, 167
Hekou Uprising, 262
Helvetic Republic, 154
Henan (China), 280, 283, 284, 299
Henningsen, Charles Frederick, 22
Henri III (king), 16
Henry VIII (king), 12
Herder, Johann Gottfried, 124, 163, 168

Herzen, Alexander, 9, 146, 189
Hesse (Germany), 159, 177
Hidalgo, Anne, 150
Hill, Christopher, 18–19, 38, 49–50, 53, 336
Hillenkoetter, Roscoe H., 288
Himmler, Heinrich, 4
Hinton, William, 295
Hiroshima, 246, 280, 286
Hispaniola, 50
Hitchens, Christopher, 5
Hitler, Adolf, 8, 11
HIV/AIDS, 332
Ho Chi Minh, 7, 23
Ho Chi Minh City, 7
Hoare, Samuel, 203
Hobbes, Thomas, 38, 39, 42–3, 53, 69, 78
Hobsbawm, Eric, 1, 4, 17, 26, 100, 336
Hochdeutsch (High German), 161
Hoffmann von Fallersleben, August Heinrich, 167
Hofman, Bert, 316
Hölderlin, Friedrich, 156
Holland, 129, 285, 334. *See also* Netherlands
Holocaust, 236
Holstein, 175, 177
Holy Alliance, 140, 167
Holy Roman Empire, 181
Hong Kong, 260, 264, 294, 312, 320, 342
Hong Xiuquan, 264, 265
Honolulu, 279
Hooker, Richard, 53
Hoover, Herbert, 229
Hopei (Hebei, China), 290
Hordynski, Joseph, 23
Horthy, Miklos, 224
Hotel des Invalides, 134
House of Commons, 28, 36, 41, 51, 53, 60, 61, 64, 74, 130, 157, 160, 329
House of Lords, 39, 41, 64, 130, 329, 330
House of Representatives, 76, 81, 82, 87, 328–9
Hoxha, Enver, 246, 248
Hsupeng, Battle of (1948), 289
Huaihai campaign, 289
Huang Xing, 262, 263, 266
Hubei (China), 260, 261
Hughes, Thomas, 156
Hugo, Victor, 84, 86, 130, 138, 139, 144, 147, 150, 156–7
Huguenots, 17, 47, 57
Huizhou Qinühu Uprising, 262
Humboldt, Wilhelm von, 167
Hume, David, 33, 51, 52, 53, 68
Hunan (China), 260
Hunan Soviet, 274
Hunan–Jiangxi border, 261
Hundred Days' Reform, 29, 263, 267
Hundred Flowers Campaign (1955), 297

Hungary, 13, 22, 36, 101, 141, 153, 158, 186, 195, 212, 223, 224, 246, 247, 250, 251, 256, 257, 265, 339, 342
Hunt, Lynn, 96, 100, 104, 131
Husák, Gustáv, 248
Hussein, Saddam, 25
Huxley, Thomas Henry, 29, 263, 267
Hu Yaobang, 307, 317
Hyndman, Henry, 4

Île-de-France, 162
Illinois, 89, 332
Indignados (movement), 343
Imperial Guard, 193
India, 13, 56, 62, 64, 66, 75, 83, 103, 108 297, 301, 304, 308, 311, 314, 319, 342
Indian Appropriations Act (1871), 90
Indian Health Service, 90
Indian Removal Act (1830), 83
Indochina, 148, 331
Indonesia, 308, 341
Inglis, John, 288
Inner Mongolia, 294
Institut de France, 134
International Monetary Fund (IMF), 315
International Women's Day, 189, 193, 229
Iran, 24, 26, 326
Iraq, 5, 25, 66, 257, 333
Ireland, 7, 17, 23, 36, 38, 42, 48, 50, 55, 64, 66, 102, 120, 141, 150, 153, 163, 188, 330, 334
Ireton, Henry, 36, 41
Irish famine (1840s), 299
Irish Free State, 23, 66, 195
Irish Rebellion (1916), 23
Irish War of Independence, 23, 66
Irkutsk (Russia), 217
Iron Curtain, 252
Irwin, Stafford LeRoy, 288
Islam, 24, 25, 26
Islamic (or Iranian) Revolution, 24, 326
Islington (London), 206
Italian penal code, 24
Italy, 2, 4, 7, 8, 15, 21, 22, 24, 27, 30, 31, 37, 50 52, 96, 100, 105, 124, 128, 129, 132, 147, 148, 153, 159, 161, 162, 163–6, 169–71, 173, 175, 178–83, 186, 188, 189, 195, 197, 208, 224–5, 239, 243, 247, 265, 305, 326, 329, 330, 332, 334–5, 337, 339
Ivanovo-Voznesensk (Russia), 200

Jackson, Andrew, 82, 83
Jackson, Thomas, 92
Jacobins, 13, 96, 98, 104, 116, 117, 118, 124, 125, 127, 130, 132, 134, 151, 175, 190
Jacobites, 48, 51, 52, 102
Jamaica, 50, 58, 67
James II (king), 43, 44, 46–7, 48, 51, 56

Jameson, Fredric, 342
Japan, 1, 4, 23
Jaurès, Jean, 97
Jay, John, 78
Jefferson, Thomas, 2, 67, 70, 71–2, 80–1, 131, 188
Jiajin mountains, 276
Jiang Qing, 307
Jiangxi (China), 260, 276, 307
Jiang Zemin, 314
Jim Crow laws, 89
Jinggang Mountains, 261, 274
Jinzaburo, Saeki, 280
Ji Xianlin, 304
Joan of Arc, 127, 134
Joffrin, Jules, 7
John Lennon Airport, 37
John Paul II, Pope, 332
Johnson, Andrew, 87–9
Johnson, Ben, 53
Johnson, Boris, 6, 329
Johnson, Hewlett, 336
Johnson, Samuel, 51, 72
Jones, Colin, 119, 120
Jowett, Benjamin, 10
Juárez, Benito, 148
July 4 (Fourth of July, US), 35
Juneteenth, 92
Jura (France), 98

Kádár, János, 248
Kaliningrad (Königsberg, Russia), 177
Kamenev, Lev, 197, 198, 201, 211, 223, 230, 231, 241
Kang Youwei, 29, 263, 264
Kant, Immanuel, 124
Kapodistrias, Ioannis, 158
Karimov, Islam, 256
Kautsky, Karl, 30, 199, 223
Kazakhstan, 234, 235, 237, 239, 256, 257
Kazatin (Ukraine), 219
Kellermann, François Christophe, 105
Kemal, Mustafa, 24, 25, 195, 224
Kennedy, John F., 87
Kennedy, Paul, 249
Kentucky, 84
Kenya, 66
Kerensky, Alexander, 192, 199, 200, 201, 208, 211
Key, Francis Scott, 83
Khachaturian, Aram, 244
Khlevniuk, Oleg, 238
Khomeini, Ayatollah, 24, 25
Khrushchev, Nikita, 233, 248, 251, 309
King, Martin Luther, Jr, 59
Kingdom of the Serbs, Croats and Slovenes (Yugoslavia), 195
Kingdom of the Two Sicilies, 31, 140, 169, 178
Kishinev pogrom (1903), 90

Kissinger, Henry, 3, 308
Kleindeutschland, 176
Knights of Labor, 91
Knox, Alfred, 217
Kolchak, Alexander, 216, 217, 218
Kollontai, Alexandra, 196, 229
Königgrätz (Sadowa, Czechia), 177
Königsberg (Kaliningrad, Russia), 177
Kornilov, Lavr, 200, 216, 217, 219
Kossuth, Lajos, 36
Kosygin, Alexei, 233, 249
Kotkin, Stephen, 234
Kravchuk, Andrei, 217, 253
Kremlin Wall, 7, 14
Kristof, Nicholas, 310
Kronstadt (Russia), 201, 227
Kropotkin, Pyotr, 9
Ku Klux Klan, 89
Kulturkampf (1871–78), 181
Kulinovo, Battle of (1380), 245
Kun, Béla, 223
Kuomintang (KMT), 262, 266, 270, 272–76, 277, 278–80, 281, 282, 283, 284–5, 286–90, 292, 294, 295
Kurdistan, 25
Kursk (Russia), 243, 245, 246
Kutuzov, Mikhail, 245
Kwangju (South Korea), 317
Kyiv (Ukraine), 5
Kyrgyz Republic (Kyrgyzstan), 5, 257

L'Année terrible (1872), 150
Labour Day, 197
Labour Party (UK), 6, 329, 343
Lafayette, Marquis de, 105, 114
Lamartine, Alphonse de, 131, 133, 135, 136, 143, 145
La Motte, François Henri de, 120
Lancashire (England), 56, 85
Languedocien (language), 162
Laos, 187, 247
Lao Tzu, 319
Laponneraye, Albert, 99
Laqueur, Walter, 184
Las Cases, Emmanuel de, 129
Laslett, Peter, 46
Latin America, 29
Latin script, 24
Latvia, 204, 213, 215, 218, 224, 239, 246, 252, 257
Lauenburg (Germany), 175, 177
Law on Co-operatives (1988), 251
Law on the State Enterprise (1987), 251
Lawson, George, 344
Lazarus, Emma, 91
League of Nations, 278
Lebanon, 66
Le Blond de Neuveglise, 124

Le Bon, Gustave, 97
Ledru-Rollin, Alexandre, 143, 145
Lee, Robert E., 86, 92
Lefebvre, Georges, 97, 134
Left Socialist Revolutionaries, 201, 211, 215
Lega Nord, 327
Lemarque, Francis, 331
Lena Goldfields massacre, 208
Lenin, Vladimir, 7, 9, 53, 96, 105, 184–7, 189, 191–2, 195, 197–202, 205–15, 220–2, 225–30, 232, 237, 239, 241, 245, 246–8, 252, 257, 258, 262, 266, 268, 274, 282, 284, 322, 336, 340
Leningrad, 7
Lenin Museum, 254
Leo X, Pope, 12
Leopardi, Giacomo, 165
Leopold I (king), 154
Le Pen, Marine, 329, 333, 334
Les Invalides, 130
Lessing, Gotthold Ephraim, 167
Les Trois Glorieuses, 137, 139
Leutze, Emanuel, 276
Levada Center, 243
Levellers, True, 18, 41
Lewin, Moshe, 230, 231, 237
Lexington (Massachusetts), 3, 70
Liberal Democratic Party, 255
Libya, 66
Ligachev, Yegor, 249
Liguria (Italy), 161, 169
Lilburne, John, 41
Lin Biao, 288, 310
Lincoln, Abraham, 84–6, 87
Lincoln Square, 85
Linton, Marisa, 117, 119
Lisle, Rouget de, 116
Lithuania, 193, 213, 215, 218, 220, 224, 240, 246, 252, 257
Little Bighorn, Battle of (1876), 90
'Little Moscow', 272. *See also* Anyuan
Little Red Book, 303
Liu Chunhua, 272
Liu Shaoqi, 105, 302, 307
Liverpool, 37, 56
Livingston, Robert, 71
Li Zicheng, 14
Lloyd George, David, 37
Locke, John, 39, 46, 49, 53, 56, 67, 68, 72, 78, 102, 267
Loire (river), 118, 119, 135
Lombardy (Italy), 128, 148, 169, 171
London, 3, 4, 30, 34, 38, 41, 45, 104, 120, 123, 136, 154, 158, 165, 203, 205, 210, 250, 260
London, City of, 38, 62, 69, 74
London Conference (1830), 154
London Protocol, 158
Long Island, Battle of (1776), 74

Long March, 261, 276, 277, 294, 318
Long Parliament, 19, 42, 49
Longyu (empress dowager), 264, 266
Lorraine (France), 148, 195
Louis XIV (king), 16, 18, 46–7, 108, 263
Louis XV (king), 20, 107, 108, 109, 147
Louis XVI (king), 6, 28, 34, 96, 97, 101, 106, 109, 113, 117, 118, 124, 134–5, 151, 153, 327
Louis XVIII (king), 134–6, 328
Louisiana, 82, 89
Louisiana Separate Car Act (1890), 89
Louis-Philippe I (king), 34, 98, 105, 130, 134, 138–9, 142–3, 147
Louverture, Toussaint, 131
Lower Saxony (Germany), 161
Luding Bridge, Battle of (1935), 276
Lugou Bridge, 279
Lukashenko, Alexander, 256
Lula, 343
Lu Min, 321
Luoyang (China), 260
Lushan Conference (1959), 300
Luther, Martin, 12, 53, 161
Luxemburg, Rosa, 5, 212, 223
Lu Xun, 271
Lvov, Prince, 194, 198, 199
Lyon (France), 140

Macau, 342
Macaulay, Thomas Babington, 28, 34, 61–2
Macaulay, Zachary, 62
Macedonia, 158, 257
Machiavelli, Niccolò di Bernardo dei, 15, 17, 40, 53, 146, 164, 167, 225
Mac Mahon, Patrice de, 150
Macron, Emmanuel, 5, 127, 134, 150, 329, 334
Madison, James, 78
Magna Carta (1215), 190
Mahler, Gustav, 163
Maidan Revolution, 5
Maidan Square, 5
Maine, 119
Maistre, Joseph de, 123
Makhno, Nestor, 219–220
Malaparte, Curzio, 337
Malaysia, 1, 319
Mallet du Pan, Jacques, 6, 123
Manchester, 63, 85
Manchu, 294
Manchuria, 218, 246, 263, 277–8, 285–6, 288, 292
Mandelstam, Osip, 241
Manhattan, Battle of (1776), 74
Mann, Michael, 77
Manteuffel, Edwin von, 160
Manzoni, Alessandro, 133, 162
Mao Dun, 271

Mao Zedong, 7, 36, 53, 105, 251, 260, 264, 267, 271, 285, 293, 303, 307, 309–10, 312, 323
Mapaoying Uprising, 262
Marat, Jean-Paul, 7, 106, 134
Marble Arch, 36, 120
March on Rome (1922), 4
Marco Polo Bridge, 279
Marcu, Valeriu, 210
Marianne (symbol of France), 127
Marie-Antoinette (queen), 101
Marinetti, Filippo Tommaso, 337
Marlowe, Christopher, 53
Marly, Anna, 339
Marshall Plan, 247
Marston Moor, Battle of (1644), 44
Martines, Lauro, 15
Marvell, Andrew, 43, 45
Marx, Karl, 3–4, 5, 21, 32, 40, 49, 53, 66, 86, 87, 96, 103–4, 105, 107, 116, 134, 140–1, 144, 145, 146, 147, 149, 150, 172, 177–8, 184–5, 188–90, 199, 205–6, 207, 223, 227, 245, 260, 264, 267, 272, 274, 296, 300, 336, 344
Mary II (queen), 46, 47, 48, 50, 51
Maryland, 70, 84
Masaniello, 16
Massachusetts, 70, 75, 76
Maupeon Revolution, 20
Maupeou, René-Nicolas de, 20
Maurras, Charles, 97, 337
Mavromichalis family, 158
Maximillian, Archduke, 148
May, Theresa, 5–6, 329, 331
Mayakovsky, Vladimir, 189
May Day, 37, 189, 291
Mayer, Arno, 96, 98
May Fourth Movement (1919), 268, 269, 270, 296, 303
Mazzini, Giuseppe, 159, 167, 169, 170, 172, 175
McDowell, Nicholas, 45
McNamara, Robert, 252
Medici, Catherine de', 16
Meiji Restoration (Revolution), 1, 4, 24–5, 263–4, 268, 271, 339
Mélenchon, Jean-Luc, 334
Melzi d'Eril, Francesco, 169
Mencius, 269
Menemen Incident (1930), 25
Mensheviks, 41, 191, 194, 198, 207, 209–10, 227
Merkel, Angela, 252
Merridale, Catherine, 235
Merseyside (England), 37
Metaxas, Ioannis, 224
Metternich, Klemens von, 161
Meurthe (France), 98
Mexican Revolution (1910), 120
Mexico, 29, 82, 101, 148, 180, 241, 305, 319
Meyerhold, Vsevelod, 192

Michael, Grand Duke, 194
Michelet, Jules, 128
Middle Ages, 11–12, 35, 54, 168
Middle East, 26
Middle English, 161
Middle French, 161, 162
Middle Kingdom, 267
Mikoyan, Anastas, 230, 233
Milan, 128, 170
Milanović, Branko, 253, 257
Mill, John Stuart, 62, 63, 86, 112, 124, 189, 267
Milošević, Slobodan, 253
Milton, John, 43, 44, 45
Milyukov, Pavel, 186, 203, 227
Ming dynasty, 14
Minin, Kuzma, 245
Minsk (Belarus), 206, 220
Mirabeau, Honoré Gabriel Riqueti, Comte de, 105, 106, 114
Miracle of the Vistula, 220
Mississippi, 82, 83
Missolonghi (Greece), 156
Mitter, Rana, 283
Mitterrand, François, 127, 328
Modena-Parma (Italy), 169
Mohammad Reza Pahlavi, Shah, 24
Moldavia (Moldova), 141, 252, 257
Mommsen, Theodor, 11
Mongolia, 219, 257, 294, 341
Mongols, 240, 245, 294
Monmouth, Duke of, 46
Montagnards, 104
Montand, Yves, 331
Monteith of Salmonet, Robert, 16
Montenegro, 154, 194
Montesquieu, 20, 21, 35, 52, 53, 54, 58, 67, 68, 102, 117, 267
Moore, Barrington, 9
Moore, Thomas, 156
Morales, Eva, 344
Moravia, 160
More, Thomas, 53, 342
Morocco, 66
Morris, William, 342
Mosaddegh, Mohammad, 25
Moscow, 7, 14, 101, 188, 192, 201, 205, 209, 213, 216, 217, 226, 237, 243, 246, 254, 260, 272, 275, 283, 286, 301, 308
Moscow, Battle of (1941), 192
Mugabe, Robert, 248
Mughals, 66
Muhammad Ali, 23
Mujahideen, 249
Murmansk (Russia), 218
Mussolini, Benito, 2, 4, 8, 11, 96, 224, 248, 274, 338
Mustafa Kemal Atatürk, 24, 195, 224

Nagasaki, 246, 280, 286
Nagorno-Karabakh (Azerbaijian), 256
Naguib, Mohammed, 23
Nanjing, 260, 264, 265, 273, 270, 280, 287, 289
Nantes (France), 118
Naples, 16, 18, 31, 37, 129, 140, 154, 169, 170, 171, 173
Napoleon I (emperor, Napoleon Bonaparte), 9, 21, 27, 37, 63, 82, 98, 105, 106, 108, 116, 119, 127–38, 151, 154, 161, 169, 172, 185, 188, 190,
Napoleon III (emperor, Louis Napoleon Bonaparte), 63, 99, 116, 144–9, 170–1, 173
Napoleonic Wars, 15, 18, 30, 65, 103, 119, 128–36, 164, 168, 175, 182, 194, 326
Narodnaia Svoboda (People's Freedom), 197
Narodnaya Volya, 208
Nassau (Germany), 177
Nasser, Gamal Abdel, 23
National Assembly (France), 111, 107, 113, 115, 119, 145, 146, 148, 150, 151, 210
National Congress, Seventh (April–June 1945), 309
National Convention, 102, 117
National Liberals, 181
National People's Congress, 320
National Revolutionary Army (China), 279
National Socialist Revolution, 4
National Statuary Hall Collection, 85
National Unity Day, 193
NATO, 247, 249, 252, 255
Naudé, Gabriel, 16–17
Navarino, Battle of (1827), 158
Navigation Acts, 50, 69
Nazarbayev, Nursultan, 256
Nazi Germany, 5, 7, 27, 96, 182, 215, 239, 240, 241–2, 246, 326, 327
Nazism, 2, 5, 26, 182, 239, 242, 335, 339
Necker, Jacques, 33, 96, 109, 113
Nelson, Horatio (admiral), 37
Neruda, Pablo, 244
Netherlands, 15, 50, 58, 141, 154, 180. *See also* Holland
Nevsky, Alexander, 245
New Economic Policy (NEP), 228, 229–30, 231, 232, 233, 297
New Jersey, 70, 332
New Marriage Law, 297
New Model Army, 40, 41, 210
New People's Study Society, 271, 272
New York, 70, 84, 197, 210, 260, 310
New Zealand, 343
Newcastle, 172
Nice (France), 148, 171
Nicholas II (emperor), 193, 216
Nicolai, Agostino, 16
Niethammer, Friedrich Immanuel, 133

Nigeria, 66
Nile, Battle of the (1798), 127
Nile Delta (1798), 129
9 Thermidor Year II, 9, 99, 126, 132
Ninety-Five Theses, 12
Ningxia Hui Autonomous Region, 294, 295, 321
Nitti, Francesco Saverio, 175
Nitze, Paul, 252
Nixon, Richard, 3, 307–8, 325
Niyazov, Saparmurat, 256
NKVD, 241
Nobel Prize, 93, 244, 252, 254
Nolan, Peter, 253, 315
Non-aggression Pact, German–Soviet (1939), 282
Normand (language), 162
Normandy, 13, 119, 242, 243
North Korea, 187, 247, 342
Northern Expedition, 273
Notre Dame Cathedral, 332
Nottingham Forest, 172
Novak, William, 77
Nove, Alec, 238
November Uprising of 1830–31, 22
Novgorod (Russia), 12
Novosibirsk (Russia), 237
Nuland, Victoria, 255
Nunn, Sam, 252
Nur-Sultan (Astana, Kazakhstan), 256

Occupy (movement), 343
October 1 (China), 35, 36, 293, 323, 340
October Revolution. *See* Great October Revolution
Odessa (Ukraine), 155, 205, 207, 218
Okhrana (secret police), 207
Oklahoma, 90
Old Supreme Court Chamber (Washington, DC), 92
Omsk (Russia), 216
Opium War, 263, 264, 267, 322
Opium War, First (1839–42), 264
Opium War, Second (1850–60), 148
Orange Order, 48
Orange Revolution, 5
Order of Suvorov, 245
Orléans dynasty, 27, 95, 98, 136, 138–40, 150, 154
Otis, James, 68
Otto of Bavaria, 22, 158
Ottoman Empire, 2, 12, 75, 141, 147, 153, 154, 155, 158, 188, 194, 195, 216, 224
Overy, Richard, 245
Owen, Robert, 5
Oxford University, 43, 49

Padua (Italy), 170
Paine, Thomas, 2, 52, 71, 75, 100, 124, 125
Palermo (Italy), 140
Palestine, 67
Palm d'Aelders, Etta, 106
Palmerston, Henry John Temple, 3rd Viscount, 64, 172, 321
Paris, 3, 6–7, 9, 33, 37, 42, 67, 74, 98, 107, 111–13, 115, 117–19, 122–4, 126, 128–9, 132, 137–8, 141–2, 144–5, 147–52, 157, 162, 167, 210, 220, 224, 260, 271
Paris Commune, 9, 63, 99, 120, 142, 148, 150, 172, 185, 189
Paris Opera, 165
Parliament, UK, 18, 29, 34, 36, 37, 38, 39–44, 47–53, 61, 67, 69, 73, 153, 189, 329
Parsa, Arlen, 93–4
Party Congress, Eighteenth, 241
Party Congress, Eleventh, 311
Party Congress, Tenth, 307
Party Congress, Twenty-Seventh, 250
Pasternak, Boris, 254
Paton, Andrew Archibald, 23
Patras (Greece), 155
Päts, Konstantin, 224
Paul, Saint (apostle), 20
Paume, Jeu de, 111
Peace of Westphalia, 15
Pearl Harbor, 242, 281, 283
Pedro I (emperor), 65
Peiping. *See* Beijing
Peking (Beijing) University, 297
Peloponnese, 155, 158
Peng Dehuai, 261, 300, 301
Peninsular Wars, 129
Pennsylvania, 70, 76, 80, 82, 84
Pennsylvania Abolition Society, 72
People's Liberation Army (PLA), 288, 289
People's Republic of China. *See* China, People's Republic of
Pepys, Samuel, 45, 56
Perestroika, 248, 249, 253, 254
Perrault, Charles, 164
Perrie, Maureen, 208
Peter I (emperor, Peter the Great), 186, 189, 191, 240, 254
Peter III (emperor), 14
Peterloo massacre (1819), 63
Pétion, Alexandre, 131
Petliura, Semen, 223–4
Petrarca, Francesco, 161
Petrograd, 36, 101, 191, 193–4, 197, 199–201, 203, 208, 209, 211–12, 216, 217, 226, 227, 228
Petrograd Soviet, 199
Philadelphia, 36, 73, 78, 260
Philippe Égalité (Louis Philippe II, Duke of Orléans), 138

Phillips, Wendell, 32
Picard (language), 162
Piedmont (Italy), 8, 141, 147, 154, 164, 169, 170–2, 175, 176, 178, 182
Piedmont-Sardinia (Italy), 147
Piłsudski, Józef, 220
Pincus, Steven, 49
Ping Liu Li Uprising, 262
Pinochet, Augusto, 324, 325
Pipes, Richard, 184, 221
Pirandello, Luigi, 337
Pisa, 37
Pisacane, Carlo, 169, 170
Pitt, William, the Elder, 69–70
Pitt, William, the Younger, 74
Pius IX, Pope, 136, 151, 163, 170
Pizzetti, Ildebrando, 337
Place de la Concorde, 117
Place de la Révolution, 117
Plekhanov, Georgi, 9, 189, 199
Plenum of the Central Committee, Sixth, 309
Plessy v. Ferguson, 89
Plessy, Homer, 89
Pol Pot, 304, 308
Poland, 14, 22–3, 117, 129, 141, 153, 158, 163, 169, 177, 195, 204, 207, 213–14, 215, 218, 220, 223, 224, 246–7, 250, 253, 256–7, 285, 291, 339, 342
Polish–Muscovite Wars, 193
Politburo Standing Committee, 215, 238, 250, 276, 297
Polo, Marco, 37
Poltava (Ukraine), 223, 224
Pomerania (Poland), 168
Pompidou, Georges, 134
Ponza (Italy), 170
Popular Front (Spain, 1936–39), 339
Popular Unity, 325
Portugal, 2, 16, 18, 56, 65, 154, 159, 180, 224, 259, 260, 334, 339
Portuguese Restoration War, 16
Potemkin (ship), 207
Potsdam Agreement, 247
Pound, Ezra, 337
Pouqueville, François, 155
Pozharsky, Dimitri, 245
Prague, 220, 248
Preobrazhensky, Evgenii, 186, 226, 230, 231
Presbyterian Church of Scotland, 38
Preston, Paul, 120
Prince, Mary, 59
Prix de Rome, 137
Protectorate Parliament, 17
Protestants, 1, 15, 16, 18, 23, 47–8, 51, 52, 53, 58, 109, 136, 163, 176, 181
Proudhon, Pierre-Joseph, 170
Provisional Government, 143, 145, 189, 191,

192, 194, 197, 198, 199, 200, 201, 202, 203, 209, 211, 216
Prussia, 8, 22, 37, 63, 99, 105, 116, 117, 140, 148, 150, 151, 159, 160, 164, 167, 168, 169, 174, 175, 176–8, 179, 182, 220
Prussians at Valmy (1792), 105
Pskov (Russia), 12
Puerto Rico, 84
Pugachev, Yemelyan, 14
Puglia (Italy), 173
Puritan Revolution, 9
Pushkin, Alexander Sergeyevich, 133, 155, 157, 243
Putin, Vladimir, 192, 217, 254, 255–6, 257, 340
Putney Debates, 41
Puyi (emperor), 264, 266
Pye, Lucian, 306
Pyrénées-Orientales (France), 98

Qingbang (Green Gang), 273
Qing dynasty, 14, 34, 65, 259, 261, 264–5, 293, 323, 327
Qinghai, 304
Qin-lian Uprising (1908), 262
Qinzhou Uprising (1907), 262
Qiu Jin, 262, 296
Queneau, Raymond, 336
Qufu (China), 307
Qu Qiubai, 105

Rabelais, François, 161
Rabinowitch, Alexander, 184
Race Relations Act (1965), 330
Radek, Karl, 223, 241
Radical Reconstruction, 88, 91
Radkey, Oliver, 209
Rahmon, Emomali, 256
Railway Protection Movement, 261
Ranke, Leopold von, 22
Rape of Nanjing, 280
Rauschning, Hermann, 5
Ravina, Mark, 25
Razin, Stenka, 14
Reconstruction Amendments, 87
Rectification Campaign (1942), 283
Red Army (China), 210, 261, 271, 274, 276, 278, 279, 288, 291
Red Army (Russia), 192, 197, 217, 218, 220, 221, 242, 243, 246, 247, 291
Red Dean of Canterbury, 336
Red Fifth Army, 217
Red Guard, 201, 202, 301, 303, 304, 305, 307
Red October. *See* Great October Revolution
Red Square, 7, 192, 248
Red Terror, 119, 221, 222, 239
Reform Club, 172
Reichstag, 179, 181

Reina, Placido, 15
Remonstrance. *See* Grand Remonstrance
Renaissance, 35, 164, 182
Renan, Ernest, 146
Representation of the People Act (1832), 28
Republican Party (US), 85
Revolutionary Insurrectionary Army, 219
Revolutionary Workers of the Hairdressing Trade, 304
Revolution of Dignity, 5. *See also* Maidan Revolution
Rhineland, 163, 178, 239
Rhode Island, 70, 75, 76, 84
Riall, Lucy, 175
Ricardo, David, 61
Risorgimento, 160, 168, 171, 172, 173, 174, 175
Rivarol, Antoine de, 78
Roberts, Geoffrey, 239, 245
Robespierre, Maximilien, 7, 96, 99, 106, 116–18, 119, 124, 127, 131, 134, 135–6
Rocard, Michel, 1
Rockingham, Charles Watson-Wentworth, 2nd Marquess of, 73
Rodzianko, Mikhail, 193
Roland, Madame (Marie-Jeanne), 117
Rolland, Romain, 336
Rolling Stones, 5
Roman Catholic Church, 12, 43, 115, 136. *See also* Catholicism; Catholics
Roman Catholic Relief Act (1829), 64
Roman History (Mommsen), 11
Romania, 154, 194, 224, 242, 246, 247, 248, 250, 256, 257, 339
Romanov, House of, 8, 188
Roman Republic (1848), 11, 172
Rome, 1, 12, 37, 39, 134, 145, 148, 162, 163, 164, 171, 172, 173, 182
Ronsard, Pierre de, 167
Roosevelt, Franklin D., 242, 243, 286, 293, 328
Roosevelt Revolution, 5
Rose Revolution, 5
Rossini, Gioacchino, 166
Rousseau, 52, 188, 267
Royal African Company, 55
Rozanov, Sergey, 218
Rum Rebellion (1808–10), 66
Rump Parliament, 41, 42
Rush, Benjamin, 80
Russell, Bertrand, 272
Russell, Conrad, 39
Russia, 5, 9, 12, 14, 22, 28, 34, 35, 37, 41, 53, 90, 96, 117, 129, 140, 141, 147, 153, 154, 157, 163, 169–70, 177, 183–85, 187–91, 193–8, 202–3, 205, 207, 210, 212–14, 216–18, 227, 239, 240, 242, 244, 245, 251–8, 261, 263, 265, 270, 272, 277, 291, 293, 298, 316, 326, 332, 335, 339–40, 341

Russian Civil War, 194–5, 206, 210, 213, 215, 216, 220–1, 223, 226, 227, 240–1, 245, 254, 291
Russian Communist Party, 215, 255
Russian Red Cross, 224
Russian Revolution, 9, 26, 34, 65, 117, 184–91, 194, 203–4, 206, 214, 269, 270, 283, 294, 323, 326, 335, 336, 339, 340, 343
Ruzsky, Nikolai, 193
Rwanda, 332

Saigon, 7
Saint Barthélemy massacre, 16
Sainte-Beuve, Charles, 108
Saint-Domingue, 119, 130, 131–2. *See also* Haiti
Saint Helena (island), 129
Saint-Just, Louis Antoine de, 106, 117, 130
Sakwa, Richard, 249
Salazar, António de Oliveira, 2, 224
Samians, 10
Samos (Greece), 158
Sand, George, 142, 144, 150
Sanders, Bernie, 343
Sans-Culottes, 107
Sapri (Italy), 170
Sardinia, 123, 141, 147, 169, 170, 172, 175
Sardinia, Kingdom of (Piedmont), see Piedmont
Sartre, Jean-Paul, 336
Savonarola, Girolamo, 12
Savoy, 148, 169, 171
Scandinavia, 334
Schapiro, Leonard, 184
Schiavone, Aldo, 11
Schiller, Friedrich, 124, 156, 167
Schleswig (Germany), 177
Schleswig-Holstein (Germany), 148, 177
Schmitt, Carl, 337
Schönerer, Georg Ritter von, 176
Schopenhauer, Arthur, 338
Schram, Stuart, 306
Schumann, Robert, 133, 162
Schwarzbard, Samuel, 224
Scotland, 17, 38, 44, 46, 47, 50, 53, 64, 188, 330
Scott, Walter, 133, 166
Scottish Enlightenment, 46, 58
Séamus an Chaca, 48. *See also* James II
Seattle, 91
Second Carlist War, 141
Second Estate, 112
Second International, 30
Second Reich, 327
Second Republic, 136
Sedan (France), 148, 173
Seeley, John, 75
Selden, Mark, 299
Semaine sanglante, 149

Semenov, Grigory, 218–19
Senate, 76, 82, 87, 89, 328, 329
Senghor, Léopold Sédar, 97
September 11 attacks (9/11), 333
Serbia, 154, 180, 194, 257
Serbian Uprising, First, 22
Seven Thousand Cadres Central Work Conference (1962), 301
Seven Years' War (1756–63), 56, 108, 110
Shaanxi (China), 276, 277, 279, 283
Shah Mohammad Reza Pahlavi, 24
Shakespeare, William, 53, 103, 138, 167, 191
Shambaugh, David, 319
Shandong (Shantung, China), 269, 290
Shanghai, 260, 264, 268, 269–70, 271, 273, 274, 275, 279, 280, 287, 289
Shanghai Communiqué, 308
Shanghai Student Union, 269
Sharp, Granville, 58, 60
Shelley, Percy, 123, 156
Shenzhen (China), 320
Shenzhen Stock Exchange, 316
Sheridan, Charles Brinsley, 156
Sherman, John, 29
Sherman, Roger, 71
Sherman Antitrust Act (1890), 29
Shimabara Revolution, 14
Shimonoseki Treaty (1895), 265
Sholokhov, Mikhail, 33, 254
Sichuan (China), 276, 281, 298
Siciliani, Vespri, 165
Sicily, 18, 31, 140, 155, 165, 171, 175, 327
Sigismund I the Old (king), 14
Sidney, Fabian, 236, 336
Sieyès, Emmanuel Joseph, 106, 113
Sighele, Scipio, 97
Sinclair, Thomas A., 10
Sinn Féin, 23
Sino-Indian War, 342
Sino-Japanese War, 283
Sino-Soviet Treaty of Friendship (1950), 286
Sioux, 90
Skocpol, Theda, 2, 6, 231, 303, 326
Slave Trade Act (1807), 60
Slavery Abolition Act (1833), 61
Slovakia, 8, 256, 257
Slovenia, 257
Smetona, Antanas, 224
Smit, J. W., 14
Smith, Adam, 50, 53, 72, 102, 267
Smith, Edmund Kirby, 85
Smith, Stephen, 323
Smith, Steve A., 184
Smyrna, 159, 195
Snegovaya, Maria, 254
Snow, Edgar, 281, 285
Soboul, Albert, 95, 97, 140

Social Democratic Federation, 4
Social Democratic Labour Party, 206, 212, 272
Social Democratic Party of Germany (SPD), 181
Socialist Revolutionaries (SRs), 189, 208, 209, 216
Socialist Revolutionary Party, 191, 199, 200, 201
Society for Effecting the Abolition of the Slave Trade, 58
Society for the Mitigation and Gradual Abolition of Slavery, 61
Society of Friends, 155
Society of the Righteous and Harmonious Fists, 265
Solidarność (party), 340
Solzhenitsyn, Aleksandr, 217, 254
Sonderbund, 154
Song Jiaoren, 266
Sons of Liberty, 70
Sophia, Duchess of Hanover, 51
South Carolina, 85
South Korea, 29, 311, 315, 317, 341
South Ossetia, 256
Soviet of Workers' and Soldiers' Deputies, 194, 197
Soviet Union (Union of Soviet Socialist Republics) 8, 34, 96, 177, 184, 185, 187, 201, 213, 215, 218, 222, 225, 228, 229, 233, 234, 236, 239, 240, 241, 242–3, 244, 246–50, 252–4, 256, 273, 275, 279, 282, 283, 284, 285, 286, 288, 292–4, 296, 297, 298, 310, 314–15, 319, 335, 336, 339, 341–3
Spain, 2, 15, 16, 22, 47, 50, 56, 65, 74, 82, 129, 141, 159, 161, 180, 224, 239, 259, 334, 339
Spanish Civil War, 120
Spartacus, 11
Spedizione di Sapri (1857), 169
Spender, Stephen, 336
Spenser, Edmund, 42, 53
Spirito, Ugo, 337
Staël, Germaine de, 54, 96, 132, 135, 137, 169
Stalin, Joseph Vissarionovich, 7, 9, 96, 105, 185, 186, 197, 198, 215, 230–48, 252, 254, 257, 276, 282–3, 286, 293, 298, 303, 304, 309, 313, 335–6, 339, 340
Stamp Act (1766), 69
Stanton, Elizabeth Cady, 87
Starmer, Keir, 6, 206
Starr, Joseph R., 236
State Planning Commission, 230
Statue of Liberty, 91, 193
Statuto Albertino (1848), 170
St Clair, William, 155
Stedman Jones, Gareth, 123
Stendhal, 134
Stephens, Alexander, 85

Stern, Daniel, 144
Stevens, Thaddeus, 87
Stilwell, General, 285
St Louis World's Fair, 90
Stolypin, Pyotr, 204, 207
St Petersburg, 7, 188, 195, 205, 206, 254, 260
St Peter's Field, 63
Strachey, John, 336
Strahan, William, 51
Straits of Messina, 171
Struve, Peter, 206
Stuart, James, 150
Stuarts, 33
Sumner, Charles, 87
Sun Yat-sen, 262, 263, 264, 266, 268, 270, 273–4, 282, 323
Sunak, Rishi, 329
Supreme Court of the United States, 89, 328, 330
Suvorov, Alexander, 245
Swabia (Germany), 168
Sweden, 21, 180
Swedish Revolution, 20–21
Swift, Jonathan, 54, 55
Swiss Civil Code, 24
Swiss Confederation, 9
Switzerland, 9, 24, 132, 141, 154, 160, 168, 175, 180, 197
Syme, Ronald, 11
Syriza, 343

Tacitus, 11
Tacky's Revolt (1760), 58
Taine, Hippolyte, 97, 104, 122, 128, 326
Taiping, 264, 265
Taiping Heavenly Kingdom, 264
Taiping Revolutionary Movement, 264
Taiwan, 29, 262, 265, 279, 288, 290, 294, 308, 310, 311–12, 315, 320, 339, 342
Taiwan Relations Act (1979), 308
Tajikistan, 256, 257
Talbott, Strobe, 255
Talleyrand, Charles-Maurice de, 105, 106, 136–37, 138
Tambov (Russia), 219, 227
Tancredi (character), 31, 32
Taney, Roger, 92
Taylor, A. J. P., 147
Taylor, John, 19
Teano (Italy), 171
Terror, the (France), 13, 27, 28, 96, 117–21, 123–4, 126–8, 130, 132, 150, 151
Teutonic Knights, 12
Texas, 82–3, 84, 92
Thatcher, Margaret, 250
Therborn, Göran, 343
Thermidor. *See* 9 Thermidor Year II

Thermidoreans (1794), 104
Thessaloniki (Greece), 20, 158, 159
Thiers, Adolphe, 142, 146, 149
Third Communist International. *See* Comintern
Third Estate, 110, 111, 112, 113, 189
Third Reich, 96, 148, 177, 179, 180, 243
Third Republic, 30, 33, 34, 63, 95, 99, 115, 136, 142, 150–1, 190
Third Rome, 187
Third War of Independence (1866), 172
Thirteen Colonies, 28, 74, 153, 189, 211
Thirty Years' War, 15, 18, 188
Thomas, Keith, 17
Thomson, James, 56
Three-Anti Campaign, 302
Three Johns pub, 206
Thucydides, 10
Tiananmen Square, 7, 96, 269, 293, 307, 310, 316–18, 323
Tibet, 281, 294, 320–1, 342
Tientsin (Tianjin, China), 287
Tilly, Charles, 324, 325
Time of Troubles (1598–1613), 14, 193
Tito, Josip, 246, 248
Tocqueville, Alexis de, 13, 30, 34, 54, 65, 83–4, 99, 103–4, 105, 108, 110–11, 112, 141, 143–6, 152, 263
Tokyo, 278, 286
Toleration Act (1689), 48
Tolstoy, Leo, 204, 254
Tomasi di Lampedusa, Giuseppe, 31
Tombs, Robert, 119, 120
Tories, 51, 73, 123
Townsend, Meredith, 86
Townshend Acts (1767), 69, 70
Toynbee, Arnold, 4
Trafalgar Square, 37
Trail of Tears, 83
Transbaikalia (Russia), 218
Treaty of Adrianople (1829), 158
Treaty of Lisbon (1668), 16
Treaty of Münster (1648), 15
Treaty of Nanjing (1842), 264
Treaty of Paris (1783), 67, 82
Treaty of Rapallo (1922), 225
Treaty of Riga (1921), 215, 220
Treaty of Shimonoseki (1895), 265
Trentino–Alto Adige (Italy), 195
Trento (Italy), 173
Trevelyan, Charles, 62
Trevelyan, George Macaulay, 172
Trevor-Roper, Hugh, 17
Trieste (Italy), 173
Trifonov, Yury, 254
Trinidad, 67
Trollope, Anthony, 160

Trollope, Theodosia, 160
Trotsky, Leon, 5, 105, 197, 201, 211, 212–13, 217, 219, 223, 227, 229, 230–2, 238, 241
True Levellers, 18, 41
Truman, Harry, 288, 289
Trumbull, John, 94
Trumbull, Lyman, 87
Trump, Donald, 76, 90, 329–30, 333
Truss, Liz, 329
Truth, Sojourner, 84
Tsvetaeva, Marina, 201, 321
Tubman, Harriet, 84
Tuileries, 98, 123, 151
Tukhachevsky, Mikhail, 217, 220, 227, 241, 245
Tulip Revolution, 5
Tulsa, Oklahoma, 90
Tunisia, 343
Turati, Filippo, 30
Turgot, Jacques, 109–10
Turkey, 25
Turkmenistan, 256, 257, 332
Turner, J. M. W., 60, 61
Turner, Nat, 84
Tuscany, 162, 171
Twin Towers (World Trade Center, New York), 333
Tyburn (London), 36, 120
Tyler, John, 13
Tyrie, David, 120–1
Tyrol (Austria/Italy), 168, 172, 195
Tzara, Tristan, 336

UK Independence Party (UKIP), 333
Ukraine, 5, 7, 207, 213–15, 216, 219–21, 223, 224, 225, 228, 233, 234–5, 252, 256, 257, 335, 340
Ukrainian National Army, 219, 223
Ukrainian People's Republic, 213, 224
Ukrainian Soviet Socialist Republic, 7
Ulam, Adam, 184
Ulmanis, Karlis, 224
Umayyad Caliphate, 13
Ungaretti, Giuseppe, 337
Ungern-Sternberg, Baron Roman von, 219
Union Army, 86
Union of Soviet Socialist Republics, 215, 257, 294
United Irishmen uprising (1798), 120
United Provinces of the Netherlands, 15
United Russia Party, 255
United States of America, 3, 4, 5, 7, 22, 25, 29, 37, 63, 72, 77, 80, 81, 82, 83, 85, 89, 92, 95, 96, 121, 169, 179, 181, 187, 188, 190, 194, 195, 208, 217, 225, 229, 240, 246, 250, 255, 264, 266, 281, 284, 286, 288, 292, 293–95, 305, 308, 317, 319, 321, 322, 324, 329–33, 334, 336, 341–2, 343

University College London, 97
University of Chicago, 325
University of Göttingen, 271
Uno Sōsuke, 317
Urabi revolt (1879–82), 23
Urals, 216, 234
Uruguay, 169
USSR. *See* Soviet Union
Uyghurs, 294, 320, 321

Van Buren, Martin, 82
Velvet Revolution, 8, 252, 260
Vendée (France), 6, 118, 119, 181
Vendémiaire insurrection, 127
Venetia (Italy), 116, 148, 169, 170, 171, 172
Venezuela, 344
Venice, 37, 170
Vercingetorix, 127, 134
Verdi, Giuseppe, 21
Verhaeren, Émile, 192
Vernet, Horace, 133
Versailles, 34, 111, 115, 122, 126, 148, 195, 212, 269
Vian, Boris, 331
Victoria, Queen, 62, 172
Vienna, 136, 154, 161, 220
Vietnam, 1, 23, 66, 187, 247, 262, 305, 307, 308, 331, 333, 341, 342, 343
Vilnius (Lithuania), 220
Virginia, 70, 74, 76, 84, 86
Virginia, Battle of (1781), 74
Vladivostok (Russia), 217
Vologda (Russia), 196
Voltaire, 21, 52, 53–4, 102, 117, 188
Volya, Narodnaya, 208
Voting Rights Act (1965), 89
Vyborg, 193, 196

Wagner, Richard, 163
Wakeman, Frederic, 259
Waldo, Pierre, 12
Wales, 50
Wałęsa, Lech, 251
Wallachia (Romania), 141
Waller, Edmund, 43
Wallerstein, Immanuel, 100
Walloon provinces, 162
Walpole, Robert, 51
Waltz, Kenneth, 249
Wang, Yuhua, 14
War of the Spanish Succession (1701–14), 56
Warsaw, 220, 248
Washington Naval Conference, 269
Washington, George, 7, 36, 70, 72, 75, 80, 100, 124–5
Waterloo, 37, 98, 129, 134, 135, 169, 242
Webbs, Sidney, 236

Webbs, Beatrice, 236, 336
Weber, Max, 48
Webster, Noah, 125
Wedgwood, Josiah, 59
Wehrmacht, 243
Weibo, 302
Weimar Republic, 2, 8, 225, 327
Wellington, Arthur, Duke of, 37, 135
Wesley, John, 58, 72
West Bank, 257
West Germany (Federal Republic of Germany), 251, 293
West Indies, 56, 67, 72, 75
Western Design, 50
Westminster Abbey, 36
Westminster Hall, 36
Westphalia (Germany), 129, 168
Wexford (Ireland), 42, 43
Whampoa Military Academy, 270
Wheatcroft, Stephen, 234, 239
Whigs, 36, 49, 51
White Lotus Rebellion (1794–1804), 264
White Revolution (1963), 24
White Terror, 119, 135, 217, 221, 222–3
White, Charles, 22
Whitehead, William, 45
Whites, 192, 205, 215, 216, 217, 218, 219, 220, 221, 225, 254
Wickham, William, 135
Wilberforce, William, 58, 61, 124, 157
Wilhelm II (emperor), 177, 182
Wilkes, John, 74
William, Prince of Denmark, 158
William II (king, William Rufus), 47
William III (king, William of Orange), 37, 46, 47, 48, 50
Williams, Eric, 56
Wilson, Woodrow, 92–3, 212
Winchester College, 330
Winckelmann, Johann Joachim, 156
Winstanley, Gerrard, 18, 41, 102
Winter Palace (Petrograd), 36, 191–2, 201, 208, 258
Witte, Count, 206
Wolfe, Bertram, 184
Wollstonecraft, Mary, 60, 114, 125
Women's Loyal National League, 87
Wood, Gordon, 65
Wood, Tony, 256
Wood, William, 66
Wordsworth, William, 60, 123, 131, 134
Workers' Union of South Russia, 205
World Bank, 257, 315
World Economic Forum, 297
World Trade Organization, 314
World War, First 2, 24, 93, 97, 173, 177, 180, 188, 194–5, 216, 218, 224, 225, 226, 269

World War, Second, 24, 27, 32, 162, 182, 187, 195, 220, 224, 242, 243, 244, 245, 247, 254, 258, 279, 281, 283, 326, 327, 335, 339
Worms (Germany), 12
Woronoff, Denis, 98
Wounded Knee Massacre (1890), 90
Wrangel, Peter N., 217
Wren, Matthew, 18
Wuchang Uprising (1911), 259, 261, 262, 263, 265, 266
Wuhan (China), 261, 273, 280
Württemberg, 148, 159, 176, 177
Wuwei, 299, 301
Wuxu Reform, 263
Wycliffe, John, 12

Xi'an, 260, 265, 278, 279
Xianfeng Emperor, 263
Xi Jinping, 307, 320, 322, 323
Xinhua, 293
Xinjiang Uyghur Autonomous Region, 294, 321
Xi Zhongxun, 307

Yagoda, Genrikh, 233, 241
Yale University, 92
Yalta, 247, 285
Yalta Conference (1945), 286
Yan'an Forum, 285
Yan'an, 261, 281, 283
Yan Fu, 267, 296
Yang, Rae, 305
Yang Su, 304
Yangzi (Yangtze, river), 261, 289
Yekaterinburg (Russia), 201
Yekaterinodar (Krasnodar, Russia), 216
Yellow Flower Mound Uprising, 262
Yellow River, 280, 284
Yeltsin, Boris, 217, 252, 253, 254, 255
Yermanés, Georgios, 155
Yevreinov, Nikolai, 192
Yevtushenko, Yevgeny, 254

Yezhov, Nikolai, 241
Yiddish, 160
Yihequan (Yihetuan, Boxers), 194, 265
Yoder, Dale, 6
Yorktown, Battle of (1781), 74, 242
Young Irelander Rebellion, 141
Young, Arthur, 110, 123, 124
Yourcenar, Marguerite, 97
Ypsilantis, Alexander, 155
Yuanmingyuan (Old Summer Palace), 264
Yuan Shikai, 266
Yu Dafu, 271
Yudenich, Nikolai, 217
Yugoslavia, 195, 224, 246, 248, 285

Zamaraev, A. A., 196
Zasulich, Vera, 9, 200
Zentrum (party), 181
Zhang Xueliang, 278, 279
Zhang Zhidong, 25
Zhangzhuangcun, 295
Zhao Ziyang, 317
Zhdanov, Andrei, 241
Zheng Guanying, 267
Zhennanguan Uprising, 262
Zhenotdel (Communist Party Women's Section), 229, 230
Zhili–Fengtian wars (1922 and 1924), 273
Zhou Enlai, 3, 105, 271, 278, 285, 298, 301, 304, 306, 307–08
Zhu De, 261, 271
Zhukov, Georgy, 246
Zhu Rongji, 316
Zinn, Howard, 3
Zinoviev, Grigory, 197, 201, 211, 223, 230, 240
Zog, King, 224
Zola, Émile, 150
Zollverein (customs union), 178, 181
Zong (ship), 60
Zunyi (China), 276
Zurich, 205
Zyuganov, Gennady, 255